EAST of the SUN

The Epic
Conquest
and Tragic
History
of Siberia

BENSON
BOBRICK

POSEIDON PRESS

New York   London   Toronto
Sydney   Tokyo   Singapore

POSEIDON PRESS
Simon & Schuster Building
Rockefeller Center
1230 Avenue of the Americas
New York, New York 10020

POSEIDON PRESS is a registered trademark
of Simon & Schuster Inc.

POSEIDON PRESS colophon is a trademark
of Simon & Schuster Inc.

Permissions Acknowledgments appear on page 517.

Designed by Karolina Harris
Manufactured in the United States of America

1   3   5   7   9   10   8   6   4   2

Library of Congress Cataloging-in-Publication Data

Bobrick, Benson, date.
East of the Sun : the epic conquest and tragic history of Siberia / Benson Bobrick.
p.   cm.
Includes bibliographical references and index.
1. Siberia (Russia)—History.   I. Title.
DK761.B6   1992
957—dc20   92-24138
                                                                                      CIP

ISBN 0-671-66755-6

Title page: A caravan of dogsleds in northern Kamchatka
(eighteenth-century lithograph)

PREFATORY NOTE
AND ACKNOWLEDGMENTS

In an obvious way, this book is a chronological sequel to my biography of Ivan the Terrible, whose reign was drawing to its close when the conquest of Siberia began. But topically its genesis was otherwise.

In 1929, my mother took the Trans-Siberian Railroad alone, at age twenty, from Moscow to Vladivostok, and from there traveled on to Seoul, Korea, to meet her father, who was then a missionary in the Far East. The year before he had been elected a Bishop of the Methodist Church with episcopal supervision over Japan, Korea, and Manchuria; four years later his jurisdiction was extended to Southeast Asia.

He had many stories to tell of still-exotic lands, and I grew up with a fascinated secondhand acquaintance—fleshed out by some wonderful old photographs—of Asia and the Far East. But missing from this panorama was always Asia's northern third—Siberia, the most mysterious of all—and a part of Russia, a land of my heritage on my father's side. My mother died before I was old enough to ask her about what she had seen, and so her journey formed part of the mystery to me of who she was. By retracing her steps, I suppose, and by learning everything I could about northern Asia, I vicariously embarked upon an imaginary conversation with her of the most far-reaching kind. My quest took me to Moscow and St. Petersburg, into Central Asia, and back and forth across Siberia from the Urals to the Sea of Japan. The rest is history.

Generally speaking, authors try to write the sort of books they like to read, and the penalty they pay for this compulsion is knowing more keenly than anyone else how far short of their own ideal their efforts fall. But whatever the shortcomings of this book, nothing can diminish the generosity of the help it received. My agent Russell Galen, Kathleen Anderson (my original and inspired editor at Poseidon), and Elaine Pfefferblit, her splendid successor, helped foster the work and carry it forward on their shoulders with their enthusiasm and encouragement; my publisher, Ann Patty, never faltered in her support. Others at Poseidon were excellent too: Toni Rachiele, Frank Metz, Ann Adelman (who copyedited the text with admirable care), and Laura Demanski, who expertly attended to numerous details. Karolina Harris developed the book's handsome design.

I am also indebted to the staffs of the Butler Library of Columbia University, the New York Public Library, the American Museum of Natural History, the Library of Congress, the Irkutsk State University Library, and the Miklukho-Maklay Institute of Ethnology in St. Petersburg.

With habitual efficiency, Loren McAuley typed up hundreds of pages of my notes; Diana Rodriguez did that and more: her faith in the project was a precious source of strength.

My brother, Jim, helped school me in useful material to consult about the Gulag.

Numerous friends and colleagues also lent a timely hand, including Vitaly Chepaukin, Justin Creedy-Smith, Larisa Glazkova, Svetlana Gorokhova, Hugh Graham, Peter Guttmacher, Brenda Horrigan, Daniel Kinnunen, Inna Kuzovenko, Steven Marks, Viktor Mernick, Jonathan Olson, Patricia Polansky, Eugenia Samoilenko, Yevgeny Shabanov, Anne Sweeney, Elena Ushakova, and Elena Yakovchenko.

Finally, I might say that as the book neared completion, I often thought of a long conversation I had four years ago with an elderly Uzbek—a man with a face like the ancient of days—one afternoon in Samarkand. We sat together under the shade of a towering fig tree for several hours outside the great Ulughbek Observatory built in 1428–29, and as he stood up to take his courteous farewell, he said to me, "You have not wasted my time." I should like nothing better than that the reader should say as much.

Brooklyn, New York
July 4, 1992

For Sherry

&

In Memory of My Mother,
who bravely crossed Siberia alone
in 1929

CONTENTS

PART FOUR

SIBERIA
AND THE ALEUTIAN ISLANDS

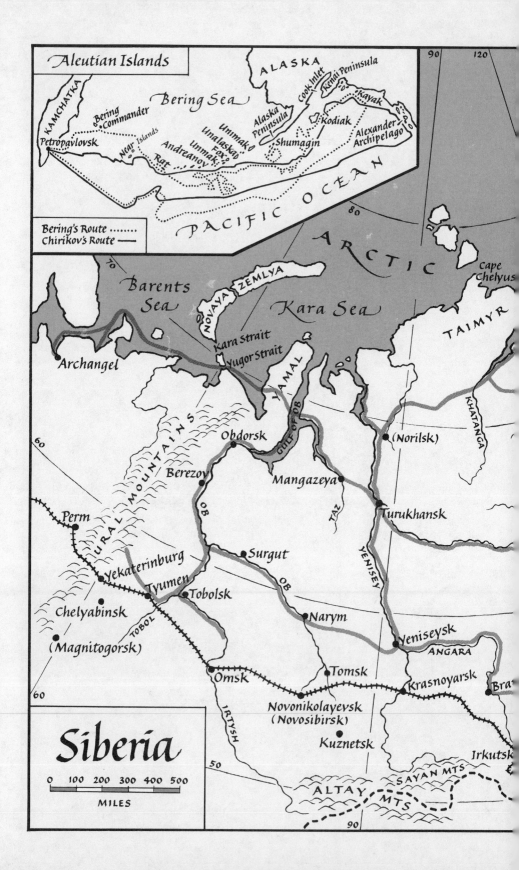

Aleutian Islands

ALASKA

Bering Sea

KAMCHATKA

Bering
Commander

Cook Inlet
Kenai Peninsula

Kayak

Petropavlovsk

Near Islands

Andreanov

Rat

Unimak
Unalaska
Fox
Umnak

Alaska
Peninsula

Shumagin

Kodiak

Alexander
Archipelago

PACIFIC OCEAN

Bering's Route ·······
Chirikov's Route ——

ARCTIC

90

120

80

70

Barents
Sea

NOVAYA ZEMLYA

Kara Sea

Cape
Chelyus

Archangel

Kara Strait

Yugor Strait

YAMAL

GULF OF OB

TAIMYR

KHATANGA

60

URAL MOUNTAINS

Obdorsk

Berezov

(Norilsk)

Perm

OB

Mangazeya

TAZ

Turukhansk

Yekaterinburg

Tyumen

Surgut

OB

YENISEY

Tobolsk

Chelyabinsk

TOBOL

Narym

(Magnitogorsk)

IRTYSH

Omsk

Tomsk

Yeniseysk

ANGARA

Krasnoyarsk

Bra

Novonikolayevsk
(Novosibirsk)

Kuznetsk

Irkutsk

Siberia

SAYAN MTS

ALTAY
MTS

0 100 200 300 400 500

MILES

50

90

60

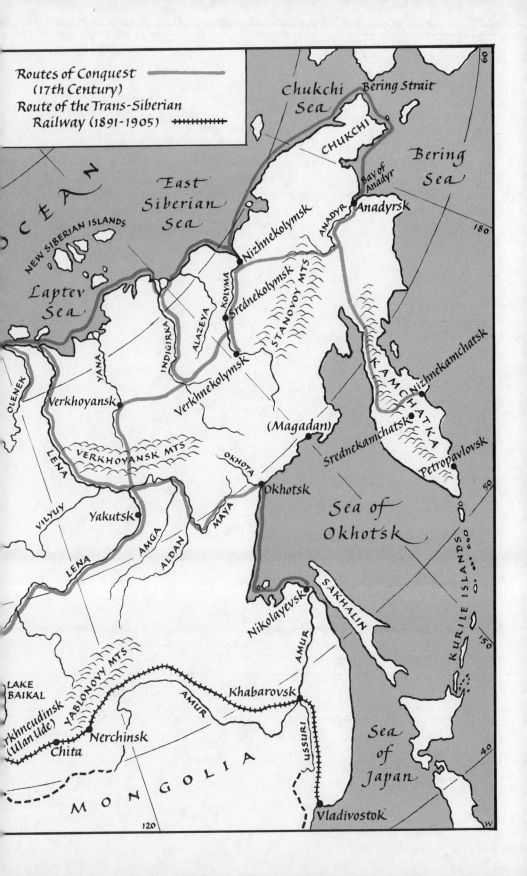

Routes of Conquest ————
  (17th Century)
Route of the Trans-Siberian
  Railway (1891-1905) +++++++++

60

Chukchi
Sea

Bering Strait

CHUKCHI

Bering
Sea

OCEAN

East
Siberian
Sea

NEW SIBERIAN ISLANDS

Bay of
Anadyr

Anadyrsk

ANADYR

180

Laptev
Sea

Nizhnekolymsk

Srednekolymsk

STANOVOY MTS

KOLYMA

ALAZEYA

INDIGIRKA

Verkhnekolymsk

OLENEK

YANA

Verkhoyansk

KAMCHATKA

Nizhnekamchatsk

(Magadan)

VERKHOYANSK MTS

LENA

OKHOTA

Srednekamchatsk

Petropavlovsk

50

VILYUY

Yakutsk

AMGA

ALDAN

MAYA

Okhotsk

Sea of
Okhotsk

LENA

KURILE ISLANDS

150

Nikolayevsk

SAKHALIN

AMUR

LAKE
BAIKAL

YABLONOVY MTS

Khabarovsk

AMUR

Sea
of
Japan

40

rkhneudinsk
(Ulan Ude)

Chita

Nerchinsk

USSURI

M O N G O L I A

Vladivostok

120

W

CHRONOLOGY

1581	Yermak crosses the Urals
1582	Capture of Isker, capital of Sibir
1585	Founding of the first Russian town in Siberia
1591	First exiles arrive in Siberia
1639	Russians reach the Pacific
1647	Invasion of the Amur River Valley begins
1648	Semyon Dezhnev rounds the northeastern cape of Asia
1682	Peter the Great crowned (as co-tsar with half-brother, Ivan)
1689	Treaty of Nerchinsk
1697	Conquest of Kamchatka
1716	First crossing of the Sea of Okhotsk
1725	Vitus Bering's First Expedition
1733	Bering's Second Expedition
July 1741	Discovery of Alaska
1743	Conquest of Aleutian Islands begins
1783	First Russian colony founded on Kodiak Island, Alaska
1799	Russian-American Company receives its charter
1803	Aleksandr Baranov sets sail for Alaska
1803	Russia's first around-the-world voyage
1804	Russia's first mission to Japan

1812	Founding of Ross Colony, north of San Francisco
1815	Hawaiian Islands claimed for the tsar
1823	Monroe Doctrine proclaimed
1825	Decembrist revolt
1847	Nikolay Muravyev appointed governor-general of Siberia
1849	The navigability of the lower Amur discovered; Sakhalin found to be an island
1853	Outbreak of the Crimean War
1856	Muravyev claims the Amur for the tsar
1858	Treaty of Aigun
1860	Treaty of Peking and the founding of Vladivostok
1867	Russia sells Alaska to the United States
1891	Trans-Siberian Railway begun
1896	Chinese Eastern Railway begun
1898	Russia leases Port Arthur
1899	Exile system declared abolished
1904–5	Russo-Japanese War
January 9, 1905	"Bloody Sunday"
1905	Treaty of Portsmouth
1908	Amur Railway begun
1914	Outbreak of World War I
February–March 1917	Fall of Nicholas II
October 25, 1917	Bolsheviks seize power in Petrograd
March 1918	Treaty of Brest-Litovsk
April 1918	Beginning of the Allied Intervention and the Russian Civil War
May 1918	Uprising of the Czechoslovak Corps
June 1918	Beginning of "War Communism"
November 1918	Aleksandr Kolchak proclaimed "Supreme Ruler of Russia"
Winter 1919–20	Defeat of Kolchak and other White armies
April 1920	Founding of Far Eastern Republic
March 1921	Adoption of New Economic Policy, or NEP
April 2, 1922	Joseph Stalin elected Party General Secretary
October 1922	Japanese withdraw from Vladivostok
October 1928	Inauguration of the First Five-Year Plan

December 1929	End of NEP; beginning of collectivization
1930	Beginning of the Soviet concentration camp system, or Gulag
December 1, 1934	Assassination of Sergey Kirov
1937–38	"Great Terror"
June 1941	Germany attacks Soviet Union
August 8, 1945	Soviet Union declares war on Japan
January 1953	"Doctors' Plot"
March 5, 1953	Death of Stalin
September 1953	Khrushchev elected Party First Secretary
1954	Construction begins on Bratsk Dam
February 1956	Khrushchev's secret report on Stalin's crimes
February 1958	Collective farm machine and tractor stations abolished
November 1962	Solzhenitsyn's *One Day in the Life of Ivan Denisovich* published by *Novy mir*
November 1963	Plans completed for a "Unified Energy System" for Siberia
October 14, 1964	Khrushchev ousted; replaced by Brezhnev
September 1966	Penal Code revised to facilitate a crackdown on dissidents
March 1969	Fighting on the Sino-Soviet frontier
February 1974	Solzhenitsyn expelled from the Soviet Union after the Paris publication of his *Gulag Archipelago*
1974	Baikal-Amur Mainline, or BAM, revived
November 1982	Death of Brezhnev; succeeded by Andropov
February 1984	Death of Andropov; succeeded by Chernenko
March 1985	Death of Chernenko; succeeded by Gorbachev
Summer 1985	*Perestroika* and *Glasnost* launched
1991	Dissolution of the Soviet Union

A NOTE ON NAMES AND DATES

There are currently in use a variety of standard systems for the transliteration of Russian names into English. Nevertheless, each one seems to require its own exceptions. In this book the soft sign, usually represented by an apostrophe, has been omitted, and anglicized (if not always English) forms have been used for ease of recognition and pronunciation. The names of rulers, however, following a sensible convention, are always given in their English form—for example, Catherine (not Katerina) the Great.

Dates throughout (until the last few chapters) are given according to the Julian calendar in use in Western Europe until 1582, but in Russia from 1700 until January 26, 1918. In the seventeenth, eighteenth, and nineteenth centuries that calendar was, respectively, ten, eleven, and twelve days behind the Gregorian calendar adopted by the West. (In Russian America, however, the lag was thirteen days until the delineation of the International Date Line in 1869.)

This desert soil
Wants not her hidden lustre, gems and gold.

—JOHN MILTON, *Paradise Lost*

If you would understand Russia, and interpret
and forecast aright the march of great events,
never forget that, for her, eastward the march of
empire takes its way; that as the sap rises, as the
sparks fly upward, as the tides follow the moon,
so Russia goes to the sunrise.

—HENRY NORMAN, *All the Russias*

PART ONE

Overleaf: Tungus family.

1

THE SLEEPING LAND

Toward the end of the sixteenth century, Russia lay in ruins. War, famine, plague, and police-state terror under Ivan the Terrible, Russia's first tsar, had depopulated the interior; Moscow itself had been burned to the ground. Its troops in retreat, contained to the west by Poland and a resurgent Sweden, and to the south by the Crimean Tartars backed by the Ottoman Turks, Russia turned to the east, where Siberia, "mysterious and far-extending, opened her arms." By an accident of history comparable to Columbus's discovery of America, a relatively minor frontier action led, within the space of a few generations, to the conquest and occupation of a territory larger than the Roman Empire.

So sudden was the acquisition that Russia never quite managed to take full account of what it possessed; yet today that vast territory—the richest resource area on the face of the earth—is the hope of Russia's desperate future and the world's last true frontier.

Siberia, as the Russians first encountered it, was a geological and anthropological wonder. Although part of it resembled the European Russian north, and its level marshlands to the south continued the endless sweep of the Eastern European plain, it was a subcontinent apart, and aside from its western margins, unknown except by name. Large mountain ranges cut across it to the south and east, majestic volcanoes on its far horizons formed part of the Pacific rim of fire, and its mighty rivers, rivals to the Mississippi and the Nile, could, if linked together, encircle the globe twenty-five times. Each one of its three major river basins was larger than the whole of Western Europe. In climate, it ranged from the Arctic to the semi-tropical, supported animals as diverse as camels and polar bears, and shared latitudes with areas as distant as Thule, Greenland, and Marseilles. Five million square miles, or about 7.5 percent of the total land surface of the globe, lay within its compass, from the Urals to the Pacific, and from Mongolia to the Arctic seas. In trying to imagine what this means, one nineteenth-century explorer remarked:

> If it were possible to move entire countries from one part of the globe to another, you could take the whole United States of America from Maine to California and from Lake Superior to the Gulf of Mexico, and set it down in the middle of Siberia, without touching anywhere the boundaries of the latter territory. You could then take Alaska and all the States of Europe, with the single exception of Russia, and fit them into the remaining margin like the pieces of a dissected map; and after having thus accommodated all of the United States, including Alaska, and all of Europe, except Russia, you would still have more than 300,000 square miles of Siberian territory to spare.

Siberia also included perhaps the oldest place on earth, north of Mongolia around Lake Baikal. At the turn of the century, an expedition to the area searched for traces of the Garden of Eden, and although the Siberian north might seem inimical to the ever-green idea of a garden of earthly delights, in its natural resources, in fact, Siberia would prove beyond compare. Two parables explain the paradoxical plenitude of its ice-bound wealth. One wittily provides that in distributing earth's bounty across the land, the hands of God momentarily froze as they passed over Siberia and let riches fall upon it in disproportionately large amounts. But another holds that when God saw that man was not worthy of the wealth he had provided, he froze it and locked it away in frosty desolation, and made the land itself lifeless in expiation of Adam's sins. "Siberia" itself is a mystical term, derived from the Mongolian *siber* ("beautiful," "wonderful," and "pure"), and the Tartar *sibir,* which means "the sleeping land."

The sleeping beauty at its heart was Lake Baikal, the oldest lake in the world, the largest fresh-water lake by volume (with about a fifth of the fresh water on the surface of the globe), and the deepest continental body on earth. Fed by some 336 tributary rivers and streams, it formed a crescent nearly 400 miles long, yet had an isolated ecosystem comparable to that of the Galápagos Islands, where the path of evolution could still be traced. Of its 1,700 indigenous species of plant and animal life, 1,200 were unique—including a fish called the *golomyanka,* which gave birth to live young. Baikal also had tens of thousands of fresh-water seals—although the nearest ocean was 1,000 miles away. To ancient Chinese chroniclers, however, it was known as the "Northern Ocean," and revered by a number of Siberian tribes as the "Holy Sea." Even the Russians, who developed various superstitions about its sudden, apparently willful storms (whipped up by winds sweeping down from its volcanic ramparts), would say that "it is only upon Baikal in autumn that a man learns to pray from his heart."

The overall topography of Siberia divided rather neatly into three broad horizontal zones. To the north lay a great treeless tundra, extending along the whole Arctic coast from Novaya Zemlya to Bering Strait; through the middle stretched a broad belt of forest from the Ural Mountains to the Okhotsk Sea; and to the south, arable land that shaded into semi-arid desert steppes from the southern Urals to beyond the Mongolian frontier.

Inhospitable and desolate, the desert-dry tundra was covered for most of the year by trackless wastes of snow. Nothing grew upon it but tufts of coarse grass or swards of moss and lichen, and fierce Arctic gales, known as purgas, drifted and packed and scored its snowy surface into long, hard, fluted waves. Underneath was a thick substratum of "geological ice" or permafrost—eternally frozen ground—that was so deep in places as to be "centrally defeated only by the heat from the earth's hot core." In summer, the ground thawed to a depth of just a few feet, and below that was impervious to water, and hard as iron. In a sense, each spring it rained upward, since evaporation was the only way water could escape. As melting snow saturated the topsoil, over time it had become covered with a dense, luxuriant growth of gray Arctic moss. "Moss had grown out of decaying moss, year after year," until the whole tundra had become "one vast, spongy bog."

Along the tundra's southernmost margins, some trees took root, but in the shallow soil they assumed grotesquely horizontal forms. The dwarf or trailing cedar grew "like a neglected vine along the ground," and other trees became remarkably gnarled and twisted from ever-turning toward the meager Arctic light. As they revolved upon themselves, their short, knotty trunks appeared in time as if entwined "with terrible growths like splints on broken bones."

Set against this arboreal grotesque was a landscape that also at times looked as though it had been designed by a fastidious Creator devoted to geometry. By a process still mysterious, but connected to the alternate thawing and freezing, expanding and contracting of the soil, the early summer melt collected into perfectly round lakes, and stones squeezed to the surface were often arranged in neat, decorously concentric circles, with the larger stones on the periphery and the smaller stones within. Ice-wedges, made by melt-water trickling into cracks or frost-fissures, also broke the soil into exactly drawn, even-sided polygons.

On the fringe of the tundra, 200 to 400 miles inland from the coast, the primeval coniferous forest, or taiga, began. Scattered larches, groping for a patch of thawed ground, appeared first; and then, by degrees, came denser stands of spruce, fir, cedar, birch, and pine, until their intertwining branches formed a thick canopy above the forest floor. The heart of the taiga was bathed in twilight even at noon, but its greater enchantment lay in the thousands upon thousands of miles of its extent—"only migrating birds," wrote Chekhov, "know where it ends." In contrast to the limited wildlife of the tundra (the reindeer, polar bear, lemming, and Arctic fox), the taiga teemed with brown and black bear, wolves, sables, squirrel, polecats, stoats, lynx, elk, hare, wild boar, badgers, wolverine, and hundreds of species of birds, including ducks and geese.

The taiga gradually passed into a mixed forest zone of poplars, aspens, elms, maples, and limes, which in turn thinned out toward the southern steppes, rich in arable and pastureland. In places the Western Siberian steppe was as fertile as the black earth of the Ukraine. On its margins, however, it turned to sand, and for 2,000 miles Southern Siberia skirted a "land of summer snow" where thick deposits of salt broiled beneath a desert sun.

Siberia's temperature variations, indeed, touched both extremes, not only north and south, but within the same locale. Even in the upper latitudes, brief summers could be almost as hot as the winters were severe, and at Oimyakon, "the world's pole of cold," on the Upper Indigirka River, temperatures could drop to −90 degrees, yet climb toward 100 in July.

Interrupting the broad horizontal zones of tundra, taiga, and steppe were several great mountain ranges—the Altay, Sayan, Yablonovy, Stanovoy, and Verkhoyansk, and the volcanic system of Kamchatka. The Altay swept from the West Siberian Plain to the Gobi Desert of Mongolia, and the Sayan from the Altay to Lake Baikal. The Yablonovy, commencing in Mongolia, crossed the frontier and divided Transbaikalia (between Lake Baikal and the upper Amur) into two great terraces of almost equal size. The Verkhoyansk formed a huge arc east of and parallel to the Lena River that reached to the Laptev Sea. In the Far East, the Stanovoy arose on the Chinese frontier, closely followed the Okhotsk Sea coast northward, and with its white peaks marked the southern boundary of Kamchatka at the head of the Penzhina Gulf. Kamchatka in turn was divided by a spine of rugged volcanic summits that formed an almost continuous ridge, culminating in "the monarch of Siberian mountains," the Klyuchevskaya Volcano, towering to 16,000 feet. Along the whole Far Eastern coast, in fact, various ranges broke off into the sea in great shattered headlands and cliffs, where violent earthquakes, volcanic eruptions, and other cataclysms and deluges of the past had severed them from summits to which they had once been joined on the Northwest Pacific Coast. In between were left chains of volcanic islands whose bare, precipitous coasts appeared similarly sundered and torn.

From the mountains of Southern Siberia, the glaciers of the Altay, and the borderlands of Mongolia arose Siberia's three great river systems—the Ob, the Yenisey, and the Lena—each among the mightiest and most majestic rivers in the world. Giving off numerous lateral tributaries to the east and west, they wound northward for thousands of miles toward the Arctic to ultimately release their torrents into ice-laden seas. Siberia's fourth great river was the Amur, which formed on the Mongolian Plateau south of Lake Baikal, and flowed east-by-northeast in a series of great bends to its outlet on the coast of the Pacific between the Sea of Okhotsk and the Sea of Japan. Opposite the Amur's mouth lay the island of Sakhalin, and to Sakhalin's south and east the Kurile Island chain.

Still other rivers of importance lay along the Arctic coast—the Indigirka, Yana, and Kolyma—and (toward the Bering Sea) the Anadyr. Extending offshore, or scattered through the Arctic seas, were also fantastic islands and huge appendages of land, like Novaya Zemlya; the Yamal Peninsula ("ultimate land," in the language of the Samoyeds); the Taimyr Peninsula (the size of California and the northernmost extension of Eurasia); and island clusters like the Lyakhov and New Siberian where the soil was nothing but "a mixture of sand and ice and ivory and the petrified remains of giant prehistoric trees."

All this was Siberia.

In 1928, a peasant digging a cellar for his house in Siberia's northeast discovered an underground Paleolithic home in which mammoth tusks and sundry animal bones "pressed down at the base with limestone plates," furnished the foundation. Reindeer antlers meshed together provided scaffolding for the roof, and in the middle of the dwelling was a hearth with an oval grave where a child had been elaborately interred. Among the many ornaments found with the remains were a headband resembling "the well-known diadems worn by ancient kings," and a carved pendant depicting a bird in flight. Examination of the skull revealed a double row of teeth, a defect that may account for the child's sepulchral splendor, since deformity was once associated with supernatural powers.

Nearly prehistoric settlements have also been discovered from the Ob to the Transbaikal, and the remnants of Neolithic abodes exist all over Siberia. Inscriptions and pictographs on the cliffs and stratified palisades of the Yenisey River are of great antiquity, as are rock drawings along the Lena River that include a giant horse, wild bison, and two elk. Such finds offer a partial (if indeterminate) glimpse into the story of Siberia's remote past.

During the Pleistocene Epoch (when mountain glaciers covered much of the territory and the whole of its northwestern plain was locked in a glacial sheet), "huge, stooping mammoths, with yellowish upturned tusks," wandered up from northern India into South-Central Siberia, where they browsed upon the greenery and flowers that had begun to come forth in patches across the steeply rolling terrain. In that prehistoric animal kingdom were also the wooly rhinoceros, wild bison, saber-toothed tiger, and steppeland antelope or saiga, the last of which survives in Central Asia to this day.

As the glaciers receded, vast inland seas formed and trees flourished in the Arctic, for the stomachs of some of the recovered mammoths contain vegetation (like buttercups) now growing far to the south of where they died. Over many thousands of years, Siberia's landscape changed. The seas disappeared, there was a reelevation of the land, and major rivers formed. People began to settle along their banks and make for themselves some kind of home. The wolf was domesticated into the dog, timber used for dwellings, and the Siberian hunter improved his stone tools, fashioning bows and arrows out of wood, harpoons out of reindeer antlers, and fishhooks out of bone. He also began to experiment with different kinds of arrowheads and spears, and along the rivers learned how to make light and highly maneuverable birchbark canoes. By the end of the Neolithic period, the whole of northern Asia was inhabited, most densely around Lake Baikal in the heart of the taiga. From the forests the hunter ventured northward into the tundra, reached the shores of the Arctic Ocean, and set up collapsible, tall conical skin tents—a prototype of the familiar tepee that later spread to America's shores.

The first metal tools appeared around 2000 B.C.—knives, needles, and fishhooks cold-forged out of native copper found by hunters in the mountains. Much later, the natives developed molds made of clay and used them to cast knives and swords. By the beginning of the second millennium B.C., tribes of cattle breeders roamed the steppes of Western Siberia and began to cultivate the soil, using a stone hoe and grinding the grain by hand. Horse cultures also developed, and during the Bronze Age, the people living in the Minusinsk Basin (an oasis in the upper part of the Yenisey River Valley between the Sayan and Altay mountains) acquired such skill in metalwork that the collection of bronze implements from their burial mounds is said to give "a more complete representation of the progress of art in the bronze age, and of the transition from the use of bronze to the use of iron, than is to be found anywhere else in the world."

In the sixth century A.D., a people of Turkic stock founded a powerful empire centered in Mongolia, dominated by the Uighurs, who headed a tribal confederation known in Chinese annals as the Nine Clans. They carried on trade with China and spread through the Yenisey Valley, where they built great tumuli, adorned with monoliths, over their dead. Although originally pastoral nomads, the Uighurs became fine agriculturists, irrigating wide tracts of land by means of canals that more modern settlers have rediscovered and utilized. In the ninth century, however, another Turkic people, the Kirghiz, coming from the upper reaches of the Yenisey, put an end to their power. Of Europoid ethnic stock, the Yenisey Kirghiz were able farmers, skilled in handicrafts, including metalware, and carried on a brisk trade with the Tibetans and Chinese. They also had a runic system of writing, which survives in fragmentary inscriptions on clay vessels, tombstones, and stone idols decorated with symbols of the sun.

In the thirteenth century, the Mongol cavalry of Genghis Khan (the legendary warrior who united scattered Mongol tribes under his mighty rule) charged into the Transbaikal and swept westward across Siberia, pillaging the local tribes and wreaking havoc on their way of life. Within a short time, the dominion of the Mongols had been extended over much of Asia, including parts of China and India, and over all of Siberia (except the extreme north). Continuing their conquest westward, the Mongols passed the southern spur of the Altay Mountains to the plains of Central Asia and drove down into "the Land of the Seven Rivers and the Thousand Springs." Overrunning Russia (at the time made up of a number of feudal principalities), their immediate legacy was one of horror and blood. After the capture of Ryazan, one contemporary wrote: "The prince, with his mother, wife, sons, the boyars, and the inhabitants, without regard to age or sex, were slaughtered with savage cruelty; some were impaled, some shot at with arrows for sport, some were flayed or had nails or splinters of wood driven under their nails. Priests were roasted alive, and nuns and maidens ravished in the churches before their relatives. No eye remained open to weep for the dead." In 1240, advancing toward Europe, the Mongols captured Kiev, razed the city to the ground, and subjected the people to indiscriminate massacre. Only the death of Ogdai, Genghis Khan's successor, brought the onslaught to an end. In the administrative division of the Mongol Empire, Western Siberia and Russia both belonged to the Golden Horde; but its imperium was too decentralized to last. Russia eventually freed itself from the Mongol yoke in 1480, and the Horde's succession states were born.

· · ·

At the time the Russians prepared to cross the Urals—the long if attenuated divide between Europe and northern Asia—140-odd native peoples had already made Siberia their home. Pastoral nomads roamed the southwestern steppes with their herds of cattle and sheep; forest nomads hunted and fished in the taiga; and in the northern tundra, reindeer nomads drove their great herds along fixed routes. Only the most elementary agriculture was practiced (in the Amur River Valley), while in the extreme northeast were primitive tribes who hunted wild reindeer or lived off whales, walruses, and seals along the shores of the Bering and Okhotsk seas. Some of the tribes roaming the steppes and forests had emerged from the Iron Age and developed links with China and Central Asia, while the inhabitants of the tundra and Arctic regions belonged to Stone Age tribes. Most of the natives (numbering altogether about a quarter of a million people) belonged to five broad ethnic, linguistic groups: Turkic, Manchu-Tungus, Finno-Ugrian, Mongol, and the so-called "Paleosiberian," of predominantly Mongoloid stock. The Paleosiberians (the descendants of the prehistoric inhabitants) were principally the Chukchi, Yukaghir, Koryak, Asiatic Eskimo, and Kamchadal in the northeast; the "Yenisey Ostyak," or Ket, on the lower Yenisey; the Gilyak (or Nivkh) on the Amur and Sakhalin; and the mysteriously Caucasian, "hairy" Ainu in southern Sakhalin and the Kurile Islands.

Most Paleosiberians tended to be short and compact, with broad, flat, beardless faces, prominent cheekbones, small, rather sunken eyes, and nasal cavities that were exceptionally narrow, apparently to protect their lungs from large draughts of freezing air. The physical, cultural, and anthropological links between these people and Native Americans are regarded by anthropologists as incontrovertible, and it is believed that perhaps 25,000 years ago Siberians crossed over from Asia to America by way of an isthmus connecting the two continents across the Bering Sea.

From the third century on, Neosiberian tribes began to join the aboriginal inhabitants—the Finno-Ugrian Voguls, Ostyaks, and Samoyeds; Turkic tribes (like the Yakuts and Tartars); the Manchu-Tungus; and the Mongol-Buryats. The semi-nomadic Ostyaks and Voguls inhabited the forests and marshes of the Ob-Irtysh Basin; the reindeer-herding Samoyed roamed the Yamal and Taimyr peninsulas and the tundra west of the Yenisey; the Yakuts inhabited the Lena Valley, with settlements along the headwaters of the Yana, Indigirka, and Kolyma rivers; and the Tungus were found from the Yenisey Valley east to the Pacific Ocean. Cousin to the Tungus were the Lamuts on the shores of the Sea of Okhotsk, and the Goldi and the Daurs in the Amur River Valley. Finally, in the thirteenth and fourteenth centuries the Buryats had established themselves in areas of steppeland around the southern end of Lake Baikal.

Aside from the Moslem Tartars, all the peoples of Siberia were pagans, and belonged to clans or other pretribal kinship groups, or to tribes linked by reciprocal marriage relations. The Buryats and Yakuts (both descendants of Central Asian pastoral nomads) were easily the most advanced; they kept cattle and horses, and had clan chiefs. But the reindeer-herding peoples had no institutionalized hierarchy and congregated regularly, as small family bands, only for councils and seasonal rituals, or to share the fruits of their hunt. Yet it often happened that "all the efforts of man were not enough to wrench from raw nature the necessary bit of food." In the far north, the domestication of the reindeer compelled a wandering life, as the Samoyeds, Koryaks, Chukchi, and other tundra nomads followed their great herds from place to place, pausing only for so long as it took the animals to paw up the snow for moss around their encampment. None led lives more lonely than the Koryak of northern Kamchatka, who roamed over the great moss-covered steppes, as one observer put it, "high up among extinct volcanic peaks, 4,000 feet above the sea, enveloped half the time in drifting clouds, and swept by frequent storms of rain and snow."

2

CROSSING THE DIVIDE

ALTHOUGH by the end of the sixteenth century, because of explorations east and west, a large part of the world had been intelligibly mapped, Siberia had escaped the broad sphere of Renaissance discoveries because the ice-laden seas along its northern coast had proved impassable to mariners searching for China or "Cathay." Contemporary maps labeled northern Asia as "Great Tartary," but gave it perfunctory dimensions without geographical detail, so that it lingered as a cartographical convention from the ancient division of the landmass of the world into the three distinct continents of Europe, Africa, and Asia. The Ob River (thought to have its source in the Aral Sea) represented the eastern limit of the known world as discovered from the west, and whatever Great Tartary held in store was imaginatively (if decoratively) depicted by mapmakers according to the stories or legends they had heard. Their arbitrary typography was filled in with images of Asiatic nomads amid camels and tents, or showed them worshipping sundry heathen idols or pillars of stone. Accompanying inscriptions occasionally identified them as cannibals, or such as "doe eate serpentes, wormes, and other filth," though other, less shocking customs ascribed to them were simply borrowed from what was already known of certain Central Asian tribes. Plausible conjecture, however, indiscriminately mingled with abiding notions of an other-worldly, strange, and mythological land that extended even to the sunrise—"to the east of the sun, to the most-high mountain Karkaraur, where dwell the one-armed, one-footed folk."

Yet all was not obscure. The territory had been mentioned in the ancient Russian Chronicles—chronological records kept by monastics from the beginning of Russian history—and a fragment of the region (known as Yugra, meaning "the land of the Ostyaks," a local tribe) had long been familiar to Russian merchants trading in furs with tribes along the Ob. In 1236, a certain itinerant Brother Julian alluded to a "land of Sibur, surrounded by the Northern Sea," where natives scalped their victims; and in 1376, St. Stephen of Perm had bravely established a church in the Kama River Valley (still west of the Urals), where a former missionary had been skinned alive. As early as 1455, the state began to give the missionaries military backing, and in 1484 soldiers swept along the frontier. A number of tribal chieftains were captured and a treaty exacted from them which acknowledged Muscovite suzerainty and entailed the payment of tribute. Subsequently the Tartar khanate of western Sibir, a semi-feudal state formed just east of the Urals in the 1420s, when the Mongol Empire was breaking up, had come within the orbit of Muscovite political and military relations. Dominated by the Siberian Tartars, who were descended from one of the Mongol fighting groups (or "hordes"), the khanate included various Turkic-Moslem, Finnic, and Samoyedic tribes and vaguely encompassed a territory that extended east to the Irtysh River and south to the Ishim steppes.

In 1555, the khan acknowledged the suzerainty of Ivan the Terrible, who promptly if prematurely incorporated "Tsar of Sibir" into the tedious roll call of honorific titles appended to his name. Meanwhile, Muscovites had become familiar with the northern sea route from Archangel to the Urals at their northern end. However, it was not until after the capture of Kazan (another Mongol succession state on the middle Volga) that a route into the khanate was opened from the south. Yet no one knew that beyond the Ob, Greater Siberia comprised the whole of northern Asia between the Urals and the Pacific Ocean. This was as unimaginable to the most daring Russian explorer as the Pacific Ocean itself had been to Balboa and his men.

Although a coherent, if loosely confederated, state, bolstered by a trade that reached along ancient caravan routes from Russia to western China, the khanate of Sibir had been living on borrowed time. As the might of its Slavic neighbor grew, Sibir was also continually torn within by strife between the Mohammedan Tartars (who had converted to Islam in 1272) and other ethnic groups. These groups in turn were plagued by intertribal hostilities (chiefly between the Ostyaks and Voguls), while from the khanate's founding there had also been a dynastic struggle among the Tartar nobility between the Sheibanids (descendants of Genghis Khan) and the Taibugids, heirs of a local prince. Nevertheless, until 1552 at least, Sibir had little to fear from the Russians because between them stood the Tartar khanate of Kazan. But in 1552, that buffer state fell to Ivan the Terrible's armies, and three years later the ruling Taibugid prince, Yediger, prudently agreed to pay Ivan an annual tribute in furs. Partly as a result of that unpopular decision, Yediger was deposed and killed in 1563 at his capital of Isker, on the banks of the Irtysh, by Khan Kuchum, who claimed descent from Genghis Khan. Kuchum surrounded himself with a palace guard composed of Uzbeks, purged the local leadership of opponents, and with the aid of mullahs from Bukhara tried to impose Islam on the restless pagan tribes. In 1571, with Russia apparently in the throes of its own dissolution, he renounced the tribute to Moscow, and two years later sent a punitive expedition against the Ostyaks in Perm (west of the Urals) who had recognized Russian suzerainty. Emboldened by Moscow's lack of response, in 1579 he also intercepted and killed a Muscovite envoy en route to Central Asia.

During the long Livonian War (1557–81), in which Ivan the Terrible tried to batter his way to the Baltic, the government had entrusted the defense of its eastern frontier and Urals dominions to the Stroganovs, a powerful family of industrial magnates and financiers. Descended— according to legend—from a christened Tartar by the name of Spiridon, who had introduced the abacus into Russia, their wealth was founded on salt, ore, grain, and furs (the mainstays of the economy), and their assets and properties, accumulated through shrewd dealing over the course of two centuries, extended from Ustyug and Vologda to Kaluga and Ryazan. They traded with the English and Dutch on the Kola Peninsula, established commercial links with Central Asia, and had foreign agents who traveled on their behalf as far afield as Antwerp and Paris.

Although their enterprise was originally centered on their saltworks at Solvychegodsk (Russia's "Salt Lake City"), a rapid series of land grants secured the family's absolute commercial domination of the Russian northeast. The charter of 1558 (which gave them access to much of Perm, on the Upper Kama River almost to the Urals) served as a model for the rest. In each case, in return for long-term tax-exempt status for themselves and their colonists, the Stroganovs pledged to fund and develop industries, break the soil for agriculture, train and equip a frontier guard, prospect for ore and mineral deposits, and mine whatever was found. They enjoyed jurisdiction over the local population, and had the right to protect their holdings with garrisoned stockades and forts equipped with artillery. Thus, a lengthening chain of military outposts and watchtowers soon dotted the river route to the east.

As colonization advanced to the foot of the Urals, the Stroganovs endeavored to subject to their authority a number of native tribes, such as the Voguls and the Ostyaks, who lived on both sides of the mountains. The natives fought back; destroyed crops; attacked villages, saltworks, and flour mills; and massacred settlers on the Urals' western slopes. Soldiers were sent in to quell these uprisings, but they could not long be spared from the tsar's beleaguered western fronts.

Daring prospectors had meanwhile located deposits of silver and iron ore east of the Urals on the Tura River, and it was supposed, not erroneously, that the same district contained sulfur, lead, and tin. Scouts had also seen the rich pastures by the Tobol River where the Tartar cattle grazed. In 1574, the Stroganovs petitioned for a new charter "to drive a wedge between the Siberian Tartars and the Nogays" (a tribe to the south) by means of fortified settlements along the Tobol and Tura rivers in return for license to exploit the resources of the land. Moscow, in reaction to Kuchum's aggression, obliged; and in a singular measure (impelled by the manpower drain of the Livonian War), the Stroganovs were also permitted to enlist runaways or outlaws in their militia, and to organize and finance a campaign, spearheaded by "hired Cossacks and artillery," against Kuchum "to make him pay the tribute." Those who volunteered for the assignment (according to the government's unblushing recommendation) were to be promised the wives and children of natives as their concubines and slaves.

By "Cossacks" the government meant independent frontiersmen

who staked out a life for themselves along the fringes of the empire. Some were solitary wanderers or half-breeds, others belonged to a turbulent border population of tramps, runaways, religious dissenters, itinerant workers, bandits, and adventurers who had been driven into the no-man's-land of forest or steppe by taxation, famine, debt, repression, and hope of refuge from the long, strong arm of Muscovite law. In the wild country, where they mingled and clashed with the Tartars, adopted Tartar terminology and ways, and gradually displaced certain tribes, they carved out for themselves a new and independent life. In this they lived up to their name, as derived from the Turkish *kazak,* meaning "rebel" or "freeman."

To protect their homesteading communities, some Cossacks had banded together under elected *atamans,* or chieftains, into semi-military confraternities along the Volga, the Dnieper, and the Don. They raided Tartar settlements or poached on Tartar land, preyed on Muscovite river convoys, and ambushed government army patrols sent out to catch them and "hang 'em high." The whole Cossack story, in fact, with its rugged individualism and worship of democracy, its "badmen," posses, cattle rustlers, and so forth, bears comparison with the folkloric picture of the American Wild West. In the simplest and most obvious configuration, the Cossack represented the American pioneer, the Tartar the Red Indian, and the Russian Army the U.S. Cavalry.

The leader of one Cossack band was Vasily (Yermak) Timofeyovich, a third-generation bandit, and the most notorious Volga River pirate of his day. He was a powerfully built man of medium height, with a flat face, black beard, and curly hair; "his associates," according to the Siberian Chronicles, "called him 'Yermak,' after a millstone. And in his military achievements he was great."

Regular army patrols, with gallows erected on rafts, sought to enforce the tsar's authority along the Volga trade route, and a series of expeditions designed to crush or subdue outlaw bands culminated in 1577 in a great sweep along both sides of the river. With the tsar's cavalry in hot pursuit, some fled downstream to the Caspian Sea, others scattered across the steppes, and a third group under Yermak (so the story goes) raced up the Kama River into the wilds of Perm, where they were enthusiastically welcomed into the Stroganovs' frontier guard.

A few years later, exceeding the tsar's commission, the Stroganovs organized an expedition to secure the Kama frontier, bring part of Siberia within their mining monopoly, and to gain access to Siberian furs.

On September 1, 1581, a Cossack army of 840 men—including 300 Livonian prisoners of war, two priests, and a runaway monk impressed into service as a cook—assembled under Yermak on the banks of the Kama River near Orel Goroduk, south of Solikamsk. The official Chronicles tell us that the men set off "singing hymns to the Trinity, to God in his Glory, and to the most immaculate Mother of God," but this is unlikely. Who knows what they sang; but their secular fellowship was given muscle by a rough code of martial law. Anyone guilty of insubordination was bundled head first into a sack, with a bag of sand tied to his chest, and "tipped into the river." Some twenty grumblers were "tipped in" at the start.

Whether the Stroganovs voluntarily provided full assistance to the expedition, or were coerced into supplying its needs, remains a matter of dispute. But they always drove a hard bargain, and evidently intended their aid as a loan, "secured by indentures." The Cossacks, rejecting this, agreed to compensate them from their spoils or, if they failed to return, to redeem their obligations "by prayer in the next world." In after years, this sarcastic pledge would be recast as religious fervor, since the Siberian Chronicles portrayed Yermak's mercenary incursion as a holy crusade against the infidel. "Kuchum," one passage assures us, "led a sinful life. He had 100 wives, and youths as well as maidens, worshipped idols, and ate unclean foods."

Though the army (organized into disciplined companies, each with its own leader and flag) seemed hardly adequate to conquer a khanate, the odds against surviving were not as bad as many thought. While vastly outnumbered, the men were well led, well provisioned (with rye flour, biscuit, buckwheat, roasted oats, butter, and salt pig), and armed to the teeth. Indeed, it was their military superiority through firearms that would prove decisive, as it had for Cortéz in Mexico and Pizarro in Peru.

In flat-bottomed rivercraft called *doshchaniks* (which could be worked by oars, towed from shore, or mounted with a sail), Yermak proceeded along a network of rivers to the foothills of the Urals, portaged 18 miles from the headwaters of the Serebryanka River to the banks of the Tagil (at a site known today as Bear Rock), and there pitched his winter camp. In the spring, floating his boats over the river's shallows by damming the water with sails, he embarked downstream, swung into the Tura River, and for some distance penetrated unmolested into the heart of Kuchum's domain. A skirmish at the mouth of the Tobol proved costly, but it was downstream where the river surged through a ravine that the Tartars laid their trap. Hundreds of warriors hid in the trees on either side of a barrier created with ropes and logs. The first boat struck the barrier at night. The Tartars attacked, but in the enveloping darkness most of Yermak's flotilla managed to escape upstream. At a bend in the river, the Cossacks disembarked, made manikins out of twigs and fallen branches, and propped them up in the boats, with skeleton crews at the oars. The others, half-naked, crept round to surprise the Tartars from behind. At dawn, just as the flotilla floated into view, they opened fire.

The result was a complete rout.

Infuriated, Kuchum resolved to annihilate the intruders before they could reach his capital, even as Yermak knew he had to take the town before winter or his men would perish in the cold. Though so far victorious, their provisions were dwindling, while ambush and disease had already reduced the expeditionary force by half. Still they pressed on, past the meadowlands whitening with hoar frost, and the hardening saltmarshes glazed with ice, toward the tall wooden ramparts of Isker.

The decisive confrontation came in late October, at the confluence of the Tobol and Irtysh rivers, where the Tartars had erected a palisade at the base of a hill. As the Cossacks charged, they fired their muskets into the densely massed defenders with devastating effect. Many of the Tartars, conscripted by force, at once deserted; more fled as the palisade was stormed. This gave the Cossacks a chance. In hand-to-hand combat, the battle raged till evening, 107 Cossacks falling before they prevailed.

On that fateful day, Kuchum is said to have had a vision: "The skies burst open and terrifying warriors with shining wings appeared from the four cardinal points. Descending to the earth they encircled Kuchum's army and cried to him: 'Depart from this land, you infidel son of the dark demon, Mahomet, because now it belongs to the Almighty.' "

A few days later, when the Russians came to Isker itself, they found it deserted, with few of its fabled riches left behind. Instead (for which they were probably more grateful), the men discovered stocks of barley, flour, and dried fish.

Immediately there were scattered defections to the Russian side as Yermak began accepting tribute from former subjects of the khan. But to consolidate his position he needed reinforcements and artillery, and to obtain them he despatched Ivan Koltso (also a renowned bandit, and his second-in-command) with fifty others to Moscow. Traveling on skis and sleds drawn by reindeer, they took the fabled "wolf-path" shortcut over the Urals (up the Tavda River to Cherdyn) disclosed to them by a Tartar chieftain who acted as their guide.

Back in Moscow, however, the expedition was in disgrace. No one yet knew of Yermak's achievement, but they knew that in retaliation for his invasion, the Voguls had been rampaging through the Upper Kama Valley burning Russian settlements to the ground. Evidently on the very same day Yermak set out, Cherdyn was attacked and neighboring villages burned. This had prompted the military governor of Perm to accuse the Stroganovs of leaving the frontier undefended, since in putting their expeditionary force together they had apparently stripped the frontier guard. And in a letter dated November 16, 1582, the tsar bitterly reproved the industrialists for "disobedience amounting to treason." Moreover, in the west, as Ivan's Livonian War was drawing to its humiliating close, Narva had just fallen to the Swedes and the Poles were tightening their blockade on Pskov. This was the situation when Koltso arrived to cheer the gloomy capital with his sensational news. Prostrating himself before the tsar, who had planned to hang him, Koltso announced Yermak's capture of Isker and proclaimed Ivan lord of the khanate. To a stunned court he displayed his convincing spoils, including three captive Tartar nobles and a sledload of pelts (comprising 2,400 sables, 800 black foxes, and 2,000 beaver) equal to five times the annual tribute the khan had paid. Ivan pardoned Koltso on the spot and Yermak in absentia, promised reinforcements, and sent Yermak a magnificent suit of armor embossed with the imperial coat of arms.

At the Kremlin, Koltso kissed the cross in obedience; back in Siberia, Yermak struggled to extend his authority up the Irtysh, as natives were made to swear allegiance by kissing a bloody sword. Those who resisted were hanged upside down by one foot, which meant an agonizing death. Yet in his own way Yermak tried to Christianize the tribes.

In one contest of power, a local wizard ripped open his own stomach with a knife, then miraculously healed the wound by smearing it with grass; Yermak simply tossed the local wooden totems on the fire.

By the end of the summer of 1584, his jurisdiction extended almost to the Ob River. In one daring sortie, he had managed to surprise and capture Kuchum's nephew, Mametkul (in effect, the khan's Minister of War), but meanwhile the Tartar raiders who had attacked Cherdyn and other Russian settlements returned, and by attrition the strength of Yermak's band declined. In November, five hundred long-awaited reinforcements tramped into Isker on snowshoes, but having brought no provisions of their own, rapidly consumed Yermak's reserves. During the long winter, part of the garrison starved, and some "were forced to eat the bodies of their own dead companions." Aware of Yermak's dire circumstances, Kuchum's adherents stepped up attacks on foraging parties in the spring. In two grievous blows to the garrison's hopes for survival, twenty Cossacks were killed as they dozed by a lake, while Koltso and forty others were lured to a friendship banquet and massacred.

In early August 1585, a trap was baited for Yermak himself. Informed that an unescorted caravan from Bukhara was nearing the Irtysh, he hastened with a company of Cossacks to meet it, but finding the report untrue, that night was obliged to bivouac on an island in midstream. A wild storm arose and drove the watchmen into their tents. A party of natives disembarked unobserved, attacked, and killed the Cossacks almost to a man. Yermak managed to struggle into his armor and fight his way to the embankment, but the boat "floated out of his reach," and as he plunged into the water after it, his armor bore him down beneath the waves.

Out of the 1,340 men who had thus advanced into Siberia, no more than 90 remained; this hard-pressed remnant rapidly retreated to the Urals, where as they made their way through a mountain pass, they met a hundred *streltsy* (musketeers) equipped with cannon moving east.

Yermak, of course (whatever the Stroganovs' long-term aims), had not set out to conquer Siberia but had executed a typical Cossack raid for spoils. In attacking Isker, he had probably not meant to hold it, but merely to sack it and withdraw before deep snow and ice prevented his escape upstream. But the way had been shown. His foray had dealt an irreversible blow to the khanate, and it was never to be reassembled from its shattered parts. Within two decades of his death, the "colorless hordes," as the natives called the Russians, would have much of Western Siberia in their grasp. An armistice with Poland and Sweden in the west allowed the Russians to plot an organized reconquest, and with river highways facilitating their advance, Isker was immediately retaken and destroyed; Tyumen was founded in 1586 to consolidate Russia's position on the Tura River; and after the founding of Tobolsk at the confluence of the Tobol and Irtysh rivers in 1587, about 12 miles northwest of where Isker once stood, no tribe could doubt that the Russians were there to stay.

By 1591 they had extended their sway southward to the Barabinsk Steppes, founding Ufa between Tyumen and Kazan to secure a new trans-Urals route for the movement of troops and supplies. Thereafter, over the next decade and a half, the march of Russian outposts eastward occurred with such regularity that its chronological tempo, in enumeration, seems almost to mark time with a rhythmic beat. Pelym and Berezov were both founded in 1593, to control the Ostyak and Samoyed population in the north, and Surgut, Obdorsk, and Narym by 1596 to strengthen the Russians' hold. In 1598, Verkhoturye—established on the Tura—became the gateway to Siberia, and two years later ground was broken for Turinsk. In 1600, a hundred Cossacks from Tobolsk sailed down the Ob in four small ships to the Arctic coast, and then northeast toward Taz Bay. Despite shipwreck and a subsequent ambush by a party of Samoyeds that reduced their company by half, the voyagers found a spot near the Taz estuary suitable for the construction of a fort, which they called Mangazeya. Thus by 1600 Moscow had a fortified route into Siberia over which Verkhoturye, Turinsk, and Tyumen stood guard; had secured the Lower Ob River Basin with Berezov, Obdorsk, and Mangazeya, and its middle and upper courses with Surgut, Narym, and (after 1602) Ketsk. Meanwhile, south of Tobolsk, the largest expedition ever sent to found a new fort in Siberia—comprising 1,200 cavalry soldiers and 350 on foot, including Tartar auxiliaries and Polish and Lithuanian prisoners of war—had broken ground for Tara in 1594 between the Ishim and Barabinsk steppes. All these forts served as headquarters for the army of occupation and as bases for further expansion. "In Siberia," wrote Giles Fletcher, the English ambassador to Russia at the time "[the tsar] hath divers castles and garisons . . . and sendeth many new supplies thither, to plant and to inhabite as he winneth ground." Russian authority was swiftly established over a thousand miles of territory. After the major outpost of Tomsk was established in 1604 to guard the Ob Basin from Central Asian nomads raiding across the borders from the south, "the cornerstone of the Russian Asiatic empire had been laid."

The Stroganovs got less out of the early conquest than they had hoped. Although additional trading privileges were bestowed upon them, and new grants of land west of the Urals in which their empire of mines, mills, and trading posts could grow, they were denied the lands into which Yermak had advanced, for once the government realized what a great opportunity had opened up, the reoccupation of Sibir became a state venture, with a "planned domination of rivers and portages by the building of blockhouses and forts."

To some extent, the Russians accelerated native recognition of their own legitimacy by selecting sites for their outposts that had formerly been used by Tartar princelings to wield their own authority. They also exploited local enmities. The local Ostyaks cooperated with the Russians in the subjugation of the Voguls, for example, in the neighborhood of Pelym, and (despite a considerable uprising of their own in 1595) on the whole remained consistent allies. But most of the natives didn't sit easily under the Russian yoke. And the Tartars least of all. Khan Kuchum had escaped to the southern steppes before the Russians retook his capital, and from that unconquered refuge continued to harass them for another fourteen years. A wily strategist, he became a kind of Tartar Sitting Bull, time and again eluding the Russians' grasp. Campaigns against him were undertaken in 1591, 1595, and 1598. Although most of his adherents and family were eventually captured or killed, he refused to concede defeat, but continued to fight a futile rear-guard action, with attacks on isolated Russian companies or posts. At one point, he offered to negotiate a just peace that would have allowed his followers to live as they pleased, according to their ancient tribal ways, in the valley of the Irtysh. The Russians sought to tempt him instead with money, property, and recognition of his royal rank.

Kuchum scornfully burned a Russian settlement in reply. But "to reverse the course of history was beyond his power," and in 1598, old and almost blind, he met his death at the hands of Nogay assassins to whom he had turned for help.

Upon Kuchum's death, Moscow moved to erase any claim his heirs might make to the khanate's throne. Settled in Russia, they were lavishly indulged as royal exiles, and adopted by the Muscovite elite as belonging to their own. Kuchum's daughters were married to young nobles, the sons anointed with aristocratic rank. One grandson received the town of Kasimov on the Oka River, long a showcase for puppet Tartars. Kuchum's nephew, Mametkul, was recognized as a prince and became a general in the Russian Army.

Nevertheless, Kuchum's own unquenchable defiance endowed his memory with a powerful mystique, especially in Western Siberia (where intertribal ties were strongest), and well into the seventeenth century risings took place in his name.

Yermak was to be posthumously canonized in both Russian and Tartar folklore, and the names of the Cossacks who had fallen in the battle for Sibir were engraved on a memorial tablet in the cathedral of Tobolsk. Legend has it that some time after Yermak's death his body was dredged up from the Irtysh by a Tartar fisherman, who recognized it at once by the double-headed eagle emblazoned on the chain-mail hauberk. Beneath the armor, Yermak's flesh was found to be uncorrupted, and "blood gushed from his mouth and nose." Miracles were subsequently worked by his body and clothing, "the sick were healed, and mothers and babes were preserved from disease." In awe, the natives buried him at the foot of a pine tree by the river, and for many years thereafter the spot was marked by a column of fire.

3

"TO THE EAST OF THE SUN"

A<small>T</small> the time the Siberian conquest began, Russia was already one of the largest nations on earth. Its numerous and once-separate principalities had been united by force and stealth under the rule of Moscow, and Ivan the Terrible's subjugation of the two Tartar khanates of Kazan and Astrakhan on the Volga had expanded those dominions into a multinational state. Beginning with Ivan, its sovereign presumed to rule by "divine right," and though most other European monarchs claimed the same benediction, the absolute, autocratic power of the Russian tsar was exceptional, for "like Nebuchadnezzar," wrote a contemporary, "he slew, had beaten, elevated, or humbled whomsoever he wished." Near the top of the growing state bureaucracy there was a royal council, or Boyar Duma (mostly men of noble birth), as well as an inner cabinet of councilors with whom the tsar might consult. But he often did so, it was said, "in the manner of Xerxes, the Persian Emperor, who assembled the Asian princes not so much to secure their advice . . . as to personally declare his will." From the Kremlin in the heart of Moscow, the tsar ruled a population of about 13 million, mostly impoverished peasants toiling on large estates, or cultivating their gardenlike plots in tiny hamlets across the land. The old aristocracy had recently been somewhat humbled, and the service gentry had arisen to take its place. In time, however, the gentry would acquire many of the prerogatives of the class they had supplanted, including titles and inheritable estates.

There was no true middle class, no independent merchant guilds, no mercantile economy of the sort that most European countries were beginning to enjoy. Even the *gosts,* or "great merchants" of the realm, owed their status to appointment by the Crown. State service, in fact, was what Muscovy was all about, and under its repressive regime, travel within the country was restricted and travel abroad almost un-known—"that Russians might not learn of the free institutions that exist in foreign lands." Police surveillance was widespread, but the hallmark of the system (as in any police state) was the "duty to de-nounce," which obliged Muscovites of whatever rank and standing to serve as political informers against each other, and to report whatever they knew or heard about disloyal acts or thoughts. Punishments under the law were savage, and torture was routine. The condemned were variously torn to pieces with iron hooks, beheaded or impaled, branded with red-hot irons, shorn of limbs, or beaten with the knout —a short whip that had at its tapered end three thongs of hard, tanned elk hide, "which cutt like knives."

In the world of the average Muscovite there were few amenities to alleviate his downtrodden state. The roads were poor, there were no inns between towns to give refuge to the weary traveler, alcoholism had long been the national scourge, sodomy was epidemic (so for-eigners charged), and intellectual curiosity driven underground. A sim-ple knowledge of astronomy could bring a charge of witchcraft—the ability, for example, to foretell eclipses of the sun and moon. Over time, the habit of oppression, noted a foreign diplomat, had

> set a print into the very mindes of the people. For as themselves are verie hardlie and cruellie dealte withall by their chiefe magistrates and other superiours, so are they as cruell one against an other, specially over their inferiours and such as are under them. So that the basest and wretchedest [peasant] that stoupeth and croucheth like a dog to the gentleman, and licketh up the dust that lieth at his feete, is an intollerable tyrant where he hath the advantage.

The overall image Muscovy projected to the world was that of a semi-barbaric and insular people and state, at once arrogantly self-assured as the sole bearer of true Christianity, yet rife with ignorance, supersti-tion, and immorality in everyday life. One visitor to the capital summed up his impressions in outrageous rhyme:

Churches, ikons, crosses, bells,
Painted whores and garlic smells,
Vice and vodka everyplace—
This is Moscow's daily face.

To loiter in the market air,
To bathe in common, bodies bare,
To sleep by day and gorge by night,
To belch and fart is their delight.

Thieving, murdering, fornication
Are so common in this nation,
No one thinks a brow to raise—
Such are Moscow's sordid days.

Such attacks on the nation's character, however, slighted the genuine religiosity of the folk, and ignored the belated but genuine renaissance that had been taking place below the coarsened surface of Russia's everyday world. In ways unique and uniquely promising to its development, Western cultural influences through trade and other contacts had begun to make themselves felt, and these combined with Russia's own rich Byzantine heritage might have brought about an awakening more natural and harmonious than the one Russia would later endure. Such embryonic currents, however, were destined to be overwhelmed by the bloody legacies of the immediate past. The experimental tyrannies of Ivan the Terrible had divided the nation in two "as with an axe." The social enmities he had sown throughout the land would long survive him, and as if to ensure that the harvest of sorrow would be full, he had doomed his dynasty in 1582 by killing his eldest son in a rage. Upon his own death in 1584, he was therefore succeeded by another son, Fyodor, an absent-minded and reluctant monarch who relied heavily on the mighty boyars appointed to be his guardians, and whose incapacities were a clear temptation to plots. A power struggle ensued, and the dominant figure to emerge behind the throne was Boris Godunov, a noble of Tartar origin, whose sister was Fyodor's wife. Before long he was universally recognized as Lord Protector (as the English called him) and de facto head of state.

Godunov proved a man of tremendous ability. Despite the numerous inherited miseries he faced, under his regency trade prospered, revenue increased, taxes were reduced, quiet and peace returned, and people seemed to find "consolation after the sorrows of the past." Fugitive peasants drifted back to their homesteads, more arable land came under cultivation, grain prices fell, and large surpluses were even recorded in granaries. Energetic building reflected the new economic growth, with the construction of stone walls around Moscow and Smolensk, the erection of many churches, expanded port facilities at Archangel, and the completion of the famed Ivan the Great Belltower in the Kremlin, which reached upward in three tapering octagonal tiers.

Godunov also made headway against the nomads in the southern steppes (between Russia and the Crimea), establishing a series of important new fortified towns; he recovered territory lost to Sweden during the Livonian War, and in Siberia pushed the conquest eastward from the Ob.

Indeed, Godunov seemed destined for national adulation, and upon Fyodor's death without heir in 1598 he was offered the crown. Like Shakespeare's Caesar he declined it thrice, to demonstrate the inevitability of his elevation, and likewise looked to the masses for his support. At his coronation, he ostentatiously declared: "As God is my witness, there will not be a poor man in my tsardom!" and tore the jeweled collar from his gown. Envious nobles called him *Rabotsar*— the "Tsar of slaves."

After Godunov was crowned in the Cathedral of the Dormition on September 1, 1598, favors were announced, officials of the army and administration received a substantial salary increase, merchants were granted tax breaks, and even the natives of Western Siberia were exempted from taxes for one year. "We take a moderate tribute," he declared, "as much as each can pay. . . . And from the poor people, who cannot pay the tribute, no tribute is to be taken, so that none of the Siberian people should be in need."

But other forces tearing at the social fabric could not be stayed by bountiful deeds. The most fundamental was the competition among landed proprietors for peasants to work their estates. The more prosperous tempted peasants away from smaller holdings, and since many of these were held on military tenure, their decline affected the security of the state. The government took drastic action and tried to solve the problem by binding the peasant to the soil. The peasant's freedom of movement had already been severely curtailed over the years, but new decrees under Godunov and his successors embedded the trend toward serfdom in the national life. The service gentry squeezed every-thing they could from their peasants, whom state taxation bent to the breaking point. Violence spread. In the heartland, bands of peasants-turned-highwaymen ransacked monasteries and manorial estates, and along the southern frontier there accumulated legions of the disaf-fected with animosities ripening toward rebellion against the Crown.

Meanwhile, over the course of three years (1601–03) Russia was beset by protracted crop failures that led to famine and mass starvation. True to his coronation pledge, Godunov distributed money and grain from the public treasury to the destitute, but widespread hoarding and profiteering by landlords and merchants (including the Stroganovs) more than undid the effects of his largesse. Whole villages were wiped out; cats, dogs, and rats were eaten, along with bark and straw; and in public markets, human flesh was sold. Every day in Moscow, wrote an eyewitness, "people perished in their thousands like flies on winter days." Men carted away the dead and dumped them into ditches, "as is done with mud and refuse," but in the morning could be seen "bodies half devoured, and other things so horrible that the hair stood up on end." One court apothecary, who had rescued a little girl from starva-tion in the snow, entrusted her to a peasant family, only to learn later that they had eaten her. Thousands of unemployed laborers, as well as peasants abandoned to their fate by indifferent masters, scavenged through the countryside or fled into the wilds. The Time of Troubles —the most turbulent period in Russian history before the Revolution of 1917—had begun.

The crisis was beyond Godunov's control, and his standing fell as the tribulations of the nation grew. Though a legitimate sovereign, properly elected, he could claim no dynastic link with Russia's "sacred" past, and popular disaffection soon cast him in the role of a ruthless usurper who had ascended the throne through violence, deceit, and crime. Rumor retroactively charged him with the murder of the tsar-evich Dmitry (Ivan the Terrible's nine-year-old son by his seventh wife) and with poisoning his own sister, and even Tsar Fyodor himself. His network of spies uncovered numerous plots, but the discontent welled up ever more powerfully from below. In 1603, bandits, fugitive slaves, and peasants coalesced into an uprising, and the people, romanticizing even the worst days of their past, began to long for the protection of a "born tsar." On the heels of the revolt (which the army quelled),

Godunov was confronted by the messianic rumor that the tsarevich Dmitry had miraculously survived his assassination and was about to reclaim the throne. The Poles, in fact, had schooled such a pretender —the first of many imposters—and he crossed into Muscovy in October 1604 at the head of an army of mercenaries and volunteers. Though "a strange and ungainly figure, with facial warts and arms of unequal length," this False Dmitry, as he was called, proved a charismatic leader, and many malcontents rallied to his cause. By mid-November, his army had swollen to sixteen thousand men, and Godunov, helpless to oppose the rising tide, turned to sorcery and divination in an attempt to alter his fate.

On April 13, 1605, however, he suddenly died, either of poison or a stroke. Within a few weeks his wife and son had been murdered and the Kremlin stormed. The cycle of bloodshed revolved at a furious speed. Within a year, the False Dmitry had been toppled by Vasily Shuisky, a noble with the right pedigree but without popular support. New uprisings and foreign invasions followed, and then another pretender, backed by the Poles, advanced on Moscow in June 1607. That confrontation led to Shuisky's deposition and the installation of a Polish tsar. The partition of Muscovy appeared imminent. At this juncture, Russian popular armies arose in the north and east, and, instilled with patriotic fervor, went forward to victory. On October 25, 1612, the Polish garrison in the Kremlin capitulated and the foreigners were driven out. Then on February 21, 1613, a national assembly elected a new tsar—the sixteen-year-old Mikhail Romanov, grand-nephew of Anastasia, Ivan the Terrible's beloved first wife. The Time of Troubles— twelve years of unremitting misery—had come to an end.

The upheaval had thrown the Russian program of conquest into disarray. Events in the "mother country" inevitably affected its progress, since the Siberian frontiersmen—however independent, enterprising, and hardy their demanding environment required them to be—ultimately also depended on Moscow for administrative, logistical, and other support. As the nation struggled to survive, the Siberian garrisons, left more or less to themselves, were steadily depleted by disease, starvation, and death. The natives, seeing their opportunity, made several attempts at a coordinated uprising, the most powerful coming in

1608 when "a Tartar Joan of Arc" by the name of Princess Anna of Koda almost succeeded in uniting the entire native population of Western Siberia in revolt. Still another attempt was made in 1612 to reestablish the old khanate of Sibir "as it had been in the time of Kuchum." Only at the eleventh hour was the plot betrayed and ten of its ringleaders rounded up and hanged.

Although Russian occupation of the Ob-Irtysh Basin had increased the size of Russia by more than a third, Siberia was still modestly enough understood as a geographical entity in Moscow to be used as a political bargaining chip. Boris Godunov had attempted to bribe an influential boyar into supporting him against the False Dmitry by offering him "the Kingdoms of Kazan, Astrakhan, and all Siberia," and the Second False Dmitry had evidently promised to reward his brother-in-law (a powerful Polish noble) with "the whole land of Siberia" for his aid. Such geographical vagueness justly occasioned a scene in Pushkin's drama about Godunov's life in which Boris actually failed to recognize a map he was shown as that of his own dominions. Yet scarcely had the Ob-Irtysh Basin been secured before the Russian advance into the next great river valley, the Yenisey, began.

The Russians ascended the eastern tributaries of the first, crossed a low plateau to streams flowing into the second, and by 1619 had gained all the important river routes and portages that connected the two. At such junctures they immediately built blockhouses or forts to subject the natives to tribute and to bring them "under the tsar's high hand." Expeditions started from Tomsk and Ketsk in the south and Mangazeya in the north, converging on the river valley from both directions. On the lower Yenisey, the Russians met the Tungus, and on the upper portions of the river, the Buryats, whom they'd never heard of before. The latter inhabited a region rich in furs, practiced animal husbandry, and were rumored to grow crops and have access to silver —a combination certain to draw the Russians on. The Tungus tribes east of the Yenisey, and the Buryats around Lake Baikal, both fought hard to prevent the establishment of bases in their territory, only to behold with dismay the founding of Yeniseysk in 1619 (where the Angara and Yenisey unite), of Krasnoyarsk in 1627, astride magnificent cliffs of red-colored marl, and Bratsk on the Angara in 1631. On the upper Yenisey, however, the Russians also met the staunch resistance of steppe nomads (the Kirghiz and the Kalmucks) whose homelands bordered Siberia in the south, and whose unyielding hostility was not to be effectively dealt with until a solidly fortified line was eventually established (over the course of two centuries) along the southern frontier.

Meanwhile, Russian mariners had developed the sea route from Archangel to Mangazeya, and there bartered goods with the local Ostyaks and Samoyeds for furs. As this "fabulous polar city," located a few miles above the Arctic Circle, prospered and grew, it attracted more and more traders, who braved the treacherous waters of the Kara Sea. "Hundreds of thousands of sable, ermine, silver and blue fox skins," one writer tells us, "and countless tons of precious mammoth and walrus ivory" were shipped each year from Mangazeya to Europe, in an illicit trade begun during the Time of Troubles that eluded the government's control. Silk, porcelain, and costly fabrics also found their way through middlemen to Mangazeya from Central Asia and China, turning the city into "a virtual Baghdad of Siberia, where big commercial deals were celebrated at fabulous feasts that lasted for days, and that featured the best European wines and local delicacies like sturgeon, caviar, mushrooms, berries, and venison and other game." By the time stability had been restored in Moscow, reports of Siberia's vast wealth in furs had spread far and wide, and inevitably attracted the cupidity of European powers seeking to acquire new colonies. The government began to fear that foreign agents might try to trade directly with the natives, and perhaps even attempt an armed invasion through the Taz estuary to seize the whole of northwestern Siberia as a rich colonial prize. At the same time, Mangazeya had aroused the envy of inland merchants working out of the Urals, Tyumen, and Tobolsk, who saw it siphoning off commerce that would otherwise have come their way. As a result, the government closed the sea route to Mangazeya in 1619—forbidding its use even by Russians, lest they betray it to foreigners—and decreed that all who disobeyed were to be "put to the hardest possible death, and all their homes and families destroyed branch and root." Navigational markings were torn up, surveillance posts established along the coast to intercept and kill all who attempted to get through, and a coastal fort built on the Yamal Peninsula, commanding the portage between the Ob Gulf and the Kara Sea. Maps were even falsified to depict Novaya Zemlya as a peninsula rather than an island—at some cost to later mariners who would rely upon them as nautical guides.

Mangazeya eventually declined, the rich merchants departed, and in 1643 its administrative apparatus was moved to Turukhansk—known for a time as "New Mangazeya"—founded at the mouth of the Turukhan River, a tributary of the Yenisey. In 1678, without official explanation, the city was burned to the ground. Among local Samoyed tribesmen, its ruins were known as Tagarevyhard, or "destroyed town," and the very site, "swallowed up by the tundra," was not to be rediscovered for almost three hundred years.

Perhaps more than any other settlement in the early conquest, Mangazeya lent luster to Siberia's name, epitomizing the enormous wealth the new colony possessed. In 1632, a former military governor of the district, inspired by the bounty to which Mangazeya had given access, exhorted the tsar to press on from the Yenisey to a conquest of the Lena River Basin, "to the east of the sun."

The Russians had first heard about the Lena from Tungus who also told them about the Yakuts, or "horse people," who inhabited its shores. Originally pastoral nomads from regions farther south, the Yakuts had fled northward during the upheavals accompanying the rise of Genghis Khan, and had eventually settled along the middle Lena, where they continued to practice cattle and horse breeding in spite of the severe climate, sheltering the animals in their own dwellings during winter months. Westward affluents of the Lena were quickly reached from eastward branches of the Yenisey as expeditions from Yeniseysk and Mangazeya raced across short portages of low rolling hills and penetrated the river basin from both north and south. Soon rival exploring parties from Tomsk and Tobolsk also showed up, but it was not until the government despatched the Cossack Petr Beketov—renowned for his subjugation of the Buryats and Tungus along the Angara—from Yeniseysk that the conquest of the Lena really began. In 1631, he portaged from Ilimsk (founded the previous year) to the Lena with about thirty men, proceeded up the river, built a fortified camp of fallen trees, and imposed tribute on the local Yakuts. In 1632, he founded Yakutsk, later a base for expeditions to the Arctic and Pacific, on a big bend of the river, and Zhigansk to the north. Amginsk, Vilyuysk, and other outposts quickly followed on tributary streams, and Olekminsk was started at the junction of the Olekma and Lena rivers in 1635.

Meanwhile, Cossack bands from the different towns had begun to fight among themselves for a share of the spoils. Infatuated with a kind of hometown pride, some of them even became involved in intertribal wars on opposing sides. Elsewhere, tribute was collected from some of the natives two and even three times, provoking uprisings where at first peoples had been easily subdued. Such clashes led to a decline of revenue for the Treasury, prompting Moscow to designate Yakutsk in 1638 as the headquarters of a separate administrative district from which servicemen from other districts were banned.

This measure had only partial success. Whereas the conquest of Western Siberia had been methodically planned, to the east a new and more rugged country had begun, with frontier fortresses constituting tiny islands of domination in a gigantic land. On the Lena, the Russians were 2,500 miles from the Urals, and so remote from Kremlin directives that the initiative inevitably passed to the local authorities, and even to individual groups. Most Cossack or exploring parties amounted to no more than twenty or thirty men, and sometimes to less than ten. These *promyshlenniks* (hunters and trappers) led the way, with the state, which had taken the lead in Western Siberia, following after them, constructing forts to command rivers and portages and to supervise the collection they had already begun to tap.

The lack of an organized military force seemed at times to give the natives a fighting chance. The Buryats, for example, continued to resist Russian incursions fiercely, and mountainous terrain enabled them to use guerrilla tactics to telling effect. It was not until 1648 that the Russians succeeded in ascending the Angara River as far as Lake Baikal, when the Cossack Kurbat Ivanov, who first discovered the lake, also crossed it, and after fierce fighting imposed *yasak,* or fur tribute, on the Buryats inhabiting its eastern shores. In the following year, Ivan Pokhabov, a commandant from Yeniseysk, renovated and strengthened the Angara fort of Bratsk (founded 1631) with parapets and moats, and led another party across the lake to the mouth of the Selenga River. He thus found himself on the Mongolian frontier. Ascertaining that the local Buryats obtained silver, silk, and other objects from Outer Mongolia in return for furs, he sought out the warlord or khan of the eastern Mongols (known as Altyn-Khan), who professed to have no silk or silver of his own except what he obtained from the Chinese. Meanwhile, new forts were erected at Verkholensk (1641), Verkhneangarsk

(1646), Verkhneudinsk (1648), and Barguzin (1648) on either side of Lake Baikal, and then at Irkutsk (at the junction of the Angara and Irkut rivers) in 1652. As part of the Russian pacification program, many natives were forcibly baptized, and "those who did not willingly consent were driven into the Stream, and when they came back, a Cross was hung around their Necks." In one still more crude procedure, two or three Buryats at a time were tied to a long pole and plunged into freezing water through a hole in the ice. Not surprisingly, this convinced them that the new faith had little of solace to offer them, and in suicidal fury they attacked the garrison at Bratsk.

In 1652, Petr Beketov was sent to restore the tsar's authority. In the course of the following year he explored the Selenga, Ingoda, and Shilka rivers on rafts, founded Irgensk, and in the spring of 1653 Nerchinsk, across from the mouth of the Nercha River.

While the Yenisey was being brought under control, progress was also made on the Lena, as the conquest from Yakutsk proceeded in three directions—northeast to Bering Strait, the Bering Sea, and Kamchatka; eastward to the Sea of Okhotsk; and southward to the Amur River Valley. Indeed, just two years after reaching the Lena, the Russians had followed up the Aldan River to its source in the Stanovoy Mountains, and in 1639 a detachment of twenty men under the command of Ivan Moskvitin went in search of what the natives called "the great sea-ocean." Proceeding up the Maya and Yudoma rivers, they made their way through a mountain pass, and descended the Ulya River to the Sea of Okhotsk, part of the North Pacific Ocean. One hundred and twenty-five years after the Spaniards had discovered the Pacific from the east, the Russians had discovered it from the west; and in just fifty-five years, while American colonists were still east of the Appalachians, they had crossed the whole of northern Asia.

In advancing from one river basin to the next, the Russians had followed the tributary headwaters of the three great river systems, which, spreading out east and west, "almost interlocked like the arching branches of a row of trees." But the principal rivers themselves—the Ob, Yenisey, and Lena—also rolled inexorably northward to the Arctic, and by following these arteries as well the Russians were soon brought to different sections of the Arctic shore.

One of the great pioneers in this exploration was the Cossack Yelisey Buza. Setting out from Yakutsk in 1617, he sailed north along the Lena to the coast, east to the mouth of the Olenek River, where he wintered in a secluded bay, and then continued overland on sledges to the Yana. Along that river he explored the valleys of the Verkhoyansk Range, the coldest inhabited region on earth, collecting *yasak* from the local Yakuts. In the following year he pushed farther east along the coast to the Indigirka River, where he encountered a new tribe, the Yukaghirs, wedged between the Yakuts in the interior and the Tungus on the coast. Returning to Yakutsk in 1642 after a five-year odyssey, he reported the discovery of three new rivers, each of considerable size, and created additional excitement by passing on rumors of a fourth where there was said to be silver ore. The prospect of silver as well as new hunting grounds whetted appetites, and several Cossack expeditions hurriedly prepared to embark.

In Buza's absence, others had made corroborative finds. In the summer of 1640, a detachment of fifteen men under another Cossack, Dmitry Zyrian, after collecting *yasak* from the Yukaghirs on the Indigirka, sailed eastward along the Arctic coast to the Alazeya, where he encountered not only Yukaghirs, but a new people, the Chukchi. From them he learned of still another river to the east, the Kolyma, the last of the major Siberian rivers flowing into the Arctic Ocean. One thousand miles east of the Lena, this river was discovered in 1644 by Mikhail Stadukhin, who founded the settlement of Srednekolymsk near its mouth. Two years later, a company of *promyshlenniks* picked their way through the ice toward the Chukchi Peninsula, entered a small bay, and there tentatively engaged in "dumb trade" with a local Chukchi clan. The Russians spread out their goods at the water's edge, and the natives took what pleased them, leaving walrus tusks or ivory objects in their place.

Such peaceful encounters were rare. Indeed, in the face of ambush, Arctic storms, shipwreck, and other perils, few expeditions had a happy end. The frontier breed was also a hard one, and (despite the common risks of their situation, which ought to have created solidarity) Russians in trouble could not always count on their own. In the summer of 1650, for example, one company under Timofey Buldakov, a Cossack from Yakutsk, worked their way along the coast until, just south of the New Siberian Islands (about halfway between the Yana and the Indigirka rivers), they were frozen in. In September, they began to drift with the ice far out into the ocean. They broke up their vessels to make sledges, and started to drag their supplies across the ice floes toward the coast. After nine days they finally made it to shore—half-naked, starving, debilitated by scurvy, and with frostbitten limbs. A little ways up the Indigirka River they came to a winter blockhouse where a company of tax collectors had encamped. The tax collectors had a sizable stock of wheat and flour, reserved for barter with the natives, but were unwilling to yield up a single morsel to their brethren, even though the latter offered to sell themselves to them as slaves.

Such were the pitiless characters with whom the hapless natives often had to deal.

In exploring the Siberian Arctic, many of the vessels used were also of extremely primitive construction, made entirely without iron from local materials, and held together by wooden nails and leather thongs. As often as not, they had only a wooden anchor to which a rock was attached, and oars and a single mast with a deerhide sail. Others, however, were of more substantial construction, related to a kind of coastal craft developed in Pomorye, the maritime region of northern Russia. It was from this region—the basin of the northern Dvina River and the coast of the White Sea—that a rather large proportion of Siberia's *promyshlenniks* and Arctic explorers came. Some had been hunters and trappers, others deep-sea fishermen (*pomorye* means "sea people," in old Russian) who had developed into seafarers by hunting sea mammals far from shore, sometimes following the pods of seals through the White Sea into the Arctic Ocean. Experience had taught them how to build boats capable of coping with floating ice, and to "follow the spring" in sailing along the coast, as the ice, thawed by the Gulf Stream, broke up progressively eastward "towards the sun." Typically, their boat was "a relatively light maneuverable vessel of shallow draft, that had a flat-bottomed hull with curved sides. The form of the hull enabled it to avoid collisions with the ice or to ride up onto it if trapped, to negotiate leads or polynias (open water channels), and to be towed across shoals." In navigating Arctic seas it was therefore more practical than "the heavier, deep-sea vessels (with flatter sides, angled at the chines, and deeper in draft)" that Western mariners used.

The Siberian version, developed in the district of Yakutsk, was somewhat larger and sturdier than its Pomorye model—up to 60 feet long,

20 wide, with a draft of 5 to 6 feet. Made of light dry pine or larch, it had a keel and a rigid frame, braced with crossbeams, and planking, "like Western ships." Iron nails, spikes, and bolts contributed to its strength. In addition, this koch, as it was called, had a large canvas sail, iron anchors, and was furnished with a rudder, tiller, capstan, and even a wind-driven pump. Copper-cased compasses and compass sundials mounted in mammoth ivory, or pieces of lodestone set in bone, completed the basic equipment. Depending on its size, such a craft could carry up to fifty people, with a cargo reaching 45 tons.

Of all the Arctic voyages of the time, the most dramatic by far was that accomplished by Semyon Dezhnev, an enterprising Cossack soldier, in his search for the River Anadyr. A native of Pomorye (from the town of Pinega, near the mouth of the northern Dvina), Dezhnev had entered the Siberian service about 1630, assigned to Yeniseysk. Subsequently, he was transferred to Yakutsk, where he married a Yakut, and was then posted with the Cossack leader Dmitry Zyrian among the Yukaghirs on the Yana River. Over the next few years, he found himself in the vanguard of the coastal explorations, participating in the discovery of the Alazeya and Kolyma rivers.

Prospects along the Kolyma soon lured many *promyshlenniks* and traders, along with servicemen from Yakutsk, who crowded into the few settlements on its shores. An annual market held in August at Srednekolymsk brought together trappers and traders from all around, but the incentives to keep pressing eastward remained. Agents for wealthy merchants were constantly on the lookout for new opportunities, and the fate of one of them, Fedot Alekseyev, became linked to Dezhnev's own. Alekseyev had originally hoped to base his operations in Yakutsk, but found upon his arrival there in 1639 that a number of other agents were already entrenched. He decided to try his luck on the Olenek, a river to the west, but the local Russian outposts were constantly under Tungus attack. He therefore headed east, making his way from the Yana to the Indigirka to the Alazeya rivers in turn, until he reached the Kolyma in 1646. Even here, the competition was already fierce, so he formed an expedition to find the Anadyr—one of the last untapped areas in the northeast. After five years on the Kolyma, Dezhnev, too, was restless for new opportunities, for despite his past energy and initiative, he had yet to be appointed to a position of command. Offering to lead the expedition as the state's representative (in charge of collecting the tribute), he promised personally to bring back several hundred sables as a pledge of his success.

Several vessels were assembled and loaded with a cargo that included beads and copper buttons for trade, traps for sables, thirteen "lodestones in bone," and crowbars to pry away the ice from the sides of their boats. After a false start in the summer of 1647, in June 1648 they set out again from Srednekolymsk in seven koches with a party of ninety men. Emerging from the mouth of the Kolyma, they sailed eastward along the Arctic coast, but lost four boats before the Chukchi Peninsula was reached, and a fifth in shipwreck on the peninsula itself. The remaining two, commanded by Dezhnev and Alekseyev, rounded the great northeastern cape of Asia, where on a bluff they saw a scaffold, like a tower, made of whalebones, and in the sea opposite two islands—the Diomedes—inhabited by Eskimo. Battling wind and storm, they disembarked on the cape, skirmished with Chukchi, once more put out to sea, and became separated in a storm. Dezhnev's boat was thrown ashore well south of the Anadyr River on October 1. Alekseyev's boat was also wrecked somewhere on the coast, where he and most of his companions eventually perished, except for his Yakut concubine.

In this astonishing voyage of one hundred days, Dezhnev and his companions had sailed over 2,000 miles through treacherous seas, evaded a whirlpool somewhere off East Cape, discovered the Diomede Islands, and had rounded the northeast tip of Asia eighty years before Vitus Bering sailed through the strait that bears his name.

Quite unaware of his achievement, however, Dezhnev knew only that his task was to survive and find the Anadyr. With twenty-five men, he ventured into the mountainous interior, and after some ten weeks of wandering found himself near the Anadyr's mouth. Prospects on the river did not live up to their expectations, for the forest was scant, sables few, and much of the area bare tundra and rock.

The men divided into two parties to hunt for food. Twelve went upriver, but turned back without much luck after twenty days. Not far from where they were to link up with the rest, nine insisted on stopping for the night—and disappeared without a trace. The following spring (1649), the sixteen survivors constructed driftwood boats and went up the river, where (rather bravely, in their dependent condition) they managed to subdue the Anauls, a local subgroup of the Yukaghirs), from whom they collected tribute. On an island in the river, Dezhnev also founded Anadyrsk.

Meanwhile, oblivious of Dezhnev's success, Mikhail Stadukhin, the veteran Cossack and explorer, also set out to find the Anadyr, proceeding overland. He had a much easier time of it. Since Dezhnev's departure it had been learned that the upper courses of the Anyuy and Anadyr rivers were not far apart, separated only by a modest mountain ridge. With the help of Yukaghir guides, in 1650 Stadukhin and another party under Semyon Motora located the fabled river after only a few weeks march.

Dezhnev and Motora joined their commands; but Stadukhin, who was unhappy to find that Dezhnev had gotten to the Anadyr first, attempted to lord it over the others and assume control. They resisted, and he established his own rival camp, interfering with their tribute collection, terrorizing the natives (with whom Dezhnev had established a rapport), and at one point even punching Dezhnev in the face. Attempting to escape from Stadukhin's abuse, Dezhnev and Motora crossed the mountains to the south by sled in search of the Penzhina River (which empties from the north into the Sea of Okhotsk) "to find new non-tribute paying people and to bring them under the sovereign's exalted hand." Lacking a native guide, however, they were unable to find the trail, and after three weeks returned rather than brave the rigors of a winter in the wilds.

The ill-will bred by Stadukhin among the natives proved costly. In the autumn of 1650, nine servicemen and *promyshlenniks* were wiped out in an ambush, and the Russians managed to resubjugate the natives only after bloody hand-to-hand combat with axes and knives. Finding his situation untenable, and the fur resources of the Anadyr in any case scant, Stadukhin in February 1651 set out himself for the Penzhina River with a band of followers, and (perhaps a better pathfinder than Dezhnev) succeeded in reaching the northern coast of the Okhotsk Sea.

Absent Stadukhin, Dezhnev and Motora set up a dual command. But late in December 1651, Motora was killed in a fight with the Anauls, and soon thereafter Dezhnev began work on two boats to carry him back to Srednekolymsk by sea. He soon realized that he lacked the means to make a vessel strong enough to cope with the hazards he would face, and in any case wanted more to show for his efforts before he returned. In June 1652, while exploring the estuary of the Anadyr, he discovered a walrus rookery on a long triangular sandspit on the south side of the entrance to the bay. Hundreds of walruses were lolling about, and the sand was strewn with tusks. Dezhnev collected as many as he could, and in 1654 returned for more, in company with Yury Seliverstov, a new arrival from Yakutsk, who subsequently tried to claim the honor and profit of the discovery for himself.

Much to his astonishment, on this second excursion Dezhnev came upon a Koryak settlement where he found the Yakut concubine of Fedot Alekseyev. She told him that after their boat had been wrecked, most of the Russians (including Alekseyev) had been killed by Koryaks or had succumbed to disease. A few others, however, including Alekseyev's son, had pushed off in boats into the unknown.

In the autumn of 1654, Dezhnev decided he'd had enough and petitioned his superiors for his back salary and a successor to relieve him of his command. He reviewed his service since leaving Yakutsk, called attention to the hardships he had endured and how much he had undertaken at his own expense. Five years were to pass, however, before Kurbat Ivanov (the Cossack who had discovered Lake Baikal) finally arrived with reinforcements to take his place. With 2½ tons of walrus ivory in tow, as well as the fur tribute collected during the duration of his stay, Dezhnev set out for Yakutsk. By the time he got there, in the spring of 1662, more than nineteen years of back salary were due him. And from Yakutsk he proceeded at once to Moscow to collect. There, in September 1664, he made sure the Siberian Department understood the extent of his long sacrifice. His body, he told them, had been scarred all over with wounds; he had collected tribute on several major rivers without "salary in money and grain"; and during this time, he had "suffered all kinds of want and destitution, ate larch and pine bark, and accepted filth for twenty-one years." On the Anadyr especially, he told them, "I risked my head, shed my blood, suffered great cold and hunger, and all but died from starvation." In the end, the government thought he deserved better, and in January 1665 he was promoted to Cossack commander and paid about 625 rubles in goods and cash—a substantial sum at the time.

Returning to Yakutsk (where his Yakut wife, Abakayada Sichyu, had given birth to their son, Lyubima) Dezhnev served with distinction in the district before retiring to Moscow in 1672. But to the end he remained oblivious to the historic importance of his pioneering voyage. Indeed, the geographical question that was later to animate cartographers, explorers, merchants, and politicians alike—whether Asia and America were joined by land—had not yet been definitely asked. In Dezhnev's own opinion, the outstanding event of his career had been the discovery of the walrus rookery, which had somewhat made up for the comparative lack of sables on the Anadyr.

Knowledge of Dezhnev's voyage soon faded in Moscow, and only a blurred memory of it remained in the Siberian northeast. But he would one day take his rightful place in the pantheon of explorers hallowed by posterity. "By answering an important scientific question," as one scholar remarks, "Dezhnev had placed himself alongside Columbus, who had discovered the new world; Vasco de Gama, who had discovered the southern limits of Africa; and Magellan, who had found the route around South America." In recognition of his achievement, his name would be given to the northeasternmost extremity of Asia (Cape Dezhnev), to a mountain range on the Chukchi Peninsula, and to a bay on the western shore of the Bering Sea.

Although Dezhnev enjoyed a posthumous fame, other unsung heroes, perhaps equally deserving of renown, lay buried forever along the Russian Arctic coast. In 1940, a topographical survey party working on the east side of the Taimyr Peninsula found, on an islet 80 miles southeast of Cape Chelyuskin (the northernmost point of Eurasia), pots, frying pans, rusty knives, beads, pewter plates, jewelry, coins, crosses, and other objects of early date. In an adjacent bay, they subsequently found the ruins of a driftwood hut and similar relics, as well as navigational instruments, a chess set, the remains of leather shoes with cleated heels, and several skeletons, including one of a woman or a boy. Dated to 1618, years before the Cossacks were believed to have reached the Lena, these objects bear witness to the anonymous triumph of a daring party of explorers who had rounded the Taimyr Peninsula and Cape Chelyuskin 125 years before a heavily equipped naval expedition barely managed to repeat the deed.

4

"SOFT GOLD"

In crossing the Urals, the Russians had "followed the route to empire," like other European powers that crossed the seas. Instead of gold or silver, spices and other prized commodities which the Europeans wrung from their overseas colonies of India, Mexico, or Peru, it was "soft gold," in the form of the world's finest furs, which excited the avarice of the Russian adventurers. Indeed, like the United States and Canada, Siberia, writes one historian, "owed its opening and first exploitation . . . to the fur trade." And its conquest was the eastern counterpart of the westward colonial march.

Furs had long been Russia's most valuable export commodity. From the time of the first Russian settlements in ninth-century Kiev, the pursuit of fur-bearing animals had animated Russian expansion, with a progressive assumption of new hunting grounds to the north and east. Marco Polo's thirteenth-century *Travels* had identified Russia as notable chiefly for possessing "the best and most beautiful" furs in the world; and from the Dnieper Basin, "the storehouse of the European trade" at that time, hunters and trappers had subsequently moved north to Novgorod, a region with a metropolitan center enjoying kontore (or commercial enclave) status in the Hanseatic League. North of Novgorod lay an enormous hinterland, extending through the basins of the Dvina and Pechora rivers to the White Sea. Trade centers developed at Kholmogory, Pustozersk, and elsewhere, and it was not uncommon for Russians and natives to meet at annual fairs. The products

Russia obtained from the West in return for its pelts were to prove a powerful and continuous incentive for new exploration.

In Russia's domestic economy, furs were also highly prized. Until the fifteenth century, they served as a currency of the realm (*kuny,* an early term for silver, meant "marten"), and all grand princes and tsars wore a bejeweled diadem that was sable-fringed. To the populace at large in a largely sub-Arctic clime, the value placed upon furs as an enveloping shield against the cold can only be measured by the value of life itself. Especially prized were sables "unripped, with bellies and feet," but quality pelts of all kinds had been exported in such abundance by 1558 to Western Europe, as well as to Bukhara and Samarkand, that a domestic shortage resulted, with hats and coats having to be pieced together out of mangy remnants of rabbit and squirrel. The price of furs rose sharply; by the 1570s, foreign consumption (which helped finance the Livonian War) had led to the near extermination of fur-bearing animals in the north. Already a large proportion of the best pelts displayed on the Volga markets or at Solvychegodsk were obtained by barter with natives, who (as no American will be surprised to hear) proved pathetically willing to part with their precious merchandise in return for a couple of trinkets or cheap manufactured goods.

Siberia emerged as an answer to the Treasury's prayers. For centuries, parallel to the Great Silk Road there had been another trade route —a Great Sable Road—that led through Southern Siberia and the Far East all the way to Byzantium. What Russia needed most, Siberia had, preeminently, and to take hold of it, the soldiers had first come in waves, followed by hunters and trappers in a "Fur Rush" as frantic as the Gold Rush of Alaska. With any luck a man could strike it rich in a season. A few good fox pelts alone, for example, could buy 50 acres of land, a decent cabin, five horses, ten head of cattle, and twenty sheep. Progressive exhaustion of the hunting grounds drove the hunters ever farther east, but in their wake would come farmers, and after the farmers, artisans and various state employees. The cornerstone of the conquest was the government's imposition of a fur tribute, or *yasak,* on the subject tribes; and the form and early evolution of the colonial administration, its allocation of resources, military strategy and disposition of troops were all fundamentally governed by this end. Such a policy was to leave its predatory mark on Siberian society long after the fur trade had ceased to dominate its economic life.

Old Turkish in origin, the word *yasak* originally meant "government" or "regulation," but came to be applied to an obligatory tribute surrendered by the conquered to their overlords in acknowledgment of their subjugation. A similar institution, the *dan,* had been imposed by the Mongols on the conquered Slavs, and in Siberia had been adopted before the coming of the Russians by some of the surviving Mongol-Tartar groups in their relations with weaker tribes. In the contested world of Siberia's interracial and ethnic relations, the Russians, in a sense, represented "merely a change of masters," and this facilitated the relatively swift acceptance of their rule.

As the Russians advanced from one area to the next, in the usual pattern a small, well-armed unit would descend upon some newfound community, assemble the village elders, take a couple of tribal leaders hostage and "imprison them in a rapidly built stronghold." Their brethren were then invited to ransom them by paying tribute and taking an oath to become loyal, *yasak*-paying subjects of the tsar. Thereafter, hostages were taken regularly and kept under constant guard (sometimes in squalid conditions) to assure that annual payments were kept up. If the natives refused to deliver the furs, or produced too few, various punitive measures were tried, such as torching their settlements, confiscating livestock or reindeer, if they had any, or taking women and children as hostages, too.

In addition to *yasak,* the Russians exacted *pominki*—supposedly voluntary gifts in furs made in honor of the tsar. But like a tip automatically included in a bill, they became a part of the mandated tribute, and wherever natives (with an understandable lack of enthusiasm) failed to make the expected donations, their recalcitrance was treated as an act of incipient revolt.

The Russians did everything they could to impress upon the natives the inevitability of their authority. In what became almost a ritual of pacification and deceit, whenever a Russian commandant was posted to an occupied area, he summoned the tribal elders to his headquarters and received them in flattering yet intimidating fashion, with volleys of cannon and musketfire in salute. A feast followed, where he made a political speech celebrating the might and mercy of the Great White Tsar and promising a better regime than the one they had just endured.

Every native had to take an oath of allegiance to the tsar, and its form wherever possible was tailored to local beliefs. The supernatural pow-

ers in which the tribe believed were invoked, so that those who broke
the oath could expect a terrible fate. The Ostyaks, for example, swore
before a bear skin on which a piece of bread, a knife, and an ax had
been placed. Whoever reneged could expect to choke to death on
food, be cut to pieces in a fight, or be dismembered by a bear. Since,
in the life of an Ostyak, these were common enough ways to die,
evidence confirming the oath's ineluctable power was not hard to find.

The Yakuts, with even less pleasant expectations, had to walk between the quartered parts of the carcass of a dog.

The manner and amount of the *yasak* varied, but in general it was
set as high as the traffic would bear. Sometimes it was levied as an
annual tax on individuals, sometimes upon a district as a whole. At the
beginning of the century it ranged from five to twenty-two sables per
man, but by the mid-1600s, the quota in Western Siberia had dropped
to about three—reflecting the decimation of the sable population. All
men from eighteen to fifty years of age were subject to the tax, and
occasionally (though at a lesser rate) even dependents and adoles-
cents. Regulations exempted "the old, the crippled, the blind, and the
dead," but attempts were made to tax even these by levies upon their
"estates." Sables were the prime pelt, but occasionally natives were
allowed to substitute other valuable furs, according to a relative scale
of value, in which so many fox, ermine, or squirrel were counted as
equal to the number of sables required. Ivory or other items might
also take their place.

To facilitate collection, the administrative units of a district were
often based on tribal units which had existed there before, just as
Russian forts and towns were often built on former village sites. In
more or less pacified districts, every year after the hunting season was
over tax collectors made their rounds, or natives brought their *yasak*
in to forts. In more remote areas, collectors had to hole up in a blockhouse, and at the appointed time allowed two or three natives to
approach and throw their furs in through the window. The Russians,
also through the window, exhibited their hostages and threw back
trinkets and bread.

Census books recorded the names of the *yasak*-paying natives in
every settlement, and receipts were kept on the amount collected from
each man. Obviously this system was more successful with sedentary
tribes than with nomadic groups, but the hostage system (based on the

natives' strong family ties) and gifts (such as trinkets, metal implements, and cloth) tended to bring them around.

In addition to *yasak,* the state also collected a 10 percent tax or tithe
on the take of private trappers and traders. In time those Russians, too,
had every reason to feel like a subject people from whom a heavy
tribute was drawn. Although the tithe was actually applied to all raw
goods produced in the colony—the fisherman had to yield up a tenth
of his catch, the salter a tenth of his salt, and so on—the official interest
in furs gave rise to numerous special regulations. In general the tithe
was exacted in the form of every tenth pelt, "with the best from the
best and with the medium grade from the medium . . . without choice
as they come." To ensure that the best were yielded up, the tithe had
to be paid before the hunter could engage in trade, and a system of
dated receipts, with a description of the furs from which the tithe had
been taken, helped prevent evasion. From lots of furs amounting to
less than ten pelts the state collected 10 percent of their monetary
value. Beyond that, an extensive network of customs posts was set up
in villages and towns and along the major roads. Certain routes to and
from Siberia were also sealed to prevent their circumvention, and in
1695 Verkhoturye was designated the sole authorized customs station
on the frontier, where passports were issued and all goods and merchandise were inspected or reinspected and received their official
seals. Many byways favored by smugglers were eventually patrolled by
guards.

Although government officials were not supposed to trade, many
did, and often forged alliances with merchants seeking to thwart the
tax. Customs agents, however, were empowered to search almost anyone at will, regardless of rank, and even military governors returning
from their posts were sometimes surprised on the frontier. Agents
went through their wagons, trunks, and baskets, shook out their bed-
clothes, opened caskets, and poked their fingers into loaves of baked
bread. Strip searches were not uncommon, and women were by no
means spared. Standard instructions specifically required agents to
look for skins sewn into their petticoats, or anywhere else they might
be concealed.

And so, by all these means—*yasak,* tithe, purchase, confiscation, and
trade—a steady stream of furs—of all conditions, sizes, and grades—
was directed each year into the district treasuries of Siberia. There they

were variously assessed, sewn together in pairs, packed in bundles, usually called "timbers" (because they were bound between two boards), and placed in boxes or sacks to which the military governor affixed his seal. Together with the customs books, they were taken under military guard to Moscow. At the Siberian Department (a major government bureau) the pelts were re-sorted, checked against the lists, and reappraised according to Moscow prices, which invariably increased their value from 20 to 500 percent. "The difference between the locally appraised price and that in Moscow," notes one historian, "represented, according to the contemporary accounting system, the profits that accrued to the State." On average, the *yasak* accounted for about 75 percent, and the tithe about 20 percent, of the government take.

In the late 1580s, when the conquest of Siberia had barely begun, the colonial income was about 20,000 pelts a year. By 1605, with Russian authority established throughout Western Siberia, some 62,400 pelts at least were collected, although indirect evidence would indicate a good deal more. And between 1635 and 1644, when the Russians were consolidating their hold along the Lena and had begun to penetrate into the basins of the Indigirka, Kolyma, and upper Angara rivers, the harvest may have been upward of half a million skins. Siberia had become a killing field. Black fox, white fox, ermine, beaver, squirrel, wolf, wolverine, and, above all, sable, the "Golden Fleece" that lured the Russian Argonauts into the Siberian wilds, flowed into the Treasury. By the middle of the seventeenth century, Siberian furs accounted for 10 percent or more of the total revenue of the state. They were also the dominant item in Russia's foreign trade, vastly surpassing leather, wax, honey, tallow, flax, hemp, grain, metalware, caviar, and silk, among other commodities. Although some of the goods exported from Russia to Asia were actually European imports—just as the silk sold to Europe came from Asia—it was fur-wealth that enabled Russia to cash in on its geographical position as intermediary between East and West.

A majority of Siberian furs were exported to Western Europe through the northern port of Archangel (built in 1585 as a haven for Dutch merchants at the mouth of the Northern Dvina River), and passed into Central Asia through Astrakhan at the mouth of the Volga, or through the Western Siberian towns of Tara and Tomsk. The chief domestic outlets of the trade were Moscow and Kholmogory. Vologda was the great transit center between Archangel and the Russian interior; the middle Volga trade was centered at Nizhny-Novgorod and Kazan.

So important were furs to the Russian economy that the Fur Treasury of the Siberian Department has been described as a kind of "supplementary mint" analogous to the gold funds kept by the mercantile countries of the West. Treasury officials sometimes referred to the colony, with affection, as their "little India"—though, in fact, it was four times India's size.

Furs also had a role to play as gifts and bribes in Russian diplomacy. In 1595, Boris Godunov made a stupendous donation to the Holy Roman Emperor, Rudolf II, in support of his planned crusade against the Turks. Unwilling to contribute men or arms, Godunov instead sent the emperor 342,883 skins worth an estimated 44,645 rubles at Moscow prices, but, as reappraised by merchants at Prague, 400,000 rubles, exclusive of 120 sables so rare as to be priceless. On display, the furs filled twenty chambers in the emperor's palace; tens of thousands of squirrel skins had to be left in wagons outside.

The little creature on which so much of this commerce and prosperity depended, *Martes zibellina*—the Eurasian sable—seemed hardly to deserve its fate. A solitary, arboreal weasel up to 20 inches long (not counting the tail), it weighed on average about 4 pounds, ranged in color from brown to black, and had a soft, dense silky undercoat with iridescent guard hairs. Sables were usually hunted during the winter when their pelts were prime, and because in the summer they ate "a kind of berry which caused them to itch and rub against trees, with damage to their pelts." It was also not until winter that the young (born in the spring) acquired coats of desirable length.

To economize on the expense of expeditions, hunters often formed into cartels of anywhere from six to sixty men. Standard equipment included snowshoes, a small sled harnessed with dogs, cooking utensils, a sack of flour, a birchbark vessel containing the leavening for bread, bedding, weapons, bait, and traps. Each hunter also carried a long staff, like a ski pole, with a spadelike upper end for shoveling snow. Operating out of winter huts, they blazed their trails by making notches in the trees, prepared pit traps baited with fish or meat, and tracked their quarry in the snow with nets and dogs. Upon their return they inspected the traps, skinned whatever sables they had caught, and smoked the pelts. Sometimes they stored them in hollowed-out logs sealed with ice and buried in the snow. Only the most expert marksmen could prevent the fur from being scarred, and few could match the natives at hitting the sable with an arrow in the nose. Since sables lived either in holes in the ground or in nests built in trees, hunters also tried to catch them in their lairs. In one technique, a hole just big enough to admit the sable's head was cut into a tree trunk, and a log was connected by a balance to the bait. When the sable rose up on its hind legs and put its head into the hole, the heavy log was released and fell, crushing the skull—"without injuring in the slightest the valuable parts of his skin."

The conquest of Siberia proceeded from one hunting ground to the next, as the fur resources in each gave out. This alone explains why explorers and pioneers sometimes rushed with such impetuosity to the farthest extremities of the territory, for it was there that the fur-bearing animals often abounded, and native populations resided whose skill could be utilized in the kill. Far from being alarmed at finding a large native population in a given area, the Russians rejoiced, because of the greater fur tax their subjugation would produce. Under Russian tutelage, natives began using systematic hunting techniques, while animals were routed from their accustomed habitats by advancing settlements as forest land was cleared. The uncontrolled hunting took a terrible toll. When the Russians first encountered Tungus on the Yenisey, sable were so plentiful among them that the natives even used the pelts to pad their skis. And around the mouth of the Olekma River in the Lena Basin, hunters in a single expedition could snare up to three hundred sables apiece. By midcentury, quality sables were no longer found in Western Siberia at all, and by 1627 along the lower Tunguska and Yenisey rivers they had been "hunted out." By 1649 along the upper Lena, only a handful of sables remained, and by century's end it was exceptional to find the animal around Yakutsk. As sables disappeared, other creatures were hunted more rapaciously—especially black and polar fox, beaver, ermine, and squirrel.

However, the Russians moved on to Eastern Siberia before the fur resources of Western Siberia were completely exhausted, with the result that parts of Western Siberia were not to be reconnoitered until long after Eastern Siberia had been crossed.

. . .

Throughout Siberia, the Russians consolidated their hold. In the army of occupation, professional soldiers made up the core, armed with muskets, swords, battleaxes, and pikes. Supplementing these were the "Litva" (literally, Lithuanians), a kind of Siberian Foreign Legion, as one scholar remarks, consisting of men of many nationalities—Germans, Swedes, Poles, Lithuanians, White Russians, and Ukrainians—by and large recruited from among prisoners of war. Ultimately more important than either were the Cossacks—not the freebooting type that belonged to Yermak's band, but town Cossacks or frontiersmen in state service, of whom there were about one thousand in 1625, and twice that number by 1631. These irregular troops were organized "entirely at the initiative of the government" and were salaried members of the military servitor class. Others, called "village Cossacks," held tax-free land as agricultural colonists but were expected to defend the ordinary peasants they lived among. Indeed, the remnants of Yermak's own band had eventually merged with the soldiers, trappers, prisoners of war, and others enlisted to police the borders and construct forts and fortified towns. They received payment for their service in money, grain, or land, and, like gentry soldiers holding service tenure estates, had to provide their own weapons and equipment when called to arms. In civilian life, they served as local policemen, firemen, couriers, carters, postmasters, customs officials, guides, or in whatever way their Siberian service required.

Whereas the regular soldiery figured most prominently in the initial phase of the conquest, their service, under increasingly raw frontier conditions, became more like that of the Cossacks, and by the middle of the century the two could hardly be told apart. *Promyshlenniks* (traders and hunters) also took on state assignments, and by the very nature of their occupation became explorers and conquerors. Their reconnaissance and hunting forays (especially in Eastern Siberia) often anticipated expeditions by regular troops, and by turning up promising areas for exploitation, prepared the way for new conquests, in which they also played a part. In an effort to control the sometimes turbulent and renegade elements of the population that made their way across the Urals, and to turn their energy to positive account, the government also elicited volunteers from among runaway serfs, ex-convicts, and so on, particularly in more remote regions, where manpower was in short supply. Native auxiliaries helped fill out the ranks.

At various strategic locations the Russians established strongholds to rivet their gains. The typical citadel was located on a high riverbank or at a portage site, surrounded by a timbered stockade with sharpened stakes. It also had parapets and embrasures for marksmen, a gate and corner towers 20 to 30 feet high, was often equipped with artillery and surrounded by a moat. Enlarged into an *ostrog,* or fort, it served as the administrative center of a given territory, both for the collection of tribute and as a military base. There were also smaller forts (*ostro-zheks*) that usually consisted of a simple rectangular wooden stockade; and winter blockhouses (*zimoves*) built in the forests, on the tundra, or on the shores of lakes as shelters for those on assignment to outlying or peripheral zones. By midcentury, a network of such outposts spanned the Siberian taiga from the Urals to the Pacific Ocean.

In the beginning, the Russians were hugely outnumbered, and around Yakutsk, for example, in 1676, there were an estimated 16,687 natives, as compared to about 670 Russians under arms. Some native groups, however, were hardly more than large family units guided by elders; others led a nomadic life, and were unable to organize a continuous defense of the lands they roamed. And all were primitively armed. Even when their guerrilla warfare tactics made masterful use of local terrain, the warriors lacked military discipline in the Western sense, seldom acted as a unit under the unquestioned command of a leader, and in battle emphasized the individual and his opportunities for personal distinction. This brought glory to their souls, but inevitable defeat at Russian hands.

The Russians, though fewer, were a generally united force, "socially and racially homogeneous," and aided and abetted by a mighty state power. Their possession of firearms, moreover, made it possible for small bands of men (seldom numbering more than one hundred) to dominate whole districts hundreds of square miles in extent. The Russians were presumptively aware of their superiority, yet in disparaging the capacity of the natives to resist, they were really no different from the Spanish conquistadores who recognized at once the overwhelming technological advantage they enjoyed. Christopher Columbus himself had a premonition of easy triumph from the moment of his landing in the New World. Shortly after he disembarked at Hispaniola, he noted in his journal on October 14, 1492, "With fifty men [the natives] can all be subjugated and made to do what is required." And he thought a fort would be superfluous.

Nevertheless, the Russian advance across completely unfamiliar and often difficult terrain might at least have been slowed if the local population had realized how much of a cumulative threat they were. But in fact many natives initially regarded the explorers as newcomers for trade, and showed them hospitality or supplied them with advice, instructions, and guides in the traditions of the clan system. In some cases they even embraced them as allies or protectors against hostile neighboring tribes, and (being used to paying tribute to someone) a few groups were as willing to subject themselves to Russian authority as to that of their former Mongol, Kirghiz, or Buryat feudal lords.

But perhaps the paramount factor was that the Siberians were hopelessly divided among themselves. In any given region, adjacent or competing groups cherished a rancorous hatred toward one another, and in haphazard retaliatory raids fought over favored hunting or fishing grounds, honor, women, and goods. This greatly eased the Russian task of establishing control. The Buryats had clashed with the Yakuts, the Yakuts with the Tungus; and the Ostyaks and Voguls, though closely related, were hereditary foes. So, too, were the Koryak, Chukchi, and Yukaghir. And of course there was no supra-ethnic association among them all since, for example, the Tungus had never heard of the Ostyaks and Voguls, or the Buryats of the Kamchadals.

Some of the blood feuds approached a genocidal scale. The Yukaghir, for example, had once occupied the whole region between the Lena and the Anadyr rivers, from the Verkhoyansk Range to the Arctic Ocean. The Yakuts called the northern lights "Yukaghir Fire," in homage to the multitudinous fires of Yukaghir encampments which in olden days had seemed as if reflected in the evening sky. But the Koryak, Chukchi, and Tungus had all become their deadly enemies, and by the time the Russians arrived, the Yukaghir population was so reduced as to make them the least of the northeastern tribes.

Although it is sometimes said (in mitigation of the conquest) that the Russians at least put an end to intertribal warfare, the opposite is true. The Russians deliberately exploited such hostilities, and otherwise endeavored to turn them to account. Ostyaks were used as auxiliary troops against the Voguls and Samoyeds, Yukaghirs against the Tungus, Koryak, and Chukchi, and Tungus against the Buryats, as a mercenary force. *Yasak*-paying natives also helped to impose the tax on their neighbors, even as the more defiant attacked their acquiescent brethren in punitive raids.

Less deliberately, but contributing to the same tempestuous results, the Russians by their exactions and campaigns put many natives to flight, driving one group into the territory claimed by another and creating animosities that had not existed before. The economic imperatives of *yasak* and trade also (as Robert Utley remarks about the American West) "gave rise to territorial ambitions in groups formerly content with the land they occupied. For now natives killed game not only for their own needs" but for *yasak,* and also "to pile up hides and furs for barter with the whites." Ironware and copper utensils, metal arrowheads and tools became an indispensable part of their lives. The Yakuts, for example, were prepared to pay for an iron pot with as many sable skins as it would hold.

Throughout the early conquest, which had seen the Russians rapidly establish their authority over the three greatest river basins of northern Asia as well as much of the Arctic coast, there had been innumerable firefights, skirmishes, ambushes, and raids; but except for the initial battle for Kuchum's capital of Isker, almost no other sizable military confrontation had taken place. And the historic stature of Yermak's campaign itself derived less from its scale than from its unforeseen results.

Then, in the valley of the Amur—the Black Dragon River—the Russians came up against the Chinese.

5

THE BLACK DRAGON RIVER

THE tsar's satraps had been feeling their way toward the margins of the Chinese Empire ever since settling Yakutsk. Increasing problems of provisionment in Eastern Siberia drove them nearer, as part of a frantic search for agriculturally productive land. In 1626, men in Yeniseysk had complained that their food was "such, that in Russia even animals would not accept it"; in 1629, the garrison at Krasnoyarsk had been driven by starvation to cannibalism; and eastward the scarcity of foodstuffs was even more severe. In the late 1630s, Russians operating along the Yenisey and Lena rivers began to hear rumors of a valley to the southeast where agriculture flourished, and where there were rich deposits of silver and other ores. Scouts collected similar information from Tungus on the Angara, and Ivan Moskvitin on the coast of the Okhotsk Sea had made the acquaintance of the Lamuts, a tribe related to the Tungus, who told him about rich lands to the south inhabited by the Gilyaks and Daurs. It was said (as it had been of the Buryats before them) that these people had prosperous and settled communities and all that the beleaguered frontiersmen in Eastern Siberia would require.

In June 1643, Vasily Poyarkov, the *golova* or "writing chief" at Yakutsk, undertook a general reconnaissance expedition to verify the various reports. With 133 men plus plenty of powder and shot (but few provisions, since he planned to requisition what he needed on the way), he ascended the Aldan River, a tributary of the Lena, crossed the

Stanovoy Range after stationing forty-nine men at a blockhouse on the divide, and descended the Zeya River to the Amur.

The first Daurs Poyarkov encountered downstream were quite hospitable. They gave him *yasak* and hostages, and confirmed that grain was locally grown; but "in spite of his insistent demands, denied knowledge of any deposits of silver, copper, or lead ore." They explained that the metal objects in their possession came by trade from the Mongols and the Chinese.

The Russians remained unsatisfied. Though generously supplied with foodstuffs, their cruelty toward the Daurs soon erased the goodwill, and their source of provisions dried up. As a result, during the winter of 1643–44 forty Russians starved to death, and some of the dead were apparently eaten by their companions. Spring at last brought some reprieve, as the detachment from the blockhouse arrived with fresh supplies; but as the Russians made their way down the Zeya, word of their barbarities preceded them, and the inhabitants prepared to fight. Near the mouth of the Sungari, an ambush wiped out a party of Russian scouts, and finding it impossible to land anywhere in safety, Poyarkov hastened downstream. At the mouth of the Ussuri (another of the Amur's great affluents) he found himself in the land of the Goldi, and two weeks later came to the territory of the Gilyaks, whose settlements extended to the coast. A month later he was at the mouth of the Amur itself, where he passed another difficult winter (1644–45), and by the end of it had only sixty men left. Not daring to return up the Amur through hostile territory, in the spring of 1645 Poyarkov sailed into the stormy Sea of Okhotsk and, following the coast northward, three months later reached the mouth of the Ulya River, where Moskvitin had built a winter blockhouse six years before. During the winter of 1645–46, he collected *yasak* from the local Lamuts; when spring arrived, he crossed the mountains, sailed down the Maya River to the Aldan, and from there into the Lena to Yakutsk.

In the course of his odyssey, Poyarkov had traversed an enormous expanse of previously unexplored territory, recorded its salient features on a serviceable map, charted part of the coast of the Okhotsk Sea, and confirmed that Dauria (the Upper Amur Valley) had a large population, dense forests full of fur-bearing animals, and soil fertile for crops. "And the warriors of the Sovereign," he declared in his report (despite his own horrid experience) "will not go hungry in this land."

Envisioning the Amur Valley as "the future granary of eastern Siberia," he optimistically conjectured that three hundred soldiers would suffice to bring the region under Russian control.

The way to the Amur traced by Poyarkov, however, was arduous because of intervening rapids and mountainous terrain, and before long a more direct route was explored by way of the Olekma River, which led almost to where the Shilka and the Argun rivers joined. This was the route chosen for the expedition of Poyarkov's successor, Yerofey Khabarov.

Born in Ustiug about 1610, Khabarov was a merchant adventurer of the swashbuckling type who had managed saltworks at Solvychegodsk for the Stroganovs before coming to Siberia in 1633. About 1636, he began to invest in fledgling farming projects on the Yenisey, and before long he became influential in local agricultural development. Diversifying, he also began his own saltworks (at Ustkut), got into the transport business, and dabbled in the fur trade. His investments flourished as the region opened up. Living and working near the Ilim portage, the main line of communication from the Lena to the west, he also had access to the latest information about the Amur explorations, and in March 1649, with the blessing of the commandant at Yakutsk, Khabarov organized and privately financed an Amur venture of his own.

With 150 men, he made his way up the Olekma that spring, crossed the Yablonovy Range in the winter of 1650, and arrived on the Amur. The natives, expecting the worst, fled in terror before him, and the Russians found village after village deserted as they proceeded downstream. Discovering an old woman hiding in a hut, Khabarov tortured her for information, but about all he could ascertain was that the Daurs paid tribute to the Chinese. After a general survey of the area, he garrisoned an outpost with fifty men and returned to Yakutsk on May 26, 1651, where he made his report. More realistic than Poyarkov in assessing Russian prospects, he estimated that it would take an army of at least six thousand to subdue the region (given the likelihood of Chinese intervention), but that the effort would be worth it because the Amur Valley could supply the whole district of Yakutsk with grain. There was, Khabarov said, "more fish in the Amur than in the Volga, and the forests along the river, with sables in abundance, are dark and grand." The local commanders were persuaded and forwarded his recommendations to Moscow, where they found an enthusiastic response. An army of three thousand was assembled under the command of Prince Lobanov-Rostovsky, a former military governor of Tobolsk, and for the first time since the conquest began, a full-fledged military campaign got under way.

Meanwhile, a second expedition of 138 men under Khabarov in the fall of 1650 had met determined resistance from the Daurs. After much fighting, the Russians founded Achansk, occupied a large settlement belonging to a Daur princeling by the name of Albaza (for whom the future fort of Albazin was named), and in June 1651 they began to fight their way down the Amur. Khabarov ravaged numerous settlements without mercy, and in this barbarous manner conquered both banks of the river as far as the Sungari. Below this tributary, the region was "completely devastated within a week's time" as the Russians looted and burned and cut down the natives "like trees." In one instance, they seized hundreds of women and children; "with God's help," recalled Khabarov, "we burned them, we knocked them on the head . . . and counting big and little, we killed six hundred and sixty one." His rampage continued into the land of the Goldi, where he again left a trail of blood. The carnage made such an impression upon the inhabitants that two hundred years later their folktales had transformed the Russians into fiends. "When the Russians first arrived on the Amur," one historian has written, "the natives cultivated fields and kept cattle. Ten years afterwards these fields had become deserts." Although Khabarov prevailed, collected hundreds of fur pelts, and established a second strategic stronghold with the founding of Achansk, he dramatically altered Russian prospects for the long term, since the natives, anticipating unending grief at Russian hands, now urgently appealed for aid to their neighbors and nominal masters, the Manchus.

As the two great powers moved toward confrontation, a form of reintroduction was also taking place. From the early days of the Mongol Empire, when both Russia and China had come under the Mongol yoke, their subjects had mingled at Karakorum, the imperial capital, where Russian and Chinese artisans were also employed at the Great Khan's court. At one time, Russian mercenaries were formed into a praetorian guard, and periodically Russian princes had also shown up, to be ritually confirmed as vassals of the khan.

Extending from the Pacific Ocean to beyond the shores of the Black Sea, Mongol overlordship had facilitated trade and communication among the numerous peoples brought within its ken, and had effectively secured a network of far-flung highways along which a constant caravan traffic flowed. Under the *Pax Mongolica* of the Middle Ages, mail was relayed by "pony express" from the Don to the Yellow River, and the Mongols boasted that "a young girl could travel alone with a bagful of gold from one end of the Empire to the other without encountering the slightest harm." After the empire's dissolution, however, coincident with the rise of Islam in Central Asia, the trade routes were disrupted, and it was not until the second decade of the seventeenth century that official contact between Russia and China was again attempted, when diplomatic and trade ambassadors, with an imperial prestige all their own, made their way from Moscow to Peking.

The renewed encounter was one of culture shock. China had a hierarchical view of the international order (with itself at the pinnacle) and a somewhat condescending view of all other states. Chinese foreign relations were accordingly based on the tribute system—ironically enough, the progenitor (via the Mongols) of the system Russia had imposed on Siberia. Gestures of homage were expected even from the representatives of other imperial powers, and in immediate economic terms, China also claimed suzerainty over certain neighboring Siberian tribes. By trade and tribute, these tribes helped meet the appetite, in north China especially, for ivory and furs.

The route from Siberia to China led in part through outer Mongolia, which enabled the eastern mongols (as distinguished from the western Mongols, or Kalmucks, of the Altay Mountains and northwestern Sinkiang) to become intermediaries in the trade. Directly and indirectly, the Russians themselves therefore also quite early on became acquainted with Mongolian politics and geography and through the reports of their envoys, learned something of Chinese power—of the Great Wall, mounted with cannon, with monumental towers rivaling those of the Kremlin, and of the contemporary grandeur of Peking. They also knew that the Chinese had an appetite for such luxury goods as satins, velvets, and silks, wore gold and silver, and cultivated fields of wheat, barley, and oats. In pursuit of the commercial bounty that might flow from relations with such a highly developed state, Ivan Petlin, Russia's first envoy to China in 1618, had returned with a letter of invitation to trade. But unfortunately the Russians were unable to find anyone able to translate it until 1675! That lapse in linguistic competence within the Russian foreign service had such drastic consequences for their later relations that seldom has the lack of a little academic knowledge meant so much. For even as hostilities arose, the negotiation of a bilateral trade agreement—the Kremlin's original objective—remained the principal motive behind Russia's bellicose acts.

Meanwhile, in 1636, the Ming Dynasty had collapsed, to be succeeded by the Ching Dynasty of the Manchus, whose homeland was Manchuria. Preoccupied with establishing their own legitimacy and consolidating their power, the Manchus devoted the whole of their attention to pacifying the widespread unrest within the empire and, secondarily, to extending their sway over the Mongol tribes.

The first task had priority but was not easily achieved. As a result, the Mongol tribes had a chance to regroup, and Russian advances in southeastern Siberia, which had continued unchecked, culminated in daring incursions on China's northern frontier. The very same year, in fact, in which the Manchus imposed their rule over the tribes of the lower Amur, Poyarkov and his Cossack band had descended the river to its mouth.

The Manchus at first were not prepared to cope with this aggression, but in the wake of Khabarov's second expedition, they decided they could no longer wait to act. In March 1652, they brought an army of two thousand men with artillery to the gates of Achansk, and began to bombard the fort. The Cossacks, taken unawares, rushed to the walls in their nightshirts, but in the battle that ensued, the Chinese failed to press their advantage, for they were restrained by orders to take the Russians alive. In truth, the last thing the Manchus wanted (given their other preoccupations) was a foreign war. And eventually the besiegers withdrew with a warning: to immediately evacuate the fort or they would return. As the Russians under Khabarov retreated upstream, they saw more Manchus gathering at the mouth of the Sungari. At the mouth of the Zeya (site of the future Blagoveshchensk), over a third of his men deserted into the woods.

Meanwhile, news of Khabarov's earlier atrocities had reached the tsar, who demanded an accounting. In the fall of 1653, a new commandant, Dmitry Zinovyev, arrived with fresh troops, awarded the Cossacks special medals, but produced an arrest warrant for Khabarov himself. When the latter resisted, Zinovyev "seized him by the beard and beat him up."

Subsequently taken to the capital under guard, Khabarov was hauled before the Siberian Department and accused of wanton cruelty, abusing his authority, and other crimes. The government, however, was reluctant to disown such a zealous son—who, despite his excesses, had "shown ability and daring, and had worked for the future of his country." Ultimately, he was exonerated, promoted to "boyar-son," and hailed as an empire builder. With this imperial blessing, he returned to Siberia as commander of the vital fortress of Ilimsk. Two hundred years later his name would be given to a major city founded on the left bank of the Amur, Khabarovsk.

Meanwhile, Zinovyev laid the groundwork for three more forts and detailed some of the troops to farming, in anticipation of the arrival of Prince Lobanov-Rostovsky's army. That army, however, never came. Instead, it was shifted to the troubled Russo-Polish frontier, as the Kremlin decided it might be more productive to try to open a dialogue with Peking.

The Russians needed money. Large state expenditures had recently been required to deal with a number of calamities, including the Stenka Razin revolt, conflict with Poland over the Ukraine, a declining balance of trade (due in part to restrictions placed on foreign merchants at the instigation of their Russian counterparts), and inroads on the fur trade from North American competition. Although Russian furs had long dominated the markets of Western Europe, by 1649 supply had begun to exceed demand—a situation that might have corrected itself but for the introduction of Canadian beaver. "The star of the Russian fur trade was setting in Europe," notes one historian, "the star of the Canadian fur trade was beginning to rise." But in China, where furs were in terrific demand, there suddenly loomed a vast new emporium (safely remote from Canadian competition) as great as the market the Russians might lose.

In 1654, the tsar appointed Fyodor Baykov as his special trade envoy to Peking. Baykov sent Setkul Ablin, a Bukharan merchant in Russian service, ahead to announce his coming, but unfortunately the Manchus mistook him for the ambassador himself, and when he was found to possess neither letters of accreditation nor gifts, dismissed him without a hearing. No preparations were therefore made for Baykov's own arrival, and when he appeared in 1656 the Manchus couldn't figure out who he was. When at length his credentials were properly construed, the Manchus nevertheless insisted, according to their own ceremonial, that Baykov present his "tribute" (i.e., gifts) immediately, and deliver his instructions and letter to the emperor through intermediaries before an audience took place. Baykov, on the basis of his own orders— "not to act in any way that might imply the inferior status of the Tsar in relation to the Emperor"—refused, whereupon they proceeded to take his gifts by force. In the test of wills that followed, Baykov was even threatened with death; eventually he was allowed to leave unharmed, although his embassy had been an unmitigated disaster.

Military action was renewed, but some of it was unofficial and without the blessing of the Russian command. Along the Lena and its tributaries wild rumors had spread about the congenial climate and wealth of the Amur River Valley. Some of the returning Cossacks flaunted their plunder, including silks and jewels, and led their compatriots to believe that the region was the El Dorado of their dreams. By 1655, a not inconsiderable portion of Eastern Siberia's official occupation force had "run away" to seek fortunes along the Amur's forested banks. Turning bandit, these renegades plundered and oppressed the natives at will (especially when their expectations of plenty were not readily met) and made new intervention by the Manchus inevitable. Barrier stations were set up to try to stem the emigration, but they were circumvented with ease. As a result, the upper Amur quickly came to resemble a den of thieves. Local agriculture was completely disrupted, and Zinovyev's successor, Onufry Stepanov, had trouble extorting enough food from the natives even to feed the 320 men left under his command.

On June 6, 1654, when Stepanov and his men tried to proceed down the Sungari, a Manchu regiment, organized into companies and smartly dressed in uniforms corresponding to the colors of their flags, cut them off and bombarded their boats with cannon from the shore. The Russians retreated upstream, where they were joined by some sixty-five compatriots who had just arrived on rafts, but during the winter of 1654–55, the Manchus built a fortress at the mouth of the Sungari to blockade it, while the Russians holed up in their own stronghold of Kumarsk. In March they had to abandon the fort under siege. Foraging expeditions yielded little relief for the half-starved Russians as they roamed through the empty villages and fields. At length, in desperation, Stepanov in the spring of 1658 led five hundred men downriver but was trapped by Manchu barges armed with cannon, and blown to smithereens. Stepanov's replacement, Afanasy Pashkov, the former military governor of Yeniseysk, arrived on the heels of this rout and decided to base his command more safely to the north at Nerchinsk. But over the next two years his forces were decimated by famine, disease, cold, sporadic fighting, and starvation, as they waited in vain for fresh supplies and reinforcements from Yeniseysk. "Barefoot and half-naked," writes one historian, "they scrabbled for roots, grasses, bark, carrion," not balking even at devouring "an unborn foal ripped from a dead mare's womb." In 1660 they withdrew to Irgensk, with only seventy-five men (out of the original four hundred) left alive. Pashkov was recalled and succeeded by Aleksey Tolbuzin.

A new diplomatic initiative was now launched but came to nothing when the Russian envoy to Peking was summarily dismissed because his letter of introduction was judged lacking in appropriate humility.

While government forces retrenched in the Transbaikal, bands of Siberian outlaws, some numbering in the hundreds, continued to fill the vacuum in the valley they had left. In 1665, Nikifor Chernigovski, a Pole in Russian service who had murdered a Siberian fortress commander, descended upon the Amur with eighty-four other mutineers, established the stronghold of Albazin, and organized a sort of free Cossack republic. Other criminals or adventurers enlisted under his flag. "They have come into our country," complained one Chinese chronicler, "only to collect sable skins and to debauch the women and girls." The charge was true enough, but since the outlaws also had no hope of returning home, in fact their settlement acquired a degree of permanency lacking in earlier colonization attempts. Some 2,700 acres of land were brought under cultivation, and when in 1672 they offered their unofficial gains to the governor of Nerchinsk in return for clemency, he was only too happy to accept.

In 1661, the first Manchu emperor died, and during the minority of his successor, K'ang-hsi, the regents were busy suppressing revolts. Tempted once more by a sporadic Chinese response to their incursions, the Russians pushed south into the valley, and from Albazin established an ever-widening circle of outposts and farms. Then, in 1667, a prominent Tungus chieftain, Ghantimur, a former vassal of the Manchus who had taken part in the earlier attack on Kumarsk, defected (with three hundred warriors, nine wives, and thirty children, "not counting daughters") to the Russians' side. By the time the Manchus could turn their attention back to their northern frontier, they found they were facing not just outlaw Cossack bands but "permanent settlements officially integrated into Russia's Siberian colony."

Peking of course recognized that the establishment of commercial relations and a solution to the Amur problem were intertwined. However, the Kremlin's new envoy, Nikolai Milescu-Spafary (a Moldavian noble in Russian service), failed to open a broader dialogue, and when he left Peking in September 1676, he had little to show for his efforts except for a decree—not a letter—issued by the emperor K'ang-hsi demanding Ghantimur's extradition and an end to Russian aggression as preconditions for talks.

Emerging from his minority with a firm grip on his realm, in 1680 K'ang-hsi was at last able to act decisively to stop the Russian advance. Realizing that diplomacy combined with intermittent fighting would not suffice, he proceeded to develop a position of overwhelming strength from which to force negotiations on his terms. A military buildup in northern Manchuria was begun, and special attention paid to the problems of supply. Starting in 1680, a chain of garrisons was established from Peking north to the Amur and along its tributary rivers and streams, and the area around the Russian settlements was carefully reconnoitered and mapped. A dockyard was built at Kirin for the preparation of a fleet, supply transports were sent upriver, and granaries were established for the troops on the upper Liao. A canal connecting the Liao and Sungari rivers was also dug. In 1684–85, military farming was introduced in Aigun and rice stockpiled in Manchuria.

Up until the end, however, K'ang-hsi hoped for a political solution without recourse to war. He made a final effort to reach a settlement with Russian officials, urging them to return to Yakutsk ("You can hunt sables and collect taxes there, but you may not come into our land to make trouble"), and offered an exchange of prisoners and border trade. The Russians wanted more and remained defiant, but their position quickly deteriorated. A new Manchu stronghold at Aigun cut them off from the Zeya, and they were evicted completely from the lower Amur and its tributaries by 1683. On the upper Amur, only Albazin remained.

In addition to the usual stockade with corner towers, this fortress was surrounded by a large moat. Beyond the moat, which the Cossacks had dug with extreme difficulty in the frozen ground, was a wooden palisade, and beyond this, pointed iron stakes in camouflaged pits. Along the top of the walls were iron baskets filled with resin, to serve as lanterns in the event of a night attack, and stacks of long poles for pushing away the ladders of besiegers. An elevated gun turret enabled the fort's artillery to revolve in any direction.

By early 1682, when Aleksey Tolbuzin took over as fortress commander, the garrison consisted of less than five hundred men, with dwindling supplies. The Manchu force in the area, variously estimated at up to ten thousand, had cavalry and artillery, and increased its logistical advantages with each day. On May 23, 1685, it appeared beneath the fortress walls and put Tolbuzin's elaborate defensive preparations to the test.

The Manchus built earthworks around the fort, including a wall to the south as a shield for their marksmen, placed cannon to the north, deployed troops to the east and west, and launched gunboats on the river. Toward evening, they piled dry wood at the base of the wooden stockade on three sides and set the tinder ablaze. With their navy holding the riverside, the Russians had no escape. After a steady bombardment by shot and incendiary arrows, initial casualties in the fort were heavy and Tolbuzin ran up a white flag. In truth, the Manchus had the Russians at their mercy, and had been provoked to the point of rationalizing slaughter, as the Russians knew. Instead, with extraordinary consideration, the Manchus allowed the defenders an unmolested retreat to Nerchinsk. But no sooner had the Manchus themselves withdrawn than Tolbuzin returned with 826 men, 12 cannon, 4,000 pounds of powder, 140 hand grenades, enough food to last a year, and one Afanasy Beiton, a German military engineer, to supervise the construction of an even more formidable fort.

In July 1686, the outraged Manchus reappeared. On a hill a third of a mile away they placed their large cannon, and drew up their light artillery to a distance of about 500 feet. They surrounded Albazin as before, opened their bombardment with a rain of incendiary arrows, and advanced toward the walls behind large wooden shields sheathed in leather and mounted on wheels. Then they rolled up ladders equipped with grappling hooks, and after that carts of firewood, resin, and straw with which to set the fort on fire. When their demands for surrender were arrogantly met by a cannonade, they relentlessly pressed their siege, and all Russian attempts to reinforce the defenders failed.

Tolbuzin and many others perished; food ran out and the rest began to starve. It is said that at one point the famished garrison, in a desperate stratagem, sent out a pie, weighing 40 or 50 pounds, to the Manchu commander to convince him that the fort was well supplied. The commander declared himself delighted, and sent for more.

Russian emissaries now hastened to Peking to announce the appointment of a new envoy to discuss frontier problems, and delivered a letter to K'ang-hsi from the tsar expressing hope for future peace. Once it was clear that serious negotiations were at last intended, K'ang-hsi lifted the siege, on November 3, 1686.

Inside Albazin, less than sixty-six men remained alive.

Selenginsk (in the Transbaikal) was designated as the site for talks. On January 26, 1687, a high-level Russian delegation headed by Fyodor Golovin, a long-standing expert in Siberian affairs and the son of the military governor of Tobolsk, set out from the capital. An equally distinguished Manchu delegation, jointly led by two members of the imperial family—Songgotu, a chamberlain of the imperial bodyguard and a former grand secretary, and Tung Kuo-kang, a military expert—assembled their entourage in Peking.

Golovin's initial instructions were to insist on the Amur River as far as the Zeya as the frontier line, enabling the Russians to maintain their settlements along the left, or north, bank. If the Chinese demanded a total Russian withdrawal from the area, he was to agree only if it was clearly understood that a broadly conceived bilateral trade agreement would then be signed. However, he was not to agree to the extradition of Ghantimur.

This overall approach had been developed before Albazin's capitulation, when the fort might have served as a bargaining chip. But since the Chinese could now destroy it at will, Golovin was reinstructed to propose the area around Albazin as a demilitarized zone. If this were rejected, he was to suspend the negotiations in order to give the Russians time to regroup.

Having decisively defeated the Russians, however, the Chinese were unwilling to settle for anything less than Ghantimur's extradition and complete control of the river valley and all its tributary streams. "If the

Russians will accede to these points," an imperial memorial to the delegates read, "we . . . will enter into commercial relations; otherwise we shall return and make no peace with them at all."

While various strategies were being hammered out, the Mongols suddenly and unexpectedly emerged as a force to tip the scales. Though far from the "world power" their ancestral hordes had been, they remained a regional power of considerable clout, and tensions had developed between them and the Russians along the Mongolian frontier. Notwithstanding overtures by both sides for more peaceful relations, skirmishing continued, and in the maneuvering just before the negotiations were to start, the Mongols for all practical purposes cast themselves as Manchu allies. This was rather pointedly brought home to Golovin and his escort when the Mongols carried out raids around Selenginsk to coincide with his arrival there for the conference in October 1687. The Manchus had every hope, therefore, of obtaining what they wished. But the situation was in extreme flux, and in the following year an anti-Manchu coalition of western Mongol tribes arose under the leadership of one Galdan, a fierce warrior-prince and self-described successor to Genghis Khan. The Chinese delegation turned back; the conference was postponed; and Nerchinsk was selected as the alternate site. When the conference finally convened in the autumn of 1689, Galdan had made himself master of most of Outer Mongolia and was preparing to go to war with K'ang-hsi himself. This gave the Russians unanticipated leverage by putting pressure on K'ang-hsi to come to terms as quickly as possible both to forestall a Russo-Mongol alliance and to free his armies to march against Galdan.

Yet the Russians still felt squeezed. Their Treasury, already depleted, had recently been strained to the breaking point by huge military expenditures on a fruitless Crimean campaign, and by a general economic depression, which perhaps only trade relations with China could ease. At Nerchinsk, they were also surrounded by a hostile native population (the Buryats), which lent additional urgency to their task.

The Manchu delegation arrived first, on July 20, 1689, escorted by a veritable army of fifteen thousand men. Its supplies were borne by several thousand camels and horses, and a fleet of armed junks carried cannon and stacks of arms. Overnight a tent city sprang up beside the Russian fortress, which itself had a garrison of only six hundred, and was implicitly under siege from the moment the Chinese arrived. Although Golovin's own military retinue, arriving on August 9, was not inconsiderable and increased the garrison by some fifteen hundred, it was scarcely enough to affect the balance of forces at hand.

As the envoys prepared to meet on the appointed day, a company of Russians paraded with a fife and drums, and behind them came the ambassador on horseback dressed in cloth-of-gold and a caftan, sable-fringed. The floor of the Russian tent was spread with Oriental rugs, and a Persian carpet covered the ambassador's desk, upon which stood an inkstand and a clock that struck the hours. The Manchus likewise appeared, recumbent in palanquins, "in all their Robes of State, which were Gold and Silk Brocade, embroider'd with Dragons of the Empire. But upon hearing of the Russians' regalia, they decided to use understatement, removing all marks of dignity except one great silk umbrella, carried before each official." In the middle of their own tent they placed a plain wooden bench.

In all other respects, however, the protocol was remarkable for emphasizing the absolute parity of the two negotiating teams. Each had to be made up of the same number of personnel, and as they stood and faced each other, they formed exactly parallel lines, with identical spaces between the members of each row. They took turns frisking each other with much solemnity for hidden weapons, and as this ceremonial reached its comical extreme, the envoys themselves simultaneously dismounted and called out their first greetings to one another in unison.

The talks got under way on August 12, and were conducted through interpreters in Latin, with the Chinese relying on two Jesuit missionaries, Fathers Francis Gerbillon and Thomas Pereyra (both long resident in Peking), and the Russians (for form's sake) on Andrei Belobotskii, a university-educated Pole, although Golovin was fluent in Latin himself.

Each side began with excessive demands. Golovin made the first, short speech, proposing the Amur as the frontier, since "the population on its left bank had already recognized the overlordship of the Russian Tsar by paying him regular tribute." Prince Songgotu countered by proposing the Lena as "fixed by Heaven itself to be the natural boundary between the two enlightened empires." That would have obliged the Russians to withdraw all the way to Lake Baikal, giving up Transbaikalia and most of Eastern Siberia.

On the following day the negotiators got down to serious business,

and focused on the Amur itself, which flowed through an area technically under Chinese jurisdiction, but which the Russians had also managed to colonize to some degree. The Chinese were willing to give the
Russians Nerchinsk as a sheltering place for their merchants and missions, provided a trade agreement was reached; Golovin agreed to
cede the Amur as far as Albazin.

The principal delegates apparently met face to face only three times:
on August 12, when the basic positions were exchanged; the next day,
which was taken up with counterproposals; and on August 27, when
the treaty itself was signed. In the interim, messengers of secondary
rank scurried back and forth between the two camps to mediate their
differences, or to pass on various bluffs and ultimatums, with Belobotskii and the two Jesuit priests effectively helping to move the process
along.

Although both Jesuits enjoyed the confidence of the emperor himself, the Manchu ambassadors distrusted them, especially after they
realized that Golovin spoke Latin too. Nevertheless, it was largely due
to their patience and tact that the two parties came to terms, and on
August 27, 1689, the Treaty of Nerchinsk—the first ever concluded
between China and a European power—was signed. After the seals of
the respective ambassadors were attached, "the Moscovites," wrote the
Jesuit Pereyra, "ordered beautiful plates full of sweets to be brought
in, including a loaf of white sugar from the Island of Madeira which
was something our ambassadors had never seen before." Their admiration got the better of them and each member of the delegation stole
what he could to show to his friends. Toasts were made with vodka
(rather too strong for Chinese taste), and the Russians presented their
counterparts with a number of gifts, including watches, a telescope,
two silver cups, and some precious furs. The Chinese reciprocated
with golden goblets, beautiful saddles, and damask.

Both sides declared themselves satisfied with the treaty, although
the Manchus perhaps had more reason to rejoice. By its terms, the
boundary between the two empires began at the Argun River and ran
to a point about 200 miles north of the Amur; it then proceeded
easterly along the summit of the Stanovoy Range to the coast of the
Okhotsk Sea. The Russians kept Nerchinsk (an inadequate base for
continuing Russian incursions into northern Manchuria), but lost Albazin (the gateway to the Amur), which was to be destroyed. Although

the two powers agreed on the handling of fugitives and criminals within the frontier zone, Ghantimur remained in Russian hands. Certain ambiguities in the text were later to cause dispute, but plainly it barred Russia from the entire Amur Valley, which no one at the time denied. For their part, the Russians secured de facto recognition of their possessions in Eastern Siberia and their suzerainty over the Buryats of the Transbaikal, and they obtained the coveted trade agreement they had sought. Copies of the treaty were exchanged, the Russians presenting transcripts in Latin and Russian to the Manchus, who reciprocated with copies in Latin and Chinese. The Latin copies were regarded as official, but in accordance with the treaty's sixth paragraph, stone slabs engraved with a synopsis of its articles in all three languages were erected on the frontier.

The Treaty of Nerchinsk inaugurated a period of peace between the two powers that lasted for almost 170 years. It freed Russia to concentrate militarily on conflicts affecting its borders in the west, and China to concentrate on the Mongols. And within a decade Galdan would be defeated at K'ang-hsi's hands.

Although loss of the Amur cost Russia its best route to the Pacific, and affected all subsequent operations in Eastern Siberia (where the fur trade drew few settlers compared with the legions agriculture might have lured), at the time the Russians evidently preferred the tangible fruits of commerce to "the uncertain benefits of trapping in the Amur basin and sailing the river's waters to an unknown sea."

And (at the time) the choice was probably right. The revolution in the European fur trade had posed a tremendous threat to the Russian economy, but it was overcome almost immediately by the new Chinese market for furs. In another fortunate coincidence (with the sable population in decline), the Chinese preferred ermine, Arctic fox, and above all squirrel, the least (but most plentiful) of the Siberian pelts. Chinese furriers were exceptionally skillful at dyeing them, and Russian specialists soon got into the business, developing a coloring made from black crowberries boiled with alum and fish blubber that imparted such dark luster to the skins that they could be sold, or exchanged, for a much higher price.

Moreover, the single most important Asian export to Europe was silk. Uniquely positioned as the intermediary between East and West, Russia became the chief beneficiary in the trade of yet another commodity the Europeans greatly desired.

In subsequent years, Russia's whole policy toward China would be aimed at the expansion of trade relations. Both Nerchinsk as the transit point, and Irkutsk as the fur emporium of Eastern Siberia, grew, as did the amount of cross-border smuggling, with unofficial caravans to Peking outnumbering those undertaken with government sponsorship by almost four to one.

The Treaty of Nerchinsk, it should be noted, had left vague the Russian-Mongolian border, but in 1727 the Chinese sought a more explicit demarcation of it in the Treaty of Kyakhta, which drew that part of the southern boundary of Siberia from the Argun River to the Yenisey. Outer Mongolia was thereby placed outside the Russian sphere of settlement, and the frontier post of Kyakhta soon replaced Nerchinsk as the hub of the Sino-Russian trade.

6

"THE YERMAK OF KAMCHATKA"

THE loss of the Amur River Valley concentrated the government's efforts once again on Siberia's northeast. Bands of *promyshlennik*-explorers fanned out along the coast of the Okhotsk Sea, from the Uda River to the Penzhinsk Gulf, and the conquest of Kamchatka (a territory vaguely known to the Russians as early as the 1650s) was begun.

About the size and shape of Italy, Kamchatka was inhabited in the north and west by Koryaks and throughout most of the rest of the peninsula (especially in the Kamchatka River Valley) by Kamchadals, with a handful of Ainu on its southern tip.

From the fort at Anadyrsk, the Cossacks for many years had imposed *yasak* upon the Koryak reindeer herders to the south, but it was not until 1695 when the Cossack Vladimir Atlasov—"the Yermak of Kamchatka," as Pushkin called him—was appointed commandant that the Russians expanded their hold.

Born of peasant stock, Atlasov had come to Siberia with his family as a boy, and entered government service on the Lena. In 1672, he helped escort the tribute from Yakutsk to Moscow, and in 1695 was dispatched to Anadyrsk. There he became interested in Kamchatka, which the Russians still believed to be an island. In 1696 Atlasov sent the Cossack Luka Morozko to the peninsula on a reconnaissance foray and a year later organized an expedition himself of 120 men (half of them Yukaghir auxiliaries) to gather tribute from the natives and annex the territory to the Crown. The Kamchadals battled Atlasov on skis, and the

Reindeer Koryaks on dogsleds, "one man driving and another using a bow and arrow," like Roman charioteers. They fought from enclaves, hurling rocks at the Russians with slings or by hand, and used spears and other primitive weapons. But the Russians, protected by shields, advanced on the native settlements, set fire to their yurts, and butchered all who tried to escape.

Traveling by reindeer, they explored much of the west coast and part of the interior, then crossed the mountains to the eastern shore, imposing tribute on the population. By mid-July 1696 Atlasov had journeyed as far south as the Kamchatka River, where he divided his company in two—one group to continue exploring the peninsula's eastern side, the other to cross back over the mountains to the west. Atlasov's Yukaghir auxiliaries rebelled, killing six of his men and wounding fifteen others. Some Koryaks also absconded with his itinerant herd of reindeer (kept for transportation and food), but he gave pursuit, overtook them, and killed them to a man. At the headwaters of the Kamchatka River the Russians found four large fortified Kamchadal settlements containing several hundred huts. To their surprise, they were greeted hospitably, exacted tribute without incident, and (learning that the community was at war with other Kamchadals downstream) won the settlers' firm allegiance by carrying out a retaliatory raid on their behalf.

Atlasov then continued his southward march, and although he did not quite reach the southern tip of the peninsula, he learned that there were several islands (the Kuriles) in the sea beyond. These he understood to be inhabited by yet another people, "the hairy Ainu"—a strange subgroup of the Caucasian race exhibiting more body hair than any other human group. More surprising still, he heard that past the Kuriles were still larger islands where people lived "in towns made of stone," and from which the Ainu obtained "costly plates and dishes, cotton garments, cotton textiles in plaids and bright colors, kitaika [nankeen] fabric and kaftans." Some of these goods, in fact, had found their way, via the Ainu, to the peninsula. At the same time (but unable to draw the right connection), Atlasov was told of an "alien" being held by the Kamchadals. He had the captive brought to him—a small, "clean," dark man, who had been shipwrecked on the Kamchatka coast. The man was tearfully grateful to be delivered from his captors and identified himself as a subject of "Hondo" or "Endo"—a Hindu from India, so Atlasov surmised. But *Hondo* meant "Tokyo"; his name was Dembei, and he was Japanese.

A merchant's clerk from Osaka, Dembei had sailed in the winter of 1695 with a fleet of thirty transports laden with goods for Edo, when his vessel, separated from the others by a typhoon, had been driven eastward into the open sea. For weeks he and a dozen shipmates had been helplessly tossed about the ocean, until at length they managed to create a mast from a floating tree, improvised sails out of damask, and succeeded in reaching Kamchatka. Sighting a river, they proceeded upstream but were immediately set upon by Kamchadals. Dembei alone had survived.

Atlasov brought him to Anadyrsk, from where he was conveyed under escort to Moscow in 1701 and presented to Peter the Great. Peter made him the nucleus of a Japanese language school in the capital, but despite a promise to the contrary, never allowed him to return home. Eventually, he was baptized under the name of Gabriel, but lived out his days in profound melancholy in St. Petersburg—the first casualty of Russia's chronically troubled relations with Japan.

Meanwhile, after founding Verkhnekamchatsk with a garrison on the Kamchatka River, Atlasov had returned to Anadyrsk in July 1699, and from there traveled to Moscow to report in person on his exploits. From the deposition he gave, the government realized that not only was the peninsula a rich new source of furs, but possibly a land (in some compensation for the Amur's loss) where crops might thrive. In gratitude, it paid him a bonus of 100 rubles and appointed him commandant of Kamchatka. This unforeseen promotion apparently went to his head. Thinking himself above the law, on his way to take up his post he and ten confederates robbed a Russian caravan laden with Chinese goods on the Lower Tunguska River. Upon reaching Yakutsk, he tried to unload his contraband, but was discovered, tried, and convicted, and thrown into a dungeon.

Over the next few years, Russia's hold on the peninsula was superficially strengthened with the founding in 1711 of Nizhnekamchatsk at the mouth of the Kamchatka River, and Bolsheretsk (later the center for the local administration) on the Bolshaya River in 1703. By that year, the entire peninsula was theoretically registered in the tax collection books. However, several senior officers were ambushed and killed by Koryaks in the summer of 1706, and the leaderless Cossacks went wild in an orgy of violence and rape. Routine caution and defensive measures were ignored, and the much-abused Kamchadals assassinated numerous tax collectors and burned down Bolsheretsk.

The government decided it needed an iron fist. Atlasov was released from prison in 1707 and given a free hand to do whatever he deemed necessary to bring things under control. Arriving in July, his method was butchery, and by December he had the natives cowed. His willful cruelties, however, extended even toward his own men, who turned against him. In a mutiny, they seized control of Verkhnekamchatsk, but finding Atlasov had escaped to Nizhnekamchatsk (where other commanders reluctantly gave him refuge), in January 1711 they gained access to the fort, executed the remaining officers, and murdered Atlasov in his bed. Afterward, they ransacked his home and found some confiscated pelts sewn into clothing belonging to his wife.

The mutineers excused their acts on the grounds of state security, claiming the murdered officials had abused their command, appropriated government income for themselves (both in cash and furs), and had aroused the natives to rebellion by their arbitrary rule. They offered to redeem themselves by bringing order to the land, and announced their own expedition to the Kurile Islands to show that they were responsibly carrying on government work. In August 1711, a party led by Danilo Antsyferov and Ivan Kozyrevsky (the two ringleaders) crossed the strait opposite Cape Lopatka at Kamchatka's southern tip and explored the nearest of the Kurile Islands. On the basis of information forcibly extracted from the Ainu, they were able upon their return in September to prepare a very rough map of the northern half of the chain.

All this had its effect. Prince Matvey Gagarin, the first governor of Siberia, commuted their death sentence on condition they continued their work, while the government, as quickly as the remoteness of the region allowed, moved to reassert control. Meanwhile, five years of *yasak* income had been lost to the authorities, and at least two hundred Russians had been killed. Koryak war parties prowled the mountains, streams, and forests, forming alliances with Yukaghirs north toward Anadyrsk and with Kamchadals in the south. Antsyferov was burned to death in a hut, and the whole service remained in such disorder that it was not until a smallpox epidemic in 1715 ravaged the peninsula that resistance to the Russians began to wane.

Meanwhile, Kozyrevsky had again visited the northern Kuriles in 1713 and returned with some Japanese swords, iron kettles, lacquered wood utensils, and items made out of paper and silk. The Russians' curiosity was greatly aroused, since they still couldn't figure out where Japan was on the map.

Rather more startling, on the peninsula itself the remains of two old Russian log cabins had been found, near a river the natives called by a Russian name. Such was all that remained of the remnant of Fedot Alekseyev's crew, which, as Dezhnev had heard from Alekseyer's Yakut concubine, had "pushed off into the unknown" after failing to find the Anadyr. At first, it was said, when the Russians landed on Kamchatka, the natives had regarded them as gods. But after they fell to quarreling among themselves and drew blood, the natives killed them all, thinking in vain "to rid themselves forever of such fearsome guests."

7

ADMINISTRATION

THE RUSSIANS, of course, had returned, but their disorderly advance gave the natives grounds for hope. Throughout the first century of the conquest, in fact, Russia was so often in a state of social and political turmoil that Moscow could give little direction and support to the colony's development. An economic recovery of sorts had occurred after the Time of Troubles passed, but extraordinary taxes periodically levied to replenish the Treasury, together with a more or less constant succession of wars (with Sweden over the Baltic littoral, and with Poland and Turkey over the Ukraine), led to violent explosions of disorder. There were salt tax riots in 1648, bread riots in 1650, and a copper coin revolt in 1662 over the debasing of the silver currency. Then, in 1670–71, a huge popular uprising took place along the Volga led by the Cossack Stenka Razin, who secured a following of 200,000 men, and for some time held in subjection the area from Nizhny-Novgorod to Kazan. Plague swept the country in 1655, taking upward of half a million lives. Meanwhile, the landmark Law Code of 1649 had increased the state's power of taxation, reduced the authority of the Church, and effectively established serfdom by making peasants (together with their families and possessions) the legal property of the lords for whom they worked. A Great Schism had also developed in the Russian Orthodox Church, reminiscent of the Protestant Reformation that had shaken the Catholic West. In Russia, however, the reformers belonged to the establishment, and the confrontation between the

two factions was immortally framed for posterity in the struggle between the archpriest Avvakum, a leader of the conservative "Old Believers," and the patriarch Nikon.

In brief, the Old Believers subscribed to the traditional Church rite,
sanctioned by national ecclesiastical councils and hallowed by the
blood of martyrs for the faith. Nikon, who wished to bring Russian
practice into conformity with the rest of Greek Orthodox ritual, was
convinced that the peculiarly Russian variations were based on scribal
errors and long-standing misinterpretations of sacred texts. In one
summation:

> The principal differences to be settled were: whether a triple hal-
> leluia should be pronounced, in honor of the Trinity, or a double
> halleluia, in reference to the double nature of Christ; whether
> processions around the churches should march against or with the
> sun; whether it was right or wrong to have a beard; whether at mass
> there should be upon the altar one or many loaves—the Russian
> used seven; whether the name Jesus should be spelled Iissous or
> Issous; whether, in prayer, the Savior should be addressed as our
> God or as the Son of God; whether it was right to say of God, "whose
> reign is eternal," or "whose reign shall be eternal"; whether the cross
> should have four or eight points; and whether the sign of the cross
> should be made with three fingers extended, as denoting the Trinity,
> and two closed, in reference to Christ's double nature, or with two
> fingers extended, in allusion to the double nature, and three closed,
> in token of the Trinity.

The Greeks observed the former, the Russians the latter forms in
their worship; and if the controversy seemed to be over an accumulation of technicalities, both sides struggled within it as if for their very
souls. For a century and more the Russian people had been told by
their own ideologists that Muscovite Russia was the "Third Rome," the
sole remaining stronghold of the true faith in the world. As dissidents,
they now proved in astonishing numbers that they were quite prepared to die for their beliefs. "For this we came out of our mother's
womb," Avvakum wrote. "Are you afraid of the furnace? . . . Fear comes
before the fire. . . . You catch fire, and here they are—Christ and the
hosts of angels." In response to such appeals, at least twenty thousand
schismatics burned themselves to death. Patriarch Nikon's ruthless per-

secutions also took many lives, but his adamant stance did not spring solely from pious conviction. As patriarch, he was the head of a state Church, and the government's determination to acquire the Ukraine and other territories could only be furthered if their Orthodox inhabitants recognized in Russian doctrine and practice a spiritual home. But the blood the patriarch helped to spill in this cause was not perhaps more than Avvakum himself might have shed if he had had the power. To the tsar, he once wrote: "I would lay all [the reformers] low in a single day as did Elijah. . . . We would begin by quartering the dog Nikon and afterwards all the Nikonites."

Exiled with his wife and family to Siberia for eleven years, Avvakum was eventually excommunicated and incarcerated in a dungeon at Pustozersk. On April 14, 1682, he was pronounced a heretic and burned at the stake.

Shock waves from all these developments reached Siberia. Religious persecution brought a flood of refugees; attempts were made to establish free Cossack "republics" in Kamchatka and on the Amur (as we have seen), but also (in 1649–50) on the upper Ob; and from time to time there were mutinies in the Siberian garrisons over salaries, living conditions, and other grievances.

The service was hard. Officers were offered a promotion in rank and double salary for three to five years in Siberia, but real salaries remained low, and ordinary recruits often found it impossible to manage on their allotments of ammunition and food. Sometimes in the payment of salaries substituted goods were appraised absurdly high—or were utterly useless, like a quantity of rusted iron wire actually distributed one year as pay to the militia at Verkhoturye. At the same time, tough regulations were enforced to keep the men in check. "Flogging without mercy" was officially recommended for insubordination and other offenses, but some of the administrators were gratuitously cruel. In 1645, servitors alleged that the commandant at Yakutsk, Petr Golovin, for instance, "beat us mercilessly with the knout, pulled our limbs out of joint, poured ice water over our heads, pulled at our veins and navels with hot pliers, scattered hot ashes on our backs, and drove needles under our finger nails." Such sadistic behavior was, if exceptional, not unique: Atlasov, Pashkov, Poyarkov, Khabarov, Stadukhin, and others were all manifestly guilty of atrocities toward their own.

These men flourished in Siberia in part because the administration of the colony had undergone such a haphazard evolution, reflecting both the military circumstances of the occupation and the inability of Moscow to take adequate account of what it had. Until 1637, the Siberian Office (located in the Kremlin) enjoyed a relatively minor status as a subdepartment of the Kazan Bureau, which was responsible for Russia's eastern frontier. But about the time Russia began to tap the fur wealth on the Lena, a separate *prikaz,* or department, for Siberia was created to oversee all matters concerning the administration and development of the colony. It had oversight over the guidance and supervision of officials, the organization and provisioning of the army of occupation, the administration of justice, the financial exploitation and settlement of the territory, and diplomatic relations with peoples along its frontiers. It sent investigators to look into official abuses and corruption, and concerned itself with native unrest, the condition of local crops or the cost of grain, how the agricultural colonists were getting along, and so forth. The department also handled passports and stage permits, and collected a special tax on imported goods. In certain areas its concerns overlapped with those of other government bureaus, like the Office of Military Affairs, the Land Office, the Department of Transportation, and the Foreign Ministry. But its unique division was the Sable Treasury, where furs from Siberia were deposited, appraised, and stored. Its particular staff included furriers and other specialists connected with the fur trade, and "sworn men"—so-called because of the sacred oath they took in connection with their responsibilities—who were selected from among the Moscow merchant elite to be custodians of the treasured vaults.

In the field, military governors appointed from Moscow took charge of each major fort or town. Principally, they occupied themselves with controlling the natives and collecting *yasak* and tithe, and even law and order were of primary concern only as they affected the flow of the colonial income into the coffers of the state. Whereas in Russia itself the state budget was devoted primarily to the military, in Siberia the military's principal purpose was to assist the Treasury. In a sense, the military governors were also chief financial officers, and their servitors were revenue officers as well as military men.

For all practical purposes, a governor enjoyed eminent domain. He was the commanding officer in his district, the chief of police, and the principal judge. He organized all local expeditions (and debriefed the leaders upon their return), provided logistical support for all major military and "civilian" tasks, heard (or was supposed to hear) all petitions and complaints, monitored changing developments within the territory of his jurisdiction, and from time to time reported to Moscow the findings he had made.

In all this he was assisted by "men under commission" assigned to him from other government departments, and by secretaries and a *pismennaya golova,* or "writing chief," who kept the records and correspondence and was entrusted with special tasks. Customs heads were also appointed from the central bureaucracy, and as part of its system of checks and balances, after 1695 (when all traffic to and from Siberia was restricted to the route through Verkhoturye), had to countersign all documents from the governor's desk.

Such restraints had comparatively little effect. The early style of Siberian governance was based on the semi-feudal system of *kormlenie,* or "feeding," whereby officials expected to be remembered with gifts on holidays and special occasions and drew part of their own income from the population they taxed. Although theoretically abolished during Ivan the Terrible's reign, it had left behind a host of administrative habits and methods, and in Siberia enjoyed a resurrected life. Before long, the inherent corruptions of *kormlenie* made Siberia notorious for its predatory personnel. Official and unofficial revenue was simply as the governors defined it, and the populace was more or less at the mercy of the exactions they imposed. Many volunteered for the appointments because of the opportunities for plunder they presented, while those posted against their will (usually to the most inhospitable areas) still hoped to find ample recompense for the hardships they endured.

There were other enticements. During his stay in Siberia a governor's estates were exempt from taxes, and lawsuits against him had to wait until his return. He was also given a travel allowance and salary in advance, provided with means of transportation (carts, boats, and other perks), and quite a retinue was sometimes sustained. In 1635, the new governor of Mangazeya set out with 33 personal assistants and a baggage train that included 200 buckets of wine, 35 pounds of honey, 35 pounds of butter, six buckets of vegetable oil, 150 hams, besides flour, grits, and other staples. In 1643, the governor of Tobolsk took a retinue of forty men with him; others were accompanied by sixty to seventy or more. They were not supposed to use the goods they brought with them for private trading, but of course they did, and eventually the Siberian Department restricted the kinds and amounts of supplies governors could take. Nevertheless, the posts were still eagerly sought, and many smoothed the path of their applications with bribes. This became common enough for the department to develop a scale of rates proportioned to the prospects associated with each town.

Initially, appointments were limited to two or three years, to enable as many candidates as possible from among the nobility to reap the rewards of office as a sinecure. But in 1695, the term was lengthened to six years, because (as the statute explained) "they try to get rich quick if in office for just a short time."

The colonial administration in Western Siberia could be more closely regulated by Moscow, but in more remote areas abuses were hard to contain. The quintessential Russian saying, expressive of long-suffering—"God is high up and the Tsar far off"—is actually Siberian in origin. Lesser officials also tended to regard their office as a financial opportunity, and one fallen courtier claimed that in his eleven years as an exile in Siberia he met only one tax gatherer who "walked the straight path." The farther from the capital, the more immune from restraint, in a sense, a man became. A man who left Moscow as a common soldier, it was said, automatically became a sergeant upon reaching Tobolsk, an ensign in Tomsk, a lieutenant on the Lena, a captain in Yakutsk, and a colonel in Kamchatka. A fair proportion of Kamchatka's "colonels" were also criminal exiles, and though some may have redeemed their past by valiant or heroic endeavor, as often as not, tempted by the circumstances in which they were placed, they compounded the degradations of their lives.

The natives suffered most from such petty despotism, and judicial redress was rare. They had difficulty in finding scribes willing to compose their complaints, and governors and other officials naturally tried to suppress any written protests that came their way. In Moscow, of course, "the wheels of justice had to be oiled by bribes." Given the two years or more required for a special courier to go from Yakutsk to the capital and back, the process was futile anyway, since by the time an investigation was begun most witnesses had been intimidated or "fixed."

Some of the natives fled: Voguls north to the tundra, Buryats to Mongolia, Tungus to the Amur, Yukaghirs to the Arctic coast. Those to the north could often be retrieved, but if they managed to find sanctuary among the formidable nomadic tribes across the southern frontier, they were quite beyond recall. From time to time major local revolts also broke out that directly threatened forts. Berezov nearly fell to the Ostyaks in 1595 and 1607, Kuznetsk to the Tartars in 1630, and Tyumen and Tara to the Tartars in 1634. In 1635, the Buryats stormed Bratsk and massacred its entire garrison. In 1641–42, the Yakuts threatened both Krasnoyarsk and Yakutsk; in 1648, Buryats besieged Verkholensk, and in 1658, Balagansk. In 1666, a Tungus uprising raged along the northern coast of the Sea of Okhotsk and into the basin of the Indigirka River, imperiling both Okhotsk and Zashiversk. And in 1679, Samoyeds attempted to overrun Obdorsk.

Most of these uprisings might have been avoided by a more enlightened colonial regime.

The Church ought to have been more of a mitigating factor than it was. Present from the start (by tradition, a field church in the form of a collapsible tent had been carried over the Urals by Yermak's band), two churches were built in Siberia at Tyumen in 1586, the year the town was founded, and at Tobolsk a temporary church was erected even before the stockade. A year later, Siberia's first monastery was established nearby, and soon thereafter others in Turinsk, Tyumen, and Verkhoturye. But until the arrival of Siberia's first archbishop, Kiprian, the clergy could claim no independent status, and were more or less shabbily treated by the military authorities, who used them as clerks. The churches were barely functioning, and the monasteries were said to be dens of vice, where monks and nuns cohabited together, or continued liaisons with former husbands and lovers outside the walls. The clergy, one ecclesiastic complained, "lived like pagans, begetting half-breeds out of wedlock, neglecting their fast days, and eating any kind of filth with the unbaptized." When called upon to consecrate a marriage, some clergy "even seemed to have forgotten the Christian rite." And generally they refused to do anything without a hefty fee in furs.

To repair the Church's prestige, Kiprian imported sacred relics from the homeland, assembled accounts of local miracles, and, in 1622, launched a campaign to canonize Yermak as a martyr for the faith.

Collecting all the material he could about the legendary Cossack, he
started the Siberian Chronicles, and in 1635, through the efforts of his
successor, Yermak was glorified. Other Siberians were also beatified,
and in one of the towns a Madonna miraculously appeared. Before
long, Kiprian had brought new discipline to the monasteries, and
started nunneries in Yeniseysk, Tyumen, and Verkhoturye. As the
Church took hold, it also began to minister more effectively to the
territory's spiritual needs. It helped pacify the natives by conversion,
strengthened colonization through its institutions, defended settlers
against the arbitrary tyrannies of secular officials, dispensed alms, and
made a significant contribution to Siberia's early agricultural development. Church rituals also provided "rich pageantry, color and mo-
ments of splendor to be found nowhere else in the bleak, remote
outposts of the colony." Whereas most American frontier churches
were austere structures, marked by a simplicity of design, their Russian
counterparts (in their own rough-hewn fashion) were innately ornate,
and even in the remotest settlement often had bronzed or brightly
painted domes.

The work of the Church was deemed indispensable by Moscow and
was initially sustained by subsidies, tax exemptions, and liberal grants
of land. But as the wealth of the Church grew, its money also made
money, through high-interest loans to individuals with land to pledge
as security. By midcentury the archbishopric controlled several thousand acres and a sizable proportion of the farming population in the
region of Tobolsk.

In time, however, the secular administration came to regard the
Church as a rival, and Moscow, as part of a larger effort to ensure the
subordination of Church to State, began to restrict its speculations.
After Patriarch Nikon was deposed in 1667 (without prejudice, however, to his reforms), the independence of the Church was further
curtailed, and in the beginning of the reign of Tsar Fyodor III (1676–
82), new prohibitions against its acquisition of land were strictly enforced. Finally, in 1698, Peter the Great declared: "There are enough
monasteries in Siberia for men and for women to take care of those
who would like to take the vows." The state, in fact, was not particularly
eager to see natives convert. While baptized men could be conscripted
into the military and baptized women could marry Russian men, as
Russian citizens they were also exempt from *yasak,* which reduced the

income the Treasury took in. It was therefore not entirely for charitable reasons that the Kremlin prohibited forcible baptism and insisted that Christ triumph "through love."

Even among its own, the Church had limited success. As late as 1662, the archbishop of Tobolsk denounced most of the priests in his diocese as "drunkards and lechers," and appealed to Moscow for a more righteous sort. One of those to arrive was the archpriest Avvakum, then beginning his Siberian exile. Avvakum, however, proved a bit too righteous for the Church's good. Although priests were not supposed to inflict corporal punishment, during his tenure he had a drunken monk flogged for interrupting his evening prayers, a clerk whipped for accepting a bribe, and an unrepentant prostitute punished "by imprisoning her without food beneath the floor of his house for three days." Somewhat less sternly, he pacified another unfortunate by the name of Fyodor, who had gone temporarily mad with guilt after having had sex with his wife on Easter Sunday. For a subsequent infraction, however, Avvakum had him "flogged and chained to the wall of the church choir," after which he went berserk, rampaged through the town, and concluded his fit by dressing up as a girl.

In Tobolsk, Avvakum also crossed swords with the legendary Cossack Petr Beketov, who despite his long and distinguished service, came, as a result, to a most miserable end. Beketov had fought in the Yenisey and Lena river valleys, had led the way in the conquest of the Buryats, and had founded Yakutsk near the Arctic Circle and Nerchinsk on the Mongolian frontier. But while living in semi-retirement in Tobolsk, he defended a clerk Avvakum had accused of corruption, and after "publicly and vehemently" attacking the archpriest in church on the first Sunday in Lent in 1655, immediately collapsed of a stroke and died. Avvakum, vengefully choosing to see in this the hand of God, "ordered the body to be thrown in the street where it lay for three days as food for the dogs."

Until 1627, Siberia was constituted as one military district; but once the conquest had advanced into the basin of the Yenisey, the colonial administration was divided between Tobolsk and Tomsk. Tomsk owed its new prominence to its strategic position, which protected the chief route between Western and Eastern Siberia by way of Ketsk and Fort

Makovsk. A decade later the Russians were on the Lena, coming chiefly from Mangazeya (subordinate to Tobolsk) and Yeniseysk (subordinate to Tomsk), which both claimed the area as their own. As we have seen, serving men of the rival towns fought each other for preeminence, oppressed and terrorized the natives and "collected a little fur tribute for the state, and a great deal for themselves." In response, the government organized the Lena River Valley as a separate district, with its headquarters at Yakutsk. In 1649, Yakutsk assumed jurisdiction over Ilimsk, commanding the portage between the Lena and the Yenisey. As more forts to the west blossomed into towns and the population grew, a fourth district was organized in 1676–77 centered at Yeniseysk, with jurisdiction over an area that included Nerchinsk, Selenginsk, and Albazin.

In each case, surrounding towns and forts were assigned to the main towns as satellites, but among the latter an order of precedence also grew up. For all practical purposes, Tobolsk became the capital of Siberia. From the first, it was the largest, wealthiest, and most populous, the principal depot of men and supplies, and a transit point for colonists and exiles. In 1621, its importance was considerably enhanced when the Kiprian had arrived to take up his residence there as head of the colonial diocese. In 1708, it also became the seat of Siberia's first governor, Matvey Gagarin, who was assisted by two vice-governors—one likewise stationed at Tobolsk, the other at Irkutsk. The latter had under him, in turn, the military governor of Yakutsk, whose jurisdiction extended to the Okhotsk seaboard and Kamchatka. The Siberian Department in Moscow was largely supplanted by these changes, and languished until its official abolition by Catherine the Great in 1763.

8

A VANISHING WORLD

THE sweep of the conquest had been matched only by its speed, as relatively small bands of tough, reckless, and determined men made their way across northern Asia on foot or horseback, dragging their supplies by cart or sledge, or darting in relatively fragile craft down unknown rivers to an unknown sea. They explored vast tracts of the interior, and sometimes wandered up to 1,000 miles from their outpost settlements across the taiga, tundra, and swamps. The weather at times was ferocious; wild animals prowled the forests; and in the tundra Cossacks "were lucky to find a few berries, mushrooms or some tree-bark on which to feed." The desperate lives they lived were not always rewarded by gain (indeed, like gold miners elsewhere, the fortunate were few), and the rough winter shelters they built for themselves became "prisons of isolation amid the raging snowstorms and the almost endless night." Although unable to calculate their positions by astronomical coordinates, they drew serviceable maps, and (lacking paper) scratched their reports on birchbark strips. Yet in a colonial triumph that stood as a counterpart to the overseas expansion by the maritime nations of the West, never in the history of the world had so few acquired so much.

At the same time, the strategy of conquest, lacking any grand colonial design, was constantly revised to accommodate the speed with which exploration and discovery was taking place. In a kind of sustained, if far-flung, fur rush, opportunity alone determined where the Russians

went, or concentrated their efforts, and how they went about consolidating control of areas they gained. They kept to the taiga, where most
of the fur-bearing animals were found, and because along the taiga's
southern flank lived the populous and relatively warlike Mongol and
Turkic nomads (in particular, the Kirghiz and Kalmucks), who were
better organized politically than most Siberian peoples and could
mount an effective fighting force. Eventually, to keep the nomads out,
Siberia's long southern frontier became a heavily fortified line.

If the fur trade fueled the juggernaut, colonial attitudes smoothed the
way. Like other European powers then expanding overseas, the Russians were "convinced of their right to dispossess inferior and barbaric
foes, to establish the true faith, and to reap the economic benefits
of dominion." For the Russians—as for the Spanish, English, or Portuguese—progress was conveniently understood as a rise from
"savagery" to "civilization," and it demanded the conquest of the
wilderness, in keeping with the divine injunction to "Be fruitful and
multiply, and replenish and subdue the earth." Strictly speaking, Siberia was not a wilderness in the biblical sense, for (like aboriginal
America) it was occupied by long-standing cultures, ceremonial sites,
trails blazed for hunting, war, or trade, and so on; but to minds steeped
in concepts of private, or state, property, the natives' communal use of
large areas of land could scarcely be regarded as a basis for true
ownership. John Quincy Adams perhaps spoke for all colonials of like
mind when in 1802 he declared: "What is the right of a huntsman to
the forest of a thousand miles over which he has accidentally ranged
in quest of prey? . . . Shall the field and vallies, which a beneficient God
has formed to teem with the life of innumerable multitudes, be condemned to ever lasting barrenness?" Although individual tribes occupied and controlled separate territories, they were baffled by such
acquisitive imperatives. Having little conception of private property,
they held to a religious notion of the land as belonging to Nature, "just
like the waters of the river and the clear skies above."

By right of inheritance, they possessed it, even as they depended on
its power to nurture and maintain. While endeavoring to live in harmony with their environment, they had also "subdued" it in their own
practical way. Their technology and applied art relied heavily on horn,

mammoth ivory, wood, and animal skins, yet from these few materials they met all their needs. And their accomplishments were simply astonishing. They made ski masks out of bear intestines, snow goggles out of birchbark or woven hair, false teeth out of wood or ivory, artificial legs from horn, "incubators for premature babies from the waterproof bladders of seals, and set broken limbs with driftwood splints." In their dress, "they had mastered the principle of air insulation, and instead of bulky coats and sweaters, wore two sets of loose-hanging, buttonless tunics that made use of trapped air as a buffer against the cold." Heavy leathers were tanned with alder bark, and lubricated with bone marrow or sour milk; softer leathers were smoked over burning pine cones and manure. Whale intestines were transformed into barrels, the vertebrae into mortars, the veins and nerves into heavy ropes. Still heavier cables were made by braiding together strips of smoked walrus hide. Knives were fashioned out of mountain crystal, fine needles of sable bone. The Kamchadals were said to be so clever at repairing needles with a broken eye that they could "keep on making a new eye right down to the point." From a single walrus tusk, they could also make a continuous chain, with links "as round and smooth as if they had been turned on a lathe." Swaddling clothes for newborn infants were made from a marsh grass resembling sedge that was carded like flax and looked like cotton wool.

In some instances where natives and Russians had created the same items, native models were not of inferior design. The dogsleds of the Kamchadals, for example, were extraordinarily strong but light, fastened together with lashings of dried seal skin, and mounted on broad, curved runners. They could bend almost in two without breaking, yet carry loads a hundred times their own weight. The dogs, harnessed in pairs, were guided entirely by voice, and for a brake the driver used a thick stick, with a spike (like a ski pole) at one end.

The reindeer culture of the tundra nomads was as remarkable in its own way as the buffalo-hunting culture that overspread the Great Plains. Besides carrying their wandering owners from place to place—by sledge or bareback, with the rider high up on the shoulder blades, holding a bridle twisted around the horns—the reindeer furnished them with meat, clothing (hides), and skin covering for their tents. The sinews were also dried and pounded into thread, the antlers made into implements, the bones burned for fuel. Stomach and intestines were transformed into storage containers; and from the stiff, bristly skin of the legs came the tops of their snowshoes.

Reindeer on the Chukchi Peninsula tended to be wilder than most, ate bird dung and even young mice or birds, and became so excited by the smell of human urine "as to charge a man making water nearby." This understandably made all the herdsmen quite circumspect, but they eventually turned the problem to account. Each wore on his belt a small leather vessel in which urine was kept, and used it as a means of retrieving strays. When separating draft reindeer from the rest, they constructed primitive sled corrals, but one method of neutering males was incredibly savage. Although other natives severed or pierced the spermatic tubes without castration, in Chukchi practice, the deer "was caught with a lariat and thrown down; two men held him, while a third crushed the testicles with his teeth."

The revolutionary mobility of the horse among the North American Indians, incidentally, had no real parallel in Russia's Wild East. The horse was already known to many Siberians, since the Tartars were heirs to the traditions of the Mongol cavalry, and the Yakuts (first identified to the Russians as "horse people") possessed a small, sturdy variety. In the southern steppes (the Siberian version of the Great Plains), the Kirghiz and Kalmucks were masterful riders. But during the conquest's early days most natives and Russians were concentrated in the taiga, where the horse was of little use. Its utility, in any case, was a relative thing, even in the south, where camels were preferred for hauling, and in other curious respects. For example, near the Mongolian border where wood was scarce, sun-dried droppings (called argols) were burned for fuel. Over time, the collecting, pounding, molding, and drying of this dung developed into an important activity, and the local Buryats seemed able to make as many distinctions between one kind of dung and another as Eskimos could with snow. The argols of goats, sheep, and camels were especially prized, because they burned "most fiercely," and the argols of horses least, because, "not having undergone the process of rumination, they present nothing but a mass of triturated straw."

Native "housing" displayed some variety, but the common dwelling among nomads was a portable yurt, or tent, with a hole at the top for light and ventilation. Some were erected of inclined poles, like a tepee, bound together toward the top and covered with birchbark and skins.

But the large, circular, felt yurts of the Kirghiz had a light wooden frame, and the communal conical tents of the Koryak and Reindeer Chukchi were divided into small, nearly airtight family compartments called *pologs,* separated from one another by heavy fur drapes. The Coastal Chukchi, on the other hand, lived in a Paleolithic type of semi-dugout, called a *valkaran,* made of the jawbones and ribs of whales. Similar in structure were the winter dwellings of the Kamchadals— timber-lined rectangular dugouts covered with earth. Being partial to variety, the Kamchadals also built summer houses that were elevated platforms with pointed roofs thatched with grass.

If the material ingenuity of the natives aroused Russian curiosity, their spiritual life was generally scorned. Yet there was much in its development to admire. The common religious system of those east of the Tartars (who were Sunni Moslems) was shamanism, whose central priest, the shaman (from the Tungus-Manchurian *saman,* "one who knows"), was an ecstatic figure, believed to have power to heal the sick and to communicate with the world beyond. Based on primitive pantheism, shamanism pictured all inanimate nature as alive or inhabited by spirits, and invested all living creatures with special powers. To interpret their wishes and decrees was the shaman's special vocation. Dressed in a long robe, marked with fantastic figures of birds and beasts as well as hieroglyphic emblems and signs, he summoned invisible spirit-helpers with wild chants, shouts, frenzied dancing and convulsions, all the while beating out complex rhythms on his sacred tambourine.

While some shamans may have been charlatans, others were gifted healers and in some cases derived their *materia medica* from the traditions of Tibetan medicine. By means of a demanding physical and mental training, they also mastered intricate rituals of song and dance, all sorts of psycho-magical tricks, and controlled fits of frenzy and inspiration, which they could deliberately produce in themselves. As ventriloquists, they could reproduce sounds like the whirring of wings or the snorting of beasts to vivify the activities of the spirits they described, and (Houdinilike) could free themselves from tightly bound cords, walk blithely over red-hot coals, and so on. The practice of stabbing oneself through the stomach with a knife and instantly healing the wound was universal in shamanistic practice—indeed, Yermak is said to have encountered it even among the natives of Sibir. One late-sixteenth-century explorer who met up with some Samoyeds near the mouth of the Ob was treated to a demonstration of this power:

> Then hee tooke a sworde of a cubite and a spanne long, (I did mete it my selfe) and put it into his bellie halfeway and sometime lesse, but no wounde was to bee seene. . . . Then he put the sworde into the fire till it was warme, and so thrust into the slitte of his shirte and thrust it through his bodie, as I thought, in at his navill and out at his fundament; the poynt beeing out of his shirt behind, I layde my finger upon it, then hee pulled out the sworde and sate downe.

Beyond the ritualistic forms of their beliefs, some natives possessed a highly developed mythology. Among the Tungus, for example, the two most powerful animals of the Siberian taiga, the bear and the elk, formed that paired unity of cosmological images, opposed in role, with which the life of nature and society was linked to religious concepts. The bear's pursuit of the elk in the upper world (a personification of the sun cycle) gave rise to the succession of night and day; and in the netherworld, the female elk at the root of the cosmic (world) tree gave birth to animals and people whose souls the bear (as the master of ancestral spirits) reclaimed after death.

Among the Chukchi, the constellation of Castor and Pollux represented the flight of elks from two hunters, both riding teams of reindeer; that of Delphinius was pictured as a seal; the Milky Way as a westward-flowing river with many islands in midstream; and Cassiopeia as five bull reindeer. They also imagined the sun (somewhat as the Greeks imagined Phoebus with his chariot) as a man in glittering clothes driving a reindeer sled across the sky. Other legends or stories similarly explained the origin and configuration of the stars as heroic hunts, and the Milky Way as the ski track which the hunters used.

In coming to terms with their mortality, various tribes, such as the Ostyaks and Voguls, believed in an underground abode of the dead (which they placed on the lower Ob, or on an island in the Arctic Ocean); others conceived of both upper and lower worlds. The Kamchadals had a superstitious dread of lizards as "spies sent by the god of the underworld to look into their actions," and regarded the volcanoes as his kingdom. When the volcano emitted flames, it meant the dead were heating up their yurts. Others, like the Yukaghirs, hoped for an afterlife in the *aurora borealis* where they might dwell "on the red blaze, and pass their time playing ball with a walrus skull." In more exalted conceptions, the motionless North Star in the canopy of heaven was imagined as the passage to a celestial place in the east "towards morning," where the Master Spirit dwelled with those who had lived good lives on earth, in a land of everlasting day.

In harmony with this "Christian resonance," the Creation myth of the Tungus portrayed the world as formed by a deity called *Seveki* (meaning "Seven") in the midst of a watery waste, and told of the attempts of his older brother (who lived in the underworld and "made all the bad things, every kind of worm and snake") to destroy it. In the myth's elaboration, temptation was followed by hereditary sickness and shame, with unmistakable resemblances to the biblical account of the Fall.

There was another story, too, which rather remarkably combined the idea of the biblical Tree of Knowledge with the evolutionary notion of Man's descent (in both senses) from a tree: "Man was born from a tree. The tree split in two. Two people came out. One was a man, the other a woman. Until a child was born they were covered with hair. People went on being born from son to son, and at first they had neither reindeer nor dogs, and did not think about how everything came to be. But then their descendants began to think."

At the same time, their storied reading of the heavens did not prevent the natives from making rigorous observations of the objective movements of the stars. The Great Bear (the nearest of the constellations to the North Star) was their indispensable celestial clock, and the Chukchi in addition distinguished more than twenty directions of the compass by the sun. They were even aware of the special movement of the planets, or "the stars which go crosswise," as they were called. Ideas of calendrical time were also rooted in daily preoccupations— the Kamchadals, for example, divided their year into ten months of varying length, with names like "The month of the red fish," "The month of the tiny white fish," "The month of the big white fish," and "The month of falling leaves." Such pedestrian notions led one Russian to declare that the Kamchadals "are so stupid in their discourse that only in their power of speech do they differ from animals. . . . They do not [even] know how old they are. They count to one hundred, but with such difficulty that they can not go beyond ten; when they come to the end of the fingers on their hands, they join hands to indicate ten, then continue using their toes; and if the number goes beyond twenty, they do not know where they are, and they cry out . . . where to take the rest from?"

Native funeral rites did even less to improve the image of the aborigine in Russian eyes. Although the Ostyaks and Voguls, for example, in a familiar procedure, fumigated the house of the deceased with a resin torch, out of fear of the body's double or ghost they also made an image of him from pieces of his clothes and hair. This doll, as it were, assumed the departed's role as guardian of the hearth, and as the double's opposite "sat" at his place at meals and even "slept" in his bed.

Among the Koryak and Chukchi, after the body was removed and all traces obliterated to prevent its return, it was dissected with some dim analogies to autopsy procedure—the breast opened, the organs inspected, and the cause of death proclaimed. But as a courtesy to future generations, it was then stabbed on the pyre—"to prevent the child who will reincarnate the soul from having the same illness as the deceased." Indeed, among the Yukaghirs, corpses were sometimes affectionately dismembered and the parts dried and distributed as amulets, called "grandfathers," to close relations. With the tenderest of considerations, the Kamchadals also gave their dead to the dogs to eat—to ensure them a good dog team in the afterlife.

All tundra nomads recognized that sickness and infirmity were incompatible with a wandering life, and regularly put their old and debilitated to death—the latter meeting their end "with perfect composure." Elaborate ceremonies, in which the whole band participated, marked their passing, and their quietus came with a swift knife or spear thrust to a vital body part. Then the bodies were burned "and the ashes suffered to be scattered and blown away by the wind."

Only their story remained. But it would be told.

Although the natives lacked a written language, their oral literature and folklore was rich, and like the Homeric bards of old, storytellers sometimes played in accompaniment to their recitations a kind of lyre called a dombra, strung with sinew and made of pine. In the songs and ballads which they sang or intoned, they recounted melancholy tales of love or grief, or celebrated heroic deeds and exploits of the chase. Some of the ancient Ostyak ballad cycles ran to hundreds of thousands of verses, and the heroic poems of the Buryats were based on strict rules of versification that required an alternation of stressed and unstressed syllables and alliteration at the beginning of each line. The sacred songs of the Tungus were also rhymed, "full of clear, beautiful metaphors, and accompanied by a rhythmic refrain."

So the culture of the Siberian peoples was not negligible, and of more than strictly anthropological note. But the Russian conquest threatened to sweep it all away, and pulverize it almost to nothing with musket and cannon shot.

In America, the Indians were systematically wrenched from their ancestral homelands and forced to abandon the hills, valleys, forests, and rivers on which their way of life was based. In Siberia, it was more through a process of assimilation that native cultures were disrupted or destroyed. In addition to having to pay *yasak*, natives were used as guides, interpreters, heavy laborers (building and repairing town fortifications and roads), and as rowers, carters, and haulers. They picked berries, caught fish, gathered wood, and had to give up their own horses, dogs, and domesticated reindeer on occasion (as well as sledges and carts) to help meet the Russians' transport needs. Such obligatory service interfered with their age-old hunting-and-gathering patterns and took them away from other traditional pursuits. Beyond that, the Russians poached on their hunting and fishing grounds, carried off their women, and rounded up children for ransom at an average rate of one sable per child. Ironically, the European technology from which they stood to benefit—the kettles, knives, axes, and other metal tools and utensils more efficient and durable than their own—also encouraged the decay of their own skills. In time, they became dependent upon the Russians even for everyday items they had once produced themselves. In the control and humbling of the natives, European diseases, against which they possessed no immunity, did the rest, combined with the pervasive ravages of alcohol. Eventually, the "drunken, reprobate savage" as a type became as much a fixture of Siberian as American folklore.

And yet, along the advancing frontier, the engagement between conqueror and conquered tended to produce a reciprocal exchange of attitudes and knowledge such that each was variously transformed. Even as the natives gave way, for example, the Cossacks found they often had to adopt native ways to survive. They emulated the manner of their encampments, native forms of shelter and dress, and their techniques of hunting and tracking game under local conditions, which they had developed from experience over hundreds of years. The Russians, in short, had to become expert in wilderness survival, at which the peoples they subdued were already adept. Living close to their environment, Siberians were finely tuned to its vagaries, and able to exploit such food and other resources as it possessed. For all their colonial scorn of the "savages" they faced, the Russians in Siberia "went native" on occasion perhaps to a greater degree than most Indian scouts and other ambiguous figures along America's untamed frontier.

Although the classic dwelling of the Russian pioneer (like that of the American) was a simple cabin made of notched log beams, in the far north where even firewood was scarce, Russians crawled like any native into skin-covered tents and rolled themselves up in sleeping bags of fur. By example, they also learned "to eat plenty of fat food; to avoid over-exertion and night journeys; and never get into a profuse perspiration by violent exercise for the sake of temporary warmth." Some feeling of what it was like to pitch winter camp in the tundra is vividly suggested by the experience of one later traveler, who found himself on a New Year's Eve, "squatting on a great snowy plain near the Arctic circle," trying to eat up his soup before it froze solidly to his plate. Huddled with his companions close to a blazing fire, hoarfrost covered their clothing, their beards became "stiff tangled masses of frozen iron wire," and their eyelids grew heavy "with long white rims of frost" and froze together when they winked. All their metal utensils, molecularly transformed by the unearthly cold, burned their hands "almost exactly as if they were red hot," while beyond the campfire a level steppe, "as boundless to the weary eye as the ocean itself, stretched away in every direction to the far horizon." All

was silence and desolation. The country seemed abandoned by God and man to the Arctic Spirit, whose trembling banners of auroral light flared out fitfully in the north in token of his conquest and

dominion. . . . We seemed to have entered upon some frozen abandoned world where all the ordinary laws and phenomena of Nature
were suspended, where animal and vegetable life were extinct, and
from which even the favor of the Creator had been withdrawn. The
intense cold, the solitude, the oppressive silence, and the red,
gloomy moonlight, like the glare of a distant but mighty conflagration, all united to excite in the mind feelings of awe, which were
perhaps intensified by the consciousness that never before had any
human being, save a few Wandering Chukchis, ventured in winter
upon these domains of the Frost King.

Wherever the Russians found themselves, they prudently experimented with local garb. Natives in the backwoods, tundra, or steppe
dressed in varieties of animal-hide or fur tunics—deer, wolf, horse,
sheep, fox, dog, and bear—and along the coast wore fish-skin garments, or those made from the hides and intestines of walrus and seal.
The Reindeer Chukchi wore a double fur shirt or frock called a *ku-
klyanka,* which reached to the knees, and deer-skin leggings with fur
stockings. Similarly, the Koryaks wore heavy hunting shirts of spotted
deer skin, confined about the waist with a belt, and fringed round the
bottom with wolverine. Fur pantaloons, thigh-length seal-skin boots,
wolf-skin hoods, and so on became standard attire in the northeast for
Russian and native alike, and only in the most settled farming communities or in major towns was Russian fashion (beyond the traditional
sheepskin jacket or fur coat) adhered to. Even there readymade fabrics
and clothes were often hard to come by, and most settlers resorted to
making shirts and trousers out of blankets or canvas sacks.

Although the Russians did less commercial hunting than the natives,
whom they exploited as surrogates, in the hinterland their own survival often depended on hunting skills. In such circumstances, their
advanced weaponry and traps were not always an advantage, as compared to methods developed by the natives precisely adapted to their
environment and prey. Aside from pressure traps, noose-snares, pit-
falls, self-triggered bows, and so on, the Ostyaks and Voguls, for example, used a variety of arrows with highly specialized points—a
forked type for hunting ducks, one honed like a spear for otters and
bears, a serrated head for fish, and a blunt tip (so as not to spoil the
pelt) for small fur-bearing animals like sable and squirrel. The feathers
attached to the arrow were also ingeniously tailored to their task. For

example, there was an arrow, "the whistling of which resembled the sound of a hawk swooping down on its prey," which made ducks or geese drop down instantly into the waters of a lake, where waiting marksmen made their kill. Fired over the head of a rabbit, it drove the animal into the nearest bush, where it was more readily snared. Again, there was a remarkable arrow developed just for killing ducks with young. As it glided over the water, its feathers ruffled the surface like those of a duckling. The mother duck, hastening with affection toward it, came right into its path.

Sables were trapped in fine-meshed nets to which little bells were attached; foxes, in nets baited in the middle with a live swallow tied to a stake. Fish under frozen rivers were stunned by hitting the ice with a wooden mallet and then drawing them up through a hole. The Yakuts caught fish with wicker traps; the Goldi, who fished with nets, protected their catch from scavengers by chaining an eagle nearby. At fishing stations near the mouths of rivers or streams, Kamchadals and other natives of the northeast built conical *balagans* mounted on stilts (to serve as a sort of elevated storehouse), and erected scaffolding on which the fish were hung to dry. When the salmon entered the river in immense numbers from the sea in early July, they were caught by gill-nets, baskets, seines, weirs, and other kinds of snares.

Coastal dwellers had their own repertoire of wiles. In winter and spring, hunters stalking seals near blowholes in the ice wore polar-bear-fur slippers to muffle their tread, or, in camouflage, from time to time scratched the ice with a special scraper to which a seal's claws were attached. In the blowhole itself, a deer bone, "slim as a knitting needle, with a colored swan feather on its forked tip," was inserted as a float, to indicate by its bobbing the seal's approach. Along the Sea of Okhotsk, polar whales were caught in leather nets weighted with large stones as sinkers and anchored to coastal cliffs and crags. Some of their harpoons had seal-skin floats attached to the ropes, and barbed heads that detached and anchored in their prey.

Perhaps the most elaborate stratagems developed around the hunting of bears. Among many natives, a special sanctity attached to the bear, and Ostyaks and Voguls not only swore their most solemn oaths over its skull, but reverently collected and buried its bones after a triumphant feast. Yet despite the awe and respect in which it was held, no animal came in for as much ridicule and abuse. And natives came up with all sorts of ways by which bears could be made to trap themselves or even beat themselves to death. The Kamchadals, for example, would pile up logs and tree trunks at the entrance to its den, which the bear, to free its exit, would pull inside—doing so repeatedly until the den was completely filled and it was trapped. Bears were also made to crush themselves by upsetting delicately constructed piles of logs, or to knock themselves senseless by batting away logs suspended by rope, near beehives or other bait.

There were nets made out of rawhide strips in which reindeer became entangled, to be dispatched with spears or an arrow through the kidney, and a movable blind behind which a hunter on skis concealed himself, shooting at the reindeer through a small hole. Animal sounds and birdcalls were mastered as a matter of course by natives from their youth, and tundra nomads were particularly adept at imitating the call of the East Siberian stag with a birchbark trumpet, luring him to his doom.

The Kamchadal bow was made of whalebone or larch; that of the Ostyaks and Voguls, of strips of cedar and birch glued and bound together and strung with nettle or hemp. The arrows (often poisoned) were tipped with crystal or bone. Extremely powerful, they required the archer to wear on his left forearm a strong bent plate of horn to deaden the blow of the string.

Few Russian frontiersmen developed into archers or ventriloquists of such skill, but the knowledge and observation of nature acquired by native example helped many survive wilderness situations otherwise beyond their powers.

Indeed, in Siberia in the early years, the Russians often faced starvation. With improvisatory skill, they resolved butter out of fish fat, ground roots and bulbs to a powder for use in place of flour and groats, boiled their tea from cowberry leaves, and tried to live on such garden vegetables—beets, carrots, radishes, onions, and leeks—as they could grow. But grown foods like grain were scarce, and the Russians as a result often relied on native cuisine.

The main diet of the West Siberian Tartars—cereals, fish, milk products, and game—was familiar; but the Ostyaks and Voguls drank the blood of elk or reindeer fresh or collected it for use in making flour pancakes or as a thickening to broth. As winter drew on, some part of the kill was preserved, the meat being cut into thin strips and dried or smoked. Fish was generally eaten raw. Birch sap was a popular Ostyak drink; flour was mixed with boiling water and some sweetbriar or peony and made into a mush; unleavened pancakes were baked on stones.

The Kirghiz devoured horseflesh and vast quantities of boiled mutton; but instead of bread they ate *balamyk,* a mass of flour fried in oil, and slaked their thirst with *kumis,* or fermented mare's milk, which sometimes made them drunk. *Kumis* was favored by the Buryats and Yakuts too, who also drank large quantities of melted butter. One Yakut specialty was "milk tar," a kind of boiled porridge made from meat, fish, roots, grass, and the underbark of trees, all ground together in a mortar and mixed with milk and flour. As a milk tar substitute in winter, they sometimes pickled fish in bark-lined pits, and then froze the "acidified and half-rotten result." More palatable to Russians (and a particular delicacy to Yakuts) was a jelly extracted from the horns of young reindeer flavored with pine.

In consuming a butchered reindeer, the tundra nomads did not overlook a single body part; they "gulped down the eyeballs avidly like olives," relished the lips and ears, and especially prized the half-digested contents of the bowels, which consisted of a mass of plant fibers resembling a greenish pulp. With the aid of fat and clotted blood, this was eagerly converted into "black puddings," or (allowed to stand for a time and congeal) smoked and eaten like sausage. Sometimes called *manyalla*—"the nearest approximation," it was said, "which native ingenuity can make to the staff of life"—among the Cossacks it also became a dish of choice.

Although the principal food among the coastal tribes was the meat and fat of walrus and seal, the mainstay of nearly all peoples of the northeast was dried and powdered fish, known as *yukola,* which could be easily stored for winter, and then used as an ingredient of any meal. Various leaves and wild vegetables like sorrel were also consumed by themselves or used as a garnish with meat; and the abundance in Kamchatka of herbs, roots, and fish helped to make up for the lack of cereal grains. The root of the sarana lily, for example, took the place of flour and porridge, and was so much in demand that the wives of Cossacks as well as Kamchadal women used to dig up fieldmice nests (which were made of the root) and dry them in the sun.

The Kamchadals also carried on a regular trade with lemmings, who "cached away grain and roots much prized and covered them with poisonous plants against the depradations of other animals." According to one account, the Kamchadals would "carefully remove the plants, extract the stores for their own consumption, [and] . . . refill the caches with caviar or fish scraps and replace the poisonous covers. Apparently, the lemmings were satisfied with this barter, for they continued to gather grain and roots and to thrive on the substitutions."

Cedar, or stone pine, nuts, found on the mountains and the tundra, were also a Kamchadal favorite, and were eaten without peeling off the husks. The Russians became quite fond of them, too; they ate them "in large mouthfuls and in silence, particularly when people went visiting," and made a fermented beverage out of them similar to kvas, or small beer. The black berries of the honeysuckle were also used to ferment a brandy made from sweetgrass that had hallucinogenic properties and caused wild and terrifying dreams.

From the start, problems of provisionment had bedeviled the early conquest because its vanguard—the traders, the explorers, and the troops that gave them protection and support—operated primarily in the taiga, and not in areas of agricultural potential where they might have proved a colonizing force. Only gradually did settlers surround the scattered military posts, or line the navigable rivers and military roads along which the traffic to distant regions had to pass. In fact, it was not until the founding of Krasnoyarsk in 1628, "in the wooded steppe astride the upper Yenisey," that a promising agricultural settlement was made. As a result, almost until the end of the first century of the conquest, the Russians had to rely rather heavily on shipments of foodstuffs (especially grain) from across the Urals. Life in the oceanic vastness of Northern Siberia, where the calorie intake required for survival was about a third higher than in warmer climes, was attended by some of the same perils as life on the high seas, where men were constantly crippled by deficiency diseases such as scurvy. Even in towns just east of the Urals, like Berezov, there were few Russians, according to a contemporary, "whose Noses, or some other Members, do not bear the marks of this raging Distemper." The "Siberian deliveries" (as the annual shipment of foodstuffs was called) involved hundreds of thousands of bushels of grain and other goods, requisitioned by the government from towns in Russia's European northeast (such as Perm, Cherdyn, and Solvychegodsk), that were carted to Verkhoturye on the Urals' eastern slopes. From there they were distributed to various depots by riverboat, cart, or sled across the whole of northern Asia. As the supply lines lengthened, the problems of provisionment increased—with convoys sometimes taking as much as three years to reach Eastern Siberia, and five years settlements on Kamchatka or the Pacific Coast. Some areas, of course, were so remote as to be beyond hope of supply.

In time, the government began to allow private trade in grain, built warehouses for laying up stock, and paid attention to the development of agriculture in a more systematic way. The scattered fields already under native cultivation were ruled off-limits to Russian colonists, while other natives were exhorted to become "tillers of the soil for the great sovereign." In place of salaries, land grants were made to serving men, coachmen, and other personnel; free peasants were encouraged to settle in Siberia with state assistance; and Crown peasants were forcibly settled in areas where agricultural prospects were slight. Eventually, prisoners of war and convict exiles were also recruited to supplement the workforce, and although all landowners, state or private, were forbidden to employ slaves or runaway serfs (and serfdom itself never flourished in Siberia, which lacked a landed aristocracy), a slave trade emerged, especially involving Central Asian children sold by their parents on the southern frontier. On the other hand, many runaway serfs struck out on their own and established isolated homesteads, or with other peasants ran off to the growing towns. Some drifted to portages to work as carters, rowers, or boatmen, or turned mountainmen and joined the quest for furs. But all voluntary colonists whom the government could keep track of were eventually classified as "state peasants," and had to voluntarily cultivate a portion of Crown land, or relinquish to the state a part of their own crops. This approach was systematized in 1624—and set at a ratio of one to five—when the military governor of Tobolsk decided that the size of a peasant's holding determined the amount of labor he owed to the state.

Yet there were few restrictions in Siberia to the acquisition of land, and this, together with governmental subsidies and loans, stimulated agricultural development. The administration helped peasants make a start, distributed seed for new planting when crops failed, and in the event of livestock epidemics, helped replenish the herds. After steppe nomads raided the districts of Tyumen and Turinsk in 1634, destroying a number of farms, the government stepped in with disaster relief. In return, colonists were obliged to till state fields on which foodstuffs for the local garrisons were grown. But in the end, the free peasant's holding became the typical form of Siberian land tenure, according to which he was allowed as much land as he could work. This gave rise to a rather different, more hardy and independent peasant than the semi-enslaved drone European Russia had produced.

Colonists first settled in the central valley of the Irtysh, built home-steads, farmed the land or raised cattle, and tried to avoid a Tartar arrow in the back. Beyond the townships and fortified stockades, many were willing to risk the utmost rigors of frontier living to make the land their own. As with the pioneers of America, they had to adapt to the wilderness or die.

In the beginning, many lived temporarily in dugouts, half-dugouts, wattle-and-daub huts, or tents, but the one-story notched log cabin almost always became their permanent home. After the timbers were firmly wedged into place, they were caulked with a mixture of dung and clay, and in winter flanked with earthen embankments against the cold. Overhead the cabin was shingled with bark, and eventually a wooden flooring covered the hard and stony ground. Glass was scarce, and most colonists stretched a translucent animal bladder over the window space or used sheets of ice or slices of mica for panes. Tables and chairs were pegged together from wooden slabs. Yet the cabin's crude construction and complete frontier simplicity were sometimes artfully disguised by remarkable embellishment: window frames dec-orated with geometrical carving, lintels with lavish fretwork, and the whole ensemble brightly painted in reds and blues and greens.

Although at times the pioneers' isolation was such as "to make lone-liness itself appalling," there were forests to clear, marshes to drain, and rocks to be wrenched from the soil. The relative freedom and the wide open spaces also got into their blood. But more than anything else it was their spirit of individual initiative and self-reliance, as in the American West, that pulled them through.

The Russian frontier town would have been recognizable to any American pioneer: a makeshift ensemble of hastily erected plank build-ings flanked by wooden sidewalks along a wide path for a main street, the latter "well-rutted by horse hooves and wagon wheels." The church, the saloon, and the general store dominated the center of town, and "crooked tree limbs and old wooden posts served as hitching rails."

Gradually, the one-horse wooden plow was ousted by the two-horse plow with wheels, and harrows with wooden teeth were replaced by those with iron. Wealthier farmers acquired winnowers and threshers; the poorer used chains or round larch logs with teeth cut into them, drawn by horses harnessed by shafts to rectangular frames. Reaping was done with a sickle and threshing with wooden chains.

In coping with injury and illness, settlers relied for the most part on home remedies, since country doctors were few and far between. Vodka and sundry brandies served as antiseptic solutions, plant roots were beaten into poultices, and herbal brews devised to ease fever or pain. Slabs of raw meat were used to draw out poison and other infected matter from wounds. The usual prescription for rheumatism was sasparilla root, bear fat mixed with breast milk for eczema and other skin conditions, sweetgrass juice for killing lice; Angelica root and sorrel was the despairing hope of those afflicted with venereal disease.

Larch resin and wild garlic were craved as antiscorbutics, although no one yet knew what a vitamin was or how it was metabolized.

More than anything else, of course, the stability of the conquest depended on family life, whether in the hinterland or on the farm. And women were in short supply. The Cossacks claimed that at the time of Ivan Koltso's triumphant visit to Moscow (announcing Yermak's conquest) they had received an imperial charter allowing them to "transport" women to Siberia—and strangely enough, this document (granted by the government in a fit of immoral gratitude) was never disclaimed. In 1630, for example, 150 women and girls were rounded up and brought to Tobolsk, and troops regularly seized for themselves scores of native girls. It was not unusual for even a poverty-stricken Cossack to have a little harem, and on the frontier women were also pawned or sold for rubles or furs. Domestic slaves and concubines were part of the lure of the Wild East, and pimping and prostitution were rampant, some "using their own wives as security in payment of debts . . . with creditors fucking these women until their husbands have paid up. If the payment is not made on time, the creditors sell them to others for debauchery or work."

Avvakum recalled in his autobiography that Afanasy Pashkov (a hero of the Amur campaign) had encountered two elderly widows on their way to enter a convent at Yeniseysk, and deeming this an unpardonable waste of their potential had forcibly "married" them off to his troops. Mercenary lust, indeed, long remained a conspicuous feature of Siberian life, but especially so toward the beginning of the conquest, when the frontiersmen advanced far beyond the Urals and few women immediately followed in their wake. Under such circumstances, the relatively loose sexual mores of the natives were quite gratifying to Russian desires. Among Siberians, group marriages and polygamy were common, and chastity not always expected of a bride. In the language of the Chukchi, in fact, there was no term for "girl" at all, but only for "married woman," "woman living alone," and "woman not yet put in use." Marriage itself was customarily by "seizure"—either by kidnapping in war or as a ceremonial act of semi-rape. In the latter case, there were preliminary courtship rituals in which the prospective groom worked for a time for the parents of the bride but, having won their consent, then awaited an opportunity to seize her, "cut and tear off her clothes, and touch her sexual organs with his hand." Other women of the clan, as a challenge to his perseverance, were supposed to attack and beat him back, but with the bride's connivance, of course, success was easily achieved.

Native customs recognized various prohibitions and taboos, but these did not necessarily run counter to Russian desires. Among the Kamchadals, for example, no one could marry a widow until she had been "purified of her sins." To do this, according to an early Russian anthropologist, she had to have intercourse with someone else, "but only a stranger, or someone beyond the prejudice of shame and infamy, since it is considered very dishonorable by other members of the tribe. Thus it was formerly only with great difficulty and expense that widows could find men to purify them, and they were sometimes obliged to remain widows all their lives. But since our Cossacks have settled in Kamchatka, widows no longer have this trouble; they can find as many men as they wish to absolve them of their sins."

Although the nomadic Koryaks were acutely jealous, and prone to kill their wives "over the slightest suspicion" of infidelity, the settled or Maritime Koryaks and especially the Chukchi (whose customs in this regard resembled those of the North American Eskimo) eagerly offered their wives and daughters as bedmates to visiting friends. "To refuse to sleep with the wife of one's host," in fact, "was to insult him so gravely as to run the risk of being killed." Whatever native custom allowed, the Russians exploited to the hilt, and in time "among the Russians and Russianized natives throughout the whole northeast from the Lena River to Kamchatka hardly any [unmarried] girl remains a virgin, and most begin sexual life with the first traces of maturity." Incest was endemic, too, "even in the families of the clergy," and other forms of depravity were commonplace. One German explorer tellingly observed that the Cossacks became most aroused when witnessing voluptuous dances that mimed the mating behavior of bears, whales, and geese because, he said, "it corresponded to their own invitation" to copulate.

Intermarriage, in fact, was practically the norm, particularly in the north and east, and in time the ethnic term "Kamchadal" even came to signify the peninsula's mixed-blood descendants, rather than the natives themselves.

The American and Russian frontier stories are not unalike, and in comparing the two, as one historian notes, the Siberian settlers "voluntarily risked all they had and left accustomed surroundings to go into a wilderness in search of a better life. They knew hunger, disease, storm and drought, deprivation, homesickness, and loneliness before they succeeded in building new homes, planting new fields, making new neighbors, and finally gaining a new prosperity and a new happiness. Some died, some returned, some gave up after a year. The overwhelming majority stayed and survived."

There was much to hold them there. Western Siberia had some of the best farmland in the world, and eastward, too, in time there were flourishing fields—between Yeniseysk and Krasnoyarsk, and throughout the "Ilimsk Plowland," as it was called, on a great bend of the Lena River. By the mid-1640s, the district of Yeniseysk had become self-sufficient and was shipping surplus grain to other parts of Siberia; after 1685, although problems of supply remained to more inaccessible areas, the "Siberian deliveries" from beyond the Urals ceased.

Meanwhile, in the Transbaikal, traces of prehistoric mines had been found near the Argun River, and after iron was discovered near Tomsk in 1624, a fledgling mining industry began to take shape. Soon deposits of copper, silver, and mica were detected in other localities. In time, plowshares, scythes, sickles, and other iron implements (previously too expensive to import) would be obtained from Siberian forges, while the mining and production of mineral dyes, rock crystal, and various building materials, such as limestone, as well as clay for making and firing bricks, gave promise of a broad-based local industry. Salt mines were started near Tobolsk, Ilimsk, anZd Yeniseysk, and in the 1680s, sulfur and saltpeter deposits around the Selenga River and in the vicinity of Yakutsk became the foundation for a munitions industry. In 1700, Greek mining engineers in Russian employ founded the Nerchinsk Works, near the Mongolian border, and one Nikita Demidov, a common blacksmith from Tula, built the first Siberian blast furnace and cannon foundry at Neviyansk in the southern Urals. Nikita's son, Akinfey, mined for precious metals on the slopes of the Altay and Ural mountains, and built extensive blast furnaces at Kolivan, as the family enterprise grew.

Farming, mining, and other aspects of the Siberian economy, which no longer depended so heavily on furs, led to increases in population and the upgrading of towns. In 1662 the Russian population of Siberia had stood at about 70,000 (including 20,000 troops); by the end of the century it was 300,000 or more—about the same as the European population of the thirteen American colonies at that time. Perhaps 40 percent of the Russians were peasants, scattered among Siberia's twenty-odd districts, although concentrated in the west. By then, the fortresslike towns of the original conquest had also undergone some evolution, and were no longer mere enclaves where the administrative offices, government storehouses for money and munitions, customs and guardhouses were kept.

A substantial military force was still needed to put down native uprisings and keep order in the new lands, but many of these men— petty nobles, Cossacks, foreign mercenaries, or prisoners of war—had settled in Siberia themselves. Even where rudimentary forts and blockhouses were maintained, most non-military personnel often lived with their families in the area below the stockades, and set themselves up as blacksmiths, tanners, soapmakers, and so on, with a gradual proliferation of shops and stores. And while regular soldiers, both mounted or on foot, might still garrison their posts on round-the-clock alert, an irregular militia, mostly of Cossack extraction, was increasingly used by the government in both civil and military work. Among the free Siberian population a kind of nobility also grew up, largely comprised of impoverished scions of the old aristocracy, who "flourished as a military and administrative elite in the colonial environment." At the same time, to a degree impossible to imagine in European Russia, the Siberian social structure was indeterminate, as one group melded with another, and in the rough democracy of the frontier few class or service distinctions held up. The exigencies of their situation required most to be jacks-of-all-trades: carpenters, boat builders, farmers, fishermen, smiths.

By 1710, Tobolsk contained about 2,500 houses and 10,000 inhabitants, and had overspread the crest of the high eastern bank of the Irtysh River, where new stone palaces and churches stood out as more imposing than the old battlemented fort. Lower down on the flats, wooden buildings of all kinds accumulated. Growing at an even faster rate was Tomsk, which had a large wooden bazaar containing more than two dozen shops, and where various foreign goods could be bought, including lacquered wares. Irkutsk, as the chief beneficiary of the enormous China trade, would soon surpass them both. The extensive dockyards of Verkhoturye—the gateway to Siberia, built on the Tura River in 1598—also turned out hundreds of rivercraft a year. Meanwhile, Russian domination had been extended into Central Asia, and eastward to the Altay Mountains. An expedition prospecting for gold in 1714 led to the founding of Omsk, and after a garrison was posted to Semipalatinsk in 1718, a long line of fortifications roughly traced the southern frontier.

A start had been made. But it was no more than that, in the preternatural vastness of northern Asia. For a long time, few of life's material necessities (and almost none of its luxuries) would be produced in Siberia, and even paper, metal utensils, and linen cloth would have to be imported from the mother country en masse. Siberia's external trade (raw materials for finished goods) remained more important than its internal commerce, and the state predictably monopolized the principal items involved.

Sheer distance also made the colony remote. Travelers entering Siberia at Verkhoturye required around two weeks to reach Tobolsk, three months to get to Tomsk, and up to four months to reach Yeniseysk, a journey of 1,300 miles. From Yeniseysk to Yakutsk took five months or more, and from Yakutsk to the Kolyma River (980 miles away) another three. Most winter roads went over frozen rivers and streams, which in summer only presented additional obstacles to the builders of overland trails. Such trails or roads were often little more than shortcuts of the most rugged kind. In 1600, the first Siberian *yam,* or post station, had been established at Turinsk, with fifty *yamshchiks,* or drivers, and by 1662, three thousand drivers or more carried the service all the way to the Lena. Still, over 8,000 miles of travel—not as the crow flies but as men moved—or one third of the earth's circumference, separated St. Petersburg, the imperial capital (after 1713), from Anadyrsk. And within the vast dominion of Siberia itself, even as the sun was setting in Tobolsk, it was rising in Kamchatka on the following day.

The Siberia of old was a vanishing world, the Siberia of Russia's future only dimly taking shape. In an emblematic image of that divided moment in time, on the site of the former Tartar capital of Isker, a saltpeter works begun during the reign of Michael Romanov lay incomplete, while all that could be seen of the town's old ruins were the remains of a rampart, and pits and hollows where its cellars had once been.

PART TWO

Overleaf: On the road to Okhotsk (eighteenth-century lithograph).

9

MAPPING THE MIND OF A TSAR

By the end of the seventeenth century it could be said that most of Siberia had been conquered, part of it settled, but none of it completely colonized. Moreover, much of its geography remained obscure, and very little of it had been carefully surveyed. In the far northeast and along the Pacific Coast, the government's hold on its latest territorial acquisitions was tenuous at best, despite the celebrity of Atlasov's Yermaklike thrust down the length of the Kamchatka Peninsula. On the Pacific Coast, virtually the only settlement worth naming was Okhotsk, a backwater *ostrog* consisting of ten miserable little Cossack huts and a stockade. Although the more palpable attractions of the Amur had diverted the Russians for a time, once that area was forfeited by treaty, the security of the Okhotsk seaboard and Kamchatka became a matter of more urgent concern. And this was one of the tasks undertaken by Peter the Great.

It would be almost surprising if, having planted himself in St. Petersburg at the westernmost extremity of his empire, and with all his self-proclaimed determination to root out the "Asiatic" in Russian life, Peter had been interested in Siberia much beyond its potential as a source of revenue. He never traveled to Siberia, in fact, although he visited every other part of his realm; and what interested him most about it (revenue aside) was what lay beyond it—China, Japan, and the continent of North America, which he knew must extend to some point near the northeastern Asiatic coast. But Siberia was a lot to look beyond, and anyone trying to do so, physically, had to endure the rites of passage through it in order to glimpse what the far horizons held.

Born on May 30, 1672, Peter had come to power after a prolonged and irregular interregnum of regents and co-rulers that reflected the fluctuating fortunes of opposed family cliques. His father, the tsar Alexis, twice married, had left behind him at his death in 1676 two sons, Fyodor and Ivan, by his first wife, and one son, Peter, by his second. Fyodor had succeeded his father, but in 1682 he died suddenly without issue and Peter, at the age of ten, was proclaimed tsar. His twenty-five-year-old half-sister, Sophia, however, immediately took power, and with the help of the *streltsy* (capital guard) established Peter and Ivan in a double tsardom with herself as regent. Ivan was soon revealed to be a simpleton; in 1689, at the age of seventeen, Peter claimed priority, banished Sophia to a convent, and emerged as "senior tsar." But for the next five years he accepted the guidance of his mother, so that it was not until 1694 that the imperial tsardom of Peter the Great began.

A tall, powerfully built, restless, and energetic monarch, of meager education but tremendous intellectual range, Peter sought to master every aspect of governance, as well as a number of practical trades. With his "half-barbarous, half-cultivated ways," he seemed, as one writer put it, "to represent Russia's own uncouth largeness," but fundamentally his policy was to repudiate the old Muscovite traditions of isolation for the sake of "intellectual and technical cooperation with the outside world." He visited Europe twice—in 1697–98, and again in 1717—and after the first of these trips returned home with shiploads of books, maps, tools, navigation equipment, and guns, and spared no effort to impose new habits and values on an unreceptive population. Despite the bitter resentment his innovations aroused in some quarters, he recruited foreign technicians, modernized the calendar, and introduced Western culture and fashions into nearly every aspect of Russian life. The technical schools he established began to train a civil service class drawn from the gentry. His efforts toward higher education also led more famously to the establishment of the Imperial Academy of Sciences in St. Petersburg, which opened shortly after his death. Peter's military program was no less grand: Russia at last acquired a navy, the army was thoroughly reorganized along Western lines, and a new array of weaponry was introduced. These changes

were particularly opposed by the *streltsy*—a once-proud corps of musketeers—who in their latter days desperately maneuvered to maintain
their privileged status against the emerging standing army. In 1698,
their treasonous rebellion gave Peter the pretext he had sought to
break their power and liquidate their ranks.

In struggling with the entrenched bureaucracy, Peter tried to root
out nepotism and judicial and administrative corruption and base promotion on merit rather than rank or pedigree. This effort reached a
culmination in 1722, when he instituted the so-called "Table of Ranks,"
which made state service the sole criterion for social advancement.
Meanwhile, in 1708 he had divided the empire into eight provinces
(Siberia being one, with its capital at Tobolsk), created the governing
Senate in 1711 as a sort of central state planning agency, and in 1717
replaced the numerous (and often redundant) *prikazy* with nine "col-
leges" or departments that more closely resembled modern ministries.
In his radical reorganization of the Church administration, he eventually replaced the office of Patriarch by a Holy Synod of Clerics (on
the Swedish model) which answered to a government official, in a
clear subordination of Church to State.

Finally, endeavoring to develop the commerce, industry, and natural
resources of his realm, Peter improved its infrastructure with new
canals and roads, and, most imposing of all, established his new capital,
St. Petersburg, on the Neva to rival the most prosperous of Western
ports. Numerous foreign architects and sculptors were commissioned
to adorn it, and the Baroque and Italianate churches, bridges, palaces,
and other buildings they designed made it one of the most beautiful
cities the world had ever seen.

Yet all this was accomplished at tremendous social cost. Although
Russia was not beleaguered as before by incessant social unrest, the
strains upon the body politic were no less frightful as the tsar attempted to mold a recalcitrant nation to his mighty will. His construction of docks, ships, fortifications, roads, and canals was done with the
forced labor of tens of thousands of peasant conscripts, and the
marshes of St. Petersburg alone claimed so many casualties that it was
said to be a city built on bones. Moreover, this domestic program was
being prosecuted while the country was continually at war. Peter
fought to secure the southern borders of his realm against Turkey and
Persia, to obtain outlets for his new navy on the Black and Caspian

seas, and above all to firmly establish Russia on the Baltic by dislodging Sweden from its coast. His Great Northern War against Sweden's Charles XII (in which Denmark and Poland were also antagonists) lasted from 1700 until 1721, when Russia's decisive triumph was confirmed by the Treaty of Nystadt, incorporating Livonia (Latvia and Estonia), Viborg, and part of Finland into the realm. In 1721, Peter was declared "Emperor" and "Great" and Russia emerged as the dominant power in the European North. As one contemporary observed, reflecting upon the course of the tsar's remarkable career: "The maritime and trading Powers, from whom he learnt Navigation, Building of Ships, and so many other Arts unknown to Russia before his Reign; and of whom he borrowed so many skilful Workmen of all kinds, perceived too late, that they had raised themselves a very potent and dangerous rival."

All of Peter's large-scale initiatives had taken money, and the near-exhaustion of Siberia's "soft gold" and other resources by the end of the seventeenth century (with the China trade just developing, and Kamchatka not yet under firm control) had inconveniently coincided with the tremendous budgetary strain. Peter's military campaigns in particular absorbed up to three-quarters of the total state revenue, a fact that led to his pithy (if myopic) pronouncement that "money is the artery of war." To raise more of it, he taxed everything from coffins to pet bears, introduced a heavy new poll tax, established state monopolies on items like tea and paper, confiscated Church lands, sold trade monopolies to the highest bidder, and so on, in order to squeeze the population dry.

Beyond that, Peter launched a series of efforts designed to "map and count" in the broadest possible way the resources of his empire. In 1718 he commissioned Daniel Gottlieb Messerschmidt, a German naturalist then resident in St. Petersburg, to survey the natural and man-made assets of both Western and Central Siberia. After nearly a decade exploring the territory from Tobolsk to Nerchinsk, Messerschmidt returned in 1727 with wagonloads of plant and animal specimens, rock samples, sketch maps, and detailed notes on the geography, population, and natural history of the little-known regions he had traversed. Of more satisfaction to the government, he confirmed that there were major deposits of copper in the Urals, iron around Tobolsk, and silver at Nerchinsk.

Meanwhile, as early as 1711, Peter had begun to demand from Siberia money, goods, and furs "over and above the amount of income already set for such sources," and laid plans to gain access to new fur-bearing lands—for example, islands off Kamchatka and the Arctic coast. But first he had to subdue the Koryak, Chukchi, and other north-eastern tribes that had refused thus far to cooperate with the tribute system. In Kamchatka and along the Anadyr, coordinated native attacks had made *yasak* collection a costly trial, while sporadic Cossack revolts continued to break out. Some of the natives had also become familiar with firearms and (in the case of the Koryaks) had even begun to fashion armor out of metal plates. In fact, the situation in the whole northeast remained dire. Five years of *yasak* income had been lost to the authorities, and at least two hundred Russians had been killed. Overland communication with Kamchatka was so slow that it was impossible to monitor the situation closely, and it soon became apparent that a sea route had to be found across the Okhotsk Sea.

In 1714, at the behest of Peter the Great, one Kuzma Sokolov supervised the construction of a 54-foot-long, single-masted galiot at Okhotsk, and in June 1716 he sailed from the mouth of the Okhota River, following the coast northward to the Ola River and crossing the stormy sea to the west coast of Kamchatka in a voyage that took two weeks. For his achievement Sokolov was christened, rather grandly, "Russia's Vasco da Gama"; but once pioneered, this route became the usual one, saving months of roundabout travel (through the northeast via Anadyrsk) and making it possible for the Russians to meet Kamchatka's various needs with more dispatch.

More ambitious plans soon followed for the occupation of the region. These took the form of the Great Kamchatka Command, a large expeditionary force that was to establish new outposts on the Arctic and Pacific coasts, annex unexplored islands reported to lie offshore, and bring the whole northeast, including Kamchatka, more firmly under Russian control. The Kurile Islands, rumored to be veined with gold and silver ore, were also to be explored, and an attempt made to determine their geographical relation to Japan. Preparations were begun at Yakutsk, Okhotsk, and Nizhnekamchatsk, but it soon became clear that the scale of the undertaking was entirely beyond the means available to carry it out. The pattern, however, had been set, and although in June 1718 the Command was disbanded, the fur-rich Shantar

Islands had at least been discovered (opposite the Uda River) as a whet to future expeditionary appetites.

At the same time, larger geographical issues began to animate the government's designs. And these became linked, directly or indirectly, with the burning geographical question of the day—whether Asia and America were joined.

Ever since Marco Polo's seductive description, in the thirteenth century, of the riches of Cathay, Europeans had dreamed of a sea route to the East; and from the mid-1400s that dream had led to the great voyages of discovery. Portugal led the way by sending ships southeast along the African coast, but others (inspired by the *Geography* of Ptolemy and some of Marco Polo's claims) believed the route could be found by sailing to the west—as was first tried by Christopher Columbus in 1492. Columbus, who wanting nothing but the "Indies" of his desire, adamantly refused to believe he had discovered a new continent, and with diplomatic letters in hand addressed to the Great Khan "searched fruitlessly for signs of vast cities and silk-clad philosophers in the jungles of Cuba." A mere six years after his discovery of America, Portuguese ships commanded by Vasco da Gama reached India by sea. With the subtropical sealanes controlled by Portugal and Spain (via Mexico and the Philippines, Africa and the Indian Ocean), other European states turned their attention to the north.

Although most medieval notions about the perils of the "vasty deep" had been dispelled by the Renaissance voyagers, their afterimage still clung to Arctic waters, which Pliny had called "accursed by nature," and others wherein "nature breeds, Perverse, all monstrous, all prodigious things, Abominable, unutterable, and worse Than fables yet have feigned or fear conceived, Gorgons and Hydras, and Chimaeras dire." Descriptions of the Arctic often spoke of "a terrible insucking whirlpool," and of Arctic cyclones equal to tropical hurricanes in force. Tusked walruses and mammoth spouting whales were still strange enough to contemporary zoology to merge with imaginary creatures into one vista of anticipated fears, and little comfort from the twilight darkness of Arctic winter nights was to be found in their unearthly displays of trembling light and form. As an antidote to all this, and to encourage mariners to press their search for a short, direct northern route to the East, optimistic maps (like that published in Sigismund von Herberstein's *Rerum Moscoviticarum Commentarii* in 1549) willfully abridged the anticipated distance "to hold before their eyes a short journey, so they would be of stout heart, and with greater dedication through the terrifying difficulties of boundless Sea of Ice." Mercator's great maritime chart of 1569 had also conjectured the distance as "short and easy"—that once North Cape had been rounded, the coast of northern Asia would slope gently down into the Pacific Ocean. Instead, of course, it continued eastward for several thousand miles and in places thrust almost impassably upward toward the North Pole.

Various early attempts were made by the English, Dutch, French, Italians, and Danes to find a Northwest Passage; these having failed, the attention of the English turned at length to the northeast. In 1553, Sebastian Cabot formed in London the "Mysterie and company of the Merchants Adventurers for the discoverie of Cathay and divers other lands," and outfitted three small ships for the expedition—the *Bona Speranza,* the *Edward Bonaventure,* and the *Bona Confidentia*— under Sir Hugh Willoughby and Richard Chancellor, the latter a protégé of the mystic mathematician and alchemist John Dee. The three ships weighed anchor on May 11, but off the Lofotan Islands they were separated in a storm. Although Willoughby's *Speranza* managed to link up again with the *Confidentia* at dawn, Chancellor's *Bonaventure* was nowhere to be seen. But it was Willoughby and his eighty-three companions who were doomed. Forced to winter in a bay on the Lapland coast without adequate provisions, they were later discovered frozen to death in their ships. Meanwhile, Chancellor had resumed his voyage, and on August 24, 1553, wandered across the White Sea to the mouth of the northern Dvina River, where he disembarked on Russian soil.

Russia was not quite Cathay (though mutually profitable trade relations were soon established between England and Russia), and in 1556, Stephen Burrough, Chancellor's one-time shipmate, continued the quest. Sailing above the White Sea, he "went in over the dangerous barre of the Pechora," but on August 22 he was nearly crushed by an iceberg after passing through Kara Gate—the strait separating Vaygach Island from Novaya Zemlya to the north. No further attempt was made to find the Northeast Passage until 1580, when Arthur Pet and Charles Jackman passed through Yugor Strait (between Vaygach Island and the mainland), but failed to get past the pack ice of the Kara Sea. For many years the observations of Burrough and Pet would represent the extreme eastern limit of what was known of the Arctic coast.

The English were succeeded by the Dutch. In two expeditions in the mid-1590s Willem Barents explored the west coast of Novaya Zemlya, and in 1596 rounded the island's northernmost point. Almost immediately, however, he found himself pinned against the land by "whole towns made of ice, with towers and bulwarks round about them," and some 80 miles down the coast sought refuge in a bay (later called Ice Haven) "in great cold, poverty, misery and grief." There the ice floes began to pinch and twist his ship to pieces, "as if in the grip of a giant wrench." The voyagers built a rectangular hut out of driftwood and planks from their ship and fashioned a chimney from a beer barrel with the bottom knocked out. Through the long Arctic winter nights, as a big Dutch clock chimed away the hours, Barents sometimes played on his beechwood flute, or read aloud from books on navigation and history to his simple mariners by the light of a bear-grease lamp. As winter drew on, however, it seemed as if the terrible fate of Willoughby and his companions would soon become their own. The sun vanished behind the horizon; snowdrifts engulfed their hut; their clock stopped. Their slippers froze about their feet as hard as horns. Supplies salvaged from the vessel barely sustained them, but in the spring waterlanes at last began to show in the open sea. Converting their rowboats into sailing skiffs, they made their way south, and five weeks later were rescued by Russian fishermen encamped at Novaya Zemlya's southern tip. Barents himself did not survive, but before departing Ice Haven he had hung in the chimney a written account of the voyage concealed in a powder horn. Two hundred and seventy-five years later, on September 7, 1871, the skipper of a Norwegian sloop hunting for walrus off the coast was driven to the same bay by a storm, and there found still standing, hermetically sealed in a thick coat of ice, Barents's shack and the miraculously preserved relics of his ordeal.

Within a few years after his voyage, that ordeal had become proverbial for the fate that Arctic mariners faced. "You are now sailed into the north of my lady's opinion," one character tells another in Shakespeare's *Twelfth Night,* "where you will hang like an icicle on a Dutchman's beard."

Barents's voyage marked the final effort of the West in the Russian Arctic for some time to come, since after 1619 (as described earlier) foreigners were forbidden to sail east of the Yamal Peninsula. But the dream of finding a sea route to the east did not die, and it was inevitably revived with the Russian conquest of Siberia, which included striking advances along the coast. By the beginning of the eighteenth century, Russia had created an eastern empire that spanned the whole of northern Asia, and she alone was in a position to explore and verify whether a Northeast Passage did exist. On several occasions, Peter the Great was urged by various European intellectuals and scientific societies to do this, and Gottfried Leibniz, the German mathematician and philosopher, wrote to him about it at least five times.

Nevertheless, at least until the end of the seventeenth century few were optimistic. The experiences of Western mariners aside, reports filtering back from Russian explorers in the Arctic provoked this exasperated conclusion of one official with geographical expertise: "From Weygats [Vaygach Island] to the Icy or Holy Cape the Sea is utterly unnavigable with Ships, and should a second Christopher Columbus appear, and point out the course of the Heavens, he could not yet drive away these Mountains of Ice: For God and Nature have so invincibly fenced the Sea side of Siberia with Ice, that no Ship can come to the River Jenisea [Yenisey], much less can they come farther Northwards into the Sea." Peter, however, had his own reasons for taking up the challenge, as he assessed the potential benefits of a Northeast Passage to his realm. Experts suggested that it would reduce the sailing time from Europe to Japan from nine months to five or six weeks, and that England, Holland, and perhaps other maritime powers would be willing to pay a substantial toll to use it—as Spain had imposed a toll in the Strait of Gibraltar and Denmark in the Danish Sound. To enforce the Russian toll, fortresses could be built on both sides of the Kara and Yugor straits, and in certain inlets and bays. In 1714, one of the tsar's advisers, Fyodor Saltykov, drafted plans for the requisite coastal survey, using iceboats starting from the mouths of the various rivers and charting the coastline in a chain.

Such proposals merely gave formal expression to Peter's already privately announced intent. For of course he realized the tremendous inside advantage Russia would enjoy, over a route he exclusively controlled, in competition for the eastern trade. Peter's western wars had delayed pursuit of the matter, but at least as early as 1712 he apparently told John Perry, engaged by Peter as a shipbuilder and engineer, that "as soon as he had Peace and Leisure to apply his Mind to it, he will search out whether it be possible for ships to pass by way of Nova Zembla [Novaya Zemlya] into the Tartarian Sea [Arctic Ocean]; or to find out some Port eastward of the River Oby [Ob], where he may build Ships and send them, if practicable, to the Coast of China & Japan."

No sooner had the fighting in the Great Northern War come to an end, in 1719, than Peter began to apply his mind to the question. In that year, he sent men "experienced in navigation, geography, and astronomy" to the mouth of the Ob to look for harbors and to explore the waters off the coast, and dispatched two geodesists, or topographers, Ivan Yevreynov and Fyodor Luzhin (both graduates of Peter's new Naval Academy), on a related mission to the Far East. Peter himself gave them their orders, dated January 2, 1719: "You will proceed to Kamchatka and thence, as instructed, and will ascertain . . . whether or not Asia and America are joined by land; and you will go not only north and south, but also east and west, and will place on a map all that you see." In addition, they carried secret instructions (part of the unfinished business of the Great Kamchatka Command) to ascertain whether the Kurile Islands had silver ore.

Luzhin and Yevreynov left the capital in July, reached Okhotsk a year later, repaired Sokolov's battered old *Okhota,* and in September 1720 crossed the Sea of Okhotsk to Bolsheretsk. That winter they surveyed the northeastern coast of Kamchatka, and in May 1721 sailed to the Kuriles, where they traced the archipelago as far as the sixth island. Upon their return, they hastened back to European Russia where, in May 1722, they reported their findings directly to Peter the Great and showed him the map of the islands they had drawn. At the time, the tsar was in Kazan, "pausing on his way to the Caspian campaign against Persia." But he spoke with Yevreynov at some length, and also "examined with satisfaction" their delineation of Kamchatka as a peninsula, which indicated no connection between it and the American coast.

Rumors of the proximity of America were widespread in northeastern Siberia, and (strangely enough) geographers of the past two centuries had the relative position of the two continents approximately right. The existence of a strait between them had long been a cartographical convention; Gerardus Mercator's famous world maritime chart of 1569 called it the "Strait of Anian," based on a passage in Marco Polo which had been misconstrued. On the "Barents map" of 1598, this strait separated the northeastern corner of Asia from a large continent that loomed above it with the superscription: "America Pars." This was long before Dezhnev's voyage, of course, which first confirmed the geographical conceit; but by Peter's time, records of the voyage had been lost, and it was only dimly recollected among the "folk." In any case, his unread petitions and reports (still buried in the archives in Yakutsk) would not have cast light on how close America was. But based on conversations with Chukchi and Asiatic Eskimo, it was vaguely realized that there was, or had been, commerce between the natives of both lands, and that America must be near. In 1673, Matvey Pushkin, the governor of Smolensk, told a French Jesuit, Philippe Avril, that the Russians believed that America was "not far off from that part of Asia which juts into the Sea of Tartary [Arctic Ocean]," and that people had first reached America accidentally on ice floes carried out to sea. In 1697, a Chukchi guide had told Atlasov of a large island opposite an "impassable cape" of ice between the Kolyma and Anadyr rivers, and said that its inhabitants sometimes crossed the ice with furs to trade. These furs, said to be "poor quality sables," with tails displaying horizontal black and red stripes, were evidently Alaskan raccoons. The Cossack Petr Popov similarly learned from Chukchi in 1711 of small islands in the sea a little to the east, and of a Big Land inhabited by "toothed ones" (Eskimos) one day's journey beyond. They meant, of course, the Big and Little Diomede Islands and the Seward Peninsula of Alaska.

Yet the highly speculative maps of contemporary geographers seldom agreed. Their representations were often primitive, with little conception of the real configuration of either the Arctic or North Pacific coasts, and like the sketch maps of Siberia in general lacked "scale and coordinates" and were "based on river systems rather than astronomically determined points." Some showed Novaya Zemlya as a peninsula, others as an island; the Luzhin and Yevreynov map had been the first to delineate Kamchatka, but omitted the Chukchi Peninsula completely; other maps depicted "one or two complete (or open-ended) peninsulas extending east northeast into the ocean." Perhaps the most influential was that prepared in 1691 by the Dutchman Nicolaas Witsen, a friend of the tsar's with access to other informed officials, who labeled the two speculative promontories Cape Tabin and Ice Cape. The former (a construction derived from Pliny the Elder, who had never been to the Arctic) was identified with the Taimyr Peninsula, and was vaguely but correctly supposed to be the northernmost point of Eurasia; the latter (sometimes called Holy Cape by the Russians) was generally represented as mountains of land or ice. According to Witsen, some believed that either or both capes were "connected to North America," but elsewhere in his text (reflecting a dim recollection of Dezhnev's voyage) he referred to "reports of mariners sailing around the northeast corner of Asia."

Guillaume Delisle, the first royal geographer of France, published a "Carte de Tartarie" (that is, a map of Siberia) in Paris in 1706 which partly copied Witsen's map, including its mountainous open-ended cape, with an inscription indicating uncertainty as to whether it joined "some other continent."

With regard to the North Pacific, the empirical evidence accruing in a piecemeal fashion to cartographers had managed to confuse the general picture even while refining it in certain details.

This process began in 1643, when one Maerten Gerritsen Vries sailed for the Dutch East India Company to the North Pacific to discover "the unknown East-coast of Tartary [Siberia], the Kingdom of Catay, and the West-coast of America, together with the Isles situate to the East of Japan, cryed up for their richess in silver and gold." Vries's foggy survey of the region led him to identify two Kurile Islands he visited as "States Land" and "Company Land" (to both of which he attributed substantial size), and to amalgamate Hokkaido and Sakhalin into one huge landmass called "Jesso" on his map. In his accompanying commentary, Company Land was also said to be the "West-corner of America." On other, later maps, Sakhalin was depicted either as a small island (labeled "Amoerse Eylandt," at the mouth of the Amur), or as a peninsula; Japan was variously portrayed as an island, as part of Jesso, or as a peninsula attached to the Asian mainland; and, on the American side, where the coast had been explored and charted no farther than 43 degrees north latitude, some maps showed California as an island. Finally there was "Juan de Gama Land," which a Portuguese navigator was alleged to have sailed along in 1589–90 from China to New Spain, and which was thought to be either a large island or part of America. Even when doubts arose subsequently about other unconfirmed sitings, the mythic Juan de Gama Land would tenaciously remain.

Not surprisingly, the North Pacific also became the natural home to imaginary literary constructions like those of Francis Bacon (Atlantis) and Jonathan Swift. In his *Gulliver's Travels* (written between 1721 and 1725), Swift placed Company Land and States Land both east of Jesso, and his imaginary Laputa between them and North America to the west. The prosperous but isolated kingdom of Brobdingnag—with its humane race of giants, and enormous animals and plants—he depicted as a huge peninsula joined to the American Northwest to the west of the Strait of Anian. The composite map he published with his amazing fable, in fact, represented a pretty good summary of where contemporary knowledge of the North Pacific actually stood.

The question arises as to what Peter the Great himself knew. As early as 1697, when visiting Amsterdam (Nicolaas Witsen serving as his host), he claimed evidence that the northeastern corner of Asia was not joined to America, at least in the Cape Tabin area, but said he didn't yet know for sure if the continents were elsewhere connected by land or ice. Within a few years, the conquest and partial survey of Kamchatka and the northern Kuriles would somewhat clarify the coastal geography of the northeast.

By 1714, in updated maps the elongated and truncated or open-ended peninsula at the northeast corner had disappeared, and in its place was drawn a crude version of the Chukchi Peninsula, washed by the ocean on three sides. Based on information personally transmitted by Peter to Guillaume Delisle in Paris in 1717, the latter revised his own map to show a cape with islands beyond it in the sea. Similarly, in 1722 the cartographer Johann Baptist Homann prepared a map at Peter's request that incorporated the results of the Luzhin-Yevreynov expedition and other official information the government supplied.

On November 5, 1724, Peter the Great waded waist-deep into the icy waters of the Gulf of Finland to help rescue some sailors whose boat had capsized. Fever and chills followed, later developing into pneumonia; his friends and advisers gathered round. Yet even as he lay dying, he made one last grand gesture, which—in keeping with a monarch who seemed incapable of any inconsequential act—would lead to discoveries of imperishable renown. Andrey Nartov, an associate, recalled:

> I was then almost constantly with the Emperor, and saw with my own eyes how eager this Majesty was to get the expedition under way, being, as it were, conscious that his end was near. When all had been arranged he seemed pleased and content. Calling the general-admiral (Count Apraksin) to him he said: "Recently I have been thinking over a matter which has been on my mind for many years, but other affairs have prevented me from carrying it out. I have reference to the finding of a passage through the Arctic Sea. On the map before me there is indicated such a passage bearing the name of Anian. There must be some reason for that. In my last travels I discussed the subject with learned men, and they were of the opinion that such a passage could be found. Now that the country is in no danger from enemies we should strive to win for her glory along the lines of the arts and sciences."

On December 23, as the expedition assumed final shape in his mind, Peter drew up brief instructions to the Admiralty College for the selection of its chief personnel. He wanted geodesists with first-hand knowledge of Eastern Siberia, hardy shipwrights, experienced mariners, and, if possible, "a navigator and assistant navigator who have been to North America. If such navigators cannot be found in the [Russian] Navy, then immediately write to Holland via the Admiralty Post and request two men who are familiar with the sea north toward Japan."

The Admiralty opted for their own and immediately settled on Vitus Bering, a Dane in Russian service, as the expedition's commander. They assigned him two lieutenants: Martin Spanberg (also a Dane, who ran the packet boat that shuttled regularly between Lübeck and Kronstadt), and Aleksey Chirikov, an instructor of cadets at the Naval Academy. None of these men had ever been to America, but Bering had been to the East Indies in his youth, and all three were exceptionally capable and expert seamen.

Bering hastened to the capital from Vyborg, where he had a small estate, and on January 26, 1725, Peter signed his orders and scrawled terse instructions to various officials to give Bering and his staff whatever help they required. The tsar's instructions to Bering himself, however, though no less imperious and brief (according to his style), were cryptically phrased:

1. In Kamchatka or some other place build one or two boats with decks.

2. On those boats sail near the land which goes to the north which (since no one knows where it ends) it seems is part of America.

3. Discover where it is joined to America, and go as far as some town belonging to a European power; if you encounter some European ship, ascertain from it what is the name of the nearest coast, and write it down and go ashore personally and obtain firsthand information, locate it on a map and return here.

Two days later, Peter died. In his place, the empress Catherine I, his widow and successor, confirmed the orders and had them conveyed to Bering on February 5, 1725, inaugurating one of the most remarkable sagas in the history of exploration.

Born at Horsens, Denmark, in 1681, Vitus Jonassen Bering had joined the Russian Navy as a sublieutenant at the age of twenty-three, and had served in the Black Sea, the Sea of Azov, and the Baltic with distinction during the Great Northern War. His direction of transport and logistical operations earned him steady advancement, and by the end of the conflict he had made captain of the second rank. Under the patronage of two fellow Danes with considerable standing in the Admiralty, Peter Sievers and Cornelius Cruys (both primary architects of Peter's new navy), Bering's future prospects seemed bright. But at the conclusion of the war he was unexpectedly passed over for promotion, a casualty of the developing struggle in the naval high command between a faction led by Sievers and another (momentarily favored by the tsar) headed by Thomas Gordon, a Scot. Gordon's star subsequently waned, and that of Sievers rose, with the support of Admiral Apraksin. But meanwhile, in disappointment, Bering had retired from the navy and withdrawn to his Vyborg estate.

Eight weeks later he was recalled to active duty, elevated to captain of the first rank, and given the assignment that was to govern the remainder of his days. At the time, he was forty-four years old.

Bering departed St. Petersburg upon receipt of his instructions and hastened to catch up to an advance contingent of the expedition which had left the capital twelve days before. From Vologda, they proceeded together across the Urals to Tobolsk, before embarking down the Irtysh River in May 1725. After pausing at Yeniseysk, where the party grew to ninety-seven with the addition of thirty carpenters and black-smiths, they worked their way up the shoals and rapids of the Yenisey and Upper Tunguska rivers to Ilimsk. There the party divided, Spanberg going overland with the heavier supplies to Ust-Kut, where he supervised construction that winter of fifteen barges for conveying men and supplies down the Lena River to Yakutsk; and Bering heading south to Irkutsk, to assemble provisions for the next stage of the expedition and to plot the best route from there to Okhotsk.

Thus far, over the course of a year, and in spite of transport difficulties and little or no cooperation from Siberian officials, Bering had managed to move his men and equipment across 4,500 miles of mountain, forest, and steppe. But a still more trying road lay ahead. In the spring of 1726, more carpenters, blacksmiths, and two coopers were added to the force, and the whole party (reunited at Ust-Kut) embarked down the Lena River to Yakutsk. They made good time with sails and sweeps, and when the wind blew against them used an ingenious device called the watersail, made of larch logs lashed together and sunk lengthwise under the boats where the current acted upon it like the wind upon a sail. At Yakutsk, it was agreed that Chirikov remain for the winter to collect additional provisions, while Spanberg conveyed the heaviest and most unmanageable materiel (like rigging, tackle, iron, and tar) by boat to Yudoma Cross (at the headwaters of the Yudoma River). Bering himself, with two thousand leather sacks of flour, among other supplies, was to proceed on horseback directly to Okhotsk at the head of a baggage train.

The Yakutsk-to-Okhotsk Track—a deadly obstacle course of forests, rapids, marshes, icefields, bogs, and crags—was the roughest in Siberia, and after a forced march in which most of his packhorses died and tons of flour had to be cached along the way, Bering barely reached his destination before winter set in. Meanwhile, in early November Spanberg's boats became ice-bound near the mouth of the Gorbeya River, short of Yudoma Cross and 350 miles from Okhotsk. The men disembarked, built dogsleds to carry the most vital stores (which they had to haul themselves), and to fend off starvation "consumed not only their horses, but their leather harness, clothing and boots." From the raw horsehide itself they made new coats and shoes, having first "burnt off the Hair from their Skins with Lime." Even so, they survived only because they found the flour Bering had cached, and because, when

Bering learned of their predicament, he immediately dispatched dog teams for their relief. Meanwhile, to make better time, Spanberg had stored his own supplies in four different locations along the uninhabited trail. "And during his whole Passage," Bering later recalled, "the poor People had no other Relief in the Night-time, or when the cutting icy Winds blew, than to cover themselves as deep as they could in the Snow." The following spring the stashed provisions were retrieved, but there was no way to salvage the materiel which had been left on the boats, despite all the effort it had taken to bring them 5,000 miles from St. Petersburg.

And there was no way to make up for them either in Okhotsk, which was a refuge only in name. Located on "a current-ridden, empty waste of water," the settlement consisted of eleven huts housing ten Russian families, a meager stock of powdered fish, and no home-grown foods, for not even rye, it was said, could ripen on its damp and windy shores. The men managed to build their own shelters, but construction of a proper ship was difficult because no stout trees like oak or elm grew in the vicinity, and the whole remote area "lacked all marine and other stores." As a result, the decked boat they built for themselves (the *Fortuna*) was tied or "sewn" together with leather strips instead of being hammered together with nails. Such makeshift craft were common enough in Siberia because of the scarcity of technical supplies, but it was not the kind of vessel the naval officers were used to, or in which they had intended to cross the Okhotsk Sea. Nevertheless, in two trips with full cargos in the hold, the *Fortuna* served to convey them in July 1727 safely across to Bolsheretsk, the "capital" of Kamchatka. Located on the north side of the Bolshaya River, Bolsheretsk itself was still scarcely more than a stockade, garrisoned with about forty-five troops. Outside the fort there was a chapel dedicated to St. Nicholas, a lodging belonging to the church, and about thirty houses on the various islands of the delta, among them a saloon and a distillery. The settlement was no place for a dockyard, so with the help of natives impressed into transport duty with their sleds and dogs, the expeditionary force crossed the rugged mountains to Nizhnekamchatsk, 600 miles away, on the eastern coast. Furious blizzards beleaguered the operation and clouds of sleet "rolled like a dark smoke over the moors." At night, "or when-ever they had a Mind to rest," they slept in deep trenches without cover which they dug in the snow.

At Nizhnekamchatsk, Bering paid off the surviving Kamchadals with a little tobacco and train oil extracted from a whale that had washed up on the beach.

After years of unrest, a period of calm had ensued on the peninsula. Government agents, furnished with comprehensive written instructions, annually came and went; priests arrived to provide spiritual guidance for the unruly Cossacks and to convert the heathen; attempts were made to regularize *yasak* collection; and a census was taken of the native population and their property. But resentment toward the Russians smoldered underneath, and order would not be completely established until the 1730s, after many of the Kamchadals and Koryaks had been decimated by epidemics and new insurrections crushed.

In 1726, Bering's overwhelming impression of Kamchatka was of a "strange place, which lies so far out of the Reach of the rest of Mankind, that it could never have been visited, much less planted and possessed by any but the Russians." He realized its potential strategic importance, but conceded it had little to attract colonists, and in a rather backhanded compliment supposed that "if a sufficient Number of People were sent thither to cut down the vast Forests with which it is incumber'd, and enabled to till, manure, and cultivate the Earth, it might be render'd a Place far enough from being despicable." At the time, the Russian presence was still pitifully small. There were only seventeen dwellings in Verkhnekamchatsk, and fifty in Nizhnekamchatsk, the two main settlements after Bolsheretsk. During the whole time Bering was there, no more than 150 servitors lived in all three forts, and their primary function was not to colonize but to collect the fur tribute from the Kamchadals. Native and Russian alike lived on fish, roots, berries, and wild birds, and the only agricultural initiative Bering could discover was at a local hermitage, where monastics had managed to coax turnips, barley, radishes, and hemp from the soil. In the spring, after working all winter on a new seaworthy vessel for the voyage, his vitamin-starved workmen frantically scrounged for wild garlic beneath the melting snow.

To provision the expedition and meet its other needs, Bering had to improvise. Hauling lumber for the ship on dogsled, he made a tar substitute from the sap of the local larch, and "instead of Meal or Corn, he furnished himself with Carrots or other Roots. By boiling the Seawater, he procured as much Salt as he wanted. Fish Oyle served instead of Butter, and dry and wet Salt-fish took the Place of Beef and Pork. Having collected a vast Quantity of Plants and Herbs, he also distilled from them a pretty strong Spirit, upon which he was pleased to bestow the Name of Brandy, and of this he laid in a plentiful Stock."

On July 14, 1728—three and a half years after leaving St. Petersburg —Bering's newly constructed ship, the *St. Gabriel,* stocked with enough food to sustain its crew of forty for a year, sailed from the mouth of the Kamchatka River. Following the coast of the peninsula northward for five days, Bering turned northeast, and on the next day encountered land again just above 60 degrees north latitude. This was the underside of the Chukchi Peninsula (not clearly delineated on his map), and with some perplexity he coasted along it for about two weeks. On August 1, he lingered to explore a bay, but a week later encountered eight Chukchi, who approached the ship in a hideskin boat. "When we invited them to come aboard," recalled Bering, "they inflated the bladder of a large seal, put one man in it and sent him out to us to converse." Later, the Chukchi brought their own boat along- side and through the two interpreters Bering had brought with him learned that the land, trending in a northeasterly direction, soon turned back to the west, and that there was an island nearby in the sea. On August 10, Bering sailed past it, noticing dwellings but no people, and named it St. Lawrence, "since it was his feast day."

By August 13 the ship had rounded the southwesternmost point of the Chukchi Peninsula. A few days later, without realizing it, Bering passed through the narrow strait between Asia and America which now bears his name. Although in clear weather (at the strait's narrowest point) it is possible to glimpse both continents at the same time, on that historic day fog hid the American coast, and as far as Bering knew, it was 1,000 miles away. Without pause he steered due north (into the Bering Sea), but after the Asiatic coast disappeared from sight on the 15th, he decided to consult with Spanberg and Chirikov as to whether to continue the voyage or return to Kamchatka before cold weather set in. It was Spanberg's advice that the expedition sail on for no more than two days, "because we have reached 65 degrees 30' of the north- ern region and according to our opinion and the Chukchi's report have arrived opposite the extreme end and have passed east of the land." And so, "what more needs to be done?" Chirikov, on the other hand, argued that they could not know with certainty whether America was separated from Asia unless they went "to the mouth of the Kolyma River," or at least until their path westward around the peninsula was blocked by ice. So they ought to follow the land, if possible (and as their instructions required), to see if it led to America.

Bering agreed with Spanberg. The Chukchi had told him the coast turned north, then west, and was surrounded by the ocean—and in fact, as Bering could see, the coast bent away to the west as he proceeded farther north. It seemed pointless to him to verify the obvious, at mortal risk to his ship and crew. Further delay might oblige him to winter among the Chukchi on the peninsula's forbidding coast, which, so far as he could tell, consisted of nothing but great ridges of snow-covered rocks quite bare of trees with which to build winter huts.

Bering turned south. Once again the coast of Asia came into view, but by an unlucky chance, as he threaded the strait, Bering failed a second time to see America through the mist, though he discovered one of the Diomede Islands. Four days later the crew bartered rather profitably with forty Chukchi who came out to the ship in boats—the Russians trading pins and needles for "a good Quantity of dry'd Flesh, Fish, Water contain'd in Whale Bladders, 15 Fox Skins, and four Narval's Teeth." Without further incident, on September 2, the *St. Gabriel* returned safely to port.

Despite apparent confidence in having accomplished his mission, Bering had misgivings, and throughout the winter he consulted with a number of Cossack veterans and others knowledgeable about the local geography. Advised by several that land was supposed to lie not far off the coast—as evidenced by birds flying eastward and unfamiliar trees floating in the sea—toward the end of June 1729 he steered the *St. Gabriel* due east from the mouth of the Kamchatka River, and explored the seas for a radius of about 130 miles. He might have ventured farther, but storms cut short his quest. That done, from Nizhnekamchatsk he sailed around Cape Lopatka at the peninsula's southern tip —"which Thing was never done before"—crossed over to Okhotsk, and began the long overland trek back to St. Petersburg, where he arrived on March 1, 1730.

While Bering and his men had been in Kamchatka, a companion expedition of sorts, with tasks resembling those given originally to the

Great Kamchatka Command, had been authorized by the Senate and the newly created Supreme Privy Council. Led by Afanasy Shestakov, a Cossack leader based in Yakutsk, it involved an army of fifteen hundred men (huge by Siberian standards) in a bid to strengthen Russian control over the entire northeast. Part of the force was placed under the command of Dmitry Pavlutsky, captain of dragoons in Tobolsk and Russia's foremost Chukchi fighter, but the results of the expedition were not commensurate with the efforts made. Quarreling between Shestakov and Pavlutsky hindered the operation, and Shestakov's attempts to pacify the Koryaks ended in disaster when he was killed in a battle in March 1730, and a contingent coming to his support was wiped out. Shestakov's dried head was preserved long afterward by the natives as a trophy of their victory.

Encouraged by these developments, some Kamchadal leaders also began to consider ways to drive the Russians from their land. Bering, it seems, had left Kamchatka just in time. Although the area had never been free of lawlessness and misrule, the transport burdens placed upon the native population by his expedition had certainly contributed to the unrest. In 1731, rebellions occurred in the vicinity of Bolsheretsk and Verknekamchatsk; and then, around Nizhnekamchatsk, the Kamchadals coalesced under a baptized native named Fyodor Kharchin and captured the fort. A few survivors managed to make their way to a Russian ship about to sail for the Anadyr, and the crew hastily disembarked and dragged their cannon to the fortress walls. When the Russians began blasting through, the defenders panicked, and Kharchin himself made his escape disguised as a girl. Others, however, fought on, until a shot ignited the powder magazine and the entire fort blew up. Enraged by the rape of their women (mostly native concubines), the Cossacks killed their prisoners to a man. A month later Kharchin himself was seized, but some of his accomplices and their families chose mass suicide rather than fall into Russian hands.

In St. Petersburg, the authorities decided that Kamchatka was too remote from Yakutsk to remain under its effective jurisdiction, and transferred responsibility for the peninsula to Okhotsk. An official was also dispatched from Tobolsk to restore order; after investigating the causes of the revolt, he executed and otherwise punished with impartial justice a number of Russians as well as Kamchadals.

Meanwhile, after Shestakov's death, Pavlutsky had taken over the

expedition's command and had made Anadyrsk his base for a conquest
of the Chukchi. Although the Russians defeated these indomitable warriors in several battles, they could not subdue them, and the most
tangible (yet elusive) result of the expedition turned out to be geographical—the search for the "Big Land" supposed to lie opposite the
East Cape of the Chukchi Peninsula. Pavlutsky organized an expedition
to find it, and placed the expedition under the direction of Mikhail
Gvozdev, a metallurgist, with Ivan Fedorov as pilot. They appropriated
Bering's *St. Gabriel* for the purpose and assembled a crew of thirty-
nine. Sailing from the mouth of the Anadyr in July 1732, they paused
briefly at one of the Diomede Islands, and then continued eastward,
apparently coming within sight of Cape Prince of Wales, Alaska. Drawing near, they saw that it was quite large and covered with forests of
poplar, spruce, and larch. After skirting the coast for several days, they
found "no end to it in sight." At one point, "a naked native paddled
out to the vessel from shore on an inflated bladder," and through their
interpreter asked them who they were and where they were going.
They replied that they were lost at sea and were looking for Kamchatka.
The native promptly pointed in the direction from which they had
come. They did not make a landing, however, and because after their
return they failed to collate their notes and make an adequate map,
their voyage did not come to official attention until a decade later, in
1743. By then the priority of their discovery had become a technicality,
since far more momentous events had transpired.

Upon his return to St. Petersburg in March 1730, Bering had reported
to the Admiralty. From that moment on, criticism of his voyage began.
Until quite recently, the consensus of posterity was that he had failed,
out of excessive caution bordering on cowardice, to fully carry out his
instructions. He had found the strait he was supposed to find, but had
not absolutely proved that Asia and America were not joined by land
—as he might have had he followed Chirikov's advice. The passions
expressed on this point for many years reflected the intense interest of
statesmen, merchants, and academicians in a Northeast Passage; but a
reexamination of the fundamental documents suggests that a very different conclusion should be drawn. As a leading scholar points out,
the orders Peter the Great drafted "say nothing about a strait or a

search for one," but rather in their own somewhat cryptic but definite fashion demand that Bering follow "the land that goes to the north," which "it seems is part of America." If it led to America, he was to proceed if possible to a European settlement, and also reconnoiter the coast. What land was Peter talking about? To fully understand his orders requires a map—the one, that is, that Bering was given on February 5, 1724.

In all probability, this was the so-called "Homann map," created around 1722 at Peter's request by Johann Baptiste Homann, a German mapmaker and copyist in his employ. It included the first printed presentation of Kamchatka as a peninsula, and two unknown lands (cut off by the frame) off the North Pacific coast of Asia. One was apparently meant to represent the "Big Island" in the sea of which the Chukchi spoke, the other "Juan de Gama Land," sometimes portrayed as being linked to America. So, depending on how Peter's orders were interpreted, "the land which goes to the north" could be the land off Kamchatka (Da Gama Land), the finger of land north of that off the Chukchi Peninsula, or the coast of Asia itself. Actually, no one knows for sure, but Bering seems to have tested all three hypotheses. He sailed north along the Kamchatka coast, then northeast in search of the Big Island (only to run into the Chukchi Peninsula, not known to project as far out into the ocean as it did), and then, the following summer, subsequently sailed east of Kamchatka where the other land was supposed to be.

In fact, the location of a strait (which Peter was already sure existed) was subordinate to his larger mission, which was to find the way to the western coast of America. Bering didn't go to America because the coast he followed to the north didn't lead there; and if he failed, it was because the cartographical information he'd been given was imprecise. Bering had followed the Homann map as best he could, but found it completely erroneous in placing the Chukchi Peninsula directly north of eastern Kamchatka, instead of projecting far to its east. In trying to make his experience fit with the map he had, which was supposed to guide him, Bering correctly assumed that he had passed the utmost part of East Asia and that the two continents were not joined.

"Having become a naval power," as one authority notes, "Russia need no longer look on the ocean as a barrier to continued eastward expansion. Other powers had to sail halfway around the globe to reach the North Pacific. The Russians were already there." Peter's secret long-range intention was colonial conquest—to reconnoiter the American coast with a view to gaining a foothold (as the French, Spanish, and English had already done) in the New World. The supposed geographical objective, as publicized to foreign ambassadors, cartographers, and others (like Andrey Nartov, who dutifully spread the word), was part of what today would be called a disinformation campaign, designed to mislead other governments by appearing to pursue the question with which they were preoccupied. "There is no doubt," remarks a student of Bering's voyage, "that Peter looked upon the annexation of the unknown lands of the northwest coast of North America as a continuation of the colonization of Siberia." Nevertheless, he had to proceed covertly, so as not to prompt other powers to block his designs.

Bering had explored and mapped the coasts of both Kamchatka and the Chukchi Peninsula, and he had confirmed the existence of a strait. Although criticized by some for not having rounded the Chukchi Peninsula westward to the Kolyma River (to prove a Northeast Passage did exist), and by others for not having been more venturesome in attempting to discover how far America actually was from Siberia's coast, posterity's grumblings have little to do with the Admiralty's own estimate of Bering's accomplishment, for he was promoted to the rank of captain-commander (the third highest rank in the Russian Navy) and given a 1,000-ruble reward.

A new map of the Siberian northeast prepared by his staff also more accurately depicted that corner of Asia as a large double-headed peninsula, shaped like a "bull's horn." As for the land he had conjectured slightly to the east of Kamchatka, and which he had sought in vain in the summer of 1729—it was, in fact, there. But it was not the "Juan de Gama Land" of the speculative maps, nor the America of which he dreamed. It was a lonely, uninhabited little island. And it would be the land where he would die.

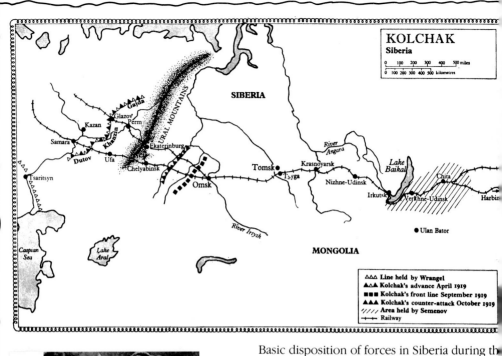

KOLCHAK
Siberia

0 100 200 300 400 500 miles
0 100 200 300 400 500 kilometres

SIBERIA

Galda
Glazov
Perm
URAL MOUNTAINS
Kazan
Khazin
Samara
Dutov Ufa Ekaterinburg
Chelyabinsk
Tsaritsyn
Omsk

River Angara
Tomsk
Tsyga
Krasnoyarsk
Nizhne-Udinsk
Irkutsk
Lake Baikal
Chita
Verkhne-Udinsk
Harbin

River Irtysh

● Ulan Bator

Caspian Sea
Lake Aral

MONGOLIA

△△△ Line held by Wrangel
▲▲△ Kolchak's advance April 1919
■■■ Kolchak's front line September 1919
▲▲▲ Kolchak's counter-attack October 1919
//// Area held by Semenov
—+— Railway

Basic disposition of forces in Siberia during th[e]
Civil War.

Siberian shaman.

Main Street in Norilsk.

Theodore Roosevelt and the plenipotentiaries from both sides at Portsmouth, New Hampshire. Roosevelt mediated; Witte, at left, skillfully negotiated for the Russian side.

Admiral Aleksandr Kolchak, leader of the "Whites" in the Russian Civil War of 1918–20.

Grigory Semyenov, terrorist ruler of the Transbaikal during the Russian Civil War and puppet of the Japanese.

Sergey Witte, Minister of Finance under the last tsar and chief mastermind of the Trans-Siberian Railway.

A cartoon anticipating an easy Russian victory over the Japanese in the Russo-Japanese War of 1904–5.

...oyeds.

Buryat woman, from the Transbaikal.

...yat man, from the Transbaikal.

Vogul man.

Engraving depicting an attempted escape.

Convict shackled to a wheelbarrow.

Prison official with a *plet,* a three-tailed rawhide lash.

Convict with branded cheek and brow. The "K" stands for *katorzhnik*—"forced labor convict."

Sergey Volkonsky, a leading
Decembrist exiled to Siberia.

His wife, Maria, the "Princess of
Siberia."

Convicts at Aleksandrovsky-Post Prison.

Nikolay Muravyev-Amursky, the governor of Eastern Siberia who wrested the Amur region from China and successfully defended Russia's Far Eastern frontiers during the Crimean War.

Tobolsk homestead scene.

Aleksandr Baranov, the first governor of Russian America.

Nikolay Rezanov, the visionary architect of Russian expansion in the New World.

Kamehameha, King of the Hawaiian Islands.

Vitus Bering.

Grigory Shelikhov, the "Russian Columbus."

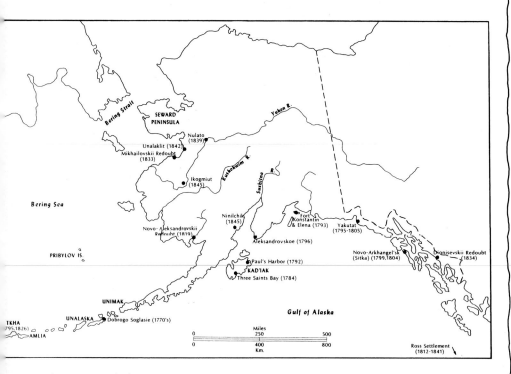

ssian settlements in Alaska.

Interior of a Kamchadal yurt (eighteenth-century lithograph).

Kamchatka volcano (eighteenth-century lithograph).

Aleuts in kayaks with hunting spears.

A winter hut near Okhotsk (eighteenth-century lithograph).

TRIBES OF NORTHERN ASIA.

130

J. HART, NUTLEY

Church of the Old Believers.

Overnight stop in the woods in Eastern Siberia (eighteenth-century lithograph).

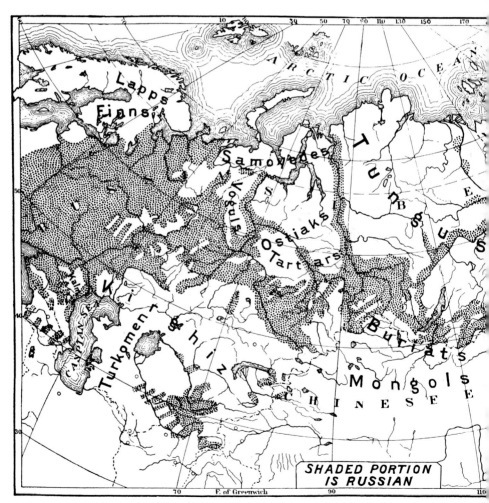

SHADED PORTION IS RUSSIAN

Distribution of the major tribes of northern Asia and principal areas of Russian settlement.

Typical town fortification.

Scenes depicting the early conquest of Sibir, as illustrated in seventeenth-century Siberian chronicles.

Tyumen, the first Russian fortress town in Siberia.

Yermak's band crossing between two rivers.

A Tartar ambush along the Tobol River (note the banner of Christ advancing of its own accord downstream).

Fighting near the Tartar capital of Sibir.

Yermak, Conqueror of Sibir.

10

THE GREAT NORTHERN
EXPEDITION

THE "covert operation" of Bering's First Kamchatka Expedition proved but the prelude to a second of far more ambitious design. Two months after his return to the capital, Bering drafted proposals for increasing Russian settlement in the Far East, and for expanded exploration and discovery in the Arctic and North Pacific. These were presented to the Admiralty and substantially adopted by the Senate, with considerable elaboration over the course of the next two years.

The First Expedition had revealed how tenuous Russian occupation of the region still was, with unmanageably long supply lines, and virtually no development of the natural resources there contributing to the maintenance of life. Bering recommended a number of improvements in all of these areas, including the introduction of agriculture and livestock (horned cattle and pigs), the development of iron-ore deposits near the Angara River and Yakutsk, saltworks near Okhotsk, factories to convert pine pitch to tar from the forests along the Yudoma and Uda rivers, the transformation of Okhotsk into a port, with a school for navigation, and other steps that would bring a measure of self-sufficiency to the Russian Far East. In addition, he saw the need for more evangelical missionary work among the natives, and for removing the local administration from the jurisdiction of Yakutsk. Such efforts seemed minimally necessary to him if the empire hoped to take full possession of the region and develop it as a foundation for an overseas Pacific trade.

This was one set of proposals. In a second (which he disingenuously called "A most humble plan"), he urged that voyages be undertaken to open that trade up—one along the Kurile Islands to explore the sea route to Japan, and another to find the way to America which he had been unable to do in his first attempt.

Despite this failure, Bering was convinced that "America or other lands" were not far off the eastern coast, for he had observed off Kamchatka "low waves which are customary in narrow seas," pine and other trees not native to the peninsula ripped out by the roots and floating in the ocean, birds flying east, and other telltale signs. The proximity of land had also been affirmed indirectly by yet another field report from one of Pavlutsky's Cossacks, who had apparently encountered two Eskimos.

Ancillary to the Pacific voyages, and with a view to establishing once and for all whether a Northeast Passage did exist, Bering further proposed a nautical survey of the Siberian Arctic coast west of the Lena River, since he thought he already knew that beyond the Lena there was a sealane (however choked with ice) that extended all the way around the Chukchi Peninsula.

On the strength of Bering's recommendations and reports, a Second Kamchatka Expedition was planned, and gradually became a huge collaborative effort involving members of the Admiralty College, the Administrative Senate, and the Imperial Academy of Sciences, recently established in St. Petersburg. Perhaps the leading figure in developing its program was Ivan Kirilov, a protégé of Peter the Great and the Senate's senior secretary, who had long been an ardent student of geography and maps, and was the organizing force behind the preparation and publication of the first Russian atlas in 1734. But the fantastic elaboration Bering's proposals subsequently underwent also owed something to the atmosphere then prevailing around the throne. During his five years absence from the capital, the empress Catherine I had been succeeded by Peter II, grandson of Peter the Great, whose brief reign as a minor ended with the enthronement of the empress Anna in January 1730. After a period of anti-Western reaction, the reformers, with Anna, returned to power. To quote Bering's biographer:

They sought to continue Peter's work . . . and Anna aimed to shine in Europe as the ruler of a great power and in Russia as a West European queen. Europe was to be awed by Russian grandeur and Russia by European erudition. She and her associates had an insatiable desire for the lustre and outward splendor of culture. One of the surest roads to this glory was through the organization of scientific expeditions. They had at their disposal an academy of sciences, a navy and the resources of an enormous empire. They saw to it that their enterprises were as big, as sensational, as amazing as possible.

And none more amazing than the Second Kamchatka Expedition became, "the like of which there never was before." To begin with, it expanded the Ob to Lena survey to cover the complete coast of the Russian Arctic, as divided into five sections—from Archangel to the Ob, the Ob to the Yenisey, the Yenisey to the Taimyr Peninsula, the Taimyr Peninsula to the Lena, and the Lena to the Anadyr—with a simultaneous advance to be made on all fronts. In preparation, provisions were to be stockpiled at strategic locations along the coast, lighthouses built at the mouths of the principal rivers, reindeer corraled for food and transport needs, and small fishing stations set up in inlets and bays. Beyond that, astronomical positions were to be established throughout Siberia; two vessels (not one) were to be built and equipped on the Pacific Coast to search for America, and three others to explore the Kurile Islands and the route to Japan. The Pacific Coast from Okhotsk south to the mouth of the Amur River and the Shantar Islands was also to be charted, as well as all the rivers in Siberia that flowed into Lake Baikal from the east, in order to find a shorter route to the coast. Whatever islands lay east or southeast of Kamchatka were also to be located and claimed (for "the collection of tribute looking to the profit and benefit of the state"), and all explored areas were to be carefully surveyed for precious ores.

Mindful of the tribulations of the First Expedition, special officers were to be sent ahead to Yakutsk at once "to build boats to expedite the transportation of materials," and Okhotsk was to be prepared for the arrival of the naval personnel. The Academy of Sciences was then brought into the planning, and proposed what amounted to a complete physical, anthropological, linguistic, and historical account of Siberia.

As the Academy of Sciences contingent of the expedition took shape, it came under the joint direction of Gerhard Friedrich Müller and Johann Georg Gmelin, two ambitious young German scholars who had been attracted to the Academy by the unusual opportunities it offered for quick advancement. Born in Westphalia in 1705, Müller had studied literature and history at the University of Leipzig. He emigrated to St. Petersburg in 1725, and was hired to teach history and Latin in the Academy's gymnasium. Two years later, in 1727, he was appointed adjunct (assistant) in history at the Academy itself, and in 1730 promoted to professor. In addition to teaching, he performed administrative and library duties, and edited and contributed to the Academy's publications. In 1730, he traveled to Germany, Holland, and England on the Academy's behalf, and while in London was elected a member of the Royal Society. But upon his return he found himself at odds with the Academy's director, and eager to get away, assumed charge of the expedition's historical and ethnographical work. Among other things, he was to examine all the extant archives in Siberia, and describe all the tribes.

Müller proved a scholar of great ability, but Gmelin was his equal. Born in Württemberg in 1709 and a kind of child prodigy, he had matriculated at the University of Tübingen at age thirteen, where he excelled in medicine and natural history. Upon his graduation, he crossed the Baltic to St. Petersburg, where he was promptly appointed adjunct in natural history at the Academy. Over the next few years, he catalogued the Academy's mineral collection, prepared several scientific papers, and published some articles in the popular press. In 1731, at the age of twenty-two, he was made professor of chemistry and natural history. A year later, he volunteered for the position of naturalist with the expedition, then apparently got cold feet and abruptly withdrew, claiming a "chronic liver complaint." However, he soon recovered remarkably after drinking two bottles of Rhine wine.

Accompanying Müller and Gmelin, but without leadership responsibilities, was the expedition's astronomer, Louis Delisle de la Croyère, the half-brother of two celebrated French scientists, Guillaume and Joseph Nicolas Delisle. A bit of a misfit, Louis had originally studied theology, but by inclination proved somewhat dissolute. After "seventeen wild years" in Canada, his family persuaded him to adopt his mother's maiden name so as not to sully their lofty reputation. But when Joseph accepted the post of professor of astronomy at the Academy in St. Petersburg in 1727, Louis (always adventurous) had tagged along. Joseph drew up some of the expedition's all-important maps, and used his influence to get Louis involved in the project, although he was not qualified for the work he was called upon to do. Louis's primary task was to determine the latitude and longitude of important points in Siberia, and, taking part in the American voyage (sailing with Chirikov), to do the same on the American coast. Two geodesists from the St. Petersburg Observatory, Semyon Popov and Andrey Krasilnikov, were assigned to help him; and an interpreter and a mechanic to repair his instruments were also attached to his retinue.

As finally spelled out in sixteen Articles, the Second Kamchatka Expedition (or Great Northern Expedition, as it came to be called) "in all its undertakings, was the largest expedition of its kind ever undertaken by any European government for the purpose of scientific and geographical research up to that time." But its aim was not only great and immortal glory through scientific achievement, but (in Kirilov's words) "expansion of the empire and for inexhaustible wealth." This was to be done by establishing Russian sovereignty in the North Pacific as far south as Japan, and on the American northwest coast—about the only part of the New World not yet claimed by other powers. The Spanish were ensconced in Mexico and southern California, the French had pushed to the headwaters of the Mississippi and the Great Lakes, and the English were building settlements along the Atlantic seaboard and had begun to compete for Canada with the French. As one Russian official remarked: "It is known what profit [these powers] receive and how important the commerce and navigation to these regions are to these kingdoms," so that "in the exploration of America there may also be such gains for the [Russian] state."

To conceal its true ambitions from the outside world, the expedition was cast as a second attempt to determine whether Asia and America were joined—the first attempt having failed. Its officers received special instructions "for public display" to that effect, and were sworn to secrecy, to which they pledged their lives. Moreover, no information pertaining to or deriving from the expedition was to be revealed "either secretly or openly, anywhere, orally or in writing," without clearance from the Crown.

Although the expedition involved three thousand men, including laborers and guards, and for logistical and administrative purposes was divided into several distinct undertakings, with Bering as its supreme head. That meant that he had to accommodate, transport, and supply over a period of several years a small army of sailors, soldiers, laborers, and academic personnel in the Siberian wilderness, and guide them all toward their myriad goals.

Associated with Bering were his two lieutenants from the First Expedition, Aleksey Chirikov and Martin Spanberg, who had both been promoted to captains of the third rank. Chirikov was to command one of the two ships to America, and to take charge (initially at least) of transporting all the necessary men and supplies to Okhotsk. Spanberg was to supervise construction of the ships for the Pacific branch of the expedition, and to command the voyage to the Kurile Islands and Japan. Neither were particularly popular officers—Spanberg was an overbearing, heavy-fisted man, and Chirikov something of a stickler, who always went by the book—but Bering (in the acknowledgment of one with whom he sometimes quarreled) was "a man of good manners, kind, quiet and universally liked by the whole command both high and low." Under almost anyone else, the whole undertaking would probably have gone to pieces, since his patience and circumspection helped overcome the innumerable obstacles he faced. Indeed, exceeding the challenge of the First Expedition, "the Accounts that he received, were such as gave him to understand that a more difficult Task could scarce be imposed on any Man, than that which had been lain upon his Shoulders." Vice-Admiral Count Nikolay Golovin—soon to be made admiral and president of the Admiralty College—was not unmindful of the problems involved and suggested sending heavy equipment, ammunition, and other material to the Pacific by sea from Kronstadt halfway around the world via Cape Horn. He estimated that it would otherwise take Bering at least two years to convey all of his supplies across northern Asia, two more to construct oceangoing craft, and two more to complete his voyage and return to St. Petersburg. Ships from Kronstadt, on the other hand, could reach Okhotsk or Kamchatka in under a year, saving time and expense. And when they got there, they could proceed independently in search of new harbors, bays, and lands, defend the empire's interests from foreign interference, and give "unruly native peoples there an impression of Russian might." Golovin's memorandum was rejected, but the Admiralty promised advance work to ease the logistical strains, and the Senate recommended double pay, with a year's pay in advance for all officers, "so that they may get their outfits and depart in a contented frame of mind."

Peter the Great's original orders to Bering for the First Expedition were incorporated into those for the Second, although instead of telling him to sail "to a town under European control" (which might unmask the expedition's secret objectives), he was to winter in America north of where any Europeans were thought to be.

By December 31, 1732, all the plans had been completed and approved, and the project was launched.

On February 1, 1733, the first naval detachment left St. Petersburg under Spanberg, who was to go directly to Okhotsk. Bering followed on March 18 and went to Tobolsk, where the rest of the expedition with its stores began to arrive. The Academy contingent, six hundred strong, did not get going until August, and did not reach Tobolsk until January 1734, where Bering was impatiently awaiting their arrival, since they had to supply him with surveyors and instruments for the Arctic coast expedition that was to sail down the Ob.

The Academy contingent, in keeping with its professorial dignity, was "right luxuriously equipped." The staff included secretaries and research assistants, draftsmen, illustrators, an animal painter, an interpreter, "whose acquaintance with all the languages of antiquity was supposed to equip him to converse with the natives of America," a surgeon, cooks, servants, an instrument maker, five topographers, a drummer, and a military escort of fourteen musketeers. In their train was a library of several hundred volumes, "not only of scientific and historical works in their specialties, but also of the Latin classics and such light reading as *Robinson Crusoe* and *Gulliver's Travels,*" large stocks of writing paper, drafting materials, artists' colors, inks, and so on. The supplies of de la Croyère alone included ten cartloads of instruments, assorted telescopes up to 16 feet long, five theodolites or astrolabes, twenty thermometers, twenty-seven barometers, "as well as bulky copper spheres, chains, magnets and clocks." Each professor was allowed ten horses and the other members of the expedition six.

In addition to familiar European foods, the Academics had also packed away kegs of their favorite continental wines. Wherever they went, they had authorization to examine any archive collection, to requisition interpreters and guides, and to purchase necessary items at the Academy's expense. Even though, within the program of the expedition, they enjoyed a more or less independent status, it was Bering's responsibility "to move this cumbersome machine, this learned republic, from St. Petersburg to Kamchatka, to care for their comforts and conveniences, and render possible the flank movements and side sallies that either scientific demands or their own freaks of will might dictate." In fact, this task eventually became too much for him, and he left them to look after themselves.

By May 1734 a ship had been built at Tobolsk to survey the Arctic coast from the mouth of the Ob eastward to the Yenisey (under Lieutenant Dmitry Ovtsvyn), enabling Bering to continue with part of his command to Yakutsk. He arrived in October, followed by Chirikov and most of the equipment the following spring. But at Yakutsk, Bering found that no preparations whatever had been made for his arrival, that none of the advance work necessary for the next stretch of the coastal surveys had been done, and that no special officers had ever shown up (as promised from the Admiralty) to build boats and expedite the transport of materials to Okhotsk. Nevertheless, with little help from local officials, he managed in the course of the next six months to oversee construction of two small ships for the Arctic expeditions, and four barges for carrying supplies. On June 30, 1735, the two ships —the *Yakutsk,* commanded by Lieutenant Vasily Pronchishchev with Semyon Chelyuskin as pilot, and the *Irkutsk,* under Lieutenant Petr Lassenius—started down the Lena on their mission, the former to make its way westward and round the Taimyr Peninsula to the mouth of the Yenisey; the latter to sail eastward and, if possible, around the Chukchi Peninsula to the Anadyr.

The desperate hardships of wintering on the Arctic coast immediately took their toll. In 1736, Pronchishchev sought shelter on the Olenek River, and Lassenius was driven by storm and ice into a bay at a latitude of 71 degrees 28'. In that uninhabited spot, he built a driftwood house, but the entire company languished from scurvy, and before help could reach them in the following spring Lassenius himself and all but eight of his fifty men had died. Bering dispatched a new command, almost as large, under Dmitry Laptev (for whom the Laptev Sea is named), and shipped supplies ahead to the mouth of the Lena to be placed at depots along the Arctic coast. Through four grueling seasons (1736–40) Laptev charted the coast eastward from the Lena River to the Kolyma, but could not get much farther due to ice.

Once the Arctic expeditions were under way, Bering could at last turn his attention to the two Pacific voyages, and in 1735–36 he began to recruit men and horses and to stockpile goods and provisions for transshipment to Okhotsk. Near Yakutsk he also set up a foundry for the manufacture of anchors, pulleys, and other articles of iron. Meanwhile, the Senate and Admiralty clamored for results. More than three years had elapsed since the expedition had set out from St. Petersburg, 300,000 rubles had been spent—an enormous sum at the time—and the expedition had already cost the lives of at least forty explorers. Lassenius was dead; his successor, Dmitry Laptev, scarcely east of the Lena; Pronchishchev, in two summers of trying, had been unable to double the Taimyr Peninsula; and Ovtsyn was still struggling in vain in the Gulf of Ob. Nor had Bering and Spanberg begun their Pacific expeditions. And Bering, they learned, had not even reached the coast.

The government demanded that the expedition be brought to a head, "so that from now on the treasury should not be emptied in vain." "Your expedition is a very protracted one," the Admiralty wrote to Bering, "and apparently it is being conducted somewhat carelessly on your part, which is shown by the fact that it has taken you nearly two years to reach Yakutsk. Moreover, it appears from your report that your stay in Yakutsk will be too long; in fact there seems to be no reason to hope that you will succeed in getting any farther. As a consequence of this the Admiralty is extremely dissatisfied, and will not let matters go without an investigation."

A year later his pay was cut in half, and "as a result of failures to send wanted information and to undertake the work assigned to him," he was threatened with demotion. In an acerbic reply, Bering noted that none of the Admiralty's own promises of help had been kept—"not a pood of provisions provided, nor a single boat built"—to help him move his company from Yakutsk to Okhotsk. Nor had the local authorities taken "a single step" on the expedition's behalf. As a result, he had had to do everything himself. Along the 750-mile Yakutsk-to-Okhotsk Track—down the Lena, up the Aldan, Maya, and Yudoma rivers, and across the Stanovoy Mountains—he had cut roads through forests and marshes, built storehouses, barracks, winter huts, and piers, improvised bridges, and had hammered, tied, or otherwise put together over seventy riverboats, with which to convey the cannon, powder, cables, hemp, spikes, hawsers, and other heavy equipment, as well as food and stores required for six or eight seagoing ships. He had had to spend two years doing this, he said, in order not to see "the whole expedition come to a complete standstill, bring upon my men the direst need, and force the whole enterprise into the most ignominious ruin." Recalling that during the First Expedition Spanberg and his baggage train had nearly perished on the trail, Bering pointedly reminded the Admiralty that compared to the men and supplies he now had to move, that convoy had been minuscule. Even after reaching Yudoma Cross—so-called from the cross erected near the Yudoma River's fording point—the going on horseback across the mountains was extremely rough. The foothills were covered with dense forests, and the riverbeds studded with so many rocks and rounded boulders that horses scrambling over them were often maimed. As they worked their way up the slopes, they often became stuck in the mire, and on the summits there were enormous bogs and quagmires. When a pack-horse broke through, one of the travelers recalled, "there was no means of getting him out, and when passing over thin places one noticed with great horror the ground shaking in waves for twenty or more yards around."

Upon reflection, the government realized that Bering was not wholly to blame. It threatened the local authorities with torture unless they gave him more help, and belatedly relieved him of further responsibility for the surveys along the Arctic coast, so that he could concentrate on the voyages to America and Japan. Special officers were also sent at last to expedite the transportation of supplies. But by the time most of this assistance reached him, it didn't matter anyway, for he had already embarked for Okhotsk.

During all this while, following behind Bering in leisurely stages, the Academy contingent had made its way to Irkutsk. Rather than press on via Yakutsk to Kamchatka—investigation of which was supposed to be the final object of their labors—Müller and Gmelin paused to explore the Selenga River Valley south of Lake Baikal, and made various excursions to the Sino-Russian frontier. There they consulted with Chinese officials, studied the border trade, and visited the silver mines near Nerchinsk. Returning in September 1735 to Irkutsk, they lingered through the Christmas holidays, which evidently consisted of one long drunken orgy; and then it was on to Ilimsk, where Easter furnished the occasion for another week-long binge. In this atmosphere of wild debauchery, Müller and Gmelin seem to have restrained themselves—

the pervasiveness of syphilis in nearly every settlement perhaps stiffened their will—but given their encyclopedic mandate, they had more than enough to do anyway, and had already accumulated a voluminous archive of documents and notes.

At the beginning of May 1736, the ice began to break up on the Lena River, and on the 27th the whole Academy group, including de la Croyère, embarked downriver in a flotilla of twelve boats. Many peasants and convict exiles had been impressed into transport duty as veritable galley slaves for the expedition's numerous detachments, but by the time the Academics set out, they had deserted in such numbers that rows of gallows had to be erected in villages all along the river to discourage further flight.

When the Academics finally strode into Yakutsk in September, most of the naval personnel had long since arrived and the city had been transformed into a central supply depot for Bering's remaining tasks. Indeed, there was no room left for anyone else, and their arrival created a logistical nightmare. Bering had already been badgered unfairly by the Admiralty for unwanted delays, and his own priorities were clear. The naval command, he told them, "had enough to do just to look after itself." And so, to whatever complaints the Academics had about housing, supplies, and transportation, he simply turned a deaf ear. All decent lodgings being taken, most of the scholars had to hole up for the winter in primitive, tentlike cabins that had a central opening in the roof for ventilation and light. These *"Schwarzstuben"* (swartrooms), as Gmelin called them, were "impossible for anyone with work to do requiring clean surroundings," as botanical specimens withered, writing paper quickly became black with soot, and the expedition's artists "had to mix their colors on entirely different principles," because so much unavoidable black got into them that they were spoiled.

Such inconveniences came to seem quite unimportant to Gmelin, however, after a fire broke out in his quarters on November 8 and burned them to the ground. All of his collections, most of his previous year's notes, and much of his library were destroyed. Remarkably, in that sub-Arctic wilderness, a copy of one indispensable volume, a highly technical work on botany, was actually discovered in the possession of an exiled Italian count, Francesco Santi (one of the talented foreigners originally invited into Russian service by Peter the Great), who at the time was confined to Shigansk, a convict settlement on the Arctic Circle north of Yakutsk.

Since the Academicians lacked any independent means to get to Kamchatka themselves, in the spring of 1737 they explored their more immediate surroundings according to their scholastic bent. De la Cro-yère went down to the mouth of the Lena to determine its latitude, Müller pored over the local archives, and Gmelin tried to reconstruct what he could of his lost collections and notes. The truth is, they were not all that eager to go to Kamchatka anyway (still the least hospitable and most dangerous place in the empire), and a modification of their plans had conveniently suggested itself in the form of Stepan Krashe-ninnikov, an enterprising young student originally assigned to Gmelin as his assistant, whom they sent ahead to prepare for their eventual arrival. He was to collect all the information about Kamchatka that he could, have houses built for them in Bolsheretsk, and start a small botanical garden for the study of local plants. All this would enable them to abbreviate their own reluctant stay there. After hasty prepara-tions were made for his departure, Krasheninnikov set out for Okhotsk on July 8, 1737, in Bering's train.

Bering's memoranda for a second expedition had envisaged a Pacific base of operations, with the development of the Okhotsk region and the transformation of the little settlement at the mouth of the Okhota River into a port. But the plans of the Admiralty had gone awry in Okhotsk just as they had at Yakutsk. Grigory Skornyakov-Pisarev, an exile who had demonstrated great ability under Peter the Great as a major general, director of the Naval Academy, and Chief Procurator (Attorney General) of the Senate, had been placed in charge of the advance preparations, but in embittered exile his considerable talents had "gone to seed." His instructions had been to settle Yakut and Tungus shepherds and Russian peasants (including three hundred convicts) in the neighborhood of Okhotsk, start them farming, and introduce into their care herds of horses, cattle, and sheep; he was to get carpenters going on accommodations for the naval personnel, and on wharves and dockyards for the ships; set up a foundry, where iron workers from Yekaterinburg could begin forging anchors and other like objects of iron; and establish a saltworks nearby on the coast. In short, he was to do for the seaboard in advance of Spanberg's arrival what the Admiralty was supposed to have done for Bering in advance at Yakutsk.

As early as July 30, 1731, orders respecting his new command had gone out to Pisarev, and in the following year he had been given jurisdiction over the newly formed Okhotsk administrative district, which included Kamchatka and Anadyrsk. But when Spanberg arrived in 1735 to direct the fitting out of vessels, he found "no Pisarev, no ships, no quarters, no food, no Russian agriculturalists with full granaries, no Tungus with herds of fat cattle, nothing but the old cheerless and bare village that he had left behind him five years before." Although Pisarev eventually showed up with a party of Cossack settlers, that was it. The two men almost immediately came to blows, tried to arrest each other, and took turns denouncing one another to the authorities. Pisarev withdrew to a stockaded fort two miles away, and from that enclave did his best to obstruct the implementation of Spanberg's emergency plans. When the latter broke ground for a dockyard, Pisarev began work on a rival site, although the unsuitability of either location soon became apparent when in 1736, with construction still under way, heavy rains caused the Okhota River to overflow, flooding the low-lying plain and washing away all their labors. Thereafter for the most part Pisarev "gave himself over to plunder, turbulence and drink," and instead of bothering with the expedition's affairs, "set up a harem and took delight in riding down the icy slopes of Okhotsk with his concubines."

Like Bering at Yakutsk, Spanberg took everything into his own hands. On a sandspit in the delta of the Okhota River, where the wharves were eventually placed, his men kneaded the clay, molded the bricks, built the houses, barracks, magazines, and other buildings, including a church, and in two years, by the time Bering arrived in the summer of 1737, had transformed Okhotsk into something like a Pacific port. Although timber and joints for shipbuilding had to be floated 25 miles downriver to the site, Spanberg had not only repaired Bering's two old boats, the *Fortuna* and the *Gabriel,* but had completed two new ships (the *Archangel Michael* and the *Hope*) for the Kurile Islands–Japanese voyage. And these lay fully equipped in the harbor. In fact, about the only thing he hadn't been able to do was build the two galliots for the American voyage.

Confronted upon his arrival with the Spanberg–Pisarev feud, Bering did his diplomatic best to keep Pisarev at bay, although the latter's "foul-tongued criticisms" soon wore even the captain-commander's patience thin. "For a correspondence with him alone," Bering complained at one point, "I might use three good secretaries." As it was, his own voyage would have to wait until Spanberg's could get under way, and the lateness of the season obliged the latter to postpone his own until the following year (1738). Meanwhile, the *Fortuna* was sent across to Bolsheretsk in Kamchatka with Krasheninnikov on board.

Used regularly since Bering's First Expedition as a cargo ship across the Okhotsk Sea, the *Fortuna* had outlived its days. As soon as it was out of sight of land, it sprang a leak, and despite the efforts of men at two pumps and some furious bailing with pots and pans, the water began to come in through the ports. To lighten the ship, the crew threw everything on deck into the sea, and when that did no good, in a frenzy jettisoned the rest of the cargo—14,000 pounds of it—to reduce the water in the hold. Ten days later, as Kamchatka came into view, a storm arose with towering waves generated by a tremendous earthquake. To save the ship, as it entered the mouth of the Bolshaya River, the pilot intentionally ran it high up on the shore. The mast was cut down, but overnight the vessel was battered to pieces and part of its wreckage swept out to sea. "We then learned," wrote Krasheninnikov, "how great was the danger we had run, for all the planks of the vessel were black, and so rotten that they were easily broken with the hand." More alarming still, their "terra firma" itself was trembling so violently that they could barely stand on their feet.

In the calamity, Krasheninnikov lost all of his belongings (including his official credentials) as well as a two-year supply of food, and the natives became convinced that his arrival was responsible for the meteorological disasters that had recently struck their land. Nevertheless, he established himself at Bolsheretsk, and in the following year explored lower Kamchatka, making notes on the flora and fauna, and gathering a mass of facts relating to the habits, customs, and beliefs of the Kamchadals.

Although mercifully spared any such ordeals, Müller and Gmelin were finding life in Siberia increasingly hard to take. Müller spent the winter of 1737–38 in Irkutsk, where he was bled seventeen times in two months for his health, and Gmelin joined him there in March. They had now been on the road nearly five years—the total amount of time they had expected to be away—and with mixed feelings began to give up on the idea of ever getting to the Pacific Coast. Returning westward, they wintered at Yeniseysk, but their joint petition to come back to St. Petersburg was denied. Meanwhile, de la Croyère, although a delightful companion, had failed to contribute anything of scientific value to the enterprise, and after five years in Siberia had been unable to determine beyond a reasonable doubt the astronomical coordinates of a single locale. Moreover, he was always in one kind of trouble or another, and the promiscuity of his wife (whom he'd brought along) was a constant humiliation to him and a distraction from his tasks. His two colleagues privately protested his shortcomings to the Academy, and tactful arrangements were accordingly made for "supplementary personnel."

The remarkable man who soon appeared in that humble guise was Georg Wilhelm Steller, "a born naturalist and botanist" (as Linnaeus would one day call him), and perhaps the greatest figure the expedition would produce. The son of a Lutheran cantor in Windsheim, Germany, Steller had come into the world still-born on March 10, 1709, only to be miraculously revived by repeated exposure to the vapors of burning sulfur. As a youth, he received a thoroughly classical education, and (much like Gmelin) displayed "a precocious inclination towards the investigation of natural things." At the University of Wittenberg he studied both theology and medicine, and attended the famous anatomical lectures of Abraham Vater (discoverer of the Pancinian corpuscles), which included the dissection of cadavers "so prepared by injections of red wax that the intestines appeared as if in life filled with blood." Less respectably, he also dabbled in the spirit world, mastering spells and incantations, and acquiring fortune-telling gifts. "Once on the night before Christmas," he reportedly confessed to a friend,

when the moon was shining, our band of divination students went to a coppice wood near the city. There we cleared a place of snow and in the middle of it marked off a circle with the requisite signs and began to mumble our incantations. Suddenly a wonderful figure appeared, dressed in a motley, ragged costume with black stockings, red boots and yellow heels. . . . I had the audacity to step close up to the fellow from behind, lift up one foot and examine the boot and heel closely. At that moment a violent storm arose. We took fright and fled in the greatest fear and dismay toward the city and were incessantly pursued with thousands of snowballs, without however suffering any injury from them. Since then I have sworn off such dangerous business, and regret my folly with the most painful reminiscence of these diabolical jugglings and horrible doings.

From Wittenberg, Steller went to the University of Halle, where natural history was taught by the medical faculty—botany, for example, as a branch of herbal medicine—and about this time developed a voracious appetite for fantasy travel literature, such as Defoe's *Robinson Crusoe* and Schnabel's *The Wonderful Fortunes of some Seafarers*, a tale of shipwreck on an island paradise in an unknown sea. Under their influence (or because, as his contemporaries believed, he had the gift of second sight), Steller had a vivid premonition of his own fate. In 1734 he predicted that he would eventually travel to a far-away place, suffer shipwreck, be cast upon an uninhabited island, and die in a desolate land. Later that same year, after briefly attaching himself as a medic to a Russian artillery regiment involved in the siege of Danzig, he sailed across the Baltic to St. Petersburg.

With just a few kopeks in his pocket (so the story goes), he found his way to the Botanical Garden. There he was befriended by a German gardener who, noting his poverty, took him to the house of Archbishop Theophan Prokopovich, primate of the Russian Church. Prokopovich, a liberal-minded, cosmopolitan cleric who had spearheaded Peter the Great's ecclesiastical reforms, recognized him at once as a man of ability and appointed him house physician. This was quite in keeping with the archbishop's character. A patron of the arts and science, he managed a learned (if epicurean) household, famous among other things for its culinary luxuries, including homemade beer.

At the time Stellar arrived in the capital, the Academic contingent was already halfway across Siberia. When in the beginning of 1735 it was decided to strengthen its scientific staff, Steller leapt at the chance to join. Prokopovich recommended him to the Academy, as did Johann Amman, the internationally acclaimed botanist with whom he had begun to work as an assistant.

While Steller waited for his application to be approved, he sought out Daniel Gottlieb Messerschmidt, who as a result of his seven years in Siberia (1720–27) collecting data and specimens relating to the region's natural and human history, "monuments and other antiquities and what other remarkable objects he might come across," probably knew more about Siberia than anyone else. His observations and writings filled nine densely written folio volumes, but the exactions of his task had left him half-deranged. In February 1728, he suddenly turned over to the Academy all his collections and notes, and became obsessed with one Birgitta Helena, the daughter of a colonel, a "wild young woman, quite his opposite, whom he believed to be the very woman he had seen in a dream while in Solikamsk." Messerschmidt married her and made arrangements to return to his native Danzig; but on October 27, 1729, he and his bride were shipwrecked, lost all their belongings, and ultimately struggled back to the capital. During the last few years of his life he was so dejected and morose as to be unemployable, and the couple lived in abject poverty until his death at the age of fifty in 1735. No sooner had Messerschmidt died than Steller, in a sense, repeated his mistake and fell in love with and precipitously married his widow, under the illusion that she would be the helpmeet of his dreams. Meanwhile, on July 28, 1736, his application had been approved, and after examining some classified documents relating to the expedition, on September 9, 1737, he took the prescribed oath.

A number of the expedition's officers (Bering, Spanberg, and de la Croyère, among others) had their wives or families with them, and Steller had also persuaded his wife to go along. She promised to go to the ends of the world with him and share his hardships, but by the time they got to Moscow she changed her mind and "decided to stay home and share his pay." He gave her part of the salary he'd received in advance, but already knew she would betray him. In the coming months (as he confided to Gmelin) he found himself willing "to undertake anything by which he could obtain oblivion from his grief."

Steller's journey to Okhotsk took three years. After pausing for the winter (1738–39) at Tomsk—where the Festival of the Archangel Michael (November 8) was celebrated by such a "rush to get drunk" that "one would be justified in believing an order had been issued for everybody to fill up with whisky on that very day"—he continued on to Yeniseysk, where on January 20, 1739, Gmelin and Müller (who were just then trying to get out of their Kamchatka obligations) warmly greeted him as their reprieve. They quickly realized that he was just the man to take over from Krasheninnikov, and Gmelin "went nearly into ecstasies in praising Steller's fitness." Roughing it was simply not their style. They were used to (and expected) creature comforts and various luxuries suitable to their professional rank, and seldom ventured far from the considerable support apparatus—with its cooks, servants, drivers, and so on—of their wagon train. Steller worked in a completely different way. "He was not troubled about his clothing," Gmelin would later write, and reduced his basic equipment

> to the least possible compass. He had one drinking cup, and only one dish out of which he ate and in which was served all his food. For this he needed no chef. He cooked everything himself, and that with so little circumstance that soup, vegetables and meat were put into the same pot and boiled together. Smoke and smell in the room in which he worked did not affect him. He used no wig and no powder; any kind of shoe or boot suited him. . . . So indefatigable was he in all his undertakings that . . . it was no hardship for him to go hungry and thirsty a whole day if he was able to accomplish something advantageous to science.

Steller volunteered to go to Kamchatka alone, and although his colleagues dutifully described to him the risks he was taking and the privations he faced, their warnings seemed only to whet his appetite for the task. Their duty done, they stripped their own resources to speed him on his way.

A letter meanwhile had arrived from de la Croyère requesting someone capable of repairing his pendulum clocks, which had been damaged during his trip down the Lena in 1738. The trip had been a hard one and his retinue had been decimated by scurvy, frostbite, and (in one case) suicide. To help him out, Gmelin and Müller tapped the best local talent, who turned out to be an exiled sex offender "with considerable experience in clock-making and other mechanical arts." He was requisitioned from Yeniseysk and sent along with Steller to Irkutsk.

Arriving on March 23, 1739, Steller found himself obliged to remain there almost a year. During the summer he explored the Alpinelike Barguzin Mountains on the far side of Lake Baikal, discovered several new plants never before described, and developed a new technique for the preservation of microscopic parasites by enclosing them between thin flakes of clear mica, as would later be done with glass. Three quarters of a century later, when the parasites were examined for the first time by another scientist, "they could [still] be drawn and described as if they were alive." All summer long Steller scarcely allowed himself any rest, assembling specimens and writing lengthy and exceedingly exact descriptions of them, as well as studies of the landscape and some of the local tribes. As a result, his supply of paper, which he also needed for drying his plant collections, ran out, and that winter he had to travel all the way to the Chinese frontier to replenish it.

Meanwhile, his wife had written to demand more money, "which nearly drove him to distraction by its lack of consideration," but (as he would repeatedly do) he arranged to send her what he could. At the same time, putting even more distance between himself and the capital, he packed up his collections and manuscripts, addressed them to the Academy, and on March 6, 1740, embarked for Yakutsk 1,624 miles away. The winter road led over the mountains southwest of Lake Baikal, then on to Kirensk, where he paused to wait for the ice on the Lena to break.

It was at Kirensk that Steller learned of Spanberg's voyage to Japan.

Five years after the first naval detachment had left St. Petersburg, the Pacific voyages had begun. Toward the end of June 1738, the *Archangel Michael*, commanded by Martin Spanberg, the *Hope,* under Lieutenant William Walton, an Englishman, and the old *Gabriel,* under Midshipman Aleksey Shelting, had sailed from Okhotsk to Bolsheretsk, and on July 15 for the Kurile Islands. A reconnaissance was made along the Kurile chain, and various islands named en route, down to Iturup, before the ships (which had not kept together) returned. The following spring, Spanberg built an eighteen-oared sloop, the *Bolsheretsk,* transferred Walton to the *Gabriel,* gave Shelting command of the *Hope,* and departed with his squadron on May 21, 1739, this time intent on finding the sea route to Japan. After passing through the strait between Shumshu and Paramushir islands, they sailed SE-SW far out into the Pacific Ocean, expecting to encounter Juan de Gama Land. When the apocryphal land failed to materialize, they altered course at latitude 42 N and headed southwest. On June 14 they spotted the northeast shores of Honshu, largest of the Japanese islands, and followed them south. Spanberg and Walton lost sight of each other in a drifting fog, and on June 22 Spanberg anchored in a bay on the east coast of Hondo and made cautious but friendly contact with the Japanese. Two junks laden with tobacco and foodstuffs pulled alongside and began a spirited trade, and when officials showed up, Spanberg produced a map and a globe to confirm his whereabouts, which they readily pointed out. The next day Spanberg made his way northward along the coast, and passing beyond it discovered three more Kurile Islands. Scurvy, however, had broken out among his crew, and by the time he reached port on August 14, thirteen of his own men and eleven on the *Hope* had died.

Nevertheless, Spanberg was more than satisfied, for he had met the full challenge of his command. He had found the sea route to Japan, had established (in effect) that States Land and Company Land were two of the Kurile Islands, had fixed the geographical positions of the east coasts of two or more Japanese islands, and had shown that Juan de Gama Land did not exist. In fact, he had every reason to believe that he had earned immortal renown. Waxing vicariously patriotic, he noted that no power as yet controlled the Kuriles, and saw a clear opportunity for the Russian Empire to add them to its domains. Meanwhile, Walton (whom Spanberg detested) returned to Bolsheretsk with news that he had independently landed on Honshu, and that a member of his crew, invited into a Japanese home, had been regaled with wine, rice, fruit, and various delicacies.

News of the voyages reached the capital by special courier on January 6, 1740, but the excitement it caused soon gave way to confusion and doubt. For one thing, the findings of the two captains ran counter to all the accepted maps; and in their competition for glory, Spanberg and Walton had impugned each other's logs. Independently, Bering found that the records of both contained a number of irregularities, and attempts by the Admiralty to rework and reconcile their calculations proved of no avail. Out of enmity toward Spanberg, Pisarev had also written to the Senate to suggest they had really been to Korea, not Japan. His evidence, he said, was based on a Japanese map reportedly found at Okhotsk. As a former director of the Naval Academy, he knew his opinion had to be given weight. In the end, not knowing whom to believe, the Admiralty decided, even as Spanberg was hastening west-ward to report in person on his discoveries, to order him to repeat his voyage. Flabbergasted, he tried to get back to Okhotsk before Bering sailed for Kamchatka, only to arrive on August 12, 1740, just as Bering (who had requisitioned Spanberg's ships and remaining stores for his own use) was about to start ferrying provisions across the Okhotsk Sea. Under the circumstances, Spanberg was told he would have to wait, build another vessel, and get new supplies of equipment and provi-sions from Yakutsk. That meant a probable delay of at least two years. About the only thing he could be thankful for was that Pisarev (on April 13, 1739) had been replaced as a port commandant by Anton Devier, another prominent exile, who more readily cooperated with the ex-pedition's staff.

Other personnel gathered, including Steller and de la Croyère. Steller had considered sailing with Spanberg to Japan, but now gave up on the idea and began to wonder how he could get Bering to invite him to join the American voyage. At their first meeting, Bering was apparently impressed with Steller's attainments, and while taking his request under advisement, made arrangements for conveying him to Kamchatka in one of his ships.

In the interim, Steller investigated the local *materia medica,* includ-ing some kind of edible clay that, when boiled with reindeer milk, relieved diarrhea, and a species of cow parsnip from which a sugar substitute could be derived. The latter was also used to make a pow-erful hallucinogenic drink. For his part, de la Croyère continued as best he could to practice the elementary procedures necessary for calculating longitudes and studying the tides. His potential contribu-tion to the upcoming voyage could hardly be overestimated, and per-haps he still hoped by a mechanical diligence to master his discipline at the eleventh hour. But other indications are that his heart was no longer in anything he did. Despite the enormous expense account with which he'd started out, he was now "so deeply in debt that he didn't know which way to turn," while his wife's incessant exploits had ren-dered him "physically ill, morally worn out, and socially dead."

Some months before, Bering had refitted the *Gabriel* and sent it ahead with a crew to select and survey a suitable harbor from which the expedition would start. They had chosen Avacha Bay, a magnificently sheltered haven on Kamchatka's eastern coast, which had a circumference of 26 miles, was large, deep, and surrounded by high green hills. Along the shores of one of its inner harbors they had built a small town, and Bering had named it Petropavlovks—or the Harbor of St. Peter and St. Paul—after his two ships. Completed in June 1740, the ships were exactly alike, after the fashion of packet boats then plying the Baltic. Each carried two masts brig-rigged, and was 80 feet long, 22 feet across, and had a 9½ foot draft. Their loading capacity was 220 tons, and fourteen small cannon bristled from their sides. Bering selected the *St. Peter* as his flagship; Chirikov was to command the *St. Paul.*

On September 1, Sofron Khitrov, Bering's first mate, started from the mouth of the Okhota River in the *Hope* bound for Avacha Bay, but immediately ran the ship aground on a sandbar and irreplaceably lost a considerable amount of the expedition's provisions, including all the hard biscuit. Bering, unable to tolerate any further delay, sailed anyway for Kamchatka a few days later, with the rest of his supplies. After arranging at Bolsheretsk for their transshipment overland to Avacha Bay by dog team, he rounded Cape Lopatka with his two command ships to Petropavlovsk.

The overland operation proved a tremendous ordeal, and bore some comparison with the miseries suffered on the Yakutsk-to-Okhotsk Trail. And because men were desperately needed to assist, once again natives were rounded up from all over the country with their sleds and dogs. The manner in which this was done was so harsh that many thought they were being herded together by the Russians for one great massacre. A rebellion broke out, but the ringleaders were soon identified, and surprised and killed in their subterranean dwellings by grenades dropped down through smokeholes in the roof.

Steller had meanwhile taken over from Krasheninnikov, who brought him up to date on his research. He had traveled to the southern end of the peninsula, up the tributary streams of the Bolshaya River, over the mountains into the central valley, and down the Kamchatka River to its mouth. He had endured interminable winter blizzards and miasmic summers in the lowland swamps, and had witnessed terrifying earthquakes and the awe-inspiring fiery eruptions of some of Kamchatka's volcanoes, including one early in 1739 that had showered the landscape with so much ash that sledges couldn't be drawn across the snow.

In January 1741, Steller himself explored the region south of Bolsheretsk toward Cape Lopatka, but shortly after his return he received an urgent letter from Bering summoning him to Petropavlovsk. Accompanied by Thomas Lepikhin, a Cossack he had recently hired as his assistant, he hurried across the peninsula by dogsled, and met with the captain-commander at his headquarters on March 20, 1741.

There he learned that Bering's chief surgeon had suddenly bowed out of the voyage, claiming to be ill, and that the Lutheran clergyman assigned to his ship had also abruptly withdrawn due to "melancholia." Aware of Steller's training as a Lutheran theologian and especially of his medical skills, Bering invited him to take their place. He was also needed as a mineralogist, since one purpose of the voyage was to assay the mining potential of any newly discovered lands. Steller, of course, was overjoyed, but it is not surprising that the enthusiasm of others had begun to wane. Aside from the sheer exhaustion of the preparations, the voyage was a dangerous one, the North Pacific an uncharted sea. Bering himself was pretty much discouraged and worn out, and his once-robust physical strength was almost gone. Over the course of eight years, the unrelenting strain of expectations had taken a terrific toll; and, wrote Steller a bit obscurely, "in the slimy environs of Okhotsk and Kamchatka, [even as] he tried to lift out and up everybody who had fallen into the mire, they leaned so heavily on him that he himself must sink."

In fact, Bering had already helped to accomplish far more than he could know. The Arctic voyages he had spent so much time preparing had begun to achieve spectacular success. The coast of the Kara Sea and the west coast of the Yamal Peninsula had been thoroughly explored; the Yamal Peninsula had been rounded; and surveys carefully continued from the Ob to the Yenisey. Both sides of the Taimyr Peninsula had at last also been charted, and the northernmost point of Eurasia, Cape Chelyuskin (named for the pilot of the voyage), had been rounded from the east. There were many sad, if heroic, stories in these endeavors, but that of Vasily Pronchishchev, who died in 1737 in one of the Taimyr expeditions, was perhaps the most poignant. "To his melancholy fate," one later explorer remarked, "there attaches an interest which is unique in the history of arctic exploration voyages. He was newly married when he started. His young wife accompanied him on his journey, took part in his dangers and sufferings, survived him only two days, and now rests by his side in a grave on the desolate shore of the Polar Sea."

In late April, the shrouding was made fast to the mainmast, and on May 4, 1741, a ship's council, attended by Bering, his senior and junior officers, and Louis de la Croyère, was held to decide what course to sail. To guide them, Joseph Nicolas Delisle had prepared a map of the North Pacific and adjacent islands, and had suggested three possible routes: (1) due east from the tip of the Chukchi Peninsula; (2) due east from Kamchatka; and (3) southeast from Kamchatka toward Juan de Gama Land. According to Lieutenant Sven Waxell, a Swede and the *St. Peter*'s second-in-command, their uncertain judgment in choosing was ultimately swayed by the map's location of Juan de Gama Land (supposed to be contiguous to America) at 46 degrees north latitude southeast of Avacha Bay. They decided to steer for it, but if no land were found at that latitude, to make an abrupt U-turn of sorts to the northeast, and after reaching America to return along the 65th parallel to the Chukchi Peninsula toward summer's end. Unfortunately, this plan replaced an earlier consensus that would have spared them many pains. "It had not been the wish of the Admiralty," notes one writer,

> that Bering should sail east to make a blind landfall on the coast of America. Their instructions required him first to sail up the Siberian shore to East Cape, cross to Alaska and trace the American shore southwards, thus providing a broad and coherent picture of the relationship of the two continents. But, fearing obstruction by ice if he reached East Cape early in the season, Bering determined to reverse this course by sailing directly to America and then circling north, giving the ice in northern waters time to disperse. He had intended to winter at a conveniently southern latitude on the American shore and devote a leisurely two seasons to his circuit of the North Pacific, but ... had been compelled to alter his purpose by the inadequate provisioning of his ships. The prudent course of deferring the voyage for another year in order to bring the ships up to the maximum

fitness in equipment and supply was ruled out by the years already wasted and the enormous costs incurred.

Rather than attempt a long winter layover somewhere on an unknown coast, the voyage in its entirety was abridged to three or four months, which meant they would have to find their way to America by the shortest possible route, almost with unerring luck, if they were to have enough time to accomplish even a part of the mission their numerous instructions required.

As Bering prepared to sail, Steller was assigned to the *St. Peter,* de la Croyère to the *St. Paul,* and each ship given a complement of seventy-six men. On May 29 they were towed out of the inner harbor into the open roadstead, and on June 4—an auspiciously bright, sunny summer's day with a high, fair wind—they set sail. Proceeding E by SE, they approached the position of Juan de Gama Land, and found nothing but the sea. "It became quite evident," wrote Chirikov, "that [the said land] did not exist, since we had sailed over the region where it was supposed to be."

Bering and Chirikov changed their course to E by N, but on the morning of June 20 they became separated in a storm. Bering spent several days searching in vain for the *St. Paul,* and after returning to 45 degrees north latitude (still looking for Juan de Gama Land) decided to proceed E by N again on the 25th. He did so over the objections of Steller, who, "observing in the water reed grass and seaweed of a type which occurs only on rocks and in shallow water, and noting also the presence of gulls and seals," thought they must be traveling parallel to a continental shelf. Steller argued with the officers about it, but his opinion was ridiculed, and the enmity that now developed between him and most of his shipmates was never to relent. Thereafter he was seldom heeded, although on all other important matters he would turn out to be absolutely right.

The price of their detour was soon felt. Rations were reduced, and by July 14 half of the ship's water was gone. What remained could not sustain them past the beginning of September. By mid-July it was surmised that either all their bearings were off, or some part of America would soon be seen. For days a heavy fog had hung upon the sea. Expectations rose on the 15th, and the following morning the crew milled about anxiously on deck. Then, a little past noon, suddenly the clouds lifted, and before them stood, as though risen from the sea, the peak of Mount St. Elias in all its grandeur. They had discovered Alaska! The rejoicing, "with great expectations of future reward," was almost universal, and although they stood in some peril at that moment, along an unknown coast in unknown seas, all their foregoing efforts momentarily seemed redeemed. But when the men eagerly congratulated Bering, wrote Steller, "the captain-commander, whom the glory of the discovery mostly concerned," merely "shrugged his shoulders while looking at the land." He had fulfilled his commission, at whatever cost. Now he wanted to be done with the whole affair as soon as possible and get safely home.

Over the next few days as they skirted the coast they sighted Kayak Island, which "stood out alone like a stone column in the sea," and Cape St. Elias due east. Noting a strong, fresh-water current in the sea, Steller correctly surmised that a river must be located nearby, and suggested the place as an anchorage. But the only reaction this drew from the crew was ridicule.

Steller's frustration increased by the hour. No one else appeared interested in drawing up plans for exploration, and the sole reason given for landing was to take fresh water on board. He could not help saying that it seemed as if their only purpose for having come there was to bring a little American water back to Asia.

On the morning of July 18, Khitrov put off in the longboat to find safe anchorage among the islands to the north, but when Steller was told he would not be allowed to go with him, he confronted Bering before the whole crew and threatened to report him to the Admiralty. Bering relented somewhat and promised to let him go ashore in the yawl with the watering party at ten o'clock; but as Steller climbed into the boat with Thomas Lepikhin, his hired Cossack, Bering sent two trumpeters to the rail and sounded a mock salute. Steller, however, understood how timeless the moment was, and when the boat struck the beach, he leapt ashore, "the first white man to set foot on Alaska." No time was to be wasted. While the watering crew attended to their task, he and Lepikhin struck out along the shore, and soon came upon traces of inhabitants who had fled hastily into the woods: a fireplace still steaming with red-hot stones, the remnants of a recent meal, including bits of meat still clinging to the bones, and pieces of dried fish, scallops, and blue mussels, which had evidently been eaten raw.

Nearby he found a bow drill for making fire, tufts of moss used as tinder, and trees that had evidently been felled with axes of stone. Without fear for his own safety—Lepikhin was armed with a gun, but Steller carried only a Yakut *palma,* or dagger, for digging up rocks and plants—he followed a path that led into the forest, and promptly discovered a covered pit containing various bark utensils, arrows, thongs of twisted seaweed, and articles of food.

Nothing escaped him. Having carefully recorded everything he'd found, he deposited numerous samples in a sack and covered the storehouse over. He sent Lepikhin to warn the rest of the party not to feel too secure and to ask Bering for more men to help him in his work. Utterly alone, he cut a path for himself through the woods until he came to a rise that also cut off the beach. From the top of a bluff he looked longingly toward the mainland, "to take a good look at least at that country on which I was not vouchsafed to employ my endeavors more fruitfully," and noticed smoke rising in the distance from a hill. Reluctantly, Steller returned with his collections to the landing stage, made himself some tea, and resting on the beach, made descriptions of the rarer plants he had discovered before they withered and died.

An hour or so later the yawl returned with some objects Bering wished to leave for the natives as indemnity for those removed, including an iron kettle, a pound of tobacco, a Chinese pipe, and a length of Chinese silk. Steller thought the natives would have appreciated knives or hatchets more, but "to this it was objected that such presents might be regarded as a sign of hostility, as if the intention were to declare war." Steller replied that if the natives tried to eat the tobacco, as they probably would, they would think the Russians had tried to poison them.

But now was "no time for moralizing," as he put it. He sent Lepikhin to bag some birds he had noticed, and went off himself in another direction to botanize as rapidly as he could. They met again at the landing place at sunset, and there Steller saw among the birds his companion had brought one that he recognized from an illustrated book he had once studied in a library in St. Petersburg. The book had been published in the Carolinas, and the engraving he remembered was of the Eastern blue jay. Its Alaskan cousin (now classified as *Cyanocitta stelleri*) was the bird he held in his hand. This proved that they were really standing on America's shores.

Posterity would judge Steller's ten hours ashore as a time of astonishing industry, even if other members of the crew could see little
value in the rock samples, carcasses of birds, and plants and other
specimens he began to haul on board. But perhaps Bering after all had
a broader view, for when Steller entered his cabin, "prepared to receive the gruff reproaches of the old commander," to his surprise he
was treated to chocolate.

An hour later Khitrov returned and declared he had discovered a
safe harbor, and not far from where he landed had seen "human tracks
in the sand." A little ways up the beach he had also stumbled upon a
wooden hut with walls "so smooth that it seemed as if they had been
planed . . . with cutting tools." Within he had found (and taken) "a
wooden vessel, such as is made in Russia of linden bark and used as a
box," a whetstone with streaks of copper on it, a wooden paddle, the
tail of a blackish-gray fox, and a hollow clay ball with a pebble in it—
evidently "a toy for small children." All these items he had brought on
board, and they were carefully described by Steller for posterity.

It had taken the *St. Peter* seven weeks to reach America; Bering prudently assumed it would take at least that long to return. So far, the
winds had been easterly, but he correctly feared a change with the
coming of autumn to southwesterly blows, directly contrary to his
course. By his calculation, that gave him three weeks at the most to
reconnoiter the American coast.

His energy for doing so was not very great. Increasingly depressed,
he kept more or less to his cabin, while throughout the day the longboat loaded with water casks shuttled to and from the shore. But on
the morning of July 21, two hours before daybreak, he unexpectedly
got up and came on deck and, without consulting anyone, gave orders
to weigh anchor. Waxell, his first officer, objected that twenty casks
remained to be filled, but Bering sensed a squall coming on and peril
in standing near the land.

For the next two weeks, the *St. Peter* zigzagged along the coast,
steering clear because of the sandbanks and continuous heavy fogs.
The voyagers missed Kodiak Island, and mistook a small island east of
Afognak for a promontory off the mainland, naming it Black Point.
Turning south, on August 4 they sighted five of the Semidi Islands,

where they observed large numbers of seals, sea lions, porpoises, and sea otters playing in the waves.

Scurvy, the terror of all long wilderness expeditions, whether on land or sea, now began its devastation of the crew, and by August 18 it had incapacitated twenty-one. A dispirited Bering called a ship's council, and all agreed that given the impending autumn storms, the developing sickness, and their distance from home, they had better abandon their examination of the coast and steer directly for Avacha Bay. At that moment, they were about 1,600 miles from port.

Pessimism had not yet completely enveloped the crew, and as the *St. Peter* steered into the open sea, the weather remained calm, and there were the diversions that mariners look for as salt to their yarns. On the evening of August 10, for example, they encountered the famous "sea-ape," faintly illuminated under the moon and stars. As its doglike head plunged upward out of the waves, it was seen to have erect and pointed ears, large eyes, thick body hair (like an ape), and long whiskers that grew out of the sides of its upper and lower lips. Instead of forefeet or fins, it appeared to have a divided flipper or tail.

> For over four hours it swam around our ship, looking, as with admiration, first at the one and then at the other of us. At times it came so near that it could have been touched with a pole, but as soon as anybody stirred it moved away a little farther. It could raise itself one-third of its length out of the water exactly like a man, and sometimes it remained in this position for several minutes. After it had observed us for about half an hour, it shot like an arrow under our vessel and came up again on the other side; shortly after, it dived again and reappeared in the old place; and in this way it dived perhaps thirty times.

Something of a riddle to later naturalists, this playful and completely charming creature would eventually be identified as "a full grown bachelor fur-seal."

The perilous realities of their situation, however, soon aroused the direst forebodings as to their fate. Battling headwinds, which grew into a westerly gale, by August 27 they were still only 60 miles from Alaska, and at that rate it would take them two and a half months to get back home. With only twenty-five barrels of fresh water left, they had to find some anchorage soon to take more on. To the astonishment of all, land kept appearing again and again to their north, as they stumbled in storm and darkness along the Aleutian Island chain. On the 30th a fire was spotted on one of the islands, and the next day Bering sent the longboat to an adjacent isle with ten empty casks to be filled. Steller went along, and found several wholesome springs, but when he returned to the beach he saw that the men had already begun filling the casks with water from a stagnant pool. He pointed out that the pool rose and fell with the sea, and therefore must be brackish, "but although in this matter I ought to have been listened to in my capacity of physician, nevertheless my proposition, most honestly made in order to preserve the life of my fellow beings as well as my own, now fallen into the power of others, was rejected from the old overbearing habit of contradicting."

The men afterward regretted their stupidity. As it was, the medicine chest of the *St. Peter* was woefully inadequate, for instead of medicines for treating scurvy, asthma, and other ailments associated with long voyages, it was incongruously supplied with plasters, ointments, salves, and other surgical remedies more appropriate to attending the wounded on a man-o'-war. Strictly speaking, of course, their expedition was a naval one, under the auspices of the Admiralty, but when Steller asked Bering for several men to help him gather antiscorbutic herbs, he was unaccountably spurned. Even as he returned to the beach with his own invaluable store of gentian, black crowberry, spoonwort, and other cresslike plants, one of the sick had been carried ashore and expired in the open air.

Steller privately resolved in the future to "only look after the preservation of my own self without wasting another word," but in fact he never ceased to do what he could for the other men. Bering himself (whose growing apathy was an early symptom of the disease) soon responded well to his ministrations, and in eight days was out of bed and back in command on deck. Rationing his supply to the rest of the crew, Steller was at least able to slow their decline.

Meanwhile, Khitrov, with five armed men and a Chukchi interpreter, had landed with the yawl on the other island and found the ashes of the fire seen the day before. A storm prevented their return to the ship, and the boat was wrecked when Khitrov beached it, so that they couldn't be rescued until September 2. As a result of the delay, the fair weather that immediately followed was lost to their return. "Everyone grumbled," wrote Steller, "because whatever that man [Khitrov] had touched from Okhotsk on had gone wrong and had brought misfortune."

Strangely enough, in the month and a half since the Russians had discovered Alaska, no encounter between a white man and a native had taken place. Yet the eeriness of their absence increased with every empirical trace. Then on September 4, 1741, at about 4:30 P.M. off Bird Island, one of the Aleutians,

> we had scarcely dropped anchor when we heard a loud shout from the rock to the south of us, which at first, not expecting any human beings on this miserable island twenty miles away from the mainland, we held to be the roar of a sea lion. A little later, however, we saw two small boats paddling toward our vessel from shore. We all waited for them with the greatest eagerness and full of wonder. . . . When yet about half a verst [⅓ of a mile] distant both men in their boats began, while still paddling, simultaneously to make an uninterrupted, long speech in a loud voice of which none of our interpreters could understand a word. We construed it therefore as either a formula of prayer or incantation, or a ceremony of welcoming us as friends.

The Russians beckoned for them to come nearer, but they, in turn, pointed toward the land and with other signs seemed to invite the crew to feast ashore. When a Koryak interpreter called out to them in his own language, they pointed to their ears. Then with startling and mysterious bravado, one of them paddled up quite close, rapidly painted his face with colored clay he drew out of his shirt, stuffed his nostrils full of grass, and tying a hawk's wing to a stick "with a laugh threw it toward the vessel." Accepting it as a gift, the Russians tied two tobacco pipes, strings of glass and iron beads, and some small copper bells to a board and lowered it into the sea. The native picked it up, looked at it, and brought it over to his companion. Then he returned and was shown a length of Chinese silk. In response, "he tied an entire eviscerated falcon to another stick and passed it up to our interpreter. . . . It was not at all his intention that we should keep the bird but that we should place the piece of silk between the claws so that it would not become wet."

After the natives had departed, the Russians lowered the longboat with a crew of armed men under Waxell and decided to attempt a landing. The beach, however, was rocky, and the wind and waves so high that the boat was nearly dashed. Waxell allowed the interpreter and two others to wade ashore, where they were received "in a very friendly way and led by the arms, quite deferentially as if they were very great personages [and] presented . . . with a piece of whale blubber." Meanwhile, one of the islanders had come out to the longboat in his kayak, where he was invited to down a cup of vodka. He spat it out immediately, in surprise, "and became very indignant." They then urged him to inhale some smoke from a pipe, after which he paddled away in disgust.

There was misunderstanding on both sides. As the interpreter on shore began to leave, some natives tried to detain him, while others seized the longboat's painter and tried to haul the boat up on the beach. Shots were fired in the air, and the natives fell down "as if hit by thunder," then a tug-of-war ensued, until Waxell gave the order to cut the cable and pull for the ship. The natives were outraged, "scolded us because we had rewarded their good intentions so badly, and waved their hands for us to be off." Some, in a threatening gesture, picked up stones.

That night the natives built a big fire on the beach, but the next day, as the St. Peter tacked about in a strong wind, seven kayaks came out in single file, two right up to the ship. In a conciliatory gesture, the Russians gave the men an iron kettle and some needles; in turn, they were given two oval-snouted caps resembling eyeshades, with rims made of bark or driftwood adorned with ivory figurines. The natives consulted with each other about the exchange, returned to shore, built another big fire, "and shouted very loudly for a while."

On the morning of the 6th, the St. Peter sailed around the northern end of the island and passed out to sea. Swept along the 51st parallel by a storm, the crew sighted a number of other islands, including Atka, which they supposed might be an appendage of the American continent. But time for further survey had long since passed. The wind rose, and "seemed as if it issued forth from a flue." Over the next several days a series of westerly gales increased steadily in force, until on the 30th one descended upon them with such violence that we could not imagine it could be greater or that we should be able to stand it out. Every moment we expected the destruction of our vessel and no one could lie down, or sit up or stand. Nobody was able to remain at his post; we were drifting, under the might of God, whither the angry heavens willed to send us. Half of our crew lay sick and weak, the other half though able-bodied, were quite crazed and maddened from the terrifying motion of the sea and ship. There was much praying, to be sure, but the curses piled up during ten years in Siberia prevented any response. Beyond the ship we could not see a fathom out into the ocean because we continuously lay buried among the cruel waves. Under such conditions no one any longer possessed either courage or counsel. They began too late to regret that matters had not been managed right and that various things had been overlooked. . . . Let no one imagine that our situation is here represented as too dangerous; let him rather believe that the most eloquent pen would find itself too weak to describe our misery.

On the following day, the sailors beheld St. Elmo's Fire and then an incredibly rapid flight of the clouds that "shot like arrows past our eyes and even met and crossed each other with equal rapidity, often from opposite directions."

Meanwhile, the scurvy showed no abatement and sharks began to swarm about the ship. Lassitude and mental depression, the earliest symptoms of the disease, had been followed by soreness and stiffness in the joints, a jaundiced pallor, blue spots on the skin, and swollen and bleeding gums with loosened teeth. By October 18, twenty-nine men were on the sick list, including Bering, as Steller's herbal remedies ran out. Snow and hail began to fall; and one by one the men began to die. Steller ministered to everyone as best he could, but as the ship reached the westernmost group of the Aleutian Island chain, "misery and death suddenly got the upper hand to such an extent that not only did the sick die off, but those who according to their own assertion were well, on being relieved at their posts, dropped dead from exhaustion."

On the 30th, they came upon two islands east of Attu which they mistakenly identified with the Kuriles and so set their course northward, with disastrous results. Steller wrote in his Journal:

It had come to this, that the sailors who used to be at the tiller had to be led to it by two other sick ones who were still able to walk a little. When one could not sit and steer any longer, another in not better condition had to take his place. They dared not carry too many sails, because there was nobody who could have taken them down in case of necessity. . . . The vessel was several days without guidance at all. It lay like a log on the water at the mercy of the winds and waves. Nothing would have been accomplished by severity against the despairing crew. It was much more effective that the command-ing lieutenant [Waxell, Bering being ill] spoke gently to the men, saying that they ought to not entirely despair of God's help but rather put forth their last strength for the salvation of all, which perhaps was nearer than they thought. In this way some were induced to stay on deck as long as it was possible for them to work.

By the morning of November 4, with their bearings and calculations gone awry, many believed, in a delirium of hope, that they must be almost to Kamchatka. Since the ship was enveloped in fog, order was even given to shorten sail so as not to run on the land. The few men who were strong enough to come up on deck peered intently about, in vain construing dissolving formations of the mist as forms of their redemption. Then, toward nine o'clock, lo and behold, a high forbid-ding coast loomed up before them, directly off the bow. "It is impos-sible," says Steller, "to describe how great and extraordinary was the joy of everybody at the sight. The half-dead crawled up to see it, and all thanked God heartily for this great mercy. The captain-commander, who was a very sick man, became not a little aroused, and all talked of how, after having suffered such terrible misery, they were going to care for their health and take a rest. Little cups of brandy concealed here and there made their appearance in order to keep up the joy."

It is doubtful whether the *St. Peter* could have managed one more day at sea. Apart from the pitiful state of the crew and their dwindling stores, the ship itself had been almost completely disabled by storms. The shrouds were breaking continuously, all the rigging was loose, the sails were falling to pieces, and the topmasts and yards were down. With the crew completely exhausted and scurvy ravaging the ship, there was no one strong enough to do any repairing, and since astro-nomical observations could not be taken because of bad weather, navigation had been virtually left to chance.

On November 4, Bering called together all those "still able to drag themselves to the cabin," and it was agreed (under the assumption that the land was Kamchatka) to winter on the coast. But as they drew nearer, they failed to make out anything familiar in the landscape, and when at noon the voyagers finally got their first observation of the sun in ten days, they discovered to their dismay that their actual latitude was 54 degrees 30'. Nevertheless, almost everyone convinced himself they must be somewhere on the peninsula, because Bering, on his First Expedition, was believed to have thoroughly explored the seas in the same latitude for 50 miles offshore. So the question arose as to whether to disembark immediately or search for the entrance to Ava-cha Bay. Bering favored the latter, but (in the democracy of the ship's council) was overruled by his officers and crew. After everyone's opinion had been asked, "at last," writes Steller,

> according to the favorite order of precedence, my turn came also; but . . . I answered: "I have never been consulted in anything from the beginning, nor will my advice be taken if it does not agree with what is wanted; besides, the gentlemen themselves say that I am not a sailor; therefore I would rather not say anything." I was next asked if I, as a person worthy of belief (being now for the first time so considered) would not at least add a written certificate regarding the sickness and the miserable condition of the crew. This I thereupon undertook to do, in accord with my conscience.

During the night of the 4th conditions went from bad to worse. Heavy winds shredded what remained of the shrouds, and two more dead were consigned to the sea. Bering was told that there were not enough men left on their feet to manage the ship; in fact, once the decision to land had been made, the relief was such that everyone simply collapsed and lay down to sleep.

Hour after hour passed, but not an officer showed on deck. Finally, anchor was dropped in view of what seemed, in the halflight of the early morning hours, a smooth span of sandy beach. Everything was quiet; the wind and sea were still. The tide went out, clouds gathered, the surf began to run; suddenly, the vessel was caught in a violent commotion of the waves, which snapped the cable and carried the ship onto a reef. Some men sprang up; a second anchor was rashly thrown, but its cable also broke, and the *St. Peter* was in danger of being smashed to pieces on the rocks. The superstitious crew, roused at last from their penumbral slumbers, blamed the sudden calamity on two new corpses in the hold. Instead of tending to the real needs of their situation, they devoted all their desperate but enfeebled efforts to dragging the bodies up to the deck and hoisting them over the side.

When all seemed lost and utter shipwreck inevitable, a huge wave providentially lifted the vessel up and over the reef into the quiet channel between it and the shore. The panic-stricken sailors suddenly found themselves "as in a placid lake all at once quiet and delivered from all fear of stranding." Their last remaining anchor was dropped in 4½ fathoms of water, and the spent crew, completely exhausted, relapsed once more into a stupor from which no further danger was likely to awaken them again.

The next morning, their situation was grimly assessed. Forty-nine men were on the sick list, twelve had died, most of the rest were prostrate, and the able-bodied remnant was barely sufficient to handle the longboat and get fresh water from shore. In its present anchorage, the ship remained precariously exposed to the fury of the sea.

Shortly after noon, Waxell, Steller, and a few companions rowed ashore. Numbers of sea otters came toward them as they neared, which at first they mistook for bears or wolverines. Upon landing, they were surrounded by packs of blue Arctic foxes, which had to be kept at a respectful distance by kicks and knocks. So many came close, however, sniffing and snapping, that on that first day alone the men killed sixty with axes and knives. Not far from their landing place they found a pure mountain stream, but except for a few small willows, the landscape was bereft of trees and seemed to consist of nothing but crumbling volcanic rock formations and sandhills mixed with driftwood and sea-animal bones. The sandhills were also pockmarked in places by deep pits, which had been dug as burrows by the foxes, and it was decided to enlarge them into dugouts and cover them over with sails. Toward evening, Steller sat down to tea with Waxell and exclaimed: "God knows whether this is Kamchatka!" to which Waxell replied, "What else can it be?" But the fearlessness of the otters and foxes had at once convinced Steller that they had been stranded on an uninhabited isle.

As the men prepared to disembark, some of them didn't realize how sick they really were, "got up, were gay, put on their clothes and thought they would soon recover. However, no sooner did they arise

from their bed in the lower part of the ship where the air was dark
and contaminated, and came into the fresh atmosphere on deck, than
their end overtook them." A particular effort was made to spare Bering
such a fate. Carefully wrapped in blankets, he was carried ashore on a
stretcher and immediately placed in a tent. A few days later a special
pit was dug for him in the sand. His situation was completely pathetic,
yet "everyone wondered," wrote Steller, "at his composure and singular contentment."

It took the able-bodied sixteen days (to November 22) to get all the
sick ashore, and their condition as they lay on the beach was appalling.
Some cried out because they were cold; others, hungry and thirsty,
were unable to eat anything because their gums were "swollen like a
sponge, brown-black, and grown over the teeth." Attracted by their
helpless cries, the foxes flocked to the camp in ever-increasing numbers, and their audacity knew no bounds. They pulled all the baggage
about, scattered provisions, stole and carried off clothes and even
objects of iron, for it was impossible to adequately guard these belongings and stores. Even the corpses were not spared, and while their
graves were being dug, foxes bit off their noses, fingers, and toes.
Some of the Russians began to look upon them as a divine retribution
for the fur trade's wanton slaughters of the past. But this moral reflection soon yielded to infuriated spite, as the men "killed young and old,
tortured them most cruelly, and did them all possible harm."

Waxell, one of the last to be taken off the ship, seemed beyond hope
of cure. Nevertheless, a great effort was made with food and medicine
to bring about his recovery, since, in the event of his death, the command would devolve upon Khitrov, whom many of the men detested
too much to obey. Discipline by this time had utterly collapsed. Distinction by class or rank was unenforceable, and the officers, fearing
mutiny, had long since ceased to issue orders and addressed the men
politely by their family names. Even Steller had to be diplomatic with
Lepikhin, who furiously upbraided his superior for having brought
him on the voyage. In other ways, too, in their extremity, their familiar
world was turned upside down. Skins or pelts had become worthless,
but other things priceless, such as needles and thread, "which in former days many of us would not have stooped to pick up."

Although the crew had been stranded about 400 miles from Kamchatka, most persisted in believing they were somewhere on its coast,

and scouting parties were sent out to determine just where. Futile
plans were also made to save the ship by hauling it up on the beach. It
remained for the sea, churned up by a storm, to accomplish this task
for them in a better way than they could have done themselves. On the
night of November 28, a powerful wave threw it forward and rather
neatly lodged it near their dugouts on its side. Despite damage to the
hold, enough of the cargo was saved to give them hope of enduring.

Bering's health continued to decline, not so much from scurvy,
which Steller's ministrations could probably have reversed, but from
"gas gangrene," as it was called, which ravaged his bowels. Although
he himself had become convinced they were cast away on a desert
island, he confided this to only a few so as not to discourage the rest.
But in his last days he also frankly admitted that the expedition had
been too much for him and ought to have been given into the hands
of a younger man. Half buried in the sand which had crumbled down
upon him from the dugout walls—but which, it is said, he would not
allow his men to remove because it gave him a sensation of warmth—
Vitus Bering died on the morning of December 8, 1741, age sixty, to
the end "in full possession of his reason and speech." Covered over as
he was, his men had to exhume him in order to give him a decent
burial.

The outlook for the survivors was not entirely bleak. Two days after
Bering a thirtieth man succumbed, but he was to be the last, and as the
men endeavored to get through the winter, they settled into salutary
routines. Meat was stored in tightly secured barrels in front of each
dwelling, to protect it from the foxes, and scaffolds were erected upon
which clothing and other effects were hung beyond their reach. In
their various dugouts, they also divided into labor teams. Some did the
cooking, others the hunting, still others gathered driftwood for fire.
The last was a particularly onerous task, since not a tree was to be
found on the whole island, and driftwood was sometimes buried
under several feet of snow. By December, all the wood in the vicinity
had already been gathered in, so that it became necessary to drag it
from more than two miles away. Yet at all times everyone knew what
his task was, and psychologically at least this lightened the burden and
improved morale. Before long the little colony, relatively speaking,
began to thrive, and as the scurvy yielded to the effects of fresh food
(seal and sea-lion meat, for example), by Christmas most of the sick
were nearly back on their feet.

This put them in a mood to celebrate. Although the only flour remaining was up to three years old and had been impregnated with gunpowder and other substances dissolved in the salt water in the hold, small Christmas cakes were cheerfully made from it and fried in seal fat, and a tea improvised by pouring boiling water over a paste compacted of butter and roasted flour.

With their health, however, the vices of the men returned. They began to gamble obsessively, and to kill sea otters for their skins to use as stakes in their games. Night and day, "nothing but card-playing was to be seen in the dwellings. . . . In the morning, at inspection, no other topic of conversation was heard." Some began to steal the skins from others, and strife spread through the ranks. Before long, their rapacious hunting had driven all the animals away, and it became harder and harder to bring in fresh game. At times, they had to search for many miles along the beach, or to scavenge for dead animals cast up by the sea. By spring, their quest took them over the mountains to the other side of the island, in a pathless scramble of about 12 miles. This was made doubly trying by the suddenness with which the weather sometimes changed. On April 1, 1742, Steller and four others, including a midshipman by the name of Ivan Sind, left camp to hunt, but toward evening a blizzard blew in from the northwest. They became separated from one another, and Steller returned to camp first. Three of the others staggered in at daybreak "out of their mind and unable to speak," and an hour later the midshipman, who during the night had fallen into a brook, was found frozen almost solid on the beach.

Four days later, Steller, Lepikhin, and two others again went out hunting, crossed over to the other side of the island, killed as many sea otters as they could carry back, and pitched camp near a cliff for the night. Another storm arose with so much snow that Lepikhin was soon completely buried under it, while the other two spent the night trying to keep themselves warm by running incessantly to and fro. Steller, by smoking almost constantly, did his best to distract his thoughts from death. At daybreak they finally found shelter in the rocks, although Lepikhin, utterly despondent, had to be "dug out of the snow by force."

As spring came on, the snow melted and the brooks overflowed, flooding the dugouts; but the deluge itself supplied the remedy, uncovering large accumulations of driftwood, which made it easier to build new shelters above ground.

While the rest of the crew gambled away the hours, Steller occupied himself making pipe stems from the wing bones of the albatross, and continuing his scientific work. In addition to maintaining his invaluable journal of the voyage, he wrote, under the incredible hardships of dugout life, a number of treatises, including a classic work on the ichthyology and ornithology of Kamchatka, based on his notes. His "field work" on the island also yielded striking results. For example, he discovered and described the flightless, spectacled cormorant (soon to be extinct), with its comically rotund body and small wings; was the first to measure, dissect, and describe a sea lion; meticulously recorded over the course of six consecutive days (while ensconced in a driftwood hut) the behavior and habits of a colony of fur seals; and preserved through his observation and anatomical study a living portrait of the "sea-cow," whom no scientist would ever see again. Distantly related to the elephant, the sea cow *(Rhytina stelleri)* was a herbivorous mammal and a northern cousin of the manatee. Of prodigious size, it grew up to 30 feet long and weighed from 3 to 4 tons; but despite its rough outer skin, which resembled "the bark of an old oak," it seemed to lead the most vulnerable of lives. "Entire families keep together," noted Steller in his attentive tribute,

> the male with the female, one grown offspring and a little, tender one. To me they appear to be monogamous. They bring forth their young at all seasons, generally however in autumn, judging from the many new-born seen at that time. Nor have I ever seen more than one calf about each cow.
>
> They eat incessantly, and because of their enormous voracity keep their head always under water with but slight concern for their life and security, so that one may pass in the very midst of them in a boat....
>
> In the spring they mate like human beings, particularly towards evening when the sea is calm. Before they come together many amorous preludes take place. The female, constantly followed by the male, swims leisurely to and fro eluding him with many gyrations and meanderings, until, impatient of further delay, she turns on her back as if exhausted and coerced, whereupon the male, rushing violently upon her, pays the tribute of his passion, and both give themselves over in mutual embrace.

Their anthropomorphic habits made sadder still their hapless fate. With food near camp grown scarce, the men fixed their hungry eyes upon them as they moved in and out along the coast "browsing on seaweed with the flowing and ebbing tides." By means of a large iron harpoon, attached to a long, thick rope held by thirty men on shore, the sea cow, hooked from the longboat, was pulled laboriously in. Sometimes members of the herd, hastening to its aid,

> tried to upset the boat with their backs [wrote Steller], while others pressed down the rope and endeavored to break it, or strove to remove the hook from the wound in the back by blows of their tail. . . . It is a most remarkable proof of their conjugal affection that the male, after having tried with all his might, although in vain, to free the female caught by the hook, and in spite of the beating we gave him, nevertheless followed her to the shore, and several times, even after she was dead, shot unexpectedly up to her side like a speeding arrow. Early next morning, when we came to cut up the meat and bring it to the dugout, we found the male again standing by the female, and the same I observed once more on the third day when I went there by myself for the sole purpose of examining the intestines.

On July 12, 1742, Steller attempted to dissect a large female that had been caught and beached. With the careless assistance of a few members of the crew (whom he had to bribe with tobacco to help), in wind and rain, between tides, and with packs of foxes "tearing with their vile teeth and stealing everything from under my very hands," he managed a nearly complete and detailed anatomical analysis that is still regarded by zoologists as a model of its kind.

During the winter, it had been decided that the *St. Peter* had suffered irreparable damage, should be broken up and out of the wreck a smaller vessel built. On April 6, 1742, after a scouting party returned to confirm (what by now everyone suspected) that they were marooned on an island, this plan was settled upon, and it gave the castaways a new purpose and will. Grindstones were dressed and placed in troughs, tools cleaned of rust and sharpened, a smithy erected, charcoal made out of driftwood, and crowbars, iron wedges, and large hammers were forged. All three of the ship's carpenters had died of scurvy, and the only remaining crew member with any mechanical knowledge of ship construction was a Siberian Cossack who had worked under Spanberg in the yards at Okhotsk. Nevertheless, by June the *St. Peter* had been dismantled and the new vessel was in frame, with a keel of 36 feet, a depth of just over 5 feet, and 12 across the beam. By mid-July all its seams had been caulked and the hull painted with tar below the waterline. Water casks were repaired, meat salted, bread baked in preparation for the voyage. Six hundred sea-otter, fur-seal, and fox pelts were also carefully stowed away in the hold. By August 8, the new vessel, christened the hooker *St. Peter* (as the off-spring of the mother ship), was ready to be launched.

Steller's baggage allowance was fixed at 360 pounds, much less than that of the regular officers, though he had assembled sizable collections of plants, animal skeletons, and stuffed skins, including one of a young sea cow, filled with dried grass. None of this was allowed. Aside from his manuscripts, all he could salvage were the dried seeds of 211 species of plants, and a pair of the horny palatal plates which served the sea cow in place of teeth.

On August 11, the forty-six survivors assembled on board. In one of their last acts before departure, a plain cross was placed on Bering's grave, both as a memorial to the man and (in sepulchral grandeur) as a sign that the island belonged to the Russian Crown. It was, of course, Bering Island, one of two in the "Commander" group, so-called in tribute to his rank.

Two days later, as the ship put out to sea, they watched from the deck as the foxes on shore ransacked their former dwellings "with the greatest glee."

Almost immediately the vessel sprang a leak, but with buckets and pumps the situation was brought under control. Over the next four days they were favored by a high, fair wind, and on the morning of the 17th, one of Kamchatka's snow-capped volcanoes came into view. Then their progress was slowed by unfavorable weather for a week. On the 25th, in a veritable frenzy of anticipation, they took to the oars, and brought the ship into Avacha Bay on the following morning.

Somewhat to their surprise, they were greeted almost with misgiving, as men risen from the dead. For months it had been assumed that they had been lost at sea, and (things being scarce on that far shore) with a kind of unseemly haste the property they had left behind had been largely given away. With considerable trepidation, they also now learned the fate of their sister ship, the *St. Paul.*

After the two ships had become separated, the *St. Paul* lingered only briefly in the vicinity before steering northeast. Three weeks later, at one o'clock in the morning, on July 15, 1741 (one day ahead of Bering), Chirikov had also discovered Alaska—north of the 56th parallel, at the panhandle's southern end. Coasting past Prince of Wales Island in search of safe anchorage, he approached Lisyansky Strait about noon on the 17th. The next day, he sent his first mate, Avraam Dementyev, with a Koryak interpreter and ten armed men in the longboat to examine the bay and make a landing if they could. Supplied with trinkets (the same assortment Bering had on board), he was to identify the land, the people, and their resources, and especially to keep an eye out for precious ores.

The longboat entered the bay—then disappeared. Chirikov waited five full days for its return. Not only was there no sign of the men, but none of the prearranged signals of distress were made from shore. Then on July 23 a blaze was spotted on the beach. Chirikov fired his guns, but the flames only grew bigger, and no answering shot was made. Thinking the longboat must have been damaged, he decided to send the boatswain ashore in the yawl with a carpenter, caulker, and sailor. Like the first, the second boat disappeared. Time passed; the ship tacked back and forth; once again Chirikov signaled, without response. Then another bonfire rose up on the beach.

At noon of the following day, two natives in kayaks came out from the bay and when still at a considerable distance stood up and shouted something twice, waved their hands, and paddled back to shore. The Russians waved white handkerchiefs to entice them back, but "it did no good." Their apparent reluctance to come closer made the crew suspect that they had either killed their shipmates or taken them hostage. Chirikov lingered for another day, but the situation of the *St. Paul* fast became desperate. Without boats, the men could not land to replenish their water supply, which was already low, let alone carry out the other instructions connected with the voyage. And by their own reckoning, at least 2,000 miles of ocean lay between them and Petropavlovsk. With extreme reluctance they therefore abandoned their missing compatriots to their fate.

What had happened to Chirikov's men? No one knows. According to one theory, both boats were swamped in rip tides, for at the entrance to Lisyansky Strait there is "a tidal bore of considerable turbulence and power." But among the local Indians the story was later told that in the long ago some white men had been lured ashore by a chief who had dressed himself up in a bearskin and played along the beach. Deceived by his masterful pantomime, they pursued him into the woods, where warriors caught and killed them to a man.

Over the next six weeks, headwinds slowed Chirikov's return. He skirted Kenai Peninsula, made his way westward along the Aleutian chain, and on the morning of September 9, the high, snow-covered mountains of Adak Island to the west came into view. When they drew near the coast, they saw "men walking through the grass across the hills from north to south." The crew called out to them in Chukchi and Russian; a little later they heard voices calling back, but the breaking of the surf drowned out their words. Then seven kayaks came toward the ship, but when still about 100 yards away, they stopped and the men in them stood up and began to shout, "turning first to one side and then to the other, not in the manner as if they wished to speak but as the Yakut and Tungus shamans do in their incantations." The Russians motioned for them to come near, but they imitated the drawing of a bow, as if afraid they might be harmed.

At length, conquering their fears, the natives came alongside to barter, and in return for four arrows, some kind of mineral wrapped in seaweed (which Chirikov identified as antimony or stibnite), and a birchbark hat, the Russians gave them an ax ("which they received gladly") and a copper kettle, which they returned. In the afternoon, fourteen more boats came out to trade. Presented with some needles, the natives, showing "no great gratitude," let them fall into the water and sink. What they really wanted were knives, which they indicated by sawing with their hands in front of their mouths, after the fashion of the Kamchadals when eating meat. When one was offered, "they were quite overjoyed and grabbed each other and begged for more." Divining that the ship needed water, they fetched some in a bladder from shore, but would not yield it until two more knives were produced.

Chirikov could not afford to dally. A thousand bladders of water might have helped him, but already his supply had to be stretched with crudely distilled seawater and rainwater wrung from the sails. By August 1, the men were on rations of buckwheat mush and biscuits, and after September 14 had only cold food. On the whole of their homeward journey, they had just three fair-weather days. Inevitably, scurvy made its appearance, and by the end of September most of the crew was down. From September 21, Chirikov himself was too ill to guide the ship, and had to rely on a heroic sailor, Ivan Yelagin, who remained on deck almost continuously despite his own debilitated state. On October 8 they sighted Kamchatka, but by the time the *St. Paul* entered Avacha Bay and anchored on the 10th, eight men had died, and the only water the ship had left had been boiled out of the brine.

Louis de la Croyère, Steller's counterpart, as it were, on the *St. Paul,* had been bedridden since September 27, and to help him forget his sufferings (physical and otherwise) had taken to drinking "large quantities of brandy every day." As the ship cast anchor, however, he got up, dressed, and merrily prepared to disembark. He broke out another bottle, and expired. "He had the best heart in the world," Gmelin later remarked, "and the greatest desire to do something important and worth while for science. . . . If he had only determined the longitude of the places where he stopped by certain and unquestionable astronomical observations, that truly would have been an important geographical achievement which would have immortalized his name."

That December (although still ravaged by the effects of scurvy) Chirikov bravely proposed a follow-up voyage, both to search for Bering and to continue the expedition's work. Winter passed into spring without word of Bering or his ship, and on May 25, 1742, with an enfeebled crew, Chirikov again sailed east from Avacha Bay. By sheer bad luck he managed to bypass Bering Island, and after exploring the nearby seas without result (except for a reconnaissance of Attu Island), he returned at the end of June. Convinced that any further search was pointless, he sailed for Okhotsk, just a few days before the survivors rowed their hooker into port.

. . .

Remarkably, during almost all this time Spanberg had been trying to assemble the necessary supplies and build the ships for his redundant Japanese voyage. Although "discouraged and disgusted at this useless and purposeless repetition of his previous achievement," he had built the *St. John,* readied the *Archangel Michael,* the *Hope,* and *Bolsheretsk,* transported supplies across the Yablonoy Mountains to Okhotsk, and finally, on May 23, 1742, set out for Japan. He landed at Shumshu, the first of the Kurile Islands, where an interpreter was taken on board, but on June 4 lost sight of the *Archangel Michael* and the *Hope* in fog. Eight days later, off Kunashir, he also lost sight of the *Bolsheretsk.* After a leak developed in the hold of his own ship, the *St. John,* he returned to Shumshu, where the other vessels had already reassembled, and sailed back to Bolsheretsk.

The voyage was a complete waste.

Back in Kamchatka, the indefatigable Steller took up his survey of the peninsula where he'd left off two years before. He explored its southern end (visiting also the first three Kurile Islands), and crossed northern Kamchatka to Anadyrsk. At one point, he hoped to travel into the Kolyma Basin down to the Arctic Ocean, in search of mammoth remains. Early in 1744, however, he started back down the coast but, constitutionally unable to resist adventure, at one point tried to cross the ice of the Bering Sea to an island 15 miles offshore. When he had gone a considerable distance, the ice broke and his dogs and sledge tumbled into the sea. With desperate agility, he somehow managed to jump from one ice floe to another all the way back to land.

Upon his return to Bolsheretsk, Steller became involved in Kamchatkan politics. A succession of petty despots had recently directed the local administration, and he lodged a formal complaint against one of them for oppressing the Kamchadals. The commandant, in turn, formally accused Steller of encouraging the natives to rebel. Given the government's continuing anxiety about regional security, this was a grave charge—and Steller would indirectly pay for it with his life.

About this time, he had evidently begun to drink heavily, and loneliness had made him nostalgic for what had never been. During his years in Siberia, he had kept up an intermittent correspondence with his wife, and the memory of his original feeling for her had created illusory images of what might yet be. From Bolsheretsk he even had written to her that he "wished nothing more than to see her again."

As the Great Northern Expedition officially drew to a close, Steller was recalled to St. Petersburg, and with sixteen packing cases full of specimens and manuscripts, he sailed to Okhotsk in August 1744. By October he was at Yakutsk, and by the following spring at Irkutsk. There he was confronted with the earlier accusations made against him, but was unconditionally acquitted once the circumstances were explained. From Irkutsk, he sped westward over the winter trail, reached Tomsk by the end of January 1746, and Tobolsk in March, where he fatefully clashed with the governor, who willfully delayed forwarding his acquittal to St. Petersburg.

This had the saddest results. After passing through customs at Ver-khoturye, in April he arrived at Solikamsk, just above the Kama River, and was there hospitably received by Grigory Demidov, an amateur botanist and heir to the family's industrial empire. Steller botanized in the vicinity and planted the seeds of about eighty species of shrubs and herbs in Demidov's garden; but on August 16, 1746, he found himself suddenly confronted by a special Senate courier, who was charged with conducting him back to Irkutsk for trial. Protestations of his innocence were useless, and after entrusting the care of his papers, notes, specimens, and other scientific effects to colleagues and friends, he set out again for Siberia on August 18, 1746. By the time he got to Tara, however, word came that he had been cleared. Reversing his course, he passed three festive weeks in Tobolsk, and then one day toward the beginning of November, he crawled into his covered sledge and set out for Tyumen 170 miles away.

En route, the story goes, his escort stopped one night at a tavern, leaving Steller drunk and asleep in the sledge outside. When they returned, they found him burning up with fever, and by the time they got to Tyumen he was barely alive. Despite the diligent efforts of two naval surgeons, he died later that day.

At the time of his death, Steller was thirty-seven years old.

As Tyumen had no Protestant cemetery, he was interred on a high bluff on the right bank of the Tura River, just outside the town. The snow-covered ground was frozen hard, so that only a shallow grave could be made. A few days later, grave robbers dug the body up and left it in the snow, a prey to wolves and dogs. Some friends reinterred it, and placed a boulder over the mound. In time, however, the river's erosion wore away the bank to where the gravesite stood, and Steller's bones, in the words of one of his great successors, Peter Simon Pallas, were "mingled with the bones of the mammoth on its farther shores."

Steller's pioneering work enriched the field for other naturalists, who went on to enjoy more lasting fame. But on Bering Island and in Alaska mountains have been named for him, and he is discreetly commemorated, in a manner that would surely have pleased him, in the Latin names for a number of animals and plants.

Unfortunately, no known portrait of him survives.

Steller's remarkable personality and gifts should not obscure what his two great colleagues, Müller and Gmelin, also achieved. Although prevented by circumstance (and to some degree, their own inclination) from exploring the wildest part of the Russian east, their wanderings took them up and down most of the major rivers and to many distant locales. Between 1733 and 1743, they traveled over 24,000 miles throughout Siberia, and in the end made contributions to their specialties which assured their international fame. Gmelin returned to Tübingen as a professor of botany and chemistry, and on the basis of his careful description and classification of 1,178 species of Siberian plants (contained in a four-volume *Flora sibirica,* printed in St. Petersburg in 1747), the great Linnaeus was moved to exclaim that Gmelin had "discovered more new plants than all other botanists combined." Müller's name would become even more widely known. His collection and description of official and unofficial archival sources proved all but exhaustive. In addition to copious notes based on his observations of the languages and cultures of various tribes, he returned to St. Petersburg with more than thirty folios filled with copies of original documents. He was the first to describe the circumstances of Siberia's early conquest and settlement, and to give some account of the pioneering voyages of discovery, including that of Semyon Dezhnev, whose story emerged from material found in the archives of Yakutsk. In his lifetime, Müller was designated "historiographer of the Russian Empire"; posterity salutes him as the "father of Siberian history."

• • •

In the aftermath of the Great Northern Expedition, the government found it difficult to suppress information that emerged about it, despite concern that if some of the discoveries became known, they might tempt other powers to act against Russia in some way. On January 27, 1746, the Senate demanded that the Academy of Sciences surrender all documents pertaining to the Japanese expeditions; on March 7, it prohibited the publication of the Pacific discoveries; and one month later, on the night of April 7, the professors were told that all remaining charts relating to the expedition, "rough drafts and clean copies, as well as those made on post-paper, all that exist, written or printed, nothing omitted, likewise the reports and descriptions from this same expedition recently sent to the Academy of Adjunct Steller, of whatever kind they may be, are to be brought to Her Imperial Majesty's Cabinet the next day in the morning." The professors made haste to comply, with Müller himself gathering up all the items required.

Meanwhile, Joseph Delisle had been placed under surveillance for sending maps and other documents to France without authorization, and after he returned to Paris in 1747, members of the Academy were forbidden to correspond with him. In 1750, Delisle published his own account of the expedition anyway, in which he claimed credit for every one of its achievements. Müller penned a withering rebuttal at the Academy's behest, which appeared in both French and German in 1753.

As for the naval personnel, Chirikov was promoted to the rank of captain-commander in 1745; Waxell to captain-commander in 1758; and Khitrov, Steller's nemesis, was made rear admiral in 1753.

At the beginning of the eighteenth century, very little had actually been known of Siberia's geographical extent. By the end of the Great Northern Expedition, not only was its configuration clear, but its human and natural history had been surveyed and assessed. Some broad, if tentative, determinations had also been made as to its needs. Moreover, the Russians had eliminated Juan de Gama Land and Company Land from their maps, had sketched in Hokkaido and several of the Kurile Islands, had charted the longest Arctic coastline in the world, and had rediscovered America from its Pacific side. The final conquest and settlement of Eastern Siberia had also begun. While the First Kamchatka Expedition had disclosed the poorly developed state of the Okhotsk seaboard and the Kamchatka Peninsula, the Second saw their settlement assume a viable form. The whole support apparatus of the expedition in the form of living quarters, storage depots, port facilities, iron foundries, saltworks, administrative offices, and so on, together with the transformation of Okhotsk into a port and the founding of Petropavlovsk, formed the nucleus of the future Russian communities on those far shores. New towns like Tigilsk and Gizhiga were born, and Okhotsk and the main Kamchatka settlements doubled or tripled in size. Peasants and others, transplanted to the region, made a start with farming and animal husbandry, and various skilled artisans set up shop and practiced their trades. Although not numerically large, the influx, proportionately, was substantial, as merchants, soldiers, Cossacks, exiles, clerics, and others all found a place for themselves in a once-desolate land.

11

RUSSIAN AMERICA

WITHIN two years of Bering's final expedition, notes one historian, "reports of the blue fox, fur seal, and sea otter abounding in the islands east of Kamchatka had spread through Eastern Siberia. Just as the sable had enticed fur hunters across the Ural Mountains and the vast Siberian plains to the Pacific Ocean, so the sea otter lured the Russians ever farther out among the fog-bound islands lying between Asia and North America." The search for skins led them first to the Commander Islands, then to the Aleutians, and finally to the mainland of Alaska. Between 1743 and 1764, there were forty-two hunting or trading expeditions from Kamchatka to the Aleutian Islands alone, most organized by small groups of traders and carried out in makeshift vessels manned by illiterate and lawless crews. The naval expeditions of Bering, Chirikov, and Spanberg had shown the way, but the scrimmage for advantage in the North Pacific thereafter was the rough-and-ready work of Cossack adventurers and *promyshlenniks*. The familiar pattern of the Siberian conquest was repeated—with a ruthless exploitation of the aborigines, and the wanton slaughter of the creatures from whom the Russians derived their wealth. Over the next several years, individual enterprise inspired by piratical greed explored the unknown waters and marked out its island dominions for the Crown. In culmination of this process, the founding of Russian America was a direct extension of the conquest of Siberia, and the natural result of the Russians' eastward drive "to meet the sun."

Extending in an 1,100-mile-long arc or pendulant chain from the tip of the Alaska Peninsula to Attu Island, the Aleutians were a partially submerged volcanic range, with mountains that rose steeply from the coast and reef-fringed rocky shores scoured by the pounding surf. For the most part, nothing grew on these rugged isles but low and creeping brush, and it was not until the Russians had almost reached the mainland of Alaska that they came to one that had any standing trees. Some of the islands had active volcanoes, others (like Atka) showed traces of their fiery birth in sulfurous boiling springs; but however inhospitable, their fur and related peltry wealth was great. On the Commander and Near islands (that is, those nearest to Kamchatka), the only land animals to be found were Arctic foxes, which had originally come from the mainland on drifting ice and had "multiplied remarkably," feeding on what the tide brought in. On other islands, in addition to foxes, there were bears, wolves, river otters, beavers, and martens, sea otters in abundance off the coasts, and in the surrounding ocean seals, sea lions, dolphins, and whales. Eventually, the Aleutians were distinguished into groups, called (from east to west): the Commander, Near, Rat, Andreanov, and Fox. Associated with them were also the Pribylov or Seal Islands (St. Paul and St. George, and the much smaller Otter Island and Walrus Rock). In all, there were seventy-odd islands, but in just thirty-five years the fur rush in the North Pacific would reveal the whole Aleutian chain.

Inhabiting most of them were the Aleuts, a people possessing little tribal organization and related to the Eskimo. So-called after the Teleuty, a Mongolian tribe of similar physique inhabiting the province of Tomsk, the Aleuts were of medium height, with long black hair, a flat and swarthy countenance, and eyes black as coal. In general, their faces were severely tattooed, and bone and bead decorations were worn in their noses and lower lips. The lip ornaments were often quite prominent, and the Chukchi called them *Zubati,* which means "men with big teeth."

Like the Paleosiberians (Chukchi, Koryak, Yukaghir, and Kamchadal), they belonged to the Stone Age and their only implements were those of bone or stone. Even so, their natural technology was worthy of note, no less than that of other tribes. Their one-man *baydarka,* or kayak—essentially a small decked canoe—was light enough to be carried with one hand yet was "a practically unsinkable" craft.

Made to the "severest symmetry of ship construction" (in the words of one naval historian), it had a light driftwood frame over which seal skin or walrus hide was tautly stretched. There was a circular opening toward the stern where the paddler sat, and about it was sewn a gutskin strip or hem that opened and closed like a purse. The Aleut tightened the hem around his body and fastened it with a bowknot, so that the water could not get in. This, in effect, made the man and the boat one. Two inflatable fur-seal bladders were kept under the deck to serve as floats, and a third, filled with fresh water, was furnished with a hollow stalk, like a straw. In such a craft, an Aleut could maneuver without fear even in the most turbulent seas.

The Aleuts lived from the sea. At different times of the year they hunted fur seals, sea otters, porpoises, sea lions, and whales. Their common garments were birdskin parkas (made from bellies of the horned puffin, with the feather side turned in) and capes of whale or seal-lion gut. Seal skin furnished their trousers, and the esophagi of sea lions their knee-length boots. Their familiar sea cap resembled an eyeshade, with a painted wooden visor projecting over the eyes "like a duck's bill." This was adorned with sea-lion whiskers strung with beads and little bone figurines. The women wore delicately embroidered headgear, and did their fine needlework in hair or fish gut with needles cut from the femoral bones of gulls. These needles had no eye, but a very narrow groove to which the thread was so artfully fastened that it followed the needle without a slip. Their yarn was made from fox sinew, and their rope from the sinews of sea lions, porpoises, and whales.

Much like the Kamchadals, the Aleuts lived in semi-underground earthen huts with a driftwood frame, roofed and thatched with long dry grass. In a communal arrangement, these were divided by short partitions into open stalls, the space in the middle serving as a latrine. Light was provided by stone lamps, which typically consisted of a stone dish filled with train oil around a wick of twisted moss. Raw fish, meat, berries, and roots made up the whole of their cuisine.

The men were polygamous, and (it was said) not prone to jealousy so long as the wayward wife was discreet. Wealthier Aleuts had up to six wives, and if a man married a widow who had a daughter, he slept with them both. But on the whole Aleut women were reputedly more chaste than the Kamchadals, and not driven by that "rank compulsion" which the Russians pretended to abhor. Among the Aleuts there were also a number of "female men," who dressed as the women did, did women's work, and "as an object of unnatural affection" sometimes accompanied men on distant hunting expeditions, "with needle and yarn."

Like other Siberian peoples, Aleut mythology about the origin of humanity vaguely anticipated the theory of evolution, yet savored of biblical themes. It held, for example, that at first a dog came and "gave birth to two humanoid creatures with very hairy backs." Successive generations gradually became less hairy and more human, but as they multiplied, wars began to develop, and they withdrew to various islands and "began to make distinctions." Reflecting their difficult lives, Aleuts called themselves by names meaning "one caught in a struggle," or "those driven from their island out of fear." Nevertheless, within their own communities, everyone shared the fruits of their labor, and the aged, sick, and orphaned were never left without care. This custom of mutual assistance was so deeply lodged that even after years of exploitation by the Russians, Aleuts still found it "very strange to see anyone begging for help."

The first Americans sighted by Bering's Second Expedition, of course, were two Aleuts in skin *baydarkas,* and when the Russians began their conquest of the islands, there were probably about 25,000 Aleuts in all. Sixty-five years later there were only 2,500 left, and these were much mixed with Russian blood.

The first trader to follow in the wake of Bering's expedition was Yemelyan Basov, a sergeant in the Nizhnekamchatsk command. In a boat named the *Kapiton,* Basov sailed in 1743 directly to Bering Island, wintered there, and returned with a rich cargo of fox, fur-seal, and sea-otter pelts. In 1745, backed by a Muscovite merchant, he led a second expedition to Copper Island (another in the Commander group), which resulted in a harvest of 1,600 sea-otter, 2,000 fur-seal, and 2,000 blue fox skins.

News of his success spread quickly. The fort commander at Bolsheretsk, who had just married the wayward widow of de la Croyère, next sponsored a drive to search for new islands, led by Mikhail Nevodchikov, the sex offender who had failed to repair de la Croyère's clocks. Nevodchikov set out from the mouth of the Kamchatka River and reached the Near Islands (Attu and Agattu), which were inhabited by Aleuts. He first attempted a landing on Agattu, but reconsidered when swarms of natives began paddling toward him in kayaks from the shore. Meeting a quieter reception on Attu, the Russians took advantage of Aleut hospitality—at a spot known to this day as "Massacre Bay"—and raped a number of the women, slaughtering the men who came to their aid. Upon his return to Kamchatka, Nevodchikov was empowered to oversee the collection of tribute from the islands he had found.

Without any larger purpose (and in complete disregard of Peter the Great's long-term aims), fur-bearing animals were gradually exterminated from the islands close to Kamchatka, as the adventurers drifted from one landfall to the next; between 1750 and 1775, up to a dozen ships a year set out on these island-hopping forays. These were not such ships as Bering and Spanberg had built, but rough descendants of the inland rivercraft used by the Cossacks in their Siberian conquest, and of the North Russian single-masted koch. As often as not, they were hastily knocked together with raw timber and wooden pegs, and "sewn" or lashed together in places with leather thongs, twigs, or roots. In such vessels, Andreyan Tolstykh had discovered the Andreanovs (named in his honor) between 1746 and 1765, and Gerasim Pribylov the Pribylovs. In 1759, the Cossack Stepan Glotov reached the islands of Umnak and Unalaska at the eastern end of the Aleutian chain. Four years later, in September 1763, he disembarked on Kodiak Island off the Alaskan Peninsula, and the following summer undertook a reconnaissance along the peninsula's southern coast.

Reports of the furry wealth of the Kuriles had also precipitated a rapacious descent down those islands, although their exploitation was a relatively minor branch of the fur trade that ensued.

Despite the daring of many individual mariners, little in the conquest would give rise to heroic song. Even where *promyshlenniks* at first lived on friendly terms with the natives, the mercenary lust and greed of the Russians finally provoked them to revenge. Unlike many Siberian peoples, the Aleuts had never paid tribute to anyone, and in the winter of 1762, feeling themselves unbearably oppressed, they seized and burned three Russian ships on Umnak and Unalaska and killed the crews. The following spring new *promyshlenniks* appeared, and when they learned of the fate of their comrades, they retaliated, destroying whole settlements without mercy to woman or child. One of the Russians, Ivan Solovyev, amused himself by binding a dozen Aleuts together in a row, one behind the other, to see how many a single musket ball would pierce. "He learned from experience," wrote one of his compatriots, "that a bullet would pass through nine and lodge in the tenth man."

Meanwhile, lack of strict government supervision, combined with reports of the fabulous profits to be made, lured merchants to Kamchatka from all over the empire. And for a time they had almost a free hand. As the seaborne trade developed, there was little attempt at first to regulate it, while Siberia's immense size, inadequate communications, and administrative character made it difficult for the capital to exercise much control. The governor was at Tobolsk, Eastern Siberia was administered by a vice-governor at Irkutsk, who left the government of northeastern Siberia to Yakutsk. Yakutsk left the seaboard and Kamchatka to Okhotsk, where petty official despotism and corruption were the rule. Since most officials looked upon service in Eastern Siberia, or Kamchatka especially, as equivalent to banishment, they sought compensation for their miseries in semi-lawless and acquisitive schemes. The dispensation of justice was capricious at best, and since colonial officials often wore many hats, the official who judged a complaint was sometimes the one against whom it had been made.

The government was not disinterested, of course. The first reports of Basov's voyages, together with Nevodchikov's maps of the Near Islands and other navigation charts, had all been sent to St. Petersburg, along with samples of copper from Copper Island which were analyzed by the Academy of Sciences and pronounced almost pure. A few years later, an official mineralogist was dispatched to the island, where on the northwest promontory, beneath shattered cliffs of limestone and slate, he found lumps of solid copper as large as an egg. But the government of the empress Elizabeth, daughter of Peter the Great, decided that heavy state investment in the remote northeastern regions had produced a poor return, and this was true enough: the Arctic expeditions (despite their ultimate success) had demonstrated the impracticality of the Northeast Passage for commercial use; and the American voyages had failed to find deposits of gold or silver, or any native peoples prepared to swear allegiance to the Crown. Only the pelts

brought back by Bering's beleaguered crew indicated the new prospects, but their extent did not become apparent until the *promyshlenniks* showed the way.

The natives in the Siberian northeast, moreover, were restless. Although the Kamchadals lacked heart for further resistance (and suicide
had begun to compete with disease in reducing their ranks), between
1745 and 1755 the Koryaks carried out a number of successful raids on
Russian outposts and burned the fort of Atlansk to the ground.

The Chukchi were harder to tame. They rejected *yasak,* survived
numerous campaigns (led by Major Dmitry Pavlutsky) against them,
virtually exterminated the Yukaghirs (whom they despised as Russian
allies), drove off herds of reindeer kept by the Russians for transportation and food, and so forth. On the night of March 12, 1747, Pavlutsky
gathered ninety-seven Cossacks and thirty-five Koryaks together for a
retaliatory strike, and at dawn on the 14th sighted six hundred Chukchi
camped on a mountainside. Without waiting for reinforcements, he
attacked. In a sort of Russian version of Custer's Last Stand, the famous
Chukchi fighter was quickly encircled and trapped. By evening he had
fallen, along with most of his companions, as the attackers captured all
their arms, a cannon, the company flag, and Pavlutsky's marshaling
drum. When news of the defeat reached St. Petersburg, the Siberian
Department dispatched five hundred dragoons to the Anadyr Basin,
and their repeated onslaughts at last obliged the Chukchi to give way.
In 1756, a Chukchi delegation came to Anadyrsk to sue for peace, and
agreed to a token *yasak* of one fox skin per man. This was acceptable
to the government, and gave it an excuse to abandon the fort at Anadyrsk, which had long been prohibitively expensive to maintain. Between 1710 and 1764, it had earned only 29,152 rubles, yet had cost
the Treasury 1,381,000 rubles, including 841,760 just for supplies. In
1770, it was reduced to the status of a trading post.

In North Pacific waters, aside from widespread efforts on the part of
traders to avoid payment of the regulation tithe, reports of the "outrage
and oppression" that marked the *promyshlennik* advance had begun
to annoy the government as further evidence that its jurisdiction was
being defied. The government was also unhappy about the contradic-
tory geographical information it was getting from the trading captains,

some of whom fudged their reports to conceal the location of various islands that were being kept as private hunting preserves. After 1760, expeditions of any size were supposed to have special government agents on board, but many secret, unauthorized voyages were still launched.

In 1762, the empress Elizabeth died, and was succeeded by her nephew, Peter III. Peter was promptly murdered by the adherents of his wife, Sophie Anhalt-Zerbst, who was enthroned as Catherine II, known to history as Catherine the Great. Catherine decided that naval expeditions were required to consolidate Russian authority in the area, assess its resources, bring order to the fur trade, and correct the maps. In May 1765, Lieutenant Ivan Sind (a veteran of the Second Bering Expedition and a member of Bering's shipwrecked crew) made an initial survey of the seas east of Kamchatka, and was followed by Lieutenant Mikhail Levashev and Captain Petr Krenitsyn, who achieved greater success. Despite groundings, shipwreck, scurvy, and other setbacks, they managed to survey and chart a number of the western Aleutians, including Unalaska (where they spent a grueling winter under virtual siege in their driftwood camp), and assembled enough data for a creditable map of the North Pacific to be made.

In the process, they also helped solve a lingering geographical puzzle: the exact identity of the coast discovered by Bering and Chirikov in 1741. It should be remembered that the latter did not know that they had discovered Alaska, but merely assumed they had found some part of the American coast. It was during their Aleutian hunting forays that the Russians first actually learned of "forested Alakshak," as the natives called it, when an Eskimo prisoner of war, held by Stepan Glotov in 1759–60 on the island of Umnak, drew a map in the sand and indicated by big and little stones the size and position of various islands. The Russians made a copy of this map, using "charred wood and colored clays," and identified Alakshak as a very large island. Four years later, Mikhail Lomonosov, Russia's great eighteenth-century polymath, correctly suggested that Alakshak "was in fact the 'cape' of North America." Part of the mission of Krenitsyn and Levashev had been to determine if this were so. They concluded that it was, and by the early 1780s there was no longer any doubt that the "Big Land" opposite the Chukchi Peninsula about which the Russians had heard for so long, and "forested Alakshak," were the same.

In partial fulfillment of their mandate, Krenitsyn and Levashev also collected invaluable information on the habits and condition of the Aleuts. But they had little anthropological patience for their subjects, and tended only to emphasize the brutish circumstance of Stone Age lives:

> In their persons we should reckon them extremely nasty. They eat the vermin with which their bodies are covered, and swallow the mucus from the nose. Having washed themselves according to custom, first with urine, and then with water, they suck their hands dry. When they are sick, they lie three or four days without food; and if bleeding is necessary, they open a vein with lancets made of flint, and suck the blood. Their principal nourishment is fish and whale fat, which they commonly eat raw. They also feed upon sea-wrack and roots, particularly the saran, a species of lily; they eat an herb, called kutage, engage in frequent and bloody quarrels, and commit murder without the least compunction. Their disposition engages them in continual wars, in which they always endeavour to gain their point by stratagem. The inhabitants of Unimak are formidable to all the rest; they frequently invade the other islands, and carry off women, the chief object of their wars. They all join in hating the Russians, whom they consider as general invaders, and therefore kill them wherever they can.

Such a report might have been used to justify a continuing Russian onslaught, but elsewhere it also unflinchingly revealed the extent of the Russian brutality, and spurred efforts to curb the exploitation and abuse.

Most of the early North Pacific trading companies were formed for single, speculative ventures, and consisted of groups of investors who banded together to finance the outfitting of a ship and crew in a simple arrangement that shared the spoils. The crews were typically half-Russian and half-Kamchadal (the latter being "compelled to the sea service" at almost no pay), and sailed from Okhotsk or Kamchatka in late summer or early fall, wintered on Copper or Bering Island, where they reprovisioned with dried sea-cow and sea-lion meat, then started for the eastern islands at the end of the following spring. Upon reaching their destination, the crew divided up into groups to hunt and trap animals on the island, supervise sea-otter-hunting expeditions by the Aleuts, or guard the ship and supplies. Such voyages lasted up to four years, or (as a rule) until enough pelts had been taken to pay at least twice the cost of fitting them out. The health and safety of the men were given little account, provisions were inadequate, and it was normal to lose about one-fourth of the men to disease. About a quarter of the cheaply built galiots were smashed to pieces on the rocks, or went down in the rough and stormy seas.

The sea otter was the foundation of the maritime fur trade, and the Aleuts, who were far more skillful than the Russians in hunting at sea, were more ruthlessly exploited than any other aboriginal group. Compulsory labor was exacted, together with tribute, even after 1788 when the latter was banned; so that, in effect, the Aleuts were enslaved. Although 350,000 pelts or so were still being taken out of Siberia each year (thanks largely to the conquest of Kamchatka), about 85 percent of Russia's vital commerce with China was based on the new sea-otter catch, since the other turned out to have the pelt the Chinese valued most. The Russians made tremendous profit by their mark-up, one skin being valued at 10 to 15 rubles in Kamchatka but at 60 to 80 rubles in Kyakhta by the Chinese. In exchange, Russians acquired silk, gems, gold and silver, ivory, porcelain, and tea, and by the 1780s up to ten thousand Russian carts a year carried Chinese goods from Kyakhta to Irkutsk.

The Aleutian fur trade and concerns associated with it, including coastal defense, sustained the growth of colonization on the seaboard and in Kamchatka which the Great Northern Expedition had begun. The streets swarmed with sailors, soldiers, natives, laborers, and exiles, while prosperous merchants attempted a rough imitation of polite society at the uttermost confines of civilization. The Russian population of the peninsula alone increased from about 500 (in 1725) to over 5,000, and in the coastal settlements life pulsed feverishly, with strenuous work by day and drinking, gambling and brawling at night. By European standards, of course, Okhotsk and Petropavlovsk didn't look like much, but their hundred or so dwellings, storehouses, and shops (however poorly stocked) compared favorably with what had been there before.

About a quarter of the Russians in the Far East were exiles, and

among those stranded was one Maurice August Benyowski, an audacious, swashbuckling adventurer and confidence man. Born in Hun-
gary, Benyowski had originally emigrated to Poland where (as part of
a guerrilla band) he had fought against the Russian occupation force.
Twice captured, at his second interrogation he passed himself off as a
Polish count, and was exiled to Yakutsk. En route, he forged new
orders assigning him to Kamchatka, from where he hoped to escape
by sea. At Bolsheretsk, he mingled with other exiles, and drew a number of them into his plans. At the same time, he contrived to ingratiate
himself with the local commandant, Captain Grigory Nilov, an inveter-
ate alcoholic, who entrusted him with the education of his son. On
April 24, 1771, Benyowski and about seventy confederates over-
powered the guards, who were "too drunk to resist," murdered Nilov,
and looted the local treasury. They then drew up a bombastic manifesto condemning the Russian occupation of Poland, high taxes, official
corruption, the state monopoly on salt and wine, and so on, and sailed
off into the Pacific on a government ship with a treasure in furs and
several women and girls.

Making their way down the Kurile Island chain, they eventually
reached Macao, where Benyowski embarked on a French frigate for
Mauritius in the Indian Ocean. From there he reached France, entered
government service, and was sent to Madagascar, where he founded a
colony in 1774. In 1777, he met the Polish general Casimir Pulaski in
Paris and tried to interest him in a project to turn Madagascar into an
American base against Great Britain. Benjamin Franklin became enamored of this scheme, and furnished him with letters of introduction
to George Washington. Benyowski (pretending to be an agent of the
French Foreign Ministry) met with Washington in 1782 and offered to
raise a foreign legion of three thousand men to fight in the Revolutionary War. Washington forwarded the plan to the Continental Congress,
where it was more soberly scrutinized and scrapped. Benyowski then
turned to the slave trade, and in Baltimore persuaded several Swiss
merchants to finance an expedition to Madagascar. He raised a corps
of freebooters, landed in 1784, and tried to set himself up as the
island's king. Two years later, he met his death when a French amphibious force stormed the stronghold he had built for himself into the
side of a hill.

Boieldieu would later write a comic opera based on his exploits, including his escape from Kamchatka, but Catherine the Great was traumatized. She immediately decided that the settlement of political exiles in the Siberian northeast jeopardized Russia's situation there instead of adding to its colonial base, and (perhaps over-anxiously) connected the incident to larger events.

The North Pacific was potentially disputed terrain. Even as the Russians were pushing their way toward Alaska from the west, the Spaniards were approaching it from the south and the English, through Canada, steadily from the east. Spain claimed the whole area as its patrimony by right of a papal dispensation dating from 1493 (which had divided the discoverable world between the Spanish and the Portuguese), and had recently dispatched a new Spanish ambassador to St. Petersburg to find out how much of the North Pacific the Russians already possessed. Although Catherine had resolved on securing not only the Kurile Islands and the Aleutians, but the American coast itself above 55 degrees 21' north latitude for the Crown, her policy of surrogate expansion (that is, acting unofficially through private traders and entrepreneurs) remained tenable only so long as it prevented a clash with other powers. Reports of Russian incursions had already spurred Spanish Jesuits in California to expand their missions up the coast, and by 1770 presidios or garrisons had been founded at San Diego and Monterey. The Russians evidently even feared a preemptive Spanish attack, and in September 1770 they began to stockpile guns, ammunition, and provisions at Petropavlovsk and to enlarge the defenses of Okhotsk, which at the time consisted of nothing but a simple square surrounded by a palisade. Benyowski had witnessed these preparations, knew their extent (or lack thereof), and had gone off with top-secret information, which he was sure to sell. In 1772, Catherine therefore declared the Aleutians under the jurisdiction of the commander at Bolsheretsk—that is, an extension of Siberia.

Declarations of sovereignty, however, were not the same as showing the flag, which was soon brought home to the government as the British entered the scene. In what was to be the final expedition of his great career, Captain James Cook, aboard the *Resolution,* sailed in 1776 with a second ship, *Discovery,* from England to the North Pacific in search of the Northwest Passage. After discovering the Sandwich, or Hawaiian, Islands, he continued north along the American coast to Alaska, rounded Kenai Peninsula to Cook Inlet, which he carefully explored for the fabled passage he sought, passed south of Kodiak Island, and near Shumagin Island met natives who, to his surprise, showed him a document in Russian. After passing Cape Prince of Wales, which he named, he crossed Bering Strait to the Asiatic coast, and arriving off East Cape, saw what Bering had missed. "The weather becoming clear, we had the opportunity of seeing, at the same moment," he wrote, "the remarkable peaked hill, near Cape Prince of Wales, on the coast of America, and the East Cape of Asia, with the two connecting islands of Saint Diomede between them." Returning to Alaska, he discovered and named Norton Bay, left reports and letters with the Russians at Unalaska to be sent to Britain by way of Kamchatka, and proceeded to the Hawaiian Islands, where he intended to winter before continuing his explorations in the spring.

On February 14, 1777, however, Cook had a bloody confrontation with the natives, and in a fatal instant, as he turned his back, a native struck him on the head with a club and plunged a dagger into his neck. When it was realized aboard the *Resolution* that England's greatest captain was dead, "a general silence ensued throughout the ship, for the space of half an hour: it appearing to us," recalled a shipmate, "somewhat like a Dream that we could not reconcile ourselves to for some time. Grief was visible in every Countenance ... for as all our hopes centered in him; our loss became irreparable and the sense of it was so deeply impressed upon our minds as not to be forgot." It was left to Cook's fellow commander, Charles Clerke, to faithfully complete his voyage. In the spring of 1779, Clerke returned to the North Pacific and in the course of his survey of coastal waters docked at Petropavlovsk. The Russians at first suspected the English of being pirates, and the size of the English ships (considerably larger than any of their own) raised alarm. When a party was invited on board, two Russian officials refused to come until two sailors were given as hostages for their own security. But eventually everything was clarified, and the Russians agreed not only to reprovision the English ships, but to safely convey copies of Cook's Journal overland to St. Petropavlovsk, and from there ship them to England. From Petropavlovsk, Clerke sailed north through Bering Strait, but was soon turned back by pack ice, and —desperately ill himself—died as he reentered the Russian port.

His lieutenants took over command of the vessels, sailing south past Japan, and anchoring at Macao, a Portuguese colony on the China coast.

There they learned that the revolt of the American colonies had led to hostilities between England and France, which put them at risk of attack from both French and American vessels on their journey home. This dramatic news, however, was quickly overshadowed by their discovery that Chinese merchants were prepared to pay large sums of money for the sea-otter pelts they had picked up for almost nothing on the Alaskan coast. Even damaged skins turned an enormous profit, and most of the sailors (in a near-mutinous state) wanted to return to Alaska for more furs.

As a result of Cook's last voyage, by 1783 the world knew of the possible fortunes to be reaped in the fur trade; within a short time numerous British traders, putting out from Macao and the East Indies, ventured into the North Pacific, inaugurating a new epoch in its history. Most sea-otter pelts were sold or bartered at the Chinese port of Canton, and this sudden competition threatened to undermine the once-secure profits of Russia's exclusive trade. Cook himself had remarked how much value the Russians placed upon it. Meeting some *promysh-lenniks* on the Alaskan coast in 1778, he noted in his Journal: "Never was there greater respect paid to the memory of any distinguished person, than by these men to that of Bering . . . whose misfortunes proved to be the source of much private advantage to individuals, and of public utility to the Russian nation."

Taken together, reports of Cook's reconnaissance along the Aleutians, his stops at Alaska and Kamchatka, his (and Clerke's) exploration of the coastal waters north and south of Bering Strait, and of "persistent British probing in an area claimed by Russia" led to a change in Russian policy. "The Empress," reported the British ambassador to St. Petersburg, "expressed a *very* earnest desire of having Copys of such Charts as may tend to ascertain more precisely the extent & position of . . . her Empire." Artillery was dragged all the way from Irkutsk to Petropavlovsk, and in 1786 the government decided that the time had come to consolidate and (if necessary) defend the coastal waters it claimed. Ambitious plans were laid for an expedition of five three-masted ships, fully equipped and armed, to sail halfway around the world from the Baltic, to officially take possession of all North Pacific territories from the Kurile Islands to Alaska. At various points along the North American coast 1,700 iron and copper plates were to be secretly buried, each inscribed with the date and proclaiming in both Latin and

Russian: "This territory belongs to the Russian Empire." Any crests or signs that might be found belonging to any other power were to be leveled and destroyed. An impending war in the West forced cancelation of this mission, but meanwhile the French had mounted their own North Pacific expedition (1786–88) under Count Jean-François de la Pérouse. In addition to discovering La Perouse Strait between the Japanese island of Hokkaido and Sakhalin Island, he took on board six hundred sea-otter pelts for the Canton trade; and right on his heels came the Boston captain, Robert Gray, sailing up the Oregon coast. Gray discovered the estuary of the Columbia River (named for his sloop), took a shipload of skins to Canton, and from there sailed westward on to Boston—the first American skipper to circumnavigate the globe.

The first contact between a Russian and an American in the Pacific, incidentally, had already taken place on October 8, 1778, when Captain Cook, docking at Unalaska, had sent the American John Ledyard, a seaman in his service, ashore. Ledyard became aware of the lucrative sea-otter trade, and hoping to profit from it, sought Thomas Jefferson's backing for a quixotic solo expedition, in which he proposed to cross Siberia (west to east) to Kamchatka, embark for Alaska on a Russian ship, and from there walk to the Mississippi with "two large hunting dogs, an Indian peace pipe, and a hatchet for chopping firewood." Jefferson thought he was crazy, but, tantalized by the "new, curious & useful information" such an adventure might produce, wrote to Catherine the Great for a passport on his behalf. Catherine refused it, but Ledyard, not to be deterred, got as far as Irkutsk, where in February 1788 (after questioning a number of merchants rather too closely about their North Pacific fur-hunting expeditions) he was arrested and expelled from Russia as a spy.

Meanwhile, Spanish claims were superficially strengthened by a series of expeditions up the California coast as far north as Prince William Sound, where Spanish captains, following the instructions of their superior officers, took possession of lands they believed they were the first to sight. The Russian effort was more substantive. Pioneering on the high seas had given way to organized business, as small traders, lacking the money to equip large-scale expeditions to the distant islands, had to bow out before wealthier ones.

The most powerful conglomerates to emerge were the Lebedev-

Lastochkin Company, led by Pavel Lebedev-Lastochkin, a merchant from Yakutsk; the Irkutsk Company of Nikolay Mylnikov; and the Shelikhov-Golikov Company, led by Grigory Shelikhov, whom Gabriel Derzhavin, court poet to Catherine the Great, would dub the "Russian Columbus."

Born in Rylsk in the Ukraine about 1730, Shelikhov had set out to make his fortune in Siberia. Employed first as a customs official in Kyakhta, where he became an investor in expeditions to the Kurile Islands, in 1778 he went into business with Ivan Golikov, a fellow Ukrainian, who had been banished to Siberia for embezzling government funds. Their alliance was strengthened by Shelikhov's marriage to Golikov's niece, Natalya Alexyevna, a businesswoman of considerable acumen and herself the daughter of a wealthy merchant of Irkutsk. With his increased assets, Shelikhov expanded his operations from the Kuriles to the Aleutians. Although most other figures in the North Pacific fur trade eventually impoverished themselves or met with only limited success, Shelikhov proved to have the Midas touch. He was the first to form a permanent company for sponsoring longer voyages— "the initial investment capital to be divided into shares with each investor receiving shares in proportion to his investment"—as opposed to financing single voyages through temporary partnerships. And in 1783, with his enterprising wife, the first white woman to visit Alaska, he sailed with three galiots to Kodiak Island to assess the trade first hand. There on the northeast coast he established Three Saints Harbor for his expanding enterprise, and explored the coast and adjacent islands. By the end of 1786, he had temporary trading stations at Afognak Island, Kenai or Cook Inlet, and Cape St. Elias. Longer voyages by his company led to more permanent settlements on the islands, which he provisioned annually with the same cargo-laden ships as were sent out to pick up the year's accumulation of furs. In this way, the number and length of the voyages was reduced, but the harvest increased, since the hunting in Alaska waters could continue year-round.

While other traders exerted themselves toward immediate gain, Shelikhov also thought in terms of "stable, long-term rewards." He was the first to urge that hunting be regulated in such a way as not to interfere with the natural reproductive cycle of fur-bearing animals, but also saw that such a policy would be impossible to implement so long as rival companies strove for the maximum profit from each new voyage. His growing credit enabled him to secure large loans from the Demidovs, the Urals industrial magnates, and in time his operations were on such a scale that he could make a plausible appeal to the empress to grant his company a monopoly on the North Pacific trade. Holding up the example of the English East India Company, in principle subordinate to the government but with jurisdiction in its own domains, Shelikhov argued that effective occupation of the North Pacific territories, and their credible defense, was beyond the means of scattered companies' pursuing their own shortsighted and competing aims. Indeed, with the Lebedev-Lastochkin Company laying claim to part of Cook Inlet and controlling the seal rookeries of the Pribylov Islands, while other agents operated in the Aleutians, a vicious competition had also arisen for control of the better hunting grounds as the resources of the islands declined. Already by 1789 sea otters were rarely seen around most of the Aleutians, having retreated to the American coast, and the sea cow, coveted for food, had become extinct. Meanwhile increasing foreign interest in the North Pacific made urgent the need to bring the whole trade under centralized control, if only to make credible Russia's claims. Shelikhov enlisted the support of the governor of Siberia for his appeal, and through court connections obtained an interview with Catherine the Great. Catherine, however, subscribed to the laissez-faire economic theories of Adam Smith, and refused his application; but (with some pontification) she bestowed gold medals upon him and his partner for their efforts in promoting Russian enterprise.

Undaunted, Shelikhov pressed his case behind the scenes, acquiring the help of two successive governors of Eastern Siberia, and working through Plato Zubov, a relative of his wife and the empress's current paramour. He also cultivated the friendship of Nikolay Rezanov, an influential young nobleman who had entered the civil service as Derzhavin's secretary and supervised the stream of petitions that wound their way through the bureaucracy to Catherine's desk. Before long, Shelikhov had engaged his sixteen-year-old daughter, Anna, to Rezanov, and her dowry was "a handsome block of shares" in the family enterprise.

In a second interview with the empress, Shelikhov repeated his earlier arguments and, in a flattering peroration, declared: "The main end of my enterprise has been to bring newly-discovered waters, lands, and islands into our Empire before other Powers occupy and claim them, and to undertake new ventures to augment the glory of our Empress and bring profit both to her and to our fellow-countrymen." Catherine blushingly replied that "a monopoly and exclusive trade are still against my principles," but did nothing to discourage Shelikhov from stepping up his activities along American shores. In addition to establishing forts or redoubts on Afognak and Atka islands and in Kenai Inlet, he founded St. Paul's Harbor on Kodiak Island in 1792, and had begun to lay plans for other settlements when he died suddenly in July 1795.

Upon his death, his gifted widow, Natalya, took up the cause and remained faithful to his grand designs for a Russian colonial empire. After successfully fending off a hostile takeover bid, she assumed direction of the company, which she merged in 1797 with a rival (the Irkutsk Company) to form the United American Company. Nikolay Rezanov, her son-in-law, emerged as majority stockholder and chairman of the board of directors and lobbied in St. Petersburg for imperial support. Although another rival, the Lebedev-Lastochkin Company, had also established permanent outposts on the Alaska Peninsula, in 1799 Emperor Paul I, Catherine's successor, recognized the paramount contribution the Shelikhov Company had made and granted the renamed Russian-American Company (a joint-stock company modeled after all on the East India and Hudson's Bay companies) a twenty-year charter with the monopoly it sought. Soon thereafter, the government acquired a third of the company's shares and, reflecting the new and direct state involvement, company headquarters were moved from Irkutsk to St. Petersburg.

With Rezanov in the capital, it was left for one Aleksandr Baranov to make the Russian presence in America viable and prove the company worthy of the mandate it had received.

Born in Kargopol on April 16, 1747, Baranov had worked for a Moscow merchant in his youth before coming to Siberia at the age of thirty-three. Married at the time, he failed to send for his wife and daughter, and never saw them again. Settling in Irkutsk, he managed glass factories and vodka distilleries, and dabbled in the fur trade, at which he prospered; but in 1788 he suffered a series of financial setbacks that induced him to accept an offer from Shelikhov to become manager of his interests in Alaska. Thus tempted to the New World at a time when his fortunes were at a low ebb, Baranov set sail to repair them as quickly as possible, but his first taste of what he was in for discouraged most of his future hopes. After a nerve-racking voyage through tempests and squalls, he was shipwrecked on Unalaska Island, where with fifty-two men he spent the winter in dugouts roofed with driftwood, living on roots and crabs and the meat of a dead whale. Leaving ten of his crew behind to guard the salvaged stores, Baranov and the others set out in three open boats in the spring of 1791 for Three Saints Bay, on Kodiak Island, 800 miles away. Upon his arrival, he at once assumed command and his work on Shelikhov's behalf really made possible the monopoly the new company won.

After surveying conditions in the colony, Baranov decided in 1792 to move his headquarters to the north side of the island, where there was a better harbor and timber for housing, fortifications, and ships. There, at St. Paul Harbor (present-day Kodiak), with the 150 or so *promyshlenniks* under his command, he began to put the fur trade on a sounder foundation. *Yasak* having been banned from the islands in 1788, he organized large hunting parties of Aleuts under Russian foremen, and in effect replaced the fur tax with compulsory labor. Under Baranov's regime, all Aleut males between the ages of eighteen and fifty were obliged to hunt for the company, and "assembled with their *baydarkas* and harpoons at predetermined locations in the spring. . . . The colonial catch was collected annually and shipped to Okhotsk for forwarding to St. Petersburg or Kyakhta." Sea otter was the most coveted pelt, but the fur seal was caught in far larger numbers, and comprised about 70 percent of the total haul. Beaver, fox, bear, lynx, sable, muskrat, mink, wolf, wolverine, and marmot were also hunted on land, and walruses were taken on the Pribylov Islands and off the coasts of the Bering Sea. Walrus hide was too thick to cure, "but tusks, which measured up to 2½ feet in length and weighed 15 pounds or more, were prized in Turkey and Persia." Pelts, walrus ivory, and whalebone were also obtained by barter with the natives at the company's forts and redoubts. In Chugach Bay (Prince William Sound), Baranov established a dockyard, where he undertook to build vessels of his own. Lacking tar and pitch, he boiled pine and fir sap together to produce a substitute gum, and launched the three-masted *Phoenix,* the first Russian-built ship in America. That autumn, two transports arrived from Okhotsk loaded with provisions, implements, and cattle, about two hundred hunters and settlers, and eight priests from the Valaam Monastery in Finland. Meanwhile, Baranov had begun to domesticate his own situation by taking the eighteen-year-old daughter of a native chief as his wife.

After 1799, all of the Aleutian and Pribylov islands as well as Alaska were placed under his jurisdiction, and as company manager he became, in effect, governor of Russian America.

The competition on the northwest coast was fierce. Although Spain had effectively bowed out (after a confrontation with the English) with the Nootka Sound Agreement of October 28, 1790, the scrimmage for advantage thereafter was left to the Russians, British, and Americans. Between the British and Americans, the Yankee traders—or "Boston Men," as they were called—soon gained the upper hand. Indeed, the American appetite for skins perhaps exceeded the Russians' own. One of the early Yankee traders off the northwest coast gave appropriate expression to his countrymen's rapacity when he exclaimed, "Next to a beautiful young woman, a prime sea otter skin, two feet by five feet with its short, glossy, jet black fur, is the finest natural object in the world."

Haunting the bays and coves of the North Pacific coast, American skippers were completely mercenary in their dealings, "always on the lookout for ways to make easy money," as one contemporary put it, and prepared to barter guns and ammunition as well as rum for skins. One captain paid a keg of powder for each sea-otter pelt he bought, and another offered four pound-caliber cannon for thirteen pelts. This didn't always work out as planned. In 1803, the Indians near Nootka Sound attacked and burned the Yankee ship *Boston* and slaughtered the crew. But whenever Baranov reproached Americans for any of their doings, their response was: "We're traders, we're after profits. There's no law against it!" And indeed in their bid to out-trade the Russians, they used every stratagem they could. Perhaps the most reprehensible was their willingness to foster a slave trade among the Indians on the northwest coast. "Whereas in Europe efforts are being made to abolish the slave-trade," one Russian captain scathingly reported,

citizens of the United States of America are exerting all their energy to strengthen it. To buy slaves, American vessels proceed to latitude 45 degrees N on the Northwest Coast, where the population is large.

Having learned by experience that they will be paid far more for men than for peltry, the natives of those parts have turned to that dreadful hunt. As American merchants have provided them all with firearms, they easily overpower the unfortunate races living in the interior, then give their captives to shipmasters in exchange for various items of clothing. Moving instances of filial love are not rarely encountered among those persecuted tribes, but their inhuman persecutors draw advantage even from this, out of avarice. When, for instance, a son hears of the captivity of his own father, he runs to the slavers to offer himself in exchange. And the barbarians readily accept this magnanimous proposal, as a young man is of more use to them than an old one. When a ship is thus sufficiently laden with slaves, she sets off north to latitude 55 degrees where the Coast Indians take the unfortunates for their own service in exchange for sea-otter skins. The [Americans] sell these for a good profit in China and rejoice at their gains, so shamefully made.

Baranov held his own. Once ensconced he won the grudging respect of natives and traders alike (including Yankees), and proved a shrewd and aggressive businessman. With approximate accuracy, Washington Irving imagined him as "a rough, rugged, hospitable, hard-drinking old Russian; somewhat of a soldier; somewhat of a trader; above all, a boon companion of the old roystering school, with a strong cross of the bear." Only Baranov didn't drink very much, prohibited gambling of any sort like a contagious disease, and was sociable after the manner of a man of courteous reserve.

Rather small and thickset, with a dignified bearing and a soft, measured style of speech, he was inclined to be somewhat surly and morose, but had eyes that "shone with a lively and penetrating gaze." To disguise his baldness he wore a wig, "held in place by a black band under his chin," but in all other respects was oblivious to fashion, and wore the same outmoded uniform for fourteen years. By his patience, self-sacrifice, and forbearance, Baranov extended Russian holdings, and with each succeeding year his reputation grew. "Even those living far away sometimes travel specially to see him," a visitor reported, "and they wonder that such great deeds should be accomplished by such a small man."

Some things were judiciously beyond his inclination to attempt. At one time, for example, Shelikhov had envisioned in the Alaskan wilderness a full-fledged colonial capital worthy of the name "Slavoros-siya" ("Glory of Russia"), with large public squares, tree-lined streets, orderly rows of houses, fenced-in gardens, and public buildings in neoclassical style. The actual conditions under which Baranov labored, of course, made such schemes preposterous, and the chief feature of all the settlements he founded was a stockade with an infirmary and barracks, a few houses, and a church outside the walls. The houses were all built of notched log timbers, caulked with moss, and had roofs thatched with grass. A few of the windows were glazed with talc, but more generally seal gut, sewed together, oiled and stretched on a frame, supplied the panes.

Unlike the Aleuts, the proud and indomitably defiant Native Americans of the Pacific Northwest were not timid at all, and in their skin loincloths and bark-fiber aprons, closely resembled the prototypical Indian figure of the American West. The Russians encountered the Chugach in Prince William Sound, the Koniags on Kodiak Island, the Kenais on Kenai Peninsula, and the fierce Thlingit (whom they referred to as *Kolosh,* a generic term equivalent to "Indian") from Yakutat Bay to the Stikine River, and on islands offshore. A mighty tribe, the Thlingit belonged to two powerful clans, the Raven and the Wolf (based on matrilineal descent); they wore rawhide tunics painted with clan crests, wooden armor tightly wound about their bodies with whale gut, thick wooden helmets, and masks made to resemble the faces of fearsome beasts. They were armed with daggers, spears, bows and arrows, and clubs, took the heads of their slain enemies as trophies, and their women and children as slaves. In general, they lived in settled communities of considerable size, in houses built of hewn planks, morticed together, with a low gabled roof supported by posts at either end. Split-level in design, these had a platformlike sleeping loft above the ground floor, and in some ways were more sophisticated than ruder Russian pioneer homes. The posts and facade were even carved and painted to illustrate stories, which rendered them more elegant and stately than any other native dwellings the Russians had ever seen. In their art, the Thlingit used highly complicated and abstracted forms, cryptic codes, hidden animal forms within geometric patterns, and so forth. Their hunting and trapping equipment—snares, deadfalls, weirs —was as ingenious as that of any Siberian tribe. The Thlingits also had portable cedar-bark tents that could be transported in their oceangoing canoes.

Their ritual system was shamanistic, and their shamans were distinguished by "their long, tangled locks, and by their haggard faces and gaunt bodies, exhausted from frequent thirsting and fasting." Before cremation, the bodies of chiefs lay in state for several days.

The first American artifacts and habitations found by Steller and Khitrov evidently belonged to the Thlingits, who were probably also responsible for the death of Chirikov's men.

Despite Baranov's precautions, from time to time the Indians killed or abducted isolated parties of Russians or Aleuts, attacked fledgling outposts, burned *baydarkas,* and so on, in a continuous war. And they were never tamed.

Besides the Thlingits, the intrusion of foreign traders, and other worries, Baranov's operations were disrupted by numerous calamities. On one occasion, a large party of Aleuts returning from a hunting expedition ate tainted shellfish washed up by the sea, and to induce vomiting their Russian foremen forced them to swallow gunpowder and tobacco mixed with soap. Over the next two hours more than a hundred died in horrible convulsions. That winter, the coast and islands were battered by unusually heavy storms. Although in any given three- to four-year period Baranov might accumulate a catch of up to a million skins, in some cases tens of thousands spoiled through overhunting, in losses perhaps more costly to the company than the new low prices fetched at Kyakhta due to stiff competition at Canton.

But above all, the Russian American outposts were frightfully isolated possessions. Although Bering Strait was only 56 miles wide at its narrowest point, St. Paul's Harbor for all practical purposes lay across some 3,000 miles of stormy waters from Petropavlovsk, which was supplied chiefly from Okhotsk. Okhotsk, in turn, was supplied ultimately from Irkutsk, via Yakutsk, which was likewise 3,000 miles away. Almost half of the company ships sailing from Okhotsk also perished in the waves. The fate of one sent to Petropavlovsk, was not exceptional. Near the mouth of the Vilyuy River, almost within sight of refuge, it was smashed by a storm against the rocks, and only three of the crew managed to climb to safety out onto the face of a cliff. When rescuers arrived, they found "for a distance of three versts along the shore the limbless and disfigured corpses of their comrades, covered in sand and seaweed; some were even caught in the branches of the trees, but most terrible of all was the spectacle of those lifted up by the waves and thrown against the cliffs and hanging there by an arm or leg, their whole body in the air.... Lumps and tatters of the cargo littered the seashore and the river's edge."

Unable to feed themselves adequately, the Russians relied for their provisioning upon an extension of the old "Siberian deliveries" system, with results less satisfactory than earlier efforts had been to supply the Okhotsk seaboard and Kamchatka. Attempts were made at agriculture at Kodiak and Yakutat Bay, but as in parts of Eastern Siberia, the harsh environment repeatedly frustrated efforts to cultivate the soil. Even in the major settlements, colonists were occasionally reduced to eating eagles, crows, and cuttlefish; scurvy was common, and food poisoning frequent from scavenging for dead animals on the beach. For those suffering from scurvy, a little millet with molasses and beer brewed from pine cones provided the only relief. Before long the Russians found themselves precariously dependent on sometimes-hostile natives for basic foodstuffs (wild goat meat and other fresh game), and also obliged to barter for their subsistence with foreign ships. In turning to foreigners, Baranov was often forced to accept "package deals," in which goods for which the Russians had no use were included in the transaction in return for furs. In this way, the company's prime source of revenue fell into the hands of competitors at the lowest possible rate.

At about this time, Captain Adam Johann von Krusenstern, a Baltic officer in company service, "developed a plan," writes one historian, "to supply the American colonies from European Russia by sea, from the port of Kronstadt on the Gulf of Finland around the world by the Cape of Good Hope or by Cape Horn." Based on observations he had made during a sojourn in 1798–99 at Canton, he also believed that Russian profits in the China trade would be immeasurably increased if furs and other products from Alaska and the islands were directly carried to that port by sea, saving two years or more on the long and toilsome transit to Kyakhta via Okhotsk. The return voyage would include stops at various South Pacific ports for the purchase of additional items for Russia's foreign trade. In this way, the colonies could be more economically supplied, trade with China increased, the cost of acquiring Oriental goods reduced, and the latter resold to European countries at prices competitively lower than those charged by other maritime powers.

Krusenstern's plan was taken up by Rezanov and "captured the imagination of both commercial and government leaders." And in the summer of 1803, two ships—the *Hope* under Krusenstern, and the *Neva* under Captain Yury Lisyansky—were readied to sail. Emperor Alexander I (who had succeeded Paul I two years before) decided to further utilize the expedition to pursue Rezanov's idea that both the colonies and Eastern Siberia might be provisioned by trade with Japan. And so as part of Russia's first around-the-world voyage, he appointed Rezanov special trade envoy, and (to enhance his standing) Imperial Chamberlain.

Grief-stricken from the recent death of his wife (Shelikhov's daughter) in childbirth, Rezanov embraced the difficult mission with resurrected zeal.

A letter from the emperor to the shogun was magnificently written in gold on a large sheet of vellum, and beautifully decorated translations of it in Manchu and Japanese were attached. The three documents were carefully bound in gold brocade, placed in a handsomely carved redwood box, in turn nestled in a case lined with emerald cloth. Rezanov's other effects included cartloads of paintings, mirrors, model boats, a thousand books, numerous trunks of clothes, and musical instruments, largely to embellish the culture of the Russian settlements in Alaska.

On August 4, 1803, the *Hope,* with Rezanov on board, and the *Neva* weighed anchor, bound for the East by way of Cape Horn and the Hawaiian Islands. After stopping at the islands to revictual, the *Hope* was to proceed to Japan via Petropavlovsk, the *Neva* to the American colonies.

When they docked at Honolulu in the summer of 1804, the Russians found that a quarter century after its discovery by Captain Cook, the archipelago had undergone a remarkable change. Western ships had habituated the natives to Western technology and ways, including luxury goods; their reigning monarch, Kamehameha, had a European bodyguard, owned schooners armed with swivel guns, and had grown quite wily in the conduct of international affairs. His overriding policy was to maintain good relations with the captains of foreign vessels to avert armed conflict (which he knew he would lose) while also obtaining weapons from them for his own inter-island campaigns. By Polynesian standards he was practically invincible.

Yet the natives themselves made a sorry sight. Though warriorlike, with tomahawk haircuts, they were naked and lean, their bodies covered with scabs. Many had front teeth missing, and syphilis and yaws had left almost everyone with running sores. They could drive a hard, commercial bargain, but their newfound skill had not particularly enhanced their lives. Moreover, as soon as a European vessel pulled into port, the women, universally inured to prostitution, swam like schools of fish around the ship. Some of the more enterprising came out to the men in boats and were not easily denied. But after a long voyage with inadequate provisions, fresh food seemed rather more appealing: when a naked girl of "matchless vivacity" leaped from a schooner onto the *Neva*'s deck, the crew immediately noted with disappointment that she hadn't brought any food to trade. Just then, in fact, another craft approached, and "some men spotted a little sucking pig, a pig that, at this moment, no one would have exchanged even for the most beautiful woman, let alone for a savage girl. . . . Everyone uttered the word 'piglet' with the keenest expression of voice. 'They've brought a piglet,' said one to another with delight. 'There it is, in that craft under the leaves! What a sweet and plump little piggy!' "

The *Hope* and the *Neva* parted company on June 10, 1804; but before sailing for Kodiak, Lisyansky strolled to the beach where Cook had fallen, and found several flattened bullets still embedded in the trees. Pausing also at the island of Kauai, he was met by Kaumauli, a local chieftain and King Kamehameha's main antagonist in the inter-island wars. Kaumauli sought Russian military assistance, but made a terrible first impression despite couching his appeal in extremely tempting terms. Coming on board with an attendant bearing a small wooden spittoon studded with human teeth (supposedly souvenirs of former friends), all during his parley with Lisyansky he ignored the attendant completely, "spitting almost constantly on deck." Nevertheless, in return for arms, he offered to make his island a Russian protectorate—an arrangement Lisyansky had no authority to accept but which he was loath to decline. For as he and all his crew could see, sugarcane, yams, watermelons, coconuts, taro, and other foodstuffs grew on Kauai and the other islands in abundance, and pigs and cattle thrived. Most of the foods could be obtained more cheaply there than from foreign ships, and from that moment on it was ambitiously hoped that through colonization and trade the company might solve not only its own provisioning needs but those of Eastern Siberia as well.

Sailing on to Kodiak, Lisyansky arrived to find the colony in crisis. One night in June 1802, when the sentries at Fort St. Michael had let down their guard, a war party of Thlingits had scaled the stockade, slaughtered the garrison, burned the fort, captured a cache of muskets, set fire to a fleet of *baydarkas* anchored nearby, and carried the women and children away as slaves. Lacking sufficient arms to retake the outpost, Baranov had struck a deal with an American captain, Joseph O'Cain, whereby he would supply him with Aleuts and kayaks to hunt sea otters off the California coast in return for weapons and a split of the catch.

O'Cain lived up to the agreement and returned in the summer of 1804, just before Lisyansky arrived. Meanwhile Baranov had assembled 120 Russians in four small ships and 800 Aleuts in *baydarkas* to try to wrest the settlement back. Lisyansky's sloop-of-war now made a considerable addition to this force. For their part, the Thlingits had built a formidable new fort upon the ruins of the old, and had constructed a network of trenchlike dugouts from which to fight.

The *Neva* approached as close as it could, anchored, and opened fire, but the barrage fell short, obliging the Russians (with Aleut auxiliaries) to land and make an infantry assault. The Thlingits smartly returned their fire, wounding Baranov among others and forcing a retreat. By expert maneuvering the *Neva* edged in closer, and a more effective bombardment of the fort began. At length, the Indians signaled a desire to negotiate, and after an exchange of hostages, vanished into the woods. Their fort was promptly burned to the ground, and the Russians set about building a more solid citadel for themselves nearby. This was furnished with a battery of cannon to guard the entrance to the bay, and was set upon a high promontory projecting out into the sea. While the fortress was under construction, Baranov lived "in a torn tent exposed to the elements," later moving for the winter into a windowless bathhouse with a rickety roof. But when his own dwelling was finished on the promontory's height, he enjoyed a spectacular view of the bay and the surrounding islands, and the high snow-capped mountains inland from the coast. New Archangel, as it was called— later to be named Sitka—was the most propitiously situated and well fortified of all the company's outposts, and became the colonial capital in 1808.

While the *Neva* was helping to reclaim Russian authority in Alaska, Krusenstern on the *Hope* had unloaded his cargo at Petropavlovsk and had sailed with Rezanov for Japan.

The willful isolation of the Japanese had long been an irritant to Western powers. In 1543, well before Peter the Great was introduced to Dembei, or Spanberg and Walton had skirted Honshu's shores, three Portuguese sailors on a Chinese junk had been swept by a typhoon across the East China Sea to Japan. In their wake had come waves of traders and priests bringing firearms, tobacco, Christianity, and venereal disease. For a time, the Japanese welcomed them—the English and the Dutch as well as the Spanish and Portuguese—and Catholic missionaries made hundreds of thousands of converts, since the shogunate allowed them to proselytize. But the Church became a threat to the new political order, which had only recently unified and delivered Japan from its feudal past, and by 1638 hundreds of missionaries had been executed, thousands of their converts killed, and all foreigners expelled from the land. To enforce the insularity of the kingdom, the shogunate made it a capital crime to travel abroad, or even to construct seagoing vessels large enough to cross the seas. Only at Deshima, a little island artificially constructed off Nagasaki in 1641, was vestigial contact with the West allowed, and then only in a trading compound surrounded by a high, roof-covered fence topped by a double row of spikes.

Such was the prickly xenophobic stance they had maintained for 150 years.

Anchoring off Nagasaki in October 1804, Rezanov and his retinue met a hostile reception, and were immediately imprisoned in another fenced and guarded compound for several months. Despite all his lofty titles, dazzling imperial gifts, and his gold-embossed epistle from the tsar, Rezanov's attempts to be recognized as a goodwill trade ambassador were spurned. Although no harm came to him, and he was allowed to depart the following spring, he nursed vengeance in his heart. And doubtless it increased when he saw first hand how much trade with Japan might have helped to shore the colony up. From Petropavlovsk, Rezanov decided to cross to New Archangel in a company ship, and at once got a shocking glimpse of the plight of the employees. Quarters were so cramped that more than fifty people had to sleep in their clothes on deck, and most of the crew, in spite of the heat of June, were dressed in greasy furs. Skilled navigators were scarce, and many "sailors," recruited from Siberian towns, had never before seen a ship or been to sea. Most of them were adventurers, drunkards, bankrupt traders, or branded criminals in search of piratical gains, and those he met at New Archangel, where he docked in July 1805, were, he wrote, "depraved, drunk, violent and corrupted to an extent that any society should consider it a great relief to get rid of them."

Rezanov also discovered that the Indians had recently wiped out another settlement at Yakutat; that there were no doctors to care for the sick; that food was rationed; that almost everybody went in rags; and that no missionary had yet learned the language of the Thlingits, and only one had bothered to learn Aleut. Baranov himself, exhausted from his efforts to establish an impregnable fortress, was suffering from arthritis, and (as the citadel at the time stood incomplete) was still living "in a kind of plank lean-to so full of damp that every day mold has to be wiped off." Rezanov found his fortitude positively heroic, and in a letter to the company directors exclaimed: "What a man! He worries only about the comfort of others, but so neglects his own comfort that one day I found his bed awash and asked if the weather-boarding had split from the wall beside his bed. 'No,' he replied quietly, 'plainly it leaks through from the square,' and he continued about his business."

Finding the settlements critically undersupplied, Rezanov purchased an American ship, the *Juno,* complete with its cargo of foodstuffs, to see the winter through, and the following spring (1806) sailed south to San Francisco Bay. There he charmed the Spanish governor, romanced the fifteen-year-old daughter of the local commandante, and secured a cargo of grain, flour, dried meat, barley, peas, lard, salt, and other provisions for the beleaguered colony. To identify themselves as they entered the Spanish port, the Russians simply shouted "Russkie," and although Madrid technically banned trade by the missions, the local friars (known to be "principal agents in exchange of contraband") bartered to their hearts' content.

Rezanov's intended, Maria Arguello de la Concepción, was said to be the most beautiful girl in northern California. Her father consented to their union, but since the lovers were of different faiths, dispensations had first to be obtained from both Rome and St. Petersburg. Promising to return within two years, Rezanov sailed over the horizon, and she never saw him again. Perhaps he had not meant to betray her; for he was fated to die the following March of pneumonia at Krasnoyarsk. For many years thereafter, it is said, Maria watched in vain for his return, and eventually, having given up hope, joined the convent of St. Catherine, Benicia, as California's first nun.

Before leaving the settlements, Rezanov had discussed with Baranov what needed to be done, and his own blueprint for the colony's survival included settlements in the Oregon Country (as the entire area between California and Alaska was called), California, and the Hawaiian Islands. Japan, he thought, might also be forced open to trade, and he wrote to the company directors that the founding of a settlement north of San Francisco might prepare the way for eventually seizing northern California from Spain.

An ardent imperialist, he dreamed of Russia as the dominant trans-Pacific power, although it seems odd for him to have such ambitions for a colonial enterprise that still contained only about five hundred beleaguered Russians in 1804.

Any hope of trade with Japan was also destroyed by his own intemperate acts. Still smarting from his captivity, Rezanov had written from New Archangel to the tsar in July 1805 that the Japanese would trade only under threat of attack, and he recommended punitive raids on their settlements on Sakhalin Island and Matsumae, a major island in the Kurile chain. Among other things, he hoped to take a number of Japanese prisoners to be exploited for company work, and chose for their resettlement a tiny island in Sitka Sound, to this day called Japonski (or Japanese) Island. Without waiting for imperial consent, he discussed his scheme with two young naval officers, Nikolay Khvostov and Gavril Davydov, who had sailed with him to Alaska. As might have been expected, given his high rank, they understood his suggestions for retaliatory raids as commands.

The first raid was carried out in the summer of 1807 in two ships, the *Juno* and the *Avos.* The Russians landed on Sakhalin Island at Aniwa Bay, confronted a bewildered group of Japanese, and read out a proclamation. Taking hostages, they pillaged and burned warehouses, destroyed fishing boats and nets along the beach, and before departing fixed a copper plaque to the wall of the local temple denouncing the Japanese prohibition on trade and threatening to devastate northern Japan. The following summer they attacked a string of Japanese outposts on the Kurile Islands over the course of forty days. Upon their return to Okhotsk, however, Davydov and Khvostov were apprehended and imprisoned for their unauthorized acts; ultimately, they were exonerated by a special committee of inquiry chaired by the Minister of Foreign Affairs.

But there the matter did not end. In the summer of 1811, Captain-Lieutenant Vasily Golovnin aboard the *Diana,* a sloop-of-war, was undertaking a survey of the southern Kurile Islands, when off Etorofu he was startled to see Japanese soldiers hastily assemble in full battle gear on shore. In a parley, the Japanese made known their rage at the recent raids, to which Golovnin replied that "such attacks upon them by two craft of tiny size could hardly have been launched at the behest of the monarch of a great and mighty State." This did not wholly appease them. When he attempted to chart the strait between the island and Hokkaido, guns suddenly boomed through the mist, and two cannonballs struck the water near his bow.

Golovnin landed at Kunashiri to clarify the situation, and was escorted into the fortress with some officers and men. They promptly found themselves surrounded by several hundred fully armed Japanese. After a brief interrogation, the Russians panicked, tried to escape, but were subdued. Tied together in such a way "that the pull of a long rope, held by a guard, would have strangled them," they were taken by boat to Hakodate and incarcerated in a set of zoolike cages in a dark and massive jail. Subsequently, they were marched to Matsumae and cast into a kind of partitioned chicken coop with doors so low they had to squirm through on their stomachs. Finally, they were transferred to a house within the fortress grounds. Meanwhile, the *Diana,* under Golovnin's second-in-command, Pavel Rikord, had briefly exchanged fire with the Kunashiri fortress and returned to Okhotsk.

The Russian government, deploring the incident, decided not to try to mount a major rescue operation. It had other things on its mind. Napoleon had crossed the Niemen; Moscow, in September, had been burned. A "second front" on the other side of the world was out of the question. After Napoleon's defeat in October 1813, however, the *Diana* returned to Hakodate with a written apology for the earlier raids, and with several Japanese whom Rikord hoped to exchange for his captive shipmates. (One of the Japanese, incidentally, was a woman, who became friendly with the wife of the doctor on board. The two ladies—the first Russian and Japanese of their sex to meet—eschewed matters of state and instead "compared makeup, tried on each other's fineries, and embraced and kissed each other" in a rare instance of national rapport.) But Japanese officials made clear that they would only release the hostages in return for a more formal document stating that the raids had been authorized. This was duly obtained, and Golovnin and his companions were finally freed.

Japan was a lost cause, but following up on Rezanov's California initiative, Baranov sent expeditions south in September 1808 to establish settlements on the Columbia River and the northern California coast. The first, under Nikolay Bulygin in the *St. Nikolay,* failed when the ship, caught by winds and currents, was driven ashore and destroyed just north of James Island. There most of its company were either killed by Indians or perished from starvation or exposure.

The second, under Ivan Kuskov, in the *Kodiak,* was more successful. Disembarking at Bodega Bay, he found the local Indians friendly, and the region otherwise unoccupied. After eight months of hunting and trading (and burying copper markers which proclaimed: "Land of the Russian Empire" along the coast), he returned to build a fort with ten cannon north of San Francisco on a high bluff above the sea. On August 30, 1812, the imperial flag was raised over its ramparts and the settlement was christened Fort Russ—a name later corrupted to Ross. The Russians also built a dockyard at Bodega Bay, and occupied the Farallones, a group of islands about 28 miles off the Golden Gate. At its California base, the company managed to carry on a regular, if somewhat covert, trade with Spanish missionaries and develop a small agricultural community.

The Oregon Country, however, passed beyond Baranov's reach. American soldiers were already starting to build barracks on the Columbia River and could be found distributing medals with Washington's portrait to the local Indians. By 1810, the British were pushing their explorations downriver to its mouth, and John Jacob Astor's Pacific Fur Company had also begun construction of the Astoria outpost on its shores.

Quite a few of the Russians were desperate characters. Although Baranov usually managed to keep order among them, inevitably there were murderous plots and feuds. The most serious of these occurred in the winter of 1809, when an exiled Pole and several confederates (inspired by the story of Benyowski's revolt at Bolsheretsk) planned to murder

Baranov, plunder the storehouse, kidnap a number of young women, and set sail for the South Seas. En route to Easter Island (their ultimate destination), they hoped to reprovision at the Hawaiian Islands by swapping sea-otter pelts for goods. The plotters, however, lacked Benyowski's gift for masquerade, and at the eleventh hour their poorly coordinated plot was betrayed.

In the bleak, gloomy* environment of New Archangel, the South Pacific had also been much on Baranov's mind. Ever since Lisyansky's visit to Hawaii, he had hoped to strike some trade agreement with Kamehameha, the archipelago's recognized king. Both shared a desire to maintain some independence from the increasingly aggressive tactics of Yankee traders, and as early as 1806 the king had proposed through an intermediary to victual Baranov's settlements in exchange for skins. In the following year, when a small company vessel detoured to the islands, the king repeated his invitation, and as a gesture of his earnest goodwill sent Baranov a royal helmet and a gorgeously befeathered cape.

In mid-November 1808, the *Neva,* now under Lieutenant Leonty Hagemeister, returned to Russian America with supplies. Baranov sent the vessel to the Hawaiian Islands for a cargo of salt, and when Hagemeister arrived at Oahu at the beginning of January 1809, he was evidently prepared to establish a fledgling colony. According to one of the sailors given passage: "The ship had a house in frame on board, and intimation was given that volunteers would be received," though none came forth. Since the voyage coincided with the dispatch by Baranov of the reconnaissance expeditions to the Columbia River and the California coast, it seems likely that it was part of a coordinated attempt to implement Rezanov's broad strategy to rescue Russian America from its semi-dependent state.

While the *Neva* lingered and its hold was stocked with foods, Kaumauli, still vying with Kamehameha for control of several islands, renewed his appeal for Russian support. Hagemeister demurred (as reluctantly as Lisyansky had before him), but confided to the company head office in June 1809 that "the king would be willing to sell us [Molokai] or some other island," and that Molokai alone could supply the wants of every Russian outpost on the Pacific rim. In his estimation, forty soldiers, a couple of cannon, and two ships were all that would be needed to annex the island to the Crown.

The continuing turmoil in Hawaiian politics momentarily discouraged the scheme, and the War of 1812 between Great Britain and the United States also intervened. Baranov, however, turned the war to good account. Several American captains, in fear of British warships or privateers, either sold their vessels to him or sailed under the company's flag, and by March 1814 he had some seven oceangoing craft at his disposal—a rather fantastic state of affairs. Company profits for 1814 climbed to a million rubles, and extra dividends were paid. In 1813, the Board of Directors also reached a promising agreement with John Jacob Astor, by which the latter was to supply the settlements with all necessities in exchange for a commission on the company's furs sold by him (as the company's sole agent) at Canton.

This agreement lapsed, however, and after Fort Ross failed to live up to original expectations as a reliable source of foodstuffs, the Hawaiian Islands appeared the last best hope of all. As his "man in Hawaii" Baranov chose Georg Anton Schaffer, an itinerant apothecary and charlatan who had taken part in an abortive project in 1812 "for the construction of balloons to combat Napoleon's invading army." Arriving in 1814 at New Archangel aboard the *Suvorov,* commanded by Lieutenant Mikhail Lazarev (a member of the Russian expedition that would later discover Antarctica), Schaffer was Baranov's candidate by default, since all his other trusted lieutenants at the time were absent on other tasks. Schaffer's double mission was to recover the cargo of the *Bering,* a company ship that had capsized in a gale off the coast of Kauai, and to initiate long-term trade. Two other ships, the *Discovery* and *Kodiak,* both armed, were to arrive later with goods to barter and, if necessary (since Kaumauli had appropriated the *Bering*'s cargo), to enforce Russian claims.

Arriving on the American ship *Isabella,* posing as a naturalist to disguise his aims, Schaffer disembarked at Honolulu early in November 1815. Within a remarkably short time he had made himself indispensable to the king and to the king's consort, whom he promised to cure of obesity, as their personal physician, and with pledges of Russian military support quickly acquired a house in Honolulu, fishing rights offshore, a tract of land on the Pearl River, herds of sheep and goats, a tobacco plantation, and a breadfruit grove.

Schaffer next sailed for Kauai, where he found Kaumauli even more eager to please. On May 21, 1816, this chieftain not only agreed to surrender the *Bering*'s cargo, but professed willingness to place his entire dominions more or less at the company's disposal, where it could erect warehouses, cultivate plantations, or otherwise establish itself as it saw fit. He offered, moreover, to sign an exclusive trade agreement with the company, to supply a workforce for its local needs, to revictual Russian ships, and to swear allegiance to Alexander I. Schaffer in return promised Kaumauli Russian protection and a fully armed ship, decorated him with a silver medal, and made him a line staff officer in the Russian Navy.

All this, of course, was quite beyond his authority, but on July 1, 1816, the two men exchanged still wider commitments in a secret pact. Kaumauli agreed to place five hundred warriors under Schaffer's command in a campaign backed by Russian ships to conquer Kamehameha's dominions, yielding in return half of Oahu and property on every other island in the chain. In anticipation, Schaffer began renaming various parts of the landscape according to his whim, and at Hanalei even named a valley after himself. On a high promontory, he also began building a stronghold with a gun emplacement out of lava blocks, and over its ramparts ran up the Russian flag.

This convinced the English and American traders that the Russians had decided to make an outright grab for the archipelago. Kamehameha, whose whole policy was to safeguard Hawaiian sovereignty, reacted with outrage, and things began to unravel for Schaffer as fast as they'd been stitched. The Russian post on Honolulu was burned down by natives and "American hot heads," and in late November 1816, the Russian-armed brig *Rurik,* under Lieutenant Otto von Kotzebue, put in and was met by an irate Kamehameha with a litany of complaints. Kotzebue promptly disowned the whole adventure and assured him the Russian government had not sanctioned anything Schaffer had done.

Expelled from Oahu, Schaffer tried to retrench on Kauai, but Kaumauli saw the balance of power swing against him and pretended indignation at having been duped. On May 8, 1817, he put Schaffer in a leaky boat and forced him to paddle out to the *Kodiak,* which had just arrived. Subsequently, Schaffer was transferred to an American ship and sailed for Macao.

The government in St. Petersburg flatly repudiated his exploits, which had threatened to bring Russia into conflict with other Pacific powers. For Baranov, the affair was a costly reverse. By overreaching himself, Schaffer had spoiled Kamehameha's initial goodwill and had even failed to recover the cargo of the company's stranded ship. The Russians were discredited and ousted from the islands in disgrace.

Schaffer emerged unscathed. Following his own remarkable star, he eventually found his way to Brazil and (confidence man extraordinaire) there persuaded the emperor Dom Pedro I and his young Hapsburg empress to give him an estate. By 1821, he had "joined the parvenu nobility of the Brazilian capital as Count von Frankenthal," and when he died in 1836 was laid to rest as a great propertied magnate and councilor of state.

Baranov's humiliation was wholly undeserved. Against all odds, he had built a commercial empire "on beggarly means," and its proceeds supported branch offices at Moscow, Irkutsk, Kyakhta, Yakutsk, and Okhotsk, besides sixteen posts throughout the colonies. The Russians had occupied much of the coast and adjacent islands south of the Yukon River, and had a chain of hunting and trading posts that extended from California to the Bering Sea. Many native tribes (if not the Thlingits) had also come under their domination and had nominally converted to the Russian Orthodox faith. However, in his haste to occupy and settle the coastal strips (it is said), he had missed the opportunity to establish firm bases in the hinterland, where he might have conducted a more balanced trade. The British, of course, eventually filled the gap, as their overland expansion through Canada brought the Hudson's Bay Company into the Yukon and other river valleys of Alaska, thus hemming the company in along the shore. But when Baranov had first arrived, it was the sea otter, not balanced trade, that counted most, and taking the coastal strips that made commercial sense. Moreover, at no time did he have more than five hundred Russians with which to secure his gains. Under his administration, the company's assets (apart from expenses and dividends paid on shares) had also doubled, notwithstanding the many misfortunes and disasters that beset his enterprise. Indeed, when all the losses (at sea and otherwise) had been discounted, exports from the colony between 1897 and 1821 were:

Sea otters—male, female, and young	*72,894*
River beavers	*34,546*
Beaver tails	*59,530*
Otters	*14,969*
Fur seals	*1,232,374*

Black and silver foxes	*13,702*
Blue foxes	*21,890*
Red foxes	*30,950*
Sables	*17,298*
Wolverines	*1,151*
Lynx	*1,389*
Minks	*4,802*
Blue polar foxes	*36,362*
White polar foxes	*4,234*
Wolves	*121*
Bears	*1,602*
Sea lions	*27*
Walrus tusks	*1,616 puds 20 pounds*
Whale bone	*1,173 puds*
Castoreum	*21½ pounds*

By the time of the founding of Fort Ross, Baranov was sixty-seven years old and had already spent twenty-three years in the colonies. With his customary stoic patience, wrote his biographer, he "awaited daily for a replacement to release him and lift from him the burden of responsibility he had borne for so long." Baranov's appeal did not go unanswered, but twice the men sent out to replace him died en route —the first, in 1811, as he was about to sail for the colonies from Petropavlovsk; the second, in 1813, when his ship went down in Norfolk Sound. In November 1817, Captain Leonty Hagemeister disembarked from the *Kutuzov* (named in honor of the Russian conqueror of Napoleon) to take over as chief manager, finally allowing Baranov to retire. After conducting a careful inventory, Hagemeister turned the colonial administration over to Lieutenant Semyon Yanovsky, a naval officer who had recently married Baranov's Creole daughter Irina. In Hagemeister's ship, Baranov sailed for home. A few months later, just short of his seventy-second birthday, he died while passing through the Straits of Sunda, on April 12, 1819. His body was lowered over the side and the waters of the Indian Ocean "closed forever over his remains."

The governors who succeeded Baranov were all officer-aristocrats of the Imperial Navy. Some had exceptional scientific training, carried out meticulous nautical surveys, and explored the interior, including the basins of the Yukon and Kuskokwim rivers. One of the more notable of the expeditions was that commanded by Otto von Kotzebue (discoverer of Alaska's Kotzebue Sound), whose vessel, the *Rurik,* "had been built in Swedish dockyards for Arctic exploration and was equipped with new scientific instruments designed in Britain. The provisions on board also included "newly invented tinned soups, vegetables, and meats."

In 1821, the company was granted a second twenty-year charter, underwent a degree of corporate organization to attract new investments, and began to pay its employees salaries instead of shares. More missionaries, doctors, and teachers were brought in in an effort to keep the colonization alive. The Church in Russian America belonged to the Eastern Siberian diocese, which included the Kurile Islands and Kamchatka, and for many years its guiding spirit was Father Ivan Veniaminov, the "apostle of Alaska."

Born in the village of Anginskoy in the region of Irkutsk, where he had begun his career as a parish priest, Veniaminov volunteered for missionary work in the Aleutians in 1823. He taught the Aleuts carpentry and other crafts, devoted himself to a study of their culture, mastered their language, and created its written form. In time, he translated the Gospel According to St. Matthew and various liturgical texts into Aleut, but also set up schools to teach the natives Russian, so that about one in six became literate under his tutelage. His own book, *The Way to the Kingdom of Heaven,* could eventually be found in many island homes. In 1833, Father Veniaminov was transferred to New Archangel, where he repeated his efforts among the Thlingits, compiling information on their rituals and mythology but making very few conversions.

Nevertheless, as a result of his great industry and devotion, in 1840 he was ordained (under the name of Innocent) the first bishop of Alaska and Kamchatka. In 1867, he was elevated to the post of Metropolitan of Moscow, the second highest office in the Russian Church.

As foreign opposition to any further growth of Russian America increased, Tsar Alexander I, in a vainglorious effort to shelter the colony from encroachment, in September 1821 banned foreign ships, under threat of seizure, from the waters of the North Pacific north of 51 degrees north latitude, from Alaska to the Kurile Islands. Both England and the United States, however, claimed territory above that line, up to the 55th parallel, inland and on the coast, and in December 1823, President Monroe (in the "Monroe Doctrine") asserted "as a principle" that "the American continents, by the free and independent conditions which they have assumed and maintained, are henceforth not to be considered subjects for colonization by any European power." Confrontation was averted, and by the end of 1825 Russia had signed protocols with both Great Britain and the United States that recognized free trade along the disputed coast and delimited the southern boundary of the Russian American colonies at 54 degrees 40′ NL.

The great nineteenth-century American naturalist Henry Wood Elliott once remarked that the Russians "did not live here [Russian America] as a people, but as a company of fur-traders only, with a single eye to the getting of skins." The meagerness of the settlements was indeed astonishing. In all of Russian America at its height there were less than a thousand Russians, and the Ross colony as late as 1832, for example, consisted of a modest wooden fortress with seventeen small-caliber cannon, thirty-eight *promyshlenniks* (twelve of them engaged in agricultural pursuits), and a few hundred Aleuts. In livestock, it had 46 horses, 213 bulls and cows, 81 pigs, and 842 sheep—hardly enough to supply all of Russia's Pacific needs. A decade later, the total population of all territories under the company's rule (excluding the Kurile Islands) consisted of 633 Russians, 1,425 Indians, 483 Creoles, and 4,287 Aleuts. Every Russian had a little plot of ground for potatoes, turnips, carrots, radishes, and other vegetables, but in the chill, damp clime (similar to that around Okhotsk) nothing much else would grow. "An inhabitant of New Archangel," wrote one visiting doctor, "can be compared to an amphibian. His body is submerged not only in a mass of air as are the bodies of other people, but also in a cold steam bath."

In other respects, New Archangel seemed a cultivated oasis in the wilderness. Its library had more than 1,200 books in several European languages, and there was a large room devoted to paintings, drawings, and maps. The local museum housed a number of scientific instruments, including chronometers, theodolites, an astrolabe, a very precise Jurgenson pendulum, telescopes, a microscope, natural and artificial magnets, barometers, thermometers, and an electricity machine. In addition, the museum had a natural history wing, with sam-

ples of the local flora and fauna as well as artifacts from the natives on
display. A meteorological observatory, constructed in 1841 on Japan
Island, formed part of a network of such installations that spanned the
empire. From time to time, activities at company headquarters faintly
imitated court life, with amateur theatricals, concerts, and masquer-
ades, and occasional soirées with ballroom dancing for the officer
corps. Within the town itself there were also three Orthodox churches,
one Lutheran church, two hospitals, and at least three schools, including one for orphans.

But culture and colonization were static, and once its boundaries
had been fixed, Russian America began to shrivel and decay from
within. Its inhospitable remoteness brought few voluntary settlers to
its shores, while measures undertaken to sustain it only contributed to
its decline. After 1821 the company prolonged the term of obligatory
service from seven to fourteen years, and after 1844 all those indebted
to the company found themselves in the position of indentured servants, unable to leave until they had repaid what they owed. More
charitably, the company had also begun to settle ex-employees (including the old and infirm) in the colonies as colonial citizens, and to
provide them with land and welfare benefits. This made Russian America at the time probably "the only place in the world," one visitor
remarked, "where there is not a single beggar." On the other hand,
the general dependency the system fostered inclined Creoles and
Aleuts especially to idleness and drink. Most Aleut and Creole women
also became veritable prostitutes, since the Russians, taking advantage
of their meekness and naivete, taught them, wrote a contemporary,
that they "cannot refuse a man, or annoy him, when it is so simple to
satisfy his demands." Among the Creoles themselves it was said that
"to marry a Creole woman means to take a wife for others to enjoy."

Sheer boredom inclined many others to profligate behavior, one
visitor finding that there was virtually nothing to do in New Archangel
"but watch ravens tear apart black cuttlefish, a pig chase a dog, or a
billy goat chomp the bark off shrubs." Not surprisingly, the extreme
isolation sometimes drove men over the edge. The Polish director of
the meteorological observatory, in the atmosphere of license that prevailed, never let his wife out of his sight, and even followed her from
room to room within their own home. He constantly looked under
couches, tables, and chairs to make sure no one was hiding there to

captivate her, bolted the shutters, drew the curtains tight and fastened them with pins. The doors were always double-locked, and spoons, irons, and other objects were balanced on or against them, as alarms. The door into the bedroom was tied with wire, and a blanket hung over it so no one could peek in. For six months his wife was unable even to go outside, and could talk to her daughter only in whispers, under threat of a beating if she so much as raised her voice. But one day her husband, "for the first time in his life, decided to take a nap after his midday meal. Scarcely had he fallen asleep when his wife grabbed the child and a small bundle which she had secretly prepared, and rushed out onto the street and ran as fast as she could."

The natives had their own madness to cope with in their own disoriented world. Although the Russians finally persuaded them to accept inoculation for smallpox, the spread of syphilis remained epidemic, especially among the Thlingits, who were constantly being infected by American traders operating in the straits. The shoreline was lined with brothels, and although they were periodically burned in raids, many natives had come to regard the disease as "an unavoidable evil," and even deliberately tried to become infected so as to get time off from work.

New Archangel was a capital in decay. At its height, it had a population of only a thousand (more than half of whom were Thlingits or Aleuts), some seventy-six dwellings, and a central fort. The fort had never been renovated, and the yellow two-story building in which the chief administrator lived and worked had been grotesquely enlarged (or elongated) by "many annexes"—servants quarters, a parlor, a billiards room built above the gate, and so on. At the base of the cliff stood the harbor facilities, which were substantial, but the settlement itself had only one narrow street, unpaved and for most of the year awash in mud from the rains. On the other side of the fort, part way up the hill, were some warehouses and workshops, and then a palisade separating the settlement from that of the Thlingits.

For all practical purposes, the fort was "constantly in state of siege" and as late as 1860 the Thlingits still manifestly controlled the land beyond the settlement's walls, where they sometimes hid with knives behind bushes and trees, or more defiantly gathered in warpaint, leather gauntlets, and wooden slat armor to brandish their weapons and shout. No Russian dared to go fifty paces out from the fortress unarmed, and from day to day the Thlingits could only be cowed by holding important tribesmen hostage and by a round-the-clock display of Russian artillery trained directly upon their village adjacent to the fort.

Yet this had scarcely tamed them. "Their hearts are filled with vengeance," one official wrote. "They seethe with open animosity, and await only an opportune time to strike." In addition to knives, some Thlingits carried their own revolvers and muskets, wore iron breastplates, and had even sequestered small cannon in the woods. One visitor, soliciting a demonstration of their martial prowess, noted "with no little surprise" that they "fired rapid volleys, like the firing of regular infantry."

The Aleuts, on the other hand, were a living reproach to the early prosecution of the fur trade. Small and awkward, with an overdeveloped upper torso and short and crooked legs (as a result of long service in the sea), they had not a trace of warlike spirit left. In remarking their pathetic condition, one official wrote: "Aleuts are very sensitive; harsh or rude words hurt them deeply, and physical punishment is considered such a degradation that to punish an Aleut means in essence to force him to commit suicide." Before the coming of the Russians, their population had stood at about 25,000. The initial *Promyshlennik* advance was devastating, and by the time the Russian-American Company brought a halt to their decimation, most of the population had already been wiped out. By 1806, there were only 5,234 Aleuts of both sexes left. A smallpox epidemic in 1836 further reduced their number, which dwindled as well from the ravages of venereal disease.

Notwithstanding Father Veniaminov's noble exertions, their general docility had made their conversion to Christianity almost meaningless, since there was little real conviction in their faith. "If they were told tomorrow that they must become Mohammedans," wrote Golovin, "then without thinking, they would attend a mosque and perform namaz just as they presently go to church and light candles in front of the icon."

The Thlingits, on the other hand, seldom attended church except out of curiosity, laughed out loud on occasion in the middle of the service (particularly if any "strange or incorrect expression" were used), or got up and walked out. A special church had been built for them, but in a revolt they attempted in 1855, they merely occupied it as a vantage point from which to inflict damage on the Russian garrison.

After the powerful Hudson's Bay Company had entered the coastal trade in the middle 1820s, the Russian-American Company rapidly lost its dominance even within the vicinity of long-established posts; in 1839 it was decided to make a virtue of necessity and lease the continental portion of the Alaska Panhandle to the English in return for regular deliveries of food. As part of this divestiture, in 1841 the company also sold Russian California for $30,000. Subsequently, the company established fish and timber industries on a modest scale, to diversify the colonial economy (as the fur trade with China failed), and began an ice trade with San Francisco. Prefabricated housing had always been a specialty of the Russians, and the Gold Rush in California created a large new market for their skills. The ice trade developed from the same impetus, since before long the going fleet of Boston iceboats was unable to meet California's needs. Most of the ice was cut from lakes on Kodiak Island, in an operation, according to one account,

performed with marvelous ease and speed. A horse is harnessed to an iron cutter with one smooth runner and one with a sawtooth edge. The horse moves along at an even gait and the saw gouges the ice about two inches deep. Then they turn it back again and set the sledge so the smooth runner goes along the cut line and the saw cuts a new one. In this manner they mark the ice with absolutely straight lines and then cut lateral marks the same way. Thus they cut a large surface and market it in perfectly uniform squares just like a checkerboard. Then along these marked lines they drag a saw-like plow, which cuts the ice about eight inches thick.

A single blow was enough to separate the blocks, which were heaved up onto the ice and dragged by ropes to the harbor along wooden rails. Indians did most of the heavy work, and showed great immunity to the cold, working all day out on the ice in below-freezing weather dressed only in capes.

New Archangel also had various facilities for the construction, repair, and outfitting of ships (it was the only ice-free port in the empire), and ventures were undertaken in whaling (in conjunction with a Finnish firm) and coal mining at Kenai.

The coal mining never got anywhere, and in the whaling business, the Russians were completely outdone. American whalers were almost as aggressive as pirates, and landed at will on Russian coasts, including islands of the Aleutian and Kurile chains. They felled trees where they wished, extracted whalebone and rendered oil on the beach, "covered the sea with blubber and the shores with carcasses and whales that had died of wounds." Occasionally, in their disorderly forays they wrecked isolated company outposts or took the lumber the Aleuts had prepared with great labor for winter, and their supplies of dried fish. By the 1850s, the New Bedford whaling fleet (America's largest) was even prowling the northern part of the Okhotsk Sea.

The survival of Russian America had become a balancing act. But its future was not to be decided wholly in New Archangel, which had ceased to have any prospects of its own, but in southeastern Siberia, in the valley of the Amur, where China's Black Dragon River promised to become Russia's "Mississippi of the East."

After the refusal of the Japanese to establish trade relations, Russian interest in the Far East had waned. The Kurile Islands, formerly valued as stepping stones to Japan, had been drawn into the fur trade, but were not yet coveted as strategic assets in their own right; Sakhalin Island was believed to be a peninsula obstructing the mouth of the Amur; and the mouth of the Amur itself was thought to be blocked by sand. The Amur in any case belonged to China, and "without an outlet to the sea," remarks one historian, "the development of the Far East seemed hopeless."

Then the Opium War between Britain and China (1839–42) revealed a Manchu Empire in precipitous decline. By the Treaty of Nanking, Great Britain (Russia's greatest enemy) obtained the island of Hong Kong and other concessions, and other nations immediately followed suit with equally "unequal treaties" that left China in disarray. Russia promptly undertook a thorough review of its own eastern policy, and among the documents that conveniently came to the tsar's attention was one by a young zoologist who claimed that natives along the lower Amur "were in feeling and fact completely independent from China, and that the Chinese delineated their frontier with Russia considerably more to the east and south than the Russians realized."

Every inch of the border between Siberia and China, of course, had never been delimited on the spot, but technical uncertainties in the Treaty of Nerchinsk now prepared the way for a broad license in interpretation, at least on the Russian side. The valley's loss, in any case, had never been totally accepted by Russian imperialists, and there was hardly a time after 1689 when the government did not have at least one eye on the prize. An original ambition of Bering's Great Northern Expedition (as conceived by the Admiralty College) had been to survey the Pacific Coast from Okhotsk to the Amur's mouth, with the idea of facilitating an attack on China from the sea. And in 1752, one of Siberia's more enterprising governors, Rear Admiral Vasily Miatlev (seeing no other way to meet Eastern Siberia's needs) had recommended that the Amur Valley be reoccupied and a shipyard built at the river's mouth. Catherine the Great is supposed to have remarked that "if the Amur were useful only to supply Kamchatka and the Okhotsk Seaboard, its possession would be important," and in subsequent years the plight of the Far East periodically tempted officials to adventurist schemes.

The paramount importance of the China trade to the Russian economy had restrained them, but the calm on the Manchurian frontier was an empty one in every respect. Russian designs were merely in abeyance; and due to an astonishing lack of geopolitical judgment, the Chinese had failed to colonize the Amur Valley in the years since the Treaty of Nerchinsk had confirmed it as their own.

Russia began to move. On May 17, 1846, a small brig under the flag of the Russian-American Company set sail from Okhotsk ostensibly to verify reports from wandering Tungus that some Russian fugitives had camped at the mouth of the Amur. In fact, its mission was to explore the navigability of the river's mouth. After failing to find a satisfactory entrance, the commander of the expedition decided that the estuary was impassable—at least for sailing ships; but within the government there was disagreement as to whether the matter should be pursued. Count Karl Robert von Nesselrode, the Foreign Minister, thought not, out of concern for Russo-Chinese relations. But with the appointment of Nikolay Muravyev as governor-general of Eastern Siberia in 1847, an aggressive Chinese policy quickly gained the upper hand.

Born on August 11, 1809, Muravyev had enjoyed a distinguished military career, with commendations for exploits during the Russo-Turkish War of 1828–29, the suppression of the Polish revolt of 1831, and several expeditions against guerrilla strongholds in the Caucasus Mountains. In 1844, upon his retirement from the army as a major general at age thirty-six due to ill health, he was appointed governor of the province of Tula, where he gained a reputation as an idealistic liberal and administrator of unusual fairness and integrity. He was one of the first (among high officials) to advocate the abolition of serfdom, and his ardent admiration of the United States reflected his relatively democratic views. But it was as one of the great empire builders of the nineteenth century that he would make his name.

When Muravyev first took up his post, he was struck by the insufficiency of the military forces at his disposal. Over the immense territory of Eastern Siberia there were only four battalions of the line, without any field artillery, and the manpower shortage among free citizens there made it impossible for him to fill in the gaps. With the tsar's approval, he therefore emancipated several thousand Transbaikal peasants from their forced drudgery in the mines of Nerchinsk, and began to mold them into new infantry Cossack battalions.

In 1849, naval Captain Gennady Nevelskoy, with Muravyev's support, undertook to survey the northern shores of Sakhalin to determine whether it was an island, as well as the far eastern coast down to the Amur's mouth. To his triumphant surprise, he found a narrow but navigable strait between Sakhalin and the mainland, and determined that the Amur could be entered by seagoing ships. This meant that Eastern Siberia was actually connected, by way of the Amur, to both the Pacific Ocean and the Sea of Japan. As guardian of the river's mouth, Sakhalin at once assumed new strategic importance, and Nevelskoy urged that Russia seize the lower Amur without delay. Under the pretense of establishing a trading post for the Russian-American Company, Nevelskoy returned in the summer of 1850, broke ground for the fort of Nikolayevsk, brought ashore a holy icon, recited a few prayers, and raised the Russian flag, claiming the estuary for the tsar. "A long clap of thunder," he recalled, "resounded immediately after our cheers; large drops of rain in bright sunshine sprinkled the ground under our feet and we involuntarily cried out: 'God is with us and no one will prevail against us.' "

A crowd of bewildered Gilyaks suddenly appeared, prepared in their own pathetic way to resist. To their surprise, they were made welcome with tea and gruel, and (after hastily conferring together) "began to eject heavy stones from inside their clothing." Each was given a tobacco leaf, and lengths of pink and blue calico print cloth, which they instantly ripped to shreds to make ribbons for their hair.

Nevelskoy's impetuous action outraged Count Nesselrode, but Nicholas I on this occasion, with imperial pride, made the memorable declaration: "Where once the Russian flag has flown, it must not be lowered again." By early 1853, the Russians had extended their occupation up the river for several miles and along the coast to De Kastri Bay, and in October the Russian-American Company, "masquerading as a private concern to camouflage state aims," took possession of Sakhalin under Nevelskoy's direction. Accompanied by a corps of prospectors, furriers, and other specialists, he assessed its diverse resources, and was not disappointed in what he found. Nor was he entirely surprised: two years before, encountering some of the island's natives, he had noticed that a button worn by one of them was a lump of coal. By the end of September, a Russian fort mounted with cannon had been built at Sakhalin's southern end (at Aniwa Bay, the site of Khvostov and Davydov's first raid); meanwhile, Muravyev had begun to press for bolder action on the Amur front. In a memorandum to Grand Duke Konstantin (his alter ego in the government) he linked the Amur to regional security and put into sweeping perspective Siberia's unique importance to the empire. He warned that if China, "now helpless in its ignorance," became a pawn of the English or the French, Russia's hold on Siberia itself would be threatened, and "in Siberia, besides gold, there is space, which is vital to us and is sufficient for all of the excess agricultural population of European Russia for an entire century. The loss of this expanse cannot be compensated by any victories and conquests in Europe." Control of the Amur emerged as indispensable to keeping Siberia and assuring a strong, if not dominant, influence over China to check the machinations of other powers.

Other events soon strengthened Muravyev's case, as the jockeying for advantage in East Asia increased. In 1852, the United States (flexing new muscle on the international scene) had dispatched a fleet of gunboats to Japan under Commodore Matthew Perry to force that nation open to trade. Moving with competitive speed, Russia's Vice Admiral Evfimy Putiatin arrived off Nagasaki on August 21, 1853, with similar aims. Two months later, the Crimean War broke out, and although Russia's far eastern possessions were remote from the main theater of war, they were directly threatened by an allied force.

The Russian outpost on Sakhalin, hopelessly vulnerable to enemy cruisers, was abandoned as a strategic liability, and every means instead devoted to protecting the shores of Siberia itself from attack. After some hesitation, the tsar in April 1854 approved Muravyev's scheme for an expedition down the Amur, to effectively reinforce the posts at its mouth, prevent the river from falling into allied hands, and enable him to maintain communications with Petropavlovsk and other fortified positions on the coast. Muravyev quickly assembled a mile-long flotilla of seventy-five barges and rafts, sufficient to carry a Cossack cavalry squadron, an infantry battalion, a division of mountain artillery, plus cattle and stores downstream. In May he embarked at its head on the *Argun,* the first steamer to be built in Eastern Siberia.

As the Russians entered the upper Amur for the first time in 165 years, a military band played "God Save the Tsar," soldiers crossed themselves, and waved their caps and cheered. Muravyev, filling a tumbler with water from the river, drank to the mission's success. An icon of the Blessed Virgin, supposedly evacuated in 1686 from Albazin when it fell, was carried in a circuit around the deck, and when the flotilla came to the site of the historic fortress, the soldiers stood in silence as the band played hymns. Muravyev, disembarking to inspect the ruins, knelt reverently in prayer. Upon reaching the beautiful promontory just below where the Amur and Ussuri rivers unite, Muravyev, surveying the heights, declared, "Here there shall be a town"—and there Khabarovsk was founded in 1858.

Although Muravyev had notified Peking that he was taking troops down the Amur to protect the estuary from attack, he had not waited for clearance to start, and his message was not even received in the Chinese capital until the flotilla had passed Aigun. The next thing the emperor knew it had reached Marinsk, a new fortified Russian settlement opposite De Kastri Bay. Marinsk, Nikolayevsk, and other strategic posts were strengthened by the new arrivals, of whom four hundred were also sent to bolster the fortress at Petropavlovsk.

Their dispatch could not have been more timely. The port was defended by meager batteries scattered about the surrounding hills, plus an armed frigate and transport anchored behind a sandspit at the entrance to the bay. In late August, an Anglo-French squadron of six ships, operating out of the Hawaiian Islands, stormed the fortress, but its amphibious assault was repulsed with a loss of three hundred men. The unexpected victory, in stark contrast to the humiliating defeats Russia was experiencing on the Crimean Peninsula thousands of miles away, was attributed directly to the reinforcements Muravyev sent down the Amur, and gave a tremendous boost to his arguments and plans. Foreseeing, however, that the following year would bring a still more determined attack, Muravyev ordered the abandonment of Petropavlovsk, so as to concentrate all his forces about the Amur's mouth. The garrison embarked in April 1855, eluded English cruisers in a dense fog, and sailed into the "Bay of Tartary." Unaware of Nevelskoy's discovery of a channel between Sakhalin and the mainland, the English commodore thought he had the Russian convoy trapped. He was therefore utterly confounded when it escaped up the Amur as if into thin air. Lacking other strategic targets in the area, the allies seized a Russian-American Company supply ship, the *Sitka,* and briefly occupied the Kurile Island of Uruppu and the harbor of Ayan on the Okhotsk Sea.

Meanwhile, under Muravyev's direction, 130 new barges had been built, sufficient to carry 7,000 tons of supplies, 3,000 more men, fortress artillery, and 5,000 settlers to the lower Amur, where they could begin to colonize. On June 8, 1855, the Manchu emperor was again startled to learn that the Russians had defied his military stations; and that winter, still more Russians arrived, boldly proceeding by land along the river's left bank. By the end of the year, Russia's hold on the estuary was established beyond the power of China to dislodge.

Nicholas I was succeeded by Alexander II in 1855, and the following March Nesselrode resigned as Foreign Minister. He was replaced by the abler Prince Aleksandr Gorchakov, to whom Alexander II (preoccupied with internal reforms) increasingly entrusted the direction of foreign affairs. A third Russian expedition went down the river in the summer of 1856, and throughout the rest of the season the Russians came and went at will, with the local Manchu authorities unable to do anything but forward estimates to Peking of the forces that passed their posts. On his way back up the Amur, Muravyev had paused at Ust-Zeysk, and amid general rejoicing renamed it Blagoveshchensk, meaning "Good News." A few weeks later, he rode into Irkutsk through a triumphal arch erected to his glory.

Although Russia lost the Crimean War, no evidence of a humiliated and defeated Russia was apparent to either China or Japan. Somewhat in recognition of this fact, on February 7, 1855, Vice Admiral Evfimy Putiatin concluded the Treaty of Shimoda, which opened several Japanese ports to Russian ships, recognized a roughly equal division of the Kurile Islands between them (Uruppu and islands to the north as Russian, Etorofu and Kunashiri to the south as Japanese), and "joint possession" of Sakhalin, with the final disposition of the island to be decided at a later date. Subsequently, in February 1857, Putiatin was appointed plenipotentiary to China, where in addition to hammering out an expanded trade agreement, he was to secure recognition of Muravyev's fait accompli.

Putiatin and Muravyev went down the Amur together with a heavy military escort in May 1857. While Putiatin continued on to China, Muravyev organized further military settlements, bringing Russian troop strength up to 22,000 on the Manchurian frontier. That winter, snow roads were also established between Nikolayevsk and other key posts.

In further acknowledgment of Russia's growing regional clout, Britain and France (its recent bitter antagonists) sought its help (as well as that of the United States) in persuading China to open its doors. The Chinese soon capitulated, and in separate treaties the Western powers gained various concessions, but none more handsome than those the Russians obtained. In addition to a substantially expanded trade agreement, the two parties agreed to negotiate an immediate redetermination of the Amur frontier in a supplementary pact.

That pact was dictated, in effect, by Muravyev in May 1858 at Aigun. On May 11, the morning after his arrival, he opened negotiations with a historical survey and justification of his actions, demanding free navigation on the Amur for Russian ships, possession of the river's north or left bank, and a new determination of the frontier line that followed the Amur and Ussuri rivers to the sea. In the afternoon he invited his Chinese counterpart aboard ship to hear singing by the Irkutsk Cavalry Choir, and the next day, May 12, his chief aide presented a draft treaty to the Manchus. On the evening of May 13, one of the Chinese negotiators came to him in tears and implored him to abandon claims to the Ussuri area, threatening otherwise to drown himself on the spot. Muravyev would have none of this, and the next day went ashore and presented all his demands as an ultimatum, giving the Manchus until morning to respond. Morning came, the Manchus yielded, and the Treaty of Aigun was signed on May 16.

Fresh from his triumph over China, Muravyev disembarked on August 10 at Sakhalin with troops and a drum and bugle corps, and claimed that because the island was "homogeneous with the Amur river," it therefore also belonged to Russia, in contravention of the recent Russo-Japanese accord. Unlike Putiatin, Muravyev did not accept the concept of joint occupation, and went to Japan in August 1859 determined to renegotiate the treaty's terms. At Shinagawa he offered to allow Japanese fishermen already on Sakhalin to remain, but the Japanese were not impressed by his magnanimity and insisted on either joint occupation or the southern half of the island for themselves. The talks ended in deadlock; but without trying to impose their claim by force, the Russians, fostering settlements, built up their own position, exerting steady pressure to squeeze the Japanese out.

Unwilling to compete with this tactic or risk war, the Japanese eventually agreed (in May 1875) to swap southern Sakhalin for Russia's half of the Kurile chain. Not all Russians at the time regarded the trade as a good one, since the Kuriles enclosed the Sea of Okhotsk, and Russia's sole possession of them would have turned the sea into a "Russian lake." Moreover, Sakhalin had no attractive harbors to speak of, and its barren soil seemed unlikely to support agricultural communities. But it had coal and other resources, potential as a penal colony (requiring, of course, a considerable military guard), and it ensured Russian command of the strait. For their part, the Japanese repossessed a group of islands they regarded as their own, thus delaying a dangerous confrontation with a mightier power, and gaining time in which to find their own direction and strength.

More immediate Russian triumphs were in the offing. In 1860, taking advantage of an Anglo-French siege of Peking, Nikolay Ignatyev, on a diplomatic mission to the capital, mediated a truce that secured the evacuation of the invaders, and as a result of Chinese gratitude succeeded in extracting the Treaty of Peking. This amazing treaty not only confirmed the terms obtained by Muravyev at Aigun, but ceded to Russia the whole region between the Ussuri River and the Pacific

Ocean, with a coastline extending southward to the Korean frontier. In the same year, the port of Vladivostok (boastfully meaning "Lord of the East") was founded on Peter the Great Bay.

Taken together, the two treaties had increased the size of Russian Siberia by over 400,000 square miles. The relatively mild climate and fertile soil of the Ussuri region immediately attracted Cossack and peasant settlers, and by the end of 1860 about forty thousand colonists had arrived. All through the river valley new military posts sprang up, while dockyards were being built at several harbors on the coast. Russia's fledgling Pacific navy began to take shape, and in March 1861 a Russian warship occupied the strategic island of Tsushima in the straits between Korea and Japan.

Ignatyev went on to enjoy a long, prominent career in state service; Muravyev, ennobled by the tsar for his achievements, quietly retired to Paris with the title "Count of the Amur," his surname becoming Muravyev-Amursky.

In the wake of Russia's dramatic expansion in East Asia, the Russian American colonies were obliged to reassess their place. A number of circumnavigatory expeditions by Russian seafarers, sailing halfway around the world to provision both the American colony and Eastern Siberia by sea, had failed to relieve the Russian-American Company's situation; Fort Ross had been abandoned under duress; and in Alaska the English were closing in on the Yukon as well as threatening Russian settlements from the sea. Baranov's successors had tried to keep the company alive by reorganizing and consolidating its corporate struc-ture and holdings, by missionary activity to tame the Thlingits, and by various attempts to lure new colonists to the American shores. But by the 1860s it had become clear that Russian America could not endure. It had become an intolerable drain on the Imperial Treasury, had failed to secure the territory under its control, and was too dispersed and distant to defend. The Crimean War, in particular, had underscored the vulnerability of Russia's maritime flanks to British seapower, even though most coastal settlements had been largely spared. (Although the fort at New Archangel, for example, was sufficient defense against Indians, a man-of-war firing from the harbor, it was said, could easily reduce it to dust.) Above all, the government had correctly determined that Russia's real Pacific future lay in the riverine highways and fertile valleys of the Amur Basin, which it once more bent all its energies to acquire.

Equal in importance to all this was the fact that Russian America found itself on the doorstep of an irresistibly expanding United States. Americans had been working their way up the Missouri River and westward to the Rocky Mountains, and Indian tribes living east of the Mississippi River had been forcibly removed to the Great Plains. Texas had been annexed in 1845; in 1846, Britain and the United States had settled on the 49th parallel as dividing their dominions, and by 1848 the Southwest and California had been wrenched from Mexico by war. Within a few days of that war's end, one James Marshall "spotted a golden glint in the millrace of a sawmill he was building on California's American River," and the California Gold Rush began. In 1856, gold was discovered in the Fraser River Valley, and the Indian Frontier (from Minnesota to Louisiana) collapsed under the wheels of wagons bearing goldseekers to the West. By 1860, California and Oregon had joined Texas in statehood, and nearly all the rest of the land west of the Missouri River had began organized into the territories of New Mexico, Utah, Washington, Kansas, and Nebraska. The Homestead Act of 1862 accelerated settlement, and after the Civil War, emigrants crowded the new transcontinental rails which crossed the prairies to the western rampart of the Sierra Nevada Mountains. The momentum was unstoppable, from sea to shining sea. Ohio Senator John Sherman (younger brother of William Tecumseh) told his colleagues in 1863, "If the whole Army of the United States stood in the way, the wave of emigration would pass over it to seek the valley where gold was to be found." And if gold were discovered in Alaska, Russia could scarcely withstand the tide. In fact, Russia's position was so weak that in 1858 even the rumor that some militant Mormons might try to settle there had "caused a momentary scare in St. Petersburg."

Muravyev saw clearly that Russia's position had become untenable, and that it ought to relinquish its colonies in favor of opportunities in the Far East. As early as March 1853, he had analyzed the situation in a memorandum to the tsar:

Twenty-five years ago the Russian-American Company urged the occupation of California, which at the time was not yet controlled by anyone, out of concern that it would soon be acquired by the United States. In Petersburg it was said this wouldn't happen for a hundred years. The Company warned it could happen in twenty-five years, and now it has been already over a year that California constitutes one of the North American States. One could not but foresee . . . that these States, once they had established themselves on the Pacific Ocean, would soon take precedence over all other naval powers there, and would require the whole northwestern coast. The sovereignty of the North American States in all of North America is so natural, that in fact we oughtn't to fret that in California we failed to consolidate our own position, because sooner or later we would have had to yield it, although we might have received greater benefits in exchange. Now, with the invention and development of railroads, it is obvious . . . that sooner or later we shall have to yield.

Almost no one in the government disagreed. And after the Crimean War and the new annexations, the idea of selling the colonies quickly took hold. In 1857, Admiral Ferdinand Wrangel, the former governor of Russian America, suggested the government sell them even at a loss out of "anticipatory prudence"—concurring with Konstantin, who wanted to resolve "amicably and for us profitably a question that may otherwise be decided in our disfavor by conquest." The Crimean War had also depleted the Russian Treasury, while colonial expenses continued to mount. By 1866, the company's administrative obligations cost the government 200,000 rubles every year (above and beyond its earnings), compounding a debt that already stood at three quarters of a million. And it was frankly hoped that the sale of Alaska would retire this debt. Already in 1860–61, a joint mission of the Finance and Naval ministries had gone to the colonies to assess their worth.

It was unlikely that Russia and America would fail to come to terms. The two powers shared a hostility toward Great Britain, and had developed other ties that bind. Russia had supported the colonies in the Revolutionary War, and during the Crimean War, American doctors had braved a British bombardment to tend the Russian wounded in Sevastopol. During the Civil War, in support of the North, Russia had sent squadrons to New York and San Francisco to forestall outside intervention. Both (almost simultaneously) had also freed millions of their subjects (serfs and slaves), and whatever conflicts had emerged between the two had ended without bloodshed in accords. In 1866, the tsar could say truthfully, "The Russian and American peoples have no injuries to forget or to remember."

And so, imagining an American Alaska would stand as a buffer between Russian Siberia and the British Northwest, on March 18, 1867, Russia abruptly sold Alaska (and the Aleutian Islands) for $7,200,000—or just 2 cents an acre—to the United States.

Edouard de Stoeckl, the Russian minister to Washington, had obtained the authority he needed from St. Petersburg the day before and had gone directly to the house of William Seward, the Secretary of State. The two worked all night to draw up the treaty, and just before dawn, in Seward's office in the Department of State, it was signed. Acre for acre, "Seward's Folly," as his detractors dubbed it, was even more thrifty than the Louisiana Purchase from Napoleon in 1803, which for 3 cents an acre had doubled the nation's size.

Seven months later, on October 18, 100 Russian and 250 American soldiers lined up on the square outside the governor's house in New Archangel to complete the transfer of power. A salvo in salute from an American vessel in the harbor was answered by honorary fire from within the fort, and then the deed of sale was read aloud. The Russians began to lower the company flag, but freezing rain had started to fall and the flag clung stubbornly to the pole. A Russian sailor had to shimmy up the staff to shake it loose. Five minutes later the Stars and Stripes flew over the cliff.

Those left behind suffered an unhappy fate. Creoles watched Russians leaving in large numbers; native women remaining with small children saw their husbands sail away. Many turned to drink, like one Vasily Shishkin, for example, a Creole deacon, who roamed "drunk in the port . . . and was beaten up in an American bar." Others committed suicide. Without just cause, the commander of the American troops also evicted a number of remaining Russians from their homes. Nothing, in fact, was done to establish a civil government, and Alaska remained under military rule for another seventeen years.

New Archangel, renamed Sitka, continued to be the capital of Alaska until 1900, and six buildings from the period (preserved by the National Park Service) still stand.

The mark left by the Russians on frontier America was by no means slight. Their *promyshlennik* vanguard had gained a foothold on Alaska's coastal islands by the time of the Revolutionary War, and Russian pioneers had established farming communities and hunting outposts in California before any white man had ventured west of the Mississippi. When they made their unofficial grab for Hawaii, "the United States was still licking the wounds of the War of 1812." Some rode with Kit Carson and John Frémont as members of the California Battalion of Mountain Volunteers in 1846, and joined the Gold Rush of 1849. One of the Indian river guides used by Lewis and Clark was a Nez Percé half-breed chief named Tetoharsky, and the most valued war medicine of one Sioux chief was a large color portrait of a Russian general who had fought in the Napoleonic Wars. Aleksandr Baranov, moreover, was one of the fundamental figures in the European settlement of North America, and was recognized by his contemporaries as belonging in the company of Peter Stuyvesant, Daniel Boone, and John Smith. Russians even participated (however slightly) in the pathetic final decimation of the culture of the Great Plains. As buffalo hunting became a popular sport (under the influence of railroad promoters), the Grand Duke Alexis, son of Alexander II, journeyed to Kansas to prove his shooting skill.

The only overseas colony ever ventured by the empire, Russian America was not destined to last. Geography and geopolitical realities were against it, and the course of history—perhaps even time itself. "It is rather difficult to come to terms with real time," one traveler to the colonies wrote in 1817, "if one looks at east-west time chronology, Greenwich time and shipboard time" (reckoned from dawn, but dated from noon to noon), "time by the sun and by the stars, the astronomical day and so forth." All other Europeans in the Pacific told their time from west to east, via Canton, while the Russians made their calculations from east to west, and were (it seemed) a day ahead of themselves.

PART
THREE

Overleaf: Early nineteenth-century view of New Archangel (Sitka); the large elevated building in the background was the home of the governor. Note the octagonal lighthouse on top that sent a beam far out to sea.

12

"THE BOTTOM OF THE SACK"

In the same year that Russian America was sold to the United States, Great Britain abolished the exile system that had colonized Australia. In Siberia, exile had long preceded the founding of Botany Bay, yet after two centuries its tide of misfortune had not yet reached its height.

There are two Siberias that everybody knows: the land of sub-Arctic wilderness and icy death; and the land of chains. Both owe their original hold on the popular imagination to accounts of Siberian life in the mid-nineteenth century largely inspired by reports of the tsarist exile system.

As with other Western powers who acquired colonial possessions overseas, the acquisition of Siberia over-the-Urals led to the establishment of "exile"—for political, judicial, or other reasons—as a common form of punishment. Siberia's sheer size and comparative desolation had always discouraged the government's half-hearted attempts at its development, while 5,000 miles and more from the imperial capital, its easternmost limits seemed as remote to successive tsars as contemporary Australia to the British Crown.

This did not spare its punitive function close examination, and one investigative journalist, George Kennan, who in the 1880s visited numerous Siberian prisons and places of exile, eloquently remarked the pathetically sad scenes that commonly took place when convict-exiles paused briefly to consider their plight at the boundary post between

Europe and Asia: "There is no other boundary post in the whole world," he wrote,

> that has seen so much of human suffering and so many broken hearts. More than 170,000 exiles have traveled this road since 1878, and more than half a million since the beginning of the present century. In former years, when exiles were compelled to walk from their places of arrest to the places of their banishment, they reached the Siberian post only after months of toilsome marching along muddy or dusty roads, over forest-clad mountains, through rainstorms or snowstorms, or in bitter cold. . . . Some gave way to unrestrained grief; some comforted the weeping; some knelt and pressed their faces to the soil . . . and collecting a little earth to take with them . . . crossed themselves hastily, and with a confused jangling of chains and leg fetters, moved slowly away past the boundary post into Siberia.

Strangely enough, the first Siberian exile was neither a common criminal nor an enemy of the state. It was a bell—the 700-pound town bell of Uglich—punished for sounding the alarm at the assassination of the tsarevich Dmitry in 1581. Those who participated in the brief uprising that followed were whipped and had their tongues cut out. The bell was likewise flogged, its "tongue" wrenched from its socket, and (to complete the superstitious elaboration of its chastisement) it was ignominiously dragged across the Urals to Tobolsk, where it was banned forever from being rung again.

A scattering of political exiles soon followed, along with colonists deported in a fledgling effort to settle the new lands. When punishment by exile was officially incorporated into the penal code in 1649, however, it was inspired by the desire of "civilized" society to banish from sight those physically mutilated by its still-barbarous criminal code. At the time, writes Kennan,

> men were impaled on sharp stakes, hanged, and beheaded by the hundred for crimes that would not now be regarded as capital in any civilized country in the world; while lesser offenders were flogged with the *knut* or bastinado, branded with hot irons, mutilated by amputation of one or more of their limbs, deprived of their tongues, and suspended in the air by hooks passed under two of their ribs

until they died a lingering and miserable death. When criminals had been thus *knuted*, bastinadoed, branded or crippled by amputation, Siberian exile was resorted to as a quick and easy method of getting them out of the way.

Although originally applied as a penalty supplemental to corporal punishment, in time exile came to be viewed more definitely as a means of populating and developing the colony. With the spread of mining and the need of forced labor to sustain it, penal servitude began to replace long prison terms, while the list of offenses meriting exile was steadily lengthened to include such petty infractions as vagrancy, prizefighting, or taking snuff. A large proportion of the early exiles were also prisoners of war, who possessed a reservoir of diverse talent the new colony could put to use, and after the Ukraine was forcibly united to Russia in 1675, for example, Siberia received the benefit of its officer corps. By the end of the seventeenth century perhaps one tenth of the total Russian population of Siberia was made up of deportees. From the beginning of the eighteenth their ranks were swelled by religious dissenters, *streltsy*, Polish rebels, nine thousand Swedes captured by Peter the Great in the Great Northern War, entire transplanted villages of Lithuanians and Byelorussians, and eventually revolutionary intellectuals of all kinds. Numerous palace intrigues also led to the banishment of statesmen, courtiers, and other high government officials, generals, princes, and counts, who could be found marking their miserable time from Berezov and Pelym to Kamchatka. In Empress Anna's time alone, perhaps twenty thousand suffered this fate, and under the Empress Elizabeth another wave followed, either in chains or by demotion to assignments at outlying posts. It was under the empress Elizabeth that the exile system underwent its greatest expansion, as a result of her decrees of 1753 and 1754, which abolished the death penalty and replaced it with exile at hard labor.

Meanwhile, in addition to throngs of common criminals—murderers, rapists, smugglers, thieves—some tens of thousands of serfs were also banished to the districts of Tobolsk and Yeniseysk, and punishment by exile was broadened to encompass a whole new galaxy of crimes, such as usury, fortune-telling, debt, lasciviousness, drunkenness, wife-beating, cutting down trees where prohibited, accidentally starting a fire, and begging when not in genuine distress. About a third of the exiles were "set free" as settlers, about a seventh sentenced to hard labor, and the rest consigned to prison terms or exile residency requirements for periods of varying length. Almost a fifth were charged with no particular offense, except that they had "rendered themselves obnoxious" to one community or another in which they had lived. Turned over by their communes or village parliament to the government for exile, their guilt was presumed, and appeals rarely heard.

In 1790, Catherine the Great sentenced Russia's first "literary revolutionary," Aleksandr Radishchev (whose *Voyage from Petersburg to Moscow* had criticized serfdom and autocracy), to exile at the primitive Siberian fortress town of Ilimsk.

By the beginning of the nineteenth century, new exiles numbered on the average about 2,000 a year; by the end of the century, 19,000— more than half a million in the course of eighty years. Of these, from 10 to 15 percent died en route. Prisons and penal settlements were established at Turukhansk, Irkutsk, Selenginsk, Akmolinsk, Semipalatinsk, Yakutsk, Omsk, Nerchinsk, and elsewhere, where sadistic wardens, rotten food, vermin, stench, thrashing with the *plet* (a three-tailed rawhide lash) or the knout (thongs laced with wire) either killed the inmates or drove them to despair. Escapees, of whom there were many —pursued by bounty-hunting natives, and facing illimitable distances, dark forests, wide rivers, rapids, swamps, trackless wastes, and killing frosts—had little chance to survive. Peasants often placed conciliatory offerings of bread, milk, or soup on the windowsills of their huts, but inevitably "during the spring thaw," wrote one nineteenth-century traveler, "when the snow commences to melt, a large number of corpses of 'unknown persons' are found in the forests. . . . And this is so common the people call them 'podsnieshniks' or 'snowflowers.' "

Exiles were divided into four classes: hard-labor convicts, penal colonists, the merely deported, and those who voluntarily followed after them, such as wives or children. The first two were banished for life, deprived of all civil rights, variously branded or tattooed, shaven lengthwise along the right side of their heads (with the left side cut short), and loaded with chains. The leg-irons weighed from 5 to 14 pounds, were fitted with an iron ring by a blacksmith on an anvil, and riveted in place. Originally, red-hot irons were used to brand male felons with tell-tale letters to indicate their crime—"K" or "KAT" for *katorzhnik* (hard-labor convict) or "в" for *brodyaga* (vagrant) on the cheek or brow. Later, the letters (as crudely formed as those carved by a knife into the bark of a tree) were replaced by deep tattoos.

Various modifications in the penal code gradually eliminated some of the more egregious forms of corporal punishment (like facial disfigurement), but retained flogging and other punitive measures for all except the nobility. The knout was replaced by the three-pronged *plet* in 1845, but this was a relatively small mercy until the maximum number of lashes was set at one hundred in 1871. The law also allowed prisoners to be chained to a wheelbarrow for up to three years.

Floggings alone could kill; in the usual procedure, the criminal was bound tightly to a thick board (called the "mare") that was tilted forward and had holes like a stock for the head and hands. The convict-executioner, as he was called, lashed the victim's back from several angles, so that the wound assumed "the shape of an asterisk or star." Fyodor Dostoyevsky, who was thrashed at the Omsk Prison for having complained of a lump of filth in his soup, wrote that it felt "like a fire burning you; as if your back was being roasted in the very hottest of fires." Prisoners everywhere tried urgently to bribe the executioner not to lay it on too hard, and eventually a fixed scale of bribes was exacted (not always with merciful result) according to the prisoner's means. In *The House of the Dead* (1862), Dostoyevsky has preserved a vivid memorial of his four years of hard labor at Omsk. More unforgiving still were the gold and silver mines in the desolate Kara and Nerchinsk districts, and, eventually reserved for the rebellious, the coal mines on the island of Sakhalin. In the degraded condition of their servitude, those who managed to survive the climate and toil were ravaged by pneumonia, diphtheria, dysentery, scarlet fever, smallpox, syphilis, scurvy, or typhus. Some camp functionaries were "so vehemently hated," writes one historian, "that escaped prisoners were known to dig up the bodies of recently deceased officials and pound stakes into their hearts."

On the other hand, a number of exiles were allowed to settle where they wished; others (if not imprisoned) were assigned to farms, towns, or to various civil or military tasks. As an ecclesiastical exile, Avvakum, for example, helped make up for the lack of priests in Tobolsk. The new territories, in need of every type of skill or labor, easily absorbed all who came.

Yet usefulness was not always a reprieve. After his stint at Tobolsk, Avvakum was sent to Yeniseysk, where he was attached as military chaplain to a regiment of five hundred men bound for the Amur River Valley. This, of course, was in the days before the Treaty of Nerchinsk, and his commanding officer, Afanasy Pashkov, was also of the hardest frontier breed. At various times, he knocked Avvakum to the ground, clubbed him with his commander's ax, had him flogged almost to death with the knout and dragged him across a rapids studded with sharp rocks. By the time the regiment reached Bratsk on October 10, 1656, the torn flesh on Avvakum's back had begun to putrefy. Nevertheless, he was thrown into "a frozen tower" and, he wrote, "I lay like a dog on the straw, some days they would feed me and some days not; and there were a great many mice." Later, in chains, he was transferred to a hut where the local Buryat hostages were kept. In the spring of 1657, Avvakum formed part of a work crew on the Ingoda River, where he floated lumber for the building of houses and forts, but many of his companions (exiles among them) starved to death, or died of exhaustion and exposure under the eyes of pitiless guards.

Eventually, he returned to European Russia through Tobolsk after a bitter sojurn of almost eleven years.

In his novel *Resurrection*, Tolstoy describes a convoy of convicts setting out from St. Petersburg:

The gates opened with a crash like thunder, the clanking of chains became louder, and the escort of soldiers in white tunics, armed with muskets, came out into the street and performed what was evidently a familiar and much practised manoeuver, posting themselves in a wide perfect semicircle in front of the gates. When they were in their places another command was given and the convicts emerged in pairs, with flat pancake-shaped hats on their shaven heads and sacks slung over their shoulders, dragging their chained legs and swinging one free arm while the other supported the sack on their backs. First came the men condemned to hard labor, all of them wearing identical grey trousers and cloaks with black marks like aces on the back. All of them—young, old, thin or fat, pale, florid or dark, those with moustaches, the bearded and the beardless, Russians, Tartars, Jews— came out clanking their chains and briskly swinging their arms, as though preparing for a long walk, but after taking ten or twelve steps they halted and meekly arranged themselves in rows of four, one behind the other. They were immediately followed through the gates by another batch with shaven heads, and dressed like the first; they had no chains on their legs but were handcuffed together. These were prisoners sentenced to deportation. They strode out just as briskly, halted as suddenly, and ranged themselves four abreast. Then came those exiled by their village communes; after them the women, also in order—those condemned to hard labor in grey prison cloaks and kerchiefs, next women being deported, and those who were going voluntarily to be with their men-folk, wearing their own town or village clothing. Some of the women carried babies wrapped in the folds of their grey cloaks.

With the women came the children, boys and girls, huddling close to the prisoners like colts in a herd of horses. Some of the women set up a wail, and the party, surrounded by soldiers in white tunics, moved off, raising the dust with their fettered feet. . . . Last of all came the carts carrying the sacks and the ailing prisoners.

The journey was a long one—on foot, by convict barge, horse-drawn cart, and later rail, over forest-clad mountains, through wind, storm, blistering heat, and bitter cold—some 1,600 miles from St. Petersburg to the Siberian frontier. And this was just the beginning of their march. From Yekaterinburg the "Convict Highway" wound its tedious way eastward from *étape* (or transit prison) to *étape,* and mile by mile accumulated untold miseries to its name. On the way to Tyumen 100 miles east of the Urals stood the tall, square pillar of plastered brick, covered with names and inscriptions, that marked the geographical divide, and as the exiles continued on, they sometimes sang the "Begging Song," a wailing sort of chant, accompanied by the jingling and clashing of their chains. "Have pity on us Our fathers," it began,

> Don't forget the unwilling travelers,
> Don't forget the long-imprisoned.
> Feed us, O our fathers—help us!
> Feed and help the poor and needy!

Until the close of the eighteenth century, the exile system was so carelessly organized and run as scarcely to merit being called a system at all. There was almost no long-range planning, and even the supervision of the exiles en route was (from both the humanitarian and logistical point of view) negligent in the extreme. Herded in droves from town to town, and forced to beg their way because virtually no provision had been made for their subsistence, some managed to provide for themselves from peasants who catered to the wayside trade, but generally their government allowance of a few kopecks a day was scarcely enough, and their mortality rate was high. Exile parties were seldom accompanied by doctors, and only four prison hospitals stood between Tomsk and Irkutsk, a distance of 1,000 miles. The lack of record keeping was such that officials often didn't know where the exiles had come from, what crimes they had committed, or what their proper destination was supposed to be. Hardened murderers, originally sentenced to the mines for life, were set at liberty as colonists; while others, exiled for the most innocuous infractions, or because their commune or landlord had simply banished them from sight, found themselves doomed to the mines.

To bring order out of this chaos, beginning in 1811, all exiles were furnished with identifying documents, including papers stating their crime, punishment, and exile destination, and after 1817 *étapes* were erected at intervals along the principal routes. In 1823, a Bureau of Exile Administration was established at Tobolsk (later Tyumen), which classified the exiles upon their arrival, and tracked their progress and distribution across Siberia to prisons, penal settlements, and places of exile.

From Tyumen, the convicts were dispersed to various towns or villages in Western Siberia, or continued by barge to Tomsk. The prison barge had a specially built deck, furnished with heavy iron-wire cages that looked like reinforced chicken coops. Armed guards patrolled the narrow catwalks on either side; and the cages were roofed with a stout wire mesh. Pitiable-looking Ostyaks would sometimes paddle up to the floating jails in their bark canoes and offer fish for barter, but the soldiers and boatmen called them all "Vanka" (Johnny), and treated them with contempt.

At Tomsk, prisoners destined for Eastern Siberia began their interminable march in guarded convoys of three to five hundred—men, women, and children—with the convicts in chains and wearing government garb that included gray overcoats with yellow, diamond-shaped patches sewn on the back. The journey to Irkutsk took about three months (and a whole year to the headwaters of the Amur); and from May to October, the exiles trod the dusty, muddy post road from six in the morning to seven at night. Marching parties were expected to make about 330 miles a month, stopping every third day for twenty-four hours rest, and up to 1883, all marched together, regardless of exile status, age, or sex.

On the march or in prison, the convicts' "body politic" was dominated by the artel, a kind of union or cooperative with elected leaders, its own severe code of laws, and financed by contributions (exacted from each member) to a common fund. It bribed executioners to go easy with the knout, hired carts to help transport the weak or weary, procured contraband like tobacco, liquor, and cards, and orchestrated the timing of escapes. The artel also upheld all agreements, such as those foolishly made by drunken deportees (derisively nicknamed "biscuits") who gambled away whatever money they had and proved willing to exchange their identities with hard-labor convicts for a little booze. This practice flourished within the convoys, where such a large proportion of the banished were vagabonds or vagrants, and many hardened criminals as a result were freed at once into the population, while their alter egos paid the price of their simplicity by enslaving themselves for twenty years at hard labor in the mines. The power of the artel over its members, in fact, was absolute, and anyone who disobeyed the organization or betrayed its secrets faced almost certain demise. "The records of Russian prisons," writes Kennan, "are full of cases in which the sentence of death pronounced by an artel was executed years afterwards, and in a place far removed from the scene of the offense."

The main hard-labor colonies were centered at the prison complexes of Nerchinsk and Kara, where about 2,500 inmates on the average (including 40 to 50 political prisoners) were interned. At Kara, all the gold mining was done above ground, for thirteen hours a day, ten months out of twelve; after the conquest of the Amur, some of the convicts who had formerly worked at state mines in the Transbaikal were transferred to its placers when the state enterprises came into private hands.

The convict mines at Kara, about 300 miles from Chita, were scattered over rough, mountainous terrain, between the headwaters of the

Amur and the Mongolian frontier. About 1,800 hard labor convicts
worked the open gold placers there in 1885, many living in barracks,
or with their families in little dilapidated cabins—"mere dog kennels
of driftwood and planks"—outside the prison walls. These convicts,
although confined to the penal settlement, belonged to the so-called
"free command." Eventually, they were distributed as forced colonists
throughout Eastern Siberia.

More dreaded than Kara was Akatui, "a lonely, cheerless, God-
forsaken place in a snowy, secluded valley" in the district of Nerchinsk.
Akatui was one of seven prisons in the Nerchinsk silver-mining complex containing three to four thousand prisoners, who labored at
mines first worked in 1760 by serfs. The air above the silver mines was
said to be so heavy that "no bird could live within a radius of a
hundred and fifty miles." But the notorious "salt mines" of Siberia in
reality were few. Indeed, although hard labor in the mines was probably the most notorious (and highly publicized) aspect of the system,
the servitude was sometimes surprisingly light. In the Kara gold placers
(c. 1882) the convicts worked alongside free laborers, and at one mine
in the Nerchinsk district (which in 1885 had about 1,000 hard-labor
convicts), Kennan, who found only 35 convicts at work, was apparently
more shocked by the antiquated equipment they were using than by
the exertions their task required: "Most of them seemed to be engaged
in carrying ore in small wicker baskets to the hoisting shaft, emptying
it into square wooden buckets holding about a bushel each, and then
raising it to the surface, a bucketful at a time, by means of a clumsy old
wooden windlass. I doubted whether methods more primitive were
employed even by the aborigines who worked these silver veins three
centuries before." Dostoyevsky, who found many aspects of his situation difficult to bear, acknowledged that the work itself

> did not seem at all like the hard, *penal* labour it was supposed to be,
> and I realized only much later on that its hardness and *penal nature*
> consisted not so much in its being difficult or unalleviated as in its
> being *forced*, compulsory, done under the threat of the stick. It is
> probable that the peasant in freedom works incomparably harder
> and longer, sometimes even at night, especially in the summer, but
> he works on his own account, with a reasonable end in view, and
> this makes it far easier for him than for the convict with his work that
> is compulsory and quite without use to him.

On occasion, even this psychological burden was eased when convicts were leased to the owners of private operations and worked, as it
were, for extra money on their own behalf. Female hard-labor convicts
were also treated with some consideration. "Their most strenuous
chore," writes one historian, "even in the notoriously oppressive Nerchinsk district was to break up and sort silver ore in a shed. Others
worked in the kitchens, laundries, and primitive hospitals of prisons
and hard-labor camps." More fortunate still were those assigned to
Aleksandrovsk, about 50 miles from Irkutsk, where a huge brandy
distillery had been converted in 1874 into the largest prison in Eastern
Siberia. This prison, the same historian writes, was the resort of the
system, at least in its latter days:

> The great square building looked forbidding enough in contrast to
> the pretty domes and spires of the convict-built, red-brick church
> nearby, but inside, the dormitories were clean and the meals mod-
> erately well prepared. The twelve hundred-odd inmates, all men
> without chains, were kept busy as shoemakers, tailors, carpenters,
> and, ironically enough, locksmiths. Besides a canteen where white
> bread, cheese, sausages, sardines, and cigarettes could be bought
> with the small prison wage, there was a joint library and adult school
> —adorned with lugubrious pictures of the evils of drink—together
> with a makeshift theater for the performance of concerts and skits by
> the felons themselves. After a certain period, good-conduct criminals
> whose wives and children had followed them were permitted to live
> with them in outside cabins, provided that they reported daily at the
> prison. For the youngsters, a matron ran a neat, cheerful school.

In this thoroughly domestic beehive of cottage industries, the felons
were even allowed to make cigarettes, and every man had a bath and
clean linen twice a week.

Aleksandrovsk was exceptional, of course, although occasionally ex-
aggerated descriptions of some aspects of the system were published
to promote outrage. "They never see the light of day," went one apocryphal account of convict miners, "but work and sleep all the year
round in the depths of the earth, extracting silver or quicksilver under
the eyes of taskmasters, who have orders not to spare them. Iron gates
guarded by sentries close the lodes, or streets, at the bottom of the
shafts, and the miners are railed off from one another in gangs of

twenty. They sleep within recesses hewn out of the rock—very kennels —into which they must creep on all fours." There were inhumanities enough in the system without having to invent them and, as Kennan stressed, it was not the hard labor but the frightful condition of most prisons and *étapes* that was most deserving of reproach.

Although an immense amount of money had been appropriated to build the *étapes*—enough, Kennan was told, to make a line of them out of solid silver along the whole route from Tomsk to Irkutsk—most of it had gone to payoffs and graft. As a result, the *étapes* were tumble-down, red-roofed barracks that looked like hastily built stockades. They swarmed with lice, bedbugs, and other vermin, and the infestation was so bad that a common method of gambling was to guess at the number of fleas that would jump within a certain length of time onto a dirty old overcoat spread on the floor. Unventilated and "saturated with miasm," their whole furnishing was a single stove, rows of bare plank beds, and an excrement tub. The roofs invariably leaked, and the floors, covered in muck, were rotted through. When prisoners crowded into them, "the scenes of debauchery to be witnessed," complained one official, "cannot possibly be described. All the shame and all the conscience that a criminal has left are here lost completely. Here go to ruin also the families of the criminals, irrespective of age or sex. In addition to debauchery, the prisoners are guilty of many other offenses and crimes."

The squalor of the *étapes* merely anticipated that of the compounds and forwarding prisons at Tyumen, Tomsk, Krasnoyarsk, and elsewhere, where the hospitals were as unsanitary as the barracks and the death rate was extremely high. In the dimly lit rooms the rough plank floors were black with hard-trodden filth, and the walls stained red where tens of thousands of bedbugs had been crushed. "Scores of men," wrote Kennan, "slept every night on the foul, muddy floors, under the platforms, and in the gangways between them and the walls." Their daily ration consisted of two and a half pounds of black bread, half a pound of boiled meat, and a quarter pound of buckwheat with tea. Occasionally, a bowl of cabbage soup was substituted for other fare. Almost no precautions were taken to protect the prisoners' health, and those with infectious or contagious diseases were seldom isolated from the rest. Some prison hospitals lacked not only nurses but even beds, and in the Tomsk forwarding prison, Kennan found three hundred sick lying in rows so close together on the floor that "a patient could not cough or vomit without coughing or vomiting into his own face or into the face of the man lying beside him." At Achinsk, the wards were completely unventilated and "pools and masses of excrement" had accumulated on the floors. Under such conditions, in the late 1880s (according to Kennan), the average daily sick rate ranged from 13 to 23 percent, and the annual death rate was 15 percent or more—with typhus alone accounting for about a third of those who languished and died. This matched or exceeded the death rate among the infamous chain gangs of the contemporary American South.

Although Kennan's method of calculation was questionable ("dividing the average daily number of prisoners by the total number of deaths throughout the year"), there can be no doubt that prison conditions were appalling, and that the documented horrors (whatever their statistical sum) were real enough. And they went hand in hand with the arbitrary injustice of the system as a whole. Of the 2,144 prisoners found in Kara in 1879, for example, aside from those guilty of specific, serious and violent crimes, 677 were classified as "vagabonds," 86 as "offenders against discipline and defaulters in public service," and 73 as "various." In other words, almost 40 percent had not been charged with a definite offense.

As a place of exile, Siberia has sometimes been compared to Australia, but some clear distinctions may be drawn. Australia was founded as a penal colony, and its early European population was made up almost entirely of convicts, whereas convicts were never a majority in Siberia, even though its criminal and exile population in absolute numbers by comparison made that of Australia seem minuscule. Moreover, Australia's convict history lasted just 80 years, from 1788 to 1868, and involved the transportation of 155,000 convicts in all, whereas exile to Siberia under the tsars spanned a little more than three centuries and ultimately involved seven times as many deportees. The Australian system overall also made a more positive contribution to the country's early development, by "converting vagabonds, most useless in one hemisphere, into active citizens of another," in the words of Charles Darwin, by no means a stony-hearted apostle of penal servitude.

The exile system, on the other hand, was not only institutionally unjust, but hindered the country's development and had a demoralizing and even ruinous effect on the Siberian population as a whole. Western Siberians in particular, as they grew more prosperous, resented the colonization of criminals in their midst, and towns just west of the Urals also objected because their neighborhood was regularly overrun by escapees. By the 1880s, from ten to thirteen thousand were exiled a year—about a third of them destined for prison, the other two thirds confined to towns or forcibly settled on the land. In addition to those who escaped from these conditions, thousands of vagrants, thieves, counterfeiters, burglars, highway robbers, and murderers were released into the colony every year as their prison terms expired. By the 1870s, more than two thirds of all crimes committed in Siberia were by deported felons, so that what had begun as a faintly rational program of colonization had developed into a systematic degradation of the social life of the Siberian community. By 1886, 48,000 or 42 percent of the forced colonists in Eastern Siberia had run away and could not be found, and only 33 percent of the exiles in Western Siberia were in the places to which they had been assigned. A not inconsiderable proportion of these runaways certainly perished in the wilds, but thousands more roamed about the countryside engaged in intermittent crime. The slang term in Siberia for a freed colonist or convict—*varnak*, meaning "vagabond"—suggests their typical career.

Perhaps comparatively few would have remained in Siberia had the choice been theirs. In any case, although many got free of their prisons and settlements, few escaped from Siberia itself. At any given time, wrote Kennan, one could speak of "a great army of brodyags [vagabonds], which is constantly marching westward through the woods in the direction of the Urals," but seldom arrived. And because Siberia itself constituted one huge prison, whose forests, rivers, swamps, lack of roads, and so on were effectively as insurmountable as towering prison walls, sooner or later a fugitive who had not otherwise perished was likely to be recaptured, or forced by cold and starvation to give himself up. "The Tsar's cow-pasture is large," noted one *étape* official, "but you can't get out of it; we find you at last if you are not dead." The Transbaikal formed a kind of cul-de-sac bounded by enormous forests to the north, the deserts of Mongolia to the south, and Lake Baikal (400 miles long and covering 12,500 square miles) to the west. In between, bounty-hunting Buryats were willing for a few pounds of flour to hunt escapees down "like vermin," and on the lower Amur Gilyaks brought them in for three rubles a head. "If you shoot a squirrel, you get only his skin," one told a traveler, "but if you shoot a *varnak* you get his skin and his clothing, too." Under such circumstances, criminals who were often quite at home in the wild woods were much more likely to survive than revolutionary intellectuals and other politicals to whom the forest ways were strange.

Although escapes in winter were relatively rare, "when convicts heard the mating call of the cuckoo in the spring," wrote Kennan, those serving lengthy terms found flight hard to resist:

When the weather becomes warm enough to make life out of doors endurable, the free command begins to overflow into the forest; and for two or three months a narrow but almost continuous stream of escaping convicts runs from the Kara penal settlements in the direction of Lake Baikal. The signal for this annual movement is given by the cuckoo, whose notes, when first heard in the valley of the Kara, announce the beginning of the warm season. The cry of the bird is taken as evidence that an escaped convict can once more live in the forests; and to run away, in convict slang is to "go to General Kukushka [Cuckoo] for orders."

More than two hundred men left the Kara free command every year to join General Kukushka's army, and in Siberia as a whole the number of runaway exiles and convicts who took to the field in response to his annual summons exceeded thirty thousand, with an average of one out of every twenty making their escape. Some of the getaways were spectacular. "All the familiar stock-in-trade of the famous great escapes was there," writes one historian,

tunnels, lock-picks, forged papers, filed bars, bribed warders, dummies in the bed and ropes of knotted sheets.... One veteran brodyaga and amateur conjurer named Tumanov brought off an audacious vanishing act in the fortress at Tobolsk by leaping over the prison's wooden palisade from the top of a human pyramid formed by fellow prisoners during a display of acrobatics and prestidigitation which was being performed before an audience of the governor and his invited guests in the gaol courtyard.... A search party failed to find Tumanov, but discovered, nailed to the prison wall where he had landed, a large false beard made of flax which he had used as one of his theatrical props. As a rather burlesque finishing touch to the story, it was later said that the provincial governor was so outraged by the whole affair that he ordered the prison commander to wear the beard "to his dying day" as a mark of his gullibility and shame!

Whether an escape artist, a member of the free command, or an exiled settler who had had enough of his confinement to a remote village or unproductive field, such a fugitive joined the great westward migration, living precariously on surreptitious charity or on what they could scrounge for themselves in the woods. By day they concealed themselves in the forests, and toward evening sought shelter in bathhouses or bivouacked under the stars. The popular song, "Holy Baikal," captures the hope and bravado of that flight:

> Holy Baikal—glorious sea,
> An old fish barrel—my glorious ship.
> Ho, North Wind, stir the waves for me,
> And hasten a brave lad's trip.
>
> Heavy chains I dragged for many a day.
> Through the hills of Akatui I went.
> An old friend helped me run away.
> I came to life with freedom's scent.
>
> Shilka, Nerchinsk, I've been everywhere.
> The mountain police didn't catch me,
> In the forests the gluttonous beast kept his lair,
> No rifleman's bullet could scratch me . . .

Even if they were eventually caught or returned, wrote Kennan, "they have had their outing, and have breathed for three whole months the fresh, free air of the woods, the mountains and the steppes. With many convicts the love of wandering through the trackless forests and over the great plains of Eastern Siberia becomes a positive mania." Such outings were not always so innocent, and the ambivalence of the Siberian population toward the convict-exiles was profound. On the one hand, they sympathized with them as fellow sufferers under tsarist tyranny, and tended to view them as fallen brethren or victims of circumstance. But some of the fugitives, after all, were hardened criminals, already guilty of savage deeds and capable of the cruelest crimes. Wayfarers made easy targets, and the by-roads of Siberia were strewn with the bodies of those who had been assaulted, robbed, murdered, or raped. Occasionally, major highways and even cities came under bold attack. The road between Tomsk and Achinsk was especially dangerous, and some areas had to be patrolled by mounted police. In February 1886, Tomsk itself was "terrorized by a band of criminals who made a practice of riding through the city in sleighs at night and catching belated wayfarers with sharp grappling hooks." In Eastern Siberia, desperadoes became such a widespread menace the government offered a bounty of three rubles for each one dead or alive. Peasants made no allowance for their predations, large or small. In the Marinsk district east of Tomsk, for example, when a thief was caught, ground glass was forced into his eyes.

Sometimes roving bands of outlaws were also trapped and executed "in acts of communal vengeance and reprisal," yet crimes of extreme violence remained so common that it was possible for a government report to say that "if they had been committed in European Russia, they would have caused a national sensation and been the talk of the reading public for a very long time, but in Siberia, they are lost among the welter of similar 'events.' "

As winter approached, many fugitives sensibly turned themselves in (despite the forty strokes of the *plet* that customarily awaited them), and they often found they had tangibly improved their lot. When interrogated, they pretended amnesia, were classified as unidentifiable vagrants, and sentenced to a flogging and only five years at hard labor—a generous reprieve from the possible twenty from which they had escaped.

A few of those who remained in the wilds and survived became notorious bandits—"the Robin Hoods, Ned Kellys and Billy the Kids of the Siberian taiga"—for whom various local forests, villages, rivers, and streams were even named. "Siberian children," writes one historian, "played not at cops and robbers or cowboys and Indians but at 'brodyagi and soldiers' and ... peasant girls were often seduced into leaving their villages by fantasies of a life of excitement and glamour in the taiga as a Siberian gangster's moll."

. . .

In the course of the nineteenth century, almost 1 million people were sent into Siberian exile, accompanied by 150,000 to 200,000 others (mostly wives and children), though comparatively few penal colonists or exile settlers comprised family groups. On average, about eighteen women were deported for every hundred men, and since few single women ventured to Siberia alone, the chronic shortage of them made the family homestead (traditionally the most successful instrument of colonization) the exception rather than the rule. In time, as we have seen, the criminal class made up a significant proportion of Siberia's population, and because it was constantly leavened and renewed, it was quite impossible for the colony's freely settled inhabitants to process this element out. Ex-convicts were not supposed to make up more than a fifth of any given community—the legal maximum, itself extremely high—but in some districts the concentration was much higher than that. By 1889, for example, exiles made up roughly two thirds of the Russian population in the province of Yakutsk.

Thus did a quite limited idea of Siberia become fixed in the public mind. One Victorian writer called the colony "the cesspool of the Tsars," and if the judgment seems harsh, the prevailing view was perhaps fairly epitomized by Count Nesselrode's emphatic pronouncement that Siberia was "the bottom of the sack." In 1882, the governor-general of Eastern Siberia lamented this notion of the territory in a report to Alexander III. Describing the exile system (not Siberia) as "an ulcer upon the Empire," he wrote in conclusion:

> Siberia is truly a beautiful country. Its people are gifted with high intellectual capacity, and are honest, industrious, and energetic. Both the country and its inhabitants deserve the most gracious consideration . . . It is time for the Government to give this country particular attention, and extricate it from the position into which it has been put by its remoteness from the center of the Empire, by its designation as a place of exile and penal servitude, and by the long-continued failure to satisfy its needs and demands.

The tsar himself, reacting to this appeal, scrawled in the margins: "I am more than troubled. . . . It is inexcusable, and even criminal, to allow such a state of affairs in Siberia to continue."

As a result of new attention paid to Sakhalin Island, a kind of preliminary solution to Siberia's woes emerged. After Russia acquired undisputed sovereignty over the island in 1875, the government decided to turn it into a penal colony to relieve mainland Siberia of its convict element. Sakhalin's economic potential, moreover, promised to make it "the pearl of Russia's eastern possessions . . . as rich in coal as Wales, in fish as Newfoundland, and in oil as Baku." And in 1881 the government went forward in earnest with its prison island scheme. After 1884, when a prison administration headed by a military governor was established, the convicts and exiles flowed in at the rate of about one thousand a year; some came via the Amur to Nikolayevsk, from which they were ferried across to the island, but most arrived by sea from Odessa after a two-month voyage via the Suez Canal, the Indian Ocean, and the East China Sea. Because the island's isolation made it an even more natural prison than Siberia's expanse, there was little chance of escape, and most hard-labor convicts, repeat offenders, and *brodyags* who refused to divulge their identities were subsequently confined there. By 1888, Sakhalin had become the most important and the biggest of Siberia's prisons.

If Siberia was Russia's Australia, Sakhalin was its Norfolk Island. One writer has eloquently summarized the dread conditions which prevailed:

On Sakhalin, the guards were more criminal than the convicts and the free settlers suffered more than the imprisoned. On Sakhalin, free women sold their children to preserve a mockery of a family, while convict women, rationed like precious commodities, were known to murder their designated spouses in hope of a better match. On Sakhalin the aborigines enjoyed an open season on escapees with a bounty for each corpse. On Sakhalin, men and women went to the woods not in search of grapes nor to gratify their lust, but for deadly toxic wolfsbane which would bring a quick end to their tormented lives. On Sakhalin, peasants talked wistfully of that same Siberia that Muscovites dreaded.

On Sakhalin, the coal-miners ate tallow candles and rotten wood while the rivers were clogged with salmon. Sakhalin infused its unfortunate residents with a special malady. Chekhov called it "febris sachalinensis" and described it as sensations of dampness, shivering fits, severe headaches, rheumatic pains, and a sinking feeling that one would never be able to leave the island. He added that "if only those who liked Sakhalin lived there, the island would be uninhabited."

At the turn of the century, Sakhalin was also the only place throughout the Russian Empire where the death penalty existed, where convicts were still chained to wheelbarrows, and floggings remained
routine. In a candid admission in 1890 by the island's military governor, "Everyone wants to escape from here—the convicts, the settlers,
and the officials." And Chekhov exclaimed: "I have seen Ceylon, which
is paradise, and Sakhalin, which is hell."

The story of Sakhalin's women is especially lamentable. As they
made up less than 10 percent of the exile population, they were processed to meet the universal demand. Upon arrival, some became the
concubines of officials and were immediately enrolled in the prison
administration as maids or domestic servants; others were "set aside
as prostitutes for the guards and minor clerks"; the majority were
distributed among the convict settlers as common-law wives. But wherever the new arrivals went, wrote Chekhov, they were followed by
crowds of hungry men, the way whales, seals, and dolphins—"hoping
to feast on the fat egg-filled herring"—followed schools of fish. That
feast was not always one the men savored for long. Most of the women
had been exiled for murdering their husbands or lovers, and an abu-
sive mate easily tempted them to repeat their crime.

There were some mitigating factors. Convict settlers were supplied
with a small homestead, seed, tools, clothing, and a modest allowance
for each child under eighteen. After six years they were eligible to
become free peasants, and could return to Russia if they wished. Nearly
everyone who could afford to did. To supplement the exile population,
develop the island's natural resources, and give it an agricultural base,
the government also made some attempt to lure free immigrants with
tax exemptions and other incentives. But the degraded atmosphere,
physically inhospitable environment, and lack of planning frustrated
most efforts to turn their labor to account. Only the large coal deposits
located around Due on the west coast were profitably mined, after
Chinese coolies were imported from Hong Kong.

Of all the notorieties of the exile system, perhaps none aroused so
much feeling in the West as its use in suppressing political dissent.
Before the revolutionary movement developed in earnest—with a proliferation of terrorist organizations and communist cells—easily the
most celebrated of the dissidents were the so-called "Decembrists,"

who in December 1825 attempted a sort of libertarian *coup d'état* in St. Petersburg.

The Decembrists on the whole were gentleman-aristocrats of liberal views who had been embittered by the failed promise of Alexander I's regime. Upon ascending the throne in 1801, Alexander had surrounded himself with a coterie of brilliant and energetic young reformers who proposed a number of plans for democratic change. The tsar himself corresponded with Thomas Jefferson, who sent him pamphlets explaining the character of American political institutions, and with Alexander's evident approval a constitution granting free speech and other civil rights was drafted as a new foundation for the rule of law. It is not clear how far the tsar was prepared to go in his reforms (except that they were to be imposed from above), but the Napoleonic Wars and the burning of Moscow expunged his enthusiasm and strengthened the forces of reaction. The government grew ever more determined to resist the "Jacobin spirit" of the West, and detected sedition in the least dissent. After 1817, dissidents were forced to whisper and secret societies began to form. Some evolved from Masonic lodges, where restless intellectuals of like mind made contact; others brought together those who through study and travel had become familiar with the French Encyclopedists, and with the revolutionary movements in France and the United States. Army officers returning from the Napoleonic Wars naturally compared what they had seen abroad "with what," wrote one of them, "confronted them at every step at home: slavery of the majority of Russians, cruel treatment of subordinates by superiors, all sorts of government abuses, and general tyranny. The masses who had been told that they were fighting 'Napoleonic despotism' came back to find at home a regime more despotic than Napoleon's had been."

The first organization to lay a basis for the Decembrist revolt was founded in St. Petersburg in February 1816 by nobles who were all officers of the Guard. Two branches of the organization evolved and underwent somewhat independent development. The northern branch, based in St. Petersburg, on the whole favored a constitutional monarchy; the southern and more radical wing, based in Tulchin in the Ukraine, wanted a republic. The former was led by Nikita Muraviev, a young officer who had been among the first to enter Paris after Napoleon's defeat; the latter, by Pavel Pestel, a regimental colonel and a veteran of Borodino and the European campaigns.

Muraviev drafted a constitution which envisioned a bi-cameral National Assembly, regionally elected legislatures, trial by jury, emancipation of the serfs, and a reorganization of the country into a federation of thirteen regions—in emulation of the original pattern of the United States. Pestel's credo, on the other hand, provided for the overthrow of the tsar—by regicide, if necessary—abolition of the monarchy, its replacement by a republican form of government, and (to ensure an orderly transition while the republic was being formed) the introduction of a "temporary dictatorship." Pushkin was one of Pestel's early admirers but later wrote that he had "Napoleon's profile but Satan's soul." Nevertheless, nearly all the conspirators, north and south, were rather naive young idealists, most of them in their mid-twenties (Pestel in 1825 was just thirty-three), and profoundly ambivalent in their aims. The age-old aristocracy to which they belonged had bred in them a certain hereditary, if reluctant, loyalty to the monarchy, which half-paralyzed their will to challenge it and see their sedition through.

Yet they were reckless at the game they played. Adam Mickiewicz, the Polish poet and a kindred revolutionary spirit, attended a meeting at one of the conspirator's apartments in St. Petersburg in October 1825:

An old servant opened the door. "They are all in there," he whispered, pointing to a room at the end of a very long passage.

There must have been more than a dozen people in the room, but at first I could not distinguish anything because of the dense blue haze of pipe and cigar smoke. They were sprawling on sofas and on the deep windowsills; [two] sat cross-legged, Turkish-fashion, on a Persian carpet on the floor. The officers had undone their tunic buttons and stiff collars, the civilians wore voluminous cravats à la Byron; some were dressed like Directoire dandies. Through the wide-open windows swirled great white puffs of St. Petersburg fog.

An intense youth, pale-complexioned, with a prominent forehead, a face like Shelley, lifts a glass—"Death to the tsar." The toast is received with emotion. . . . Everyone drinks except me, a Pole and a guest. . . . They sing. . . .

"One, two knives,
One, two, three,
Long and sharp. . . ."

The rhythmic chant flows through the open windows for all to hear. A glow of a lantern out on the quay suddenly lights up the room. The chant stops abruptly, as fear sobers them up. . . . I can almost hear the sinister cry of a raven, a raven circling the gallows.

Rather more scathingly, Pushkin remarked:

> 'Twas all mere idle chatter
> 'Twixt Château Lafite and Veuve Cliquot.

The die, however, was cast. On November 19, 1825, Alexander I died unexpectedly at Tagenrog in southern Russia, and in the confused interregnum that followed—in which Alexander's two younger brothers, Nicholas and Konstantin, swore allegiance to each other but neither assumed the throne—the conspirators had their chance. But the moment had come before they were prepared to take advantage of it, and the uncertainty about the succession itself proved both a temptation to and a ruin of their plans. In the first place, the conspirators were not immediately sure how to frame their rallying cry, or against whom to frame it; and secondly, they had only the vaguest notions as to whom they could count on outside their own circle for support. Nor had they settled on the degree of violence they were prepared to use. As a result, although Alexander's death had long been imagined as a pretext for action, their hastily improvised plot was crippled at once by misgiving and doubt.

On December 14, the conspirators mustered their adherents (about two thousand strong) in St. Petersburg's Senate Square, hoping to prevent the accession of Nicholas I, in whose favor it had been learned that the elder, Konstantin, had abdicated in advance. But the tsar had already been sworn in secretly, and the poorly organized rebels were easily dispersed by loyal troops. A subsequent insurrection in the south was also crushed. Trials for high treason followed in which 121 were charged, 31 imprisoned, and five (including Pestel) hanged. The rest were sent in chains to Siberia—some to distant towns like Turukhansk, Berezov, Pelym, and Narym, but most in penal servitude to the silver mines of the Transbaikal in the district of Nerchinsk.

History might not have accorded the Decembrists any particular glory except for the luster that, in the aftermath of their debacle, attached to their name. Although they had faltered in Senate Square, they would prove steadfast in exile, and it was there that their legend was really made. Most demonstrated a determination to make the best of their situation, showed conviction in defeat, and scorned the idea, as one put it, of exchanging their fate "for a gilded yoke." But neither their fate, nor history's recollection of it, would have been quite the same had not eleven Decembrists also been followed into exile by their wives and fiancées. This act of brave devotion did more than anything else to romanticize their cause, and although tsarist officials tried in every way to dissuade the women from their purpose—by depriving them of all their titles, privileges, and civil rights, by making their banishment permanent, and obliging them to leave their children behind—they would not be deterred. Six of the women abandoned a total of thirteen children to the care of relations, and seven would eventually lose eleven or more children in exile. Even Nicholas I was moved, and confessed, "Their devotion is worthy of respect."

One of the women was Katerina Trubetskaya, the daughter of a count. Raised in stupendous splendor, she had lived with her husband, Sergey Trubetskoy, in a house in St. Petersburg furnished with marble floors that had come from the emperor Nero's Forum in Rome. In Chita, she cheerfully rented a room in the dilapidated shack of a local Cossack with fishskin windowpanes and dirty mud floors. More remarkable was Maria Volkonskaya, a descendant of Mikhail Lomonosov and the daughter of a hero of the Napoleonic Wars. A beautiful young woman with a smooth, olive complexion, dainty figure, and lustrous curly black hair, she had many suitors (including Pushkin), but at the age of eighteen had married Prince Sergey Volkonsky, an officer who could trace his bloodline back to Rurik but was twice her age. In their first year of marriage, they were seldom together, and Maria knew nothing of the conspiracy in which he was involved. But a few days after she gave birth to their first child, Sergey was arrested and subsequently remanded to Siberia. Without hesitation, Maria packed up all her belongings in a sledge and followed after him, leaving her newborn child behind. The morning after she reached the silver mines of Nerchinsk in Eastern Siberia, 4,000 miles from home, she set off for the shaft where her husband was toiling, escorted by the prison commander and two guards. "I stepped down into total darkness," she recalled.

Gradually, as I extended my hands, I began to feel that I was in a tiny cell, like a kennel, and that someone was slowly dragging himself toward me; I heard the clanging of iron on the stone floor. My husband stood before me and I saw that his legs were bound by heavy chains. No words can ever describe what I felt when I saw the immensity of his suffering. Only then did I fully realize the sacrifices required to fight for liberty in our country. A feeling of exaltation and great pride swept over me. To the bewilderment of the guards, I knelt on the filthy floor and kissed the chains.

The tsar, however, didn't want martyrs on his hands, and the lives of the exiles came to include a remarkable number of amenities. Their situation was also eased considerably by the indulgent supervision of their "warden," General Stanislav Leparsky, an elderly cavalry officer with a humane consideration for their plight. The wives were permitted to visit with their husbands twice a week, and (in Maria's view) the work the men had to do, five hours daily in two shifts, was "not excessive and was good for them, because it allowed them exercise." At Chita, where many of them were gathered together, and were able to draw upon each other for intellectual companionship, comfort, and strength, the prisoners worked at the local flour mill, cultivated the prison garden, attended to sanitation, repaired the buildings, or dug or filled ditches by the roads. As one jauntily described their routine:

Every day except on Sundays and feast days the sergeant on duty would enter the prison early in the morning and call: "Gentlemen, to work." In general we were eager to get out, and left with songs on our lips and energy in our hearts. No force was ever used on us. Our column would then amble forth toward the Devil's Grave. Peasants enlisted by the guards carried our picks and shovels and pushed the wheelbarrows, while we ourselves fastened our chains to our belts and jingled our foot fetters to the rhythm of some stirring revolutionary tune.

These relatively informal work details were transformed into social outings when the women joined them on the march. "The guards," we are told, "then carried the ladies' folding chairs, rugs, samovars, hampers with food, newspapers, chessboards, and reading material. A shady spot would be found on the edge of the forest near the Big Ditch. The ladies settled comfortably under the trees, sewing or reading, while the prisoners would dig for a couple of hours, and then everyone would have lunch and relax. Some played chess; [others] sketched; some soldiers played cards, others stacked their muskets and went to sleep."

In the annals of the exile system, such a trusting and idyllic convoy must have been unique.

Whenever the work proved more strenuous than some could handle, their hardier comrades were always willing to lend a hand. And by otherwise sharing with one another just about everything they had, no one lacked for food, clothing, books, and so on, despite the fact that each prisoner was granted only 114 rubles 23 kopecks a year from the state.

"Our life in Chita has really become quite tolerable," Maria wrote to a relative. "We explore the lovely countryside around us; we have even managed to engage local servants, who though raw and untrained, help to shift the burden of domesticity from our shoulders. I lead an active and occupied life."

In Chita, the Decembrists organized themselves into a school, or "academy" as they called it, in which each member lectured in the field of his expertise. One taught military science; another, physics, chemistry, and anatomy; a third, Russian history; a fourth, literature; a fifth, foreign languages; and so on. With Leparsky's permission, books, magazines, and newspapers in French, German, and Italian started to arrive from abroad, and during the prisoners' three years in Chita and later at Petrovsky Zavod, near Nerchinsk, a substantial library was built up. They also established a carpentry workshop and forge, formed Siberia's first string quartet, and organized musical soirées, with Maria as occasional "guest" pianist, playing on the clavichord she had brought along. Sometimes their Academy lectures were attended by outsiders, and in other ways too they contributed to the knowledge and welfare of the community. Nikolay Bestuzhev, a gifted painter, compiled a Buryat-Russian dictionary and collected native legends; others made agricultural experiments, taught the natives the art of hothouse cultivation, and introduced barley, asparagus, cucumbers, melons, and cauliflowers to the Transbaikal. Those individual Decembrists unlucky enough to be scattered to outlying settlements also left their mark. One published a local newspaper in Kyakhta, another made an outstanding map of the northeast, a third gathered material on local folklore and native customs, and the Borisov brothers, Petr and Andrey, "developed a system of entomological classification that was later adopted by the French Academy of Sciences."

Whereas almost all educated officials or aristocrats before them had regarded their time and tenure in Siberia as a temporary circumstance, the Decembrists knew they were in Siberia to stay, and so committed themselves to the life and development of the country. As Siberia's first true resident intelligentsia, they also represented the best and brightest that tsarist Russia had yet produced. "One can definitely say," wrote Nikolay Basargin, rather modestly, "that our long stay in various parts of Siberia was of some use."

After two years, the prisoners were allowed to remove their leg-irons, and Pauline Annenkova (who had followed her lover to Siberia and married him in prison) kept those belonging to her husband and fashioned them into bracelets so comely that the other wives found in them an emblem of defiance and insisted on copies of their own.

In August 1830, the prisoners were transferred to Petrovsky Zavod near Nerchinsk, but it is obvious they all knew in advance that the hard labor associated with those mines was not to be their fate. Indeed, the march to the new prison (at an unforced rate of about ten miles a day) could almost be compared to a leisurely camping trip. "The convoy would start off," writes Maria's biographer, "as a rule, at 3 A.M., so as to avoid the hottest hours of the day. Camp was pitched about 9 A.M. and a short rest followed after lunch. [One exile's] task was to ride ahead at dawn each day with the servants and some of the guards to pitch camp for the night, preferably in a picturesque location, and have supper ready when the main parties arrived. On warm days, the prisoners were allowed to bathe in the rivers or lakes along the way."

At Petrovsky Zavod, the cells were dark but otherwise quite commodious, and handsomely furnished by their inmates with rugs, pictures, couches, and the like. Married couples were allowed to live together in a separate wing of the prison, and others had their own private cells. Nearby, Maria Volkonskaya had a small house built for herself, where she employed a maid and a cook. After Sergey's prison sentence expired in February 1835, the Volkonskys moved to Urik, a little village near Irkutsk, where they had a two-story country house with glass windows, servants' quarters, and a veranda built on a scenic bluff overlooking the Angara River. In 1844, they also acquired a small mansion in Irkutsk, retaining their Urik dwelling as a summer retreat.

In Irkutsk, Maria helped finance local schools and hospital facilities, and became a patron of the arts. Through her efforts, the city acquired a new theater and concert hall, and her son Mikhail, born in exile, became a prominent member of Muravyev-Amursky's staff. Denied her royal rank as a Decembrist's wife, it was nevertheless reclaimed for her by a grateful public in Irkutsk who christened her "the Princess of Siberia."

In August 1856, thirty years after their revolt, an imperial amnesty brought the Decembrists' exile to an end.

The comparative comforts allowed to many Decembrists contrast so remarkably with what was suffered by political prisoners in Stalin's Gulag that some of the luster of their fortitude has since worn off. One of the characters in Solzhenitsyn's *The First Circle* exclaims: "The wives of the Decembrists—do you think they performed some heroic feat?" And the actual conditions of their exile (with certain exceptions) were not very harsh. Even within the exile system itself, their treatment was notably indulgent, in obvious deference to their former pedigree and rank. Yet it cannot be denied that they had stood up to the autocracy on behalf of democratic ideals, were deprived of the splendor to which they had been born, and endured without recanting. And their own sacrifices were ennobled by those made voluntarily by wives and lovers on their behalf.

In time, the Decembrists were perceived as kinds of martyrs, as one of them, Dmitry Zavalishin, had foreseen this in advance. "I am certain that we shall perish," he declared, "but the example will remain." And Pushkin, looking beyond their bungled plot, paid tribute to a future he imagined would be theirs:

> Deep in the Siberian mine,
> Keep your patience proud;
> The bitter toil shall not be lost,
> The rebel thought unbowed. . . .
> The heavy-hanging chains will fall,
> The walls will crumble at a word;
> And Freedom greet you in the light,
> And brothers give you back the sword.

Indeed, to some degree by their example the coming revolutionary struggle in Russia was legitimized. In the same year that Nicholas I died, Aleksandr Herzen founded his revolutionary journal, *Polar Star*, which featured portraits of the five hanged Decembrists on the cover and claimed to inherit their cause. The standard code used by prisoners to communicate with one another through cell walls also became known as the "Decembrist alphabet" (although no Decembrist may ever have used it) in which the letters were mentally pictured as a square and indicated by tapping their coordinates.

The government did what it could to delay the new day. The deportation of dissidents to Siberia increased, and in 1833 the death penalty was decreed for any exile who committed a serious political crime. A "Statue on Punishments" in 1845 also made "corrective" exile more common for political offenses.

Literary societies and other gatherings where opinions might be freely exchanged were considered seditious, and in 1836, for example, one writer was declared insane by the authorities for challenging the official view "as set forth by the Minister of Education, to the effect that 'Russia's past is admirable, its present more than magnificient; as for its future, it is beyond anything that the boldest imagination can picture.' " But "thinking is like gunpowder, dangerous when pressed," as the Decembrist Aleksandr Bestuzhev remarked, and, inevitably, secret political societies began to form. Fyodor Dostoyevsky, for example, belonged to the small Petrashevsky Circle which debated Utopian Socialist ideas. The group posed little immediate threat to the tsar, but on the night of April 23, 1849, several members were rounded up, imprisoned, and eventually tried for crimes against the state. Fifteen were condemned to death, including Dostoyevsky, who found himself one morning at the Semyonovsky Drill Grounds with a hood over his head, facing a firing squad. In a cruelly orchestrated denouement, his sentence (and that of the others) was commuted at the last moment, to penal servitude in exile. Some were sent to the mines of Nerchinsk, others to distant Siberian towns. Dostoyevsky spent four years at hard labor at the prison at Omsk, after which he also had to serve for a time as a private in the frontier guard at Semipalatinsk.

Nevertheless, the views of Utopian Socialists like Fourier and Saint-Simon found increasing numbers of disciples on Russian soil. Russia's defeat in the Crimean War had revealed its glaring backwardness and did much to finally discredit the oppressive rule of Nicholas I. The accession of Alexander II in 1855 brought a general desire for change, and in response the tsar embarked upon a series of modernizing reforms. He granted an amnesty, allowed the press (in a limited way) to comment on controversial issues, and on February 19, 1861, freed some 23 million serfs. Subsequently, the emancipation was extended to about 8 million peasants settled on state and Crown lands. A number of judicial abuses were also eliminated, restrictions on foreign travel eased, and military rule in Poland relaxed. But even as progress was being made, the extremely circumscribed and conditional way in which the emancipation of the serfs was carried out embittered reformers throughout the empire, and popular discontent increasingly acquired a more revolutionary cast. After its leaders supported the Polish revolt in 1863, the tsar reacted harshly, imposing martial law, and empowering the police to break up any gathering in a private house where more than seven people were assembled. More than 18,500 Poles were also exiled to Siberia.

Some of these staunch Polish patriots refused to accept their fate. In June 1866, seven hundred staged an uprising in the Transbaikal where they hoped to liberate other political prisoners working in the mines and escape through China to the sea. Taking several lakeside villages and stations as far as Mysovaya, they seized carts, horses, arms, money, and food, and destroyed some bridges and the telegraph line. But the tsar's troops caught up with them, defeated them in a pitched engagement, and hunted down those who scattered into the woods.

After an attempt on the life of Alexander II in 1866, there was a new wave of arrests and deportations, but in the early seventies a more radical generation of dissidents emerged. One of the more celebrated was Nikolay Chernyshevsky, who during his incarceration in the Fortress of Peter and Paul had written *What Is to Be Done?* (1863), a semi-socialistic novel that became the touchstone text of Russia's restless youth. Exiled to Siberia, Chernyshevsky did time at the Usolye salt mines near Irkutsk, then at the silver mines of Nerchinsk. After his term at hard labor came to an end, he was transferred to Vilyuysk, a remote northern settlement of four hundred Yakuts and "Yakutized Cossacks" surrounded by swamps.

The attempt to suppress progressive ideas was useless. In the spring of 1874, thousands of young idealists left their revolutionary circles, study groups, jobs, schools, and homes to "Go-among-the-People," as they called it, in a peaceful effort to educate the populace about issues of political and economic change. In the ensuing crackdown almost a thousand were arrested, and two mass trials were staged in the capital, which resulted for many in imprisonment and exile. Four years later, on January 23, 1878, Vera Zasulich shot and fatally wounded General Fyodor Trepov, the military governor of St. Petersburg, and an era of revolutionary terror began. The following August the main underground revolutionary group, Land and Liberty, split into two factions, with the majority reuniting in *Narodnaya Volya*, or the People's Will, a terrorist organization inspired by the Fenian Irish revolutionaries and their use of dynamite tactics to win independence from Great Britain. Making no secret of their aims, the People's Will issued a manifesto that condemned the tsar—"for all the blood he has spilled and for all the torment he has caused"—to death. All sorts of security precautions were taken to protect him—the timetables of his specially fortified train were repeatedly changed, and he drove around in several armorplated carriages (acquired from Napoleon III) so heavy they killed the horses that had to pull them. Nevertheless, after several failed attempts to shoot him, to derail his train, and even to blow up the Winter Palace in St. Petersburg, the inexorable day of execution, March 31, 1881, finally arrived.

> Dismounting from his carriage to inspect the damage caused by a bomb which had missed him but landed among his Cossack escort, the Tsar became an easy target for a second assassin. A Polish student named Grinevitsky rushed out of the gathering crowd and threw his bomb between himself and the Tsar. Grinevitsky died immediately, but Alexander, his legs nearly severed from his body and his stomach ripped open, had just enough strength to mutter, "Take me to the Palace—to die there."
>
> His last wish was granted, in the presence of his son, the new Alexander III and his 13-year-old grandson, the future Nicholas II. Unknown to his subjects the dying Tsar's last official act had been that morning to consent to the establishment of a national representative council to advise on legislation. The project died with him.

Six years later, the People's Will concocted a plot to assassinate his successor, Alexander III, with bombs made extra-lethal by lead pellets filled with strychnine. One member of the assassination team was Aleksandr Ulyanov, a university zoology student and Lenin's elder brother. Also implicated were Bronislaw and Jozef Pilsudski—the latter destined much later to emerge at the head of a resurrected Polish state. To help pay for the dynamite, Ulyanov pawned a gold medal he had just won for his research on fresh-water *Annelida* (a variety of earthworm), but the plot went awry and the conspirators were brought to trial. When Ulyanov took the stand he tried to take complete responsibility for the fiasco and, it is said, "astonished his mother and the court with his volubility." But his statement did no one any good. Bronislaw was sentenced to fifteen years of hard labor on Sakhalin; Jozef was exiled to Eastern Siberia; Ulyanov himself and four others were hanged.

Most Russian dissidents weren't terrorists, of course; and although politicals made up only about 1 percent of the exiled population, their plight attracted particular attention because many belonged to the educated classes, and had been sentenced for their political views. Moreover, the miserable conditions under which some of them were forced to live aroused widespread indignation. Easily the most thorough account of their plight was given by George F. Kennan, who had first come to Siberia during 1865–68 as part of a survey team in connection with a round-the-world telegraph scheme promoted by Western Union. In 1885 he returned to write a series of investigative articles about the exile system for the *Century Magazine*. Skeptical of the more shocking accounts reaching the West of political repression (he had already defended the system in an address before the American Geographical Society), Kennan set out as a "friendly observer" and found the Russian authorities eager to provide assistance for what they expected would be a positive report.

In the course of his travels, however, Kennan found that mental activity was "officially regarded as more dangerous to the state than moral depravity," that every newspaper published in Siberia had been periodically suspended or suppressed, and that almost every foreign traveler who made a serious attempt to study local conditions in Siberia was liable to arrest—like one English cleric who was detained as a distributor of revolutionary pamphlets, even though his polylingual material consisted entirely of Scripture and religious tracts. Unfamiliar scientific investigations also aroused alarm. When the German naturalist and explorer Alexander von Humboldt surveyed the Siberian countryside around Ishim in 1829, the local police chief wrote anxiously to the governor-general:

A few days ago there arrived here a German of shortish stature, insignificant appearance, fussy, and bearing a letter of introduction from your Excellency to me. I accordingly received him politely.... [But] I disliked him from the first. He talks too much and despises my hospitality. He pays no attention to the leading officials of the town and associates with Poles and other criminals. I take the liberty of informing your Excellency that his intercourse with political criminals does not escape my vigilance. On one occasion he proceeded with them to a hill overlooking the town. They took a box with them and got out of it a long tube which we all took for a gun. After fastening it to three feet they pointed it down on the town and one after another examined whether it was properly sighted. This was evidently a great danger for the town which is built entirely of wood; so I sent a detachment of troops with loaded rifles to watch the German on the hill. If the treacherous machinations of this man justify my suspicions, we shall be ready to give our lives for the Tsar and Holy Russia. I send this despatch to your Excellency by special messenger.

Kennan comments wryly: "A letter more characteristic of the petty Russian police officer was never penned. The civilized world is to be congratulated that the brilliant career of the great von Humboldt was not cut short by a Cossack bullet or a police saber, while he was taking sights with a theodolite in that little Siberian town."

With his official clearance, Kennan was able to travel to numerous locales otherwise barred to visitors and met about five hundred political exiles, including a number of so-called "Nihilists," living under police surveillance or in the penal settlements. He soon discovered that the term "Nihilist" (popularized by Turgenev in *Fathers and Sons*) was indiscriminately applied by the authorities to almost all dissidents, regardless of their views. Confronted with this official caricature, Kennan was led, by reaction, into a kind of naive enthusiasm and admiration for most of the political exiles he met. He never got over his amazement and (being an educated man himself) his horror at seeing "well-bred" individuals obliged to do common or menial work. That somewhat patrician bias aside, he produced a remarkably broad, statistically provocative, and powerfully felt portrait of the exile system. Indeed, as his views changed and his research grew in scope, he found himself in a constant cat-and-mouse game with the police. Accumulating important and compromising documents, he grew remarkably in girth, as he attempted to conceal them in a leather belt around his waist. Still others were bound into the covers of books, or sequestered in the hollow sides of boxes and trunks. Five years after safely returning to the United States, he published his monumental *Siberia and the Exile System* in two volumes (1891), the classic exposé and indictment of the system.

Kennan broadly divided the political exiles into three classes: Liberals ("men of moderate opinions, who believe in the gradual extension of the principles of self-government"); Revolutionists (in favor of the overthrow of the autocracy by conspiracy and armed rebellion); and Terrorists, or "embittered revolutionists." Although government propaganda had attempted to dismiss the terrorists of 1879–81 as nothing but "an insignificant gang of discharged telegraph operators, half-educated school-boys, miserable little Jews, and loose women," Kennan considered most of them people of extraordinary ability and essentially noble nature, who had been gradually radicalized by the government's arbitrary acts.

Hard-labor politicals began arriving at Kara in significant numbers after 1879, as the revolutionary movement grew and the prisons of European Russia became crowded with political offenders. At Kara, they were imprisoned in buildings intended originally for common felons. Beginning in 1880, their situation grew more dire, as their privileges were increasingly curtailed, ending in the abolition of the free command. Half-shaven heads, chains, and leg-fetters became the lot of all.

Conditions in the women's prison for politicals at Ust-Kara were somewhat more humane; each prisoner had a cell to herself, and doors were left unlocked during the day so that the inmates could socialize whenever they wished.

As with the Decembrists, the government was in a quandary as to how best to contain the spread, in exile, of subversive ideas. In prison, politicals were isolated from common criminals (whom it was feared they would corrupt). To make it more difficult for them to escape, they were generally distributed in small groups among remote towns and villages, in forced colonization, or assigned residences under police surveillance. This arrangement, however (according to the governor-general of Eastern Siberia), had also spread "anarchistic ideas" where they had never been known before.

However dispersed, it was exile by "administrative process" which allowed the government to do with them what it wished. In brief, this most egregious aspect of the penal code allowed the arrest, detention (for up to two years), and eventual banishment without hearing or trial for up to ten years (after 1888) of any individual judged by the local authorities to be "prejudicial to public order" or "incompatible with public tranquillity." Under this authority, people could be picked up suddenly, without warning on the street, for reasons as impalpable as the air—as in the case of a man who was "suspected of an intention to put himself into an illegal situation." Although primarily aimed at suppressing political dissent, in fact anyone known to wish a change of regime was liable to exile for life. So was anyone aware of anyone contemplating such a wish who did not report it to the police.

Although the use of administrative exile as a state weapon had preceded by several years the first attempt on the life of a government official, its application was redoubled as Russia's pre-revolutionary struggle intensified. Hundreds of people, wrote Kennan, "representing all classes and all social grades," were "swept into the prisons by the dragnet of the police," and before the end of 1889 "there was hardly a town or large village in Western Siberia that did not contain administrative exiles." Their individual treatment varied according to the luck of their locale, but in the wave of repression that followed the assassination of Alexander II, a newly promulgated statute of police surveillance and its companion "standard" code of exile regulations (both set forth in March 1882) more strictly circumscribed an exile's life.

Among other things, they effectively deprived him of any independent means of support. In Kennan's inventory, he was

forbidden, under pain of imprisonment, to act in the capacity of teacher, doctor, chemist, photographer, lithographer, librarian, copyist, editor, compositor, reporter, lecturer, actor, lawyer, bookseller, or clerk. He cannot hold any position in the service of the state or of society; he cannot be an officer or a partner in any commercial company; he cannot be a member of any scientific body; he cannot have anything to do with drugs, medicines, photographic or litho-graphic materials, books, weapons, or newspapers; and, finally, he cannot "exercise any public activity."

"What," expostulated Kennan, "is there left for an educated man to do?"—especially since most administratives were professional men or intellectuals, and generally unfit for farming or other manual trades.

Beyond this, the administrative was a captive of his place of banish-ment; had to report at intervals to the police; and his residence was subject to search and seizure at any hour. His correspondence was so strictly censored that all letters were tested with a solution of chlorate of iron, to see whether any entries had been made with invisible ink.

Of course, the rules were not always strictly enforced, despite the tsar's bureaucratic effort to make them uniform. But apart from the humiliating restrictions, some exiles were also subjected to the harsh-est conditions of Siberian life. At Surgut, a small town on the Ob just south of the Arctic Circle, and Berezov at the river's mouth, Turu-khansk, Verkhoyansk, and Srednekolymsk (the usual destination "for all Jewish suspects" after 1888), and other miserable little native settle-ments so small or remote as not to be on the map, exiles languished among the aborigines and sometimes found that for hundreds of miles around there was not a single person with whom they could converse. Nikolay Chernyshevsky, the radical social theorist and writer exiled to Vilyuysk, wrote to his wife: "People here are so used to travelling endless distances that Yakutsk, which is 700 versts [464 miles] away, seems to them a town you could reach out and touch." For lack of anything else to do, he spent his time "collecting mushrooms and drying them by a method developed by my experiments and deep cogitation."

Another exile complained to a friend that he was followed by a suspicious Yakut everywhere he went—"for fear that if I escape they will have to answer for it to the Russian authorities." Inside the com-munal tent (where he was forced to dwell) there was invariably some Yakut

who has stripped himself naked, and is hunting for lice in his cloth-ing. . . . The excrement of the cattle and of the children; the incon-ceivable disorder and filth; the rotting straw and rags; the myriads of vermin in the bedding; the foul, oppressive air, and the impossibility of speaking a word of Russian—all these things taken together are positively enough to drive one insane. The food of the Yakuts can hardly be eaten. It is carelessly prepared, without salt, often of tainted materials, and the unaccustomed stomach rejects it with nausea. I have no separate dishes or clothing of my own; there are no facilities for bathing, and during the whole winter—eight months—I am as dirty as they. I cannot go anywhere. . . . I have nothing to read— neither books nor newspapers—and I know nothing of what is going on in the world.

The Decembrist Muravyev-Apostol spent a year of his exile (1828) at Vilyuysk, which at the time consisted of a little shacklike church with a dome, four houses, and a few dozen yurts. The church had been built during the reign of Catherine the Great, but the priests had spent most of their time engaged in the fur trade, and few Yakuts had been evangelized. The surrounding landscape was barren, relieved by only a few coniferous trees, and Apostol's attempt to plant potatoes completely failed. He had more luck at first with millet, which grew quickly, but before it could ripen it was nipped by frost. After a long and bitterly cold winter, summer came in a brief blaze of heat and with a swarm of giant midges that bred out of the swamps. These midges, he wrote, were

to be compared with the Egyptians' boils in the time of the Pharoah . . . I could not even poke my nose outside my yurt. Whole clouds of midges of great size stick to you cruelly. The Yakut wear masks against them, woven from hairs from horses' manes. In the yurt they protect themselves by means of smoke from a dung fire. There is a large pot containing coal, and they put into it pieces of dried dung paste, and this they also use in autumn to smear on the outside of the yurt. This fumigation, far from fragrant, continues day and night.

Under such circumstances, the return of the frightfully cold winter, with temperatures that dropped to up to 50 below, seemed to him a "saving frost."

One of the most famous of the women revolutionaries sent into exile was Katerina Breshkovskaya, who had first "gone among the people" in 1874, and in punishment for this (after nearly four years in preliminary detention before her trial) was sent first to Ust-Kara, then to a prison camp near the eastern shores of Lake Baikal. "I was like a wild falcon in a narrow cage," she recalled. "I grew almost frantic with loneliness and to keep my sanity I would rush out in the snow shouting passionate orations, or, playing the prima donna, sing grand opera arias to the bleak landscape—which never applauded." She managed one spectacular, if short-lived escape, making her way across the rugged mountains with two companions for 600 miles toward the Pacific Coast before being caught. After several years near the Arctic Circle, she was transferred as a forced colonist to Selenginsk, a half-Buryat village of wooden huts in the desolate valley of the Selenga River. Seven years later, she became a "free exile," and in 1896 was finally released.

When Kennan met her at Selenginsk in 1885, he was much impressed with her character and fortitude, but predicted she would die in captivity, leaving only an unpainted wooden cross in a bare graveyard in the Transbaikal. In fact, after her release, she returned to Russia, and ("an embittered revolutionist") helped plan the assassinations of Count Vyacheslav von Plehve, Minister of the Interior in 1904, and of Grand Duke Sergey in 1905.

Although most administratives were exiled as *neblagonadyeshny*—literally "those of whom nothing good can be expected"—when given the least opportunity to manifest their industry and gifts, quite the opposite was often true. From the beginning, in fact, Siberian exiles had made significant contributions to the life and culture of the empire. The exiled seventeenth-century Croatian priest Yuri Krizanich was usefully consulted by early trade envoys to China; Johann Tabbert von Strahlenberg, a Swedish prisoner of war, drew some of the best contemporary maps of Siberia and "compiled polyglot tables of aboriginal languages"; and a number of Poles pursued studies that earned them lasting renown. Two mountain ranges in Northern Siberia are named after Polish geologists; other exiles (such as Waldemar Bogaras, Waldemar Jochelson, and Dmitry Klementz) added enormously to the knowledge of native cultures and folklore. Their compatriot, Aleksandr Tschekanovsky, devised a magnifying glass for himself from a broken decanter, and developed into an acclaimed entomologist. He also made geological studies along the Angara River, and (again with instru-

ments of his own making) meteorological observations at Irkutsk. The
Siberian-born Grigory Potanin, a founding father of the movement for
Siberian autonomy, was actually exiled *from* Siberia to the European
Russian north, but returned in 1876 to lead naturalist expeditions to
Mongolia, Tibet, and the Central Asia Plateau. Bronislaw Pilsudski did
pioneering work among the Ainu, Gilyak (Nivkh), and Oroks on Sak-
halin Island.

Among the exiles Kennan met at Tomsk was Prince Alexander Kropotkin (brother of the famous Socialist), who had first been arrested
as a student for possessing a copy of Emerson's essay on "Self-
Reliance." Arrested again in 1877, he was banished to Minusinsk, north
of Mongolia on the Yenisey, where in conjunction with a dedicated
local naturalist he founded an outstanding museum devoted to the
geology, botany, and archeology of the region.

Yet the repression that created the exile system ultimately negated
even some of these gains. In 1822, for example, the Polish scholar,
Jozef Kowalewski had joined a secret patriotic society organized by the
poet Adam Mickiewicz. He was arrested, after the society was broken
up by the police, banished to Kazan, where he studied Oriental languages for six years, and in 1828 was transferred to Eastern Siberia.
From there he was allowed to travel to Peking. He returned with many
books in Manchu, Mongolian, Tibetan, and Chinese, and did such brilliant work in his field as to become the preeminent Orientalist of his
day. Ultimately allowed to return to Warsaw, he happened to be living
in a house from which a bomb was thrown at the Russian governor on
September 19, 1863. In reprisal, the authorities burned everything the
house contained, including a piano that had once belonged to Chopin,
and all of Kowalewski's priceless manuscripts and books.

Three centuries after the town bell of Uglich had been exiled, it received an imperial pardon, on May 20, 1892. Reconsecrated and repaired, it was duly restored to its original abode, where, we are told,
"the people lined the piers and river embankment to give a rousing
welcome to the steamer that was bringing the alarm bell home. The
bell was placed on special stretchers and borne into the city to the
loud cheers of the crowd. The city's dignitaries stood as a guard of
honor over the bell till the following morning, when in the presence

of five thousand fellow townsmen, the sexton rang it." Seven years later, on May 6, 1899, the system itself was declared abolished, and the announcement (according to an official publication) "removed from Siberia that shameful stain attached to it as a place of exile, by putting it on the same footing with other countries of the Empire." A few months after that, with great fanfare, the Russian delegate to the International Prison Congress in Brussels declared: "The Middle Ages left to Russia three legacies: torture, the knout, and exile. The eighteenth century abolished torture, the nineteenth the knout, and the first day of the twentieth century will be the last of a penal system based upon exile."

The imperial edict of June 12, 1900, however, failed to sweep it away. Imprisonment replaced exile as the punishment in a number of cases, and Siberian exile (as distinguished from banishment to Sakhalin) was more or less limited to political or sacrilegious crimes. But the penal colonization of Sakhalin continued, and communes could still turn undesirables over to the authorities for deportation, even if they now had to readmit those who had served their term. In 1900, 287,000 exiles remained in Siberia, not counting convicts at hard labor; and over the next several years the vagrants and vagabonds of old would be supplanted by new revolutionary intellectuals deported in continuing waves.

13

THE NEW FRONTIER

No matter how many exiles were poured into its flatlands, valleys, or Asiatic alps, or were forcibly lodged in the most recessed nooks of its terrain, in the settlement of Siberia it was the potential of the region that was most conspicuous, and among its many growing communities, the vast empty spaces that remained.

At the beginning of the eighteenth century there were approximately 300,000 Russians in Siberia, and by the beginning of the nineteenth, 1 million or more. The colony produced millions of bushels of grain and potatoes, and sent annually to European Russia enormous quantities of raw products, such as hides, tallow, bristles, furs, birds' skins, flax, and hemp. Cottage industries also turned out rugs and carpets, fish netting, linen cloth, barrels, telegas and sleighs, leather goods, stockings, mittens, belts, and scarves. Beekeeping was started in the eighteenth century by Old Believers around Ustkamenogorsk. The breeding of marals (a species of red deer) began at the beginning of the nineteenth century in the southern Altay and subsequently spread to the Transbaikal. Their horns, ground to a powder, were coveted by Chinese apothecaries for all sorts of remedies, their fat as a medicine for ulcers, and their bone marrow as a lubricant for guns.

A significant increase in commerce with China had come after 1762, when Catherine the Great abolished the Crown monopoly on the fur trade and on the privilege of sending caravans to Peking. One million chests of tea a year were imported through Kyakhta, where the leaves were carefully repacked and sewn up in rawhide satchels for transport west. Silks and rhubarb (valued as an antiscorbutic) were also brought in, along with powdered sugar, paper, and great quantities of compressed or "brick" tea—a mixture of coarse leaves and stems that sometimes used ox blood as a binding agent when stamped into bricks. Russian convoys, in turn, wound their way southward to Peking with woolens, linens, leather goods, tinware, and furs.

For 150 years the fur trade had dominated the Siberian economy, and its various needs had defined the colony's relationship to the state. In the middle of the nineteenth century, some 10 to 15 million squirrels were killed in Siberia every year, along with tens of thousands of ermines, rabbits, martens, foxes, sables, lynx, and wolverine. Along the Arctic and Pacific coasts the chief prey were walrus, seal, and polar bear.

The ivory trade had also grown. The refrigerated carcasses of hairy mammoths—second only to the African imperial elephant as the largest land animals ever hunted by man—had lain imperishably preserved in frozen Arctic crevices and riverbanks for tens of thousands of years. Long before the coming of the Russians, in fact, their recovered remains had "excited the wonder and curiosity of men, to follow in their footsteps and traffic in their bones." There is evidence that such bones found their way through China in late antiquity to Khiva, Khorezm, and Greece as commodities, and early Russian settlers (identifying the mammoth with the Behemoth of the Bible exterminated during the Flood) called the ivory "Noah's wood." The contemporary Chinese, who valued powdered ivory as a medicinal base, believed the mammoth to be a giant Arctic rat (*yin shu*) whose immense subterranean stirrings were responsible for earthquakes. This notion spread to Europe, where it persisted at least until the latter part of the seventeenth century, when a learned burgomeister of Amsterdam repeated it in his own monumental book on northern Asia. Mammoths, it was thought, were always discovered half-buried simply because they expired on contact with the air. And Catherine the Great expressed the hope in a letter to Voltaire that a live mammoth might one day be found.

Under the Russians, digging up mammoths became a kind of heavy industry, and between 1650 and 1900 the tusks of an estimated 40,750 mammoths (each tusk weighing from 150 to 200 pounds) were taken out of Siberia. Between 1825 and 1831, the annual shipments exceeded 60,000 pounds as great quantities of fossil ivory were collected with each summer's thaw from crumbling embankments along the Arctic coast, and especially from two islands in the New Siberian group, known as the "isles of bones." On the international market, Russian ivory, as it was called, competed successfully with that from Africa, India, and Ceylon.

Mining interests also developed apace. Early in the eighteenth century, the mines of the Altay, the Transbaikal, and the eastern Urals had begun to assume importance; in 1726, copper mines were opened around Tomsk and Kuznetsk. The Altay mines led to the development of the Zmeinogorsk mines and their accompanying smelters in Kalyvansk and Barnaul—the latter founded in 1738 on the banks of the Ob. About 1745, prospectors from Chelyabinsk discovered the magnetic mountain of Eye-Derlui (near present-day Magnitogorsk), rich with iron, and two years later mining operations were begun with serfs, who dug the ore out of the side of the hill. The work continued year round, and in winter the ore was transported on sledges over the steppe to a foundry where it was smelted with charcoal in little "teapot" blast furnaces, which yielded a few tons of iron a day. Subsequently, in the late 1750s, the mine and smelting plants were sold to a metallurgical corporation controlled by stockholders in Belgium and France. Gold deposits were also found in the Urals, mines started in the Sayan Mountains (both east and west of the Yenisey), while the mica quarries along the Vitim River supplied the colony with its windowpanes. By 1740 Siberia's mines had made the Russian Empire the foremost producer of precious metals in Europe and the world's leader in copper production. By the end of the century, the Altay region was also yielding up to 18 tons of silver and 1,300 pounds of gold per year. In 1832, dredging for gold began on the Chulym River; gold strikes were made on the upper Zeya; and in 1863, prospectors reached the Vitim (a tributary of the Lena) and Olekma rivers, and began tapping the renowned Lena gold fields. Gold production in Siberia grew so rapidly that by the end of the century it reached 40 tons and accounted for 75 percent of the total gold output of the empire.

All this stimulated the building of cart roads and cattle-driving routes, postal relays, river commerce, and so on, and brought the first steamers to the Yenisey, Lena, Vitim, and Shilka rivers. Copper works, cast-iron foundries, and iron works sprang up, new industries emerged in the upper valleys of the Ob and Irtysh rivers, and in the vicinity of Barnaul and Semipalatinsk. The skilled workers and craftsmen they brought to the region paved the way for the growth of towns and the flourishing of trade. The town of Yeniseysk, for example, developed into a thriving center for silversmithing and related crafts.

The demand for agricultural products naturally increased, and could be met. Despite enormous stretches of forest and tundra, Siberia had about 500,000 square miles of arable land, over a third of it in Western Siberia. This bounty was only slightly less than the cultivable land found in the twelve north-central United States. In Western Siberia the predominant crop was wheat, in Eastern Siberia, rye. In the north, barley was important. The technical crops grown, mostly for local use, were flax and hemp. The region of Yeniseysk yielded considerable tobacco, and throughout southwestern Siberia, especially around Krasnoyarsk, peasants annually harvested tens of millions of bushels of grain. In their vegetable gardens, they also grew cucumbers, carrots, onions, radishes, turnips, beets, cabbages and rutabagas, potatoes (after 1840), melons and cantaloupes around Minusinsk, and fruits like apples, cherries, and pears.

Farming developed rapidly among the Buryats in the mining districts of the Transbaikal, and by the end of the eighteenth century the variety of their crops included rye, wheat, hemp, and oats. By the middle of the nineteenth many Yakuts too lived in large agricultural communities, and like the Buryats tended herds of cattle or flocks of sheep and goats.

Most of the land in Siberia was owned by the Crown, and at first peasants tilled it under the so-called "plowed land subject to the sovereign's tithe," paying rent in kind to the state. This system eventually gave way to a money quitrent (by the 1730s about half of the peasants in Siberia tilled land on that basis), and since the Siberian peasant was not enserfed, he was pretty much free to buy and sell his land, or rent or mortgage it as he chose. Although technically 96 percent of the land belonged to the state, in fact, most of the settlers simply worked as much land as they could occupy. In European Russia, serfdom had grown up as a means of maintaining the gentry class, which the government needed for both civil administration and military campaigns. In northern Asia, however, there was no need for such a class, especially after the Kirghiz had been pacified, and because there was practically no armed friction with China once the border was fixed. Resident Cossacks and small regular army detachments were all that Siberia required to police its conquest or as a frontier guard. So instead of gentry estates, worked by serfs, Siberia had Cossack estates, worked by free men.

This system of colonizing Southern Siberia had begun under Peter the Great. In 1716, a fortified line on Siberia's southwestern frontier had been established as a protection from the raids of nomads, and by 1800 it consisted of about 124 fortresses, redoubts, and outposts manned by several thousand Cossacks, most of whom had been enlisted from Western Siberian towns. Ten cavalry regiments and two companies of artillery were added in 1808, and in the 1820s all their members received substantial allotments of land along the frontier. New land grants as well as other privileges followed in 1846, and by midcentury the Cossack Host's military complement (including men on active service and in the reserve) had risen above 12,000 men. The protected territory behind the fortified line attracted more peasants, and in this way Southern Siberia was colonized.

After the treaties of Aigun and Peking, military villages were also established along the Amur and Ussuri rivers, on the Manchurian border, and in the Transbaikal. In such areas, the Cossacks emerged as a privileged caste, since they were awarded the richest land, in larger allotments (typically, 100 acres) than the 20 to 40 acres regular settlers received.

There were also agricultural communes, whose members lived in compact villages rather than on individual farms, and took their cattle to a common pasture, instead of to fenced-in fields. Although the village commune enjoyed what the land produced, without legal title it could not dispose of it nor reduce any part of it to individual ownership, but, instead, periodically divided it up among its members into individual plots. This system of rotation discouraged development— the building of barns, farmhouses, and so on—since each peasant eventually had to abandon whatever improvements he made.

Nevertheless, Siberian peasants overall were the most prosperous in the empire. Indeed, most migrants ended up with more land in Siberia than they had abandoned, and those who stayed outnumbered those who could not adapt by ten to one. Free settlers, in any case, always outnumbered those officially resettled or exiled, and their proportion increased after 1822, when Alexander I allowed all state peasants (as opposed to serfs on private estates) so inclined to migrate to Siberia. Careful surveys of tillable land were begun in 1837, and about 40 acres offered to every adult male. Beginning in 1843, migrant families received up to 95 acres apiece, together with monetary aid and freedom from all obligations, including military service. Perhaps 350,000 peasants took advantage of this beneficence over the course of the next twenty years. Irregularly, other colonists kept coming too, until the abolition of serfdom in 1861 opened the gates. The possibility of securing unlimited land by emigration to Siberia was comparable to the opening of the Great West in the United States. "The migration," writes one historian,

> became elemental. The government issued decrees and regulations uselessly and, so to speak, after the event. Belatedly it tried to introduce some order into the "human rush" and, if possible, to foresee its effect upon the land problem, living conditions, and political development. It worked to direct a flood it could not dam up, by encouraging settlement into the Far Eastern regions, along the Amur, and in the Altay and Kirghiz country. . . . Because people of all nationalities and races poured in from European Russia, and because in Siberia they lived among many others, Siberia became the melting pot of Russia.

As long as Siberia could be regarded as a single fur colony economically, it had made a kind of sense to govern it as a single unit politically. But in 1719 (in recognition of its evolving character), the territory had been subdivided into five regions. During the reign of Catherine the Great, a new idea of Siberia took shape: not as dependent on the homeland, but as "a colonial realm capable of supporting itself as well as rendering tribute"—a sort of "India to Russia's England." The territory was split administratively into Western and Eastern Siberia, with their capitals at Tobolsk and Irkutsk, and in 1802 Alexander I established a governor-generalship for the whole region.

Nevertheless, the government long failed to formulate a coherent Siberian policy. No monarch (or even heir) bothered to cross the Urals to take a look for himself, and Siberia remained an administrative backwater where powerful officials did as they pleased. When Anton Devier succeeded Skornyakov-Pisarev as commandant of Okhotsk in 1740, he found only 12 rubles 22 kopeks in the treasury and 108 pounds of provisions in the magazine. Ivan Koch, commandant of Okhotsk from 1789 through 1794, was even more presumptive and arbitrary in his rule, and the time-honored proverb, "God is high up and the Tsar far off," was popularly revised to "God is in Heaven and Koch is in Okhotsk." Siberia's first governor, Prince Matvey Gagarin, tried to create an independent kingdom for himself beyond the Urals, and eventually it was discovered that he was siphoning off into his own treasury a considerable portion of the China trade. After a decade of amassing an illegal fortune with impunity (including a diamond-studded icon of the Virgin worth 130,000 rubles that hung over his bed), he was arrested, confessed, and appealed for clemency, but Peter the Great decided to make a public example of him and had him hanged in March 1721. Yet few of his successors (or their lesser appointees) quailed, perhaps because it had taken so long for Peter to bring his satrap to account. One dissolute noble in charge of the mines at Nerchinsk, for example, unable to persuade a local merchant to give him a loan, surrounded the man's house with artillery, and was about to give the order to fire when the merchant suddenly appeared on the porch with money on a silver plate.

The appointment in 1802 of a governor-general for Siberia was a first step toward acknowledging the colony's neglect. But the first man designated to fill the office—Ivan Pestel, father of the Decembrist leader—was not the happiest choice. Together with his devoted assistant, Nikolay Treskin, civil governor at Irkutsk, he imposed his will upon the population without regard to legal restraints, and tried to make up in energy what he lacked in administrative tact. Yet the policies he enacted reflected the tsar's clear mandate for change. Committed to the development of Siberian agriculture, he guaranteed peasants a greater return on their crops through generous state purchases of grain, settled new areas, and with land grants, loans, and other kinds of assistance encouraged the Buryats to take up farming. As an example of the industriousness Pestel hoped to foster (among Russians and Buryats alike), he pointed to the success of the Old Believers, whose thriving farms were the mainstay of the Verkhneudinsk and Nerchinsk districts. At the same time, as a cushion against famine, he expanded the system of state granaries. To promote competition and free trade, Pestel also abolished internal customs and tariffs, refused to acknowledge the exclusive monopoly privileges prominent local merchants had long enjoyed, and liberalized the grain trade with China by lowering export requirements. Beyond that, he built new roads, improved navigation on the rivers, and demolished and rebuilt whole sections of towns.

Although the aims were progressive, the methods used to attain them were despotic, and gave both Pestel and Treskin an evil name. Merchants who resisted their schemes were severely punished by fines, lawsuits, and exile to remote areas, and the sweep of their persecutions reached such a scale that eventually Alexander I (prodded by the Ministry of Finance, which objected to the substitution of state monopolies for commercial ones) had to rein them in.

Pestel himself, not incidentally, acted almost entirely through Treskin, while luxuriating throughout most of his tenure amidst the splendors of St. Petersburg. In this, as one writer remarks, he was rather like the old Roman proconsuls who eschewed the boredom of the provinces they governed for the pleasures of imperial Rome. Pestel, however, was also known to have an intricate network of spies. One evening he happened to be dining with Tsar Alexander I, when the tsar pointed out the window and asked, "Look there, what is that black speck on the cathedral tower? " "I can't make it out, your majesty," one of the other guests replied, "but you might ask Pestel. He has amazing eyes and can see from here all the way into Siberia."

A more thorough reexamination of Siberian affairs soon followed, and the man of the hour was Mikhail Speransky, an official of exceptional intellectual range. The son of a priest (in Russia the lower clergy were free to marry), Speransky was familiar with the philosophical and scientific thought of the Enlightenment, and had taught mathematics, rhetoric, and philosophy before entering politics in 1796. Hardworking and articulate, he earned rapid advancement: from secretary to the Attorney General of the Senate he rose to Assistant Minister of Justice, held posts in the Interior Ministry, and in 1808 accompanied the tsar to his critical meeting with Napoleon, who afterwards described him as "Russia's only clear head."

In January 1810, Speransky emerged from among a number of more prominent candidates as state secretary to the newly established State Council, and in this capacity, for four years, seemed destined, through a series of proposed constitutional reforms, to revolutionize Russian political life. But in the general reaction following the outbreak of the Napoleonic Wars, Speransky fell from favor and, summarily dismissed in March of 1812, returned home at midnight to find a police carriage waiting at his door. Four years of exile (to provinces west of the Urals) ended with his appointment as governor of Penza Province in 1816, where his skill in administration once again caught the monarch's eye. Three years later he was appointed governor-general of Siberia, and after an extensive tour of the colony, returned to the capital in 1821 to draft and supervise the implementation of a number of far-reaching reforms.

Speransky had traveled to places in Siberia where no previous governor had gone, and although, as his biographer observes, he had come to Siberia "with the stereotype picture of a backward, cold, dreary, and unpromising country, fit to be only a penal colony, deprived of any serious economic and social value to Russia," he discovered "a hard-working, patient, and resolute people." He was also struck by Siberia's potential, its great agricultural and mineral wealth, and the untapped possibilities of the China trade. That nothing should stand in its way, he ferreted out corrupt and arbitrary officials—681 in all were charged with various misdeeds—established Lancaster schools of mutual instruction (in which brighter or more proficient children were used to teach others under the direction of an adult), sought more humane working conditions for the mines, began the systematic survey of the province of Yakutsk (a territory the size of India), and took an interest in the cultural life and customs of the natives, whose villages and festivals he made part of his regular tour.

Although he pressed the campaign against merchant monopolies (while abolishing their state equivalents), he maintained the state granaries as a safety net for those in need, established new markets and fairs, and tried to come up with a rational scheme for the settlement of exiles, although their steadily increasing tide would eventually overwhelm his plans. To increase agricultural production, he freed Cossacks of the line from many of their military obligations, and peasants from irregular labor drafts.

With regard to native affairs, he could see that the smaller and more

backward tribes, isolated and subjected to disease and periodic famines, had become "stepchildren of the empire" and were dying out,
while among the more prosperous groups (principally the Buryats and
Yakuts) the old clan system was breaking down and a kind of class-
consciousness evolving among them, based on economic activity and
wealth. In recognition of these changes, Speransky divided the native
peoples into three groups: settled, nomads, and vagrants. He recommended that the settled be grouped administratively with the Russian
peasantry (with whom they now had much in common), but that the
latter two groups be administered as nearly as possible according to
their own laws. Each encampment (*ulus*) of fifteen families or more
was to form a clan administration, and several encampments a native
administration, to which the clan administration was subordinate. Several clans together were entitled to a Steppe Duma, or nomad forum,
made up of prominent members of the community. These institutions
(although subject to Russian authority, of course) allowed for a considerable degree of self-government and helped keep the thread of their
cultural traditions alive.

As a result of his various recommendations, a special Committee on
Siberian Affairs was set up as an oversight body in the capital, two
governor-generalships were created for Western and Eastern Siberia,
and advisory councils were established to assist the governor-generals
in executing their tasks.

Speransky's reforms were long-lasting, even as the colony's organization evolved. In 1838, the special oversight committee was
superseded by a Siberian Bureau; in 1879, Western Siberia was divided
into four provinces (Tobolsk, Tomsk, Semipalatinsk, and Akmolinsk),
and Eastern Siberia into six (Irkutsk, Yakutsk, Yeniseysk, Transbaikal,
Amur, and Maritime). By the end of Muravyev-Amursky's tenure, the
larger geopolitical subdivisions had also been fixed: "Western Siberia,"
as extending from the Urals to the Yenisey; "Eastern Siberia" from the
Yenisey to the Yablonovy-Stanovoy mountain ranges of the Transbaikal;
and the "Russian Far East" as that portion of Siberia—the Transbaikal,
Amur, and Maritime provinces—that drained to the Pacific Ocean.
(The Maritime Province, created in 1857, comprised the coastal area
down to Vladivostok.) In 1882, the Western Siberian governor-generalship was abolished, Tomsk and Tobolsk provinces came directly under
the jurisdiction of the Interior Ministry, and a new governor-general-

ship of the steppe was created out of portions of both Western Siberia and Turkestan. In 1884, the government of the Amur Province assumed responsibility for the Russian Far East and Sakhalin Island.

Three years after drafting his Siberian reforms, Speransky was appointed to the special tribunal that tried and sentenced the Decembrists. At the tsar's behest, he personally drew up the rules of procedure, but the task was a torment to him, for a number of the defendants had been his friends. One of them recalled that when he was summoned to answer the questions put to him by the court, Speransky, standing nearby, "looked at him sadly, and a tear rolled down his cheek." It subsequently became known that the Decembrists had once considered Speransky as a possible interim head of state.

Never an anti-monarchist, in fact, Speransky had always been less interested in changing the structure of the state than in improving its functioning. His life-long passion was legal procedure, and in his twilight years he became the leading force in the project for the codification of Russian laws. In 1830 his career was crowned with the publication of the first *Complete Collection of the Laws of the Russian Empire.*

With the reappearance of the Amur River Valley as the hope of the Russian Far East, the importance of the Okhotsk seaboard and Kamchatka had declined. And it was not long before the very name of Petropavlovsk was uttered with disgust by Europeans and Russians from St. Petersburg. Despite its heroic reputation from the Crimean War, and monuments to Bering and La Pérouse commemorating the town's role in the history of navigation and discovery, in 1866 it consisted of little more than a cluster of log cabins thatched with bark, a church with a green painted dome, a crumbling wharf, and vaguely cut paths that meandered like sheepwalks among the scattered houses and slumbering cows.

The monument to La Pérouse was scarcely a tourist attraction. Inaccessibly set on a steep slope between the harbor and the bay, it was nothing but a frame of wood covered with sheet iron, painted black, and looked, wrote Kennan, "like the tombstone over the grave of a criminal." Along the crest of a ridge dividing the inner and outer bays and commanding the western approaches to the town could still be seen traces of the fortifications which had repelled the allied attack. Yet the batteries were already overgrown with grass and flowers, and "only the form of the embrasures distinguished them from shapeless mounds of earth." One hundred twenty-five years after the founding of Petropavlovsk as Russia's major Pacific port, its whole population consisted of a few hundred natives and Russian peasants, along with a handful of merchants drawn there by the sable trade.

Although the economy of the coastal population had been devastated by the mass extermination by Americans of whales and walrus in adjacent seas, the overall failure of Russian settlement in the area had allowed American traders to become an increasing presence on the Asiatic coast. After the sale of the Aleutians to the United States, the traders instantly acquired a string of island ports that led inexorably back to Kamchatka, as they had once led to Alaska a century before. Settlements like Tigil and Gizhiga, which controlled the residual fur trade and other regional commerce, received annual visits from American captains, who landed large quantities of flour, tea, sugar, cloth, copper kettles, tobacco, vodka, and other goods.

After 1849, American whalers also showed up along the Chukchi Peninsula and found that for a gallon of rum (which cost them 40 cents) they could get a hundred dollars' worth of bone or fur. This trade touched the Alaskan side of Bering Strait as well, but after it was curbed by Congressional legislation in 1873, American skippers redoubled their efforts to sell their alcohol on the Siberian coast. In the mercenary machinations of the trade, they dispensed diluted whiskey, adulterated tobacco, or defective goods. But they sometimes got as good as they gave. "It was relatively common," one writer tells us, "to find fox tails sewn [by natives] on rabbit skins, or damaged fox skins cleverly patched with rabbit fur; broken walrus tusks riveted together with lead and the joints concealed by smeared reindeer fat; and stones set in the root canals of walrus tusks to increase their weight." Natives even began to make their own moonshine to sell to visiting ships—and one American sailor swore that he obtained "the hottest stuff" he ever tasted from a Siberian Eskimo. "Wherefore," he added, "there was, for a time, joy in the forecastle." Later, on the beach, the crew found a little distillery, ingeniously devised:

The still itself was an old tin oil can; the worm, a twisted gun barrel; the flake-stand, a small powder keg. The mash used in making the liquor, we learned was a fermented mixture of flour and molasses obtained in trade from whale ships. It was boiled in the still, a twist of moss blazing in a pan of blubber oil doing duty as a furnace. The vapor from the boiling mash passed through the worm in the flake-stand and was condensed by ice-cold water with which the powder keg was kept constantly filled by hand. The liquor [called "kootch"] dripped from the worm into a battered old tomato can.

Some of the Yankee trading vessels were "floating general stores," stocked with guns, ammunition, cloth, sewing machines, thimbles, thread, tobacco, flour, chewing gum, dried apples and prunes, molasses, sugar, tea, clocks, scissors, mirrors, harmonicas, knives, hammers, saws, canned milk, compasses, opera glasses, spy glasses, and even phonographs and phonograph records, among other wares. For all intents and purposes, by the 1880s the economy of the region was largely run out of San Francisco and Seattle, not Bolsheretsk or Okhotsk. The quality of the American items was much higher on the whole (yet about half as expensive) as those the Russians could supply, and included a number of things in addition which the Russians themselves had never seen. As a result, coastal natives came to depend on the Americans for virtually all of their manufactured goods. One Russian visitor to Uelen reported that "nothing there was Russian, not even the language," and that all the wares (from gramophones to assorted statuettes) in the local store were of American make. He even discovered a native sewing overalls with a sewing machine in his tent, while a less pragmatic companion, captivated by a typewriter, "enthusiastically tapped out symbols" that he couldn't read.

Not surprisingly, the Russian government began to feel that its sovereignty was being threatened, and sent more and more supply steamers into the area to try to wrest the commerce back.

Throughout Siberia, the fate of the natives had been mixed. Some had done well enough under the Russians, but epidemics of measles, smallpox, and other diseases prevented the smaller nomadic groups from gaining any ground. In 1876, for example, there were said to be only about 1,600 Yukaghirs left, roaming land between the Yana and Kolyma rivers—the pitiable remnant of a once-powerful tribe. Here and there their ancient burial mounds could still be seen, containing skeletons with bows, arrows, spears, and shamanistic drums, but the descendants of these mighty warriors had fallen into such indolence and addiction that their chief delight was a coarse Ukrainian tobacco stretched with dung. Children were taught to smoke as soon as they could toddle, out of a belief (fostered by the Russians) that it was good for the throat and lungs.

Natives drank with predictable abandon, too, and in a spirit of communal generosity even shared their brandy with babes-in-arms. One skipper who visited a small Chukchi settlement on the Asiatic shore found every person, including the smallest children, in such a state of drunkenness they were on the verge of insanity.

The Yukaghirs, Kamchadals, and other natives in the northeast had also discovered the narcotic delights of the fly-agaric mushroom, which made them "lightheaded, more lively and gay, more daring and bold." When immoderately consumed, however, it produced convulsions, followed by fever and delirium. "A thousand chimeras, happy or sad, seize their imagination," wrote one observer. "A small hole seems a great door to them; a spoonful of water, a sea." Although such psychedelic illusions acquired a semi-religious cast, simple addiction to the drug was undeniable, especially among the Koryaks, who to conserve their supply (or stretch it to the utmost) went so far as to drink the urine of those intoxicated, and even to reingest what they threw up. The Russians tried to ban the mushroom's consumption, but that only increased its black market rate of exchange.

In matters of hygiene, it must be said, the natives could not teach the Russians much. The Yukaghirs regarded lice as a sign of good health, and the Kamchadals methodically combed lice out of their hair and ate them. As part of their annual housecleaning, the Tungus dug up nests of ants and brought them into their huts. These killed off all the other vermin but intolerably infested the premises until the ants perished themselves with the first frost. With less ambiguous results, the Gilyaks domesticated ermine to rid their dwellings of rats and mice. Subsequently the Manchus supplied them, at a high price, with cats, castrated to keep the monopoly in their hands.

The half-Russified natives, however, adapted as best they could. Kamchadal women and girls began to dress in Russian styles, wearing camisoles, skirts, blouses, bonnets, and ribbons; and to better please their men, improvised cosmetics—rouge from a sea plant mixed in seal oil, powders from worm-eaten wood. They also began to live in log cabinlike houses and went through worshipful motions at the inevitable village church, which allured them with its green sheet-iron roof surmounted by onion-shaped sky blue domes of tin.

The Orthodox enthusiasm for icons was also emulated by the half-converted natives in a worship of graven images of any kind. In one hut near Anadyrsk, for example, a portrait cut from *Harper's Weekly* was posted up in a corner and adored as a Russian saint. "A gilded candle was burning before his smoky features," writes Kennan, "and every night and morning a dozen natives said their prayers to a major-general in the United States Army." In another hut he found the walls transformed into a kind of secular iconostasis with cut-outs from the *Illustrated London News.*

The natives were also introduced to high finance. Because famines were common throughout the Siberian northeast, where widely scattered settlements seldom husbanded supplies against an unlucky year, the government established a sort of "Fish Savings Bank," where 100,000 dried fish were initially deposited as the capital stock. To maintain and increase its surplus funds, each year every male inhabitant had to pay into this bank one tenth of all the fish he caught, which entitled him to a loan in time of need. By 1867, this bank (which proved a great success) had 3 million dried fish in reserve.

If the natives took readily to icon worship and banking, they were utterly defeated by the mystery of canned foods. On one occasion, Kennan revenged himself upon some unruly Koryak drivers by indulging their curiosity about a pickle, which he miraculously produced from a tin.

Knowing well what the result would be, I gave the whole cucumber to the dirtiest, worst-looking vagabond in the party, and motioned to him to take a good bite. As he put it to his lips his comrades watched him with breathless curiosity to see how he liked it. For a moment his face wore an expression of blended surprise, wonder, and disgust which was irresistibly ludicrous, and he seemed disposed to spit the disagreeable morsel out; but with a strong effort he controlled himself, forced his features into a ghastly imitation of satisfaction, smacked his lips, declared it was "akhmel nemelkhin"—very good, and handed the pickle to his neighbor. The latter was equally astonished and disgusted with its unexpected sourness, but, rather than admit his disappointment and be laughed at by the others, he also pretended that it was delicious, and passed it along. Six men in succession went through with this transparent farce with the greatest solemnity; but when they had all tasted it, and all been victimized, they burst out into a simultaneous "ty-e-e-e" of astonishment, and gave free expression to their long-suppressed emotions of disgust. The vehement spitting, coughing, and washing out of mouths with snow, which succeeded this outburst, proved that the taste for pickles is an acquired one, and that man in his aboriginal state does not possess it.

Kennan's drivers belonged to the sedentary or Coastal Koryaks who, like the Kamchadals, had been thoroughly debased by the coastal trade. It was said without praise of the Kamchadals that they would "suffer and endure any amount of abuse and ill-treatment" yet remain "as faithful and forgiving as a dog. If you treat them well, your slightest wish will be their law."

The Wandering Koryaks, on the other hand, were still wild and independent, and roamed with their vast reindeer herds in solitary bands along the great desolate steppes to the north. Although they acknowledged the sovereignty of "the Great White Chief," as they sometimes called the tsar, they were not overawed by earthly rank per se, as one American major in an exploration party found out. Endeavoring to impress a local elder with his own "general importance in the world," the officer summoned the Koryak to his tent,

and proceeded to tell him through an interpreter, how rich he was; what immense resources, in the way of rewards and punishments, he possessed; what high rank he held; how important a place he filled in Russia, and how becoming it was that an individual of such exalted attributes should be treated by poor wandering heathen with filial reverence and veneration. The old Koryak, squatting upon his heels on the ground, listened quietly to the enumeration of all our leader's admirable qualities and perfections without moving a muscle of his face; but finally, when the interpreter had finished, he rose slowly, walked up to the Major with imperturbable gravity, and with the most benignant and patronizing condescension, patted him softly on the head.

By the sheer inaccessibility of their homeland these natives had, to some degree, been spared intrusion by the whites. Civilization and its full array of discontents lay over the horizon, but in the late nineteenth century at least, much of their world remained unchanged. And a timeless picture of the Koryak reindeer herdsman still squatting through the night under a little brushwood hovel, watching for wolves, could still be drawn.

Alone and almost unsheltered on a great ocean of snow, each man ... patiently endures cold which freezes mercury into solid lumps, and storms which sweep away his frail shelter like chaff in a mist of flying snow. Nothing discourages him; nothing frightens him into seeking the shelter of the tents. I have seen him watching deer at night, with nose and cheeks frozen so that they had mortified and turned black; and have come upon him early cold winter mornings, squatting under three or four bushes with his face buried in his fur coat, as if he were dead.

The even more independent Chukchi (who had reluctantly agreed to become Russian subjects only in 1789) had staunchly resisted Russification, and about all one renowned ethnographer could identify as Russian about them was that they had adopted a few Slavic sayings and the Russian chimney in their huts. Of course, they had grown used to ironware and guns, colored beads, and so forth; but on the whole (as late as the 1860s) when they occasionally showed up at trading posts and annual fairs, they preferred to deal with Russians only at the end of a spear. As Kennan describes this commerce (which was similar to how some natives had dealt with one another of old),

A Chukchi would hang a bundle of furs or a choice walrus tooth upon the sharp polished blade of a long Chukchi lance, and if a Russian trader chose to take it off and suspend in its place a fair equivalent in the shape of tobacco, well and good; if not, there was no trade. This plan guaranteed absolute security against fraud, for there was not a Russian in all Siberia who dared to cheat one of these fierce savages, with the blade of a long lance ten inches from his breast bone.

Even after years of Russian rule, during which a number of their other skills decayed, it was still possible to find Ostyaks, for example, who could "mark an arrow in the middle with a piece of charcoal and discharge it in the air, while a second man, before it reached the ground, shot at the descending shaft and struck it on the mark."

Among settled natives, perhaps the Buryats maintained the strongest ties to their heritage and roots. Russian clerics had been unable to convert them, and in 1814 the London Missionary Society, founded "to spread the knowledge of Christ among the Heathen and other unenlightened Nations," decided to send its own missionaries among them to evangelize. Rather grandly, these Protestants secretly hoped to extend their efforts into Outer Mongolia, and eventually to make a spiritual conquest of China itself.

Most Buryats were devotees of Lamaism, a form of Buddhism with Tibetan roots, and although the majority of Siberia's non-Moslem peoples had superficially converted to Christianity, the Buryats were swept during the eighteenth century by a Buddhist revival generated by missionaries from Mongolia and Tibet. The monastic temples of the lamas (or priests) were known as *datsans*, or lamaseries, where the sacred white elephant was worshipped, as in contemporaneous Siam. In the early nineteenth century, the great lamasery at Goose Lake, with its Sino-Tibetan architecture, lama orchestra, images, and so on, was an exotic tourist attraction. Located near Selenginsk (a garrison town founded in 1666 on the far side of Lake Baikal), it had an impressively large library of sacred books, and was the residence of the Grand Lama of Eastern Siberia. In 1885, when Kennan visited the town, he respectfully sought him out, but the lama's pretended lack of sagacity left him somewhat miffed: among other things, the Grand Lama adamantly insisted that the earth was flat, and claimed never to have heard of the United States.

The melting pot of Russia—Siberia—was being constantly stirred. From the end of the seventeenth century, some portion of the empire's ever-increasing diversity of ethnic groups had fled or been deported to its wide-open spaces, where they mingled with the polyglot world that was already there, and left their individual or hybrid mark on the character of Siberian life.

There were, for example, unique religious communities, where Old Believers, *Skoptsy*, Sabbatarians, and others dwelled. The Sabbatarians were Russian by birth, but Jews by conversion and faith; the *Skoptsy* made up a fanatical sect that believed in sexual abstinence and self-castration (based on Matt. 19:12) as a means to Paradise. Like the Old Believers, however, they also endeavored to live devout and energetic lives (with some analogies to the Puritan ethic), prohibited stimulants of any kind, including tobacco, coffee, and tea, and proved extraordinarily industrious as farmers and craftsmen. Exiled for the most part to the province of Yakutsk, their determined industry was particularly valuable in making progress against the hard and bitter clime. Unfortunately, the built-in obsolescence of their communities could not do Siberia much lasting good. One of their settlements near Turukhansk was described as "a model village and without crime"; but the inhabitants, noted a visitor, had a remarkable appearance. They were all sallow; the men were beardless, with squeaky voices; and no inhabitant was less than forty years of age." There were also the *bezpopovtsy*, or "priestless ones"; the *dukhoborty*, or "spirit warriors" (the so-called "Quakers" of Siberia); the *molokans*, or "milk drinkers," a vegetarian cult; the *khlysts*, or "flagellants"; and the *kamenshchiki*, who sought refuge in remote mountain fastnesses to isolate themselves from the rest of the sinful world. The *bezpopovtsy* were almost indistinguishable from these; they believed the priesthood had been fatally corrupted and that the end of the world was at hand. Like certain radical Protestant sects in the West that subscribed to a priesthood of all believers, they administered the sacraments to one another, or in theatrical demonstrations of their direct contact with the powers above, could sometimes be seen kneeling "by the roadside or in the market for hours with their mouths wide open and turned upwards to receive the invigorating drops of spiritual blessing that they supposed distilled from the skies."

But whatever the schismatic cut of their convictions, all hoped to find in Siberia a freedom of worship and social expression akin to the promise that had driven European dissenters to America's eastern shores. Their exceptionally well-organized communities generally combined a spirit of self-reliance with a belief in mutual aid, and could be found in the secluded swamps and forests of the middle Ob, in mountain hideaways along the Mongolian frontier, on the fertile prairies around Tobolsk, Tomsk, and Barnaul, and in the north toward the tundra, where their hermitages formed valiant enclaves of their faith.

But of all sectarians, the most numerous by far were the Old Believers, some thirty thousand of whom had settled in the Transbaikal during the reign of Catherine the Great alone. By the 1870s they accounted for about 10 percent of the population in the Amur River Valley, where not only were their farms among the richest, but the steamboat traffic on the river was largely in their hands as well.

The Russian Orthodox Church tolerated other creeds, and both Protestant and Roman Catholic churches could also be found in all the principal cities of Siberia, alongside Russian churches and Islamic mosques. In certain areas, Jews and even moderate Raskolniks (dissenters) achieved a measure of legal recognition, with Jews making up a third of the population of Sretensk. Verkhneudinsk also had a Jewish synagogue, and the city of Kansk on the Baraba Steppe was so predominantly Jewish in the 1880s that it was known as the "Jerusalem of Siberia."

From town to town one moved as if from world to world. On Siberia's westernmost frontier stood Yekaterinburg (the gateway to the Kingdom), founded by Peter the Great in 1720 and named for his wife, Catherine. By the mid-1730s it had become a mining town of some importance, and began to resemble a modern European city, with regularly spaced, broad streets, and houses "nearly all built after the German fashion." By the 1880s, it had tramways and electric lights, and in keeping with its cosmopolitan air, nuns painted icons while sitting at easels in an artist's studio, and in their own candle manufactory, with their sleeves tucked up, gave the candles a final polish with their elbows, using the forearm as a rolling pin.

Omsk and Semipalatinsk, on the other hand, located on the fringe of the Central Asian steppes, were decidedly Moslem. Over half their population was Kirghiz and Tartar, Jews (in Omsk at least) were discriminated against and Christian churches were outnumbered by mosques. A city of thriving shops and tea gardens, Omsk was the principal fortress and headquarters of the general staff of the Siberian Fortified Line. But every day without fail at the designated hours the "wailing cries of the muezzins could be heard from the minarets," while beyond the town, "wild-looking" Kirghiz boys, wearing "immense goggles of horsehair netting" against the sun's glare and smoking cigars, "rode fiercely among their herds of cattle on small hardy-looking" steeds. In winter, long lines of camels could be seen dragging Kirghiz sledges across the snow, their legs swathed in wool and rags to protect them from the cold. Although most of the houses were colorfully painted green, red, or blue—in part to add color to the barren landscape, where the soil was unable to support trees along the unpaved streets—on the town's outskirts the Kirghiz lived in bee-hive-shaped portable yurts, made partly of wood and a kind of trellis-work covered with hides and felt. There the women (shrouded in linen headdress and veil) stored *kumis* in goatskin bottles and plaited horse-hair into ropes.

Semipalatinsk to the south was even more Mohammedan and was popularly known as "the Devil's Sandbox" because of its hot climate and desertlike terrain. A bit more eclectic was Ulbinsk, which contained a handful of Tartar mosques, Orthodox churches with colored domes of tin, and a high quadrangular fortress surrounded by a dry moat.

At Tomsk, on the other hand, not far from the Sino-Russian frontier, "everyone received us according to good Chinese custom," one eighteenth-century traveler recalled, "and treated us to many kinds of tea-water without milk and to Chinese confections, which consisted of preserved or candied fruits." Chinese silk shirts were the fashion (because they absorbed sweat in such a way as to keep the skin dry), while throughout the Transbaikal most Russian homes had Oriental chests, Chinese porcelain, and other furnishings of similar decor. Chinese brick tea, boiled with butter and salt, was common fare, and pig-tailed Manchus, for example, made up about half the inhabitants of Sretensk (on the Shilka River), where Chinese opium dens were also to be found down many alleyways and lanes. In Irkutsk, as well, a number of summer houses were adorned with galleries in the Chinese style, and the governor there kept a Chinese jackdaw that was profusely bilingual, welcoming guests with streams of Russian and Chinese.

Oddly enough, Kyakhta on the frontier itself more closely resembled the typical Russian fortress town, built as a square and surrounded by palisades and a moat. Inside was a wooden church, the commander's residence, a rhubarb storehouse, barracks, a large bazaar, a distillery, and a few houses of spacious design where wealthy merchants lived. But just to the south, perhaps 250 yards away, lay the completely Chinese village of Maimachin, a name meaning "Buy and Sell" in Chinese. Its streets were laid out straight from gate to gate, very clean and lined with bamboo houses spread over with sizing; within, the floors were covered with clay, and the walls papered over with colorful prints. The windows (generally large, with painted paper panes) had a grating made of small, delicately chased rods. Smoke from the kitchens was ingeniously diverted downward through a pipe that passed into a smokestack built onto the street. Between the two towns stood a boundary post neatly etched with parallel inscriptions. One, in Russian, read: "Here ends the Russian Empire." The other, in Mongolian, "Here begins the Chinese domain." There was considerable friendly interchange between the two towns, but toward evening each day a bell would ring, and according to a strictly observed regulation, Chinese and Russian citizens alike would promptly withdraw.

Of all Siberian towns, however, Irkutsk was unquestionably the most cosmopolitan. In the middle of the eighteenth century, when its configuration was still that of a palisaded square, its chief attractions were a bazaar, a meat market, several all-night saloons, and a bathhouse for traveling merchants. By the beginning of the nineteenth it had grown into a pleasant little city of some fifteen thousand inhabitants, with a cathedral, a dozen churches, several mansions, and numerous stately private homes. By 1875, a Russian ethnographer could enthusiastically describe Irkutsk as "chic: in no other Siberian town will you find shops with such luxurious goods and exquisite taste, such magnificent carriages, such dazzling society. . . . Now you are in an academic circle, now at a meeting where economic issues are being solved, now at a charity committee meeting, now at a literary soirée."

Then in July 1879 a hayloft was accidentally set on fire, and the conflagration that followed destroyed three quarters of the town. The "Fire Department" failed miserably, as "many were drunk," wrote an eyewitness, and the firemen had no means of conducting water by hose from the river, but carried it in large barrels on wheels. When the inner city was rebuilt, many new brick and stone structures went up, but the result was a strange mixture of squalor and grandeur, since the streets were still unpaved and the sidewalks nothing but plank causeways over open sewers, and a full ten years later traces of the devastation remained.

These contrasts permeated the city's life. Many settlers straggled into town with little more than the clothes on their backs; others, triumphant at the head of a caravan of steamer trunks loaded with handspun linens, chastened dinnerware, silver samovars, and crystal. Every society residence had a grand piano (even if it was used only for decoration), drawing rooms stocked with books and even foreign magazines, and rare prints and fashion plates on the walls. Some had tall porcelain stoves and large double windows, too, courtyards with riding stables, servants' quarters, and perhaps an enclosed verandah or porch. On the Angara River stood a palace designed in 1804 by the Italian architect Jacomo Queringgi and financed by the gold merchant and shipping magnate Aleksandr Sibiryakov. Known later as the "White House," it became the residence of the governor-general of Eastern Siberia. The old bazaar had been replaced by a market hall of stone, with rows of shops stocked with goods from both Europe and China, and some of the public buildings would not have seemed out of place in London, Paris, and Rome. Irkutsk, in fact, was respectfully christened the "Paris of Siberia"; nor was its citizenry out of touch with continental tastes. Just a few years after Weber's opera *Der Freishütz* had its debut, the local military band could play selections upon request.

Outwardly, indeed, the city was gay and prosperous—even a little too worldly to be entirely pleasing to some of the Victorians and their families who passed through. One visitor found the ladies of high society "lazy, indolent creatures, with no ideas beyond immoral intrigues," who lay around all day smoking cigarettes, and stayed up until dawn. They spent lavishly on clothes, read "yellow-backed French novels," and created "perfumed little nests" for themselves in their boudoirs with low, luxurious couches, Turkish embroideries, and Persian rugs. Yet a few blocks from the "White House" a solitary pedestrian was liable to be strangled "with a short stick and a noose of twine" or lassoed in a blizzard by a criminal in a passing sleigh. In some streets, "pigs wallowed in liquid filth"; and in the restaurant of the Old Metropole Hotel, guests might be entertained by "a troupe of girls from Warsaw [who] sang lewd songs, and then came and drank champagne with the audience."

In back rooms, Chinese gold smugglers, posing as tea merchants, plied a sepulchral trade. Whenever one of their brethren died, they insisted on sending him home for burial, and as part of their embalming operation, blew gold dust up his nostrils through a tube into the empty skull.

Siberia's rapid transformation had made for some extraordinary incongruities elsewhere too. Because of its central location, Tomsk, for example, was one of Western Siberia's main import-export hubs. The city had learned from the fiery calamity that had befallen Irkutsk and erected several fire stations, each with a high turret surrounded by a balcony, where watchmen with field glasses were posted day and night. It had electric lights and other contemporary conveniences, but the streets remained unpaved and every droshky raised a cloud of dust or (after a rainfall) splattered through swamps of mud. In winter, milk was often delivered to the houses in frozen blocks; yet in summer, oranges and lemons could be had from as far away as Sicily.

Although Tomsk was home to some of Siberia's richest merchants, and its intellectual and cultural life, revolving around the university, was vibrant, its elite remained hopelessly gauche. At a typical day-long feast at one of the great houses, according to one participant,

> You sit around and take a hand at cards or from one in a dice party. Ten minutes elapse, the host comes round, pats each one of his guests on the shoulder, and at the same time flicks his third finger against his neck. This is the Siberian invitation for a drink. The crowd collects around the table, each takes a glass filled with vodki [sic], or with some one or other of the many mysterious compounds which go under the name of Siberian liqueurs, tosses it off, makes a grimace, sometimes the sign of the cross, gulps down a bit of bread and sardine, and wanders back to the card table.
>
> In another ten minutes a huge sturgeon, smoking hot, is brought in on a dish. The host comes round again, again pats shoulders, but this time moves his jaws convulsively, as if in the action of eating. Up rises the crowd once more, in order to make a combined attack upon the sturgeon with finger or with fork, washing down toothsome morsels with more vodki. Back again to card-playing, and up again to eat or drink—so the day wears on.

In 1876, when about one tenth of the world's gold came from Siberia, Tomsk was also the repository of much of what was mined north of the Altay in the western regions, just as Irkutsk was the depot for what Eastern Siberia produced. At Tomsk, it was sequestered in deep, medieval-like dungeons, "guarded by heavily armed soldiers; ponderous gates and doors; keys a foot long; rusty hinges, bolts." In the inner sanctum, enormous iron safes let into the walls had locks specially sealed with wax, and in the smelting room was a little scale "so true that a piece of paper was weighed against so many hairs." "I afterwards wrote my name on the paper in pencil," one visitor recalled, "and the weight of my signature was clearly shown." The Siberians also developed some of the best gold-washing machines in the world.

Yet the Tomsk exile-forwarding prison, which processed all exiles and convicts destined for Central and Eastern Siberia, resembled to the end of the century "a small prairie village on the frontier, surrounded by a high stockade of sharpened logs to protect it from hostile Indians." And in some small riverside settlements not far distant, the mail was delivered in a corked glass bottle dropped by a passing steamer into the water near the quay.

There were other curiosities. One traveler encountered a Mississippi River pilot on the Ussuri River; another, a Negro minstrel from South Carolina in Irkutsk. In the southern Transbaikal, Kennan encountered all sorts of luxury American items that had been shipped from California, and a well-thumbed copy of Bret Harte's *The Luck of Roaring Camp*. Minusinsk, a town of just five thousand, 150 miles from the Mongolian frontier, contained the largest and most important museum of archeology and natural history in Siberia. Its display of two hundred prehistoric skulls, and plaster death masks of great antiquity, in fact, were world-famous, along with the knives, helmets, and other artifacts unearthed from burial mounds. The museum also had life-sized models of men and women from various tribes in native dress.

The even smaller town of Nerchinsk (which had a population of just four thousand in 1885) was incongruously dominated by the palatial residence of a wealthy mining proprietor, who had adorned its forty-odd rooms with hardwood marquetry floors, silk curtains, stained-glass windows, crystal chandeliers, soft Oriental rugs, and white-and-gold furniture upholstered with satin. The hallways were lined with marble statues; old Flemish masters hung on the walls. A large greenhouse attached to the mansion was "filled with palms, lemon-trees, and rare orchids from the tropics"; and in another museumlike chamber could be seen the principal minerals and ores of Siberia handsomely displayed. That was not all. In a huge semicircular gallery above the ballroom stood an orchestrion, as big as a church organ, which furnished music for the host's extravagant entertainments, and the ballroom itself boasted the largest mirror in the world. Bought at the Paris

Exposition of 1878, the mirror had been transported halfway around the world by sea, before being towed up the Amur River on a special barge.

Elsewhere, Krasnoyarsk (in the same longitude as Calcutta) had the best public gardens in Siberia, but after the local opera house burned down, performances were held in a cowshed—"Tchaikovsky and Pushkin," as one critic wrote, "to the smell of manure." Real pistols with bullets were used on stage in the duels, but the players carefully shot at the ceiling. The town's most famous feature was a unique belltower, built over the main street, under which everybody entering the city passed.

The exile and prison culture of Siberia added its own peculiar spice to the variety of life. In more accessible places, the solidarity among criminal exiles was such that not to have a criminal record was considered a liability, even a barrier to respectability. One Siberian-born merchant at Krasnoyarsk, whose business was faring poorly, journeyed all the way to St. Petersburg to commit a felony, returned to Siberia in chains, served time in the Aleksandrovsk prison outside Irkutsk, and reopened his business at Krasnoyarsk, where his now thoroughly blemished reputation at last enabled him to thrive.

Along the Great Siberian Post Road or Highway, many villages became known as "thieves' towns": Tara on the Irtysh specialized in moonshine and most of the inhabitants had their own illegal stills; Mysovaya was virtually an outlaw haven; and between Tomsk and Krasnoyarsk, there were numerous little villages inhabited entirely by convict settlers who had established enclaves in the swamps and in the middle of the deepest woods. Everywhere one turned there were people "whose past could not bear inspection," even among the elite. One queen of society in Irkutsk in the late 1870s had done five years at the mines for poisoning her niece, a rich heiress, and was living quite nicely on the proceeds; others, though grown prosperous in legitimate circumstances, were still unable to give up their compulsion to crime. Once, in the middle of a banquet given by the military governor of Chita, the mayor (an ex-con) politely excused himself on important business "and went straight from table to waylay the passing night-mail." With his friends, he galloped after the coach, murdered the driver, seriously wounded the guard, and seized the bag containing the registered letters and cash.

Ex-cons were also pervasive among the hired help. At Akatui, the warden was waited upon by a chambermaid who had split her husband's skull in two, and when a guest expressed unease, he explained: "But I always employ assassins. They make far better servants than thieves. My 'Yamshchik' [driver] is also a murderer."

The domestic arrangements of a warden at a maximum security prison might be viewed as exceptional, but in the world of Siberia in fact they were not. Probably no group was so heavily infiltrated with ex-convicts as the special confraternity of *yamshchiki,* or drivers, upon which all Siberia depended for the long-distance transport of people and goods. In summer or winter, their sleighs and carts formed great caravans drawn by reindeer, horses, or camels, carrying furs, silks, spices, and tea from the heart of Siberia or the Mongolian frontier to the great Russian trade fairs in the west. They also operated out of post stations, of course, for the transport of individual travelers, and in addition to their official duties, often engaged in illicit trade. The line between a *yamshchik* and a bandit or black marketeer was razor-thin and, not surprisingly, escaped felons favored the occupation as a way to begin a new life. One company of Americans, for example, who crossed Siberia in 1876, engaged six drivers for their journey, only to discover on the way that every one of them had been convicted of murder. Subsequently, it was revealed that their interpreter (on whom they most relied) had been convicted for murder twice, and that his wife, engaged as the cook, had butchered her former husband with an ax.

Into the late nineteenth century, Siberia had few schools and nothing even remotely resembling an educational system. Missionary and trade schools were scattered here and there, but by and large there was no stepped curriculum of primary, secondary, and higher education. In 1724, Peter the Great had established a school of Oriental languages in Irkutsk, and the great naval expeditions along the Arctic coast and in the North Pacific had led to the founding of a navigational school for future seamen. Here and there seminaries sprang up, but in 1826, there were still only 31 schools with 1,588 pupils throughout the whole territory. A few English missionaries had set up tutorial classes in their own homes for native children, and had founded an institute at Selenginsk "for the Instruction of a Select Number of the Youth of the Heathen Tribes of Siberia," but neither had any lasting effect. Indeed, not long after the mission's dissolution in 1840, popular superstition among the Buryats had transformed the missionaries into "spooks."

Siberia's first university finally opened in Tomsk in 1888. Largely financed at the outset by money donated by the Demidovs (the Urals' industrial magnates) and Aleksandr Sibiryakov, the university rather pretentiously aspired to be "the intellectual center of Asia." But it did become the intellectual center of Siberia, with a vast library of some 97,000 volumes assembled in an effort spearheaded by Petr Makushin, a merchant and devoted bibliophile, who had previously opened the first Siberian bookstore in 1873. The rare book division of the library housed a number of treasures, including a unique, complete set of the *Moniteur Universale,* a newspaper published during the French Revolution; a sixteenth-century book of psalms; and an album with views of Egypt that had once belonged to Napoleon. The "House of Science" in Tomsk today is appropriately named after Makushin, though a predictably tasteless and secular monument to him nearby features a rail (symbolizing the way to knowledge) and an electric valve above it (symbolizing constant study) that shines both day and night.

Eastern Siberia, however, was not to have an institute of higher learning until Irkutsk University was founded in 1918.

Meanwhile, public libraries and museums had begun to open in most of the major towns, and some independent private collections were also outstanding. Perhaps the most famous was that of the Krasnoyarsk gold mine and distillery magnate Gennady Yudin, which contained about 80,000 volumes, and was subsequently obtained by the Library of Congress of the United States, where it formed the nucleus of the Slavic Collection.

If Siberian education was slight, health care was woefully inadequate. Smallpox vaccination had been introduced into Siberia in 1771, but Siberia's first medical society was not formed until 1858 in Irkutsk. And it was not until the mid-1880s that major towns like Omsk and Krasnoyarsk had medical societies of their own. In 1830, there was only one doctor for every forty thousand inhabitants, and operations and autopsies could be as primitive as anything a Paleolithic native might perform. After the learned Decembrist Mikhail Lunin died at Akatui in December 1845, the examining physician, lacking proper instruments, opened his head with an ax.

Even some important settlements like Selenginsk had only a regimental surgeon, who interpreted the scope of his responsibilities so narrowly that he refused to treat anyone outside the garrison. Russians as well as natives often had to rely on shamans and other "witch doctors" (when home remedies did not suffice), but this wasn't always detrimental to their health. The lama doctors of the Buryats in particular had the august traditions of Tibetan medicine behind them (which favorably compared with much of what a Russian doctor might know). They procured most of their medicines in powdered form from China, performed acupuncture, and knew how to read a pulse. The use of amulets, ritual spells, surrogate sacrifices (using effigies of the sick), and so on were sometimes resorted to, but reluctant Europeans in need could not always afford to scoff at their expertise. One English missionary whose copyist suffered from an intermittent fever took him to a Buryat physician who effectively prescribed a body rub with a medicinal ointment, followed by a four-day cycle of drugs that alternately knocked the patient out and purged him. At the end of the treatment, he felt as good as new.

Steadily, the Russian population of Siberia increased—from a third of a million in 1700, to over 1 million by 1812, to 3 million by 1854. Between 1815 and 1854, the size of the Siberian merchant class tripled, and the monetary value of the goods being carried across Siberia by waterway and road virtually quadrupled. Although a total of 27,800 miles of Siberia's rivers were navigable, and paddlewheel steamers began to make their appearance in the 1840s, the value of river transport in general was limited by the fact that all but the Amur flowed northward into ice-bound Arctic seas.

Siberia's economic life was fundamentally constrained by the distances between its mines and fields and the European markets where products could be exchanged for manufactured goods. The Urals (like the Allegheny Mountains in the United States until the beginning of the nineteenth century) remained a great divide. Had the mighty rivers of Siberia run east-west and not "poured their superfluous waters into an Arctic Sea," the transportation problems might not have been so great, but "the whole country was kept waiting," writes one historian (drawing an analogy to the United States), first for the advent of steam, and then the iron horse.

When we remember that, with all the facilities offered for transportation on the Great Lakes, Chicago was but a village in 1830, and that twenty years later it was considered doubtful whether Minnesota could be profitably settled, and twenty years later still it was a problem whether the Dakotas and the valley of the Red River of the North could offer permanent inducements to agricultural industry, we need not wonder that Western and Central Siberia were left practically unsettled until the dawn of the new era at the beginning of the twentieth century.

Siberia's internal commerce on the whole was "natural" (or in kind), and local, carried on mostly along the north-south river routes. The government's various canal-building schemes over the years had come to nothing, and although the Ob was a fairly well developed artery of trade, the Yenisey and Lena, which emptied into the Arctic at higher latitudes, could only be utilized in their middle course. Thus, the commerce was concentrated at Krasnoyarsk, Yeniseysk, Minusinsk, and Irkutsk. (Moreover, Adolf Nordenskiöld's famous expedition of 1878, which would bring the *Vega* through the Northeast Passage to Bering Strait, was attended by so many difficulties as to demonstrate how frankly impractical for regular communication the Northeast Passage was.) As things stood, without a more rapid means of crossing Siberia from west to east, the cost of importing heavy machinery to eastern regions would remain prohibitive, and the mines (outside of those owned by the tsar himself, which could draw on convict labor) were doomed to be worked by antiquated and wasteful methods.

The Roman Empire in the time of Hadrian had 53,000 miles of roads, many of them paved; Siberia (larger than Hadrian's dominions) in the late nineteenth century had only dusty roads and trails. A network of postal and other routes connected many villages and towns, but even in the taiga west of Irkutsk in the 1890s there was still on the average only one inhabitant per square mile. Moreover, it took the mail three and a half months by pony express to get from the Urals to Okhotsk, and half a year from Moscow to Kamchatka. Although roads had been cut and maintained with relative ease across the level plains of Western Siberia, Eastern Siberia was rugged and mountainous, and in the middle of it lay enormous Lake Baikal, which stretched north-south for more than 400 miles. Although the Great Siberian Post Road, or *Veliky*

Trakt, ran around the southern end of the lake, the detour was so long that goods bound to or from Kyakhta as part of the China trade sometimes rotted on the wharves.

Three routes from Tyumen led eastward: the northern or river route, by way of the Irtysh and the Ob, to Tomsk; the middle or winter route, which followed the Great Siberian Post Road through Omsk; and the southern steppe, via Omsk, Semipalatinsk, and Barnaul. At Omsk the routes from Orenburg, Semipalatinsk, and Central Asia converged, the main road continuing east to Irkutsk, where one fork went northeast to Yakutsk, another around the southern end of Lake Baikal to Verkhneudinsk. There it divided again, leading on to Kyakhta or Sretensk. Verst posts erected every two-thirds of a mile from the Urals to Vladivostok kept reminding the traveler, in a sometimes annoying fashion, how far he was from St. Petersburg—2,543 versts at Tyumen, 4,053 at Tomsk, 5,611 at Irkutsk, and finally, at Vladivostok, 9,877 versts (6,250 miles).

In the preternatural vastness of Siberia, space became time—or time was absorbed into it—and measured from place to place. One emblematic story was told, for example, of six Kamchadal virgins who set out under imperial escort for the capital, 7,000 miles away. Before they reached Irkutsk, each had given birth to a child fathered by their military chaperon, and by the time they arrived at St. Petersburg, where they were to be presented at court, each was nursing a second babe-in-arms. Aside from what this story may imply about the chastity of Kamchadal maidens (or the reliability of Russian escorts), it was as much as to say that St. Petersburg was a lifetime away.

In the mid-nineteenth century, in fact, it was still possible to reach the capital from Kamchatka more quickly by sailing eastward across the Pacific Ocean to California, traversing the United States by rail, embarking on a ship across the Atlantic Ocean for Europe, and from there continuing on to St. Petersburg by horse or rail.

Although the Great Siberian Post Road spanned the distance overland, it was little better than "a mere track cut by caravan traffic," pitted and unpaved. The seatless, springless carts in which wayfarers were customarily obliged to travel (with their knees squeezed up to mitigate the joint-wrenching jolts) were notoriously uncomfortable, and even the stalwart Kennan found traveling by telega, as such vehicles were called, almost too much for him. "On a bad, rough road," he wrote, it "will simply jolt a man's soul out in less than twenty-four hours. Before we had travelled sixty miles . . . I was so exhausted that I could hardly sit upright; my head and spine ached so violently, and had become so sensitive to shock, that every jolt was as painful as a blow from a club." In spring, the roads were also awash in mire, and roughened by daily thaws and nightly frosts. Still worse was the Yakutsk-to-Okhotsk Track, which had been reconstructed in the mid-1750s by convicts, but somehow to no avail. Corduroy roads (or wooden causeways) had been laid over some of the bogs at the beginning of the nineteenth century, but so many horses floundered in the snow or slipped and fell where rain and other weathering had caused the wood to rot that scarcely one of every hundred survived. One traveler reported seeing more than two thousand horse skeletons between Okhotsk to Yudoma Cross, some with their heads grotesquely protruding from the mire.

Aside from a telega, all that could be had for travel was a rudimentary, poorly sprung carriage called a tarantass. In either case, to travel by post station meant to travel "by transfer," that is, having to change vehicles and horses at every stop, unloading and reloading one's luggage perhaps hundreds of times in the course of a trip.

> Boxes and cases with sharp edges had to be discarded, and all one's gear packed in flat leather bags. Bedded in hay, these formed the foundation for what was to be the traveler's bed for the duration of the journey. On top of this layer came a fur sleeping bag, or a mattress and rugs and blankets. Soft pillows were needed to line the whole of the back part of the vehicle, and in the front part, under the driver's seat, space had to be found for all the odds and ends needed for a journey of several weeks—food, teapot, cutlery, and so on. . . .
> To repeat the packing process as well, over two hundred times, at all hours of the day and night, in the depths of a Siberian winter, was not something to be looked forward to.

It was much better to buy or hire one's own carriage, if possible, for the duration, and sleep on it at night rather than in one of the miserable inns.

Siberia's fame, of course, attracted all sorts of wilderness enthusiasts, missionaries, scientists, ethnographers, geologists, journalists, world travelers, and Victorian dilettantes. Toward the end of the nineteenth century, in fact, Siberian travel literature became almost the rage. One

American, who set out to cross Siberia on foot, wore a hat that was telescopic and could be used as an umbrella. Even so, before his journey was half done, his hair had become as bleached as sheep's wool. Another came to rough it on a holiday, and John Dundas Cochrane, a captain in the Royal Navy, proposed to walk around the globe via Siberia "as nearly as could be done by land." Setting out from London, he crossed the English Channel to Dieppe, traveled on to Moscow, and from there all the way across northern Asia to the Sea of Okhotsk. Still unspent by his exertions, he embarked for Kamchatka, but soon after his arrival fell in love with a Kamchadal maiden and returned with her westward the way he had come. There were also priggish Anglican clerics who disapproved of everything aboriginal, investigative journalists like Kennan, tsarist apologists, and scientists like Adolph Erman, a Prussian physicist who had studied in Berlin and Königsberg and later became a professor at the University of Berlin. In 1828, he crossed Siberia as part of a journey around the world, and made magnetic and other scientific observations along the Lena River that earned him a gold medal from the Royal Geographical Society.

Travelers of whatever sort were prudently advised, in one inventory, to equip themselves with "a revolver, heavy woolen underwear, well-lined rubber boots, warm furs, a mosquito veil, a pillow or an air cushion, bed linen, a coverlet or a rug, towels, soap, a portable india-rubber bathtub, and 'remedies against insects of a vexatory disposition.' To avoid police suspicion as a disseminator of subversive propaganda, one should . . . never use anything but unprinted paper for wrapping fragile personal belongings in trunks and handbags."

None of this was superfluous. Most inns were wayside huts almost without accommodations, and for some reason often run by invalids. One wayfarer recalled that between Tomsk and Yeniseysk, he stopped first at an inn run by a peasant who turned out to be deaf, and the following night at another whose keeper was dumb. A porter then appeared who was blind. Between Tomsk and Krasnoyarsk, houses swarmed with large blackish-red and small white cockroaches that filled all the chests and cupboards, and at dinner it often happened that thousands of them fell into the bowls and plates as the result of the ascending smoke. Even at Tomsk the lodgings were dismal. At one "hotel," some Americans couldn't even get utensils with their meals. "We carved our bread with a bowie knife," one wrote, "and ate our eggs, not with a spoon, but by jerking all that would come out into our mouths, before breaking the shell and sucking away what remained attached to the skin." At the Hotel Europe, where another guest stayed, the headwaiter apologized for the fearless mice and said: "We keep twelve cats, but they seem rather afraid of the mice themselves."

As late as 1897, many of the hotel rooms in Omsk lacked even a washstand, and were thronging with blackbeetles and other vermin, like an *étape*. Anticipating the entomological assault, one guest had imaginatively brought along with him four saucers and a can of kerosene. The legs of the bed were placed in the saucers, into which the kerosene was poured; but "with a sagacity which one would hardly credit in so small an insect," he wrote, "the bugs detoured up the walls on to the ceiling," and then, "having accurately poised, drop down upon their victim."

From Verkhneudinsk to Kansk, summer travelers were plagued by gnats, horseflies, and other blood-sucking insects that bred in such swarms that they enveloped the ground "in a sort of haze." Everyone wore delicate horsehair nets over their faces, high boots and leather gloves, and even cattle hid themselves during the day in stables and barns,.venturing out to pasture only at night. "And people," one bitter traveler exclaimed, "can't be too careful when they have to attend to the necessaries of life. I myself was stung so severely that for three days I didn't know where to turn on account of pain, and I had the greatest trouble to prevent the setting in of gangrene at this delicate portion of my privy parts infected by the sting."

In nature, Siberia also found its redemption. In 1764, Catherine the Great ordered rows of silver birches planted along the open road from Yekaterinburg to Tyumen, and had them set so closely together that as they grew to an imperial height their branches intertwined to form an elegantly arched canopy of leaves above. Entering Siberia through this noble arboreal arcade, one could easily imagine that the territory possessed exceptional natural beauties in compensation for the sorrows of its fame. And almost everywhere one turned, that expectation was confirmed. The mountains surrounding Lake Baikal were reminiscent of the Scottish Highlands, and the environs of Minusinsk on the Yenisey compared in scenic beauty to parts of Switzerland or the Italian

Lakes. High up in the snow-capped, rugged Altay lay alpine pastures filled with flowers, while the broad, fertile valleys below them were clothed in aspen, larch, and pine. Those seeking harsher vistas would not be disappointed, for Kamchatka offered many spectacles of wild rocky canyons, and swollen mountain torrents "foaming around sharp black rocks, and falling over ledges of lava in magnificent cascades." The peninsula's great volcanic range itself compared to the Sierra Nevadas for savage wildness, with spurs and foothills that broke the landscape up into deep sequestered valleys of the most picturesque kind. Volcanic eruptions occasionally sent columns of smoke and flame blazing up from the craters, and molten lava flowing in broad fiery rivers down the snow-covered slopes. Yet Kamchatka could also appear quite idyllic, as it did to Kennan in 1866 when, having sailed from America, he first viewed its coast from the other side:

> The fog was beginning to break away, and in a moment it rose slowly like a huge gray curtain, unveiling the sea and the deep blue sky, letting in a flood of rosy light from the sinking sun, and revealing a picture of wonderful beauty. Before us, stretching for a hundred and fifty miles to the north and south, lay the grand coast-line of Kamchatka, rising abruptly in great purple promontories out of the blue sparkling sea, flecked here with white clouds and shreds of fleecy mist, deepening in places into a soft quivering blue and sweeping backward and upward into the pure white snow of the higher peaks. Two active volcanoes, 10,000 and 16,000 feet in height, rose above the confused jagged ranges of the lower mountains, piercing the blue sky with sharp white triangles of eternal snow, and drawing the purple shadows of evening around their feet.

At the entrance to Petropavlovsk, Kennan beheld (to his own surprise) green grassy valleys that stretched away from the rocky coast, rounded bluffs covered with clumps of yellow birch, and a profusion of flowers nestled in "the warm sheltered slopes of the hills." Herds of black and brown bears roamed everywhere over the plains and through the valleys, wild sheep made their home in the mountains, and swarms of ducks, geese, and swans gathered near every marsh and lake. In the Kamchatka River Valley, the strangely opposite yet harmonious autumnal blend of "snow and roses, bare granite and brilliantly colored foliage" challenged the most romantic images of the sublime.

Kamchatka was not alone in evoking such emotions. Far to the southwest, the Sayan Mountains—their great peaks "divided into many tall masses of rock and cliffs of varied shape and size"—conjured up in the mind of one traveler the battlemented citadels of late medieval romance. As he crossed the fertile Baraba Steppe, he also saw congregating on the shores of lakes "an enormous quantity of swans, cranes, pelicans, ducks and wild geese," and in the woods and swamps bittern and snipe, grouse, mountain cock, and other fowl. When he came to Krasnoyarsk, it seemed to him "a place where everything is to be found that beautiful Nature brings forth for the enjoyment and the use of Man." A century later, Chekhov unhesitatingly agreed. Though he had found little to cheer his passage across Western Siberia until he came to the Yenisey, he declared it the most magnificent river he had ever seen—"a powerful, turbulent giant which does not know what to do with its enormous power and its youth." Krasnoyarsk on its banks, set against misty and dreamlike mountains, he judged "the best and most beautiful of all Siberian towns. I stood there and I thought: what a full, intelligent and brave life will some day illuminate these shores!" The road from Krasnoyarsk to Irkutsk led through fruitful valleys, forests, and fir-clad hills, and "one beautiful view after another," wrote another traveler, "appeared everywhere before my eyes." Then along the Angara (in Maria Volkonskaya's rapturous description),

> as May advances, night entirely disappears, and as the twilight draws near, swans, geese, and duck appear in clouds and the air resounds with the flapping of their wings; their numbers surpass anything that can be imagined, and must be seen to be believed. Each species of bird has its own particular note, and it struck me as a chant, marvelously solemn, a hymn raised by so many millions of creatures in tones which the Creator himself had taught them. Around me, as far as the eye could reach, were countless chains of duck, geese, and graceful Siberian cranes traversing the sky without any interruption, like so many streams all in the same northerly direction; there wasn't a clear space in the air, and all the expanse of water below, the river and the islands, was completely covered with them, as thickly as the stars stud the firmament on a clear night.

Perhaps the beauties of such a Siberian summer evening were surpassed only by the transformations wrought by the *aurora borealis* upon an Arctic winter night. "No other natural phenomenon," wrote Kennan of his sojourn to the Siberian northeast, "is so grand, so mysterious, so terrible in its unearthly splendor as this; the veil which conceals from mortal eyes the glory of the eternal throne seems drawn aside, and the awed beholder is lifted out of the atmosphere of his daily life into the immediate presence of God." Awakening one night, in the midst of such a display,

the whole universe seemed to be on fire. A broad arch of brilliant prismatic colors spanned the heavens from east to west like a gigantic rainbow, with a long fringe of crimson and yellow streamers stretching up from its convex edge to the very zenith. At short intervals of one or two seconds, wide, luminous bands, parallel with the arch, rose suddenly out of the northern horizon and swept with a swift, steady majesty across the whole heavens, like long breakers of phosphorescent light rolling in from some limitless ocean of space. Every portion of the vast arch was momentarily wavering, trembling, and changing color, and the brilliant streamers which fringed its edge swept back and forth in great curves, like the fiery sword of the angel at the gate of Eden.

From one end of the territory to the other, Siberia's melancholy reputation was belied. The "fervent heat" of its summer sunshine took almost every traveler by surprise, as did "the extraordinary beauty and profusion of Siberian flowers." In the Siberian Arctic, summer was sudden yet complete. "There is no long, wet lingering spring," remarked an admirer, "no gradual unfolding of buds and leaves. . . . The vegetation, which has been held in icy fetters for eight long months, bursts suddenly its bonds, and with one great irresistible sweep takes the world by storm."

In time, a more precise knowledge of the landscape was acquired and gaps in the map of the Siberian Arctic were filled in. The New Siberian Islands, a collection of four large and several smaller islands, had been discovered in 1761. In 1770, the four Lyakhov Islands became known after explorers followed the footprints of a herd of reindeer northward across the ice of the East Siberian Sea. In 1819, Alexander I authorized an expedition to trace the northeastern coast of Siberia from the Kolyma River eastward to East Cape, and a young naval officer, Lieutenant Ferdinand Wrangel (later governor of Russian America), undertook to do this by land. Starting in 1820, he made his way from the Kolyma to Cape Shelagsky, which he doubled, but only, he wrote, with

> great difficulty and danger. We had often to ascend steep icebergs ninety feet high and to descend at great risk to the sledges . . . at other times, we had to wade up to our waists through drift snow, and if we came to smooth ice it was covered with sharp, crystallized salt which destroyed the ice-runners and made the draught so heavy that we were obliged to harness ourselves to the sledges, and it required our utmost efforts to drag them along. . . . Both men and dogs were completely exhausted. We had only three days' provisions left, and it appeared very doubtful whether we might venture further. . . . The want of provisions now obliged us to return; and I was forced to content myself for the present with having ascertained that for forty miles to the east of Cape Shelagsky, the coast trended in a southeast direction.

Three years later, he succeeded in rounding Cape Shelagsky all the way to East Cape, covering 1,530 miles in seventy-eight days. In so doing, he demolished any lingering theory (as espoused by an English admiral as late as 1817) about a land bridge connecting Asia and America. It was Wrangel who provided incontrovertible and final proof that the continents were nowhere joined.

Although the map of the Arctic coastline had been completed by Wrangel, the difficulty of penetrating the ice of the Kara Sea, and the shortness of the period during which the mouth of the Yenisey was ice-free, long prevented any shipping between Central Siberia and European ports. As late as 1840, the Russian Admiralty concluded that a commercial passage through the Kara Sea was "altogether impracticable." But in the 1870s attempts to establish a route were pioneered by Captain Joseph Wiggins, an Englishman, and Baron Adolf Nordenskiöld, a Swede. After several attempts, Wiggins succeeded in 1874 in reaching the mouth of the Ob, and in the following year, Nordenskiöld the mouth of the Yenisey. Two years after that, Wiggins reached and ascended the Yenisey for 1,000 miles to Krasnoyarsk. Not to be outdone, Nordenskiöld in a 350-ton steamer, the *Vega*, originally built for the northern whaling trade, proceeded right through the Northeast

Passage and rounded the tip of Asia in 1878–79. As a result of that historic voyage, a Siberian Trading Syndicate was optimistically formed in England, with the Russian government granting it the right to ship goods to the heart of Siberia, duty-free. But even as the *Vega* was completing its mission, another began that would bring home to the world how treacherous for shipping the Russian Arctic was.

This was the voyage undertaken to the North Pole by U.S. Navy Lieutenant George Washington De Long in the *Jeannette*. Sailing from San Francisco on July 8, 1879, De Long passed through Bering Strait to Wrangel Island, and followed its coast to the north. On September 5, the ship became trapped in pack ice, and for the next twenty-one months drifted helplessly with it through Arctic seas. On June 12, 1881, still 750 miles south of the North Pole (and 600 miles north of the Siberian coast), the ice began to tighten its grip, until "the deck bulged upward and the oakum and pitch were squeezed out of the seams." On the following day, the *Jeannette* sank, leaving a shipwrecked crew in three open boats to find their way through a maze of narrow sea-lanes and hummocks of rotten ice. After nine weeks of scrambling, they found themselves off Faddeya Island, one of the three large islands of the New Siberian group, and at last beheld the open sea. They now desperately rowed southwestward toward the Lena Delta, more than 100 miles away, but before they could make much progress, a storm smashed one of their boats and separated the other two.

Under De Long's chief mate, one crew reached the mouth of the Lena safely and proceeded upriver for help. The other under De Long also made it to shore, but ultimately perished; they were not found until the following spring, when on March 23, 1882, De Long's arm was discovered sticking out of the snow. It was the grisly fate of this expedition that evidently first gave the American public its abiding (and somewhat distorted) notion of what Siberia was like.

From the beginning of the conquest, of course, there were those who had borne witness to Siberia's potential as a "virgin land." In this view, it enjoyed a kinship with the "promised land" of America—a land of opportunity, relatively free of tsarist despotism and serfdom, where a man had a fighting chance to make a new life. Dostoyevsky observed that those "who are adept at solving life's problems nearly always remain in Siberia and gladly put down roots there," whereas the others returned home with slanders against it as a savage place. But he thought it possible whatever one's vocation "to be supremely happy" there and to prosper over time. "The young ladies bloom like roses," he wrote in *The House of the Dead*, "the wild game flies about the streets and comes to meet the hunter of its own accord. An inordinately large amount of champagne is drunk. The caviar is marvellous. In some localities the crops give a fifteen-fold yield." The relative freedom Siberians enjoyed also gave them an appreciation of human dignity and civil rights, and it was not uncommon for travelers to note with surprise and admiration that Siberians somewhat resembled Americans "in their manners, customs, and even in their mode of life."

The notion, or feeling, that Siberia and its people were distinctive fostered an impulse toward regional autonomy and even a movement toward the creation of a separate state. Its adherents championed the cause of democratic freedoms, and made common cause with the Siberian natives against colonial rule. At the very least, the Siberian Autonomist movement (secretly formed in 1864) demanded local self-government through elected representatives and an end to using Siberia as a dumping ground for criminals. But others went further: they envisioned throwing off the colonial yoke entirely and establishing a new, independent, prosperous Siberian "nation," free to follow its own peculiar path of development. Sympathizers (secret and otherwise) existed in some of the highest councils of government, and the promise of Siberia seems to have taken possession even of Muravyev-Amursky's soul. "Like all men of action of the government school," Peter Kropotkin tells us in his *Memoirs of a Revolutionist* (1885), "he [Muravyev] was a despot at the bottom of his heart; but he held advanced opinions, and a democratic republic would not have quite satisfied him. . . . He had gathered around him a number of young officials, quite honest, and many of them animated by the same excellent intentions as himself. In his own study, the young officers . . . discussed the chances of creating the United States of Siberia, federated across the Pacific Ocean with the United States of America." Muravyev's white colonnaded mansion overlooking the Angara River in Irkutsk, in fact, was sometimes called the "White House" (as noted earlier) in unmistakable tribute to such ideas. In 1878, a journal published in Geneva by Russian populists predicted that Eastern Siberia's economic interests would eventually link it more naturally to Washington than to St. Petersburg, and it was the fantasy of one would-be assassin of Alexander II that Siberia would secede from the empire and join itself outright to the United States.

Partly to counteract such notions, the Imperial Russian Geographical Society (with branches in Eastern and Western Siberia) began to disseminate a good deal of ethnic and geographical data to encourage the idea of an overarching imperial community and to make educated Russians more aware of the scope and diversity of the empire. And toward the end of the nineteenth century even native Siberians began to be recognized as "citizens" with equal status under the law.

But the problem remained as to how to make Russia and Siberia one.

14

THE IRON ROAD TO WAR

MURAVYEV-AMURSKY's vision of Siberia as a land of opportunity with unlimited potential may have been shared by some other officials, yet nothing lasting had been done to lend substance to the dream. Not until almost the end of the century did the economic and social development of Siberia at last became a priority of the government. And the chief means used to advance it was the building of the stupendous Trans-Siberian Railway (1891–1905).

After the emancipation of the serfs in 1861–63, emigration to Siberia had increased enormously. The one great road across Siberia—the Great Siberia Post Road, or *Veliky Trakt*—was an unpaved relic of the conquest and early settlement, and though coordinated with a growing river traffic, could scarcely accommodate the new torrent of humanity or meet the basic economic and communication needs of the region. Nor was the network sufficient for the region's defense, now that neighboring Manchuria and Korea were both coveted by an awakening Japan.

The United States had opened the world's first transcontinental railway in 1869, followed by the Canadian Pacific in 1885. The binding of British Columbia to eastern Canada seemed especially analogous to what Russia needed to do to at last make European Russia and Siberia one.

The idea was not entirely new. Muravyev-Amursky had suggested linking the Amur River Valley with the sea by rail, and in 1857 an

American millionaire and world traveler, Perry McDonough Collins, had proposed a short line from Irkutsk to Chita, to join the Amur River Valley with that of the Yenisey. "Reflecting on the vast extent of the country, its mighty rivers ... the magnitude of its natural resources, and with its possible value to the commerce of the world," he pictured the Amur River as "the destined channel by which American commercial enterprise was to penetrate the obscure depths of Northern Asia, and open a new world to trade and civilization."

Collins's enthusiasm found a sympathetic ear at the U.S. Department of the Treasury—well connected, he had made his fortune in banking with the brother of Ulysses S. Grant—which vaguely appointed him "Comercial Agent of the United States at the Amoor River." In 1856 he sailed for St. Petersburg, met Amursky (who gave him every encouragement), and after a winter journey of 3,500 miles (in which he had to change horses 200 times), became the first American to set foot in Irkutsk since the Connecticut Yankee John Ledyard had been arrested there as a spy. From Irkutsk he went to Chita, visited the silver mines of Nerchinsk and the gold deposits near the Onon River, and boarded a steamer down the Amur to Nikolayevsk. As he passed through the river valley, he admired the "majestic cliffs streaked with iron, the shore well-timbered with pine and, somewhat farther downriver ... meadows carpeted with shoulder-high grass." All around he beheld wild game in abundance. Although the area was Russian by treaty, its wilderness suggested a no-man's-land, and in fact the Chinese still pretended to some jurisdiction. From time to time a Manchu official, "distinguished by a cap sporting a peacock feather, two black squirrel tails, and a white ball," would row out to the barge and, passing his hand repeatedly across his throat, indicate Collins had better turn back if he didn't want to lose his head. But on July 10, 1857, he reached Nikolayevsk safely, took an opium pill to ensure a good night's sleep, and called on the Russian rear admiral in charge of the region the following morning.

Meanwhile, Amursky had received Collins's "Amoor Railroad Company" proposal, and had referred it to the Minister of Ways of Communication in St. Petersburg with his endorsement. The Siberian Committee, however, recently created to study major questions bearing on Siberian affairs, decided the undertaking was "premature," in part because its fanciful cost estimates omitted any serious discussion of logistical or technical problems to be encountered in the engineering task.

Disappointed, Collins sailed home to the United States, only to return a few years later with another grandiose Russian project to promote. Backed by Western Union, it was Collins who became the driving force behind the round-the-world overland telegraph scheme that first brought George Kennan to Siberia in 1865.

The debate about a Siberian railway went on without result in the Russian government for several years, but by 1875 it was accepted in principle that there should at least be a through trunk line from Moscow to Irkutsk. A first link in that line, from Perm on the Volga through Yekaterinburg in the Urals to Tyumen, was completed in 1885, and in 1886 construction was also begun on a line from Samara northeastward through Zlatoust to Chelyabinsk. Thereafter it was more or less agreed to eventually connect the major towns and cities, located on the major rivers, in Southern Siberia by rail. Some urgency was lent to the matter by increasing reports of Chinese infiltration into the Transbaikal, but the strategic vulnerability of the region was also recognized more clearly than ever now as a consequence of its general neglect. On the three hundredth anniversary of the conquest of Siberia by Yermak, Alexander III suggested that "the vast and rich Siberian region" would soon be "in a position indivisibly together with [Russia] to enjoy similar institutions of state and society, the benefits of enlightenment, the increase of industrial activity to the general good and glory of our beloved fatherland." But four years later (1886), in the margin of a report from his governor-general of Eastern Siberia, he exclaimed: "I must own with grief and shame that up to the present the Government has done scarcely anything to meet the needs of this rich but forsaken country. It is time, it is high time!"

In fact, it was too late. For the pace of events would now outrace all that the imperial will could do.

Surveys of possible routes were hurriedly begun; to keep construction costs down (Alexander III was an exceptionally tight-fisted monarch), it was decided to adopt building standards well below those used elsewhere in Russia and the West. The line was to have one track, and corners were to be cut on the quality and quantity of all materials used, including ties, rails, and roadbed ballast. This also meant bridges of wood rather than steel or stone—except across the widest rivers, which required long, costly metal spans—and depots and stations of the crudest design. Steep gradients and sharp curves were also tolerated to avoid tunneling or cutting through hills.

The preliminary design of the route was: from Chelyabinsk in the Urals (designated the first station of the great new railway), eastward in a nearly direct line through the heart of Southern Siberia, linking all the principal towns that had grown up along the original post road from the Ural Mountains to Irkutsk. Then the line was to loop around Lake Baikal, descend the Stanovoy Mountains through the Transbaikal to Sretensk, and down the Amur River Valley all the way to Vladivostok.

The one anomaly in the route was that it bypassed Tomsk—at the time Siberia's fastest-growing city—but did so by design: Tomsk was a hotbed of regionalist sentiment, and by disconnecting it, in a sense, from the mainline of Siberia's future communication and growth, the government punitively hoped to keep the separatist movement from gathering force.

On May 12, 1891, an imperial edict authorizing construction of the Trans-Siberian Railway was promulgated on the shores of the Pacific at Vladivostok by the tsarevich, Grand Duke Nicholas, hier to the throne. On May 19, Nicholas pushed a wheelbarrow full of dirt along a plank and emptied it upon an embankment: the work had begun.

No tsar or tsarevich before him had ever visited Siberia, and Nicholas's very presence seemed to herald the end of official neglect. "Every town he passed through erected a triumphal arch to commemorate the occasion," we are told, and Cossacks "crowded on the cliffs of the Amur to shout hurrahs as he passed." Wherever he performed the slightest official function, or paused to dine, or spent the night, brass plates would later mark the spot, and "on a hill outside Chita, a pillar was inscribed: 'Here our master deigned to accept bread and salt.' " All this must have been quite gratifying to the tsarevich, whose recent grand tour of Greece, Egypt, India, Indochina, and Japan had been brought to an untriumphant conclusion when a saber-wielding fanatic in Tokyo had nearly struck him down.

Because of different geographical conditions obtaining along the line, and to facilitate and speed construction, the Trans-Siberian was also divided into six sections, which allowed work to be carried on simultaneously at different points. These were: the Western Siberian section, from Chelyabinsk to the Ob River (880 miles); the Central Siberian, from the Ob to Irkutsk (1,162½ miles); the Circumbaikalian, from Irkutsk to Mysovsk, around the southern end of the lake (194 miles); the Transbaikalian, from Mysovsk to Sretensk (669 miles); the Amur section, from Sretensk to Khabarovsk (1,326 miles); and the Ussuri section, from Khabarovsk to Vladivostok (483 miles)—for a total length of 4,714½ miles. The most difficult areas, around Lake Baikal and flanking the Amur, were reserved until last.

Though most of the tsar's advisers were lukewarm to the idea of a railway (largely because of its prohibitive expense), Sergey Witte, the new Minister of Finance, overcame their resistance and remained the guardian angel of the enterprise. Easily the most capable official in the imperial government, he was a man of extraordinary self-discipline and spartan habits who worked sixteen hours a day throughout his professional life. Though of eccentric appearance, with "a massive head, a long and heavy torso, and weak and oddly short legs," he had a commanding presence, a rigorously analytical mind, and the kind of prophetic insight into political matters that gave him the reputation of a seer.

Born in Tiflis, Georgia, in 1849 to Dutch and Russian parents of high social standing and substantial means, Witte's privileged origins did not entirely favor his prospects in life, since the turmoil of his childhood left him deeply scarred. It is said that he "held it as a grievance against his mother that she did not suckle him herself, and his early precocious recollections were of his family's eighty-four servants and of ugly scenes between his wet nurse and his nursery-maid and her drunken husband." A series of besotted or erratic tutors—"a retired Caucasian veteran, who also drank heavily; a retired officer in the French navy, who was deported by the authorities after a scandalous love affair; and a Swiss who became enamored of his governess"—did not ease his development, although something like a rage for order was kindled in him in reaction to the chaos of his formative years. His first ambition, in fact, was to become a professor of pure mathematics, but a precipitous decline in the family fortune induced him to enter railway administration instead. Within a very short time he had mastered all the technical details that bear upon the efficient management of freight, and at the time of the Russo-Turkish War (1877–78), he happened to be in charge of all traffic passing along the Odessa Railway to the front. Witte's exceptional management of the line brought him to the attention of high government officials, including the tsar, who also noted the remarkable system of tariffs which lowered rates yet increased the revenue. In February 1892 he was made Minister of Ways of Communication, and six months later, Minister of Finance.

Witte moved briskly to rehabilitate the Russian economy. To restore confidence in a declining ruble, he established the gold standard, accumulated financial reserves, lured large blocks of foreign investment capital to new industrial initiatives, assisted industries with government subsidies, introduced the state liquor monopoly, taxed staples like tobacco, sugar, and kerosene, and selectively imposed or eliminated tariffs to foster foreign trade. Yet his policies involved sacrifice, and because the Trans-Siberian Railway was the most visible of his great undertakings, Lenin was not absolutely mistaken in depicting him as a "conjurer" who, while disclaiming a deficit, "plundered the treasury to see his railway through."

Extending eventually 5,500 miles through seven time zones from Chelyabinsk in the Urals to Vladivostok on the Sea of Japan, the Trans-Siberian Railway was destined to be by far the longest railway in the world. It would not only facilitate colonization but also defense, spur development in the territory through which it passed, and spread Russian influence throughout the Far East. As a by-product, the construction and heavy industries of Russia stood to gain, and within Siberia itself the railway could be expected to lead to improved waterways, expanded metallurgical plants, more efficient mining and agricultural enterprises, a growing trade with China, and the transport of "tons of Siberian grain, timber, hides, butter, and minerals to bolster the mother country's internal and export trade." It would also help build up a solid base for Russian power on the Pacific and facilitate the maintenance of Russia's Pacific Fleet. Beyond that (in Witte's opinion) it might even create a new world order by opening up "new horizons not only for Russia but for world trade ... resulting in fundamental alterations in the existing economic relations between states." And relations with the United States were among those uppermost in his mind. Indeed, the railway excited so many expectations that it deserved to be called, as it was, one of the wonders of the world.

More than anything else, however, the government was counting on the line's ability to serve as a "safety valve" to ease the rural overpopulation of European Russia, beleaguered by famine and seething with inchoate revolutionary discontent. Although these huddled masses were yearning to breathe free (if that is what the promise of Siberia meant), the difficulties of the journey by barge and cart were sufficient to discourage even the hardiest of peasant families, among whom disease and other perils of the journey took a terrible toll. Before the coming of the railway, some 10 percent of the children of emigrants, it is said, died en route. Most migrants settled in southwestern Siberia, where most of the arable land could be found. Indeed, the known resources—outside of Pacific fishing—justifying construction of a railway east of Omsk were obscure, and strategic and political considerations emerged as paramount for carrying the Trans-Siberian through to the sea.

At Witte's urging, a special Trans-Siberian Committee was established—made up of the tsar's chief ministers or cabinet, presided over by the tsarevich—to coordinate construction with land distribution schemes, and medical, veterinary, and various other services to ease the emigrant's plight. The committee's expanded powers subsequently gave it jurisdiction over all matters bearing on Siberian development, including "the right to allocate funds, fix expenses, expropriate land, timber, and buildings, requisition convict and military labor, establish a separate railway police force, select routes, and determine where and when construction should begin."

Built with astonishing if reckless speed, within a month of the groundbreaking ceremony in Vladivostok, the road began to cross the wastelands of Siberia, spanning the widest rivers and manned by an army of up to 100,000 laborers and technicians of all kinds.

The western division—from Chelyabinsk to the Ob—was carried forward under the direction of Constantine Mikhailovsky, designer of the great Alexander Bridge over the Volga and Russia's greatest civil engineer. Although the track was laid through level plains, including the Ishym and Barabinsk steppes, he faced wholly inadequate supplies of wagons, horses, barges, and basic materiel, and had to recruit skilled workers from as far away as Turkey and Persia. Steel had to be imported from the Urals, cement from St. Petersburg, other supplies from Warsaw. His line passed through swamps, peat bogs, and jungles of nettles; and to prepare the way, he had to improvise dikes, dig canals, and sink trestle pilings into beds of slime. Even hardwood had to be brought in, since the local timber was unsuitable for bridges and ties. And every wooden tie had to be hand-cut. In addition, he had to build lime kilns for the brickwork of his bridges, and drill artesian wells. Since no shelters had been prepared for the laborers in advance, they bivouacked on the open plains until the early frosts came, and then moved into makeshift log cabins, boxcars, or "crude huts thrown together with railway ties and partly covered by sod."

Despite such obstacles and the primitive equipment at his disposal (including shovels of plain wood "without even a strip of tin on the digging edge"), by March 1896 Mikhailovsky had built a great stone-piered steel bridge over the Irtysh (which still stands) and carried his track all the way from Chelyabinsk to the Ob.

The central portion—from the Ob to Irkutsk—was supervised by Nikolay Mezheninov, "a plumpish railway veteran with a small, pointed gray beard, bushy eyebrows, and thinning hair en brosse." Laid largely through mountainous taiga, where wolves and bears abounded but human habitation was scarce, its six thousand rails had to be brought in from England by way of the Kara Sea, then up the Yenisey to Krasnoyarsk. From December until July, permafrost gripped the ground to a depth of six feet, and then dissolved into a swamp. Since local manpower was lacking, convicts were requisitioned from Aleksandrovsk Prison northwest of Irkutsk, and an incentive system was tried, counting eight months' work as a year at hard labor and reducing periods of exile. To help build some of the more substantial bridges (over a hundred were required on this section alone), Italian stonemasons were enlisted from Milan. Winter construction on the bridges was particularly hazardous, with a routine calculation of three to four deaths for every million rubles spent, and before the great seven-spanned steel bridge over the Yenisey was complete numerous workmen had slipped to their death from the icy spans. Recessed alcoves were later built into either end where icons (above a receptacle for contributions) were placed to allay the wayfarer's fears.

To expedite the transportation of supplies, various waterways were deepened, widened, dredged, and blasted free of obstructions, but to avoid the expense of tunnels and cuttings, the line followed a meandering path. In carrying the final section over the mountains to Irkutsk, Mezheninov took remarkable risks in his perfunctory construction of embankments, and in the dramatic gradients and curves. But like Mik-hailovsky he completed his task well ahead of schedule (if not within the estimated cost), so that by August 1898, Russia had a Trans-Siberian Railway that went all the way to Irkutsk.

The Transbaikal portion—from Mysovsk on the eastern shore of Lake Baikal to Sretensk—was variously delayed by floods and other calamities, and when construction was finally attempted, dynamite had to be used just to open the frozen ground. Encounters with the twisting torrent of the Angara River required fifty bridges over ravines and tributary streams, while the loop around the southern tip of Lake Bai-kal, almost inaccessibly recessed by overhanging cliffs, was to prove one of the most difficult in railway engineering history. Still, good progress had been made on the line throughout until July 1897, when

> mountain torrents and extraordinary heavy downpours flooded the whole river system from the eastern shore of Lake Baikal to Sretensk and beyond. Rampaging waters demolished embankments and re-taining walls and overturned locomotives and other rolling stock. Entire settlements were obliterated at uncounted loss of life. More than two hundred and thirty miles of track were damaged in the Ingoda and Shilka valleys. Near Sretensk, the Shilka undermined a mountain flank and released a landslide that buried newly laid track under tons of earth. Fifteen bridges vanished without trace, while two others were wrecked irreparably. West of Verkhneudinsk, the surging Selenga River swept away great piles of lumber stored on its banks for pier caissons of a future steel bridge.

Another three years were required to repair all the damage done.

Farther east the problems seemed to mount. On the Ussuri line—from Khabarovsk to Vladivostok—sub-Arctic cold in winter and torren-tial rains at the onslaught of spring frustrated construction, horses perished from anthrax, men from fever and disease. From time to time, Manchurian outlaws also beleaguered the railway campsites, despite the posting of Cossack guards. Nevertheless, under chief engineer Orest Vyazemsky, regiments of soldiers impressed into service as nav-vies, three thousand convicts from Sakhalin (granted reduced sen-tences in return for their labor), and fifteen thousand coolies brought in by sea from North China every spring "cleared a path through dense forests choked with undergrowth and vines, built access roads, drained broad swamps, and blasted cuttings" through basalt cliffs. By November 1897, the easternmost portion of the great Trans-Siberian was done.

In the process, Khabarovsk had been transformed from an insignificant hamlet into an important military town; Blagoveshchensk ("Annunciation"), founded in 1858, had acquired a population of twenty thousand, tree-lined streets, and official buildings of whitewashed brick; and Vladivostok had begun to live up to its name—"Lord of the East." In 1885, it had been a mean frontier town with a population of about 13,000 Russians, Chinese, and Koreans. By 1897, when the Ussuri line opened, that had grown to 30,000, with "frowning earthworks, huge barracks, and bustling warehouses. From dawn to sunset," wrote a visitor, "the low green hills around the harbor swarm with white-clad soldiers at work on the fortifications. Snake-like torpedo-boats glide noiselessly in all directions, and wicked-looking guns of modern and deadly type peer out of the most unlikely places, for defensive precautions are being carried on with a restless persistence that must eventually crown Vladivostok Queen of Fortresses in the Far East." Many of its buildings were of brick and stone, and in spite of the fact that over the doorway of the railway station it was dolefully printed in old Russian characters: VLADIVOSTOK TO PETERSBURG, 9877 VERSTS (about 6,250 miles), within a few years the city would boast wide paved streets, electric lights, telegraph wires, and railway trains running down to the wharves.

Only the long Amur Valley section and that around Lake Baikal's southern rim remained to be built. But time was of the essence. By the mid-1890s, a number of colonial powers had begun to consider how China might be divided up into colonies or spheres of influence, after the fashion of Africa. The Pacific had already, in a more general way, been parceled out. Australia and New Zealand belonged to the British, who, with the Germans and French, had "snapped up little chains of islands stretching from New Guinea to Pitcairn." Sakhalin belonged to the Russians, the Kuriles to Japan. The United States was in full possession of Wake, Midway, Honolulu, and Hawaii, and was about to annex the Philippines (in 1898) from Spain. But China was an enormously more appetizing prize. Acting to stake their own claim to the region before a completed Trans-Siberian Railway facilitated the movement of Russian troops and arms to the Far East, in the summer of 1894 the

Japanese had attacked and defeated China over their competing claims
on Korea, and by the Treaty of Shimonoseki (1895) forced China to
agree to a large indemnity, and to cede both the island of Formosa
(Taiwan) and the Liaotung Peninsula, with the ice-free port of Port
Arthur at its tip. Germany, France, and Russia united at once to pressure Japan to divest itself of its territorial gains in return for an enlarged indemnity.

"Like vultures," writes one historian, "the European powers now
clawed for their own cut of the carcass." And Russia, not least. As it
moved into position between 1892 and 1895, almost 400 miles a year
on the average were built on the new railway; and after the Japanese
attack on China, construction pressed urgently forward with 836 miles
in 1895. The difficult Circumbaikal section was indefinitely delayed,
and large icebreakers capable of ferrying entire trains with all their
passengers across the lake were commissioned from British dockyards
to bridge the gap. The first such vessel produced, appropriately called
the *Baikal*, was 290 feet long, 57 feet wide, and displaced 4,200 tons.

> Her hull, belted with inch-thick steel plates and reinforced by a two-
> foot inner sheathing of timber, was designed to crunch through three
> to four feet of ice. She could accommodate the coaches of an entire
> express train, or from twenty-five to twenty-eight fully loaded freight
> cars, on three pairs of rails parallel with the keel. Above this deck, a
> towering superstructure contained a luxurious lounge and a buffet;
> cabins for a hundred and fifty first- and second-class passengers; a
> special suite for consequential dignitaries; a chapel; quarters for
> ships' officers and crew; and deck space for six hundred and fifty
> persons in third class.

If any vessel could make up for the lack of a Circumbaikal section,
the *Baikal* was surely it, especially in conjunction with a smaller sister
ship, the *Angara*. Meanwhile, instead of the proposed Amur Railway to
link the Transbaikal and Ussuri lines, an alternative route through
Manchuria to Vladivostok was chosen, subsequently known as the
Chinese Eastern Railway. Despite initial expectations, the Amur had
never lived up to its promise as a granary, and disillusionment had set
in. The region was still largely uninhabited, and (as Chekhov described
it in June 1890) an "utter wilderness."

To the south, Manchuria (China's northernmost province) emerged as a "rich economic and strategic prize." It had the ice-free ports of Port Arthur and Talienwan, which the Japanese had almost gained, but also gold, iron, and coal, grasslands with thriving cattle, and a fertile soil. By means of the proposed railway (which would shorten the Trans-Siberian by 350 miles) Russia therefore began the takeover of Manchuria "by commercial subterfuge." Having appeared (in conjunction with Germany and France) to defend Chinese territorial integrity, Russia now offered Peking a loan toward the payment of its indemnity obligations (which it was too impoverished to meet without outside help) in return for a railway concession through northern Manchuria 900 miles to Vladivostok. This concession, however, which included the right to secure and defend the railway with armed guards, was not granted directly to the Russian government but to the Russo-Chinese Bank, a private concern conceived by Witte and financed mainly by the French bankers who had facilitated the China loan. The bank in turn transferred the concession to the Chinese Eastern Railway Company, a subsidiary corporation created by Witte and controlled by the Russian Treasury, but with a Chinese diplomat as chairman of the board.

The terms of the concession allowed the railway to operate the line for eighty years, after which it would automatically revert without charge to the Chinese government, although the latter had an option to buy it after just thirty-six years, if it could afford to do so. The terms of the arrangement, however, noted Witte, who had devised them, "were so burdensome that it was highly improbable that the Chinese Government would ever attempt to effect the redemption." This secret agreement between Russia and China (which also included a defensive alliance against Japan) was signed in the spring of 1896, when Li Hung-chang, China's elderly and notoriously corrupt First Chancellor, attended the coronation in St. Petersburg of Nicholas II.

Taking over the negotiations from Prince Lobanov-Rostovsky, the Foreign Minister, who, Witte remarked sarcastically, "was entirely ignorant of our Far Eastern policy," Witte received the Chinese dignitary in his own office at the Finance Ministry, where everything was settled over a hookah pipe and tea. As a reward for his acquiescence, Li is believed to have received surreptitiously over time about 3 million rubles in bribes.

In an age of railroad imperialism, the Chinese Eastern Railway was an exceptionally bold and clever coup. But in all other respects, it was typical of the way in which the European powers were methodically carving up China. From the various beachheads they established, railways immediately extended their acquisitive arms. By 1898, Belgian financiers were planning track from Peking to Hankow; their German counterparts were capitalizing lines in Shantung Province; the British were forging a line from Shanghai to Nanking; and the French were spiking down railroad ties in the three southern provinces of Kwangtung, Kwangsi, and Yunnan. The Russo-Chinese Bank was also subsidizing a French branch line to the Belgian track. Not to be left out, an American syndicate had obtained a concession for 1,000 miles of railway from Hankow, the "Chicago of China," to Canton, the principal seaport in the south. When connected, all these lines would quarter the empire.

Indeed, even before construction of the Chinese Eastern Railway had begun, Germany in the summer of 1897 had seized Kiaochow Bay; Russia responded by occupying Talienwan and Port Arthur, to "protect" China from further German encroachment; Britain landed at Weihaiwei, and France at Kwangchow in the south. The complete disintegration of China seemed at hand. The dual role inadequately filled by Vladivostok as a military and commercial port was now neatly divided by the Russians between Port Arthur, which was turned into a powerful fortress and naval base, and Talienwan (rechristened Dalny, or "Far Away")—both obtained from China on lease.

In the summer of 1898, thousands of railway construction workers and about three thousand armed escorts, or "Matilda's Guards," as they were called after Witte's wife, marched into the sleepy hamlet of Harbin, on the banks of the Sungari River in north-central Manchuria, and set up the administrative headquarters of the Chinese Eastern line. Under their chief engineer, Aleksandr Yugovich, they built a kind of pilot line first, rudimentary even by Trans-Siberian standards, to convey laborers and materiel swiftly to the building sites. Then they pushed their track eastward to meet construction crews proceeding from the Ussuri to the west. This required a number of substantial bridges and eight tunnels, including one about two miles long bored through the desolate, windswept Great Khingan Range. Meanwhile, a South Manchurian line, with branches to Port Arthur and Dalny, was also begun.

As elsewhere, severe winter frosts, summer floods, and granite-hard ground created such obstacles that only the most grueling effort could overcome them. This was especially so because all mechanical equipment was lacking, and after stretches of the frozen ground had been blasted loose or thawed by fires, the laborers, having hacked away at the soil with shovels and picks, carried it off in baskets on their backs. Bands of Manchurian outlaws, called *hunghutzes* (literally, "red beards"), were far more formidable in their own homeland, of course, than along the Ussuri line, and exacted protection money from merchants and traders operating within their domain. River convoys and campsites were also constantly subject to attack. Although they were usually struck by small guerrilla bands, some of the assaults were on a larger scale. Southwest of Harbin, for example, seven hundred red beards completely sacked the town. "Matilda's Guards" proved insufficient protection against them, and Cossack cavalry squadrons were brought in and set up a system of defense.

Still other problems arose, most notably in the summer of 1899 when bubonic plague broke out at Yingkou, a town on the South Manchurian branch near Dalny. To contain its spread, troops cordoned off land approaches to the port and quarantined steamers and junks in the harbor. Before these measures could take effect, at least 1,400 had died in the nearby construction camps.

Nevertheless, by the spring of 1900, it appeared that nothing could prevent the completion of the line. Some of the temporary wooden bridges had even been replaced with structures of metal or stone, a number of stations had been built, and more than half of the Chinese Eastern's 1,575 miles of track had been laid. Harbin was developing into a full-scale metropolis, military and naval installations were increasingly fortifying Port Arthur, and Dalny seemed likely to fulfill its promise as a great commercial port.

Within a few months, however, all the optimism created by Russia's gains would begin to fade.

Unwilling to countenance the partition of China so as to be excluded from the China trade, the United States in September 1899 had spelled out its "Open Door" policy, and in the following July pledged to protect China's territorial integrity. This was in no way consoling to Japan, which had triumphed over China only to see its hard-won treaty rights revoked and redistributed to rival European powers. Nor was it convincing to the Chinese, who wanted the foreigners off their soil. The

Russians were neither more nor less hated than the rest, but, as one historian puts it, "the leasehold appropriation of Port Arthur and Dalny —to say nothing of the imminent incursion of a 600-mile Chinese Eastern branch down the full length of Manchuria's most prosperous and densely inhabited valley—infuriated Chinese nationalists." Li Hung-chang was exiled to South China, and the leaders of the delegation who had approved the lease of the ports were put to death. A secret society of fanatical patriots arose, calling itself the "Righteous and Harmonious Fists" (or "Boxers"). They practiced martial arts as a physical and spiritual discipline, grew rapidly in numbers, and (with the tacit approval of the Empress Dowager) spearheaded the anti-foreign reaction. Chinese regulars covertly cooperated with them, as xenophobic fury swept the land. Foreigners everywhere in China were in danger, and many massacres occurred.

In the summer of 1900, the Boxers began to derail trains, burn bridges, and destroy miles of telegraph and railway installations in the Mukden region. Chinese troops, covertly working with the Boxers, blew up a Russian ammunition dump and killed about thirty officers and men. They tried to blockade the Amur River, destroyed the Russian railway near Harbin, and interdicted rail transport to Port Arthur. Harbin came under attack, but a disciplined contingent of Witte's paramilitary railway police fended the Chinese off until a detachment of Russian regulars arrived. When War Minister Aleksey Kuropatkin heard of the Boxer Rebellion, he is said to have remarked, "I am very glad. This will give us an excuse for seizing Manchuria."

A direct pretext was found in the pretended plans for a Chinese attack on Blagoveshchensk, one of the major Russian settlements on the Amur's left bank. The attack had supposedly been set for July 2, and rumors spread that there was a large Chinese force gathering nearby at Aigun. When shots were fired from Aigun at a passing Russian steamer, panic seized the Russian community. Manchu insurgents were said to have infiltrated the town, each provided with a length of rope with which to strangle a Russian in his bed. The Russian commander ordered the immediate expulsion of all eight thousand Chinese residents (more than half the town), who were rounded up in house-to-house searches—including old men, cripples, invalids, women, and children—and on July 14 driven at bayonet point into the river. Those who resisted were killed on the spot. Nearly all the rest were drowned.

In fact, five days before this completely premeditated massacre, Kuropatkin had secretly authorized the invasion of Manchuria. Some
200,000 troops were hurriedly mobilized, and six army corps poured
across the border, occupying the whole province, north and south.
Sixty-eight Chinese villages were burnt to the ground, leaving nothing
but blackened posts and crumbling ruins. "Nothing and nobody was
spared." In September, Russian battalions converged on Mukden and
other Manchurian strongholds held by rebels and drove them out.

Meanwhile, every other power that had a stake in the country had
sent expeditionary forces to suppress the uprising and to rescue besieged foreign legations in Peking. The capital and its environs were
occupied in August 1900, and the imperial palaces looted, the foreigners (having united into an International Force) not withdrawing
until December, when the rebellion had been completely suppressed.
The Russians, however, remained in Manchuria, in effect as an army of
occupation, under the pretense of protecting the Chinese Eastern and
its South Manchurian extension while they were being rebuilt. Two
thirds of the railway, including the junction stations at Mukden and
Liaoyang, had been destroyed or damaged in the turmoil, and the flight
of Chinese workers had reduced the labor force by almost half. As
reconstruction began, Russians filled the gap. Despite an outbreak of
cholera that swept through almost every camp on the line, and even
struck Harbin, on July 1, 1903, the Chinese Eastern, with stone bridges
of "Roman massiveness," and otherwise probably the most solidly built
stretch of the whole Trans-Siberian, opened to Vladivostok, with its
branch lines to Port Arthur and Dalny. Of course, construction costs
had soared well beyond the original estimates, but Witte's budgets
somehow managed to conceal the losses incurred. In trying to deci-
pher his figures, hapless analysts in the British Embassy in St. Petersburg were reportedly driven to tears.

But a different kind of price would be paid. By strengthening its bid
for standing as a Pacific power, and especially by extending its influence into Manchuria, Russia had upset the strategic balance in East
Asia; and so to forestall any further Russian advance, Britain now
sought collaboration with Japan.

It was Britain that Russia feared most. While Russia had been acquiring dominion over Poland and Finland in the west, extending its sway
down the Amur River Valley in the east, and into the Caucasus and

Central Asia, Britain was establishing its hold on India and Upper Burma, Malaysia, North Borneo, and Hong Kong. It was poised on the borders of Afghanistan, Persia, Nepal, and Tibet, and dominated two thirds of China's coastal export trade. "Russian and British expansion," notes one historian, "had produced a situation where the spheres of influence of the two Empires were so contiguous that if either stirred they were bound to collide." In the Far East, Britain had little man-power strength, but the French Foreign Minister prophetically re-marked in 1901 that England might seek in Japan the soldier that she lacked. Just one year later Japan entered into a full-scale defensive alliance with England; moreover, Russia failed to realize that Japan had become a major world power in its own right.

The once-insular island empire had recently undergone an astonish-ing modernization along Western lines. Formerly xenophobic, it now welcomed foreigners in every port, sent officers to German military academies for training, and future admirals to Great Britain, where Japanese warships were being built. Japan's aspirations as an area power inevitably stretched to the mainland, where in part in response to growing Russian hegemony, it had attacked China in 1894. Subse-quently obliged under international pressure to relinquish Port Arthur and other strategic gains, it had seen Russia acquire some of them by a secret convention with Peking. In addition, a group of adventurers at the Russian court had begun to promote a scheme for timber conces-sions on the Yalu River, with designs on Korea. Japan immediately began to enlarge its own Korean holdings with thousands of new settlers and to insist, in secret negotiations, on spheres of influence that would cede Manchuria to Russia but gain Korea for itself.

The negotiations made little headway, producing an atmosphere of crisis in which neither side dared yield; but Russia never expected Japan to go to war. After all, Japan was a newly emergent country, and the Russian military the most powerful in the world. Moreover, the Russians thought of the Japanese almost as children, incapable of man-aging large military equipment because of their diminutive size. One Russian admiral seriously described Japanese sailors on a battleship as struggling like infants with an oversized toy, and Russia's military at-taché in Tokyo (supposedly a Japanese expert) thought the Japanese "would need about a century to develop a modern army comparable to that of the weakest army in Europe." Needless to say, such benighted notions also clouded Russian estimations of the Japanese capacity for strategic thought.

The Russians had not always been so blind. Although Admiral Krusenstern had thought (perhaps correctly) in 1805 that "two [Russian] cutters of sixteen guns and sixty men would be sufficient . . . to sink the whole Japanese fleet," others had read more clearly between the lines. Vasily Golovnin, for example, despite the humiliation and abuse he had suffered during his Japanese captivity of 1814, had emerged with a healthy appreciation of the military potential of his captors. "Japanese seamen put on a European footing could," he warned, once the nation came out of its self-imposed isolation, "in a short time match their fleet with the best of Europe. . . . One must not provoke the Japanese, a populous, intelligent, patient and imitative people. For if ever there ruled over that people a monarch like our own Peter the Great, it would not be many years before Japan was lording it over the whole Pacific Ocean." Japan delayed the day, but just fourteen years after it was forcibly opened to the world economy by gunboat diplomacy, when Commodore Perry sailed into Yedo Bay, Japan began its remarkably rapid transformation from a semi-medieval, feudal society into a largely Westernized modern industrial and military state.

The transformation began with the rapid adoption of European cultural habits and styles, such as public lavatories, Western garb, and building materials of brick, plaster, and plate glass. In 1871, a post and telegraph office was opened; in 1872, the first railway, linking Tokyo and Yokohama, "with an imported Englishman to drive the train." In 1873, Japan adopted the solar calendar, and in the same year introduced universal conscription, sounding the death knell for the Samurai. By 1877, the Japanese military had also put together a Prussian-style general staff. Japan's soldiers began to be trained by the Germans, British, and French, and by 1903 it had an army of thirteen divisions, six first-class battleships, and six armored cruisers built in British yards. The government's China indemnity had helped pay for all this, but Japan's growing economy sustained the military growth. During a single decade (1893 to 1903) the value of its imports trebled, the tonnage of its merchant marine quadrupled, and the combined deposits in all its banks increased by more than six times. Although the emperor was declared to be sacred and inviolable, Japan's constitution allowed the election of a national Diet, modeled on that of Bismarck's Germany.

Even after Japan had embarked on its program of modernization and development, Russia failed to take its measure. As late as 1896, at a commercial fair held at Nizhny-Novgorod, Japan was given a mere room in the Chinese pavilion; and in 1903 there was no general book about Japan (other than monographs on exotica) in the whole Russian Empire. "To most Russians," one writer observed, "Japan was a fairy-book sort of place, filled with fascinating little people who lived in paper houses, indulged themselves with geishas, and wasted hours on flower arrangements and tea ceremonies."

At the beginning of February 1904, the Russian Army had 1,100,000 men under arms, compared with Japan's 180,000. Russia's active reserve also totaled 2,400,000, and it was believed that in that category Japan could muster no more than 150,000 men. In fact, since all Japanese males between the ages of seventeen and forty were liable to military service, the Japanese could muster 850,000 men—six times the Russian estimate—and these were much closer than their Russian counterparts to the potential theater of war. Nevertheless, aside from greatly underestimating the number of fighting men Japan could put into the field, it was also axiomatic in the racist court circles of Nicholas II that "one Russian soldier was the equal of three Japanese." Even ordinary Russians sometimes referred to the Japanese as "Makakas," a zoological term meaning "related to the monkey or baboon." Man for man, of course, the manpower reserve of the empire appeared to give Russia overwhelming might. But it was in fact in a disciplined infantry that Japan had its secret strength. "With the invention earlier in the nineteenth century of breech-loading rifles using metallic cartridges," explains one historian, "muskets and muzzle-loaders had been cast aside, but the Russians had not appreciated the value of the new weapon. In training, they spent most of their ammunition rations on unobserved fire. The Japanese trained on the range. The Russian soldiers shot badly, the Japanese excellently. The Russians fired in volleys. The Japanese learned to aim and to shoot to kill."

As for the comparative naval strengths of the two powers in East Asian waters, Japan was numerically inferior in battleships but superior in cruisers. Its warships were also equipped with the newly developed Whitehead torpedo, powered by a propeller-driven compressed air engine, while some of the Russian ships in Port Arthur were relatively old and in disrepair.

Strengthened by their alliance with Great Britain, the Japanese, in fact, believed they could prevail in a limited war. Russian land forces in the Far East were as yet inconsiderable, and the one-track Trans-Siberian Railway for a number of reasons was incapable of rapidly hauling heavy supplies. The Russian general staff, however, estimated that the Trans-Siberian and Chinese Eastern railways could carry six to eight troop trains to Manchuria a day, effectively matching Japan's capacity for amphibious landings on the Korean coast. Moreover, the six or more Russian divisions already in Manchuria were well positioned should war break out. Nevertheless, War Minister Kuropatkin later claimed, "I thought that a rupture with Japan would be a national calamity and did everything in my power to prevent it." As to the first half of his statement at least, he was right.

Russia steadily increased its troop strength in the Far East during 1903, raised additional battalions in the homeland, and toward the end of January 1904 moved three battalions of the East Siberian Rifle Regiment toward the Yalu River. Four artillery brigades stationed in European Russia and Western Siberia were also dispatched to Manchuria. In March, one battleship, seven cruisers, and four torpedo boats left the Red Sea for Port Arthur, a voyage of six or seven weeks.

Meanwhile, the Japanese drilled regiments of troops in subzero weather on Mount Hakkoda in northern Japan in preparation for a Siberian campaign.

With the completion of the Chinese Eastern, all that now remained for a railway through to the Pacific was the formidable stretch designed to round the southern tip of Lake Baikal. Thousands of Central Asian, Persian, Turkish, and Italian navvies joined the Russian construction crews, but the problems they encountered were more daunting than on any other segment of the line. The only access roads were meandering goat trails along the steep walls of the cliffs, and timber baulks had first to be built along the overhangs to prevent rockslides from crushing workers on the track. Along Baikal's eastern shore, the heights came down to the water, and a long tunnel was required to bring the track out along a road bed cut in the solid rock. From there the line described a great semicircle through hills and tunnels to Verkhneudinsk. With hostilities looming on the horizon,

Russian engineers worked desperately all summer and fall to blast their tunnels through the mountains, but when winter descended in its frozen fury they were still far short of their goal. Lake Baikal was still the unbridgeable gap in the line.

By the end of December ice had already begun to form on the surface of the lake. By the end of January, the *Baikal,* which had been ferrying five troop trains a day, and a smaller ferry, the *Angara,* which was not equipped to take troop trains, could no longer break through, and Russian troops heading for the East were obliged to march across the ice, halting at four-mile intervals in heated shelters to recover from exposure.

Storms were frequent and the ice often cracked, leaving immense fissures into which the unwary troops often fell. With a growing sense of urgency as the war clouds added their threat to the winter storms, the Russians had mobilized 3,000 horses to draw sledges loaded with supplies across the lake. Since supplies were often lost in mountainous quantities, engineers experimented with a line laid across the ice. Though the ice would not stand the weight of a locomotive, it was found that horses could be used to draw loaded trucks. In the first two weeks that the new system was in use, however, only twenty trucks reached the eastern side of the lake.

Witte's devotion to the development of the Trans-Siberian had inevitably involved him deeply in Far Eastern affairs, and for a time he was the chief architect of the government's policy in that sphere. The negotiations concerning the Chinese Eastern had been entrusted to his care, and he had always been aware that any overly aggressive move might lead to military confrontation with Japan. For that reason, he had opposed the outright military occupation of Manchuria, and had also objected to the acquisition of Port Arthur and Dalny, since a policy of gradual economic penetration promised more solid and enduring gains. In 1898, he had been astonished to hear Russia's Foreign Minister suggest that to secure Port Arthur and the peninsula, all that was required was "One flag and one sentry, the prestige of Russia will do the rest." Witte didn't think that would be quite enough. Foreseeing war, he wrote in November 1901 to Count V. N. Lamsdorf:

An armed clash with Japan in the near future would be a great disaster for us. I do not doubt that Russia will emerge victorious from the struggle, but the victory will cost us too much and will badly injure the country economically—in the eyes of the Russian people a war with Japan for the possession of distant Korea will not be justified and the latent dissatisfaction may render more acute the alarming phenomena of our domestic life, which make themselves felt even in peacetime. Between the two evils, an armed conflict with Japan and the complete cession of Korea, I would unhesitatingly choose the second.

Witte's apprehensions were exactly right, and Lamsdorf shared them. But the war party was on the rise, and their adventurism completely jeopardized all that Witte had achieved.

Under international pressure, on April 8, 1902, the Russian government formally agreed to gradually withdraw its forces from Manchuria —in three phases over eighteen months—"provided that no disturbances arise and that the action of other Powers should not prevent it." Since "disturbances" could include banditry, for example, with which the area was plagued, the Russian gesture was recognized almost at once as a delaying tactic, and indeed the Russians never moved to carry the agreement out. But Witte saw the writing on the wall. After visiting the Far East during the summer of 1902 to study the situation, he bluntly advised Nicholas to evacuate Manchuria and restrict subsequent efforts to extend Russian influence in the region to peaceful means. His candor was not appreciated, and quickly led to the decline of his influence, as intrigues against him by reactionaries increased at Nicholas's court. In that court's corrupted atmosphere, the fact that Witte's wife was Jewish was also held against him, for the tsar's own special hatred, it was said, "was reserved for Englishmen, Jews and Japanese."

One of the tsar's more trusted advisers at this time was Vyacheslav Plehve, a former secretary of state for Finland, who became Minister of the Interior in 1902 after the assassination of his predecessor. Among other things, Plehve's anti-Semitic convictions included the belief that revolutionary and socialist ideas were largely "Jewish in origin." To demonstrate his zeal against dissent, Plehve even arrested his own foster parents on suspicion of treason and deported them to Siberia. His views on foreign policy reflected a similar delicacy of feeling. In 1903, he remarked to Kuropatkin: "What this country needs is a short victorious war to stem the tide of revolution."

On August 28, 1903, Witte was summarily dismissed as Minister of Finance. The tsar had long felt overshadowed by Witte's reputation and influence, and perhaps already sensed, as Witte later put it, that "he was not born for the momentous historical role which fate had thrust upon him." As if the former's abilities would automatically pass to him by default, Nicholas rather pathetically wrote in his diary: "Now I rule."

He didn't, in any effectual sense. Conflict with Japan eventually became inevitable because of a reckless brinkmanship in Russian diplomacy, and because by all accounts the manner in which policy was formulated at the time was negligent in the extreme. "The stagnation in the Foreign Ministry is indescribable," one official wrote. "Everybody is asleep." And the German ambassador reported: "In my whole life I have never seen so much laziness as in the ministries here. All officials arrive at 11 or 12 o'clock and disappear at 4 never to be seen again. During office hours they do nothing but smoke and promenade in the corridors." Nicholas himself was often away on long holidays, and the British ambassador, Sir Charles Scott, in any case judged him "incapable, either from want of sufficient experience or by natural diffidence, of taking a decided initiative on his own judgement."

Such a state of affairs allowed Far Eastern policy to be concentrated in the hands of the militant new viceroy at Port Arthur, Yevgeny Alekseyev, and of a special committee headed by an extremist adventurer, Aleksandr Bezobrazov, who had won the tsar's confidence. Bezobrazov had "masterminded" the Yalu River timber concession; Alekseyev reportedly owed his early advancement to having once taken the blame for a brawl in Marseilles started by a member of the imperial family. The purpose of the viceroyalty, with its headquarters in Port Arthur, was to consolidate the administration, including regional defense, of all Russian territories to the east of Lake Baikal. Japan interpreted the new post (created in August 1903) as a preparation for war.

Taking advantage of the favorable climate in world opinion which had coalesced on their side, on February 8, 1904, the Japanese (without a declaration of war) launched a devastating, surprise attack on the Russian fleet at anchor in Port Arthur. Subsequently, the port itself was besieged and taken; and gradually, in spite of bitter engagements near Mukden and elsewhere, the Russians were routed from the Liaotung Peninsula and pushed deep into Manchuria. The land war as it developed was enormously costly for both sides, with the two huge battles for Port Arthur and Mukden alone costing each side over 100,000 dead.

The Japanese had deliberately struck before the Trans-Siberian could be strengthened, and when the crippling rail-gap at Lake Baikal had still to be closed. The equipment and rolling stock proved inadequate for moving heavy artillery and other modern war materiel; in addition, only a fourth of the bridges were of metal construction, the wooden bridges sagged, and the overlight rails (rolled from low-grade steel) bent under the weight and strain of the trains. Because of the sharp curves and extremely steep gradients, locomotives were severely limited in the amount of freight they could haul, and in some mountainous areas of the east slowed to a crawl. In places, the underballasted track also tended to "creep sideways," rails buckled and sank in the permafrost, and many of the raw, untreated ties had already begun to decay. One visiting engineer remarked that "after a spring rain, the trains run off the track like squirrels." Finally, there were simply not enough sidings, water-supply depots, and marshaling yards. As a result, Russian forces reached Manchuria only after five to six weeks of interrupted, fatiguing, and sometimes alarming travel. The Lake Baikal bottleneck continued to cause many delays, and in the spring and summer of 1904 whole regiments piled up while awaiting passage on the *Baikal* and the *Angara*.

With the outbreak of the war, no further hesitations in construction were allowed. Blasting their way through the rocky spurs that close in on the water around the lake's southeastern end, the engineers threaded the line through thirty-nine tunnels from Baikal to Kultuk. On September 25, almost seven months after the beginning of the war, the loop was done.

Meanwhile, throughout the line, an army of workers laid heavier rails and ballast in critical sectors, modified curves and inclines, added two hundred sidings, and rerouted track. Supplementary rolling stock was rounded up from other parts of the empire, and new locomotives were being produced at record speed. By March 1905, 300,000 men had already been carried by rail to the front, and 400,000 more were on the way, which swung the preponderance of land forces in Russia's favor. As the war entered its second year, Russia's solitary advantage, its vast manpower reserve, began to be felt, as reinforcements continued to arrive at the front.

But command of the sea had been won by the Japanese at the outset, and in a series of hard-fought engagements in southern Manchuria the Japanese had been victorious, preeminently in the capture of Port

Arthur in January 1905. Finally, in May, Russian naval reinforcements, dispatched all the way from the Baltic, were annihilated by Admiral Togo in the Battle of Tsushima Strait.

The Japanese, however, feared an exhausting war of attrition, and in response to their secret request, President Theodore Roosevelt arranged a peace conference between the belligerents at Portsmouth, New Hampshire. To strengthen their bargaining position before the conference convened, the Japanese attacked and occupied Sakhalin Island in July, as most of the free settlers and part of the small improvised convict army fled. The tsar now summoned Witte, whom he was constrained with some humiliation to appoint head of the Russian delegation. Witte proved the man of the hour. In a treaty signed on September 5, 1905, Russia acknowledged a paramount Japanese interest in Korea, ceded to Japan its lease of the Liaotung Peninsula and the southern half of Sakhalin Island, but retained its position in northern Manchuria as the dominant power. Although Russia lost, with the Liaotung Peninsula, the branch lines to Port Arthur and Dalny, Witte had salvaged for Russia the rest of the Chinese Eastern, and against all odds, had overcome Japan's insistence on an indemnity. International opinion regarded it as a stunning diplomatic victory. *The New York Times* wrote: "A nation hopelessly beaten in every battle of the war, one army captured and another overwhelmingly routed, with a navy swept from the seas, dictated her own terms to the victors."

In the aftermath of the Russo-Japanese War, the two powers reconciled. In opposing the Open Door policy of the United States, both realized that there was more to be gained through collaboration, and through a series of secret agreements (in 1907, 1910, and 1912) they created two exclusive spheres of influence in China north of the Great Wall—the Russian sphere comprising northern Manchuria, Outer Mongolia, and Sinkiang, the Japanese southern Manchuria and Inner Mongolia. Without Russian opposition, Japan in 1910 also annexed the prize for which it had fought—Korea.

In the ensuing years, the Russians and Japanese also developed their respective halves of Sakhalin Island—its fisheries, forests, coal and oil reserves—although the Japanese worked with more efficiency and zeal. In the north, the Russians faced a daunting task of reconstruction, with a population that had dwindled from 40,000 to 7,000 as a result of the war. The island's penal colony was abolished in April 1906, forty-

seven years after its founding, but Sakhalin still suffered from its reputation, so that it wasn't until the outbreak of World War I, when the
government announced that its inhabitants would be exempt from
military service, that over fifteen thousand prospective colonists suddenly rushed across Siberia to settle there. Meanwhile, the demise of
the Manchu Dynasty in 1912 facilitated Russian domination of Outer
Mongolia, whose people were kindred to the Buryats, and which was
physically separated from China proper by the Gobi Desert. At Russian
insistence, China granted Outer Mongolia autonomy, thus preparing
the way for its later emergence as a satellite of the Soviet state.

Yet between rival powers cooperation seldom, if ever, leads to genuine trust. Russia remained wary of Japan's ultimate intentions, and
because the Chinese Eastern (now partly under Japanese control) lost
its value as a military road, the government revived its plans for an
Amur line, along a route somewhat to the north of where it had originally been drawn. Aside from helping to provoke a disastrous war, the
Chinese Eastern Railway had (as its original critics predicted) merely
helped develop a territory Russia did not truly own. As a result, it had
contributed to the impoverishment of the Amur region by diverting its
fledgling river traffic (as well as new colonists) to Manchuria. Vladivostok had also atrophied as a port, since its military and commercial
functions had been transferred to Port Arthur and Dalny. One visitor
to the lower Amur reported that the typical settlement there consisted
of "a collection of dilapidated log huts, one or two decent houses
belonging to officials, a handful of filthy-looking skin-clad natives, and
some mangy dogs and attenuated pigs wallowing in the mire." In short,
the welfare of a Russian province had been sacrificed to that of a
Chinese, and the government now sought through the Amur Railroad
to redirect Russian enterprise and capital back to the Russian Far East.

Inevitably, the line also became part of a new overall defensive
strategy for the region, which included the taming of the wilderness
through colonization, the expansion of the Pacific Fleet, construction
of new military and naval bases, and the fortification of the harbors at
Vladivostok and Nikolayevsk.

Construction began in the spring of 1908, along a route that ran
from a junction near Sretensk in an irregular arc to Khabarovsk
through a forbidding, unpopulated wilderness of mountains, forests,
bogs, and marshy plains. The supply roads the workers built became

the highways of the region; the swamps they drained and the bogs they filled became its fields. Artesian wells were drilled in the permafrost; forest land was cleared. Rice and flour mills, sawmills, tanneries, soap, brick, cement, candle and match factories were established, along with railway shops and large shipping plants. Emigrants were moved down the Amur on huge rafts—a method found to be just as efficient and more economical than by steamer—built of rough-hewn logs, with a shed at either end for the accommodation of people and horses. Families had all their household goods and domestic animals on board, and upon reaching their destination, dismantled the raft and used its timber to build houses without delay. At Khabarovsk, a bridge nearly a mile and a half long was built—Russia's longest span.

Whereas the Trans-Siberian in its eastern stretches had relied heavily on the use of low-paid Chinese and Korean labor, Asians this time were deliberately excluded, as Russian laborers were brought in at great expense. This hastened the Russification of the area, although the roughnecks working the line were not the ideal colonizing sort. To maintain order, fourteen companies of troops were attached to the project to reinforce the railway guards.

Vladivostok again came into its own, refortified with massive masonry bulwarks, new heavy artillery, and a garrison of 80,000 men. About 120,000 more were stationed throughout Eastern Siberia. The small Cossack settlement of Sretensk became a booming railhead of ten thousand people; Chita grew from its wartime reputation as the favorite halting place for officers and troops on their way to Manchuria. Along the Ussuri line, villages were also "springing up like mushrooms," and soon became towns of considerable size.

Renovations extended down the line. Part of the Trans-Siberian was double-tracked, a branch line laid from Omsk to Tyumen, new warehouses and other storage facilities were built, and wooden bridges were gradually replaced by those of stone and steel. Gradients were also eased, and overall improvements made in the construction and maintenance of the track.

The government was so impressed with the result that it decided to try to lure international travelers to the Trans-Siberian with special, luxuriously appointed trains. These featured locomotives of the latest design, plushly furnished lounge and restaurant cars, where a piano, easy chairs, writing tables, a library, and board games could all be found, carpeted sleeping coupés, a gymnasium car equipped with dumbbells and a stationary bicycle, electric reading lights in each compartment (powered by a steam-driven dynamo in the baggage car), porcelain baths, a darkroom, and even a church car, or "ambulatory basilica," complete with priest, icons, and a little belfry on the roof.

Such a train was reproduced in amazing miniature (just over a foot long) in the workshop of Peter Carl Fabergé in 1900. The tiny locomotive that pulled the cars was gold and platinum, "with a ruby gleaming from its headlight," and started up with the turn of a gold key. More grandly, at the Paris Universal Exposition of 1900 a simulated State Express, as it was called, was displayed in the Palace of Russian Asia. Conceived as a kind of diorama of Siberia, the exhibit included photomurals of Siberian landscapes, a scale model of the icebreaker *Baikal*, "stuffed seals and polar bears perched precariously on papier-mâché icebergs," and "reindeer-drawn sledges with fur-clad dummies of Ostyak hunters beside them." Visitors were invited to dine in the restaurant cars, where they could behold a panorama of steppes, mountains, virgin forests, gold mines, churches, and towns sweeping past, courtesy of a mechanized rolling strip of painted canvas produced by set designers at the Paris Opera.

Oddly, the imaginary Trans-Siberian journey took the diner all the way to Peking (perhaps revealing Russia's ultimate ambitions), where a Chinese porter suddenly appeared to announce the end of the line.

In reality, these trains were never as luxurious as advertised, nor did they attract the hoped-for clientele. But the State Express won some admirers. In 1900 Annette Meakin, the first Englishwoman to travel across northern Asia to Japan by rail, found the private compartments quite comfortably furnished, and at dinner one evening was agreeably entertained by a tenor and a pianist. Another traveler, however, complained that in his train at least the piano served "primarily as a shelf for dirty dishes," and that the only porcelain tub he could find was in the baggage car, where it was used for the storage of ice, vegetables, and meat.

In his charge to Nicholas in 1891 as president of the Trans-Siberian Committee, Tsar Alexander III had exalted the railway as a project "to facilitate the peopling and industrial development of Siberia," and to bring "peace and enlightenment to the East." This theme was repeated in the railway's official *Guide,* which proclaimed it part of "the civilizing mission of the Russian government" and the vanguard of "Christianity in Asia." Although it might be wondered what the civilizing mission was of a country that had an illiteracy rate of 80 percent, the lowest standard of living of any nation in Europe, the highest infant mortality rate, and the greatest incidence of syphilis, drunkenness, famine, and epidemic disease, there is no doubt that at the time it was built, the railway itself seemed like "a rainbow joining West and East" and one of the wonders of the world. "Whether he looked on it from the political, the strategic or the economic point of view, nobody could deny," one historian remarked, "that the Trans-Siberian Railway had a certain greatness, a certain exotic nobility of conception, a touch, almost, of Jules Verne."

Upon the abolition of serfdom in 1861, many peasant families in the crowded central Russian provinces had set out for Siberia to establish larger homesteads, and to escape the recurrent famines that stalked the land. Before the coming of the railway, they had proceeded miserably on foot on an interminable journey beside horse-drawn carts loaded with all their worldly goods. Once in Siberia, land was plentiful and easily claimed, since large manorial or monastic estates were rare, and most of the land belonged to the Crown, which welcomed almost anyone willing to settle on it and turn it to some account. On the other hand, the migrants were pretty much left to shift for themselves. From 10 to 30 percent of them perished in an attempt to establish a new life, and a rather large proportion of the remainder eventually lost heart and returned home.

By the mid-1880s, the government had decided to intervene. To relieve the overpopulation of parts of European Russia and accelerate the colonization of Siberia's expanse of untamed land, it established a new and more generous typical family allotment of 140 acres, with tax breaks, an exemption from military service, and long-term interest-free loans to heighten the allure. But more needed to be done. Like exiles they belonged to the world of the forlorn, and en route at least camped in such conditions that typhus and other epidemics spread through their ranks. A large samovar was kept boiling at every station to provide them with hot water for tea, but otherwise they had to provide their own food. "The filth, the rags, the utter woe-begone aspect of the

Russian emigrant," wrote a contemporary American traveler, "is something inconceivable." Moreover, as the numbers increased geometri-
cally with each succeeding line of track, government supervision
became more urgent, as thousands were stranded at various wayside
stations or encampments, became vagrants, or died.

Beginning in 1893, the government instituted a crash program to
improve the transit facilities and entice the emigrants on their way. At
the major stations, hospitals, soup kitchens, heated barracks, laundries,
bathhouses, and other facilities were established where most of the
services were virtually free of charge. By 1898, mortality among migrants of all ages had been reduced tremendously, to perhaps 1 percent, from the 20 percent average of former days. Moreover, the
migrant fare was so low (originally ⅕ of a cent per mile, later less, with
children under ten traveling free) that for a handful of rubles a family
could travel halfway across Siberia.

For those hoping that Siberia would absorb Russia's surplus population, the traffic volume as far as Irkutsk initially exceeded all expectations. Some 275,000 immigrants crossed the Urals by rail in 1896 and
1897—mostly in seatless, fifth-class boxcars marked: "For twelve
horses or forty-three men." Indeed, even with increased government
assistance, the going was hard. One eyewitness recalled:

There were cars for families and cars for single men. The former
were simply stables on wheels. In them, three human generations—
grandparents, the man and his wife in their prime, the children—
and the population of their little farmyard back in Russia. Three cows
and half a dozen sheep lie in straw and knee deep filth, munching
hay and green stuff. Bales of hay and straw are stacked to the roof,
the home of the wandering fowls and turkeys and ducks. A couple of
big lean dogs crouch in a corner. . . . Goods and chattels are disposed
here and there, chairs are placed around the rude table, a lamp and
even a pair of religious prints hang on the wall. . . . The single men's
quarters are populated by an intimidating band of ruffians, bare-
headed, barefooted, shaggy bearded creatures with flat animal faces
and wild, bloodshot eyes, one's conception of a shipwrecked crew
after ten years on the desert island.

Some 3.5 million acres in the Barabinsk Steppe—"in summer, a
mosquito-infested jungle of reeds, sedge grass, and stagnant lakes and

ponds between Omsk and Novonikolayevsk"—was cleared and drained by the government; more arid areas were irrigated by canals.

In 1894, about two-thirds of the emigrants that year settled in Tomsk Province and most of the rest in the steppe region of Akmolinsk and Semipalatinsk. A few thousand others ventured east as far as Irkutsk, or embarked at the Black Sea port of Odessa for the Ussuri Valley by sea. By 1896, the valley of the Yenisey had also become popular, with many settling around Minusinsk and Kansk; and by 1900, others were prepared to brave an overland journey all the way to the Far East— formerly a two- to four-year trek by road, but by rail reduced to just a few weeks. Even so, to encourage settlement the government divided the area into 80-acre lots (about twice the size of the average homestead), with 20 percent of all the migrants who crossed the Urals in 1907 making the trip. In some cases the allotments were as much as 160 acres—equal to the generous norm established in America under the Homestead Act. By 1914, almost 2 million Russians had settled in the Far East, the majority in Transbaikalia, but over 300,000 in the Amur River Valley as well.

Altogether, up to 7 million peasants entered Siberia from 1823 to 1914, with 750,000 making the trip in 1908 alone. This mass migration over the Urals, as one historian has pointed out, was "one of the greatest such movements in history . . . surpassed only by the greatest of all historic time which brought 35 million people in a century from Europe across the Atlantic to the United States." The Trans-Siberian brought most of them in, and sustained them as well, with seed grain, food to tide them over until the harvest, implements, lumber for cabins on Siberia's great southern plains—in short, with all the supplies and materials they required to establish a new life.

Not only did the railway vastly increase the population, but it changed its complexion, as the proportion of Russians to other ethnic groups reached 86 percent. Economically, it encouraged specialization and facilitated the exchange of goods over large areas. The sudden accessibility of distant markets stimulated agriculture and dairy production, led to an expanded fishing industry on the Pacific Coast, and enabled innumerable cottage industries to thrive. It also helped to open the country to competition, which meant an end to long-standing monopolies exercised by Siberian merchants on some consumer goods, and a more rapid development of Siberian industry because the cost of importing machinery and equipment was no longer prohibitively high. Factories and workshops sprang up where none had existed before; new firms began to work rich mineral deposits, especially iron and coal. Millions of pounds of surplus grain from Siberia went for export, as did millions of pounds of surplus high-grade, clarified butter, which was a major Siberian industry even before the Trans-Siberian Railway was built. Danish settlers in Western Siberia introduced new and improved dairy methods, and the increased output soon led to special refrigerator cars and eventually complete butter trains. By 1900, there were more than one thousand dairies in operation, and in 1913 more than four thousand. By 1913 Siberian butter production had exceeded that of Australia and the Netherlands, and had begun to rival Denmark itself.

In short, the Trans-Siberian Railway dramatically transformed the entire area through which it passed, fostering agriculture and industry along the line, and effectively ending Siberia's colonial status by bringing Vladivostok to within ten days' journey of the capital. A vast new influx of settlers virtually doubled the population to 10 million in as many years; and after 1907, about a fifth of these settled in the Far East. In parts of Western Siberia (around Tomsk, for example) the population increased nine times. Meat, dairy, and grain production, and prodigious shipments of timber, minerals, and hides all helped bolster Russia's import and export trade, and in Moscow and St. Petersburg food from Siberia could be found on every plate.

Although Siberia remained rural (only about 12 percent of its population lived in towns) and its industry comparatively small (3.5 percent of the industrial population of the empire in 1908), some of this lag began to be made up by foreign investment. Large gold-mining companies were foreign-financed—by the British, primarily, but also the Germans, Belgians, and French—and the industrial expansion likewise attracted American capital, which participated in railway building and in the manufacture of trolleys, bridges, dry docks, and ships. The International Harvester Company supplied agricultural equipment of all types to Siberia; the Westinghouse Company made air brakes for Russian railway cars in a factory it had opened in Petrograd; the Singer Sewing Machine established itself in Krasnoyarsk and other Siberian railway towns. Parke Davis & Company and Victor Talking Machine were other companies that played a role in Siberian industry and trade.

· · ·

In 1905, Nicholas II was the only remaining monarch in Europe who did not share power to some degree with a parliament or other representative assembly. Article I of the Fundamental Laws of the Russian Empire declared his sway absolute, and (with the encouragement of his wife, Alexandra) Nicholas clung to medieval notions of his autocratic power. He was, in fact, far more medieval in his thinking than his grandfather, Alexander II, who (though only vaguely apprehending Russia's perilous future) had introduced tentative reforms "from above"—most notably, the abolition of serfdom in 1861 and the creation of *zemstva*, or locally elected provincial and county councils in the following year—which happily coincided with the beginnings of an industrial and commercial revolution.

But the abolition of serfdom did not emancipate the peasantry from its desperate poverty, while a new class of poor—the urban proletariat —emerged with Russia's burgeoning factories and mills. As for representative government, only nobles and bureaucrats were granted a voice, and then only in an advisory capacity, which bred some dissatisfaction even among society's most privileged coteries. The hopes raised by Alexander's initial reforms in any case faded as his own enthusiasm for modernization seemed to wane. Frustrated by his inability to relieve the exasperating state of domestic affairs, foreign policy adventures increasingly absorbed him, while day by day revolutionary organizations found a deepening soil in which to thrive. After his assassination, the tsardom under Alexander III had reverted to its age-old insular, Caesaro-papist form; "Nationalism," "Absolutism," and "Orthodoxy" were its talismanic words; the national and religious minorities of the empire felt the full weight of the imperial yoke.

Nicholas in turn did nothing to relieve the strain. Infatuated with the autocratic aura and legacy of his forebears, he made clear at the outset of his reign that he regarded popular aspirations for a voice in national policy as "senseless dreams." On this matter alone, perhaps, he and Witte saw eye to eye. "I am an enemy in principle—and I have been so since my youth—to any kind of constitutionalism, parliamentarism, or granting of any measure of political rights whatsoever to the people," Witte flatly declared. In Witte's adamant opinion, Alexander II's *zemstvo* reform of 1864, which had introduced the principle of representative self-government into Russia, was fundamentally at variance with the principle of autocracy, and would ultimately lead to anarchy.

In the 1890s, the first Marxist exiles arrived in Siberia. Lenin spent three years (1897–1900) in Eastern Siberia, at Krasnoyarsk and in the village of Slushenskoye, described by one writer as "a typical Siberian backwoods village, five hundred versts from the railway, with a tiny primary school and six pubs." At the end of 1903, Stalin was exiled to the tiny Buryat village of Novaya Uda.

The Russo-Japanese War had been intensely unpopular, and every new and costly defeat increased the popular rage. Anti-war demonstrations in St. Petersburg were echoed across the land. "Conditions in Russia are overshadowing the war," wrote *The New York Times* on June 6, 1905. "There is fear of revolution." Indeed, the "short victorious war" to stem its tide was proving ingloriously short and hastening the day. In Siberia, the discontent was perhaps even greater than elsewhere. It had borne the brunt of the costly and unsuccessful conflict, which had exposed it directly to attack, and in Central Siberia had led to famine, since food shipments normally meant for the interior had been diverted to the front. Inadvertently, the war had also fostered literacy in the countryside, as the demand for newspapers in the villages increased. Those who read the latest news could also read the latest revolutionary pamphlets, which often seemed to articulate their malaise.

With the war on their list of grievances, just three weeks after the fall of Port Arthur, on Sunday, January 9, 1905, columns of workers and their families, led by a priest and carrying placards, icons, and banners, marched in a peaceful protest to the Winter Palace in St. Petersburg to present a petition to the tsar. A phalanx of troops moved to cut them off, ordering the assembly to disperse. When the marchers refused, they fired point blank into the crowd. On "Bloody Sunday" (as it came to be known), hundreds were killed and wounded; and the day marked the beginning of the Revolution of 1905. In the following weeks disorders spread through the empire, with riots, strikes, and a mutiny on the *Potemkin*, the flagship of the Black Sea Fleet. Socialist Revolutionary assassins also killed Grand Duke Sergey and Count Shuvalov, the military governor of Moscow.

Russia's humiliating defeat in the war heightened the crisis. There were mutinies by troops returning along the Trans-Siberian, and the railway repair shops became hotbeds of unrest. In the tumult, Witte's relative triumph over the Japanese at Portsmouth, New Hampshire, was scarcely remarked. Toward the end of October all the main Russian cities were paralyzed by a general strike. Junction towns became the principal seats of revolutionary ferment. Propaganda leaflets appeared in profusion; there were strikes and demonstrations at Tomsk, Omsk, Krasnoyarsk, Irkutsk, Chita, and elsewhere; many protesters were shot by government troops. Peasant uprisings occurred in most of the southern regions of Siberia. In December, open revolt broke out in Moscow.

A few years before, Marxist organizations had been formed in various Siberian cities and had begun to coordinate their activities. Although rival ideologies emerged, Siberian Marxists as a whole were scornful of the Social Democratic Party's split into Bolshevik and Menshevik, and to some degree their relative isolation had kept them pure. They had sent delegates to both the Bolshevik Third Party Congress in London, and its Menshevik counterpart in Geneva, but within their own ranks at least affirmed their essential solidarity. Together, they worked to undermine the tsarist regime.

In response to all this turmoil, Nicholas vacillated, as was his wont. In March 1905, he issued a manifesto reaffirming the autocracy, but this went over so badly that in August he felt obliged to announce the eventual formation of a parliament—though not on the basis of universal suffrage. By October, soviets (or councils of workers) had begun to spread from St. Petersburg to other villages and towns, including Krasnoyarsk and Chita. On October 17, as a device for buying time, the tsar issued a proclamation granting broad constitutional rights to the people and establishing a representative legislature, or Duma, after the fashion of a constitutional monarchy. This shrewd maneuver (concocted by Witte) won over the professional middle class and left the more radical demands of the soviets without broad support. Their call for a general strike failed and many ringleaders were arrested. A few months later, in January 1906, Nicholas felt secure enough to revise his manifesto in such a way as to emasculate its original thrust, giving him the power to dissolve the Duma at will. The First Duma, in fact, was quickly dismissed; as was the Second, as arrests, secret trials, and banishments resumed in greater volume than before.

In 1906, Pyotr Stolypin was appointed Minister of the Interior and then prime minister, a post he held until 1911, when he was assassinated at the opera. During his tenure, he sought to use agrarian reform as a buffer against revolution by abolishing communal land tenure and by subsidies to peasants from the Peasants' Land Bank. His goal was "to make every peasant a proprietor and give him the chance to work quietly on his own land, for himself." To relieve the land hunger in European Russia, he encouraged internal colonization by further migration to Siberia. Conditions in Siberia favored the strong. "Throughout the Empire," writes one historian, "peasant agriculture was being transformed into independent farming, and that economic change was accompanied by social consequences. A thaw was attacking the frozen agricultural system of communal tenure and extensive cultivation, as well as the apparent moral inertia of the Russian village. Siberia was leading the way." Stolypin hoped that those peasants who could not make a go of it would be absorbed by the developing industry.

In the cities, the government attempted to counteract the Labor movement by instituting "legal" trade unions, each controlled by a government representative and infiltrated by the secret police. These for a while served their purpose of pacifying discontent by engendering the hope of some redress of workers' grievances; at the same time they were used to identify agitators, who were deported by administrative order to Siberia or other outlying provinces of the empire. A number of future Bolshevik leaders—among them Ordzhonikidze, Frunze, Dzerzhinsky, Sverdlov, and Kuibyshev—were also exiled to Siberia at this time, and were scattered from the Ob to the Yenisey to the province of Yakutsk.

Although Trotsky later described the Revolution of 1905 as "a dress rehearsal for 1917," a world of political development (or regression) was to take place in the intervening years.

The unrest ebbed and flowed. On November 28, 1910, Yegor Sazonov (the assassin of Plehve) committed suicide in the men's prison of Gorni Serentui to protest the conditions of his incarceration. When his suicide became known, mass demonstrations took place in nearly every city of Russia. In Moscow, thirty thousand students marched. In January 1912, workers at the Lena goldfields, the site of vast gold-dredging operations, staged a protest against conditions at the mines. Troops were sent in, and on April 4, 1912, the demands of the strikers were met with volleys of rifle fire that left 270 miners dead and another

250 wounded. This massacre inspired a tidal wave of sympathy strikes. There were also peasant uprisings, also crushed by soldiers, in most of the southern regions of Siberia. At a conference in Prague in the same year, the Social Democratic Party confirmed its split into Bolshevik and Menshevik. Two years later, "the lights went out all over Europe" and the entire continent was engulfed in World War I.

Russia's entry into the war (a "just war," it seemed, not an autocratic adventure) briefly rallied the nation behind the tsar, and gave the government a short reprieve. But by the end of 1916 the initial enthusiasm had disappeared with the realities of the carnage and was completely buried along with Russia's 5 million dead. In Siberia, all of the regular troops stationed in the Far East had been sent to the European front, and most of the Siberian Cossacks had left their farms. Simple peasants too were mobilized, and the industrial workers in the towns were called up. Farms lay idle, factories were shut down. But up to the very end, Nicholas refused to cooperate with the reconstituted Duma, and assumed personal command of the armed forces over the vehement objections of his cabinet. The reins of civil government were surrendered to his wife Alexandra, whose judgment was perversely guided by Grigory Rasputin, a mystic Siberian peasant and self-styled *starets,* or holy man, from Tyumen, whose ability to ease the hemophilia of the tsarevich Alexis placed her under his power. State and ecclesiastical officials were appointed or dismissed according to his whim, and domestic policy was narrowly shaped to protect his own exalted position in the imperial household. Even military affairs received some inflection through his intuitive advice (not always, by the way, inferior to that of the tsar's); but no private scandal or public mistrust could shake Alexandra's faith in him, and toward the end of 1916 he was murdered at a banquet by a conservative clique. A few weeks later the autocracy itself was swept away in the tide of revolution.

PART
FOUR

—

Overleaf: Ainu man.

15

THE RED AND THE WHITE

THROUGHOUT the land, war weariness, resentment against the corruption of the imperial court, the food shortages in Petrograd, and all the abiding, intractable problems of the realm which seemed destined to sustain unrest even in more pacific times led to escalations in the violence. Bread marches began in the capital on February 23, 1917, and three days later a mutiny took place in the Fourth Company of the Pavlovsky Regiment of the Imperial Guard. Within twenty-four hours thirty thousand soldiers had gone over to the side of the demonstrators and some clashed with the mounted police. On March 2, Nicholas abdicated, and on the 8th he was arrested at his general headquarters at Mogilev.

A Provisional Government was immediately set up under Prince Georgy Lvov, with a Socialist, Aleksandr Kerensky, as Minister of Justice; it announced plans for the election of a fully democratic Constituent Assembly as well as various reforms. But the Provisional Government also affirmed its intention to remain in the war. Most Russians in fact were reluctant to unilaterally desert the Allied cause, and in general the Petrograd Soviet of Workers' and Soldiers' Deputies, a revolutionary committee with broad popular support, cooperated with the new regime.

Siberian Marxists were in the forefront of these developments. They favored a broad-based tolerance of diverging opinion, accepted traditional ideas of national defense, and hoped to unify "all the vital forces in the country," not excluding the bourgeosie. It was in Siberia, in fact, that the groundwork was laid for the Menshevik–Socialist Revolutionary coalition that dominated the Petrograd Soviet in 1917—and which might have led the Soviet Union down a completely different road.

The Provisional Government, however, failed to preserve law and order and even basic services within the empire, and proved unable to lead the Russian armies to victory against the Central Powers. Nor could it arrest the economy's decline. The transportation system had almost completely broken down, and the Trans-Siberian was in such a decrepit state that it was said that it would require three hundred ships over the course of six months to ferry all the rolling stock and equipment needed from across the seas to bring the line back up to standard.

Meanwhile, in April 1917, the German high command granted Lenin safe passage in a sealed train through Germany in the hope, as Winston Churchill expressed it, that he would enter Russia like a "virus" and undermine its will to remain in the war. Upon arrival, he found that the new workers' soviets by and large supported the Provisional Government—"the bourgeois constituent assembly," as Lenin saw it—and he tried to shake their allegiance by simple emotional slogans like "All Power to the Soviets" and "Bread, Land, and Peace." As Russia's losses at the front continued to mount, the army's morale deteriorated, industry foundered, unharvested crops remained standing in the fields. The government reshuffled its cabinet and brought more Socialists in. Kerensky emerged as prime minister, but faced a Bolshevik attempt to topple him in July. Lenin, denounced as a German spy, fled to Finland, but by summer's end had returned, incognito, to urge the revolution on. On October 25, his adherents seized strategic locations—railroad stations, bridges, telephones, and so on—throughout the capital, stormed the Winter Palace, arrested members of the Provisional Government, and installed Lenin at the helm.

In power, the Bolsheviks acted with dispatch. They nationalized banks, turned factories and other industrial enterprises over to the workers, introduced price regulations, and expropriated large estates. Soviet power was rapidly extended across the Eurasian landmass with relatively little resistance, but at the moment of their triumph, the Bolsheviks were still very much a minority party in the land. In the elections to the Constituent Assembly in November, in fact, they won only 25 percent of the seats, and both the Socialist Revolutionaries and the Mensheviks (the majority of the left) distrusted the despotic presumptions of the professional revolutionary vanguard. Their mistrust was not misplaced. To consolidate his hold on the government—and to "combat counterrevolution and sabotage"—almost the first act of Lenin's regime was to dismiss the Constituent Assembly and establish the Secret Police.

The "dictatorship of the proletariat" had begun.

On the international stage, the Bolsheviks had also managed to antagonize the Allies. The new government canceled its foreign debt, unilaterally withdrew from the war, and signed the Treaty of Brest-Litovsk in March 1918 with Germany, yielding up, in return for peace, the Baltic states, Byelorussia, the Crimea, and the populous and industrially developed Ukraine. That promised to breathe new life into Germany's war machine.

Indeed, Russia's early contribution to the Allied cause had been tremendous, and by forcing the Central Powers to divert considerable forces from the Western Front, had indirectly saved Paris, prevented German victories at Verdun and Ypres (as General Von Hindenburg acknowledged in his memoirs), and helped win the Battle of the Marne. In 1917, its great Eastern Front extended from the Baltic through Romania all the way to the Black Sea, tying up from 2 to 3 million troops of the Central Powers. The Treaty of Brest-Litovsk allowed forty German divisions to roll westward as part of the last great German offensive, and the looming disaster faced by the Allies at this juncture brought a reluctant United States more forcefully into the war.

In Siberia, the turmoil leading up to and following the October Revolution had produced a flood of new refugees—some of them ordinary people seeking a haven, others linked to a cause: members of the privileged or educated classes, army officers, moderate Socialists, anti-Communist revolutionaries, conservatives, right-wing extremists, anarchists, Cossacks, and counterrevolutionaries of every stripe. There were reactionary legitimists, who hoped for the restoration, constitutional monarchists willing to accept any figurehead of adequate pedigree, and those who believed that only a military dictatorship could rescue Russia from the morass into which it had sunk. Secret officers' organizations existed in all the major cities, and intrigue hovered over every encounter in the street. Although Lenin had once thought to locate his fledgling regime behind the Urals (when negotiations with the Germans at Brest-Litovsk had stalled—"from the borders of our Uralo–Kuznetsk Republic," he had declared, "we will spread out again and return to Moscow and Petersburg"), Siberia in general was not fertile ground for the Reds. The area had a very small industrial proletariat, and only a few peasants who were desperately poor. Most peasants—"well-fed, solid, and successful," as Lenin himself had noted—in any case were of no particular political persuasion, and in the cities democratic socialism and a lingering movement for Siberian autonomy were entwined.

In August 1917, even before the October coup, a coalition of Mensheviks, Socialist Revolutionaries, and others opposed to Bolshevism had come together in Tomsk as the First Siberian Congress and voted for autonomy. It adopted as its banner a green and white flag, representing the forests and snows of Siberia, and sent delegates to Kiev where another regional government was taking shape. Two months later, the Congress reconvened to lay the groundwork for the creation of a provisional government for Siberia along parliamentary lines. Bolshevik agents, however, broke up the governing committee; subsequently its members regrouped as the Provisional Government of Autonomous Siberia and transferred from Tomsk to Harbin in Manchuria, where they set up their headquarters in a railroad car. In the elections to the Constituent Assembly, moreover, the Bolsheviks had done less well in Siberia than elsewhere, receiving only 10 percent of the vote (and just 20 percent in the Urals), as compared to their 25 percent showing overall. An anti-Bolshevik government was formed by the Committee of Members of the Constituent Assembly at Samara on the Volga on June 8, 1918; another, the Provisional Siberian Government, in Omsk at the end of June. The former was dominated by the Socialist Revolutionaries; the latter by much more conservative factions. In the Far East, in addition to the Provisional Government of Autonomous Siberia, General Horvath, the manager of the Chinese Eastern Railway, tried to establish the nucleus of a conservative administration based in Manchuria.

The governments at Samara and Omsk jockeyed for jurisdiction over the Urals, and engaged in a minor customs war, with Omsk refusing to

ship grain westward and Samara blocking the movement of manufactured goods to the east. But the future of the White (or anti-Bolshevik)
movement as it developed in Siberia was principally to depend on one
wholly unforeseen event.

This was the uprising of the Czechoslovak Corps at the end of May
1918. And it marked the beginning of the Russian Civil War. The Corps,
or Legion, was composed of approximately forty-five thousand Czechoslovak ex-prisoners of war who, at the time of the October coup, had
been fighting for the Allies on the Eastern Front. After that front was
abandoned, the French government and the Czechoslovak National
Council, led by Thomas Masaryk, had arranged to evacuate these men
from the Ukraine and dispatch them to the battlefront in France. In so
doing, Masaryk hoped to win Allied recognition for the establishment
of a new Czechoslovak state. Since German battle-lines prevented the
Corps from proceeding overland, it was decided to send it halfway
around the world by sea from Vladivostok through the Panama Canal.
The Soviets (as the Communists now called themselves) agreed to
provide safe passage through Siberia, provided the Czechs surrendered most of their arms at Penza, a town along the route. Joseph
Stalin telegraphed the Czech National Council in Paris: "The Czechoslovaks will travel not as fighting units, but as groups of free citizens,
who carry with them a specified number of weapons for defense
against counterrevolutionary attacks."

Toward the end of March 1918, the first of eighty trainloads departed eastward. Twelve thousand men reached Vladivostok by mid-
May (fifty-seven days after setting out), but the greater part of the Corps
was strung out in groups at broad intervals along the Trans-Siberian
line. Progress had been slow, with many inexplicable delays, and misgivings began to arise about the way in which the Corps had been split
up. Meanwhile, in consultation with War Commissar Leon Trotsky, the
Supreme Allied War Council had decided to more expeditiously evacuate the westernmost units through Archangel, thus dispersing the
Corps to an even greater degree. The Czechs (attributing the idea to
the Bolsheviks) suspected it as a scheme to further divide them, with
the most malevolent aims. Lenin had made almost every imaginable
concession to the Central Powers in the Treaty of Brest-Litovsk, and
among the Czechs the fear grew that they were being disarmed as a
prelude to being handed over to the German government.

The Bolsheviks, of course, had their own apprehensions, and had delayed the Czech anabasis for fear that, among other things, the Corps might be used in an Allied conspiracy with the counterrevolutionaries to seize Siberia. The Czechs had maintained their discipline as a fighting force while the rest of the Russian Army was in disarray, and already in early April 1918 a small Japanese naval contingent had landed at Vladivostok (allegedly to protect the Japanese community there), and counterrevolutionary (or "White") forces based in Manchuria had begun to operate in the Far East. Although Masaryk himself had originally insisted that the Corps not be used in Russia's internal conflicts, by the time it got to Penza, many Czechs had begun to hide their arms.

"Under these circumstances," writes one historian, "a small incident led to big consequences." On May 14 (about the time the first Czech train was pulling into Vladivostok), a westbound convoy of released Austrian and Hungarian prisoners (to be repatriated under the terms of the Treaty of Brest-Litovsk) paused opposite a trainload of restless Czechs at Chelyabinsk in the foothills of the Urals. Insults were furiously exchanged, and as the westbound train began to leave the station, one of the Hungarians hurled a piece of cast iron across the tracks, knocking a Czech soldier to the ground. His enraged companions boarded the train and lynched the culprit on the spot. The local Bolsheviks intervened to arrest the vigilantes, but were in turn disarmed by the other legionnaires, who occupied the station, capturing two thousand Red Guards almost without a fight. The skirmish also yielded a stockpile of weapons, including twelve thousand rifles and thirty pieces of light artillery.

Moscow overreacted and (in an uncoded telegram sent by Trotsky) ordered the local soviets to disarm the Czechs, remove them from their trains, and disband them as a corps. He added, rather intemperately, that any Czech found with a weapon in his hands should be shot. The Czechs intercepted this message at the telegraph office at Chelyabinsk, and concluded that their only chance to escape entrapment and slaughter was to turn their exodus into an expeditionary campaign. They relayed their intention to their compatriots, and before long the Corps had seized control of the Trans-Siberian line. Fighting their way eastwards, they routed any Bolshevik garrisons that tried to stop them, and within a few weeks had taken several major Western Siberian towns—Novonikolayevsk on the 26th, Penza on the 29th, Tomsk on the 31st. Omsk fell at the beginning of June, and Krasnoyarsk on the 20th. The munitions stockpiled at Krasnoyarsk furnished them with new pistols, rifles, hand grenades, light artillery, and even an armored train.

By the end of the month the Bolshevik government in Vladivostok had also been overthrown. Some resistance was met at Barnaul, and there was especially heavy fighting around Lake Baikal, centered on the thirty-nine railroad tunnels bored through the rugged escarpments that curve along its southern shore. The Bolsheviks tried to demolish the tunnels with a trainload of explosives, but the Czechs anticipated their strategem and blew the train up. On Lake Baikal, heavy log rafts mounted with guns also defeated Bolshevik armed steamers, and elsewhere the Reds proved unable to rally a strong defense. An armored train and a small excursion steamer converted by the Czechs into a gunboat helped take Irkutsk in mid-July; the Soviet government for Siberia retreated to Chita. Meanwhile the Czechs in Vladivostok had marched westward to link up with units pushing eastward from Irkutsk, and those on the Volga and at Chelyabinsk had joined to advance on Yekaterinburg, where the imperial family was being held. Their threat to this stronghold probably hastened the family's massacre on July 11, before the Reds withdrew to the west. Yekaterinburg fell to the Whites on July 25, and a fortnight later the Legion helped to take Kazan, where they captured the Imperial Gold Reserve, valued at more than $330 million. Ironically, this fund had originally been evacuated from Petrograd to Samara for safekeeping, and from there (when Samara was about to fall to the Czechs) to Kazan by barge.

By mid-September all of Siberia was White, and Red loyalists had dispersed into the mountains and forests to form partisan bands.

Lenin was convinced that the Allies had colluded in the Czechoslovak mutiny; and Trotsky declared, "Here' was a malicious, precisely worked out plan." Their theory gained credibility when (as if in reward for the Legion's actions) France promptly recognized an independent Czechoslovak Republic on June 30, followed by Great Britain, the United States, and Japan. The Soviets also knew that Allied warships had gathered at Vladivostok, ostensibly to guard the huge stockpiles of war materiel assembled there for transshipment to the Eastern Front, yet no troopships to evacuate the Czechs had ever arrived. They therefore interpreted the Czech revolt as part of a larger design, in which Vladivostok was to serve as a supply depot for an interventionist campaign.

And that, in fact, is what it became.

The temptation to intervene was considerable. Munitions, rifles, armored vehicles, truck wheels, barbed wire, field guns, rubber from Sumatra, harvesting machinery, lathes, ship and airplane parts, rope from the Philippines, jute from India, and even sugar from Cuba and wine from France had been laid up by the Allies for the war effort, not only at Vladivostok but at Archangel and Murmansk. There was genuine concern that some of it might find its way into German hands; partly to prevent this, a company of British Royal Marines had landed in Murmansk at the beginning of March. Then, on April 5, the Japanese began landing at Vladivostok, followed by troops of other powers. Schemes to repossess these stores, using a more or less token force, began to give way to others designed not only to rescue the Czechs but to punish the Bolsheviks and reopen the Eastern Front. The British (especially War Secretary Winston Churchill) were the most ardent advocates of intervention, and it was even suggested that a joint Allied expedition be sent across the whole of Siberia to fight the Germans in the Ukraine.

President Woodrow Wilson regarded the scheme as impractical, which of course it was, but by June 1918 the Siberian question had begun to cost him sleep. Loath to involve America in the growing Civil War, Wilson confided to an aide: "I have been sweating blood over the question what is right and feasible to do in Russia. But it goes to pieces like quicksilver under my touch." Finally, he evolved the desired formula and embodied it in a document which he tapped out on his own typewriter, and which became known as the *Aide-Mémoire*. This stated the intention of the United States to intervene with the rest of the Allies militarily, but only "to steady any efforts at self-government or self-defense in which the Russians themselves may be willing to accept assistance." And he called upon the others to forswear "any interference of any kind with the political sovereignty of Russia, any intervention in her internal affairs, or any impairment of her territorial integrity either now or hereafter." Although he suggested Japan send troops not in excess of the seven thousand America was prepared to commit, the Japanese volunteered to send a good many more than that, and did. For they intended to do everything the Americans had forsworn.

Secret agreements had already been signed between Japan and China in mid-May, which virtually allowed the Japanese to occupy northern Manchuria; the northern half of Sakhalin Island, Vladivostok, and other coastal strips also tempted them to wider imperialistic designs. On August 2, they landed two more divisions at Vladivostok, occupied Khabarovsk, and in October poured tens of thousands of troops into Manchuria, the Amur and Ussuri river valleys, and the Transbaikal. As justification for this beyond the official Allied mandate, they argued (rather fantastically) that since Eastern Siberia was adjacent to Manchuria and Inner Mongolia, which in turn were contiguous to Korea, they were therefore all "in very close and special relation to Japan's national defense and her economic existence." Meanwhile, a French colonial battalion of 1,100 from Indochina had also disembarked at Vladivostok, followed by two American infantry regiments on August 16 from the Philippines. By August 21, Japan had brought the whole of the Chinese Eastern Railway under its control. By the end of September, in a campaign that would eventually include 14 nations, the Allies had 44,000 men in the Far East, and by the end of October over 125,000, of which 75,000 or more were Japanese.

The American force was commanded by Major General William S. Graves, a West Point graduate who had served on the Mexican border and in the Philippines, and in Washington, D.C., as Secretary of the General Staff. He was an educated and highly trained officer, but was given little official guidance as to American aims. After having carefully read the government's studied declaration of neutrality, he later recalled, "feeling that I understood the policy, I went to bed, but I could not sleep; I kept wondering what other nations were doing and why I was not given some information about what was going on in Siberia." His sendoff did little to clarify the case. In a memorandum given to him in the course of a ten-minute briefing held in a room at the Kansas City railway station, Secretary of War Newton D. Baker had warned: "Watch your step; you will be walking on eggs loaded with dynamite. God bless you and goodbye!" All Graves had to go on was, as Baker later acknowledged, the vaguest of imperatives, namely, not to "create situations demanding impossible military exertions on the part of Allies and particularly of the United States, and involve our country in complications of the most unfortunate kind." Graves steered a resolutely neutral course, to the chagrin of the Whites and even the other, far more partisan Allied commanders, while his own State Department (influenced by Churchill) tried to have him replaced. In the whole sad debacle, he may have been the only honorable man.

Aside from the war materiel stockpiled there, Vladivostok—"Russia's back door"—formed a natural stronghold for the Allied troops. Before the revolution, the port had been steadily strengthened by fortifications and scores of great cannon mounted on concrete blocks set upon the crests of the hills that half-encircled the town. Caverns and vaulted tunnels linked these emplacements, and huge underground shelters carved out of solid rock protected the stores of powder and shell. Near-impregnable quarters for the gunners had also been dug into the sides of the hills.

Meanwhile, the intervention elsewhere had become more substantial: the British sent troops into the Caucasus and Transcaucasia; the French landed at the port of Odessa on the Black Sea. With the Soviet regime at bay, counterrevolutionary armies arose, often with foreign backing, to challenge its rule: in southern Russia, under Anton Denikin, whose power was based in the northern Caucasus and the Ukraine; in the west, under Nikolay Yudenich, based in Estonia; in the north, under Yevgeny Miller, based in Archangel; and in the east, in Siberia. At the same time, the Bolshevik regime showed signs of destroying itself from within. Its new economic policy of "War Communism," in which the state took over all means of distribution and production, had severely restricted private ownership and trade, and had begun to militarize the labor force, as citizens were assigned to compulsory labor gangs. The economic life of the country rapidly declined, there were uprisings in the twenty central provinces which the Bolsheviks controlled, and the anxiety aroused by the intervention had led to paranoid repressions and mass executions that from June 1918 to the end of the Civil War killed an average of one thousand people a month.

As the anti-Bolshevik campaigns merged with the greater war against the Central Powers (the Bolsheviks being viewed as de facto German agents), the early Czech escapades, when seen against the stalemate on the Western Front, had "the glamor of a fairy tale." At one time or another, the Czechs controlled almost two hundred trains, which they converted into rolling citadels. Some of the cars were reinforced by wooden baulks and iron plate, were buttressed by sandbags banked along their sides, and had circular steel gun turrets as well as machine guns bristling through embrasures. A flatcar with artillery anchored on a concrete base was attached to the front of the train (preceding the locomotive), both to protect it and to cover operations of the Czech brigades.

A large number of the legionnaires were men of education and ability—doctors, lawyers, poets, civil engineers—who could build or repair roads, tracks, and bridges, prepare aspirin and other medicaments for the sick or wounded, and meet various special needs. They maintained (and in some cases reconstructed) their own trains, set up an itinerant bank and a postal service that ran from Omsk all the way to Vladivostok, and even printed their own stamps. They published a military newsletter, established cigarette and soap factories, mobile bakeries, laundries, and canteens. To keep up their spirits, they organized musicales and painted their boxcar quarters with colorful, nostalgic scenes evoking their homeland. About 1,600 of them married Russian girls and "carried them along through all the subsequent campaigns" and thereafter home to some Czechoslovak farm or town.

Three months after the Czechoslovak uprising began, representatives of the two anti-Bolshevik governments based at Samara and Omsk met at Chelyabinsk and agreed to call an "all-Russian" conference. The conference met in Ufa, halfway between the Urals and the Volga, in mid-September, and settled upon a coalition government of sorts seated at Omsk that immediately took possession of the Imperial Gold Reserve captured at Kazan. Overall, its five-man Directory was made up of men of moderate left-wing views, but the compromise lasted eight weeks—from September 23 until November 18. On the 18th, it was overthrown in a *coup d'état* when Admiral Aleksandr Kolchak, "a small, highstrung, and humorless former commander-in-chief of the Black Sea Fleet," proclaimed himself "Supreme Ruler of Russia" and assumed dictatorial powers.

A vice admiral in the Russian Navy, Kolchak was familiar with the Siberian Arctic (where he had taken part as a young staff officer in naval explorations to Novaya Zemlya, the Taimyr Peninsula, and the New Siberian Islands), and had shown heroism in both the Russo-Japanese and First World wars. His stewardship of the Black Sea Fleet had lasted from August 1916 to June 1917, but unwilling to acknowledge the authority of the fleet committees after the tsar's abdication, had thrown his sword overboard at a mass meeting on the deck of his flagship, to protest the democratization of the command. Something of an Anglophile, Kolchak had both personal and professional ties to the British military and business establishment, and at the time the Bolsheviks took power, he was on a special mission to the United States, where he had met with President Wilson and was consulted about a planned Allied attack on the Dardanelles. From the United States, he had gone directly to Harbin in Manchuria, where he conferred with General Horvath, administrator of the railway zone. The two then traveled together to a conference in Peking, called at the end of April by the Russian Minister (and attended by Allied representatives) to help plot an anti-Bolshevik regime. The original Allied plan had evidently been to make the French General Maurice Janin the commander of all forces, Russian and foreign alike, in Siberia. But doubting that Russians would rally to a foreign officer, Janin was restricted to an advisory role (assuming technical command of the Czechs), and Kolchak emerged in his place.

Returning through Manchuria, he had been brought to Omsk in the private car of the head of the British military mission, General Alfred Knox, in mid-October, and after serving for fourteen days as Minister of War in the new coalition government, took the reins of power forcibly into his own hands. "I considered it to be my duty," he afterwards explained, "as one of the representatives of the former Government, to fulfil my obligation to the Allies; that the obligations which Russia had assumed to the Allies were my own obligations also." In an appeal to the population, Kolchak briefly summed up his program of action thus: "I set as my main objective the creation of an efficient army, victory over Bolshevism and the establishment of law and order, so that the people may choose the form of government which it desires without obstruction and realize the great ideas of liberty which are now proclaimed in the whole world."

He also agreed to reassume Russia's prewar debt.

Omsk, as the capital of the new regime, had much to recommend it. It was the center of navigation on the Ob–Irtysh river system, a Trans-Siberian junction, and had extensive railroad and machine shops, enormous barracks, and several good military hospitals. But it had nothing around it to compare to the industrial heartland over which the Soviets still ruled. "The thought kept running through my head," one Czech officer recalled,

how lonely and how dreary was the stage which Kolchak had selected for his empire-building. In the midst of this treeless steppe, six feet deep with snow in winter, windblown and brown in summer, when the only break in the endless monotony is an occasional horse-shaped cluster of Turkish yurts, Omsk is cut off from civilization. This is merely accentuated by the thin steel ribbon of the Trans-Siberian. The log huts on every hand and the unpaved street down which gallop Mongols on unclipped ponies, bumping into caravans of camels, heighten the impression of the frontier.

By contrast, the Reds had the advantage of interior communications and a growing spirit of national resistance against invaders given to them by the policy of the Allies. Indeed, the collapse of Germany and the end of World War I in November 1918 (coincident with the Omsk coup) eliminated the original excuse for intervention, which now assumed an avowedly counterrevolutionary aim. President Wilson, uncomfortably aware that his promise not to become involved in Russia's internal affairs was now automatically contradicted by the presence of American troops, proposed to mediate a peace, but the French and British rejected the idea, landed more soldiers, and stepped up their logistical support of the Whites. Eventually, Wilson was persuaded to go along, provided Kolchak guaranteed to establish a democratic regime in the event of victory. Kolchak did so, in a reply reputedly drafted for him at Omsk by French and English advisers. Nevertheless, there was a wavering will behind this Allied show of resolve, which reflected a profound uncertainty as to what the intervention could achieve. Perhaps none was more apprehensive than an American colonel, John Wood, who warned: "The Allies had better be cautious how they proceed in the diagnosis and dismemberment of this great people or they may one day find themselves on the operating table with this giant holding the knife."

Nevertheless, the Allies were initially optimistic. And not without cause. Kolchak successfully created a well-equipped army of nearly 250,000 men, as weapons and equipment from the vast surpluses in Allied arsenals poured in. Over the next twelve months, an estimated 97,000 tons of supplies would arrive by ship, including 600,000 rifles, 346 million rounds of small-arms ammunition, 6,831 machine guns; 192 field guns, plus hand grenades and other explosives originally designed to annihilate the Germans in the west. The French sent advisers to Omsk, a token Italian force took up posts at Krasnoyarsk, and British officers trained Siberian recruits. Poles, Romanians, and others maintained some kind of military presence in the semblance of a united front. Protection of the Trans-Siberian from Vladivostok to Lake Baikal was assigned by Allied accord to America and Japan. American forces were concentrated in the Vladivostok and South Ussuri regions, and stationed at intervals along a 100-mile stretch between Verkhneu-dinsk (present-day Ulan Ude) and Mysovsk. The Japanese took charge of other sectors to the east, either with their own soldiers or with mercenaries raised by the Cossack warlords in their pay. The Czechs, no longer stateless men (the new Czechoslovak Republic, with Masaryk as president, had been born on October 28), declined to fight further as a vanguard and accepted the duty of guarding the Trans-Siberian between Omsk and Irkutsk. Exhausted by months of combat and re-sentful of the Allied failure to bring their own forces (not just advisers) to the front, they saw no point in further sacrifices, especially since Kolchak had surrounded himself with decadent reactionaries with whom the Czechs (most of them Socialists) felt no accord. Yet however Russian Kolchak's fighting units actually were, they could not escape the impression of being a mercenary force, as driven home by the refrain of a popular Siberian song: "Uniform, British; boot, French; bayonet, Japanese; ruler, Omsk." Nor would the British allow Kolchak to forget to whom he was most beholden for his power. General Knox reminded him at the moment of his greatest success: "Every round of rifle ammunition fired on the front has been of British manufacture, conveyed to Vladivostok in British ships and delivered at Omsk by British guards."

In December 1918, the army's northern wing caught the Reds by surprise and captured the key town of Perm, northwest of the Urals. Maintaining the initiative, it went on to take the vital Perm–Vyatka Railway intact, along with 30,000 prisoners, 260 locomotives, 4,000 railway trucks, 50 heavy guns, ten armored cars, and much other booty besides. Strategically, Perm created the possibility of linking up with the White and British forces in Archangel for an advance on Petrograd. In the spring, Kolchak took Ufa, made a drive toward the Volga, cut off Turkestan from Soviet Russia, and inflicted heavy losses on the Red Army. At the same time, in the south, General Anton Denikin was pushing from the Don toward the center of Russia, and General Niko-lay Yudenich was approaching Petrograd from the northwest. By May, much of North Russia was under White control, and Denikin's Cossacks had advanced on a broad front to within 200 miles of Moscow. In the Civil War, both sides knew they were approaching the moment of truth. Lenin was convinced that unless the Urals could be retaken before winter, the revolution would be crushed. And Kolchak similarly declared: "Within a year one of two things will have happened; either the Constituent Assembly will have met in Moscow or I shall be dead."

In retrospect, the odds were not in Kolchak's favor. The Whites failed to establish a common, coordinated military strategy, and their four fronts—South Russia, Western Siberia, North Russia, and the Baltic—were all so distant from one another that it was said that practically no place on the globe was more inaccessible than Kolchak's forward line. The compact and central position of the Reds, however, made it possible for them to shift their forces rapidly from one front to another and deal with each in turn. Moreover, although the size of Kolchak's army and the territory under his nominal rule had continued to grow, his effective authority had not, for Eastern Siberia was largely dominated by the Japanese and two cutthroat Cossacks in their employ: Grigory Semyenov and Ivan Kalmykov.

Born in the Transbaikal of Russian-Buryat parentage, Semyenov had fought in the Caucasus in 1916, earning the St. George's Cross for valor, and was subsequently commissioned by the Provisional Government to recruit a special detachment of Buryats for the Eastern Front. When the Bolsheviks took power, he established a base for himself in Manchuria with the small army he had managed to raise. Beginning in January 1918, he started to carry out cross-border raids, but made little headway until the Czechs put the Bolsheviks to flight. Meanwhile, the British and the French in succession had put him on their payroll, but the Japanese outbid them both, and he soon became their creature and the chief instrument of their policy in the war. After Chita fell to his band, he rapidly extended his jurisdiction over much of the Transbaikal. Along the line of the Trans-Siberian, he patrolled his fiefdom in armored railway cars (bearing names like *The Merciless* and *The Destroyer*) equipped with machine guns and light artillery and made semi-impregnable (in emulation of the trains of the Czechs) with steel plate and reinforced concrete.

Although as a cavalryman he had once shown courage and dash, Semyenov had grown into a most dreadful man. One American colonel described him as "of medium height, with square, broad shoulders, and an enormous head from which gleam two clear brilliant eyes that rather belong to an animal than a man. The whole pose is at first suspicious, alert, determined, like a tiger ready to spring, to rend and tear." Lavishly funded (he was paid up to $152,000 a month by the Japanese), and with anti-Bolshevism as an excuse to do as he pleased, he fostered an atmosphere, wrote an eyewitness, "of laziness, rodo-montade, alcohol, lucrative requisitions, dirty money and the killing of the innocent." He robbed banks, pillaged villages, plundered passing trains for supplies, and on one occasion allowed a subordinate to shoot ten boxcars full of prisoners just to show that "shootings can be carried out on Sunday as well as any other day." By his own admission, he couldn't sleep at night unless he had killed someone during the day. About all that could be said in his favor was that (unlike a number of other White officers) he refrained from Jewish pogroms, apparently out of deference to his Jewish mistress, "a very pretty woman with huge black eyes."

Ivan Kalmykov, Semyenov's no less bloody compatriot, had served with him in the Caucasus and on his mission for the Provisional Government to the Far East. When the Japanese moved north from Vladivostok in August 1918, Kalmykov had gone with them, setting up his own headquarters under their protection in Khabarovsk. By the end of the intervention he was reported to have shot without trial at least four thousand people. Inclined to pose with his hand thrust into his tunic in imitation of Napoleon, his myrmidons all wore on their sleeves the letter "K" superimposed absurdly on a heraldic shield.

Both men were a law unto themselves and Semyenov, established at the junction of the Chinese Eastern and Amur railways, had a large, independent fighting force, controlled most of the Transbaikal, and could, if he wished, sever Kolchak's eastern supply lines at will. This he periodically did at the behest of the Japanese, who had a vested interest in anarchy. "The last thing they wanted," notes one historian, "was a strong, stable Russian administration in Siberia" that could eventually challenge their own designs on Manchuria, Mongolia, and the Far Eastern coast. Their whole plan, in addition to stirring up nationalist hatred for the Russians among the Buryats, was to create such chaos through Semyenov, Kalmykov, and others that Japanese soldiers would be called upon to assure law and order in just those areas they sought to acquire. But in the end they overplayed their hand: by helping to make impossible a White triumph in Siberia, they inadvertently brought about a Soviet victory.

Perhaps if Kolchak had proved an outstanding leader, there might have been some hope for his cause. But no one could say exactly what that cause was. "He possessed," wrote Churchill, "neither the authority of the Imperial autocracy nor of the Revolution." Kolchak was completely without the requisite knowledge or experience to direct a land campaign, and his mostly young and inexperienced general staff was almost as incompetent as he in this respect. None of his corps or division commanders had been pre-revolutionary generals, and only a few were genuinely qualified for the commands they held. Never more than a remote figurehead to his population and even his troops, it was "one of the oddities of the anti-Bolshevik movement," one historian remarks, "that it should have been led by an admiral without a fleet, head of a government in a town 3500 miles from the nearest port."

Military issues aside, it was imperative for Kolchak to establish a viable political administration that could win the support of the people whose territory he ruled. Otherwise, he could not but appear as the Allies' pawn.

But Kolchak inspired so little confidence even among wealthy Siberians his natural constituency, that they gave him little help. Donations came, one minister exclaimed, "like milk from a billy goat." Widespread corruption also reduced many of the front-line units to a state of near destitution. "The soldiers were dressed very badly," wrote a Russian naval officer whose gunboat was supporting a bridgehead on the Kama River in the spring of 1919, "some were literally in rags. Only a few had boots, the majority were wearing bast shoes or had sacking wrapped around their feet. Some of them had bags sewn together in lieu of uniforms." Many carried their munitions over their shoulders in potato sacks.

Meanwhile, among the people at large, the mercenary activities of White officers gave the partisan movement ever-increasing strength. There had been no partisans to speak of in the Selenga River Valley, for example, until Semyenov, in December 1919, sent five hundred Cossacks and about two thousand Mongols on ponies and camels into the area, where they carried on an orgy of violence and absconded with four thousand sledloads of loot of all types, much of it to stock a chain of retail stores Semyenov owned in Chita. Another White general, searching for partisans and weapons, upon entering a village would shoot every fifth male, regardless of age, and burn every home, if a list of resident partisans was not promptly produced.

Anyone left or right was automatically labeled a "Bolshevik," and one American official wrote in alarm from Omsk: "All over Siberia there is an orgy of arrest without charges; of execution without even the pretense of trial; and of confiscation without color of authority.... Fear—panic fear—has seized everyone. Men suspect each other and live in constant terror that some spy or enemy will cry 'Bolshevik' and condemn them to instant death." The entire White movement was also rank with anti-Semitism, and pogroms, persecutions, and other atrocities followed in the wake of all its armies. Some two thousand Jews were killed in Yekaterinburg, for example, in July 1919. The propaganda term "Jewish Bolshevism" (later adopted by Hitler) was also coined by the Whites, who had inherited the idea of the "revolutionary Jew" from people like Plehve in the tsar's last government. Kolchak himself was not immune. Frustrated at America's relative neutrality, he accused the troops under Graves's command of being "Jewish emigrants" and "the offscourings of the American Army." Meanwhile, partisan bands hostile to Kolchak behind White lines had grown so numerous that by July 1919 the spread of red dots used to show uprisings on the staff maps was "beginning to look like advanced spotted fever." Even in Vladivostok, an American officer recalled, "the Russian officers were frightened to death that their own men would murder them." To venture out into the city at night was "as safe as going to sleep in the mouth of a cannon.... Each morning found some new victims of the growing discontent lying butchered in the alley or the gutter where all who saw could understand." When the victim was a Russian officer, it was customary to find, among other cruelties, that a long spike had been driven into his body through each star on the epaulettes he wore.

A comparable state of affairs obtained even in the field. "You could never tell who was who. One day a farmer would be selling you cabbages at your camp and the next day he would be leading an attack on your positions. Or a band of them would come to town from the hills, hide their rifles in a straw sack just out of town, and then come in and hang around the camp for an hour or two, like disinterested peasants; and the first thing you knew they had all disappeared, re-covered their arms and opened fire upon you." Not that the Peasants' Partisan Army, as it came to be called, was formidably equipped. Some were armed with old hunting rifles or unwieldy elephant guns, and their crudely made grenades—filled with dynamite, stones, and bolts —had to be lit with a match.

The Red regulars had also grown in force. Recovering from their shock at the Allied Intervention, the Bolsheviks had abandoned their plans to raise an army of volunteers and began a regular mobilization. Determined at first to increase the army from 330,000 to 1 million in a year, on October 4, 1918, Lenin had declared: "Now we need an army of three million. We can have it and we will have it." And he did. The Red Army grew rapidly, improved as a fighting force, and at the begin-ning of May 1919 counterattacked and prevented a possible junction of Kolchak's forces with those of Denikin to the south. Throughout the month of May, the Reds steadily rolled the Whites back from the Volga. On June 9, having crossed the Belaya River, they recaptured Ufa and Orenberg, and on July 1 also took Perm. Breaking through crumbling White defenses in the Urals, they marched on to Zlatoust and Yekaterinburg, which were gained by mid-month. Kolchak re-placed Rudolph Gaida (commander of his army's northern wing) with Mikhail Diterikhs, who advocated a swift retreat from the Urals so that the Whites could regroup on one of the riverbanks and make a stand.

But Kolchak's young chief of staff, Dimitry Lebedev, instead opted for a complicated maneuver designed to envelop and destroy the Reds at Chelyabinsk. In this plan, the Reds would be allowed to issue unop-posed from the Urals and occupy the West Siberian Plain around the town as the Whites outflanked them on the neighboring heights. But the disciplined training required to make the stratagem work was lacking among the raw and reluctant recruits brought forward to do it, and the Reds held firm. As a result, fifteen thousand Whites were taken prisoner, and the entire Urals industrial region was lost. In mid-August, the Reds crossed the Tobol River, pushed on to the Ishym 150 miles to the east, and were briefly driven back by Cossack cavalry. But on November 4 they regained their momentum and having reached the two rail crossings over the Irtysh River, began to close in on Omsk. It had taken the Red Army two and a half months to get from the Tobol to the Ishim, but from the Ishim to the Irtysh, less than two weeks. Where the Tartars had once been routed by Yermak and his successors almost three and a half centuries before, the Whites were biting the dust. There were mutinies and desertions on a tremendous scale, and tens of thousands of railway cars were clogged with refugees. The population of Omsk increased fivefold almost overnight with the beleaguered and forlorn.

"Well authenticated reports justify the statement," General Graves cabled the War Department during an on-the-spot assessment of the situation at Omsk in July and August 1919, "that officers are leaving the troops and fleeing to the rear, staff officers preceding line officers in this flight, soldiers are throwing away their arms and ammunition and in some cases their heavy clothing so as to enable them to move more rapidly to the rear. I have been unable to discover any enthusiasm for the Kolchak Government."

Kolchak desperately appealed for popular support with hollow promises of democracy, while Diterikhs (something of a religious fanatic) organized semi-medieval orders of "warrior-knights" and a detachment of priests to face the enemy with crosses and banners in a Holy Crusade. But by early November, Diterikhs had concluded that Omsk could not be held. Kolchak replaced him with a more optimistic underling—to no avail. Two Red regiments dashed across the ice and on November 14 caught the garrison at Omsk by surprise. Some thirty thousand demoralized White soldiers surrendered, as Kolchak's army completely collapsed.

Partisan bands converged with ever more bold and devastating attacks on supply lines, depots, and strategic junctions, and in some areas no train could move at night. At times, whole stretches of the track fell into the hands of insurgents; toward the end of the year the countryside was largely in partisan hands.

The Allies were helpless to prevent the precipitate retreat. They had sent no troops to the front in the winter of 1918–19, and although some thought was given to the formation of an Anglo-Russian brigade in Yekaterinburg in the summer of 1919, Allied intervention had not been massive or resolute enough to carry the day. Nor, at the end of World War I, were there resources enough to have prevailed. "I would rather leave Russia Bolshevik than see Britain bankrupt," Lloyd George told Churchill curtly, when the latter called for reinforcements. And

Churchill, in his own inimitable way, summed up the denouement. "The snows of winter war had whitened five-sixths of Red Russia," he wrote in *The Aftermath*, "but the springtime of Peace, for all others a blessing, was soon to melt it all again."

One by one the White armies were turned back. By the winter of 1919–20 Denikin's drive toward Moscow had been reversed, Yudenich checked short of Petrograd, Kolchak's armies smashed. Even as they were reconquering Siberia, other Red divisions were repossessing territory ceded under the Treaty of Brest-Litovsk to the Central Powers— the Ukraine, Byelorussia, Georgia, Armenia, and Azerbaijan.

Under the strain, Kolchak's own intermittent self-control gave way. In a confrontation with one general, he ranted, raved, "broke several pencils and an inkpot"; General Janin reported that he showed symptoms of drug addiction, had become "emaciated, worn out, and haggard," and was a mass of nervous tics: "Suddenly he stops speaking, jerks his neck back while twisting it a little and, as he closes his eyes, becomes rigid. . . . I am told that on Sunday he broke four glasses at a meal."

In Siberia, the great frozen rivers became highways to the Red advance. A planned defense of the Ob (400 miles east of Omsk) proved impossible to mount; Novonikolayevsk fell on December 14, and regiments attempting to reform behind the Ob at Tomsk "simply disintegrated through mass desertion." Farther east on the Yenisey, Krasnoyarsk was in revolt, and after the insurgents took control of it in early January 1920, the White Army could no longer retreat by rail. Three days later, on January 7, the Reds entered the city, and now had more than 100,000 White prisoners in their hands. Farther east, the railway and the roads beside the railway were clogged with the exhausted, the starving, the dying, and the dead.

Only that part of the army's remnant now under the command of General Vasily Kappel held together and, abandoning their trains, in a five-week retreat—or "Ice March," as it came to be called—fought their way past partisan bands toward Lake Baikal. On January 26, Kappel himself succumbed to frostbite and pneumonia.

Meanwhile, after the Red Army had entered Omsk on November 14, Kolchak's government had fled toward Irkutsk, but Kolchak's effort to join his ministers there was stalled by his decision to attach thirty-six freight cars laden with the Imperial Gold Reserve (including seven full of platinum, silver, and jewels) to his train. The competition for use of the line was tremendous. The Czechs had filled their own trains with valuables and commodities, and numerous White generals at Omsk, Novonikolayevsk, and other centers had appropriated trains for themselves. In the general confusion, factions fought over coal supplies, telephones, and other facilities, in terror that the approaching Red armies would overtake them in their flight. Once again the Czechs, who had maintained their discipline, took matters into their own hands. To keep their own trains ahead of the rest, they confined everyone else to the down-line and cleared the up-line for themselves. By December 18, 180 trains had fallen to the Reds. Thousands of White soldiers were being captured daily; desertion was almost universal; typhus swept the ranks. Soldier and civilian alike mingled in one miserable river of humanity that streamed beside the railway along the old Siberian Trakt. From time to time, "the dead were thrown along the tracks to rot and contaminate the district," reported one eyewitness. "Every station was a graveyard, with hundreds and in many places thousands of unburied dead." When Red troops crossed the Ob in mid-December 1919, they found more than thirty thousand bodies strewn through the ruins of Novonikolayevsk.

Kolchak's trains made slow progress, as others given priority accumulated up ahead. At Krasnoyarsk, reached on December 17, his convoy was stalled for almost a week. Kolchak telegraphed Semyenov in code to halt the Czech withdrawal at all costs, if necessary by the demolition of bridges and tunnels, but the Czechs decoded the message, and trapped Kolchak's trains for two weeks west of Irkutsk. Then on January 4, 1920, seeing there was no help for him, Kolchak abdicated as "Supreme Ruler" in favor of General Denikin and appointed Semyenov commander of all Russian armed forces in Eastern Siberia. He stepped into a second-class car emblazoned with the flags of the Allied powers, formally placed himself under Allied protection, and proceeded to Irkutsk under a Czech guard. As soon as he arrived on January 15, the guard was withdrawn on the orders of General Janin, and Kolchak calmly remarked: "This means that the Allies have betrayed me." He was turned over to the "Political Center"—a Socialist Revolutionary–Menshevik coalition which had briefly assumed authority in Irkutsk—and the gold reserve was shuttled into a blind alley surrounded by barbed wire. The railway siding leading to it was torn up, a round-the-clock guard was posted, and ball bearings removed from the wheels of the train cars.

A few days later, the Political Center yielded power to a Bolshevik Committee, even though the Red Army itself was still several days away. But with White forces in retreat rapidly drawing near, "siege law" was declared by the Committee in Irkutsk on February 2, land mines laid in the ice on the Angara River, and ammunition and other military stores cached in the taiga for renewed guerrilla warfare if Irkutsk could not be held. The Bolsheviks had meanwhile been interrogating Kolchak closely for over two weeks, but toward dawn on February 7, to prevent his rescue, he was executed by a firing squad on an embankment of the river and pushed through a hole in the ice.

The White Army, however, bypassed Irkutsk and retreated into Eastern Siberia. The Czechs promptly negotiated an unmolested retreat of their own, in exchange for the gold reserve; and on March 5, the Red Army entered the city and had all of Central Siberia in its grasp.

Most of the Allies were hastily evacuated from Vladivostok by ship, including the Americans, who sailed away in April, leaving two hundred dead behind. After their departure, the Japanese (who had their own long-term agenda) increased their forces across the border in Manchuria to 200,000 men, and occupied northern Sakhalin Island and much of the Siberian Pacific Coast. A Bolshevik atrocity furnished the excuse. On March 25, 1920, the Japanese garrison and all Japanese civilians at Nikolayevsk were massacred on the orders of a partisan leader and his chief of staff and mistress, Nina Lebedeva, a 25-year-old Communist who liked to dress up in dark red leather and gallop about on her charger armed to the teeth. Before Japanese reinforcements arrived, they also burned the town to the ground. Both were later executed by other partisans for these brutal acts, but the Japanese seized upon the incident to justify their new occupation force. Indeed, had the massacre not occurred, another would probably have been contrived. In early 1920, for example, the Japanese had warned everyone in Khabarovsk that it would be dangerous to remain once they withdrew. To prove it, they secretly armed a band of two thousand Chinese brigands (the Japanese were on excellent terms with Manchurian warlords) who were to pillage the city as soon as they left.

The situation in Eastern Siberia, however, was unquestionably cha-
otic, and early in April 1920 the foundations were laid for a sort of
buffer state between the Bolsheviks and the Japanese. This was known
as the Far Eastern Republic, which gradually asserted its authority over
most of the territory between Lake Baikal and the Pacific Coast. Despite
its superficial resemblance to an independent democratic state, the
new republic was actually supervised by the Far Eastern Bureau of the
Bolshevik Central Committee, and its "People's Revolutionary Army"
was composed of Red Army units commanded by Major Robert Eikhe,
formerly of the Red Fifth Army and later Party Secretary for Siberia.
Semyenov, based in Chita, continued to plunder the Transbaikal for a
few more months, but Chita fell to the Far Eastern Republic on October
22, and he escaped to Manchuria in an airplane. By November 1920,
when the Crimean army of Peter Wrangel (Denikin's successor) was
also being crushed, most of Eastern Siberia had come under Far Eastern Republic control.

One final, bizarre attempt to establish a White enclave occurred
when one of Semyenov's bloodiest lieutenants, a Baltic noble named
Roman Ungern-Sternberg, took about a thousand cavalry in early October 1920 south into Outer Mongolia; claiming descent from Genghis
Khan, he rallied the Mongols around him and drove out the hated
Chinese. Flushed with this success, he married an obscure princess
of the Chinese imperial house and declared himself heir to the
Chinese throne and the living Buddha. In this exalted incarnation,
Ungern-Sternberg indulged in a reign of terror over the population,
but was pursued by the Red Army, defeated on July 7, 1921, and abandoned by his own Mongol troops in the desert to die. The Reds
picked him up and he was shot at Nikolayevsk on September 15. A
pro-Soviet government was set up at Ulan Bator, which became the
capital of the Mongolian People's Republic, a Soviet satellite state.
General Diterikhs, who had escaped to Vladivostok and tried to
revive it as a counterrevolutionary beachhead, was also defeated in
February 1922, bringing to an ignominious end the last of the White
campaigns.

In October 1922, the Japanese withdrew; Soviet troops entered Vladivostok on the 25th; and on November 14, the Far Eastern Republic
was incorporated into the Soviet Union.

The isolated northern front in European Russia had gone the way of the rest. Although the Whites had managed to raise a force of about fifty thousand men divided between Murmansk and Archangel, they posed little threat to the Soviets, and after the Allies abandoned them in October 1919, they were doomed. The Red Army began an offensive up the northern Dvina in February 1920, took Archangel on the 21st, and a month later trapped and annihilated the remaining White division defending Murmansk.

When the last Allied battalion had set sail from Archangel, an American lieutenant wrote: "Not a soldier knew, no, not even vaguely, why he had fought, or where he was going now, or why his comrades were left behind beneath the wooden crosses."

In Siberia, pockets of resistance here and there remained. There was skirmishing between Reds and Whites in Kamchatka until 1922, and Soviet power was not firmly established on the Chukchi Peninsula or in the province of Yakutsk until 1923. In that year the Whites were also expelled from the Commander Islands, where (like Bering almost two centuries before) they had dug foxholes for themselves in the hard and barren sand.

One of those who participated in the Russian Civil War in the Far East was Vselvolod Sibirtsev, whose accelerated career and dramatic fate were not untypical of many of his compatriots, although notable in our story for its all-Siberian stamp. The grandson of a Decembrist and the son of a member of the People's Will, he had studied economics in St. Petersburg, joined the Social Democratic Party in 1913, and had fought in 1917 on the Western Front. As a Bolshevik he had also agitated among the troops, before taking part in the October coup in Petrograd. A few months later, he was sent to Vladivostok on a Party assignment, but in June was arrested and imprisoned by the Czechs. Six months later he escaped, edited an underground Bolshevik newspaper, fought the Whites as a partisan in the mountains of the Far East, and was subsequently appointed military commissar of the garrison in Vladivostok in 1919. But the wheels of fate kept turning, and on April 4, 1920, he was captured by the Japanese and burned alive in the firebox of a locomotive near Muravyev-Amursky station. At the time of his death, he was twenty-seven years old.

"In all our centuries," wrote Aleksandr Solzhenitsyn, "from the first

Rurik on, had there ever been a period of such cruelties and so much killing as during the post–October Civil War?" The Civil War was the iron forge in which the outlines of the new Soviet state were given their preliminary form.

16

THE DEVIL'S WORKSHOP

Aт the end of the Civil War the Bolsheviks faced the awesome task of reconstituting a country covering a sixth of the land surface of the globe. The old bureaucracy was gone; industry was paralyzed; and the transportation system was in a state of complete collapse. There were no manpower or material reserves on which to draw for building a new nation, and few remaining professionals of acceptable ideological stripe. In Siberia, agriculture had been wrecked, mines abandoned, roads and railways destroyed. At least 56,000 peasant homesteads had been laid waste.

Lenin's "War Communism," established in 1918, had intensified after the victories over Kolchak and Denikin early in 1920, in a vain attempt to wrench the whole economy toward a Communist system of production and distribution. His methods had guaranteed the Red Army its supplies, but in other respects the nationalization of land and industry, the ban on private trade, the establishment of universal compulsory labor, and the requisitioning of grain had embittered virtually every stratum of the nation. "The onrush of revolutionary events," one participant later recalled, "changed our social relations to such an extent that we considered it best to nationalize absolutely everything, from the biggest factories down to the last hairdressing shop run by one hairdresser owning a clipper and two razors, or down to the last carrot in a grocery store. Roadblocks and checkpoints were put up everywhere so that no one could get through with food. Everyone was put on government rations."

The requisitioning of grain made the catastrophe complete. Peasants resisted, rose up, and were slaughtered; in the ensuing famine, millions of men, women, and children died. In Western Siberia, a ragtag peasant army of sixty thousand briefly occupied twelve districts, cut Soviet communications, and captured a number of towns. Strikes immobilized factories across the new Soviet Empire, and even at Kronstadt naval base, an original stronghold of the Revolution, the sailors rebelled. To forestall a popular uprising against the Party itself (which, after all, had never been popular, and had taken power by a coup), Lenin abandoned "War Communism" and in March 1921 instituted the so-called "New Economic Policy," or NEP, which restored a small measure of capitalism to the land. It suspended the requisitioning of grain (substituting for it a fixed tax in kind), tolerated small businesses and other entrepreneurial endeavors, a certain differentiation in wages, and abolished compulsory labor and labor armies; but it kept transport, heavy industry, and banking under state control. This experimental mixed economy (or "State Capitalism," as it was also called) was supposed to be transitional to state socialism, and with its help over the next several years the country struggled back to its feet.

The going was hard. In 1922, for example, Red Army rations (the most liberal in the land) were two to three pounds of bread and one pound of meat or fish for two to three days. About 20 ounces of lard, 20 ounces of sugar, and some salt were also given out per month. Meager as this was, there was seldom any meat at all available, and the fish, wrote one visitor to Moscow at the time, was

always scrawny and dripping with water when weighed out. One day the fish had little white worms crawling all over them. On the way to Tsedom, I held the wrapped parcel in the palm of one hand raised above the shoulder. By the time I got halfway across the bridge over the Moscow river, the soaked wrapper fell apart, and the fish stuck out. Right then and there, a young man clad in a technician's outfit tapped me from behind on my shoulder and said, *prodayosh, tovarisht?* (are you selling, comrade?) I pointed to the worms, but he shrugged his shoulders, said *nichevo* (doesn't matter). More protein into the bargain, he added. He shoved a handful of rubles into my hand, thrust the bundle into a shopping bag and went on his way.

After Lenin's death in January 1924, there was a struggle for control of the Party machine, from which Stalin emerged triumphant. And after a brief period of collegial pretense among his colleagues, by 1928 he had begun to impose upon the nation the manifold and heavy perversions of his will. By then the half-measures of NEP had run their salutary course and were proving insufficient to sustain economic growth. Many Bolshevik leaders advocated a gradual transition toward socialism, but in the midst of the uncertainty as to how to proceed, Stalin thrust his own agenda to the fore. Against every reasonable objection, he insisted on a rapid, spectacular development of industry through mammoth engineering projects at the expense of consumer needs, and on the collectivization of agriculture (against near-universal peasant opposition), which renewed the famine of the "War Communism" years. Evidently convinced that the disorganized Allied Intervention in the Civil War had been the prelude to another, more concerted effort by the same powers "to dismember and destroy the first Socialist State," Stalin proclaimed in February 1931 to an assembly of factory managers:

> To slacken the pace would mean to lag behind; and those who lag behind are beaten. We do not want to be beaten ... old Russia was ceaselessly beaten for her backwardness. She was beaten by the Mongol Khans, she was beaten by Turkish Beys, she was beaten by Swedish feudal lords, she was beaten by Polish-Lithuanian Pans, she was beaten by Japanese barons, she was beaten by all—for her backwardness. ... If in ten years we do not cover the distance that other, more advanced countries have taken fifty or a hundred years to traverse, we will be crushed.

This strangely pathetic view of Russia's history—after all, by the time of the Revolution Russia had become the world's greatest empire as well as its fourth largest industrial power—boded ill for its people, since their future was now in the hands of a man whose personal insecurities were the paramount facts of their political life.

"Determined to transform a mainly agrarian economy into a self-sufficient industrial behemoth," as one writer put it, Stalin at once embarked on a program of forced industrialization based on Five-Year Plans. Individual entrepreneurs were once more eliminated, private enterprise in agriculture replaced by large mechanized collective farms, and wildly unrealistic labor and production quotas set. The central economic planning commission called for coal and oil production to double, iron production to triple, and (within the same five years) for the biggest power plant in Europe to be raised on the Dnieper. A 1,000-mile railroad was also to be constructed from Siberia to Turkestan, and numerous dams, metallurgical plants, and tractor works built. Stalin approved the plan, then decided it wasn't ambitious enough. "Tempos decide everything," he announced, and pressed for the goals to be met in four, even three years. The figures infatuated everyone, even the poet Mayakovsky (as expressed in "Forward, Time!") shortly before his own disillusionment and suicide. Stalin's opponents suggested that light industries be built up first, to meet the basic consumer needs of the nation, but he purged the Party hierarchy of all dissent and forged ahead.

The rebuilding of the devastated European part of the country, with its existing industrial capacity and skilled labor force, had priority, and assured a more rapid return on investment, since the Siberian economy was still largely agrarian, centered on small craft industries, and lacked the means and infrastructure to exploit its resources. Overall, it accounted for less than 2 percent of the national industrial output, and by 1923 had dropped to about half the level it had reached before 1917.

That, however, was destined to change with the development of the Kuznetsk Coal Basin and of major industries along the line of the Trans-Siberian Railway. Monolithic iron foundries and steel mills were built at Magnitogorsk, an immense tractor plant at Chelyabinsk, a huge locomotive works at Ulan Ude, electric power stations at Irkutsk, and numerous other factories for the production and handling of glass, chemicals, processed foods, and so on, at Omsk, Novosibirsk, Krasnoyarsk, Irkutsk, and Khabarovsk. Under Lazar M. Kaganovich, Stalin's Commissar for Heavy Industry, the Trans-Siberian Railway was extended southwestward from Semipalatinsk through Alma Ata into Turkestan, thoroughly renovated with new rolling stock and other equipment, variously extended with branch lines (most notably, from Vladivostok to the commercial port of Nakhodka and from Ulan Ude toward Ulan Bator), and double-tracked throughout. Wooden bridges were also replaced with spans of steel. "Industrialization was the new faith," said one commentator, "factories were its cathedrals, its priests were the elite workers who smashed production targets and led the way to the future."

In the early days, at least, the heart of the Siberian program sought to exploit the rich surface iron deposits at Magnitogorsk in the Urals, and the seemingly inexhaustible coal deposits (which in some places lay in strata 300 feet thick) of the Kuzbas in Central Siberia. By connecting these two great untouched sources of raw material into one immense metallurgical combine, Stalin hoped to acquire an iron and steel base equal to that of the United States. Centuries before, Genghis Khan's own prospectors are said to have set up in the region smithies that forged the arsenal of swords, knives, and lances that advanced his armies to the west. And on August 27, 1734, Gmelin had noted in his diary: "This whole Neighborhood between the Irtysh and the Ob is so full of the most costly Ores that, even if the Work be mightily pressed forward, nevertheless several Centuries may pass before this Treasure is exhausted. Whereby it must be regarded as a crowning Mercy in these Parts there is no need to lay out costly Mines with costly Machines. The Ores do all lie on the Surface of the Earth." During World War I, some exploration of the Kuzbas had finally begun, and by 1928 coal output was double what it had been in 1917. By 1932, the iron and steel plants at both Stalinsk (later Novokuznetsk) and Magnitogorsk had gone into production, and by the end of the decade their mammoth blast furnaces together were producing about 3 million tons of pig iron, or 20 percent of the national total a year. By 1940, coal production had reached 22.5 million tons. Other Siberian projects concentrated on the mining of gold, tin, tungsten, molybdenum (used in special alloy steels), as well as minerals like mica and fluorspar. In the Far East, investment went into the oil fields of northern Sakhalin, port development, aircraft and shipbuilding, munitions plants, and other defense-oriented manufacturing, as Russia kept a wary eye on the Japanese occupying Manchuria to the south.

Across Siberia and elsewhere—in Central Asia, the Volga Basin, and the Ukraine—not only traditional industries were expanded but numerous others created which Russia had never before possessed. Plan by Five-Year Plan, Stalin continued his frantic industrial march. In time, cotton combines, electrical stations, and other new structures went up, with an increase in Siberia of industrial production of over 13 percent. The populations of many cities increased by two to three times, and all

the primary minerals and fuels—coke, coal, oil, and sundry ores—
were forced in ever greater quantities from the ground. In 1940 alone,
Siberia produced 3.2 billion kilowatt-hours of electrical energy,
smelted 1,536 tons of cast iron and 2 million tons of steel, mined 39
million tons of coal, and exported 51.9 million treble meters of wood.

Everything went to fuel this industrial juggernaut, and in its wake
the Russian countryside itself was devoured. Although the government's original agricultural policy had envisaged a gradual collectivization of farms—whereby individual, privately owned holdings would
be amalgamated into large state cooperatives—Stalin became impa-
tient to impose state controls in order to ensure the supply of food to
cities, factories, and mills. Peasant resistance provoked official wrath
and furnished an excuse to accelerate the pace. Stalin accused the so-
called "kulaks," or prosperous peasants, of hoarding grain, and (as
Lenin had done ten years before) dispatched requisition squads to the
countryside to take it by force. Some of the "hidden" grain they found
was seed, but they took it anyway, ensuring that famine would return.
Many outraged peasants chose to destroy their holdings rather than
yield them up for nothing to the state, and in reaction, on December
27, 1929, Stalin decided to liquidate the kulaks as a class.

Although some kulaks were usurious moneylenders who also exploited the field hands they employed—justifying their epithet, "the
tight-fisted ones"—most were simply thrifty and industrious members
of village communities, who, wrote a contemporary, "had worked
hard, saved money, and acquired not only some property but skill in
certain trades." A number had been able to give their children a good
education, producing doctors, lawyers, accountants, and other professionals which (in the eyes of the state) linked them with the old bourgeosie. But in practice, in fact, it was hard to say exactly who a kulak
was. "Anyone who employed hired labor," write the authors of *Utopia
in Power*, "was considered a kulak, but so was anyone who owned two
horses, two cows or a nice house." Before long, the state found it
convenient to brand as a kulak anyone, rich or poor, who resisted
collectivization. Local Party organizations were also directed to round
up draft animals and cattle, pigs, poultry, and sheep. Some 25,000
operatives were sent to the villages to force compliance, but in yet
another act of collective defiance, thousands of peasants slaughtered
their livestock rather than give in.

On August 7, 1932, Stalin issued a decree defining all collective farm property as state property, and making "unauthorized" use of it a capital crime. This was followed on January 11, 1933, by a resolution of the Central Committee warning against "anti-Soviet elements, penetrating the kolkhozes (collective farms) in the capacity of accountants, managers, storekeepers, brigadiers and so on, often in the capacity of leading officials of kolkhoz boards." Such elements were said to be "trying to organize wrecking, putting machines out of order, sowing badly, squandering kolkhoz property, undermining labor discipline, organizing the theft of seeds, secret granaries and the sabotage of the grain harvest." By the end of the year about a third of the supervisory or technical personnel involved in agriculture was under arrest. Over the next two years, 50 to 60 percent of the homesteads in Siberia had been collectivized, and by 1934, about 75 percent of all peasant holdings throughout Russia had been similarly transformed. In Siberia, eight hundred state machine tractor stations also equipped the huge new state farms.

In some respects "dekulakization" hit Siberia harder than anywhere else. The comparatively prosperous Siberian peasantry made a natural target, and whole hamlets as well as individual homesteads were seized as kulak nests. In one Western Siberian region alone, in just one year (1932), 43,000 families were "removed" (most to concentration camps or Arctic settlements in the Siberian north), while hundreds of thousands of "kulaks" were also deported to Siberia from other provinces of the empire. "I will never forget what I saw," wrote one eyewitness. "In the waiting room of the railroad station there were nearly six hundred peasants—men, women, and children—being driven from one camp to another like cattle. . . . Many were lying down, almost naked, on the cold floor. Others were obviously dying of typhoid fever. Hunger, torment, and despair were written on every face."

It had taken a long time for Siberia to develop agriculturally, and for its promising arable lands to be populated by an enterprising and capable peasantry. The territory had even recovered remarkably after the Civil War, and proved able to feed much of the country in the first decade of Soviet rule. And now this structure was destroyed at a single stroke.

At least fifty thousand once-productive Buryats and Mongols fled south to Inner Mongolia and China, and the Amur and Ussuri Cossacks, long established along the frontier, abandoned their villages and crossed en masse into Manchuria—joining others who had fled before. Like peasants elsewhere, many Buryat, Mongol, and Yakut herdsmen slaughtered their own livestock rather than see them incorporated into collective herds, and throughout Russia the grain harvest also fell dramatically, with the most tragic results. Famine spread across rural Siberia as well as the Ukraine, the Kuban, and areas of the Don and Volga rivers, and it is estimated that up to 7 million died.

By 1934, some of Stalin's colleagues had become convinced that the country itself might not survive his rule. The Leningrad Party chief, Sergey Kirov, seemed a promising candidate to replace him, but Stalin had him assassinated, then proclaimed his death a catastrophe in order to use it as a pretext to launch a terror campaign. Show trials of prominent figures were followed by the arrest, execution, and exile of countless others for alleged complicity in a vast anti-Communist conspiracy. "Every morning," writes Robert Conquest, "Stalin would initial numbered lists of named victims"—3,182 such death warrants were signed by him on December 12, 1937, alone—"while his henchmen were issuing massive quotas for the random killing of 'enemies of the people' in every region and city. Since every person arrested was forced to denounce dozens of accomplices, the tally of the condemned soon swelled to unmanageable proportions. The purpose was to destroy through fear not just the opposition, such as it was, but the very idea of dissent." In the year of the Great Terror (1937–38), more than 1 million were executed and an estimated 7 million sent to concentration camps.

There was method to this madness. From the very beginning of his Five-Year Plans, Stalin, in an elaboration of Trotsky's system of compulsory labor, had striven to assemble a vast forced labor pool that, as one writer put it succinctly, "could be rigidly controlled, employed under harsh environmental conditions, and easily maneuvered from place to place according to need." Hundreds of "corrective labor" camps were established in European Russia, Central Asia, and Siberia, and eventually dotted the hinterland as numerously as the old Cossack forts. In theory, "corrective labor" was supposed to reeducate all those who failed to accept a socialist way of life, but the Gulag (an acronym for the Chief Administration of corrective labor camps) ran a system of *lags*, or camps, which in fact were devoted only to the fulfillment of various "plans" and "norms." Over time, the camps pitilessly took the lives of millions, and many of Stalin's so-called "socialist achievements" were accomplished with their blood, sweat, and tears.

Stalin's primary initial challenge, as he saw it, was rapid development without foreign investments. Foreign loans were almost impossible to obtain because the government had ruined its credit by repudiating its foreign debt in 1917. And the loans the government could get (at usurious interest) were small. Since the government had no capital to invest in the new industrialization, it invested human lives. Forced labor became the "fixed capital" of the effort, and the concentration camp the major economic institution of the state. The result was a slave-labor economy.

The theoretical precedent for Stalin's methods of detention and imprisonment was administrative exile under the tsars. Most political prisoners were sentenced under Article 58 of the Criminal Code of 1927—an article so broad in its application, Solzhenitsyn noted, that "in all truth, there is no step, thought, action, or lack of action under the heavens that could not be punished by its heavy hand." Any mistake (like the misalignment of a pipe in a construction project), or the failure to satisfy an expected result (say, in the delivery of grain) could be seized upon and punished (even with execution) as a crime against the state. Investigations into an explosion in the Tsentralnaya Mine at Kemerovo in September 1936 exposed a whole "nest" of Trotskyites in Western Siberian industry; a series of pit fires in the nearby coal mines of Prokopyevsk likewise turned up evidence of sabotage. Again, any complaint could be considered "anti-state propaganda"; and the mere acquaintance with a foreign language could lead to the charge of espionage. One man was sentenced to fifteen years at hard labor just for studying Esperanto; another, a geologist, for failing to find conjectured deposits of ore. Priests, shamans, or other religious figures, or anyone with ethnic pride unwilling to be homogenized as a "Soviet person," were automatically guilty of capital crimes.

No one was safe. Indeed, Party faithfuls were among the first to be rounded up—men like Karlo Stajner, a Viennese Communist, who in his idealistic youth had helped establish an underground revolutionary press in Yugoslavia, and was subsequently transferred to publishing duties in Moscow. In 1932, when he came to the Soviet Union, he was, he tells us, "the happiest man on earth. Nothing was more precious to me than the Communist Party. . . . At long last, I was in the land of my dreams." In November 1936, however, he was suddenly arrested, and discovered, to his perplexed surprise, that a large proportion of his fellow political prisoners were actually dedicated Communists like himself. Almost no one knew why they had been taken into custody, and almost everyone was sure it was some absurd mistake. In time, they learned that everyone arrested was ipso facto guilty—otherwise, why had they been picked up? After a long pre-trial detention and then a trial that lasted about twenty minutes without benefit of attorney, Stajner was sentenced to ten years "under severe regime." "Arrests rolled through the streets and apartment houses like an epidemic," wrote Solzhenitsyn. "Just as people transmit an epidemic infection from one to another without knowing it, by such innocent means as a handshake, a breath, handing someone something, so, too, they passed on the infection of inevitable arrest." Before long, the whole country was covered with labor camps, "as if with a mysterious rash."

After sentence, the prisoners were crammed into navy blue Black Marias—prison vans disguised to look like grocery trucks, and often emblazoned with the words "Bread" or "Meat"—and taken to railroad depots or docks. There they were transferred to unheated cattle trucks or "Stolypin cars"—the latter divided into windowless compartments with wire-grating doors—or thrown into the holds of barges, to be carried in torment to their destinations. Some of the prison trains were "virtual cities on wheels," with fifty or more 60-ton freight cars, carrying six or seven thousand prisoners at a time. On top of every car a machine gunner was ensconced in a raised compartment, while searchlights mounted at either end of the train lit it up completely at night.

Even before the camps were reached, transport conditions were such that many perished from starvation or exposure. With four thousand others, for example, Stajner was herded into a freighter designed to carry lumber and taken to Dudinka (at the mouth of the Yenisey) through Arctic seas. "A cattle transport," he wrote, "would have been organized more humanely. The most elementary necessities, things to which every human being, even a captive, has a right, were lacking; only monsters could have planned something like this. We couldn't even stretch out on the damp, naked boards." Fights broke out over morsels of food; and in the stormy seas, overflowing barrels of excrement and urine splashed over the prisoners in the hold. Water, moreover, was rationed so sparely that a number of the captives died. "One night," recalled another eyewitness at Tayshet, "a goods train arrived, crammed with people, in terrible sub-zero temperatures. They opened one carriage, and a whole pack of dogs and soldiers with machine guns came rushing out into the snow. But when they opened the sixth carriage, no one jumped out. When we looked inside, we saw a horrifying picture. Everybody inside was stuck together, frozen solid in batches of two, three, four people. . . . They were just blocks of ice."

Sentimentality being cruelty's obverse side, it seems grotesquely fitting that during this exceptionally savage time some of the Trans-Siberian locomotives were adorned on the front with the tender features of Lenin as a baby. And while prisoners were being transported in veritable torture chambers, Stalin and his henchmen had built for themselves a "Lux Blue Express," which whisked them to and from their pleasure resorts:

> The first requisite [of this specially constructed train] was that no noise of the wheels be heard inside the cars, and that they move smoothly. To achieve this a thick coat of lead was poured over the floor of each car; this was covered with a layer of felt, a layer of cork, another layer of felt, a wooden flooring, and yet another layer of felt. Over this was laid a covering of linoleum, and on top of everything a soft rug. The resulting floor was like a feather bed. The rugs laid in the lounge cars cost 5,000 rubles apiece in a special restricted store in Moscow. They could not have been bought in the open market for 50,000. In testing a car a glass brim-full of water was put on a table in one of the compartments; not a drop must spill on the table during the entire trial run. On the outside the cars were painted a deep azure and the roofs sky blue. The paint was covered with a coat of lacquer and polished until not a rough spot or a scratch could be found.

Every compartment had its special luxuries. The dining car, for example,

> provided a wide selection of exquisite delicacies, a great variety of fruits, and the choicest drinks. Before every trip the conductor passed

from compartment to compartment, spraying eau de cologne and putting flowers on the tables. During the journey he brought around fruit, candy and the best cigarettes. The most extravagant whims of the generals, marshals, people's commissars, secretaries of regional party committees were to be satisfied.... Stalin's car had two bedrooms, a sitting room, an office, another office for his secretary, a compartment for the persons accompanying him, a bathroom, and a kitchen. The walls and all the furniture were of mahoghany....

The NKVD kept two girl agents permanently in the train. It was their duty to strike up an acquaintance with the passengers, engage them in conversations in the dining cars, and generally keep their ears open. They were good looking, always well dressed, knew how to behave in society and were always accessible to the important passengers.... There was such an abundance of goods around the train that no one kept any account of them. One could bring home from these trips whole cases of caviar, canned goods, wines, and cigarettes.

Meanwhile, prison barges choked Siberia's rivers; "strings of carts rolled endlessly through Novosibirsk Province, flanked by convoy troops, emerging from the snow-bound steppe and vanishing into the snow-bound steppe again"; and Soviet courts throughout the country continued to mete out arbitrary sentences at forced labor just to fill the prison trains.

"One day Larisa Fedorovna went out and did not come back," wrote Pasternak of his heroine, in the conclusion to *Doctor Zhivago*. "She must have been arrested in the street at that time. She vanished without a trace and probably died somewhere, forgotten as a nameless number on a list that afterwards got mislaid, in one of the innumerable mixed or women's concentration camps in the north."

In Stalin's slave-labor economy, three types of camp were developed: factory and agricultural colonies; camps for work like lumbering and mining; and "punitive" compounds for the special punishment of prisoners from other camps. The actual development of the Gulag system had begun in 1930 with the reorganization of the Northern Camps of Special Designation, created in the early 1920s for White prisoners of the Civil War. Their core was the camp network on the Solovetsky

Islands, where a great monastery fortress had been established in the sixteenth century, and where Ivan the Terrible had once confined leading foes of his own despotic regime. Under the tsars, the monastery had continued to double as a prison until 1905. In its Bolshevik transformation it became the prototype of the camps that followed in its wake. "There was hardly a nationality of Russia, a creed, a profession, a class, or a trend of thought that was not represented at Solovki [the main island]," write David Dallin and Boris Nikolayevsky in their classic work on the Gulag, *Forced Labor in Soviet Russia*:

> Socialists, Anarchists, so-called "counterrevolutionists," that is, former members of the "white" movement and rightist enemies of the regime; common criminals and prostitutes; former tradesmen and Soviet merchants who had trusted the NEP; people sentenced as "spies" (actual spies were shot without ado); clergymen of all denominations, especially the Greek Orthodox; workers guilty of striking and peasants accused of rioting; Soviet officials who had served their country body and soul and had been charged with wrecking; delinquent GPU agents; at the end of the 'twenties Trotskyites and members of other opposition groups within the ruling party—all were present at Solovki. Very few of them served sentences imposed by regular courts. The function of Solovki consisted not so much in punishing lawbreakers as in terrorizing the population into silence.... From the Solovetsky Islands the camps spread back to the mainland and, in the course of a few years, expanded far to the east and south.

Stalin's economic "pilot project" had been the building of the Baltic–White Sea Canal, where between 1931 and 1933, 250,000 prisoners had labored on a 168-mile-long strategic waterway to join the lakes of Soviet Karelia by canals to link the White and Baltic seas. In order to hoard its hard currency, the government decided not to purchase the appropriate machinery from abroad, but to build the canal by hand. Pile drivers, normally powered by steam, were driven by people, forced into giant human treadmills; food was rationed according to output; cold and hunger killed up to seven hundred a day. Anyone trying to escape was shot. By the time it opened in August 1933, it had cost over sixty thousand lives.

On the Solovetsky Islands, the main camp industries were lumbering, livestock farming, and the processing of fish; elsewhere, the camps developed as clusters for farming, logging, tanning, railroad construction, port work, mining, making bricks, quarrying stone, constructing roads and aerodromes, building hydroelectric plants, metallurgical combines, and even cities—such as Norilsk, Magadan, and Komsomolsk-on-the-Amur, founded in the middle of a swamp 180 miles north of Khabarovsk. In Vorkuta, coal was mined; on Vaygach Island, zinc; at Yugor Strait, fluorite; on Novaya Zemlya, lead. There were camps and camp clusters in and around Tobolsk, Novosibirsk, Narym, Kemerovo, Tomsk, Barnaul, Krasnoyarsk, Irkutsk, Yakutsk, Tayshet, Olekminsk, Chita, Khabarovsk, Nikolayevsk, Vladivostok, Gizhiga, and throughout Sakhalin Island, the Kamachatka and Chukchi peninsulas, and the Kolyma Basin—by no means an exhaustive list. There was no province, it has been said, not only in Siberia but throughout the Soviet Empire, "which did not give birth to its own camp."

The result was an "archipelago," in Solzhenitsyn's famous description; or (in Karlo Stajner's) "an actual political state," with 21 million inhabitants and 800,000 administrative employees. "The structure," Stajner once explained to a fellow inmate, "is very similar to that of the regular government. . . . There's a forestry Gulag, a Gulag of roads and bridges, a Gulag of nonferrous metals, a mining Gulag, and so on. Each of these sections has its own boss, and these leaders form a sort of council of Ministers." Stalin, in other words, had "come up with a totally new [economic] system," that was neither socialistic nor based on private capital, but a slave-labor economy unique unto itself. State investment was minimal. And although prisoners and guards had to be provided for, watchtowers constructed, and so on, the prisoners were often made to build their own camps, and other cost-cutting measures applied. "The experience of all ages and nations demonstrates," wrote Adam Smith with confidence in the heyday of the Enlightenment, "that the work done by slaves, though it appears to cost only their maintenance, is in the end the dearest of any. A person who can acquire no property can have no other interest but to eat as much and to labor as little as possible." Karl Marx, Smith's theoretical opposite, agreed, noting further that because "the slave had no interest in raising the productivity of labor," the system was detrimental to a national economy that sought a higher level of development.

The Bolsheviks, as Dallin and Nikolayevsky observe, found

a way out of this apparent impasse. Marx had naively assumed that a slave must receive the subsistence minimum of rations below which neither life nor work is possible. Now it was found that a differential could be introduced in food rations in slave labor camps and that the smallest ration, i.e., that allowed to "slackers" and "shirkers" and in general to inefficient laborers, might well fall below the minimum required for subsistence. Moreover, this deliberate undernourishment would of itself compel all in the labor camps to do their utmost for the national economy.

The plain threat of starvation, that is, became the main incentive to productivity; at the same time, it deliberately led by stages through ever lower levels of nutrition (since to work well you have to have strength) to progressive debilitation and death. Everyone suffered from deficiency diseases like scurvy and pellagra, from undernourishment, swelling of the feet, face, and eventually the abdomen, and in the northern camps, from frostbite and gangrene. To keep the system going, these laborers had to be replaced. As one camp doctor told a victim in 1949: "You are not brought here to live but to suffer and die.... If you live... it means that you are guilty of one of two things: either you worked less than was assigned you or you ate more than was your proper due."

Because terror and repression made any kind of economic enthusiasm almost impossible in the economy at large, the camps were perhaps the only enterprises that brought in any gain. Their profits subsidized industrial plants and farms, and financed the cost of grandiose projects like BAM (the Lake Baikal–Amur Railroad), big hydroelectric power plants, the Southern Siberian railway line from Chelyabinsk via Abakan to the Mongolian border, and a great northern line projected along the Arctic coast. Part of the camp profits accrued through an elaborate system of plunder. Every time someone was arrested, he forfeited his entire estate. All his hard cash was confiscated, and millions more poured into the government coffers through the sale of his possessions—jewelry, rugs, clocks, whatever—left behind. Once prisoners arrived in camp, relatives naturally tried to send them money or other items to alleviate their situation. Most of this in turn was automatically appropriated by the Secret Police. One Soviet writer tells us (thinking to impress) that "the working men of Siberia" contributed 13.5 billion rubles to the government during World War II alone, "along with a huge quantity of gold, silver, platinum, and millions of items of great value." Incrementally (given the number of victims) the proceeds indeed were astronomical: in 1928, there were 30,000 people in the camps; by 1931, nearly 2 million; by 1934, about 5 million; then in 1937–38 alone (the year of the Great Terror) 7 million more were added to the rolls. No one really knows how many millions joined them in subsequent years, as forced labor became not only the basis of the economy but numerically the main social class: the inmate was the new proletarian in the Utopian classless state. "Well, I agree this isn't socialism," one victim remarked to another in discussing their situation. "But we don't have private capital. So what is it?" His companion replied: " . . . Only the devil knows what it is."

In approaching the horrors of the Gulag, one must brace as against those of the Nazi concentration camps. So terrible were they that by comparison the exile system of the tsars seems positively humane. That is not to say that the sufferings of tsarist exiles were not great; nor are they lessened by the cruelties of another age. But with all the injustices the tsars allowed, there were sometimes great and tender mercies in the application of the laws. Mass murder had not yet blighted humanity's capacity to feel in proportion, by taking all proportion away: capital punishment was still regarded as a frightful thing, and hunger strikes often overcame the malice of the authorities rather than spurring them on to more sadistic deeds. Solzhenitsyn among others has shown in the most terrifying way how enormously evil has increased in modern times, with the idea of the secular perfection of a "mass man."

In Dostoyevsky's hard-labor camp at Omsk, floggings were sometimes fatal, but otherwise the regime was comparatively mild. Each convict was allowed numerous private effects, could keep domestic animals, enjoyed Sundays, feast days, and even his own name day as days of rest, was fed (if not always well) at least above the starvation level, could occasionally go into town to buy tobacco, tea, or beef; and on Christmas Day might even be served goose and suckling pig. Moreover, the work itself was such that Dostoyevsky could feel it as his "salvation," since it got him out of the barracks, relieved his nervous tension, and strengthened his physical health. Except for about a dozen political prisoners, all the convicts had also actually committed some crime—horrendous crimes, too, like infanticide.

On Sakhalin, those doing heavy road work or toiling in the mines received up to 56 ounces of bread, 14 ounces of meat, and 8¾ ounces of cereal a day; and at Akatui, the worst of the tsarist hard-labor prisons, 43 ounces of bread and 7 ounces of meat—six to seven times the daily Gulag norm. As for the work itself, the Decembrist prisoners in Nerchinsk had a daily quota of 118 pounds of ore to mine and load, whereas those in Kolyma had a norm into the thousands. And if it wasn't met, the brigade had to remain for as long as it took, "in the woods by the light of searchlights," sometimes barely returning to camp to eat dinner and breakfast together before they went out again into the woods. At Norilsk, those quarrying stone for roadmaking even in the midst of blizzards were granted only one ten-minute warm-up break in the course of a twelve-hour shift.

Under the Bolsheviks, the "pure moral weapon" of the hunger strike was designated "a continuation of counterrevolutionary activity in prison," and in mid-1937 the prison administration absolved itself of any responsibility for resulting deaths. Torture also became normal in interrogation, and anyone over the age of twelve was liable to execution as an adult. Then the state found it suitable to take the relatives of its "enemies" as hostages, and ultimately even to execute them, if it wished. In the exile system, a real distinction had been made between the common criminal and the political exile; and as Leo Deutsch, a convicted terrorist, remarked in 1903, "Every official, high or low, knows well that he cannot go beyond a certain point with [politicals], and that he must behave with courtesy." In the Gulag, all this was reversed. Actual criminals were more leniently treated, indeed, became lords of the camps; they were the elite, and as a rule, enjoyed privileged positions as orderlies or trusties. Among them, most politicals were like lambs thrown to the wolves.

Under the tsars, moreover, the death penalty had been an exceptional measure, and even between 1876 and 1904, when revolutionary terrorism was at its height, only 486 people were executed, or an average of 17 per year, including criminals. From 1905 to 1908, the number dramatically increased to 45 a month, but was as nothing compared to what ensued. After the Bolsheviks took power, by 1938 the annual average reached 28,000 or more. And "by early 1939," one

historian tells us, "at least one in 20 of the population had been arrested; some 8 million were being held in prisons and camps, where
90 percent of them would die. Two million inmates had already died
in the previous two years, not counting another million that had been
executed." In just one camp cluster during the year of the Great Terror, fifty thousand prisoners were "tied up with wire like logs, stacked
in trucks, driven out to a selected area, and shot." Prisoners were also
shot to "check epidemics"; others herded into barges and sunk in the
Arctic seas.

From Solzhenitsyn we may draw their epitaph:

We divide, we multiply, we sigh, we curse. But still and all, these are
just numbers. They overwhelm the mind and then are easily forgotten. And if someday the relatives of those who had been shot were
to send one publisher photographs of their executed kin, and an
album of those photographs were to be published in several volumes, then just by leafing through them and looking into the extin-
guished eyes we would learn much that would be valuable for the
rest of our lives. Such reading, almost without words, would leave a
deep mark on our hearts for all eternity.

Those transplanted as "special settlers" to agricultural, factory, or
other work colonies did not fare much better in the end. The climate
alone of the Northern Siberian settlements was enough to kill Central
Asians, and one eyewitness paints a most pathetic picture of their
fate:

Brought from the subtropical climate of their homelands to the coldest regions in the world, they died like flies. All their vital forces were
numbed as soon as they went out into the terrible cold. . . . They
stood motionless, their arms crossed, their bowed heads hunched
between their shoulders, waiting for the end. They made no response at all to orders and curses. Blows were useless—it was as
hopeless as asking tin soldiers to bestir themselves . . . they simply
stopped functioning.

Around Kuznetsk in Western Siberia, deportees lived in holes dug
out of the ground, which they covered with boards; other dwellings
consisted of earthen pits supported by wooden poles and low plank

ceilings covered by dry clay and manure. People crawled in and out of them. One German Communist, married to a Russian, was arrested in June 1938 and sentenced to five years of "corrective labor" in Siberia's southern steppes. "We lived in clay huts," she recalled, "with thousands of lice, bugs, and fleas, fully on the level of the Kazakh nomad but without his mutton steak and kumis; we spent the short hours of the night lying on wooden boards or on the ground, without straw sacks, without blankets, only to line up for work at sunrise.... How one learns to hate the pitiless Siberian sun, to hate every morning that it rises." In settlements to the north, wrote another, people were driven to "eat the bark of trees and grasses. Children, women and old men run and grovel around in the forest and feed like animals or wild beasts."

During World War II the camps were swelled by deported armies of "socially hostile" Poles, various minorities, and thousands of German and Japanese prisoners of war. Whole peoples (or large proportions of them), such as the Latvians, Estonians, Ukrainians, Crimean Tartars, Kalmucks, and Volga Germans, were forcibly transplanted to join their ranks. As a snapshot in time, it is known that in October 1946, 126,423 special settlers were sent to the Kemerovo district, 112,316 to that of Krasnoyarsk, 35,381 to the Altay, 92,968 to Novosibirsk, 83,276 to Tomsk, 56,611 to Tyumen, and 44,767 to Omsk. Natives like the Oroks on Sakhalin who found themselves under Japanese occupation and obliged to serve in their military or at various strategic installations were also arrested, and (in an inexcusable act of treachery) up to 1 million fugitives from the Soviet Union were returned to the Soviets by Allied authorities after the war. If the Russian Empire, in Lenin's description, was "a prison house of nations," the Soviet Empire became its concentration camp. "For every nation exiled, an epic will someday be written," writes Solzhenitsyn, "on its separation from its native land, and its destruction in Siberia. Only the nations themselves can voice their feelings about all they have lived through: we have no words to speak for them, and we must not get under their feet."

From 1928 to Stalin's death in 1953, the life of Siberia was bound up with the Gulag, when the majority of the population in effect lived in one kind of prison compound or another, or behind barbed wire.

Soviet and pro-Soviet books and articles celebrated the great building up of Siberia since the Revolution, and extolled the pioneering exuberance exemplified by the overnight creation of populous new towns. Even Western surveys sometimes spoke admiringly of how "entire cities rose in the wilderness" with an "uprush of towns on an ultra-American scale." The truth behind this picture is that any forced-labor camp with a population above five thousand constituted a town, and that the fastest growth of "towns" occurred not in industrial areas but in the far north and east because that was where most of the large labor camps were placed. In 1926, Eastern Siberia had a total urban population of only 891,000; within thirteen years it had more than tripled, and even in regular towns the majority comprised "special settlers" or other deportees. Eighty percent of the population of Ust-Kem, for example, were exiles, half of them Germans from the Ukraine. This clarifies the reality behind a simple statistical boast (such as appeared in an encyclopedia as late as 1968) that "the number of people in the workforce in Siberia increased three and one-half times during the first Five-Year Plan." A fuller appreciation of the phenomenon can be had by looking closely at two touchstone achievements: Magnitogorsk and Norilsk.

Founded in 1929, Magnitogorsk, one writer tells us,

instantly became the symbol of the revolutionary transformation of society that the October Revolution had promised. At the site of an iron-ore deposit just beyond the southern tip of the Urals, as far to the east of Moscow as Berlin is to the west, the Soviet government decided to build not just a steel plant, but one that rivaled (indeed that was modeled after) what was then the largest and technologically most advanced steel plant in the world, the Gary (Indiana) Works of the US Steel Company. When completely finished, the "Soviet Gary" was to produce as much steel annually as the entire Soviet Union had produced in the year before the beginning of the first Five-Year Plan! ...Brigades of young enthusiasts from every corner of the Soviet Union arrived in the summer of 1930 and did the groundwork of railroad and dam construction necessary before work could be begun on the plant itself.... The first dam across the Ural River was finished the sixth of April, 1931, and the lake began to fill up. Within two years it was five miles long and assured an adequate water supply to the city and plant for the first half of the construction work.

Meanwhile, the brigades of young enthusiasts had been fleshed out with tens of thousands of compulsory laborers and deportees, including 18,000 kulaks, thousands of Bashkir, Tartar, and Kirghiz shepherds, and up to 35,000 criminals. Most of the kulaks, from Kazan and its environs, had been "shipped like cattle to Magnitogorsk at the point of bayonets in closed box cars in which a small window had been cut"; they were fed only black bread, and forced to use a hole in the floor as a latrine. Upon arrival, they were taken under guard to the city's outskirts and bivouacked in nothing but tents through the winter, when the temperature often fell to -40 degrees. By spring, almost every child in these families had died, and a large proportion of the rest had perished from exposure and malnutrition.

By the following winter, barracks had been constructed to replace the tents, but they were so overcrowded that the normal advantages of shelter were lost. Meanwhile, new arrivals took the place of the four to five thousand dead. The Central Asians among them lived in a part of Magnitogorsk known as "Shanghai," which consisted of "a collection of improvised mud huts huddled in a sort of ravine overlooking the railroad yards." These semi- and unskilled workers furnished the labor power needed to dig foundations, wheel concrete, shovel slag, and do the other heavy work necessary in making the biggest steel *combinat* in Europe in the middle of the barren Ural steppe. By 1932, the plant was producing pig iron; and by 1933, steel. Four years later it was approaching full-scale production, and during World War II, it turned out half the steel used to make Soviet tanks.

Despite this industrial triumph, no one was secure. The director of the "Communist University" in Magnitogorsk was preoccupied with deviation hunting, and replaced his Dialectical Materialism teacher four times in one year. Two of those dismissed were taken away by the Secret Police. In the university's one history course, wrote the young American idealist John Scott, who had joined with initial enthusiasm in the enterprise, "every experience was black or white, trends and tendencies were simplified. Every question had a perfectly definite answer," yet in the long run no one really knew what that answer was. "The managers at Magnitogorsk," another writer observes, "spent about half their time trying to wheedle the rivets to fulfill the impossible plans decreed from Moscow, the other half trying to devise ideologically correct excuses for falling short. Workers tumbled from blast furnaces because the scaffolding had been stripped for firewood. And as Stalin's paranoia played itself out in merciless purges . . . the victims of political repression were stacked atop the victims of cold and deprivation." In the general purge of 1937, a third to a half of the specialists were either shot or deported to camps, and revisiting the city in early 1938, Scott found their replacements as well as the local officials "frightened half out of their wits." Most of Magnitogorsk's population (now 220,000 strong) still lived in wooden barracks or sod-covered huts, had no sanitation system to speak of, and were decimated by seasonal rounds of typhus, malaria, and other diseases. While the flourishing plant grew ever more productive, its "human resources" declined on rations of cabbage, potatoes, and black bread. "I would wager," Scott wrote, "that Russia's battle of ferrous metallurgy alone involved more casualties than the battle of the Marne."

The making of Norilsk was worse.

In 1922, copper nickel sulfide ore had been found near the mouth of the Yenisey River, and further geological probing revealed enormous deposits of nickel, copper, cobalt, and coal. Eventually, more systematic testing turned up over half the elements of Mendeleyev's periodic table, eighteen of which were important for industry. Reserves of polymetallic ore, coal, and natural gas all lay next to one another in the ground, "as if ordained by nature to facilitate large-scale iron and steel production." Although the region's forbidding cold and isolation clearly rendered the area unfit for ordinary human habitation, in 1935 the NKVD marked off a square of polar tundra for a camp, arrested several hundred mining engineers to supply the requisite technical personnel (since almost no one would go there voluntarily), a few doctors to look after them, arbitrarily charged them all with sabotage and sentenced them to ten years. In the summer of 1936, the first five thousand convicts (selected for youth and strength of constitution) were shipped up the Yenisey with tools, food, and tents.

In this way, industrial development began. The men cleared an area of snow and ice with pickaxes, crowbars, and spades, built barracks, and began to mine. But climatic conditions were so severe that despite uncharacteristically generous rations (by Gulag standards), more than half the men died of exhaustion, exposure, and disease. In 1937, 20,000 new prisoners arrived, and the following year 35,000 more, exceeding the capacity of the barracks and requiring a city of tents. Meanwhile, work had also begun on a narrow-gauge railroad to link Norilsk with the port of Dudinka at the mouth of the Yenisey. Despite the continuous stream of new transports, the inmate population remained virtually constant, since the death rate was so high. Stalin drove everyone, including the overseers, to despair. He needed the non-ferrous metals quickly in his preparations for war, but didn't have enough hard currency to buy them on the world market. From time to time, the camp's directors, failing to meet his quotas, were shackled, taken away, and shot.

When Norilsk was only three years old, wrote Karlo Stajner (who was there), its cemetery compared with that of a city that had been in existence for a hundred years.

The new directors realized that an enterprise of such magnitude could not "be pushed to completion by simple terror," and decided to encourage the technical personnel with material incentives (like edible food), and even allowed political prisoners to work at drawings and calculations in heated rooms. This had its effect. By 1942, the rail link to Dudinka had been completed, a refinery and a thermal-electric power station built, the factory's chimneys were smoking, and the production of nickel could begin. All the mining operations were conducted from open pits located on a high plateau above the city, and the ore was delivered to the smelting plants by inclined tunnels cut into the frozen soil.

Success brought no rewards. The guards arbitrarily shot up to thirty persons a day. The starvation rations were such that anyone who dropped a crumb would carefully pick it up and eat it; some prisoners got up in the middle of the night in order to catch mice and cook them in tin cans. "Once," recalled Stajner, "as dinner was being served, a young fellow was shoved and spilled his soup. At first, he stood there, perplexed, then he threw himself to the ground and lapped it up like a dog." To ward off scurvy, the prisoners were allowed only an occasional carrot, a bit of sauerkraut, some kvas, or a few drops of oil. And all the time their exhausted constitutions had to contend with the special miseries of an Arctic clime. When the polar blizzards erupted, wrote Stajner, "it felt as if the world was coming to an end. Darkness fell and all you could hear was the shrieking of the storm: 'Sheee . . . sheee . . . sheee,' like a thousand devils. . . . It was so cold that I sometimes feared my brain would freeze inside my skull."

Hardly a day passed when someone did not deliberately subject his hands or feet to frostbite to get into the infirmary, even at the risk of losing a limb. Self-mutilation with an ax became "popular," according to Stajner; in the usual procedure, "one of the men would set up a wooden block and position himself, ax in hand; the others stood in line, stepping forward one by one to have two or three fingers chopped off." Eventually, the camp refused to hospitalize such amputees and had a doctor bind them up on the spot.

An alternative way out of the camp (favored by criminals) was murder, since it automatically entailed another trial. More than four hundred murders were committed at Norilsk in one winter alone.

Yet the city grew. Stajner was transferred for a time to Dudinka, where he survived on food stolen from the docks. When he returned a few years later, he found the metal foundry transformed into a huge plant that stretched

> as far as the eye could see, with giant chimneys, workshops, sheds, warehouses. A network of railroad tracks covered the entire area, and smoke was billowing from every chimney. Lorries filled with the hot ore tailings were pulled to the slag heap by locomotives. And there were new construction sites where prisoners were digging the earth with the same kinds of tools my friends and I had once used.
>
> Yes, great things had been achieved in Norilsk. But where were the builders of this vast enterprise? Where were Ondratschek, Kerosi, Feldmann, and thousands of other foreign communists who, together with hundreds of thousands of Russians, Ukrainians, Uzbeks, Georgians, and members of other nations, raised these mighty structures out of the frozen earth? Were they enjoying the fruits of their labor? No, they were rotting in the mass graves of Norilsk, and most of the men I saw working that day would eventually join them there.

Within the context of the Gulag, Magnitogorsk and Norilsk were not unique. A survey of some of the Siberian projects on which forced labor was used makes plain that the atrocity was enacted in every region and clime: highways in Mongolia; the double-tracking of the Trans-Siberian; the railway spur to Ulan Bator; a hydroelectric power station at Ust-Kamenogorsk; the port of Nakhodka; oil pipelines from Sakhalin to the mainland; the mining of various ores and (after 1950) of radioactive elements like uranium and radium near Chelyabinsk,

Sverdlovsk, and Tura in connection with the nuclear industry; rare-metals mining in the province of Akmolinsk; logging operations almost everywhere, and so on. Not all the projects were useful, and among the more costly and ill-conceived was an attempt to build a railway along the Arctic coast. Beginning in 1947, hundreds of thousands of forced laborers, with a huge investment of technical equipment, toiled at more than eighty Arctic campsites along a 2,000-mile stretch to lay a line from Vorkuta through the uninhabited tundra to Yakutsk. Another line was supposed to connect Igarka and Norilsk. Millions of ties were riveted in place, but in the end had to be torn up as useless and removed thousands of miles away to other projected lines.

Of all the island clusters of the Gulag, the most infamous by far were the Dalstroy Camps of the Far Eastern Construction Trust, established by the NKVD in the winter of 1931–32. Altogether, Dalstroy governed about 160 camps, including numerous gold-mining operations in the Kolyma Basin. Soviet propaganda depicted the basin as a sort of Russian Klondike, but it was an atrocity unto itself.

Before the Revolution, the region had been regarded as a wasteland, and as late as 1925 had only 7,580 inhabitants. Known mostly for its considerable deposits of mica, big sheets of which were bartered in the town of Srednekolymsk by nomads, it wasn't until a White officer who had been hiding in the taiga emerged in 1925 with a few ounces of platinum that economic interest in the area began to grow. Two years later prospectors discovered gold on the Aldan River, and commercial mining began in 1927, under the auspices of Soyuz-Zoloto (Union Gold), a government trust, which dissolved in 1938 to become the Far Eastern Construction Trust or Dalstroy. Administered by the NKVD, Dalstroy eventually controlled the whole of northeastern Siberia east of the Lena, even to the Chukchi Peninsula, but most of its camps were in the Kolyma Basin, which was almost as large as the Ukraine.

For the labor force summoned to do the government's will, the deep-water harbor of Nagayev—possibly the most inhospitable place on the coast of the Okhotsk Sea—was chosen as the principal port of disembarkation, and here, surrounded by steep ridges of overhanging rock sparsely covered with larch, Magadan was founded on a swamp as Dalstroy's base of operations. En route to Nagayev, prisoners were brought to the huge transit camps on the Pacific Coast, located near Vladivostok, Nakhodka, and Vanino. One survivor, who passed through Vanino, recalled:

> When we came out on to the immense field outside the camp I witnessed a spectacle that would have done justice to a Cecil B. DeMille production. As far as the eye could see there were columns of prisoners marching in one direction or another like armies on a battlefield. A huge detachment of security officers, soldiers, and signal corpsmen with field telephones and motor-cycles kept in touch with headquarters, arranging the smooth flow of these human rivers ... 100,000 were part of the scene before us. One could see endless columns of women, of cripples, of old men and even teenagers, all in military formation, five in a row, going through the huge field, and directed by whistles or flags.

Assembled into transport battalions, they were herded onto freighters—up to twelve thousand prisoners at a time, and under such terrible conditions that Andrey Sakharov justly called them "death ships of the Okhotsk Sea." Women (who made up from 10 to 15 percent of the Gulag population) were not spared. Michael Solomon, a deported Romanian on board, later wrote:

> We climbed down a very steep, slippery wooden stairway with great difficulty and finally reached the bottom. It took us some time to accustom our eyes to the dim light of the dingy lower deck.
> As I began to see where we were, my eyes beheld a scene which neither Goya nor Gustave Doré could ever have imagined. In that immense, cavernous, murky hold were crammed more than 2000 women. From the floor to the ceiling as in a gigantic poultry farm, they were cooped up in open cages, five of them in each nine-foot-square space. The floor was covered with more women. Because of the heat and humidity most of them were only scantily dressed; some had even stripped down to nothing. The lack of washing facilities and the relentless heat had covered their bodies with ugly red spots, boils, and blisters. The majority were suffering from some form of skin disease or other, apart from stomach ailments and dysentery.
> At the bottom of the stairway we had just climbed down stood a giant cask, on the edges of which, in full view of the soldiers standing

on guard above, women were perched like birds, and in the most incredible positions. There was no shame, no prudery, as they crouched there to urinate or to empty their bowels. One had the impression that they were some half-human, half-bird creatures which belonged to a different world and a different age. Yet, seeing a man coming down the stairs, although a mere prisoner like themselves, many of them began to smile and some even tried to comb their hair. Who were these women? And where had they come from? I soon learned that they had been arrested all over Russia and in those countries of Europe overrun by Soviet armies.

Upon landing at Nagayev (after an eight- to nine-day voyage), the prisoners were put to work building or enlarging the harbor facilities or on the construction of Magadan. Their meager rations of bread, dried fish, soup, and hot water were typical Gulag fare, and their tents and brushwood huts (which they had to put up themselves) did little to ameliorate their fate. With little more than their bare hands they constructed piers for ocean steamers, cut broad roads through the stone leading down to the piers, felled trees, built sawmills, brickyards, drydocks, and a power station. In the winter they worked in icy water up to their knees, and in summer their nakedness was a feast to swarms of "disgusting, fat Kolyma mosquitoes" that could sting through horsehide and "resembled tiny bats." In time they also built the houses of their oppressors, with a special house for the police dogs, and cold-resistant barracks with double walls filled in with sawdust for the troops. Last of all they erected simple plank accommodations, without insulation, for themselves. During this time, prisoners shipped from Archangel were also disembarked at the mouth of the Kolyma River in the Arctic Ocean, to be dispersed to the mines or put to work on a long highway through the taiga to the gold fields and Magadan. On the Chukchi Peninsula, thousands of other prisoners were mining lead.

Continuous prospecting extended the Kolyma mining to the Lower Yana River on the Arctic Ocean, and after the surface deposits were exhausted, veins deeper down were reached by shallow shafts. Finally, true underground mines were blasted 120 to 150 feet deep into the rock-hard ground. The gold dust was put into 20-kilogram bags, and sent in special wooden crates to Moscow. As year succeeded year, the inhumanity of the camp regime became fixed, and it is estimated that every kilogram of Kolyma gold cost one human life. Starvation drove prisoners to eat the rotting corpses of animals, lubricating grease, or "Iceland-moss, like deer." Those unable to march to work themselves were dragged there on sledges by their compatriots, and those who lagged behind were beaten with clubs and torn by dogs. Although working in −50 degrees Fahrenheit, "they were forbidden even to warm themselves by a fire." One prisoner who worked as a nurse in the prison hospital in Magadan remembers that the surgeon routinely went down the line of cots snipping off the frostbitten fingers and toes.

In some camps, there were no medical personnel at all; and in the women's compound at Elgen (a Yakut word meaning "dead"), the professional experience of the local medical orderly was limited to that of veterinary assistant on a collective farm.

By 1938, the prison population had reached half a million, a level maintained only by constant new arrivals in the face of a death rate of 25 percent. Of the estimated 12 to 15 million killed by the labor camps as a whole, Kolyma was responsible for about one fifth. One of the camps, the Serpentinnaya, existed exclusively for mass executions, and in 1938 some 28,000 prisoners there were shot. This, writes Solzhenitsyn, was more than "the total executions throughout the Russian Empire for the whole of the last century of Tsarist rule."

As if all this were not hellish enough, in the punitive camps for special punishment the annual mortality rate was reported to exceed 30 percent. There were even rumors of a mysterious camp where men had to work in mines under the floor of the Arctic Ocean, and lived twenty-four hours a day underground. "Not one of the inmates has ever come out alive," it was said. "Every day the great elevators bring up a number of corpses for burial." Who knows what went on beyond the known horrors that are already beyond comprehension? In April 1990, a photographer for a Magadan museum, visiting a campsite 780 miles northwest of Magadan, found skulls "with the bone sliced through, for which there is no explanation."

To Siberians, European Russia was the mainland. To the denizens of Kolyma, an island within an island, the mainland was Siberia. It was almost impossible to escape. Every unit was accompanied by wolfhounds, and anyone slipping away soon fell into the taiga's fatal grip. Most of the northern camps were separated from the country as a whole by vast stretches of empty marshland, sparsely inhabited by tribal hunters such as the Chukchi, Yakut, and Samoyed. As in days of old, they welcomed wanderers, served them green tea, and sometimes offered their women to them at night, but (to alleviate their own desperate circumstances) most had also come into the unofficial employ of the Secret Police. While a guest was being regaled, a courier sped to the nearest post, and soon agents would appear on dogsleds to make an arrest.

In 1942, camp authorities got sacks of vitiated white flour, cartons of Spam, and a huge new bulldozer from the United States courtesy of the "Lend-Lease" program extended to Russia during World War II by the Allies. The flour and Spam (served up in infinitesimal quantities) scarcely improved the prison diet, and was additionally resented as tasteless. But the barrel of American machine grease for the bulldozer, wrote Varlam Shalamov, an inmate, was "immediately attacked by a crowd of starving men who knocked out the bottom on the spot with a stone." The first thing the American bulldozer was used for was to dig a mass grave.

In this way, by the mid-1940s, Magadan had established itself, with a population of 70,000, as one of Siberia's "miracle towns."

Foreign apologists of Stalinism sometimes went to extraordinary lengths to paint an idyllic picture during these years of camp life. In one particularly grotesque attempt from 1944, the author, George Borodin, claimed that:

> There is all the difference in the world between the Tsarist convict toiling in the mines of Nerchinsk and the Soviet convicts working on, say, the Dudinka-Norilsk Railway in Arctic Siberia. To start with, the fact they are in this part of the world at all is purely incidental. Conviction does not automatically carry with it transportation to Siberia. . . .
>
> The offenders are condemned by one of the courts of Soviet Russia —those courts which, incidentally, have roused so much admiration in Harold Laski. They are then assigned to one or other of the prison camps then in being. When the men arrive, they are given accommodation, not in cells but in huts or tents—accommodation that is neither worse nor better than that afforded workers on any other pioneer enterprise. From now on, the convict has to make his choice. He has shelter in the hutment. He is given food—a daily peasant ration of soup and bread. With that the responsibility of the State ceases, and everything now depends upon himself and his comrades.
>
> All around him, work is going on. In most cases, as in Siberia, it is

pioneer work, work being waged in a spirit of a crusade. The whole
atmosphere is charged with an urgency to get it done. The convict
has his choice: he may spend the day in sleeping, lazing, and drawing
his frugal rations. He may even beg a little extra food if he is that way
inclined. But—and this is the point—he may also join the work. No
immediate pressure is put upon him, though efforts are made to
induce him to see the superiority of work over crime, and the greater
pressure comes from those of his fellows who have already volunteered for labour. . . . No hours are imposed on them. They may, if
they choose, work only an hour a day or four or five hours a week.
. . . Little by little they work more and more hours, drawing larger
money, and becoming useful citizens. In their turn they proselytize
new-comers. And so the tale goes on. . . . Though when at work the
men are free, they are, of course, under surveillance by "administrators," whose job is rather that of the court missionary than the prison
governor. . . . These [also] see to it that there are no untoward inci-
dents. The settlements themselves, too, are guarded. Each is surrounded by a barbed-wire fence, and here and there are guards. But
there is nothing exclusive about these precautions. The wire fence is
by no means a shutter between the prisoners and the outside world
as a prison wall is. On the contrary, at various points the wire fence
is pierced by gateways—usually of the turnstile pattern—and local
residents wishing to do so pass freely across the settlement. The
whole arrangement reminded me of the gates and fences round an
English farmer's fields.

Perhaps the author really didn't know what was going on (though
elsewhere he shows himself informed about collectivization); certainly
Stalin did everything he could to conceal the reality from the West. Yet
the truth was undoubtedly known to the German Nazis, who to some
degree developed their own concentration camp system from Stalin's
paradigm; and when Hitler said he had learned a lot from the Soviets,
there is not much doubt as to what he meant. As Robert Conquest
points out, lists of camp clusters were published as early as 1937, and
by the mid-1940s numerous survivors, escapees, defectors from the
NKVD, released prisoners of war, and so on had reported in sufficient
detail on their experiences in articles, letters, and books that by 1947
it was possible for a complete survey of the camp system to be made.
    Nevertheless, in a famous incident in 1944, United States Vice Presi-
dent Henry Wallace and Professor Owen Lattimore (representing the

Office of War Information) visited Magadan and found much to praise. Wallace described the gold miners at Kolyma as "big husky young men" and "pioneers of the machine age, builders of cities." Lattimore cheerfully compared Dalstroy to the Hudson's Bay Company and the Tennessee Valley Authority. So far as he could tell, it resembled a public works project under FDR. Wallace described one camp director —a Soviet counterpart of Adolf Eichmann—as "a very fine man, very efficient, gentle and understanding with people"; Lattimore in turn was impressed by local greenhouses "where tomatoes, cucumbers, and even melons were grown to make sure that the hardy miners got enough vitamins." Of course, the whole thing was a charade. They never saw a genuine camp, and even the farm they visited, notes Conquest, had "fake girl swineherds, who were in fact NKVD office staff."

When the plight of Soviet prisoners was brought up before the United Nations, Deputy Prime Minister Anastas Mikoyan declared that "there were no labor camps in Russia and the prisoners there were so well provided for that English and American workers had every reason to envy them."

Boris Pasternak once suggested (through a character in *Doctor Zhivago*) that World War II came to the Soviet people at first almost like a breath of fresh air compared to the inhuman power of Stalin's Lie.

The Germans attacked on June 22, 1941, and advanced rapidly on three main fronts: through Minsk and Smolensk due east, on to Moscow; in the north, across the Baltic states toward Leningrad; and toward Kiev in the Ukraine. Over the next five months 322 large industrial enterprises were dismantled and evacuated into Western Siberia from the Donets Basin to prevent their falling into German hands. Hundreds of thousands of skilled workers went with them as the Kuzbas became the forge of the Soviet war effort, and Omsk, Novosibirsk, and other cities developed into industrial giants remote from the threatened frontiers. They turned out warplanes, tanks, and tractors and produced the fuels, weaponry and other military equipment, including the spare parts and replacements, necessary to sustain Stalin's divisions in the field. By 1945, Siberia accounted for 21 percent of the country's steel, 18 percent of its cast iron, and 32 percent of its coal.

Stalin was also determined to reestablish Russia as a Far Eastern power, and in anticipation of war with Japan doubled the industrial output of his eastern provinces between 1937 and 1940. Forty Russian divisions were stationed in the region, to guard against an attack from the Japanese forces in Korea and Manchuria.

It was Stalin's professed belief that Russia's defeat in the Russo-Japanese War had left "grave memories in the minds of our peoples. It was a dark stain on our country. Our people trusted and awaited the day when Japan would be routed and the stain wiped out." Since then, Russia had been further humiliated. In September 1931, the Japanese had invaded and conquered Manchuria, incorporating it with other Chinese territory into the puppet state of Manchukuo. Russia relinquished control of the Chinese Eastern Railway, but Stalin had every intention of taking it back. Other disputed territory was also on his list. In a top-secret dispatch to President Roosevelt, Averell Harriman (U.S. ambassador to Russia at the time) described a meeting he had with Stalin on the night of December 14, 1944:

> [Stalin] went into the next room and brought out a map. He said that the Kurile Islands and lower Sakhalin controlled the approaches to Vladivostok, that he considered that the Russians were entitled to protection for their communications to this important port and that "all outlets to the Pacific were now blocked by the enemy." He drew a line around the southern part of the Liaotung Peninsula, including Port Arthur and Darien [Dalny], saying that the Russians again wished to lease these ports and the surrounding area. Stalin said further that he wished to lease the Chinese Eastern Railway.

Japan's impending defeat in 1945 provided Stalin with the opportunity he sought. In the final days of the conflict, the Soviets poured thousands of troops into Manchuria, took many prisoners of war, and seized millions of dollars' worth of raw materials and Japanese industrial equipment. They also invaded and took southern Sakhalin; reacquired the four disputed Kurile Islands of Habomai, Shikotan, Kunashiri, and Etorofu; and upon the unconditional surrender of Japan (September 2, 1945) concluded a treaty with the Chinese Nationalist government of Chiang Kai-shek, which gave the Russians effective control of the Chinese Eastern Railway, Port Arthur, and Darien. (After the Chinese Communists came to power in 1951, however, the Soviets agreed to yield these acquisitions to the new regime.)

•   •   •

During World War II, Siberia itself never became a significant battle-field. An occasional German cruiser prowled the Arctic coast, Allied food depots on Novaya Zemlya were shelled, there was Lend-Lease aid, and from 1942 to 1945 Soviet and American pilots worked together to ferry American warplanes from Alaska through Siberia to the German front. Dozens of gravestones scattered along the route from the Yukon to the Yenisey bear names in both Russian and English of the fliers who lost their lives.

One of the few German plans for an attack on Siberia was called "Operation Wunderland," in which a German battleship was to land a party on Dikson Island at the mouth of the Yenisey, overcome the local garrison, destroy the power station, and explore routes of invasion behind Soviet lines. In 1942, the twenty-eight guns of the battleship *Admiral Scheer* were trained on the Arctic settlement, but to the aston-ishment of the Germans, Russian shore artillery and the light guns of the cruiser *Dezhnev* beat off the attack.

No one was released from the camps during the war, and a promised amnesty after it applied only to criminals. In 1948, Stalin ordered all former political prisoners still alive rearrested, usually without even the formality of a new charge.

In Siberia at that time, however vast (a whole new mountain range was discovered as late as 1936), it seemed impossible to find refuge anywhere from Stalin's police. The experience of one small, indus-trious Baptist community, originally exiled to Siberia in 1907 by the tsar, is a striking case in point. The Baptists, led by one Nikifor, had settled near Achinsk, farmed and raised livestock, practiced their faith, and with rare good fortune, had survived World War I, the Revolution, and the Civil War intact. But then, writes Stajner, "the drive for collec-tivization began. This, too, would have been acceptable to them, for they were used to collaborative farming; but when one day an agitator came into the village to talk about the poisonous nature of religion, people started to get upset; and when their prayerhouse was turned into a clubhouse (which no one went to), the peasants decided to move elsewhere." After careful preparation, the entire community— nearly two hundred men, women, and children—set off with their livestock, tools, household goods, and some provisions. They went deep into the forest, marching for ten days almost without rest, and on a meadow by the side of a river built their new homes. Improvising to supply their needs, they made thread out of hair and needles out of bone, found an herb that served as a salt substitute, fueled their lamps with resin, and made their clothes out of hides. For more than twenty years they lived and prospered in almost complete isolation, and didn't even hear about World War II until six years after it was over. Then one day, recalled Nikifor,

> in the winter of 1951, our dogs started to bark louder than usual. We were frightened, because we realized it couldn't be the wild animals which sometimes came close to the village. Eventually, the barking stopped and we calmed down. A week later—we happened to be in the prayerhouse—the dogs started barking like crazy again. Some people came rushing in so scared they couldn't say anything; all they could do was point out the door. Outside was a detachment of soldiers on skis. We stood facing each other without talking for a few moments; there the soldiers were, and here was I with four other men and my only daughter. One of the soldiers came up to us and asked who was our leader. I told him we didn't have a leader, that we were all equal, that our only leader was God. When I said this, one of the soldiers laughed.

The villagers were interrogated for three weeks, accused of making contact with American spies by radio (the radios were never found), taken to Achinsk, and sentenced to twenty-five years at hard labor. All their children were taken away to special camps.

Perhaps the most bizarre of all Stalin's nationality experiments was the creation of a Jewish Autonomous Region in Siberia in 1934 as a Jewish national "home." Popularly known as Birobidzhan, after the name of its administrative center on the Bira River (a tributary of the Amur), it was supposed to attract Jews with a pioneering spirit then living within restricted administrative areas of Jewish Settlement, or the Pale. Stalin had originally toyed with the idea of designating the Crimea as their homeland, as part of a larger plan to destroy the Crimean Tartar nation.

Jewish agricultural communes were set up on the Crimean Peninsula, but the Tartars resisted, and a large tract of land (twice the size of Palestine) was selected in Siberia instead. The climate, however, was harsh, and the region remote and about as far from biblical Judea as one could get. Nevertheless, widespread propaganda urged young Jewish enthusiasts to migrate there and start building their own state —based, of course, on Communist, not religious, principles.

Most Jews correctly recognized the scheme as an attempt to create a new Pale by another name, through the voluntary Siberian exile of the whole Russian Jewish community. Nevertheless, a little army of seven thousand die-hard pioneers set out; when they arrived, they found a small railway depot off the Trans-Siberian and a few wooden shacks surrounded by swamp. No roads led to the world beyond. In time, through extraordinary effort, the settlers established a town, furnished it with electric power, built facilities for making textiles, clothing, and prefabricated housing, and in reclaimed plots of ground sowed oats, buckwheat, and rice. Some of the local mineral wealth was also tapped. Their progress, however, never led to a general migration, and eventually the Jews became just another minority in their own state. Of course, it was never intended that they cohere into a truly national force. So Birobidzhan remained, as one enthusiast about Soviet Siberia was constrained to put it, "a sterile political idea devoid of any economic or emotional attraction to Soviet Jewry."

Having failed to induce the Jews to "concentrate" themselves, Stalin, in the Gulag's last gasp, undertook to do it by force. This produced the so-called "Doctors' Plot" of 1953, which recapitulated the Kirov assassination as a pretext for another purge. In effect, it alleged that a number of doctors (mostly Jews) had murdered Andrey Zhdanov, head of the Leningrad Party Organization, in 1948, and planned to murder other Party and government leaders, including Stalin himself. The authorities took steps to prepare the Soviet public psychologically for a massive resettlement of Jews to "reservations" in Siberia, supposedly in order to protect them from "popular anger," but in fact a large-scale operation had already begun two years before, "the purpose of which," wrote one witness, Stajner, "was to complete what Hitler had begun." In 1951, fifty thousand Jews had been deported to the banks of the Lena, and in the following spring, "Jewish transports" began to arrive at Tayshet. The public announcement of the "Doctors'

Plot" was merely the signal for a pogrom. Jews were thrown out of offices and factories, dismissed from universities and trade schools, and imprisoned as "Zionists," "terrorists," and "American spies." Only the death of Stalin in March 1953 spared them an unspeakable end.

Stalin hated poets even more than he hated Jews or Baptists, and his whole terror machine, as Osip Mandelstam once remarked, was designed "to destroy not only people, but the intellect itself." Anna Akhmatova's former husband, the poet Nikolay Gumilyev, was shot as a counterrevolutionary in August 1921; the Leningrad poet Nikolay Zabolotsky, arrested in March 1938, ended up after numerous interim torments at Komsomolsk-on-the-Amur, at hard labor; the theater director Vsevolod Meyerhold was arrested, tortured, and finally shot on February 2, 1940, and his wife was later found brutally murdered in their apartment with her eyes cut out. The poet Marina Tsvetaeva's husband and daughter both fell victim to the repressions, as did Tsvetaeva herself, driven to suicide in August 1941. Osip Mandelstam, already under suspicion as an "internal émigré," was arrested in 1934 for having written an epigram critical of Stalin, and after a fierce interrogation was sentenced to three years' exile at Cherdyn, a small provincial town in the Urals. There he suffered a nervous breakdown and attempted suicide. Allowed to complete his exile at the more hospitable Voronezh on the Don, he returned to Moscow in May 1937, only to be rearrested and sentenced to five years' forced labor in the Far East. On December 27, 1938, starved and half-demented, he died at Vtoraya Rechka Transit Camp near Vladivostok, and was buried in a common grave.

Less well known is the fate of one of his colleagues, the remarkable Ukrainian poet and scholar Mikhaylo Dray-Khmara. Born in Kiev on October 10, 1889, Dray-Khmara had studied at the University of St. Petersburg, and there came under the influence of both Aleksandr Blok and Mandelstam, whose varying examples helped him to imagine what an indigenous Ukrainian literature might achieve. In 1917, he returned to Kiev, taught philology at the first all-Ukrainian university, and (fluent in nineteen languages) translated a number of classic works into his native tongue. "Like Yeats in Ireland," wrote Padraic Colum in tribute, he "aimed at creating a poetry free of propaganda and national self-glorification."

Such a man could not remain free for long. In February 1933, Dray-

Khmara was arrested on a vague charge of counterrevolutionary activity, released but dismissed from the university, and forbidden to publish his work. Two and a half years later, on September 4, 1935, he was rearrested, slandered at the instigation of the NKVD, and condemned to five years' hard labor in Siberia. Among the specific accusations made against him was that he had received correspondence from abroad, based on a postcard found in his apartment with a Bulgarian stamp. When Dray-Khmara pointed out that the date on the postcard was 1912, before the Soviet government had begun to exist, he was told: "It is not important if it existed or not; the fact remains that you had correspondence with our enemy Bulgaria."

Among the few personal effects he managed to take with him was his own unfinished translation of Dante's *Purgatorio*.

Almost all testimonials about the Gulag come from those who survived it. Dray-Khmara did not survive, but a surprising number of his remarkable letters did, and this correspondence, recently come to light, gives rare voice to a great man's demise.

"Dearest and beloved," he wrote to his wife and daughter on May 27, 1936, "at the beginning of June I shall probably be in Vladivostok. . . . From Vladivostok I will write to you. I will be going with a convoy of about 1,500 prisoners. Twice a day we receive hot water. On the way to Mariinsk (before Krasnoyarsk) I was in a 'stolypin' car (a freight car adapted for the movement of prisoners) with only dry rations in the way of food. I shall have enough sugar to Vladivostok; in Novosibirsk I bought one kilogram of fat for 5 rubles."

After he got to Kolyma, his ultimate destination, he put the bravest face on things. "In Kolyma one year counts as two; that is why I hope to be free earlier," he wrote on June 2, 1936, and a few months later asked his wife to send him only "bacon, garlic, and dried fruits. . . . What I really need are fats and Vitamin C." Meanwhile, he was put to work in the mines, forced to stand knee-deep in icy water washing gold, and sent on logging details. Somehow under these extreme conditions he managed to read sequestered works by Dickens, Balzac, Shakespeare, Sholom-Aleichem, and others—including Dostoyevsky's *Notes from the House of the Dead* (which he found somewhat self-indulgent)—and had begun to teach himself English. He made light of the cold: "Now the temperature reaches −45 degrees, but I don't feel it; that is the same as −15 degrees in Kiev. This is because of the absence of wind, and the continental climate." At night, he slept on a mattress stuffed with woodchips, and a pillow filled with grass. "But after the work," he wrote, "one goes to sleep quickly and does not feel whether the bed is soft or hard."

Although he had arrived a relatively robust man, after a year in the camps his health began to break. A front tooth had come loose, he developed boils on his face (which made it impossible for him to shave), and he had lost a great deal of weight. In a vain attempt to ward off scurvy, he was drinking a tea called *slanyk,* prescribed by the camp personnel and made from the needles of a low-spreading evergreen that was supposed to contain a lot of vitamin C. (It didn't, as Varlam Shalamov, a survivor, would explain in his *Kolyma Tales.*)

By October 1937 he had begun to have rheumatic pains in his hands and feet; by November he had a bad back from lifting heavy buckets, as well as a bodywide rash for which he was given ineffectual camphor pills. Five months later, he confessed: "My chest—that is only skin and bones; all my ribs are showing. The veins on my hands and on my feet are swollen like those of old people, like those of my grandmother at which I wondered as a child. . . . Sometimes, especially after lunch, I can hardly drag myself along to work, thinking how I shall handle the miner's pick or shovel, but later, overcoming this weakness and starting to move, I am able to do it."

At this point, his daily food ration was just 400 grams of bread, 50 grams of fish, and a spoonful of watery soup. The occasional potato he got a hold of was frostbitten; the compôte sour. "Often I dream about tasty things and think mostly about food. . . . Before I used to think about philosophical matters and now—about my stomach." Sometimes in loving detail he recalled his favorite homemade dishes, and their very description gave him nourishment; at that penultimate moment of his life, he literally lived on words.

By June 1938, Dray-Khmara's legs were swollen (from heart disease) and as a "treatment" for it, he was "hung upside down." By autumn, he also had blisters on his hands and legs from scurvy and a tumor above one hip "caused by a fall from a truck," and he was suffering from "heartburn and nausea." Meanwhile his wife and daughter had been evicted from their apartment in Kiev and exiled to the little town of Belebej, in the Bashkir Republic. His wife complained about her situation, and in one of his last, brave letters to her, he gently rebuked her for it:

One thing I don't understand is why you torment yourself so. . . . If I, besides the heavy physical work that I do, were to torment myself and "deeply suffer" as you express yourself, there would be an end of me. . . . Anguish can increase your strength, but only when you make the effort to control it, to rise above it, when you refuse to let it take possession of your soul. . . . Rid yourself of this melancholy, forget the very word "suffering."

As he tried to convey to her some shadow of what his anguish was, his own words failed him, and he asked her to recall the opening stanzas of Aleksandr Blok's "Autumnal Love":

> When, in the damp and russet foliage,
> The rowanberry clusters burn like flame,
> When the executioner's own sepulchral hand
> Drives the last nail into my palm—
>
> When, above the leaden rippling waters
> On some anonymous, damp Golgotha, I,
> Before the stern tribunal of my country
> Am hung for nothing upon the cross to die;
>
> Then, from that forsaken height,
> Through my last tears of blood, I'll see
> Upon the wide expanse of water
> Christ floating in a little boat to me.
>
> With the same hopes his eyes are shining,
> He wears the same torn, tattered clothes;
> A nail-pierced hand pathetically extending
> From underneath his outcast's robes.
>
> Christ! My country everywhere is sad!
> My worn-out will itself begins to fail!
> And your little boat—will it ever come to anchor
> Upon the height of this crucifixion hill?

Sometime in the winter of 1938–39, Dray-Khmara died. His widow did her best to preserve as many of his poems as she could, but in Belebej one night some Tartars stole the manuscripts and sliced the thin paper into strips for rolling cigarettes.

17

HORIZONS

DESPITE Lenin's ringing characterization of the Russian Empire as a "prison house of nations," and early Bolshevik promises to redress imperial wrongs, the fate of the Siberian native population under the Soviets was not kind.

On November 1917, the Council of People's Commissars had boldly proclaimed equality, sovereignty, and free cultural and political development for Russia's different nationalities, in a "Declaration of Rights of the Peoples of Russia" signed by both Lenin and Stalin, the latter at the time People's Commissar for Nationality Affairs. Nothing was done until after the Civil War to lend credence to this proclamation, but in 1924 a Committee of Assistance to the Peoples of the North was set up, and at first acted to improve the material conditions of native life. Six years later, the administration of Siberia was reorganized as part of the Russian Soviet Federative Socialist Republic (RSFSR), on a single day, December 10, 1930, six "national regions"—Koryak, Nenets (Samoyed), Chukchi, and so on—were set up in addition to the already existing Yakut and Buryat Autonomous Republics, established respectively in 1922 and 1923. These "Autonomous Republics," not incidentally, were of enormous size—the Yakut, encompassing an Arctic and sub-Arctic area the size of India; the Buryat, with its capital at Ulan Ude (formerly Verkhneudinsk), one and a half times the size of Great Britain. The Chukotka National District encompassed the whole of the Chukchi Peninsula. Although their names appeared to give imposing recognition to the aborigines and their rights to ancestral lands, in substance the new Soviet federal structure allowed them little real autonomy.

Nevertheless, improvements in hygiene and health care were made, and an educational system was set up with all levels of schooling; but the Soviets never followed through on promises to develop textbooks in all the native languages, and after the Cyrillic alphabet replaced Roman-based alphabets in 1936, the effect was to encourage the study of the Russian language rather than the natives' own. Meanwhile, many shamans and other leaders accused of being "kulaks" were eliminated, Tartar mosques were closed, and all but one of the Buryat temples were destroyed. Buryat open-pasture animal husbandry, as we have seen, was forcibly replaced by collective-farm cattle breeding, and when Soviet collectivization reached Arctic Siberia, the Samoyed nomads were organized into work units, each bossed by a *brigadir,* who made sure that their roamings with reindeer to patches of lichen followed an official plan. Although at first the government supposed that primitive native communism would make concepts of modern communism easier to apply, native ideas of sharing were found to be too generous, notably disconnected from the labor theory of value, and their failure to distinguish between work and leisure judged to be "unproductive" and "ideologically wrong."

Wrong or right, they were never so valued as in World War II, when about 20 percent of the total native population was conscripted and sent to the front. One whole division was made up of Buryat-Mongol cavalry; others served with great distinction as snipers or scouts; and Siberian riflemen played an important part in the defense of Moscow and in the Battle of Stalingrad. Yakuts especially proved able to remain hardy under the harshest conditions, and were said to be the Red Army's best marksmen because of their skill, as hunters, in shooting their quarry in the eye.

After Stalin's death, large numbers of prisoners were released under amnesties—perhaps 8 million out of an estimated 12 million interned at the time—but most of the reprieved were common criminals, and in 1956 there were still over 1 million political prisoners in the Kolyma-Magadan camp complex alone. Dalstroy was dissolved and "corrective labor" camps officially abolished as a separate category in

1958, but the Gulag structure, not completely dismantled, was adapted to serve the modified penal code. In May 1961, a decree on "parasitism" was passed under Khrushchev, which stipulated that "anyone who had not had a proper job for more than a month could be exiled for two to five years to one of the traditional Russian places of exile . . . and forced to do physical work. This punitive measure," one writer observes, "was evidently meant to kill several birds with one stone: liquidate unemployment, provide a labor force for the remote areas, and cleanse the large cities of their 'antisocial elements.' " It was also a useful way of dealing with " 'awkward' intellectuals," although the decay of the totalitarian bureaucracy made the uniformly ruthless application of arbitrary laws less efficient than before.

Up until the dissolution of the Soviet Union, dissidents suffered exile, and even under Gorbachev, drunks and other "vagrants" could still be rounded up in the cities, given pro forma trials (without legal counsel, or the presentation of evidence) lasting no more than a couple of minutes, and sent to camps. Without question, the camp regime was much less severe than had been known under Stalin (so much so that comparison is scarcely to be made), and in August 1990 Gorbachev, to his credit, issued a sweeping decree to restore the rights of unrehabilitated victims of Stalin's repression. Huge memorials have been planned for Vorkuta, Sverdlovsk, Magadan, and elsewhere, but "the phenomenon of the Gulag," Solzhenitsyn has stated, has yet to be "overcome either legally or morally."

In the aftermath of World War II, reconstruction was initially focused on European Russia and the Ukraine. Some of the transplanted industries and their labor force were returned to their original locations in a major, if temporary, blow to such cities as Omsk and Novosibirsk; after Stalin's death in 1953, the abolition of the use of forced labor on a large scale obliged Siberia to depend on free labor. This led to a more natural organization of the economy in the sense that European Russia reassumed its historic role of shouldering labor-intensive industries, with Siberia tending toward those having large fuel and energy requirements. Major regional resource-based development programs (inspired by the Urals-Kuznetsk Combine) were the order of the day. Under Stalin, the iron and steel industry in the Urals and Western

Siberia had been greatly expanded, with additional manufacturing stemming from the war. Beginning in the 1950s, work went forward on several hydroelectric power plants and dams designed to harness the power of the Angara and Yenisey rivers—at Irkutsk, Bratsk, Krasnoyarsk, and elsewhere. Construction on the Bratsk Dam began in 1954, and for 13 years an army of 54,000 labored to build the country's largest hydroelectric plant. "For Siberians," wrote one enthusiast of Soviet development,

> dams symbolize Russian might, just as do troops and rockets. They embody man's conquest over nature and they are an article of the Communist faith. In his drive to modernize Russia, Lenin preached: "Communism is Soviet power plus electrification of the entire country," and his apostles took him so literally that they have zealously been erecting what the poet Yevgeny Yevtushenko called "temples of kilowatts." . . . Bratsk epitomizes the New Jerusalem, the Soviet blueprint for Siberia—a huge hydroelectric project feeding a cluster of new industries, a new city hacked out of pine forest beside a gorge on the rushing Angara River at an isolated spot 750 miles further north than Montreal.

It remains to be seen whether the new Russia will adapt that blueprint as its own. Among Siberians, however, enthusiasm for the project was not universal. A number of riverside villages were deliberately flooded as a result of the construction, and as their remnants floated to the surface they were bombed from the air. The inhabitants were resettled in forestry camps nearby, but (like the Siberian environmentalist and writer Valentin Rasputin, whose village was among those to disappear) many came to regard themselves as "belonging to the ranks of the drowned." The original hamlet of Bratsk, founded in 1661, is itself buried at the bottom of the Bratsk Reservoir or "Sea." Twelve miles wide and 350 miles long, the reservoir is the largest man-made body of water on earth.

Other industrial works—an aluminum factory and a large timber combine, for example—grew up nearby, and railroad connections were forged to Zheleznogorsk (meaning "mountain of iron"), a mining center 100 miles to the northeast, Ust-Kut, and other towns. Before long, the 4.1 million-kilowatt capacity at Bratsk was surpassed by a still larger dam at Krasnoyarsk powered by ten gigantic turbines, each weighing over 200 tons, made in Leningrad and shipped to the mouth of the Yenisey via the White Sea–Baltic Canal.

Such projects were followed in the mid-1960s by other undertakings on a similarly Promethean scale to develop the newly discovered oil and gas reserves of Western Siberia, both for export and to fuel the manufacturing centers of the western Soviet Union. In the mid-1970s, two additional programs were launched: one, to develop the large lignite reserves of the Kansk-Achinsk Basin "to feed a power-generating complex for high-voltage electricity transmission westward"; the second, the Baikal–Amur Mainline project, or BAM, to open up new resource areas in Eastern Siberia and the Far East for export through the Soviet Union's Pacific ports. In magnitude, the Baikal-Amur line was almost a second Trans-Siberian, extending for 2,000 miles with tunnels through seven mountains, from Tayshet north of Lake Baikal to Komsomolsk-on-the-Amur north of Vladivostok. Originally begun in the thirties with slave labor to provide a line of communications beyond the range of aerial attack by the Japanese, BAM was to have been the most important undertaking of the Third Five-Year Plan (1938–42). As World War II began, track had been laid as far as Tynda, but during the Battle of Stalingrad the rails were torn up and hauled to the Volga to create a supply line to the besieged city from Saratov. When the project was revived in 1974, strategic consideration once more assumed importance because of the vulnerability of the Trans-Siberian to attack by the Chinese. But its paramount aims were economic—to relieve the overburdened Trans-Siberian (the world's busiest track), and give access to Eastern Siberia's huge untapped deposits of strategic minerals and fossil fuels.

Much understandably was hoped for, and BAM was cast as a "Hero Project" in the tradition of the Urals-Kuznetsk Combine and the Bratsk Dam. Some $25 billion was poured into it, and like the Trans-Siberian itself, it had to traverse some of the world's most difficult terrain. In 1984, the track-laying brigades finally met near Kuanda and bolted down the last sleeper. Film footage, we are told, "showed tears of joy on the weather-beaten faces of the thousands of people who had rallied together to mark the occasion," but their jubilation and relief were premature. The road remained inoperable for another five years due to repair work, and when traffic eventually opened in December 1989 between the Amur and Lake Baikal, the track proved almost useless because the infrastructure needed to support it—the forty-five towns, settlements, and industrial complexes envisaged by the plan to make it pay—had not yet come about. As a result, there was practically nothing for the line to haul. Its only industrial fruit thus far (thanks to a $3 billion Japanese investment) has been the emergence of the coal-mine city of Neryungri on a northern spur known as Little BAM.

Meanwhile, the South Siberian Railway, begun during the war, was completed between the southern Urals and the Kuzbas; extensions of the Trans-Siberian were forged in the 1960s to Magnitogorsk in the west and to Tayshet; and the line was electrified as far as Novosibirsk. Another line was pushed across the northern Urals to the mouth of the Ob. Yakutsk (until recently without a regular highway to the outside world) is now linked to the Trans-Siberian by all-weather roads, which also connect the mines of the Kolyma and Indigirka valleys to the port of Magadan.

The development of the Northeast Passage as a route for commercial shipping likewise edged closer to reality. In 1932, the Soviet icebreaker *Sibiryakov* had made its way from Murmansk through Bering Strait to Vladivostok in a single season; and in the following year, the *Chelyuskin* proved the navigability of the route for steamships. Subsequently, the Soviet Union built six nuclear and several dozen conventional icebreakers, 150 other ice-capable ships, and commissioned "universal dry-load carriers" from Finland. Nevertheless, even with a long string of intermediate ports along the Arctic coast—Salekhard, Dudinka, Tiksi, Providenniya, and so on—and the help of the largest fleet of icebreakers and Arctic reconnaissance aircraft in the world, the 7,000-mile-long route can only be used for three to four months of the year.

Although Stalin had more or less exhausted the surface gravel deposits and placer mines in the northeast, the deep lodes of ore beneath had scarcely been touched. Subsequently, large deposits of natural gas were discovered under the permafrost of the Yamal Peninsula and the adjoining Kara Sea. Novy Urengoy, a company town near the Arctic Circle, grew up to accommodate tens of thousands of workers transplanted to the area, as millions of tons of equipment were flown in for constructing docks, houses, roads, power stations, and drilling pads. Meanwhile, Nizhnevartovsk and Surgut, situated in the midst of the frozen marshland, had been transformed by the oil boom of the mid-sixties from sleepy villages into cities as large as Anchorage, Alaska. Derricks sprang up on the tundra, drill after drill bored down through the geological ice, and power and pipelines crisscrossed the barren terrain. Omsk, far to the south, became the center of the oil-refining industry, and a sizable chemical and synthetic textile manufacturing business arose at Barnaul.

Some twenty-three hydroelectric plants have also proliferated on the Yenisey; the district of Irkutsk is heavily studded with aluminum, chemical, wood pulp, and other plants; and in the Transbaikal, Ulan Ude (the capital of Buryatia) has the largest locomotive and rolling stock manufacturing and repair works in Siberia. Other factories produce such items as airplanes, rivercraft, electric motors, truck cranes, and steel and iron castings. The region also boasts prodigious supplies of bauxite (all-important for the aluminum industry), and the Barguzin River is flanked with lodes of gold. Around Chita, miners still carve up the earth for silver and iron, but throughout the Transbaikal there are also flourishing fields of grain, herds of cattle, and great flocks of sheep and goats. Off the Pacific Coast, the fisheries of the northern Kurile Islands and Kamchatka are abundant—with salmon, herring, lobster, cod, and king crab—and an American-Japanese consortium has undertaken to develop the large oil and natural gas fields off Sakhalin's northeastern shores.

More than half of Sakhalin is covered with forest, which large factories turn to paper and cellulose. At Norilsk, the northernmost industrial city in the world, the Mining and Metallurgical Combine refines copper, nickel, cobalt, silane, platinum, and other strategic metals with up-to-date equipment—furnaces, converters, and electrolytic baths—and produces its own steel, cement, and ferroconcrete panels and brick. In tandem with its growth, Soviet planners attempted to give Norilsk a new civilized veneer. Traces of its Satanic origins were superficially erased, and buildings in neoclassical style went up on concrete pilings that did not preclude amenities (like hot and cold running water, central heating, etc.) found in few Arctic settlements in the world. In addition to its fifty large metallurgical, chemical, and food-processing plants, Norilsk has also taken on a pompous scientific air with several industrial and research institutes, such as the Norilsk Research Institute of the Agriculture of the Extreme North, the Laboratory of Polar Medicine, and the Polar Aerospace Physics Proving Ground for the Academy of Sciences. Perhaps another learned institute may one day be erected in memory of all the knowledge that was lost.

Sable is still the world's most valuable fur, and the international fur trade continues to depend heavily on Siberian pelts. By and large, these are the bounty of a corps of licensed, professional hunters who turn in their catch at regional collection depots, which process several hundred thousand skins a year. The sable population has been carefully regulated with the help of the Barguzin Sable Reserve, but ermine and mink are also valued, together with muskrat, bred from some fifty pairs imported from Canada in 1935. A number of silver fox farms were also started in Yakutia in 1936 as part of a broader program for the experimental breeding of fur-bearing animals in captivity. Altogether, the Siberian fur industry is said to be worth about $62 million a year.

More grandly, Siberia's gold and diamond deposits rival those of South Africa; its natural gas fields surpass those of the United States; the Samotlor oil field compares to any on the Arabian Peninsula; the fishing grounds of Sakhalin match those of Newfoundland; and the timber reserves exceed those of Brazil. Siberia is also endowed with the world's greatest reserves of coal, iron ore, manganese, lead, nickel, cobalt, tungsten, molybdenum, bauxite, antimony, sulfur, apatite, and asbestos. Rare metals like platinum and wolfram—in fact, every element in the periodic table of Mendeleyev—are also amply contained in the inexhaustibly rich soil.

The material promise of Siberia, indeed, was prefigured by the exiled Archpriest Avvakum in the fall of 1661. Having come to the rocky shores of Lake Baikal, he rigged up a sail with a woman's old smock, and crossed its stormy waters in an open boat. On its farther side, he beheld "such high mountains as I had never seen before. And their summits are crowned with halls and turrets, pillars and gates, and walls and courts, all made by the hand of God." In the midst of this palatial splendor, he was amazed by the natural bounty of the land—by the great bulbs of wild onion and garlic that grew upon mountain slopes, by the green valleys, sweet-smelling flowers, Baikal's abundance of fish, and "wild fowl in great number: geese and swans floating on the lake like snow. . . . And all this had been created by Christ for man, that he should find pleasure in it and praise his Redeemer."

· · ·

The population of Siberia today is about 32 million, according to official figures released in 1989. Just under half of the inhabitants live in Western Siberia (15,003,000); under a third in Eastern Siberia (9,155,000); and under a fourth in the Russian Far East (7,941,000). Natives make up about 3 percent of the total, and about 60 percent overall live in cities or towns. Although it is supposed that Siberia may one day support a population of 250 million or more, that day is very far off. Certain areas have grown enormously, of course, especially in Western Siberia; and Novosibirsk, not so long ago a dusty railroad junction town, is today larger than Paris or Berlin. Once known especially for the production of machine tools, hydraulic presses, hydroelectric turbines, and gigantic pumps, its special stature today is closely tied to Akademgoroduk (or "Science City") 18 miles south on the Ob, where in 1958 a forest of birches and pines was transformed into a university research center with thirty branch institutes. Chekhov's prediction in 1890 that "a full, brave and intelligent people" would one day illuminate the shores of the Yenisey has certainly come true at Krasnoyarsk, despite all of Russia's travails.

Yet until quite recently at least, Siberia suffered a proportionate population decline, as more people began to leave Siberia than arrived. Many were attracted by the relatively better living conditions in other parts of the Soviet Union, and in response the government used higher wages, housing privileges, longer vacations, better pensions, cost-of-living allowances, and other material incentives to give the harsher localities allure. This strategy made a difference, but eventually yielded diminishing returns, since the costs outstripped the gains. Although Soviet planners had once envisaged weather-controlled, enclosed towns dotting the tundra, and railroads on steel pylons sunk into the permafrost extending along the entire length of the Arctic coast, the retrograde idea took hold that Siberia should simply be exploited as a powerhouse and source of raw materials. Energy-intensive industries like aluminum smelting or those concerned with the primary processing of raw materials, such as lumber, were located in Eastern Siberia; those concerned with manufacturing and consumer goods in Western Siberia, where the manpower and markets lay.

Much of Siberia's once and future building, of course, must take place on permafrost, and strategies for coping with its anomalies have chiefly been devised at the Eternal Frost Institute in Yakutsk, the world's most important center for permafrost research. It was at Yakutsk that the extent of the phenomenon was first clearly glimpsed, when in the mid-1800s a merchant tried to drill a well, and with enormous effort over ten years bored without result to a depth of 380 feet. Today, this pioneering shaft enjoys the status of a national monument. Although permafrost has incidental advantages—for example, cellars and caverns hewn out of it can serve without any lining as natural deep-freeze storage vaults for foods—in general it adds enormously to the costs of building because of problems due to soil creep, rock slides, frost heave, earth flows, talus cones, thermokarst (when surface melt turns to mire), and other changes resulting from the alternate thawing and refreezing of the ground. Roads laid across permafrost require thick layers of gravel and other materials as insulation, and structures of any size have to be erected, as it were, on stilts. A building will gradually thaw the topsoil beneath it, by even the slight temperature rise created by its own weight, and, settling unevenly, will totter and lean. Throughout Siberia there are clusters of old houses that thus resemble "dismasted ships rolling and tumbling about in a high sea, some with their sterns high up out of the water, others buried with their bows in the waves." Iron pylons were first tried as building supports, but they themselves conducted heat into the ground so that, to enable the air to cool the iron, it became necessary to raise the buildings about six feet into the air. Today, the preferred method uses reinforced concrete piles jack-hammered to a depth of 30 feet.

Siberia today has about 25,000 schools with 6 million students, thousands of theaters, theater groups, opera and ballet companies, hundreds of newspapers in several languages, and so on. But despite the many colossal projects for Siberian development, on the whole housing, food, medical facilities, day care, and other social needs have been ignored. As one Siberian writer recently complained, Siberia was like "a barge moored to Russia that brings in its wealth of goods and then is pushed away from the shore." Its products were taken out of the region at low wholesale prices, while consumer goods from the European sectors were delivered at a mark-up. Until the Union's dissolution, Siberia's resources accounted for about half of all Soviet hard cash receipts, which is one explanation as to why the state wrung the territory for all the profit it could get.

Many of the gigantic undertakings were also carried forward without the slightest regard for their impact on the environment. In the Kuzbas, lung cancer rates, respiratory infections, eye diseases, and other ailments are very high due to the sulfur dioxide and other industrial wastes in the water and air, and the great aluminum smelter and pulp mill adjacent to the Bratsk Dam has so befouled the air of that city that cars and trucks often have to use their headlights at midday. Around Nizhnevartovsk and Lake Samotlor, oil spills have tainted many rivers and streams; heavy metals and other industrial waste, pesticides and human sewage contaminate the Ob down to its mouth at Salekhard. To the north, Norilsk "on windless days," wrote a recent visitor, "smells like hellfire," and at Magnitogorsk, John Scott's miracle city of steel, the open-hearth smelting system (unchanged since the war) produces every year 865,000 tons of air pollutants, including extremely toxic levels of benzine and sulfur compounds. Lung cancer rates have doubled in the past decade, and the majority of children have chronic bronchial diseases.

The flooding of river valleys for gigantic hydroelectric dams, the construction of BAM, oil and gas exploitation, and so on have also altered the geography and distribution of many native peoples. The cost to the Samoyeds on the Yamal Peninsula has been especially keen, since half of their reindeer pastures have been appropriated and the delicately sustained existence of the peninsula itself—"an iceberg with a green skin"—threatened by the reckless haste with which drilling has been done. Not content with city-sized *combinats* or artificial seas, in the mid-1960s Soviet planners also came up with "the project of the century," as they called it, to reverse the course of Siberia's rivers by building a gigantic earthen dam hundreds of miles long along the Arctic coast. All of Central Siberia was to be flooded to form a huge inland sea, and the waters then directed southward through new river channels, blasted through the mountains, to irrigate arid land. Environmentalists, already galvanized by the transformation of the Aral Sea in Central Asia into a desert by a kindred project, rallied to thwart this catastrophic scheme.

Another idea involved the building of a huge hydroelectric power plant and dam on the Katun River (the source of the mighty Ob), which rises in the perennial snows and glaciers of the Altay. Beginning in 1983, construction gangs built a wide highway to the proposed site to bring in heavy equipment, and enormous gashes were cut through masses of bedrock in the gorge. A concrete plant and a prefabricated housing factory immediately went up, but by luck the excavations also uncovered some two thousand burial mounds, with cave drawings dating back to Neolithic times. This caused a delay in the project and led to a closer look at its wisdom, with the realization that the very survival of the agriculturally rich Katun Valley was at stake.

The Cold War also visited Siberia with a vengeance. Novaya Zemlya and Semipalatinsk were used as test sites for thermonuclear blasts in the 1950s, and the Kyshtym Industrial Complex on the shore of Lake Irtyash, 50 miles northwest of Chelyabinsk, became the home of the Soviet atomic bomb. The first plutonium plant was built there in a crash program (with the help of prison labor). Workers were exposed to unsafe levels of radiation, and subsequent negligence led to meltdowns, cracking in the reactor core, and the reckless dumping of toxic wastes into nearby rivers and lakes. One of the lakes accumulated curies to an amount two and a half times that released by the Chernobyl catastrophe, and eventually, traces of radioactive material showed up in the Arctic Ocean nearly 1,000 miles away. In 1957, an accidental nuclear explosion on the southern shore of Lake Irtyash required the evacuation of thousands of people and sent "a plume of toxic isotopes" over the countryside. Today, the Kyshtym Complex also operates a reprocessing plant for separating plutonium from spent reactor fuel, and (possibly) for assembling nuclear warheads. There are nine known military reactors distributed throughout Siberia, not counting a number of civilian plants; in recent years the only Cold War monument to be dismantled on its territory was the notorious radar station complex near Krasnoyarsk, which, as Eduard Shevardnadze noted with chagrin, was "equal in size to the Egyptian pyramids."

None suffered more than the Chukchi, of whom eleven thousand or so remain. Their homeland was used as a proving ground for nuclear testing in the fifties and sixties, and almost all have very high accumulations of radioactive elements, such as lead and cesium, in their bone tissue. As a result, one in five have high blood pressure, and practically the whole population suffers from tuberculosis or chronic lung dis-

EAST OF THE SUN

ease. The lung cancer rate is two to three times above the Soviet average, and the incidence of stomach and liver cancer has doubled in the last twenty years. The death rate from cancer of the esophagus is the highest in the world. Moreover, new forms of malignant tumors—affecting connective tissue and the thyroid glands—have recently appeared. All this has produced a death rate of 70 to 100 per 1,000, and an average life expectancy of only about 45 years.

A number of large nature preserves have rescued part of Siberia from blight. The first (650,000 acres in extent) was established under Tsar Nicholas II in 1916 in the Barguzin Valley, originally to protect the sable but now extended to all wildlife and flora within its perimeters. Under the Soviets, a preserve was also created on Wrangel Island, where walrus, fox, polar bear, and snow geese can find a refuge; a huge Central Siberian Preserve encompasses some 2.5 million acres of taiga; the Zeya National Forest in the Amur Region includes an enormous bird sanctuary; and other preserves protect large parts of the Altay, the Kurile island of Kunashir, and the Taimyr Peninsula. An international park may soon flank Bering Strait. Some of these preserves only superficially resemble national wildlife refuges as we know them in the West, since (except in a few instances) they prohibit public access, and aim at the protection of an overall environment—including its soil and mineral resources—from every possible infringement. This is wonderful for the ecosystem of a natural habitat, and gratifying to the scientific study of specialists, but perhaps something of a loss for the general public, who cannot share in the enjoyment of such a pristine wilderness even under restricted conditions.

Yet in crossing the length and breadth of Siberia, it is the vast emptiness of the inhabited land that remains astonishing, the hundreds of miles of nothing but taiga and plain. In between the towns are rickety old wooden village farmhouses, dusty unpaved streets, and solitary harvesters (portraits in Russian Gothic) standing bewildered in their fields with simple scythes. Old peasant huts consisting of one large room are still warmed by great enamel-covered brick ovens, which double as sleeping platforms; indoor plumbing in many settlements is lacking, and in winter, excrement often accumulates in the outhouses in frozen mounds. People shop for a handful of necessities at local general stores, grow what they can in their little garden plots, and in winter get their milk in frozen blocks and chop their meat like wood with an ax in the yard. Whenever the Trans-Siberian stops at a station, local residents rush to negotiate supplements to their usual fare from the dining car. On the platforms, Russian, Tartar, or Buryat peasants cheerlessly wait behind their little improvised markets and bazaars, where they offer sheep's milk cheese, pickled cucumbers, eggs, roasted chickens, and flat maize cakes for sale. In the hinterland, Yakuts, scornful of more modern housing, prefer hexagonal, yurtlike cabins, with a central chimney hole in the roof: Tungus, who long ago gave up their nomadic ways to live in houses, still spend much of their time in tents in their yards.

Although Tyumen, Siberia's first fortress town, is now an industrial center of about 350,000, Tobolsk to the north has lost all its former glory (although its ancient citadel remains) and the vast frozen wilderness beyond it is home to a population thinly scattered along the tributaries of the Ob. Remote Yakutsk, inhabited by 125,000, has a thriving university, movie theaters, and a satellite disk, but Wrangel Island, surrounded by drifting icefields between the East Siberian and Chukchi seas, has only one small settlement clinging to a coastal hill. Anadyr (founded as Novo-Mariinsk in 1889 and renamed in 1920) has a population of 16,000, but the tiny Eskimo settlement of Uelkal is three days away by dogsled, and at Egvekinot, another Eskimo village (pop. 1,300) on Krestovaya Bay, planes land on packed snow rather than concrete runways.

In many Arctic and sub-Arctic settlements, the windows in the houses, buses, and cars are double or triple thick, and the entrances to buildings have a chamber between two doors that, somewhat like an airlock, mediates between the bitter cold without and the heat within. Mere body heat envelops everyone in little clouds of steam, which rise and accumulate into a blanket of fog above the town. Despite the most concerted efforts, agriculture has been unable to make much headway against the climate; but in some cases experimental farms equipped with hothouses have succeeded in forcing the upper level of the permafrost down six or eight feet, enabling fruits as well as vegetables to grow. The Taimyr Peninsula (an area as large as California) also has its own meat and dairy farms, but the region of Magadan has to import more than 60 percent of its food. "Man," one traveler wrote recently,

is an interloper here, alien. From the air, the occasional roads, pipelines, and railroad tracks he has managed to construct are only the

slightest scratches across the great expanse of snow. In the mornings
I've seen men drink cognac for breakfast to wash down piles of kasha
and plates of horse meat. The oilmen in Surgut board the bus out of
town before there is a hint of dawn in the black Siberian sky. Bundled
in rough, padded coats, they leave like fishermen setting out from a
snug harbor into a sea of wind and wilderness.

Travel across Siberia is still often spoken of as a voyage, out of
tribute to its oceanic vastness, and although all-weather roads and river
highways link various industrial centers to each other and to the Trans-
Siberian, the network remains relatively scant. All the roads radiating
out of Yakutsk are unpaved, and Norilsk can be reached during the
winter only by air. Moreover, aside from the Trans-Siberian Railway
and (in the east) BAM, the length of Siberia is traversed today as it was
a century ago by only one unpaved transcontinental highway, "in summer, a dusty, potholed strip reminiscent of stagecoach days in the
American West." The American West is readily evoked by the Soviet
Far East, which remains an untamed territory with "raw new towns,"
in one description, "as rough as Dodge City in its early days." Its
relatively few major cities, like Blagoveshchensk and Khabarovsk, are
surrounded by wilderness, and across the mile-wide Amur at Khabarovsk, the headquarters of Russian military forces in the Far East, can
be seen the distant Manchurian hills.

Andrei Amalrik, a dissident playwright exiled to Siberia in 1965 for
having "systematically avoided socially useful work" (as an artist, he
supported himself by odd jobs), encountered first hand the relatively
primitive character of Siberian country life. His first stop was Krivosh-
eino, 100 miles south of Tomsk on the Ob, a dusty, muddy village of
mostly one-story wooden houses with wooden sidewalks and two
major streets. Subsequently, he was transferred to an even smaller
village, Guryevka, five miles away, largely made up of ruined houses
with thatched roofs located along the side of a ravine. The houses had
whitewashed walls and ceilings, small windows that could not be
opened, large vaulted stoves, and two rooms: in one of them (the
kitchen), fodder was also prepared for the livestock, and newborn
calves and pigs were kept throughout winter instead of in the barn.
Each house had a vegetable garden, berries were gathered in the
woods, and two old men in the village kept bees; but for the most part,

the villagers lived on sugar, bread, butter, and eggs. Electricity had been brought to the village three years earlier, but was reliably supplied only at milking time to run the machines. As a result, although a number of houses had radio sets, they frequently didn't work.

Amalrik was put to work digging pits for poles that were supposed to carry power lines. In the hot Western Siberian summer, he was assaulted by clouds of midges, his face became swollen with their bites, and in order to urinate in peace he had to climb to the top of a tree. When resting in the shade, he lit a fire to keep the midges away, but the moment he sat down, huge Siberian ants beleaguered him with even more powerful stings. All this discomfort, however, was both unnecessary and useless. The pits were dug with a spade because no one had bothered to fix a drill, the wooden supports for the poles were untreated and doomed to rot, and "in the end ... there was no wire!" In other tasks, too, a little machinery would have gone a long way, but the Stalinist psychology of the 1930s had trickled down to levels where it no longer made even tyrannical sense. Why buy a tractor or a mechanical mower, for example, when labor was free?

The ethnic patchwork of the countryside likewise reflected the Gulag years. Guryevka's settlers had come from Byelorussia; neighboring villages were inhabited by Latvians, Tartars, and Poles. They all had to cut wood at the nearest lumber camp, where they were treated like common prisoners, and in the spring they labored with the same lack of enthusiasm at the local collective farm. Shaped by collectivization, they had lost their proprietary attachment to the soil. In fact, the spirit of enterprise had been so rooted out of them that they worked just as inefficiently on their own private plots as on the farm. And in winter, they drank themselves into a stupor nearly every day.

The fact that exiles were sent to live among them merely served to remind them of what a limited life they led. "Baffled and hurt," wrote Amalrik, "that their town should be used as a prison, they said, 'Why is our life, which we live all the time, considered a punishment?' " which didn't do very much for local morale.

At the same time, prison camp culture (like exile culture before it) had left an indelible imprint on Siberian life. With familiar improvisation, many Siberians in remote hamlets devised homemade, gas-fume lamps out of copper tubes soldered to tin cans, or created playing cards out of sheets of paper glued together with starch. Sometimes the starch was produced by straining masticated bread through a rag. Others drank chifir, an extremely bitter, densely brewed coarse tea that was once used as a camp amphetamine and is now favored by long-distance truck drivers in the north as a completely reliable means of staying awake. Peasants make their own muddy-green vodka from rye, but fortify it with ethyl or denatured alcohol. The higher the latitude, the stronger the brew—for it is "a Siberian tradition," we are told, "to have the percentage of pure alcohol in vodka match the latitude of the place where it is consumed." Eau de cologne, and even turpentine and anti-freeze filtered through bread and cotton, are sometimes used by Siberian alcoholics' to keep their spirits up.

Unable to rely on Russian medicine to cure their ailments, Siberians also tend to fall back on home remedies, such as suppositories made of raw potatoes for treating hemorrhoids and compresses made of sauerkraut for migraine. Vodka, of course, is often liberally consumed for medicinal purposes (to kill any harmful bacteria, it is said, that might inadvertently be ingested at a meal), and sugar serves as a general antidote to poisons. Official prescriptions dispensed by a local pharmacy are not necessarily more effective or safe.

Lacking the technology to exploit the resources it possessed, by the 1980s the Soviet Union had begun to face an energy crisis, with its oil and coal industries unable to increase production. Some parts of the Trans-Siberian had yet to be electrified; tankers commissioned for the transport of petroleum in the Arctic seas proved too big for their designated ports; other problems stalled the economy. *Perestroika* seemed to promise a way out. Dozens of foreign companies—Amoco, Mitsubishi, Hyundai, PalmCo., among others—signed "protocols of intent" with Soviet state concerns, covering possible joint ventures in oil and gas development in Western Siberia, lumber and gas-pipeline projects in the Far East, the building of cold-storage and other facilities for processing, packaging, and transporting food, port development, housing, ski resorts, hotels, discos, and so on; yet few real deals were struck. The risks seemed extravagant, and Soviet organizations were notorious for reneging on agreements, bills, and the delivery of promised goods. In the last days of the Union, as the internal distribution system broke down completely, the barter economy within and between republics, districts, cities, towns, factories, and individuals reached new heights. Timber was swapped for grain, shoes for tractors, sugar for cement. In some cases, goods were exchanged for expertise —the Amur District, for example, supplied soybeans to a butter-and-fat combine in Khabarovsk in return for help in its garment industry. Under such circumstances, the border trade along the Sino-Siberian frontier (based in part on the barter system, but also using Swiss francs as the currency of exchange) flourished, with Siberians obtaining finished Chinese goods like towels, blouses, shirts, and flashlights for such things as fertilizer and wood.

History is long, and "whosoever in writing a modern history shall follow truth too near the Heels," cautioned Sir Walter Ralegh in his *History of the World,* "it may happily strike out his Teeth." Ralegh (subject to a sovereign's wrath) had more than the problems of veracity in mind, but in attempting to fathom Russia's future one could do worse (for once) than appropriate an enigmatic sentence from *Tass* on a recent attempt by a research team to determine the deepest point of Lake Baikal: "Data on the magnetic declination of Baikal's anomalies was specified." Perhaps only one thing can be said for certain, and it recalls a prediction made over two centuries ago by Mikhail Lomonosov who, in a fit of enthusiasm for Russia's early eastern expansion, wrote: "Russia's might will grow by way of Siberia." He said this before the empire of the tsars had been largely established; now that that empire, inherited by the Soviets, has dissolved, it is true beyond any dream he could have had.

When the Russians first plunged across the Urals, there had been, aside from the tenuously confederated "state" of Sibir, no national political entity to oppose them; and as they rapidly extended their conquest across the land, none emerged until they were confronted in the Amur Valley by the Chinese. The Chinese never claimed any part of Siberia for themselves (beyond the suzerainty owed to them by a few of the tribes), and what interest they had in the land north of Mongolia was readily relinquished in 1689 by the Treaty of Nerchinsk. So, aside from the hereditary rights of the aboriginal population, Russia's possession of this huge territory faces no plausible challenge from any other power. Nor are the natives sufficiently numerous (in proportion to the Russians) to mount a collective nationalist movement of any force. All today are minorities in their own homelands, and few would be likely to agitate for some kind of independent statehood where none existed before. Only if Siberia itself as a "colony" of the mother country were to declare its independence could it join in the pattern of separation that has dissolved the USSR.

Local sentiment, in any case, scarcely supports such a move. A quarter to a third of the Russian population now lives in Siberia, and it has been left for the nationalities to declare their republican autonomy within a Russian federation. In May of 1990, a Latvian-born Russian lieutenant, remonstrating with other pro-independence Latvians, reportedly asked: "Where will it all end? So the Baltics want to get out of the Soviet Union. Do you think this will make things better? Then the Chukchis will want their own territory. They have all the gold. They could live like Arab princes." Most Chukchis would find that surprising. What native (and Russian) Siberians do want is more political say in the direction of their lives, and more control of the land in which they live. And now that all the empire's artificially appended states have split away, Siberia remains. With Siberia, Russia will continue to be by far the largest, and potentially the richest, nation on earth.

SOURCE NOTES

For abbreviations used in the notes, and for full titles and other bibliographical information on books, articles, and other materials cited, the reader is referred to the Bibliography.

PART ONE

CHAPTER 1: THE SLEEPING LAND
27 "mysterious and far-extending": Waliszewski, *Ivan the Terrible,* p. 349.
28 "If it were possible": Kennan, *Siberia and the Exile System,* vol. 1, p. 56.
28 Lake Baikal: To compound the mysteries of this lake (where chronology, in a sense, has been reversed), in 1991 it was discovered that it was actually an ocean in the making, with hydrothermal vents, like those in mid-ocean ridges, along its floor.
29 "it is only upon Baikal": Meakin, *A Ribbon of Iron,* p. 158.
29 "centrally defeated": Bruemmer, "Life upon the Permafrost," p. 32.
29 "Moss had grown": Ibid.
30 "like a neglected vine": Kennan, *Tent Life in Siberia,* p. 310.
30 "with terrible growths": Shalamov, *Kolyma Tales,* p. 62.
30 "only migrating birds": Quoted in St. George, *Siberia. The New Frontier,* p. 108.
32 "a mixture of sand": Mirsky, *To the Arctic!,* p. 4.
32 All this was Siberia: The southern Kuriles are still disputed territory, of course, and may or may not be considered part of Siberia; eventually, they will probably be ceded to Japan.

32 "pressed down at the base": Shinkarev, op. cit., p. 16.

32 "the well-known diadems": Ibid.

32 "huge, stooping mammoths": Ibid., p. 17.

33 "a more complete representation": Wright, *Asiatic Russia,* vol. 1, p. 253.

34 "the Land": Ibid., p. 217.

34 "The prince": Quoted in ibid., p. 5.

36 "all the efforts": A. F. Anisimov, "Cosmological Concepts of the Peoples of the North," in Michael, ed., *Studies in Siberian Shamanism,* p. 159.

36 "high up among": Kennan, *Tent Life in Siberia,* p. 124.

CHAPTER 2: CROSSING THE DIVIDE

37 "doe eate serpentes": Morgan and Coote, eds., *Early Voyages and Travels in Russia and Persia,* vol. 1, p. cxxxi.

37 "to the east of the sun": Sumner, *Survey of Russian History,* p. 458n.

38 known as Yugra: cognates survive, as in the "Yugrian Strait" between Vaygach Island and the mainland.

38 "land of Sibur": *Istorichesky arkhiv,* vol. 3, 1940, p. 93.

39 the Livonian War: The sixteenth-century state of Livonia roughly comprised modern Latvia and Estonia. When the Russians first invaded, the Livonians, ruled by an obsolete and degenerate order of medieval knights, didn't put up much of a fight, but Ivan was ultimately defeated by a coalition of Baltic powers.

40 saltworks at Solvychegodsk: literally, "the saltworks on the Vychegda River," located near a salt lake.

40 "to drive a wedge": Lantzeff and Pierce, *Eastward to Empire,* p. 89.

40 "hired Cossacks": Ibid.

41 "his associates": Vvedenskiy, *Dom Stroganovykh,* p. 88.

41 (so the story goes): A letter to the king of Poland in 1581 mentions Yermak (both by his nickname and patronymic) as the deputy commander of a Cossack contingent on the Lithuanian frontier. Some scholars are convinced that Yermak was officially transferred to the Urals by the tsar early in 1582.

42 a Cossack army of 840 men: 840 is the traditional figure. The Yesipov Chronicle (chapter 7) mentions that Yermak's band numbered 540. The Stroganov Chronicle (chapter 11) adds to these 300 men recruited on the Chusovaya, making an army of 840. The New Chronicle has 600 men coming from the Volga, afterwards joined by 50. The Remezov Chronicle (chapter 6) claims an army of 5,000.

42 "singing hymns": Longworth, *The Cossacks,* p. 53.

42 "tipped into the river": Ibid.

42 "secured by indentures": Lantzeff and Pierce, op. cit., p. 95.

42 "led a sinful life": Remezov Chronicle, chapter 23; see Armstrong, ed., *Yermak's Campaign in Siberia,* p. 117.

43 "The skies burst open": Ibid., p. 99.

44 the fabled "wolf-path": Ibid., p. 117.

44 on the very same day: Both the circumstantial background and conven-

tional chronology of the campaign have recently been challenged by the formidable Soviet scholar R. G. Skrynnikov. Skrynnikov holds that "all documents compiled in the early 1580s that are preserved in the original indicate accurately and categorically that Yermak began his campaign not on 1 September 1581, but on 1 September 1582." See "Ermak's Siberian Expedition," p. 12.

44 "disobedience amounting to treason": Lantzeff and Pierce, op. cit., p. 101.

45 "were forced to eat": Ibid., p. 105.

45 "floated out of his reach": Armstrong, op. cit., p. 211.

46 "colorless hordes": So-called not only from their pale complexion, but to distinguish them from the Mongol spectrum of fighting groups. The Mongols had assigned colors to different points of the compass and "white," not incidentally, was the color of the West.

47 "In Siberia . . . [the tsar] hath": Bond, ed., *Russia at the Close of the Sixteenth Century,* p. 83.

47 "the cornerstone": Lantzeff and Pierce, op. cit., p. 127.

47 "planned domination of rivers": Kerner, *The Urge to the Sea,* p. 13.

48 "to reverse the course of history": Shinkarev, *The Land Beyond the Mountains,* p. 44.

48 risings took place in his name: In 1654, one traveler found "the whole Urals area terrorized by a confederation of tribes led by Kuchum's grandson."

48 Yermak's flesh was found to be: Baddeley, *Russia, Mongolia, China,* p. lxxiii.

48 "the sick were healed": Armstrong, op. cit., p. 223.

CHAPTER 3: "TO THE EAST OF THE SUN"

49 "like Nebuchadnezzar": Olearius, *The Voyages and Travels . . . ,* p. 13.

49 "in the manner of Xerxes": Ibid.

50 "that Russians might not": Bond, ed., *Russia at the Close of the Sixteenth Century,* p. 56.

50 "which cutt like knives": Olearius, op. cit., p. 13.

50 "set a print into": Bond, ed., op. cit., p. 151.

51 "Churches, ikons": Quoted in Kelly, ed., *Moscow,* pp. 260–61.

51 "as with an axe": Quoted in Avrich, *Russian Rebels 1600–1800,* p. 12.

52 "consolation after the sorrows": Povroskii, *History of Russia,* p. 140.

52 "As God is my witness": Hingley, *The Tsars,* p. 75.

52 "We take a moderate": Quoted in Levin and Potapov, eds., *The Peoples of Siberia,* p. 115.

53 "people perished": Massa, *Short Account of Muscovy at the Beginning of the XVII Century,* p. 54.

53 the murder of the tsarevich Dmitry: On May 15, 1591, the tsarevich Dmitry, while playing with a knife in the courtyard of his residence at Uglich, reputedly cut his own throat in an epileptic fit. This unlikely demise understandably aroused grave suspicions, but there must have

been a number of political figures not eager to see him come to power. As a child he had already begun to manifest "sadistic traits reminiscent of his father's" (Vernadsky, "The Death of Tsarevich Dmitry," p. 16), liked to watch as animals were slaughtered, and for his own sport decapitated snowmen fashioned in the likeness of various aristocrats.

54   "a strange and ungainly": Hingley, op. cit., p. 78.
55   "the Kingdoms of Kazan, Astrakhan": Massa, op. cit., p. 91.
56   "Hundreds of thousands of sable": St. George, *Siberia. The New Frontier*, p. 264.
56   "a virtual Baghdad": Ibid., p. 265.
56   "put to the hardest": Ibid., p. 254.
57   "destroyed town": Ibid., p. 267.
57   "to the east of the sun": See source note for page 37.
59   "those who did not willingly": Georg Gmelin, quoted in Huppert, *Men of Siberia*, p. 33.
59   "almost interlocked like": Neatby, *Discovery in Russian and Siberian Waters*, p. 13.
61   to "follow the spring": St. George, op. cit., p. 263.
61   "a relatively light": Fisher, *The Voyage of Semen Dezhnev in 1648*, p. 162.
62   "like Western ships": Ibid., p. 164.
64   "to find new": Ibid., p. 58.
65   "salary in money and grain": Ibid., p. 106.
65   "I risked my head": Ibid., p. 247.
66   "By answering an important": Ibid., p. 276.

CHAPTER 4: "SOFT GOLD"

67   "followed the route to empire": Lantzeff, *Siberia in the Seventeenth Century*, p. 1.
67   "owed its opening": Fisher, *The Russian Fur Trade, 1550–1700*, p. 34.
68   "unripped, with bellies and feet": Ibid., p. 21.
69   "merely a change of masters": Ibid., p. 51.
69   "imprison them": Dmytryshyn, Vaughan, and Crownhart-Vaughan, eds. and trans., *Russia's Conquest of Siberia, 1558–1700*, p. lv.
70   "the old, the crippled": Lantzeff, *Siberia in the Seventeenth Century*, p. 125.
71   "with the best from the best": Fisher, op. cit., p. 61.
71   Strip searches: see Golder, *Russian Expansion on the Pacific, 1641–1850*, p. 21.
72   "The difference between": Mancall, *Russia and China*, p. 18.
72   the dominant item: Kerner, *The Urge to the Sea*, p. 67.
73   "supplementary mint": Bassin, "Expansion and Colonization on the Eastern Frontier," p. 11.
73   Godunov instead sent the emperor: Fisher, op. cit., p. 138.
73   "a kind of berry": Ibid., p. 155.
74   "without injuring": Kennan, *Tent Life in Siberia*, p. 159.

75   "entirely at the initiative": MERSH, vol. 35, p. 99.

76   "With fifty men": Quoted in Utley and Washburn, *Indian Wars,* p. 9.

77   "Yukaghir Fire": Levin and Potapov, op. cit., p. 788.

78   "to pile up hides": Utley, *The Indian Frontier,* p. 13.

CHAPTER 5: THE BLACK DRAGON RIVER

79   "such, that in Russia": Lantzeff, *Siberia in the Seventeenth Century,* p. 78.

80   "in spite of his insistent demands": Lantzeff and Pierce, *Eastward to Empire,* p. 156.

80   "And the warriors": Quoted in ibid., p. 158.

81   "the future granary": Tupper, *To the Great Ocean,* p. 28.

81   "more fish in the Amur": Bassin, "Expansion and Colonization on the Eastern Frontier," p. 13.

82   "completely devastated": Lantzeff and Pierce, op. cit., p. 163.

82   "with God's help": Golder, *Russian Expansion on the Pacific, 1641–1850,* p. 45.

82   "When the Russians first arrived": Ravenstein, *The Russians on the Amur,* p. 13.

83   "a young girl could": Sebes, *The Jesuits and the Sino-Russian Treaty of Nerchinsk, 1689,* p. 134.

84   "seized him by the beard": Lantzeff and Pierce, op. cit., p. 166.

85   "shown ability and daring": Tupper, op. cit., p. 29.

85   "The star of the Russian fur": Fisher, *The Russian Fur Trade, 1550–1700,* p. 209.

86   "not to act": Sebes, op. cit., p. 59.

87   "Barefoot and half-naked": Wood, "Avvakum's Siberian Exile," in Wood and French, eds., *The Development of Siberia,* p. 28.

87   "They have come into": Mancall, *Russia and China,* p. 314.

88   "not counting daughters": Lantzeff and Pierce, op. cit., p. 171.

88   "permanent settlements": Mancall, op. cit., p. 31.

88   "You can hunt sables": Quoted in ibid., p. 127.

90   "If the Russians will accede": Quoted in Sebes, op. cit., p. 73.

92   "in all their Robes of State": Mancall, op. cit., p. 155.

92   "the population on" and "fixed by heaven": Quoted in Semyonov, *The Conquest of Siberia,* p. 127.

93   "the Muscovites . . . ordered": Sebes, op. cit., p. 52.

94   "the uncertain benefits": Foust, *Muscovite and Mandarin,* p. 7.

95   which drew that part of the southern boundary: The map used by the Russian and Chinese negotiators was evidently based on the one prepared in 1678 by Nikolai-Milescu Spafary, the Russian envoy (1675–76) to Peking. See Fisher, *Bering's Voyages,* p. 33.

CHAPTER 6: "THE YERMAK OF KAMCHATKA"

97   "one man driving": Ogorodnikov, *Ocherhii istorii sibiri,* II, 1, p. 280.

97   "in towns made of stone": Dmytryshyn, Vaughan, and Crownhart-Vaughan, eds. and trans., *Russia's Conquest of Siberia,* p. 13.

98   his name was Dembei: In Moscow, officials of the Siberian Department correctly identified Dembei as Japanese by means of an illustrated German book describing Japan.

100   "to rid themselves": Fisher, *The Voyage of Semen Dezhnev in 1648,* p. 193.

CHAPTER 7: ADMINISTRATION

102   "The principal differences": Wright, *Asiatic Russia,* vol. 2, p. 280.

102   "For this we came out": Riha, ed., *Readings in Russian Civilization,* vol. 2, p. 146.

103   "I would lay all": Ibid.

103   "beat us mercilessly": Lantzeff, *Siberia in the Seventeenth Century,* p. 80.

106   "they try to get rich": Ibid., p. 172.

106   "walked the straight path": Stejneger, *Georg Wilhelm Steller,* p. 141.

106   "the wheels of justice": Lantzeff, op. cit., p. 108.

107   "lived like pagans": Quoted in Levin and Potapov, eds., *The Peoples of Siberia,* p. 118.

108   "rich pageantry, color": Dmytryshyn, ed., *Russia's Conquest,* p. xlix.

108   "There are enough monasteries": Quoted in Lantzeff, op. cit., p. 187.

109   "by imprisoning her": Wood, "Avvakum's Siberian Exile," in Wood and French, eds., *The Development of Siberia,* p. 29.

109   "publicly and vehemently . . . ordered": Ibid., p. 22.

110   "collected a little": Instructions to Golovin, quoted in Lantzeff, op. cit., fn., p. 36.

CHAPTER 8: A VANISHING WORLD

111   "were lucky . . . prisons of isolation": Longworth, *The Cossacks,* pp. 68–69.

112   "convinced of their right": Lantzeff and Pierce, *Eastward to Empire,* p. 226.

112   "What is the right": Quoted in Utley, *The Indian Frontier,* p. 36.

112   "just like the waters": Ibid., p. 35.

113   "incubators" . . . "they had mastered": Rasky, *The Polar Voyagers,* p. 23.

113   "keep on making a new eye" . . . "as round and smooth": Krasheninnikov, *Explorations of Kamchatka, 1735–1741,* p. 217.

114   "as to charge a man": Levin and Potapov, eds., *The Peoples of Siberia,* p. 807.

114   "was caught with a lariat": Ibid.

114   "most fiercely" . . . "not having undergone": Lansdell, *Through Siberia,* p. 368.

116   "Then hee tooke": Richard Johnson, in Hakluyt, *The Principal Navigations,* vol. 1, 284.

116   "spies sent by the god": Krasheninnikov, op. cit., p. 188.

117   "on the red blaze": Czaplicka, *Aboriginal Siberia,* p. 312.

117   "made all the bad things": G. M. Vasilievich, "Early Concepts About the Universe Among the Evenks (Materials)," in Michael, ed., *Studies in Siberian Shamanism,* p. 68.

117   "Man was born from a tree": Ibid.

117   "the stars which go crosswise": A. F. Anisimov, "Cosmological Concepts of the Peoples of the North," in ibid., p. 212.

117   "are so stupid": Krasheninnikov, op. cit., p. 206.

118   from pieces of his clothes and hair: As in the biblical story of Samson, essential vitality was believed to reside in the hair. Ostyak and Vogul warriors scalped their victims to prevent the reincarnation of their souls.

118   "to prevent the child": Czaplicka, op. cit., p. 161.

118   called "grandfathers": *A Handbook of Siberia and Arctic Russia,* vol. 1, p. 104.

118   "with perfect composure": Kennan, *Tent Life in Siberia,* p. 215.

118   "and the ashes": Ibid., p. 14.

119   "full of clear": Levin and Potapov, op. cit., p. 13.

119   "drunken, reprobate savage": Utley, op. cit., p. 17.

120   "to eat plenty of fat food": Kennan, op. cit., p. 276.

120   "squatting on a great snowy plain": Ibid., p. 275.

120   "as boundless to": Ibid., p. 253.

120   "was silence and desolation": Ibid., p. 267.

122   "the whistling of which" and "dive into": Potapov and Levin, op. cit., p. 520.

122   "slim as a knitting needle": Rasky, op. cit., p. 36.

124   "acidified and half-rotten": Levin and Potapov, eds., op. cit., p. 269.

124   "gulped down the eyeballs": Ibid., p. 35.

124   "the nearest approximation": Kennan, op. cit., p. 180.

125   "cached away grain" . . . "carefully remove": Tupper, *To the Great Ocean,* p. 7n.

125   "in large mouthfuls": Levin and Potapov, op. cit., p. 157.

125   "in the wooded steppe": Gibson, op. cit., p. 46.

125   "whose Noses": Ibid., p. 47.

128   "well-rutted by": *Pioneer Women,* p. 187.

128   to "transport" women: See Lantzeff and Pierce, *Eastward to Empire,* p. 102.

128   "using their own wives": See Lantzeff, *Siberia in the Seventeenth Century,* p. 180.

129   "woman not yet put in use": Czaplicka, op. cit., p. 70.

129   "cut and tear off": Krasheninnikov, op. cit., p. 266.

129   "purified" . . . "but only a stranger": Ibid., p. 267.

129   "over the slightest suspicion": Ibid., p. 283.

130   "To refuse to sleep": Ibid.

130   "among the Russians": Bogaras, quoted in Czaplicka, op. cit., p. 70.

130   the mating behavior: Carl Heinrich Merck in Pierce, ed., *Siberia and Northwestern America, 1788–1792,* p. 27.

130   "voluntarily risked": Treadgold, *The Great Siberian Migration,* p. 6.

132   "flourished as": Lantzeff, op. cit., p. 177.

PART TWO

CHAPTER 9: MAPPING THE MIND OF A TSAR

138   "half-barbarous, half-cultivated": Baring, *The Russian People,* p. 137.

138   "intellectual and technical cooperation": Riha, ed., *Readings in Russian Civilization,* vol. 2, p. 147.

140   "The maritime and trading Powers": Aubry de la Mottraye, quoted in Urness, *Bering's First Expedition,* pp. 1–2.

141   "over and above the amount": Fisher, *Bering's Voyages,* p. 163.

142   "searched fruitlessly": Utley and Washburn, *Indian Wars,* p. 9.

142   "nature breeds, Perverse": Mirsky, *To the Arctic!,* p. 13.

142   "a terrible insucking whirlpool": Tracy, *True Ocean Found,* p. 61.

143   "to hold before their eyes": Ibid.

143   "went in over the": Hakluyt, *Principal Navigations,* vol. 2, p. 334.

144   "whole towns made of ice": Rasky, *The Polar Voyagers,* p. 163.

144   "as if in the grip": Ibid.

145   "From Weygats [Vaygach Island] to the Icy": Isbrand Ides, quoted in Urness, op. cit., p. 45.

146   "as soon as he had": Quoted in Barratt, op. cit., p. 9.

146   "experienced in navigation": M. de Camprédon, French ambassador at St. Petersburg, 1719–26, quoted in Barratt, *Russia in Pacific Waters, 1715–1825,* p. 48.

146   "You will proceed": Quoted in Fisher, op. cit., p. 59.

146   "pausing on his way": Ibid.

147   "not far off from": Quoted in Urness, op. cit., p. 57.

147   "poor quality sables": Polevoi, in Starr, ed., *Russia's American Colony,* p. 18.

147   "based on river systems": Fisher, op. cit., p. 26.

147   "one or two complete": Ibid., p. 29.

148   "reports of mariners": Quoted in Urness, op. cit., p. 44.

148   "the unknown East-coast": Quoted in ibid., p. 14.

150   "I was then almost constantly . . .": Quoted in Golder, *Bering's Voyages,* vol. 1, p. 9.

150   "a navigator and assistant": Quoted in Dmytryshyn, Vaughan, and Crownhart-Vaughan, eds. and trans., *Russian Penetration of the North Pacific Ocean, 1700–1797,* pp. 66–67.

151   "In Kamchatka": Quoted in ibid., p. 69.

152   "consumed not only": Golder, op. cit., vol. 1, p. 16.

152   "burnt off the Hair": Quoted in Urness, op. cit., p. 305.

153   "And during his whole Passage": Ibid., p. 306.

153   "a current-ridden": Barratt, op. cit., p. 5.

153   "lacked all marine": Ibid.

153   "rolled like a dark": Dobell, *Travels in Kamchatka and Siberia,* vol. 1, p. 102.

153   "or when-ever they had": Urness, op. cit., p. 308.

154 a "strange place": Ibid., p. 309.
154 "if a sufficient Number": Ibid., p. 312.
154 "instead of Meal or Corn": Ibid., p. 313.
155 "When we invited them": Dmytryshyn, et al., op. cit., p. 85.
155 "because we have reached": Quoted in Fisher, op. cit., p. 83.
156 "a good Quantity": Urness, op. cit., p. 316.
156 "which Thing was never": Ibid.
158 "no end to it . . . a naked native": Dmytryshyn, et al., op. cit., p. 132.
158 "say nothing about a strait": Fisher, op. cit., p. 23.
159 the location of a strait: A primary source for the Homann map—the sketch maps of Johann Philipp Tabbert von Strahlenberg, a Swedish prisoner of war who spent a decade in Siberia (1711–21) before his repatriation in 1722—confirm this. A work based upon his maps and published in Leiden in 1726 (two years before Bering sailed) also flatly states: "It has been believ'd till the present that Asia was joined on the N.E. to North America, and that for this Reason it was impossible to sail from the Icy Sea into the eastern Ocean; but since the Discovery of the Country of Kamtzchatka, 'tis known for certain that America is not contiguous to Asia." Quoted in Urness, op. cit., p. 151.
159 "Having become a naval power": Fisher, op. cit., p. 170.
160 "There is no doubt": Ibid., p. 158.

CHAPTER 10: THE GREAT NORTHERN EXPEDITION
162 "low waves which are customary": Fisher, *Bering's Voyages,* p. 113.
162 "They sought to continue": Lauridsen, *Vitus Bering,* p. 92.
163 "the like of which": Kirilov, quoted in Fisher, op. cit., p. 184.
163 "the collection of tribute": Quoted in ibid., p. 130.
163 "to build boats": Golder, *Bering's Voyages,* vol. 1, p. 31.
165 "in all its undertakings": Hulley, *Alaska,* p. 53.
165 "expansion of the empire": Fisher, op. cit., p. 184.
165 "in the exploration": Ibid., p. 131.
165 "for public display": Ibid., p. 75.
165 "either secretly or openly": Dmytryshyn, Vaughan, and Crownhart-Vaughan, eds. and trans., *Russian Penetration of the North Pacific Ocean, 1700–1797,* p. 125.
166 "a man of good manners": Golder, op. cit., vol. 2, p. 154.
166 "the Accounts that he received": Urness, *Bering's First Expedition,* p. 303.
166 "unruly native peoples": Quoted in Barratt, op. cit., p. 24.
166 "so that they may get": Golder, op. cit., vol. 1, p. 31.
167 "right luxuriously equipped": Lauridsen, op. cit., p. 69.
167 "whose acquaintance": *Alaska. The Great Land,* p. 22.
167 "not only of scientific": Lauridsen, op. cit., p. 69.
167 "as well as bulky": Barratt, *Russia in Pacific Waters, 1715–1825,* p. 38.
167 "to move this cumbersome": Lauridsen, op. cit., p. 70.
169 "so that from now on": Stejneger, *Georg Wilhelm Steller,* p. 117.

169 "Your expedition is a very": Quoted in Lauridsen, op. cit., p. 209.

169 "as a result of failures": Barratt, op. cit., p. 33.

169 "not a pood": Ibid., p. 195.

169 "the whole expedition come": Ibid., p. 196.

170 "there was no means": Krasheninnikov, quoted in Stejneger, op. cit., p. 117.

171 "had enough to do": Ibid., p. 114.

171 "impossible for anyone": Ibid., p. 111.

172 "gone to seed": Lensen, *The Russian Push Toward Japan,* p. 46.

173 "no Pisarev, no ships": Golder, vol. 1, p. 13.

173 "gave himself over": Lensen, op. cit., p. 46.

174 "For a correspondence": Lauridsen, op. cit., p. 100.

174 "We then learned": Quoted in Stejneger, op. cit., p. 120.

175 "a born naturalist": Ibid., p. 19.

175 "a precocious inclination": Ibid.

175 "so prepared": Ibid., p. 25.

175 "Once on the night": Quoted in ibid., p. 43.

177 "monuments and other antiquities": Ibid., p. 83.

177 a "wild young woman": Ibid.

177 "decided to stay home": Golder, op. cit., vol. 2, p. 13.

177 "to undertake anything": Stejneger, op. cit., p. 392.

177 "rush to get drunk": Quoted in ibid., p. 144.

178 "went nearly into ecstasies": Ibid., p. 145.

178 "He was not troubled": Quoted in ibid., pp. 146–48.

178 "with considerable experience": Ibid., p. 150.

179 "they could [still]": Ibid., p. 169.

179 "which nearly drove him": Ibid., p. 175.

181 "so deeply in debt": Ibid., p. 174.

183 "in the slimy environs": Golder, op. cit., vol. 2, p. 157.

183 "To his melancholy fate": Wright, *Asiatic Russia,* vol. 1, p. 101.

184 "It had not been the wish": Rasky, *The Polar Voyagers,* p. 108.

185 "It became quite evident": Golder, op. cit., vol. 1, p. 200.

185 "observing in the water": Rasky, op. cit., p. 74.

186 "with great expectations" and "shrugged his shoulders": Golder, op. cit., vol. 2, p. 35.

186 "stood out alone": Ibid., vol. 1, p. 113.

186 "the first white man to set foot on Alaska": Stejneger, op. cit., p. 267. Khitrov, searching for an anchorage, may or may not have landed before Steller did, but one would like to accord Steller the honor.

187 "to take a good look": Golder, op. cit., vol. 2, p. 50.

187 "to this it was objected": Ibid., p. 52.

188 "prepared to receive": Stejneger, op. cit., p. 271.

188 "human tracks": Ibid., vol. 1, p. 99.

188 "so smooth," etc.: Ibid., vol. 2, p. 53. .

189 Scurvy, the terror: Scurvy was not definitely recognized as a deficiency disease until 1753 (a decade after Bering's voyage), when the Scottish naval surgeon James Lind showed that it could be cured and prevented

by eating oranges, lemons, or limes. After the English Admiralty included the latter in regular shipboard fare (along with sauerkraut and cress), English sailors came to be known as "limeys."

189   "For over four hours": Golder, op. cit., vol. 2, p. 55.
189   "a full grown bachelor": Stejneger, op. cit., p. 281.
190   "but although in this matter": Ibid., p. 291.
190   one of the sick: The surname of this sailor, Shumagin, was later given to the island group.
190   "only look after": Ibid., p. 86.
191   "Everyone grumbled": Golder, op. cit., vol. 2, p. 88.
191   "we had scarcely": Ibid., p. 90.
191   "with a laugh": Ibid., p. 92.
191   "he tied an entire": Ibid.
192   "in a very friendly way": Ibid., p. 94.
192   "scolded us": Ibid., p. 97.
192   "and shouted very loudly": Ibid., p. 98.
193   "we could not imagine": Ibid., p. 116.
193   "shot like arrows": Ibid.
193   "misery and death": Ibid., p. 128.
193   "It had come to this": Ibid.
194   "It is impossible": Ibid., pp. 129–30.
194   "still able to drag": Ibid., vol. 1, p. 276.
195   "at last, according": Ibid., vol. 2, p. 134.
196   "as in a placid lake": Stejneger, op. cit., p. 315.
196   "God knows whether": Golder, op. cit., vol. 2, p. 139.
196   "got up, were gay": G. F. Müller, quoted in ibid., p. 321.
197   "swollen like a sponge": Golder, op. cit., vol. 2, p. 149.
197   "killed young and old": Ibid., p. 149.
197   "which in former days": Ibid., p. 150.
198   "in full possession": Ibid., p. 159.
199   "nothing but card-playing": Steller, quoted in Stejneger, op. cit., p. 338.
199   "out of their mind": Golder, op. cit., vol. 2, p. 171.
199   "dug out of the snow": Golder, op. cit., vol. 2, p. 173.
200   "Entire families keep": Quoted in Stejneger, op. cit., pp. 355–56.
201   "browsing on seaweed": Ibid., p. 353.
201   "tried to upset": Steller, quoted in Stejneger, p. 356.
201   "tearing with their vile": Ibid., p. 365.
202   "with the greatest glee": Golder, vol. 2, p. 183.
203   "it did no good": Ibid., vol. 1, 296.
204   "a tidal bore": Murphy, The Haunted Voyage, p. 209.
204   "men walking through" and "turning first": Golder, op. cit., vol. 1, p. 304.
204   "no great gratitude". . . . "they were quite overjoyed": Dmytryshyn, et al., op. cit., p. 137.
205   "large quantities of brandy": Stejneger, op. cit., p. 379.
205   "He had the best heart": Quoted in ibid., p. 150.

206   "discouraged and disgusted": Ibid.
207   "wished nothing more": Quoted in ibid., p. 391.
207   Grigory Demidov: The Demidovs were the regional successors of the
       Stroganovs, whose political and economic fortunes had declined under
       Peter the Great. One Salt Lake City (Solikamsk) replaced another (Sol-
       vychegodsk) as the local seat of industrial power.
208   "mingled with the bones": Quoted in Stejneger, op. cit., p. 488.
208   "discovered more new plants": MERSH, vol. 12, p. 204.
209   "rough drafts": Quoted in Stejneger, op. cit., pp. 496–97.

CHAPTER 11: RUSSIAN AMERICA
211   "reports of": Hulley, *Alaska*, p. 29.
211   "to meet the sun": Boris P. Polevoi, in Starr, ed., *Russia's American
       Colony,* p. 31.
212   "multiplied remarkably": Pallas, in Masterson and Brower, eds., *Bering's
       Successors, 1745–80,* p. 34.
212   "men with big teeth": Krasheninnikov, *Explorations of Kamchatka,
       1735–1741,* p. 70.
212   "a practically unsinkable": Barratt, *Russia in Pacific Waters, 1715–1825,*
       p. 46.
213   "rank compulsion": Carl Heinrich Merck, in Pierce, ed., *Siberia and
       Northwestern America, 1788–1792,* p. 172.
214   "as an object of": Masterson and Brower, *Bering's Successors,* p. 59.
214   "with needle and yarn": Ibid., p. 104.
214   "gave birth to": Ibid., p. 167.
214   "began to make": Ibid.
214   "very strange to see": Golovin, *Civil and Savage Encounters,* p. 70.
216   "He learned": Ibid., p. 103.
217   "outrage and oppression": Barratt, op. cit., p. 46.
218   "was in fact the 'cape' ": Polevoi, in Starr, op. cit., p. 25.
219   "In their persons": Quoted in Masterson and Bower, eds., *Bering's Suc-
       cessors, 1745–80,* pp. 58–59.
222   the Sandwich Islands: named by Cook in honor of the earl of Sandwich,
       First Lord of the Admiralty.
223   "The weather becoming clear": Quoted in Neatby, *Discovery in Russian
       and Siberian Waters,* p. 89.
223   "a general silence ensued": Withey, *Voyages of Discovery,* p. 388.
224   There they learned: In fact, writes one historian, "the French had issued
       orders that Cook's ships were not to be molested because of the scien-
       tific importance of their mission, and Benjamin Franklin, the colonies'
       agent in France, had drafted similar orders to commanders of American
       ships. Franklin asked American ship captains to treat Cook and his crew
       with " 'Civility and kindness . . . as common Friends to Mankind.' "
       (Withey, ibid., p. 399.) The Continental Congress, however, that bastion
       of the new Enlightenment, rejected Franklin's guidelines, in what was
       not their most enlightened hour.

224   "Never was there greater": Quoted in Gibson, *Feeding the Russian Fur Trade,* p. 17.

224   "The Empress . . . expressed": Quoted in Barratt, *The Russian View of Honolulu, 1809–26,* p. 3.

225   "This territory belongs": Ibid., p. 88.

225   "two large hunting dogs" and "new, curious": Lavender, *The Way to the Western Sea,* p. 6.

226   "the initial investment": Wheeler, in Starr, op. cit., p. 45.

226   "stable, long-term rewards": Polevoi, in Starr, op. cit., p. 29.

227   "a handsome block": Barratt, *Russia in Pacific Waters,* p. 105.

227   "The main end": Ibid., pp. 100–01.

228   "a monopoly and exclusive trade": Polevoi, in Starr, op. cit., p. 29.

229   "assembled with their": Gibson, *Imperial Russia in Frontier America,* p. 33.

229   "but tusks, which measured": Ibid., p. 36.

230   "Next to a beautiful young woman": Quoted in Hulley, op. cit., p. 108.

230   "always on the lookout": Khlebnikov, *Baranov,* p. 68.

230   "We're traders": Ibid., p. 29.

230   "Whereas in Europe": Quoted in Barratt, *The Russian View of Honolulu,* p. 147.

231   "a rough, rugged": Quoted in Gibson, *Imperial Russia in Frontier America,* p. 15.

231   "shone with a lively," etc.: Khlebnikov, op. cit., p. 117.

233   "their long, tangled locks": Fitzhugh and Crowell, *Crossroads of Continents,* p. 62.

233   "for a distance of three versts": Khlebnikov, op. cit., p. 77.

234   "developed a plan": Lensen, *The Russian Push Toward Japan,* p. 126.

234   "captured the imagination": Ibid., p. 127.

236   "some men spotted": Barratt, *The Russian Discovery of Hawaii,* p. 92.

236   "spitting almost constantly": Ibid., p. 38.

237   "in a torn tent": Quoted in Senkevitch, "Early Architecture," in Starr, op. cit., p. 181.

239   "depraved, drunk": Quoted in Gibson, "Russian Dependence," in Starr, op. cit., p. 100.

239   "in a kind of plank lean-to": Rezanov, quoted in Khlebnikov, op. cit., p. 106.

239   "What a man!": Ibid.

239   "principal agents": Barratt, *Russia in Pacific Waters,* p. 149.

239   the most beautiful girl: Gibson, *Imperial Russia in Frontier America,* p. 178.

241   "such attacks upon them": Barratt, *Russia in Pacific Waters,* p. 165.

241   "that the pull": Lensen, op. cit., p. 207.

241   "compared makeup": Ibid., p. 227.

243   "The ship had a house": Pierce, ed., *Russia's Hawaiian Adventure, 1815–1817,* p. 4.

243   "the king would be": Quoted in Khlebnikov, *Baranov,* p. 155.

244   "for the construction": Pierce, op. cit., p. 6.

245   "American hot heads": Ibid., p. 14.
246   "joined the parvenu": Ibid., p. 31.
246   table of exports: Tikhmenev, *A History of the Russian-American Company*, p. 161.
247   "awaited daily": Khlebnikov, op. cit., p. 85
247   "closed forever over": Ibid., p. 100.
248   "had been built in": Hulley, op. cit., p. 153.
249   "as a principle": Ibid., p. 149.
249   "did not live here": Quoted in Gibson, *Imperial Russia in Frontier America*, p. 32.
249   "An inhabitant of New Archangel": Tikhmenev, op. cit., p. 421.
250   "the only place in the world": Golovin, *Civil and Savage Encounters*, p. 136.
250   "cannot refuse a man," etc.: Ibid.
250   "but watch ravens": Ibid., p. 94.
251   "for the first time": Ibid., p. 121.
251   "an unavoidable evil": Golovin, *The End of Russian America*, p. 64.
251   "constantly in a state of siege": Golovin, quoted in Gibson, "Russian Dependence," in Starr, op. cit., p. 84.
252   "Their hearts are filled": Khlebnikov, op. cit., p. 101.
252   "with no little surprise": Sergey Kostlivtsev, quoted in Starr, op. cit., p. 85.
252   "Aleuts are very sensitive": Golovin, *End of Russian America*, p. 21.
252   "If they were told tomorrow": Golovin, *Civil and Savage Encounters*, p. 108.
252   "strange or incorrect expression": Golovin, Ibid., p. 55.
253   "performed with marvelous": Golovin, *Civil and Savage Encounters*, p. 99.
254   "covered the sea": Tikhmenev, op. cit., p. 319.
254   "without an outlet to the sea": Lensen, op. cit., p. 262.
255   "were in feeling and fact": Aleksandr Middendorf, quoted in ibid, p. 263.
256   to determine whether Sakhalin was an island: The Japanese already knew it was, since the noted explorer, Mamiya Rinzo, had charted and described the island in 1809. The Chinese had once known (but perhaps had forgotten) that it was, based on information gathered by a surveying party sent down the Amur in 1699 by the emperor K'ang-hsi. The party had learned from natives of a large island opposite the river's mouth, which they called *Saghalien anga hata*, which meant "cliffs at the mouth of the black river" in Manchu. Ironically, the Russians had even earlier evidence that Sakhalin was an island from Poyarkov's report.
256   "A long clap of thunder": Quoted in Tikhmenev, op. cit., p. 287.
257   "began to eject heavy stones": Ibid., p. 289.
257   "masquerading as a private": Gibson, "Sale," in Starr, op. cit., p. 288.
257   "now helpless in its ignorance": Ibid., p. 290.
258   "Here there shall be": Quoted in Golder, *Russian Expansion*, p. 209.
261   "homogeneous with the Amur": Lensen, op. cit., p. 375.

263 "spotted a golden glint": Utley, *The Indian Frontier,* p. 3.
263 "If the whole Army of the United States": Quoted in ibid., p. 101.
263 "caused a momentary scare": Hulley, op. cit., p. 194.
263 "Twenty-five years ago": Quoted in Lensen, op. cit., p. 300.
264 "amicably and for us": Gibson, "Sale," in Starr, op. cit., p. 285.
264 "The Russian and American peoples": Quoted in Gibson, "Sale," in Starr, op. cit., p. 291.
265 "drunk in the port": Shalkop, in Starr, op. cit., p. 217.
266 "the United States was still licking": Lensen, op. cit., p. 464.
266 "It is rather difficult": Barratt, *Russian Discovery of Hawaii,* p. 46.

PART THREE

CHAPTER 12: "THE BOTTOM OF THE SACK"
270 "There is no other boundary": Kennan, *Siberia and the Exile System,* vol. 1, pp. 420–22.
270 "men were impaled": Ibid., vol. 1., p. 75.
272 "during the spring thaw": Stadling, *Through Siberia,* p. 13.
272 [numbers of exiles] In official figures: 1823–1832 (98,725 exiles), 1833–42 (86,550), 1843–52 (69,764), 1853–62 (101,238), 1863–72 (146,380), 1873–82 (175,918), 1883–88 (106,326).
273 *Katorzhnik:* A cognate of *katorga,* meaning "galley," and inspired by Peter the Great's use of convict oarsmen in galleys constructed on the Sea of Azov. By association, *katorga* came to mean forced labor (penal servitude), and *katorzhnik* a forced laborer—literally, "a galley slave."
273 "the shape of an asterisk": Landsdell, *Through Siberia,* p. 93.
273 "like a fire burning": Dostoyevsky, *The House of the Dead,* p. 241. The title Dostoyevsky gave to this faintly fictionalized account of his own Siberian internment was meant to be literally understood. After the abolition of capital punishment, the condemned were still often obliged to undergo "civil execution," a procedure that stripped them of all their rights and rendered them legally "dead men."
273 "so vehemently hated": Tupper, *To the Great Ocean,* p. 155.
274 "I lay like a dog": Riha, ed., *Readings in Russian Civilization,* vol. 1, p. 133.
274 a bitter sojourn: Avvakum's ordeal was far from over. In 1666, he and other Old Believers were excommunicated by a Church Council, and for the next fifteen years he was confined in a dungeon at Pustozersk. On April 14, 1682, he was pronounced a heretic and burned at the stake.
274 "The gates opened": Tolstoy, *Resurrection,* pp. 420–22.
275 "Have pity on us": Kennan, op. cit., vol. 1, p. 400.
277 "The records of Russian prisons": Ibid., p. 392.
278 "mere dog kennels": Ibid., vol. 2, p. 152.
278 "a lonely, cheerless": Ibid., vol. 1, 290.

278   "Most of them seemed": Ibid., p. 316.
278   "did not seem at all": Dostoyevsky, op. cit., p. 43.
279   "Their most strenuous chore": Tupper, op. cit., p. 147.
279   "The great square building": Ibid., pp. 302–03.
279   "They never see the light": Quoted in Lansdell, op. cit., p. 462.
280   "the scenes of debauchery": Quoted in Kennan, op. cit., vol. 2, p. 547.
280   "Scores of men": Ibid., p. 87.
281   "a patient could not": Ibid., vol. 1, p. 318.
281   "dividing the average": Wright, *Asiatic Russia,* vol. 2, p. 323.
281   "offenders against discipline": Ibid., p. 329.
281   "converting vagabonds": Quoted in Armstrong, *Russian Settlement in the North,* p. 87.
282   "a great army of brodyags": Kennan, vol. 1, p. 407.
282   "The Tsar's cow-pasture": Ibid., p. 382.
283   "If you shoot a squirrel": Landsdell, op. cit., p. 40.
283   "when convicts heard": Tupper, op. cit., p. 157.
283   "When the weather": Kennan, op. cit., vol. 2, p. 152.
283   "All the familiar": Wood, ed., *The History of Siberia,* p. 122.
284   "Holy Baikal—glorious sea": Tupper, op. cit., p. 158.
284   "they have had their": Kennan, op. cit., vol. 2, p. 152.
285   "terrorized by a band": Ibid., p. 462.
285   "if they had been committed": Wood, "Crime and Punishment in the House of the Dead," in Edmondson, ed., *Civil Rights in Imperial Russia,* p. 231.
285   "the Robin Hoods": Wood, ed., op. cit., p. 130.
285   "Siberian children played": Ibid.
286   "the cesspool of the Tsars": Borodin, *Soviet and Tsarist Russia,* p. 31.
286   "the bottom of the sack": Quoted in Mazour, *Women in Exile,* p. 89.
286   "Siberia is truly a beautiful": Quoted in Kennan, op. cit., vol. 2, p. 554.
287   "the pearl of Russia's": Stephan, *Sakhalin,* p. 66.
287   "On Sakhalin, the guards": Stephan, op cit., p. 65.
288   "Everyone wants to escape": Ibid., p. 65.
288   "I have seen Ceylon": Quoted in ibid., p. vii.
288   "set aside as prostitutes": Ibid., p. 71.
288   "hoping to feast": St. George, *Siberia. The New Frontier,* p. 290.
289   "with what confronted them": Mikhail Fonvizin, quoted in Mazour, op. cit., p. 55.
290   "Napoleon's profile": Quoted in Sutherland, *The Princess of Siberia,* p. 86.
290   "An old servant": Quoted in ibid., p. 92.
291   " 'Twas all mere": Quoted in ibid., p. 88.
292   "for a gilded yoke": Quoted in Mazour, op. cit., p. 222.
292   "Their devotion is worthy": Ibid., p. 10.
292   "I stepped down": Quoted in Sutherland, op. cit., p. 158.
293   "not excessive and was good": Mazour, op. cit., p. 13.
293   "Every day except on Sundays": Andrey Rozen, quoted in Sutherland, op. cit., p. 193.

293 "The guards then carried": Ibid., p. 193.
294 "Our life in Chita": Quoted in ibid, p. 202.
295 "developed a system": Ibid., p. 264.
295 "One can definitely say": Quoted in Sergeyev, *Irkutsk,* p. 14.
295 "The convoy would start off": Quoted in Sutherland, op. cit., p. 224.
296 "I am certain that we": Quoted in Yarmolinsky, *Road to Revolution,* p. 55.
296 "Deep in the Siberian mine": Translated by Max Eastman, and quoted in Mazour, *The First Russian Revolution, 1825,* p. 222.
297 "as set forth by the Minister": Yarmolinsky, op. cit., p. 58.
297 "thinking is like gunpowder": Quoted in Mazour, op. cit., p. 275.
299 "for all the blood": Quoted in Belyakov, "Terrorism Rejected," p. 50.
299 "Dismounting from his carriage": Quoted in Walder, *The Short Victorious War,* p. 45.
300 "astonished his mother": Warner, *The Tide at Sunrise,* p. 63.
300 "officially regarded as more": Kennan, op. cit., vol. 1, p. 36.
301 "A few days ago": Ibid., p. 31.
301 "A letter more characteristic": Ibid.
302 "embittered revolutionists": Ibid., p. 438.
302 "an insignificant gang": Ibid., p. 439.
303 "suspected of an intention": Ibid., p. 246.
303 "representing all classes" and "there was hardly": Ibid., vol. 2, p. 30.
303 "forbidden, under pain": Ibid., p. 39.
304 "for all Jewish suspects": Ibid., p. 25.
304 "People here are so used" and "collecting mushrooms": Ibid., p. 100.
304 "for fear that if" and "who has stripped": Ibid., p. 22.
305 "to be compared with": Quoted in Armstrong, op. cit., pp. 98–99.
306 "I was like a wild falcon": Quoted in Maxwell, *Narodniki Women,* p. 137.
306 "compiled polyglot tables": Lansdell, op. cit., p. 297.
307 "the people lined the piers": Shinkarev, *The Land Beyond the Mountains,* p. 57.
308 "The Middle Ages left": Quoted in Wright, vol. 2, p. 340.

CHAPTER 13: THE NEW FRONTIER
310 "excited the wonder and curiosity": Wright, *Asiatic Russia,* vol. 1, p. 515.
314 "The migration became elemental": Kerner, in Sherwood, ed., *Alaska and Its History,* pp. 9–10.
314 "a colonial realm": Treadgold, *The Great Siberian Migration,* p. 20.
315 "God is in heaven and Koch": Gibson, *Feeding the Russian Fur Trade,* p. 44.
316 "Look there, what": Huppert, *Men of Siberia,* p. 110.
316 "Russia's only clear head": MERSH, vol. 11, p. 88.
317 "with the stereotype picture": Raeff, *Mikhail Speransky,* p. 258.
318 "stepchildren of the empire": Raeff, *Siberia and the Reforms of 1822,* p. 111.

319 "looked at him sadly": Ibid., p. 316.

319 "like the tombstone over": Kennan, *Tent Life in Siberia,* p. 36.

320 "only the form of the embrasures": Ibid., p. 37.

320 "It was relatively common": Bockstoce, *Whales, Ice, and Men,* p. 196.

320 "the hottest stuff"; Bockstoce, op. cit., p. 199.

321 "The still itself": Ibid., pp. 199–200.

321 "floating general stores": Ibid., p. 202.

321 "nothing there was Russian": Bockstoce, op. cit., p. 204.

321 "enthusiastically tapped out": Ibid., p. 204.

322 "lightheaded, more lively" and "A thousand chimeras": Krasheninnikov, *Explorations of Kamchatka, 1735–1741,* p. 220.

323 "A gilded candle was burning": Kennan, *Tent Life in Siberia,* p. 330.

323 "Knowing well what the result": Ibid., pp. 383–84.

324 "suffer and endure": Ibid., p. 129.

324 "and proceeded to tell": Ibid., p. 183.

325 "Alone and almost unsheltered": Ibid., pp. 217–18.

325 "A Chukchi would hang": Ibid., p. 287.

326 "mark an arrow": Lansdell, *Through Siberia,* p. 126.

326 "to spread the knowledge": Quoted in Bawden, op. cit., p. 201.

327 "a model village": Lansdell, *Through Siberia,* p. 205.

327 "by the roadside": Wright, op. cit., vol. 2, p. 284.

328 "nearly all built after": Stejneger, *Georg Wilhelm Steller,* p. 144.

328 "wailing cries of the muezzins": Kennan, *Siberia and the Exile System,* vol. 1, p. 158.

328 "immense goggles of horsehair": Ibid., p. 279.

328 "rode fiercely": Meakin, *A Ribbon of Iron,* p. 13.

329 "Everyone received us": Kirchner, ed., *A Siberian Journey,* p. 110.

330 "chic: in no other Siberian town": Quoted in Sergeyev, *Irkutsk,* p. 15.

330 "many were drunk": Lansdell, op. cit., p. 113.

331 "lazy, indolent creatures," etc.: Quoted in Tupper, *To the Great Ocean,* p. 211.

331 "with a short stick": Quoted in ibid., p. 198.

331 "pigs wallowed in liquid": St. George, *Siberia. The New Frontier,* p. 144.

331 "a troupe of girls": Tupper, op. cit., p. 95.

332 "You sit around": Jefferson, *Roughing It in Siberia,* pp. 90–91.

332 "guarded by heavily armed": Ibid., p. 95.

333 "so true that a piece": Ibid., p. 96.

333 "I afterwards wrote my name": Ibid., p. 97.

333 "a small prairie village": Kennan, op. cit., vol. 1, p. 311.

333 "filled with palms": Kennan, *Siberia and the Exile System,* vol. 2, p. 323.

334 "Tchaikovsky and Pushkin": Meakin, op. cit., p. 83.

334 "whose past could not bear": Deutsch, *Sixteen Years in Siberia,* p. 174.

334 "and went straight": Ibid.

335 "But I always employ": De Windt, *Through the Gold-Fields of Alaska to the Bering Straits,* p. 261.

336 "for the Instruction": Bawden, op. cit., p. 251.

336 "the intellectual center": *Guide to the Great Siberian Railway,* p. 42.
337 "poured their superfluous": Wright, op. cit., vol. 1, p. 182.
338 "When we remember that": Ibid., p. 183.
339 "a mere track cut": De Windt, op. cit., p. 239.
339 "On a bad, rough road": Kennan, *Siberia and the Exile System,* vol. 2, p. 68.
340 "Boxes and cases": Bawden, op. cit., p. 125.
341 "as nearly as could be done": Lansdell, op. cit., p. 282.
341 "a revolver, heavy woolen": Tupper, op. cit., pp. 284–85.
341 "We carved our bread": Jefferson, op. cit., p. 83.
342 "We keep twelve cats": Meakin, op. cit., p. 31.
342 "with a sagacity": Jefferson, op. cit., p. 113.
342 "And people can't be": Kirchner, op. cit., p. 137.
343 "foaming around sharp": Kennan, *Tent Life in Siberia,* p. 137.
343 "The fog was beginning": Ibid., p. 24.
343 "the warm sheltered slopes": Ibid., p. 28.
344 "divided into many tall": Kirchner, op. cit., p. 116.
344 "an enormous quantity": Ibid., p. 100.
344 "a place where everything": Ibid., p. 115.
344 "a powerful, turbulent giant": Quoted in St. George, op. cit., p. 102.
344 "one beautiful view after another": Kirchner, op. cit., p. 116.
344 "as May advances": Quoted in Sutherland, *The Princess of Siberia,* pp. 259–60.
345 "No other natural phenomenon": Kennan, *Tent Life in Siberia,* p. 331.
345 "the whole universe": Ibid., pp. 331–32.
345 "fervent heat": Kennan, *Siberia and the Exile System,* vol. 1, 63.
345 "There is no long, wet": Ibid., p. 345.
346 "great difficulty and danger": Quoted in Rasky, *The Polar Voyagers,* p. 93.
346 "altogether impracticable": Johnson, *The Life and Voyages of Joseph Wiggins,* p. 19.
347 "the deck bulged upward": Hoehling, *The Jeannette Expedition,* p. 52.
347 "who are adept at solving," etc.: Dostoyevsky, *The House of the Dead,* p. 17.
348 "in their manners, customs": Mazour, *The First Russian Revolution, 1825,* pp. 223–24.
348 "Like all men of action": Quoted in Tupper, op. cit., p. 37.

CHAPTER 14: THE IRON ROAD TO WAR
351 "Reflecting on the vast": Quoted in Tupper, *To the Great Ocean,* p. 44.
351 "majestic cliffs" and "distinguished by a cap": Ibid., p. 55.
352 "the vast and rich": Quoted in Treadgold, *The Great Siberian Migration,* p. 23.
352 "I must own": Quoted in Tupper, op. cit., p. 72.
353 "Every town he passed": Golder, *Russian Expansion on the Pacific, 1641–1850,* p. 340.

353 "on a hill outside Chita": Ibid., p. 341.
354 "a massive head": Von Laue, *Sergei Witte and the Industrialization of Russia,* p. 13.
354 "held it as a grievance" and "a retired Caucasian": Warner, *The Tide at Sunrise,* p. 72.
355 "tons of Siberian grain": Tupper, op. cit., p. 91.
355 "new horizons not only": Sumner, *A Short History of Russia,* p. 301.
356 "the right to allocate": Tupper, op. cit., p. 94.
357 "crude huts thrown": Ibid., p. 102.
357 "without even a strip": Ibid., p. 106.
357 "a plumpish railway veteran": Ibid., p. 125.
358 "mountain torrents and": Ibid., pp. 189–90.
358 "cleared a path": Ibid., p. 178.
359 "frowning earthworks": De Windt, *Through the Gold-Fields of Alaska to the Bering Straits,* pp. 140–41.
359 "snapped up little": Walder, *The Short Victorious War,* p. 23.
360 "Like vultures": Warner, op. cit., p. 110.
360 "Her hull, belted": Tupper, op. cit., p. 227.
360 an "utter wilderness": Karlinsky, *Anton Chekhov's Life and Thought,* p. 167.
361 "rich economic" and "by commercial subterfuge": Tupper, op. cit., p. 319.
361 "were so burdensome": Quoted in ibid., pp. 239–40.
361 "was entirely ignorant": Quoted in Warner, op. cit., p. 141.
364 "the leasehold appropriation": Tupper, op. cit., p. 242.
364 "I am very glad": Quoted in White, *The Diplomacy of the Russo-Japanese War,* p. 54.
365 "Nothing and nobody": Deutsch, *Sixteen Years in Siberia,* p. 345.
366 "Russian and British expansion": Walder, op. cit., p. 23.
366 with designs on Korea: A Russian trader by the name of Julius Bryner (the grandfather, incidentally, of Yul Brynner, the actor), operating out of Vladivostok, had acquired a timber concession along the river covering an area of 3,300 square miles. In May 1897, when Bryner put the concession up for sale, the government bought it under the auspices of the East Asiatic Company in order to advance its own imperialistic designs.
366 "would need about a century": Nish, *The Origins of the Russo-Japanese War,* p. 168.
367 "two [Russian] cutters": Krusenstern, *Voyage Round the World,* p. 66.
367 "Japanese seamen put": Quoted in Barratt, *Russia in Pacific Waters, 1715–1825,* pp. 170, xvii.
367 "with an imported Englishman": Warner, op. cit., p. 25.
368 "To most Russians": Ibid., p. 158.
368 "one Russian soldier was the equal": Ibid., p. 159.
368 "With the invention earlier": Ibid., p. 167.
369 "I thought that a rupture": Quoted in ibid., p. 132.
370 "Russian engineers worked": Ibid., p. 137.

370 "One flag and one sentry": Quoted in Walder, op. cit., p. 53.
370 "An armed clash": Quoted in ibid., p. 53.
371 "provided that no": Ibid., p. 140.
371 "was reserved for ": Ibid., p. 48.
371 "What this country needs": Quoted in Warner, op. cit., p. 75. (This is an odd echo of U.S. Secretary of State John Hay's characterization of the Spanish-American War in a letter to Theodore Roosevelt [July 27, 1898] as "a splendid little war.")
372 "he was not born for": Quoted in ibid., p. 63.
372 "Now I rule": Ibid., p. 55.
372 "The stagnation" and "In my whole life": Quoted in Nish, op. cit., p. 6.
372 "incapable, either from": Ibid., p. 5.
373 "after a spring rain": Tupper, op. cit., p. 248.
374 "A nation hopelessly": Quoted in Warner, op. cit., p. 535.
375 "a collection of dilapidated": De Windt, op. cit., p. 281.
376 "springing up like": Deutsch, op. cit., p. 349.
377 "with a ruby": Tupper, op. cit., p. 269.
377 "stuffed seals and": Ibid., pp. 273–74.
377 "primarily as a shelf": Quoted in ibid., p. 281.
377 "to facilitate the peopling": Westwood, *A History of Russian Railways,* p. 110.
377 "the civilizing mission": *Guide to the Great Siberian Railway,* p. 47.
378 "a rainbow joining": Warner, op. cit., p. 138.
378 "Whether he looked": Fleming, *The Fate of Admiral Kolchak,* p. 170.
378 "The filth, the rags": Jefferson, *Roughing It in Siberia,* p. 28.
379 "There were cars": Quoted in Tupper, op. cit., p. 360.
379 "in summer, a": Ibid., p. 363.
380 "one of the greatest": Treadgold, op. cit., p. 13.
382 "senseless dreams" and "I am an enemy": Quoted in D. Turnbull, "The Defeat of Popular Representation, December 1904," *Slavic Review,* 48, no. 1, 1989, p. 64.
383 "a typical Siberian": Shinkarev, *The Land Beyond the Mountains,* p. 75.
383 "Conditions in Russia": Quoted in Warner, op. cit., p. 521.
385 "to make every peasant": Stolypin's daughter, quoted in Treadgold, op. cit., p. 156.
385 "Throughout the Empire": Ibid., p. 236.

PART FOUR

CHAPTER 15: THE RED AND THE WHITE
389 "all the vital forces": MERSH, vol. 35, p. 116.
392 "from the borders": Quoted in Mawdsley, *The Russian Civil War,* p. 101.
392 "well-fed, solid, and successful": Quoted in Pereira, "White Power," p. 50.

393 "The Czechoslovaks will travel": Quoted in Chamberlin, *The Russian Revolution, 1917–1921,* vol. 2, p. 3.
394 "Under these circumstances": Chamberlin, op. cit., vol. 2, p. 6.
395 "Here was a malicious": Mawdsley, op. cit., p. 47.
396 "I have been sweating": quoted in White, *The Siberian Intervention,* p. 230.
396 "to steady any efforts": Quoted in Fleming, *The Fate of Admiral Kolchak,* p. 65.
397 "in very close and special": Japanese memorandum, quoted in White, op. cit., p. 130.
397 After having carefully read: Graves, *America's Siberian Adventure,* p. 4.
397 "Watch your step": Quoted in Luckett, *The White Generals,* p. 171.
397 "create situations demanding": Secretary of War Newton D. Baker, quoted in Lengyel, *Siberia,* p. 237.
398 "Russia's back door": Channing, *Siberia's Untouched Treasure,* p. 108.
398 "the glamor of a fairy tale": Quoted in Fleming, op. cit., p. 79.
399 "carried them along": Baerlein, *The March of the Seventy Thousand,* p. 141.
399 "a small, high-strung": Tupper, *To the Great Ocean,* p. 381.
400 "I considered it": Quoted in Fleming, op. cit., p. 33.
400 "I set as my main": Quoted in Chamberlin, op. cit., vol. 2, p. 178.
400 "The thought kept running": Baerlein, op. cit., p. 235.
401 "The Allies had better": Quoted in White, op. cit., p. 416.
402 "Uniform, British": Quoted in Chamberlin, op. cit., vol. 2, p. 162.
402 "Every round of": Quoted in Mawdsley, op. cit., p. 143.
403 "Within a year": Quoted in ibid., p. 230.
403 "of medium height": Quoted in White, op. cit., p. 198.
404 fostered an atmosphere: Quoted in Fleming, op. cit., p. 52.
404 "shootings can be carried": Quoted in Baerlein, op. cit., p. 180, from the testimony of Col. Charles H. Morrow before the Senate Committee on Education and Labor in 1922.
404 "a very pretty woman": Fleming, op. cit., p. 53.
404 a vested interest: Ibid., p. 71. The Japanese intervention may also have been intended as a preemptive strike against American attempts to control the Chinese Eastern Railway. Toward the end of World War I, the Allies considered the Trans-Siberian Railway system indispensable to their effort, and the Provisional Government had brought over a number of American railroad experts to help maintain it, since its steady deterioration had brought about near collapse. Japan had also become hostile toward the growth of American business in Siberia, as encroaching on its economic sphere of influence.
405 "He possessed neither": Quoted in White, op. cit., p. 117.
405 "one of the oddities": Mawdsley, op. cit., p. 108.
405 "The soldiers were dressed": Quoted in Fleming, op. cit., p. 137.
405 "like milk from": Quoted in Mawdsley, op. cit., p. 137.
406 "All over Siberia": Quoted in White, op. cit., p. 119.

406   "Jewish emigrants" and "the offscourings": Quoted in Chamberlin, op. cit., vol. 2, p. 163.
406   "beginning to look": Quoted in Mawdsley, op. cit., p. 150.
406· "the Russian officers": Channing, op. cit., p. 115.
406   "as safe as": Ibid., pp. 108–09.
406   "You could never tell": Ibid., p. 169.
407   "Now we need an army": Quoted in Chamberlin, op. cit., vol. 2, p. 29.
408   "Well authenticated reports": Quoted in Tupper, op. cit., p. 396.
408   "I would rather leave": Quoted in John Sharnik and Isaac Kleinerman, CBS documentary, *The Unknown War,* 1970.
409   "The snows of winter war": Churchill, *The Aftermath,* p. 97.
409   "broke several pencils": Baerlein, op. cit., p. 231.
409   "emaciated, worn out": Ibid., p. 233.
409   the great frozen rivers and "simply disintegrated": Mawdsley, op. cit., p. 231.
410   "the dead were thrown": Quoted in Tupper, op. cit., p. 401.
410   "This means that the Allies": White, op. cit., p. 347.
413   "Not a soldier knew": Quoted in Sharnik and Kleinerman, op. cit.
413   "In all our centuries": Solzhenitsyn, *The Gulag Archipelago,* vol. 1, p. 13.

CHAPTER 16: THE DEVIL'S WORKSHOP
415   "The onrush of revolutionary": Quoted in Heller and Nekrich, *Utopia in Power,* p. 60.
416   "always scrawny and": Morris Sharnoff, *An Unforgettable Odyssey,* p. 51.
417   "to dismember and destroy": Scott, *Behind the Urals,* p. 63.
417   "To slacken the pace": Heller and Nekrich, op. cit., p. 113.
417   "Determined to transform": Tupper, *To the Great Ocean,* p. 409.
418   "Tempos decide everything": Quoted in Heller and Nekrich, op. cit., p. 225.
418   "Industrialization was the new": *Stalin,* Part 1 ("Revolutionary"), produced by Jonathan Lewis and Tony Cash, WGBH-TV, 1990, p. 5.
419   "This whole Neighborhood": Quoted in Huppert, *Men of Siberia,* p. 97.
420   "had worked hard": Scott, op. cit., p. 283.
420   "Anyone who employed": Heller and Nekrich, op. cit., p. 234.
421   "anti-Soviet elements": Quoted in Conquest, *The Harvest of Sorrow,* p. 184.
421   "I will never forget": Quoted in Heller and Nekrich, op. cit., p. 235.
422   "Every morning, Stalin": Conquest, *The Great Terror,* p. 127.
422   "employed under harsh": Shabad and Mote, *Gateway to Siberian Resources,* p. 1.
423   "in all truth": Solzhenitsyn, *The Gulag Archipelago,* vol. 1, p. 60.
424   "the happiest man on earth": Stajner, *Seven Thousand Days in Siberia,* p. 144.
424   "Arrests rolled through": Solzhenitsyn, op. cit., vol. 1, p. 75.

424 "as if with a mysterious rash": Quoted in Dallin and Nikolaevsky, *Forced Labor in Soviet Russia,* p. 32.

424 "virtual cities on wheels": Stajner, op. cit., p. 315.

424 "A cattle transport": Ibid., pp. 64–65.

425 "One night, a goods train": Quoted in *Stalin,* Part 2 ("Generalissimo"), p. 12.

425 "The first requisite": Dallin, *The New Soviet Empire,* p. 113.

425 "provided a wide": Ibid.

426 "strings of carts": Solzhenitsyn, *The Gulag Archipelago,* vol. 3, p. 359.

426 "One day Larisa Fedorovna": Pasternak, *Doctor Zhivago,* p. 506.

427 "There was hardly": Dallin and Nikolaevsky, op. cit., p. 174.

427 "Socialists, Anarchists": Ibid.

428 "which did not give birth": Solzhenitsyn, op. cit., vol. 2, p. 138.

428 "The structure is very similar": Stajner, op. cit., p. 200.

428 "The experience of all ages": Quoted in Dallin and Nikolaevsky, op. cit., p. 100.

428 "the slave had no interest": Ibid.

429 "a way out": Ibid.

429 "You are not brought": Quoted in Conquest, *Kolyma. The Arctic Death Camps,* p. 64

430 "along with a huge quantity": MERSH, vol. 53, p. 67.

430 "Well, I agree": Stajner, op. cit., p. 64.

431 "in the woods by the light": Solzhenitsyn, op. cit., vol. 2, p. 201.

431 "Every official, high or low": Deutsch, *Sixteen Years in Siberia,* p. 136.

431 "by early 1939": Norman Davies, *New York Times Book Review,* May 14, 1990, p. 20.

432 "tied up with wire": Conquest, *The Great Terror,* p. 322.

432 "We divide, we multiply": Solzhenitsyn, op. cit., vol. 1, p. 442.

432 "Brought from the subtropical": Elinor Lipper, quoted in Conquest, *Kolyma,* p. 95.

433 "We lived in clay huts": Quoted in Dallin and Nikolaevsky, op. cit., p. 24.

433 "eat the bark": Quoted in ibid., p. 45.

433 "a prison house of nations": Quoted in Borodin, *Soviet and Tsarist Russia,* p. 42.

433 "For every nation exiled": Solzhenitsyn, op. cit., vol. 3, p. 392.

434 "entire cities rose": Sumner, *Survey of Russian History,* p. 55.

434 "the number of people": MERSH, vol. 53, p. 67.

434 "instantly became the symbol": Scott, op. cit., pp. xviii and 70.

435 "shipped like cattle": Ibid., p. 281.

435 "a collection of improvised": Ibid., p. 233.

435 "every experience was black": Scott, op. cit., p. 45.

435 "The managers at Magnitogorsk": Keller, *New York Times Book Review,* March 15, 1990, p. 37.

436 "frightened half out": Scott, op. cit., p. 303.

436 "I would wager": Quoted in Keller, op. cit., p. 37.

436 "as if ordained": Chertkov, "Taimyr," p. 48.

437 "be pushed to completion": Stajner, op. cit., p. 78.

437 "Once, as dinner was": Ibid., p. 167.

437 "it felt as if": Ibid., p. 86.

438 "one of the men would": Ibid., p. 90.

438 "as far as the eye": Ibid., p. 231.

440 "When we came out": Michael Solomon, quoted in Conquest, *Kolyma*, p. 23.

440 "death ships": Quoted in Conquest, *The Great Terror*, p. 326.

440 "We climbed down": Solomon, *Magadan*, p. 85.

441 "disgusting, fat" and "resembled tiny bats": Ginzburg, *Journey into the Whirlwind*, p. 319.

442 "Iceland-moss": Solzhenitsyn, op. cit., vol. 2, p. 126.

442 "they were forbidden": Ibid., p. 138.

442 "the total executions": Conquest, *Kolyma*, p. 216.

442 "Not one of the inmates": Dallin and Nikolaevsky, op. cit., p. 113.

442 "with the bone sliced": SUPAR, no. 9 (July 1990).

443 "immediately attacked by": Shalamov, *Kolyma Tales*, p. 175.

443 "There is all the difference": Borodin, op. cit., pp. 51–53.

445 "big husky young men" and "pioneers": Wallace, quoted in Conquest, *Kolyma*, p. 140.

445 "a very fine man": Ibid.

445 "where tomatoes, cucumbers": Conquest, *The Great Terror*, p. 329.

445 "fake girl swineherds": Ibid.

445 "there were no labor camps": Stajner, op. cit., p. 238.

446 "grave memories": Quoted in Warner, *The Tied at Sunrise*, p. 549.

446 "[Stalin] went into": Ibid.

447 "the drive for collectivization": Stajner, op. cit., p. 351.

448 "in the winter of": Ibid.

449 "a sterile political idea": St. George, *Siberia. The New Frontier*, p. 330.

449 "the purpose of which": Stajner, op. cit., p. 355.

450 "to destroy not only people": Quoted in Conquest, *The Great Terror*, p. 291.

450 "Like Yeats in Ireland": Quoted in Asher, *Letters from the Gulag*, p. i.

451 "It is not important": Ibid., pp. 21–22.

451 "Dearest and beloved" and on passim: Ibid., pp. 21ff.

CHAPTER 17: HORIZONS

456 "anyone who had not": Amalrik, *Involuntary Journey to Siberia*, p. 14.

456 "the phenomenon of the Gulag": Quoted in *New York Times*, December 14, 1990, article by Roger Cohen.

457 "for Siberians, dams": St. George, *Siberia. The New Frontier*, p. 450.

457 "belonging to the ranks": Quoted in *New York Times Book Review*, p. 25, article by John B. Dunlop, December 17, 1989.

458 "to feed a power-generating": Shabad and Mote, *Gateway to Siberian Resources*, p. 3.

458 "showed tears of joy": SUPAR, no. 8 (July 1989).

461 "such high mountains" and "wild fowl": Quoted in Riha, ed. *Readings in Russian Civilization,* vol. 1, p. 136.

463 "dismasted ships": Tupper, *To the Great Ocean,* p. 5.

463 "a barge moored to Russia": Rasputin, quoted in *National Geographic Magazine* (June 1990), p. 10.

464 "on windless days": Ibid., p. 34.

464 "an iceberg with": Ibid., p. 10.

465 "a plume of toxic": *New York Times,* August 16, 1990, p. A3.

465 "equal in size to": Quoted in *New York Times,* October 24, 1989, p. A14.

467 "Man is an interloper": Shipler, *Russia. Broken Idols, Solemn Dreams,* p. 186.

468 "in summer, a dusty": Tupper, op. cit., p. 5.

468 "raw new towns": St. George, op. cit., p. 455.

469 "in the end": Amalrik, op. cit., p. 162.

469 "Baffled and hurt": Ibid., p. 170.

470 "a Siberian tradition": St. George, op. cit., p. 148.

471 "Data on the magnetic": *Tass,* November 16, 1990, quoted in SUPAR, no. 10 (January 1991).

471 "Russia's might will grow": *A Brief Description of Various Voyages,* p. 31.

472 "Where will it all end?": Quoted in *New York Times,* May 19, 1990, p. A5, article by Celestine Bohlen.

BIBLIOGRAPHY

BIBLIOGRAPHIES

Haycox, Stephen and Betty. *Melvin Rick's Alaskan Bibliography: An Introductory Guide to Alaskan Historical Literature.* Portland, OR, 1977.

Jakobson, Roman. *Paleosiberian Peoples and Languages: A Bibliographical Guide.* New Haven, 1957.

Kerner, Robert J. *Northeastern Asia: A Selected Bibliography.* 2 vols. Berkeley, 1942.

Mezhov, Vladimir I. *Sibirskaia Bibliografiia [Siberian Bibliography].* 3 vols. in 2. St. Petersburg, 1903.

Pierce, Richard A. "Archival and Bibliographic Materials on Russian America Outside the USSR," in *Russia's American Colony,* ed. Frederick Starr. Durham, 1987, 353–65.

Polansky, Patricia. "Published Sources on Russian America," in *Russia's American Colony,* ed. Starr, 319–52.

———, and Robert Valliant. *Siberia: A Bibliographic Introduction to Sources.* Honolulu, 1980.

Tomashevskii, V. V. *Materialy k bibliografii Sibiri i dalnego vostoka, XV—pervaia polovina XIX veka [Material for a Bibliography of Siberia and the Far East, Fifteenth to the First Half of the Nineteenth Century].* Vladivostok, 1957.

ATLASES AND MAPS

Atlas International Larousse Politique et Economique. Paris, 1950.

Chew, A. F. *An Atlas of Russian History: Eleven Centuries of Changing Borders.* New Haven, 1967.

Efimov, A. F., ed. *Atlas geograficheskikh otkrytii v Sibiri i v severo-Zapadnoi Amerike XVII–XVIII vv [Atlas of Geographical Discoveries in Siberia and*

Northwestern America of the Seventeenth and Eighteenth Centuries]. Moscow, 1964.

Gilbert, M. *Russian History Atlas*. New York, 1972.

Levin, M. G., and L. P. Potapov, eds. *Istoriko-etnograficheskii atlas Sibiri [Historico-Ethnographical Atlas of Siberia]*. Moscow and Leningrad, 1961.

BOOKS

Ackerman, Carl W. *Trailing the Bolsheviki; Twelve Thousand Miles with the Allies in Siberia*. New York, 1919.

Adamov, A. G. *G. I. Shelikhov*. Moscow, 1952.

Afonsky, Bishop Gregory. *A History of the Orthodox Church in Alaska, 1794–1917*. Kodiak, AK, 1977.

Alekseev, A. I. *Kolumby russkie [Russian Columbuses]*. Magadan, 1966.

———. *Osvoeniia russkimi liudmi dalnego vostoka i Russkoi Ameriki do kontsa XIX veka [The Conquest by the Russian People of the Far East and Russian America up to the End of the Nineteenth Century]*. Moscow, 1982.

Amalrik, Andrei. *Involuntary Journey to Siberia,* trans. Manya Harari. New York, 1970.

Anderson, M. S. *Britain's Discovery of Russia*. London, 1958.

Andreev, A. I. *Ocherki po istochnikovedeniiu Sibiri, XVII v [Survey of Sources for Siberian Studies, Seventeenth Century]*. Leningrad, 1937.

———, ed. *Russian Discoveries in the Pacific and in North America in the Eighteenth and Nineteenth Centuries,* trans. Carl Ginsburg. Ann Arbor, 1952.

Andrews, Clarence L. *The Story of Alaska*. Caldwell, ID, 1938.

Armstrong, Terence E. *The Northern Sea Route; Soviet Exploitation of the North East Passage*. Cambridge, England, 1952.

———. *The Russians in the Arctic*. Fairlawn, NJ, 1958.

———. *Russian Settlement in the North*. Cambridge, England, 1965.

———, ed. *Yermak's Campaign in Siberia: A Selection of Documents,* trans. Tatiana Minorsky and David Wileman. London, 1975.

Asher, Oksana Dray-Khmara. *Letters from the Gulag. The Life, Letters and Poetry of Michael Dray-Khmara*. New York, 1983.

Atkinson, Thomas Witlam. *Oriental and Western Siberia*. London, 1858.

———. *Travels in the Regions of the Upper and Lower Amoor and the Russian Acquisitions on the Confines of India and China*. New York, 1860.

Avrich, Paul. *Russian Rebels 1600–1800*. New York, 1972.

Avvakum, Archpriest. *The Life of Archpriest Avvakum by Himself,* trans. V. Nabokov. New York, 1960.

Baerlein, Henry. *The March of the Seventy Thousand*. London, 1926.

Baddeley, John F. *Russia, Mongolia, China*. 2 vols., London, 1919.

Bagrow, L., ed. *The Atlas of Siberia by Semyon U. Remezov*. Supplement to *Imago Mundi*. 's-Gravenhage, 1958.

———. *A History of Russian Cartography up to 1800,* ed. H. W. Castner. Wolfe Island, Ontario, 1975.

Bain, R. N. *Slavonic Europe: A Political History of Poland and Russia from 1447 to 1796*. Cambridge, England, 1908.

Baker, John N. L. *A History of Geographical Discovery and Exploration*. London, 1945.

Bakhrushin, S. V. *Kazaki na Amure [The Cossacks on the Amur]*. Leningrad, 1925.

———. *Nauchnie Trudy [Scientific Works]*. 4 vols., Moscow, 1955.

Balzer, Marjorie M., ed. *Shamanism. Soviet Studies of Traditional Religion in Siberia and Central Asia*. Armonk, NY, 1990.

Banno, Masataka. *China and the West*. Cambridge, MA, 1964.

Barber, Noel. *Trans-Siberien*. London, 1942.

Baring, Maurice. *The Russian People*. London, 1911.

Baron, S. H. *The Travels of Olearius in Seventeenth Century Russia*. Stanford, 1967.

Baron, S. W. *The Russian Jew under Tsars and Soviets*. New York, 1964.

Barratt, Glynn. *Russia in Pacific Waters, 1715–1825: A Survey of the Origins of Russia's Naval Presence in the North and South Pacific*. Vancouver, 1980.

———. *The Russian Discovery of Hawaii. The Ethnographic and Historic Record*. Honolulu, 1987.

———. *The Russian View of Honolulu, 1809–26*. Ottawa, 1988.

Barsukov, Ivan. *Graf Nikolai Nikolaevich Maravev-Amurskii [Count Nikolai Nikolaevich Maravev-Amurskii]*. 2 vols., Moscow, 1891.

Barthold, V. V., ed. *La Découverte de l'Asie; Historie de l'Orientalisme en Europe et en Russe*. Paris, 1947.

Bater, J. H., and R. A. French, eds. *Studies in Russian Historical Geography*. 2 vols., London, 1983.

Bau, Mingchien J. *The Foreign Relations of China: A History and a Survey*. New York, 1921.

Bawden, C. R. *Shamans, Lamas and Evangelicals. The English Missionaries in Siberia*. London, 1985.

Beaglehole, John C. *The Life of Captain James Cook*. Stanford, 1974.

Beazley, Raymond. *The Dawn of Modern Geography*. 3 vols., London, 1906.

———. *The Texts and Versions of John de Plano Carpini and William Rubruquis*. London, 1903.

———, Nevill Forbes, and G. A. Birkett. *Russia from the Varangians to the Bolsheviks*. Oxford, 1918.

Belov, M. I. *Istoriia otkrytiia i osvoeniia severnogo morskogo puti [History of the Discovery and Development of the Northern Sea Route]*. 4 vols., Moscow, 1956–69.

———. *Semen Dezhnev*. Moscow, 1955.

Benyowsky, Mauritius Augustus, Count de. *Memoirs and Travels*. London, 1790.

Berg, L. S. *Istoriia russkikh geograficheskikh otkrytii [History of Russian Geographical Discoveries]*. Moscow, 1962.

Berkh, Vasily N. *The Chronological History of the Discovery of the Aleutian Islands,* ed. Richard A. Pierce and trans. Dimitri Krenov. Kingston, Ontario, 1974.

Beveridge, Albert J. *The Russian Advance*. New York, 1903.

Blackwell, W. L. *The Beginnings of Russian Industrialization, 1800–1860.* Princeton, 1968.

Blum, Jerome. *Lord and Peasant in Russia from the Ninth to the Nineteenth Century.* Princeton, 1961.

Bobrick, Benson. *Fearful Majesty. The Life and Reign of Ivan the Terrible.* New York, 1987.

Bockstoce, John R. *Whales, Ice, and Men.* Seattle, 1986.

Bogaras, Waldemar. *The Chukchee.* New York, 1904–09.

———. *The Eskimo of Siberia.* New York, 1913.

Bolkhovitinov, Nikolay N. *The Beginnings of Russian-American Relations, 1775–1815,* trans. Elena Levin. Cambridge, MA, 1975.

———. *Russko-amerikanskie otnosheniia, 1815–1832 [Russian-American Relations, 1815–1832].* Moscow, 1975.

Bolshaia Sovetskaia entsiklopediia [Great Soviet Encyclopedia]. 2nd edn., Moscow, 1949–57.

Bond, E. A., ed. *Russia at the Close of the Sixteenth Century.* London, 1856.

Bookwalter, John W. *Siberia and Central Asia.* Springfield, OH, 1899.

Borodin, George. *Soviet and Tsarist Russia.* London, 1944.

Brooks, Jeffrey. *When Russia Learned to Read.* Princeton, 1985.

Brown, Arthur Judson. *The Mastery of the Far East.* New York, 1919.

Bunje, E. T. H., H. Penn, and F. J. Schmitz. *Russian California, 1805–1841.* San Francisco, 1970.

Burney, J. A. *Chronological History of the North-eastern Voyages of Discovery and of the Early Navigations of the Russians.* London, 1819.

Bush, Richard J. *Reindeer, Dogs, and Snow-Shoes.* New York, 1871.

Butsinski, Petr N. *Mangazeia i mangazeiskii uezd, 1601–1645 [Mangazeia and the Mangazeia uezd, 1601–1645].* Kharkov, 1889.

Chamberlin, Henry. *The Russian Revolution, 1917–1921.* 2 vols., Princeton, 1987.

Channing, C. G. Fairfax. *Siberia's Untouched Treasure. Its Future Role in the World.* New York, 1923.

Chard, Chester S. *Kamchadal Culture and Its Relationships in the Old and New Worlds.* Madison, 1961.

Chekhov, Anton. *The Island: A Journey to Sakhalin,* trans. Luba and Michael Terpak. New York, 1967.

Chen, Vincent. *Sino-Russian Relations in the Seventeenth Century.* The Hague, 1968.

Chevigny, Hector. *Russian America: The Great Alaskan Venture, 1741–1867.* New York, 1965.

Chronicle of Novgorod, 1016–1417, trans. Robert Michell and Nevill Forbes. Hattiesburg, MS, 1970.

Churchill, Winston. *The Aftermath.* London, 1929.

Clark, Francis E. *A New Way Around an Old World.* New York, 1901.

Clark, Henry W. *History of Alaska.* New York, 1930.

Clubb, O. Edmund. *China and Russia: The "Great Game."* New York, 1971.

Cochrane, Captain John Dundas. *Narrative of a Pedestrian Journey Through Russia and Siberian Tartary, from the Frontiers of China to the Frozen Sea and Kamtchatka; Performed During the Years 1820, 1821, 1822, and 1823.* Philadelphia, 1824.

Colby, Merle. *A Guide to Alaska, the Last Frontier.* New York, 1950.

Coleman, Frederic. *Japan Moves North. The Inside Story of the Struggle for Siberia.* London, 1918.

Collins, Perry McDonough. *Siberian Journey: Down the Amur to the Pacific, 1856–1857,* ed. Charles Vevier. Madison, 1962.

Conolly, Violet. *Siberia Today and Tomorrow.* London, 1976.

Conquest, Robert. *The Great Terror. A Reassessment.* Oxford, 1990.

———. *The Harvest of Sorrow.* New York, 1986.

———. *Kolyma. The Arctic Death Camps.* Oxford, 1980.

Conroy, Hilary. *The Japanese Seizure of Korea, 1868–1910.* Philadelphia, 1960.

Cook, Captain James. *The Journals of Captain James Cook on His Voyages of Discovery,* ed. John C. Beaglehole. Cambridge, England, 1967.

Cook, Warren L. *Flood Tide of Empire: Spain and the Pacific Northwest, 1543–1819.* New Haven, 1973.

Cottrell, Charles Herbert. *Recollections of Siberia.* London, 1842.

Courant, Maurice. *La Siberie colonie russe jusqu'à la construction du Trans-sibérien.* Paris, 1920.

Coxe, William. *Account of the Russian Discoveries between Asia and America; to which are added, The Conquest of Siberia and The History of the Trans-actions and Commerce between Russia and China.* London, 1804.

Cressen, W. P. *The Cossacks, Their History and Country.* New York, 1919.

Cross, A., ed. *Russia Under Western Eyes, 1517–1825.* New York, 1971.

Czaplicka, M. A. *Aboriginal Siberia.* Oxford, 1914.

Dall, William H. *Early Explorations to the Regions of the Bering Sea and Strait.* Washington, DC, 1891.

Dallin, David J. *The Rise of Russia in Asia.* New Haven, 1949.

———. *The New Soviet Empire.* New Haven, 1951.

———, and Boris Nikolaevsky. *Forced Labor in Soviet Russia.* New Haven, 1947.

Davydov, G. I. *Two Voyages to Russian America, 1802–1807,* trans. Richard A. Pierce. Kingston, Ontario, 1977.

DeLesseps, M. *Travels in Kamchatka, during the Years 1787 and 1788.* 2 vols., London, 1790.

Deutsch, Leo. *Sixteen Years in Siberia: 1884–1900,* trans. Helen Chisholm. London, 1903.

De Veer, Gerrit. *The Three Voyages of William Barents to the Arctic Regions.* London, 1876.

De Windt, Harry. *Through the Gold-Fields of Alaska to the Bering Straits.* New York, 1898.

Divin, V. A. *Russkie moreplavaniia na Tikhom okeane v. XVIII veke [Russian Voyages in the Pacific Ocean in the Eighteenth Century].* Moscow, 1971.

Dmytryshyn, Basil, and E. A. P. Crownhart-Vaughan, eds. and trans. *Colonial Russian America: Kyrill T. Khlebnikov's Reports, 1817–1832.* Portland, OR, 1976.

————, eds. and trans. *The End of Russian America. Captain P.N. Golovin's Last Report, 1862.* Portland, OR, 1979.

Dmytryshyn, Basil, E. A. P. Crownhart-Vaughan, and Thomas Vaughan, eds. and trans. *Russia's Conquest of Siberia, 1558–1700: A Documentary Record.* Portland, OR, 1985.

————, eds. and trans. *Russian Penetration of the North Pacific Ocean, 1700–1797: A Documentary Record.* Portland, OR, 1988.

————, eds. and trans. *The Russian American Colonies, 1798–1867: A Documentary Record.* Portland, OR, 1989.

Dobell, Peter. *Travels in Kamtchatka and Siberia; With a Narrative of a Residence in China.* 2 vols., London, 1830.

Dostoyevsky, Fyodor. *The House of the Dead,* trans. David McDuff. New York, 1985.

Dotsenko, P. S. *The Struggle for Democracy in Siberia, 1917–1920.* Stanford, 1983.

Dubnow, S. M. *History of the Jews in Russia and Poland.* 3 vols., Philadelphia, 1916.

D'Wolf, Captain John. *A Voyage to the North Pacific and a Journey Through Siberia.* Cambridge, MA, 1861.

Edmondson, Linda, ed. *Civil Rights in Imperial Russia.* Oxford, 1989.

Eden, Charles Henry. *Frozen Asia: A Sketch of Modern Siberia.* London, 1879.

Efimov, A. V. *Iz istorii velikikh russkikh geograficheskikh otkrytii v severnom ledovitom i tikhom okeanakh, XVII-pervaia polovina XVIII v [History of the Great Russian Geographical Discoveries in the Northern Arctic and Pacific Oceans from the Seventeenth to the First Half of the Eighteenth Centuries].* Moscow, 1950.

Emmons, Terence. *The Russian Landed Gentry and the Peasant Emancipation of 1861.* Cambridge, MA, 1968.

Erman, Adolph. *Travels in Siberia,* trans. W. D. Cooley. 2 vols., Philadelphia, 1850.

Esthus, Raymond A. *Double Eagle and Rising Sun. The Russians and Japanese at Portsmouth in 1905.* Durham, NC, 1988.

Fedorova, Svetlana G. *The Russian Population in Alaska and California: Late Eighteenth Century–1867,* ed. and trans. Richard A. Pierce and Alton S. Donnelly. Kingston, Ontario, 1973.

Figner, Vera. *Memoirs of a Revolutionist.* New York, 1927.

Fischer, J. E. *Sibirische Geschichte [History of Siberia].* 2 vols., St. Petersburg, 1768.

Fisher, Raymond H. *Bering's Voyages: Whither and Why.* Seattle, 1977.

————. *The Russian Fur Trade, 1550–1700.* Berkeley and Los Angeles, 1943.

————. *The Voyage of Semen Dezhnev in 1648: Bering's Precursor.* London, 1981.

Fisher, Robin, and Hugh Johnston, eds. *Captain Cook and His Times.* London and Vancouver, BC, 1979.

Fitzhugh, William W. and Aron Crowell. *Crossroads of Continents.* Washington, D.C., 1988.

Fleming, Peter. *The Fate of Admiral Kolchak*. New York, 1963.

Fletcher, Giles, and Jerome Horsey. *Russia at the Close of the Sixteenth Century,* ed. E. A. Bond. London, 1856.

Florinsky, Michael T. *Russia: A History and an Interpretation.* 2 vols., New York, 1953.

————, ed. *McGraw-Hill Encyclopedia of Russia and the Soviet Union.* New York, 1961.

Florovsky, George. *Ways of Russian Theology.* Belmont, MA, 1979.

Foust, Clifford M. *Muscovite and Mandarin: Russia's Trade with China and Its Setting, 1727–1805.* Chapel Hill, 1969.

Garrett, Paul. *St. Innocent. Apostle to America.* Crestwood, NY, 1979.

Geyer, D. *Russian Imperialism, 1869–1914.* New Haven, 1987.

Gibson, James R. *Feeding the Russian Fur Trade: Provisionment of the Okhotsk Seaboard and the Kamchatka Peninsula, 1639–1856.* Madison, 1969.

————. *Imperial Russia in Frontier America: The Changing Geography of Supply of Russian America, 1784–1867.* New York, 1976.

Ginzburg, Eugenia Semyonovna. *Journey into the Whirlwind.* New York, 1967.

Gmelin, Johann G. *Flora Sibirica [Siberian Flora].* 4 vols., St. Petersburg, 1747–69.

————. *Reise durch Sibirien von dem Jahr 1733 bis 1743 [Travels in Siberia, 1733–43].* 4 vols., Göttingen, 1751–52.

Goldenberg, L. A. *Semen Ulianovich Remezov: Sibirskii kartograf i geograf, 1642–posle 1720 gg. [Semen Ulianovich Remezov: Cartographer and Geographer, 1642 to after 1720].* Moscow, 1965.

Golder, Frank A. *Bering's Voyages: An Account of the Efforts of the Russians to Learn the Relation of Asia and America.* 2 vols., trans. Leonhard Stejneger. New York, 1922 and 1925.

————. *Russian Expansion on the Pacific, 1641–1850.* Cleveland, 1914.

Golovin, Pavel N. *Civil and Savage Encounters,* trans. and annot. Basil Dmytryshyn and E. A. P. Crownhart-Vaughan. Portland, OR, 1983.

————. *The End of Russian America. Captain P. N. Golovin's Last Report, 1862.* Portland, OR, 1979.

Golovnin, V. M. *Around the World on the Kamchatka, 1817–1819,* ed. and trans. Ella Lury Wiswell. Honolulu, 1979.

Graves, William S. *America's Siberian Adventure 1918–1920.* New York, 1931.

Guide to the Great Siberian Railway, compiled by the Imperial Ministry of Ways and Communications, ed. Dmitriev-Mamonov and A. F. Zdziarski. St. Petersburg, 1900.

Hakluyt, Richard. *The Principal Navigations Voyages Traffiques & Discoveries of the English Nation.* First published 1589. 12 vols., New York, 1964.

Halde, Jean Baptiste du, S.J. *The General History of China Containing a Geographical, Historical, Chronological and Physical Description of the Empire of China and Chinese Tartary.* London, 1736.

Hale, J. R. *Renaissance Exploration.* New York, 1968.

Handbook of Siberia and Arctic Russia, A. Vol. 1, compiled by the Geographical Section of Naval Intelligence, Naval Staff, Admiralty. London, 1920.

Hargreaves, R. *Red Sun Rising: The Siege of Port Arthur.* London, 1962.

Heller, Mikhail, and Aleksandr Nekrich. *Utopia in Power. The History of the Soviet Union from 1917 to the Present.* New York, 1986.

Hellman, Lillian, ed. *The Selected Letters of Anton Chekhov,* trans. Sidonie Lederer. New York, 1955.

Herberstein, Sigismund von. *Notes Upon Russia,* ed. and trans. R. H. Major. 2 vols., London, 1851–52.

Hill, S. S. *Travels in Siberia.* 2 vols., London, 1854.

Hingley, R. *The Tsars.* London, 1968.

Hoehling, A. A. *The Jeannette Expedition.* London, 1967.

Howard, B. D. *Life with Transsiberian Savages.* London, 1893.

———. *Prisoners of Russia: A Personal Study of Convict Life in Sakhalin and Siberia.* New York, 1902.

Howorth, H. H. *History of the Mongols from the Ninth to the Nineteenth Century.* 5 vols., London, 1876–88.

Hrdlicka, Ales. *The Peoples of the Soviet Union.* Washington, DC, 1942.

———. *The Aleutian and Commander Islands and Their Inhabitants.* Philadelphia, 1945.

Hulley, Clarence C. *Alaska: Past and Present.* Portland, OR, 1953.

Hummel, Arthur W. *Eminent Chinese of the Ch'ing Period, 1644–1912.* 2 vols., Washington, DC, 1943.

Huppert, Hugo. *Men of Siberia. Sketchbook from the Kuzbas.* New York, 1934.

Imrey, Ferenc. *Through Blood and Ice.* New York, 1930.

Istoriia Sibiri [History of Siberia]. 5 vols., Leningrad, 1968–69.

Ivanov, Vsevolod V. *The Trans-Siberian Express.* Moscow, 1933.

Jefferson, Robert L. *Roughing It in Siberia.* London, 1897.

Jochelson, Waldemar. *History, Ethnology and Anthropology of the Aleut.* Washington, DC, 1933.

———. *Peoples of Asiatic Russia.* New York, 1928.

Johnson, Henry. *The Life and Voyages of Joseph Wiggins.* New York, 1907.

Kaiser, Robert G. *Russia. The People and the Power.* New York, 1984.

Karlinsky, Simon. *Anton Chekhov's Life and Thought, Selected Letters and Commentary,* trans. M. H. Hein. Berkeley, 1973.

Karpovich, Michael. *Imperial Russia, 1801–1917.* New York, 1932.

Keene, Donald. *The Japanese Discovery of Europe, 1720–1798.* New York, 1954.

Kelly, Lawrence. *Moscow.* New York, 1984.

Kennan, George F. *Tent Life in Siberia.* New York, 1910.

———. *Siberia and the Exile System.* 2 vols., New York, 1891.

Kerner, Robert J. *The Urge to the Sea.* Berkeley and Los Angeles, 1942.

Khlebnikov, K. T. *Baranov: Chief Manager of the Russian Colonies in America,* ed. Richard A. Pierce and trans. Colin Bearne. Kingston, Ontario, 1973.

———. *Colonial Russian America: Kyrill T. Khlebnikov's Reports, 1817–1832,* ed. and trans. Basil Dmytryshyn and E. A. P. Crownhart-Vaughan. Portland, OR, 1976.

Kirchner, W. *The Commercial Relations Between Russia and Europe, 1400–1800.* Bloomington, 1966.

———, ed. *A Siberian Journey. The Journal of Hans Jakob Fries, 1774–1776.* London, 1935.

Klose, Kevin. *Russia and the Russians. Inside the Closed Society.* New York, 1954.

Kolarz, Walter. *The Peoples of the Soviet Far East.* New York, 1954.

Kotzebue, O. von. *A Voyage of Discovery into the South Sea and Bering Straits for the Purpose of Exploring a North-East Passage, Undertaken in the Years 1815–1818.* 3 vols., London, 1921.

Krasheninnikov, Stepan P. *Explorations of Kamchatka, 1735–1741,* trans. and annot. E. A. P. Crownhart-Vaughan. Portland, OR, 1972.

Krausse, A. S. *Russia in Asia, 1558–1899.* New York, 1899.

Kropotkin, P. *Memoirs of a Revolutionist.* Boston, 1899.

Krusenstern, Captain A. J. von. *Voyage Round the World in the Years 1803, 1804, 1805, and 1806,* trans. R. B. Hoppner. 2 vols., London, 1813.

Krypton, Constantin. *The Northern Sea Route. Its Place in Russian Economic History Before 1917.* 2 vols., New York, 1953–56.

Kuropatkin, A. N. *The Russian Army and the Japanese War.* 2 vols., London, 1909.

Kushnarev, Evgenii V. *In Search of the Strait: The First Kamchatka Expedition, 1725–1730,* trans. E. A. P. Crownhart-Vaughan. Portland, OR, 1989.

Langsdorff, Georg Heinrich von. *Voyages and Travels in Various Parts of the World During the Years 1803, 1804, 1805, 1806, and 1807.* London, 1814.

Lansdell, Henry. *Through Siberia.* Boston, 1882.

Lantzeff, George V. *Siberia in the Seventeenth Century: A Study of the Colonial Administration.* Berkeley and Los Angeles, 1943.

———, and Richard Pierce. *Eastward to Empire.* Montreal, 1973.

Lauridsen, Peter. *Vitus Bering: The Discoverer of Bering Strait,* trans. J. O. Olson. Chicago, 1889.

Lavender, David. *The Way to the Western Sea.* New York, 1988.

Ledyard, John. *John Ledyard's Journal of Captain Cook's Last Voyage,* ed. J. K. Munford. Corvalis, OR, 1963.

Lengyel, Emil. *Siberia.* New York, 1943.

Lensen, George A. *Balance of Intrigue: International Rivalry in Korea and Manchuria, 1884–99.* 2 vols., Tallahassee, FL, 1982.

———. *The Russian Push Toward Japan; Russo-Japanese Relations 1697–1875.* Princeton, 1959.

———. *The Russo-Japanese War.* Tallahassee, FL, 1967.

Lomonosov, Mikhail. *A Brief Description of Various Voyages.* St. Petersburg, 1764.

Leroy-Beaulieu, A. *Empire of the Tsars and Russians.* 3 vols., New York, 1902–03.

Lesseps, Jean Baptiste Barthelemy, Baron de. *Travels in Kamchatka, during the Years 1787 and 1788.* 2 vols., London, 1808.

Lessner, Erwin. *Cradle of Conquerors: Siberia.* Garden City, NY, 1955.

Levin, M. G., and L. P. Potapov, eds. *The Peoples of Siberia,* trans. Scripta Technica, Inc. Chicago, 1964.

Lobanov-Rostovsky, Prince Andrei. *Russia and Asia.* New York, 1933.

Longworth, Philip. *The Cossacks.* New York, 1970.

Lower, J. Arthur. *Ocean of Destiny: A Concise History of the North Pacific, 1500–1978.* Vancouver, BC, 1978.

Luckett, Richard. *The White Generals*. London, 1971.

Lyaschenko, Peter I. *History of the National Economy of Russia to the 1917 Revolution,* trans. L. M. Herman. New York, 1949.

———. *Russia and China: Their Diplomatic Relations to 1728*. Cambridge, MA, 1971.

Makarova, Raisa V. *Russians on the Pacific, 1743–1799,* ed. and trans. Richard A. Pierce and Alton S. Donnelly. Kingston, Ontario, 1975.

Malia, M. *Alexander Herzen and the Birth of Russian Socialism, 1812–1855*. Cambridge, MA, 1961.

Malozemoff, Andrew. *Russian Far Eastern Policy, 1881–1904*. Berkeley, 1958.

Mancall, Mark. *Russia and China. Their Diplomatic Relations to 1728*. Cambridge, MA, 1971.

Martin, Christopher. *The Russo-Japanese War*. London, 1967.

Massa, Isaak. *Short Account of Muscovy at the Beginning of the XVII Century,* trans. G. Orchard. Toronto, 1982.

Massie, Robert K. *Peter the Great*. New York, 1980.

Masterson, James R., and Helen Brower, eds. *Bering's Successors, 1745–80: Contributions of Peter Simon Pallas to the History of Russian Exploration Toward Alaska*. Seattle, 1948.

Mavor, J. *An Economic History of Russia*. 2 vols., New York, 1925.

Mawdsley, Evan. *The Russian Civil War*. Boston, 1987.

Maxwell, Margaret. *Narodniki Women*. New York, 1990.

Mazour, Anatole G. *The First Russian Revolution, 1825: The Decembrist Movement*. Stanford, 1937.

———. *Women in Exile: Wives of the Decembrists*. Tallahassee, FL, 1975.

Meakin, Annette M. B. *A Ribbon of Iron*. London, 1901.

Mehlinger, H. D., and J. M. Thompson. *Count Witte and the Tsarist Government in the 1905 Revolution*. Bloomington, 1972.

Mendelsohn, Ezra, and Marshall S. Shatz, eds. *Imperial Russia, 1700–1917. Essays in Honor of Marc Raeff*. DeKalb, IL, 1988.

Michael, Henry N., ed. *The Archeology and Geomorphology of Northern Asia*. Toronto, 1964.

———. *Lieutenant Zagoskin's Travels in Russian America, 1842–1844*. Toronto, 1967.

———. *Studies in Siberian Shamanism*. Toronto, 1963.

Mirsky, Jeannette. *To the Arctic! The Story of Northern Exploration from Earliest Times to the Present*. Chicago, 1970.

Moore, Frederick F. *Siberia Today*. New York, 1919.

Müller, G. F. *Istoriia Sibiri [History of Siberia]*. 2 vols., Moscow and Leningrad, 1937–41.

———. *Sammlung Russicher Geschichte*. 9 vols., St. Petersburg, 1732–64.

———. *Voyages from Asia to America, for Completing the Discoveries of the North West Coast of America*. London, 1761.

Murphy, Robert. *The Haunted Voyage*. New York, 1961.

Naske, C. M., and H. E. Slotnick. *Alaska: A History*. Norman, OK, 1970.

Neatby, L. H. *Discovery in Russian and Siberian Waters*. Athens, OH, 1973.

Newby, Eric. *The Big Red Train Ride*. New York, 1978.

Nish, Ian. *The Origins of the Russo-Japanese War.* New York, 1985.

Noble, Algernon. *Siberian Days.* London, 1928.

Nolde, Boris. *La Formation de l'Empire Russe.* 2 vols., Paris, 1952–53.

Nordenskiöld, A. E. *The Voyage of the "Vega" Round Asia and Europe, With a Historical Review of Previous Journeys Along the North Coast of the Old World,* trans. Alexander Leslie. 2 vols., London, 1881.

Norton, Henry Kittredge. *The Far Eastern Republic of Siberia.* London, 1923.

O'Brien, C. Bickford, ed. *Fort Ross: Indians, Russians, Americans.* Jenner, CA, 1978.

Ogden, Adele. *The California Sea-Otter Trade, 1784–1848.* Berkeley, 1941.

Ogorodnikov, V. I. *Ocherki istorii Sibiri do nachala XIX v. [Essays on the History of Siberia Before the Beginning of the Nineteenth Century].* Vladivostok, 1924.

Okladnikov, A. P. *Ancient Population of Siberia and Its Cultures.* Cambridge, MA, 1959.

———, ed. *Istoriia Sibiri [History of Siberia].* Vol. 2, Leningrad, 1968.

Okun, S. B. *The Russian-American Company,* ed. B. D. Grekov and trans. Carl Ginsburg. Cambridge, MA, 1951.

Olearius, Adam. *The Voyages and Travels of the Ambassadors Sent by Frederick Duke of Holstein to the Great Duke of Muscovy and the King of Persia,* trans. John Davies. London, 1662.

Owens, Kenneth N., and Alton S. Donnelly, eds. and trans. *The Wreck of the Sv. Nikolai.* Portland, OR, 1985.

Pallas, Peter Simon. *Neue Nordische Beytrage.* St. Petersburg, 1787–93.

Pares, Bernard. *A History of Russia.* New York, 1947.

Parker, E. H. *China: Her History, Diplomacy and Commerce.* London, 1901.

Parker, W. H. *An Historical Geography of Russia.* London, 1968.

Parry, J. H. *The Age of Reconnaissance.* London, 1963.

Pasternak, Boris. *Doctor Zhivago,* trans. Max Hayward and Manya Harari. New York, 1958.

Phillips, G. D. R. *Dawn in Siberia: The Mongols of Lake Baikal.* London, 1942.

Pierce, Richard A. *Georg Anton Schaffer, Russia's Man in Hawaii, 1815–1817.* Kingston, Ontario, 1976.

———, ed. *Sitka. The Wreck of the Neva,* trans. Antoinette Shalkop. Anchorage, AK, 1979.

———. *Documents on the History of the Russian-American Company,* trans. Marina Ramsay. Kingston, Ontario, 1976.

———. *Rezanov Reconnoiters California, 1806.* San Francisco, 1972.

———. *The Russian Orthodox Religious Mission in America, 1794–1837,* trans. Colin Bearne. Kingston, Ontario, 1978.

———. *Russia's Hawaiian Adventure, 1815–1817.* Berkeley, 1965.

———. *Siberia and Northwestern America, 1788–1792. The Journal of Carl Heinrich Merck, Naturalist with the Russian Scientific Expedition Led by Captain Joseph Billings and Gavriil Sarychev,* trans. Fritz Jaensch. Kingston, Ontario, 1980.

Platonov, S. F. *Boris Godunov.* Gulf Breeze, FL, 1973.

———. *The Time of Troubles,* trans. J. Alexander. Lawrence, KS, 1970.

Pokrovskii, A. A. *Ekspeditsiia Beringa: Sbornik dokumentov [Bering's Expeditions: A Collection of Documents].* Moscow, 1941.

Pokrovskii, M. N. *History of Russia from the Earliest Times to the Rise of Commercial Capitalism,* ed. and trans. J. D. Clarkson. New York, 1931.

Polevoi, Boris P. *Grigorii Shelikhov—"Kolumb russkii" [Grigorii Shelikhov—The Russian Columbus].* Magadan, 1960.

Price, Julius M. *From the Arctic Ocean to the Yellow Sea: Narrative of a Journey, 1890–1891, Across Siberia.* London, 1892.

Price, Morgan Phillips. *Siberia.* London, 1912.

Prothero, G. W., ed. *Eastern Siberia.* London, 1920.

Pushkarev, S. G. *A Source Book for Russian History from Early Times to 1917.* 2 vols., New Haven, 1972.

Quested, R. K. I. *The Expansion of Russia in East Asia, 1857–1860.* Kuala Lumpur, 1968.

Raeff, Marc. *Imperial Russia: The Coming of Age of Modern Russia.* New York, 1971.

————. *Mikhail Speransky. Statesman of Imperial Russia, 1772–1839.* The Hague, 1957.

————. *Siberia and the Reforms of 1822.* Seattle, 1956.

————. *Understanding Imperial Russia,* trans. Arthur Goldhammer. New York, 1984.

Rasky, Frank. *The Polar Voyagers. Explorers of the North.* New York, 1976.

Ravenstein, E. G. *The Russians on the Amur.* London, 1861.

Rawicz, Slavomir. *The Long Walk.* New York, 1988.

Ray, Dorothy. *The Eskimos of Bering Strait, 1650–1898.* Seattle, 1975.

Rezanov, Nikolai Petrovich. *The Rezanov Voyage to Nueva California in 1806,* trans. Thomas C. Russell. San Francisco, 1826.

Riasanovsky, N. V. *A History of Russia.* New York, 1963.

Ricks, Melvin B. *The Earliest History of Alaska.* Anchorage, AK, 1963.

Riha, T., ed. *Readings in Russian Civilization.* Vol. 1, Chicago, 1969.

Rogger, Hans. *Russia in the Age of Modernization and Revolution, 1881–1917.* London, 1983.

Romanov, Boris A. *Russia in Manchuria, 1892–1906,* trans. Susan Jones. Ann Arbor, 1952.

Rondière, Pierre. *Siberia,* trans. Charles Duff. New York, 1967.

Rowbotham, Arnold H. *Missionary and Mandarin. The Jesuits at the Court of China.* Berkeley, 1942.

Russia. Arkheograficheskaia kommissiia. *Akty istoricheskie [Historical Acts].* 5 vols., St. Petersburg, 1841–42; Index 1843.

————. *Dopolneniia k aktam istoricheskim [Supplements to Historical Acts].* 12 vols., St. Petersburg, 1846–72; Index, 1875.

————. *Sibirskaia letopisi [Siberian Chronicles].* St. Petersburg, 1907.

————. *Sbornik imperatorskoe russkoe istoricheskoe obshchestvo [Collection of the Russian Imperial Historical Society].* 148 vols., St. Petersburg, 1867–1916.

Russian Primary Chronicle, ed. and trans. Samuel H. Cross. Cambridge, MA, 1930.

Sarychev, Gavriil A. *Account of a voyage of discovery to the north-east of Siberia, the Frozen ocean, and the North-East sea.* London, 1806.

Satow, Ernest M. *Korea and Manchuria between Russia and Japan,* ed. George A. Lensen. Tallahassee, FL, 1966.

Sauër, Martin. *An Account of a Geographical and Astronomical Expedition to the Northern Parts of Russia.* London, 1802.

Scott, John. *Behind the Urals.* Bloomington, 1989.

Sebes, Joseph. *The Jesuits and the Sino-Russian Treaty of Nerchinsk, 1689; the Diary of Thomas Pereira.* Rome, 1961.

Seebohm, Henry. *Siberia in Asia: A Visit to the Valley of the Yenesay in East Siberia.* London, 1882.

Semyonov, Yuri. *The Conquest of Siberia.* London, 1944.

Sergeyev, M. *Irkutsk.* Moscow, 1986.

Seton-Watson, Hugh. *The Russian Empire, 1801–1917.* Oxford, 1960.

Shabad, Theodore, and Victor L. Mote. *Gateway to Siberian Resources (The Bam).* London, 1977.

Shalamov, Varlam. *Kolyma Tales.* New York, 1980.

Sharnoff, Morris. *An Unforgettable Odyssey.* Privately printed, 1988.

Shelikov, Grigorii I. *A Voyage to America, 1783–1786,* trans. Marina Ramsay and ed. Richard A. Pierce. Kingston, Ontario, 1981.

Sherwood, Morgan B., ed. *Alaska and Its History.* Seattle, 1967.

Shinkarev, Leonid. *The Land Beyond the Mountains. Siberia and Its People Today.* New York, 1973.

Shipler, David K. *Russia. Broken Idols, Solemn Dreams.* New York, 1983.

Shoemaker, Michael Myers. *The Great Siberian Railway from St. Petersburg to Pekin.* New York, 1903.

A Short Outline of the History of the Far Eastern Republic. Published by the Special Delegation of the Far Eastern Republic to the United States of America, Washington, DC.

Simpson, Sir George. *Narrative of a Journey Round the World, During the Years 1841 and 1842.* London, 1847.

Simpson, James Young. *The Present-Day Significance of Siberia.* New York, 1918.

———. *Side-Lights on Siberia. Some Account of the Great Siberian Railroad, the Prisons, and Exile System.* Edinburgh, 1898.

Skrynnikov, R. G. *Boris Godunov,* trans. Hugh F. Graham. Gulf Breeze, FL, 1987.

Smith, Hedrick. *The Russians.* New York, 1984.

Smolka, H. P. *Forty Thousand Against the Arctic. Russia's Polar Empire.* London, 1937.

Solomon, Michael. *Magadan.* Toronto, 1971.

Solzhenitsyn, Aleksandr I. *The Gulag Archipelago.* 3 vols., New York, 1974–78.

St. George, George. *Siberia. The New Frontier.* New York, 1969.

Stadling, J. *Through Siberia,* ed. F. H. H. Guillemard. London, 1901.

Stajner, Karlo. *Seven Thousand Days in Siberia,* trans. Joel Agee. New York, 1988.

Starr, Frederick, ed. *Russia's American Colony.* Durham, NC, 1987.

Stejneger, Leonhard. *Georg Wilhelm Steller: The Pioneer of Alaskan Natural History.* Cambridge, MA, 1936.

Steller, G. W. *Reise von Kamchatka nach Amerika.* St. Petersburg, 1793.

Stephan, J. J. *The Kuril Islands, Russo-Japanese Frontiers in the Pacific.* Oxford, 1974.

———. *Sakhalin. A History.* Oxford, 1971.

Stratton, Joanna. *Pioneer Women.* New York, 1981.

Sumner, B. H. *Survey of Russian History.* London, 1944.

Suslov, S. P. *Physical Geography of Asiatic Russia,* trans. Noah D. Gershevsky. San Francisco, 1961.

Sutherland, Christine. *The Princess of Siberia.* New York, 1984.

Swearingen, Roger, ed. *Siberia and the Soviet Far East: Strategic Dimensions in Multinational Perspective.* Stanford, 1987.

Taft, Marcus Lorenzo. *Strange Siberia. Along the Trans-Siberian Railway.* New York, 1911.

Tang, P. S. H. *Russian Policy in Manchuria and Outer Mongolia, 1911–1917.* Durham, NC, 1959.

Tikhmenev, P. A. *A History of the Russian-American Company,* ed. and trans. Richard A. Pierce and Alton S. Donnelly. Seattle, 1978.

———. *Supplement of Some Historical Documents to the Historical Review of the Formation of the Russian-American Company,* trans. Dimitri Krenov. 2 vols., Seattle, 1938.

Tilley, Henry Arthur. *Japan, the Amoor, and the Pacific.* London, 1861.

Titov, Andrei A. *Sibir v XVII v. Sbornik starinnykh russkikh statei o Sibiri i prilezhashchikh nei zemliakh [Siberia in the Seventeenth Century. A Collection of Old Russian Articles About Siberia and the Lands Adjacent to It].* Moscow, 1890.

Tolstoy, Leo. *Resurrection,* trans. Rosemary Edmonds. London, 1966.

Tompkins, Stuart R. *Alaska: Promyshlennik and Sourdough.* Norman, OK, 1945.

Tooke, William. *View of the Russian Empire, During the Reign of Catherine the Second, and to the Close of the Eighteenth Century.* Vol. 3, London, 1800.

Tracy, James D. *True Ocean Found.* Minneapolis, 1980.

Treadgold, Donald W. *The Great Siberian Migration.* Princeton, 1957.

Trotsky, Leon. *My Flight from Siberia.* New York, 1925.

Tupper, Harmon. *To the Great Ocean: Siberia and the Trans-Siberian Railway.* London, 1965.

Urness, Carol. *Bering's First Expedition: A Re-examination based on Eighteenth-Century Books, Maps, and Manuscripts.* New York, 1987.

———, trans. G. F. Müller's *Bering's Voyages: The Reports from Russia.* Fairbanks, AK, 1987.

Utley, Robert M. *The Indian Frontier of the American West 1846–1890.* Albuquerque, 1984.

———, and Wilcomb E. Washburn. *Indian Wars.* Boston, 1987.

Vainschtein, Saryan. *The Peoples of Southern Siberia.* Oxford, 1980.

Vernadsky, George. *The Mongols and Russia.* New Haven, 1953.

————. *The Tsardom of Moscow, 1547–1682.* New Haven, 1969.

Vladimir (pseudonym of Zenone Volpicelli). *Russian on the Pacific and the Siberian Railway.* London, 1899.

Von Laue, Theodore H. *Sergei Witte and the Industrialization of Russia.* New York, 1963.

Vucinich, Aleksandr. *Science in Russian Culture (to 1800).* Stanford, 1963.

Vvedenskiy, A. A. *Dom Stroganovykh v XVI–XVII vekakh [The House of Stroganov in the Sixteenth–Seventeenth Centuries].* Moscow, 1962.

Walder, David. *The Short Victorious War. The Russo-Japanese Conflict 1904–5.* London, 1973.

Waliszewski, K. *Ivan the Terrible,* trans. Lady M. Lloyd. Philadelphia, 1904.

Wallace, Donald MacKenzie. *Russia.* New York, 1905.

Wallace, Henry A. *Soviet Asia Mission.* New York, 1946.

Ward, John. *With the "Die-Hards" in Siberia.* London, 1920.

Warner, Denis and Peggy. *The Tide at Sunrise: A History of the Russo-Japanese War, 1904–5.* London, 1974.

Watrous, Stephen, ed. *Fort Ross: The Russian Settlement in California.* Jenner, CA, 1978.

————, ed. *John Ledyard's Journey Through Russia and Siberia, 1787–1788. The Journal and Selected Letters.* Madison, 1966.

Waxell, Sven. *The Russian Expedition to America,* trans. M. A. Michael. New York, 1962.

Westwood, J. N. *A History of Russian Railways.* London, 1964.

————. *The Russo-Japanese War.* London, 1973.

White, J. A. *The Diplomacy of the Russo-Japanese War.* Princeton, 1964.

————. *The Siberian Intervention.* Princeton, 1950.

Wieczynski, J. L., ed. *The Modern Encyclopedia of Russian and Soviet History* [MERSH]. 47 vols., Gulf Breeze, FL, 1976–88.

Withey, Lynne. *Voyages of Discovery: Captain Cook and the Exploration of the Pacific.* New York, 1987.

Witte, Sergius Yu. *The Memoirs of Count Witte,* ed. and trans. Avrahm Yarmolinsky. London, 1921.

Wood, Alan, and R. A. French, eds. *The Development of Siberia. People and Resources.* New York, 1989.

————, ed. *The History of Siberia. From Russian Conquest to Revolution.* London, 1991.

Wrangell, Ferdinand Von. *Narrative of an Expedition to the Polar Sea, in the Years 1820, 1821, 1822 and 1823,* ed. Major Edward Sabine. London, 1840.

Wright, George Frederick. *Asiatic Russia.* 2 vols., New York, 1902.

Wright, Richardson L., and B. Digby. *Through Siberia. An Empire in the Making.* New York, 1913.

Yakhontoff, Victor A. *Russia and the Soviet Union in the Far East.* London, 1932.

Yarmolinsky, Avrahm. *Road to Revolution: A Century of Russian Radicalism.* Princeton, 1957.

Zonn, J. G. *Through Siberia by Train.* San Francisco, 1976.

ESSAYS AND ARTICLES

SUPAR Report, 1988–91. A digest of information published by the Center for the Soviet Union in the Pacific-Asia Region. University of Hawaii, Honolulu.

Ames, E. "A Century of Russian Railway Construction 1837–1936," *American Slavic and East European Review,* 6 (1947).

Andreev, Aleksandr I. "Trudy G. F. Miller o Sibiri" ["The Works of G. F. Müller on Siberia"], in Müller, *Istoriia Sibiri [History of Siberia],* Vol. 1, 57–144.

Andrews, Clarence L. "Alaska Under the Russians—Industry, Trade, and Social Life," *Washington Historical Quarterly,* 7 (1916).

Armstrong, Terence E. "Cook's Reputation in Russia," in *Captain James Cook and His Times,* ed. Robin Fisher and Hugh Johnston, pp. 121–28, and 248–50.

Ault, Philip. "The (Almost) Russian-American Telegraph," *American Heritage,* 26 (1975), 12–15, 92–98.

Baikalov, Anatole V. "The Conquest and Colonization of Siberia," *Slavonic Review,* 10 (1932), 557–71.

Bakhrushin, Sergei V. "G. F. Miller kak istorik Sibiri" ["G. F. Müller as Historian of Siberia"], in Müller, *Istoriia Sibiri [History of Siberia],* Vol. 1, 5–55.

Bassin, Mark. "Expansion and Colonization on the Eastern Frontier: Views of Siberia and the Far East in Pre-Petrine Russia," *Journal of Historical Geography,* 14 (1988), 3–21.

Belyakov, Vladimir. "Terrorism Rejected," *Soviet Life* (June 1987), 49–50.

Boxer, Charles R. "Jesuits at the Court of Peking, 1601–1775," *History Today,* 7 (1957), 580–89.

Blomkvist, E. E. "A Russian Scientific Expedition to California and Alaska, 1839–1849" (trans. Basil Dmytryshyn and E. A. P. Crownhart-Vaughan), *Oregon Historical Quarterly,* 73 (1972), 101–70.

Bolkhovitinov, Nikolay N. "The Adventures of Doctor Schaffer in Hawaii, 1815–1819," *Hawaiian Journal of History,* 7 (1973), 55–78.

Bradley, Harold Whitman. "The Hawaiian Islands and the Pacific Fur Trade, 1785–1813," *Pacific Northwest Quarterly,* 30 (1939), 275–99.

Bruemmer, Fred. "Life upon the Permafrost," *Natural History,* 96, no. 4 (April 1987), 31–38.

Chard, Chester. "Soviet Scholarship on the Prehistory of Asiatic Russia," *American Slavic and East European Review,* 22 (1963), 538–46.

Chertkov, Vladimir. "Taimyr," *Soviet Life* (March 1988), 48–53.

Dall, W. H. "A Critical Review of Bering's First Expedition 1725–1730, Together with a Translation of His Original Report Upon It," *National Geographic Magazine,* 2 (1890), 111–66.

Dmytryshyn, Basil. "Russian Expansion to the Pacific, 1580–1700: A Historiographical Review," *Slavic Studies,* 25 (1980), 1–25.

Dufour, Clarence John, E. O. Essig, et al. "The Russians in California," *California Historical Quarterly,* 12 (1933), 189–276.

Dumond-Fillon, Remy. "Historique de l'exploration scientifique du Pacifique par les Russes," *Cahiers d'histoire du Pacifique* (1978), 13–37.

Dunlop, John B. Review of Valentin Rasputin's *Siberia on Fire* in *New York Times Book Review,* December 17, 1989, 25.

Edwards, Mike. "Siberia: In from the Cold," *National Geographic,* 177, no. 3 (March 1990), 2–39.

Fisher, Raymond H. "Mangazeia: A Boom Town of Seventeenth Century Siberia," *Russian Review,* 4 (1944), 89–99.

Frank, V. S. "The Territorial Aims of the Sino-Russian Treaty of Nerchinsk, 1689," *Pacific Historical Review,* 16 (1947), 264–70.

Golder, Frank A. "The Purchase of Alaska," *American Historical Review,* 25 (1920), 411–25.

———. "Russian-American Relations During the Crimean War," *American Historical Review,* 31 (1926), 462–76.

Hirabayashi, Hirondo. "The Discovery of Japan from the North," *Japan Quarterly,* 4 (1957), 318–28.

Kerner, Robert J. "The Russian Movement Eastward: Some Observations on Its Historical Significance," *Pacific Historical Review,* 17 (1948), 135–48.

King, Jonathan F. "Nature Reserves of the U.S.S.R.," *Sierra* (May–June 1987), 38–45.

Kinloch, Alexander. "Trade and the Siberian Railway," *Monthly Review,* 2 (1901), 60–71.

Kirby, E. Stuart. "The Trail of the Sable: New Evidence of the Fur Hunters of Siberia in the Seventeenth Century," *Slavic Studies,* 27 (1981), 105–18.

Kropotkin, P. "The Great Siberian Railway," *Geographical Journal,* 5 (1895), 146–54.

Kushner, Howard. "The Russian-American Diplomatic Contest for the Pacific Basin and the Monroe Doctrine," *Journal of the West,* 15 (1975), 65–80.

Lantzeff, George V. "Russian Eastward Expansion before the Mongol Invasion," *American Slavic and East European Review,* 6 (1947), 1–10.

Lattimore, Owen. "New Road to Asia," *National Geographic Magazine,* 86 (1944), 641–76.

Lin, T. C. "The Amur Frontier Question Between China and Russia, 1850–1860," *Pacific Historical Review,* 3 (1934), 1–27.

Liubimenko, Inna I. "A Project for the Acquisition of Russia by James I," *English Historical Review,* 29 (1914), 246–56.

———. "The Struggle of the Dutch with the English for the Russian Market in the Seventeenth Century," *Transactions of the Royal Historical Society,* 7 (1924), 27–51.

Luthin, R. "Russian Opinion on the Cession of Alaska," *American Historical Review,* 48 (1943), 521–31.

———. "The Sale of Alaska," *Slavonic and East European Review,* 17 (1937), 168–82.

Marks, Steven G. "The Burden of Siberia: The Amur Railroad Question in Russia, 1906–1916." Presented at the AAASS Conference, Honolulu, November 1988.

Mazour, Anatole G. "Dimitry Zavalashin, Dreamer of a Russian-American Empire," *Pacific Historical Review,* 5 (1936), 26–37.

McAleavy, Henry. "China and the Amur Provinces," *History Today,* 14 (1964), 381–90.

McCarten, E. F. "The Long Voyages: Early Russian Circumnavigation," *Russian Review,* 22 (1963), 30–38.

Nichols, Robert, and Robert Croskey, eds. "The Condition of the Orthodox Church in Russian America," *Pacific Northwest Quarterly,* 63 (1972), 41–54.

Pereira, N. G. O. "White Power During the Civil War in Siberia (1918–1920): Dilemmas of Kolchak's War Anti-Communism," *Canadian Slavonic Papers,* 29 (1987), 45–62.

Sherwood, Morgan B. "Science in Russian America, 1741–1865," *Pacific Northwest Quarterly,* 58 (1967) 33–39.

Skrynnikov, R. G. "Ermak's Siberian Expedition" (trans. Hugh F. Graham), *Russian History/Histoire Russe,* 13 (1986), 1–39.

Somov, Yuri, and Oleg Makarov, "Buryatia. A Republic on Lake Baikal," *Soviet Life* (March 1988), 41–47.

Stutz, Bruce. "Hurricanes of the Arctic Night," *Natural History,* 96, no. 12 (December 1986), 67–73.

Turnbull, D. "The Defeat of Popular Representation, December 1904," *Slavic Review,* 48, no. 1 (1989), 62–72.

Vernadsky, George. "The Death of the Tsarevich Dmitry," *Oxford Slavonic Papers,* 5 (1954), 1–19.

Vickers, C. E. "The Siberian Railway in War," *Royal Engineers Journal,* 2 (1905), 130–38.

Voichenko-Markov, Euphesimia. "John Ledyard and the Russians," *Russian Review,* 11 (1952), 211–22.

Wheeler, Mary E. "Empires in Conflict and Cooperation: The 'Bostonians' and the Russian-America Company," *Pacific Historical Review,* 40 (1971), 419–41.

———. "The Origins of the Russian-America Company," *Jahrbücher für Geschichte Osteuropas,* 14 (1966), 485–94.

Wildes, Harry Emerson. "Russia Meets the Japanese," *Russian Review,* 3 (1943), 55–63.

———. "Russia's Attempts to Open Japan," *Russian Review,* 5 (1945), 70–79.

Wiren-Garczynski, Vera von. "Russian America," *Soviet Life* (May 1990), 55.

Yarmolinsky, Avrahm. "A Rambling Note on the 'Russian Columbus' Nikolai Petrovich Rezanov," *Bulletin of the New York Public Library,* 31 (1927), 707–13.

———. "Shelikhov's Voyage to Alaska. A Bibliographical Note," *Bulletin of the New York Public Library,* 36 (1932), 141–48.

Zavalishin, Dimitri. "California in 1824" (trans. and annot. James R. Gibson), *Southern California Quarterly,* 55 (1973).

PERMISSIONS
ACKNOWLEDGMENTS

The author is grateful for permission to quote from Karlo Stajner, *Seven Thousand Days in Siberia,* translated by Joel Agee, and published by Farrar, Straus, & Giroux, Inc., © 1988; Christina Sutherland, *The Princess of Siberia,* published by Farrar, Straus, & Giroux, Inc., © 1984; Leo Tolstoy, *Resurrection,* translated by Rosemary Edmonds, and published by Penguin Classics, Penguin Books, Ltd., © 1966; John J. Stephan, *Sakhalin: A History,* published by Oxford University Press, © 1971; and Alan Wood, ed., *The History of Siberia,* published by Routledge, © 1991. The author is also grateful for permission to reproduce the map of Kolchak's Siberia from Richard Luckett, *The White Generals,* published by Routledge, © 1971; and the map of Russian America, from James R. Gibson, *Imperial Russia in Frontier America,* published by Oxford University Press, © 1976. Finally, the author wishes to thank G. P. Putnam's Sons for permission to extensively extract material from pages 330–38 of the author's own *Fearful Majesty: The Life and Reign of Ivan the Terrible,* © 1987.

INDEX